Law in Society: Reflections on Children, Family, Culture and Philosophy
Essays in Honour of Michael Freeman

Law in Society: Reflections on Children, Family, Culture and Philosophy

Essays in Honour of Michael Freeman

Edited by

Alison Diduck, Noam Peleg, and Helen Reece

BRILL
NIJHOFF

LEIDEN | BOSTON

Library of Congress Control Number: 2015946665

This publication has been typeset in the multilingual "Brill" typeface. With over 5,100 characters covering Latin, IPA, Greek, and Cyrillic, this typeface is especially suitable for use in the humanities. For more information, please see www.brill.com/brill-typeface.

ISBN 978-90-04-26148-8 (hardback)
ISBN 978-90-04-26149-5 (e-book)

This book is printed on acid-free paper.

Printed by Printforce, the Netherlands

Table of Contents

Introduction

Alison Diduck
Faculty of Laws, University College London

Noam Peleg
Faculty of Law, University of New South Wales, Australia

Helen Reece
Department of Law, London School of Economics and Political Science

We are delighted to offer this collection of papers written by legal scholars from around the world on a range of topics from children's rights to criminal law, jurisprudence, medical ethics and more. Indeed, at first glance this range is broad in the extreme. What, a reader may ask, links cricket, fairy tales, children's views on education, barristers' views on relocation, and family law in Italy, the Netherlands, South Africa and England? One answer is that these are all elements of what can broadly be called 'law and society', that enterprise that is interested in law's place or influence in different aspects of real lives and understands law to be simultaneously symbol, philosophy and action. The other answer, of course, is Professor Michael Freeman.

Professor Michael Freeman, FBA, joined the UCL Faculty of Laws in 1969 after teaching for some three years at the University of Leeds. He retired from UCL in 2011 after a distinguished career in which he published more than 85 books and countless articles, including pioneering work on children's rights, domestic violence, religious law, jurisprudence, law and culture, family law and medicine, ethics and the law. His law and society approach is clear in all this work as is his international vision. Another of his most enduring and innovative contributions to legal scholarship in England and Wales, that arguably comes with his 'law and society' sympathies, is his commitment to interdisciplinarity. Michael recognises that no discipline is truly autonomous, or at least that studying its meaning for real people can be enhanced by and benefit from combining its approaches and perspectives with those from other disciplines. As creator and convenor of UCL's annual Current Legal Issues Colloquium, Michael gave us 16 such combinations, including law and language, law and neuroscience, law and sociology, law and anthropology, law and popular culture, law and geography, law and philosophy, law and psychology, law and science, law and bioethics, law and global health, law and childhood studies, and law and literature.

In recognition of Michael's vision, the Current Legal Issues Colloquium 2013 was entitled 'Law and Michael Freeman'. We invited scholars and practitioners working in fields in which Michael was interested to present their current work. The response was overwhelming. In July 2013 over 100 participants heard papers from over 40 presenters. Contributors and participants came from five different continents.

It is in the Current Legal Issues' spirit of interdisciplinarity that we offer this collection of papers from the Colloquium 'Law and Michael Freeman'. Combining these two 'arenas'[1] of learning produces a whole that is astonishing not only in its breadth, but also in its commitment to understanding incidents of justice and injustice, pain and joy, hardship and advantage in everyday life. Michael's commitment to understanding the effects of law and social policy on the lives of the vulnerable has led him to think about the myriad sources not only of the norms which affect us, but 'from which we derive our learning' about law and legal concepts (Menkel-Meadow: 658). To be sure, there is 'law', in the form of legal doctrine, legal policy and the state institutions that create and enforce it, but our understanding of the meaning and effects of law are enhanced also by tropes of law and justice found in discourses of religion, culture (popular or otherwise), medicine, philosophy, 'politics' (however broadly or narrowly defined) and the day-to-day of our increasingly international and global lives. As Carrie Menkel-Meadow writes in her contribution to this collection, Michael's 'sources for analysing law range among all fields of human endeavour – science, medicine, children's literature, sports, opera, religion and ethics, among other fields and he looks beyond Anglo culture to do so' (654). When law and Michael Freeman, these two 'spheres of public or energetic action' combine, we have interdisciplinarity at its most exciting.

We have divided the contributions to this collection as they reflect the different domains in which Michael sees that law, broadly defined, impacts on people's lives. These chapters by distinguished international scholars are a testament to Michael's broad range of vision. We begin with work on law in its philosophical, cultural or symbolic realm (Part I: Law and Stories: Culture, Religion and Philosophy), including its commitment to the normative ideal of 'rights' (Part II: Law and Rights) before we move on to offer work on law as coercive state action (Part III: Law and the Coercive State) and as regulator of personal relationships (Part IV: Law and Personal Living). We continue with papers that reflect the importance of globalisation, both of law and of 'doing family' in personal and public life (Part V: Law and International Living) before we close with two papers which offer reflections on Michael Freeman's body of work generally, including one from Michael himself (Part VI: Law and Michael Freeman).

In Part I contributors explore beyond the boundaries of that which many traditionally understand to constitute law's conceptual apparatus. Roger Cotterrell issues a challenge to orthodox understandings of 'jurisprudence'. He criticises a 'jurisprudence' that packages itself as the distinct pedagogical enterprise of Anglo-American legal philosophy, searching for 'ultimate truth about law's nature, or timeless, "essential" or "necessary" characteristics of the legal' (16). Instead, Cotterrell argues with the characteristically incisive social (and historico-political) grounding he shares with Michael, that the modern juristic project, *jurisprudence,* ought better to be conceived as 'at best, a patchwork of insights related to the idea (and ideal) of law as a practice of regulation to serve social needs and social values, as these are recognised in particular times and places.' (16) John Eekelaar also is keenly aware of the potential pitfalls of timelessness and universalism in the quest for the philosophical foundations of

1 The *OED* defines arena as a 'sphere of public or energetic action'.

legal concepts such as human rights. He joins Michael in rejecting both relativism and monism, instead suggesting that cultural practices can be evaluated by reference to the well-being of the individual members of the culture. Defending himself against prior criticisms proffered by Prakesh Shah, Eekelaar insists that such evaluation is not a 'western practice', but can be used to critique western practice and indeed any cultural practice.

Questions about the sources of legal norms and the ways in which not obviously *legal* stories contribute to our understanding of law continue in contributions by Bernard Jackson and David Nelken. In the context of calls for accommodation of religious norms within the secular system, Jackson finds that models of secular jurisprudence (which tend to privilege objectively determinable truth) are not always helpful in understanding the rules of Jewish law (which tend to privilege secondary rules based upon trust), by which many live and which govern family life in particular. He raises conceptual and epistemological questions about the nature of legal reasoning; he looks to both Jewish and secular positivist-jurisprudential understandings of concepts such as truth, trustworthiness, discretion, public, private, charisma and rationality and shows how they complicate yet enrich our understanding of the interaction of state and religious law. Nelken also uses Jewish law as a lens through which we can understand stories or narrative as law or at least the relationship between them. He draws upon Talmudic stories of forgiveness which he identifies as a crucial concept that touches 'not only on issues in the sociology of law and criminology but also legal philosophy', family law and criminal justice (63). He wonders if modern legal scholars might appreciate the insights drawn from these stories for more than one reason. Nelken suggests, for example, that they might blur the line between what we see as the secular and the religious or indeed offer us fruitful ways of thinking about domestic or international criminal justice ethics and systems. Part I then concludes with two papers that also explore the connection between stories, culture and law. Lawrence Friedman and Anne McGillivray, however, are interested in popular culture and children's literature.

Friedman's wide ranging review of the ways 'law and the image of law percolate into movies, novels, plays, television shows, songs, graphic arts, magazines, and the like' (83) highlights law's ubiquity in popular cultural representation. Friedman does more than illustrate law's presence in, or *as*, popular entertainment, however. He argues not only that popular culture, including, importantly, news reports, often misrepresents the 'reality' of legal concepts and legal practice, but also raises questions about the effects of the evolving and reciprocal relationship between law and popular culture. If each has an impact upon the other, can we possibly measure that combined impact on peoples attitudes or behaviour? Anne McGillivray is also interested in the potential of literature – stories – as law. Her sensitive exploration of early 20th century children's literature as 'myth' which was 'central to constituting the child as legal subject' (103) shifts to trace a move toward the corporatisation of childhood. Whereas once children's stories may have contained advertisements, now they are advertisement. McGillivray laments this new New Childhood and proposes meaningful attention be paid to children's rights, particularly the right to be heard 'from the legislature to the courtroom to the boardroom' (119) to counter the attenuation of myth. She says 'the mythic element of stories for children bring law into the child's shaping of her self and empowers her to cope with the complexities of the everyday. As tales of origin and return, betrayal and reconciliation, justice and love, these stories constitute the legal texts of childhood' (102). But if the mythic has now become the corporate, corporations tell the stories in which children make their childhoods.

The papers in Part II focus on children's rights, fittingly. As John Tobin recognises in his chapter, 'few scholars, if any, have done as much over such a sustained period both to advance and to defend the case for children's rights' (127). Indeed, Tobin starts by paying tribute to Michael's ground-breaking 1987 article in which Michael takes Ronald Dworkin to task for not taking children's rights seriously, while Lucinda Ferguson acknowledges that it is out of Michael's acute concern with children's rights that her argument – which turns away from rights discourse – is born. But from this starting point, both Ferguson and Tobin then ask some critical questions about children's rights discourse. What unites their chapters is an emphasis that what matters is children's flourishing – the betterment of children's concrete lives – and Tobin chastens us that while children's rights discourse may have become increasingly accepted, there are serious shortcomings in the ways in which we have improved children's real lives, globally and locally. Lucinda Ferguson, in a complex argument, wonders whether children's rights are the best vehicle – and she sees them as a vehicle – to improving children's living conditions. The first tranche in her argument is to justify the proposition that children's interests deserve special prioritisation. Having made a coherent case for that proposition based around the vulnerability of children as a class, she moves on to compare the effectiveness of three tools for achieving that special status for children: the best interests principle; children's rights; and finally duty. Unusually perhaps, she finds reasons to prefer a duty-based approach that is based around the concept of virtue. In the final section of her chapter, she uses discrete case studies to argue that the duty approach has distinct advantages over the other tools for promoting children's flourishing. While Ferguson is primarily concerned with the way in which lawyers should think about children's well-being, Tobin broadens out the discussion to ask how we should respond to the fact that other disciplines have developed their own ways of talking about improving children's lives. He concludes that if children's rights discourse is to have integrity, then it needs to avoid accusations of colonisation, and it needs to be reflective. What unites Ferguson and Tobin is an openness towards a range of ways, from a range of disciplines, of theorising their – and our – unshakable concern with substantively improving children's concrete lives.

Priscilla Alderson and Mark Henaghan also advocate the importance of thinking about children's rights from a solid theoretical foundation and a range of disciplines that pay attention to differences among children. Henaghan traces the evolution of Michael's theory of children's rights and ultimately characterises it as a radical one: "liberal paternalism, grounded in the reality of a particular child's life' (193). Michael's theory contains a number of primary principles drawn from different ideas of rights, he says, including the right to equal concern and respect for dignity and personality and crucially, centres not on a child's age, but on the particular activity in question and the particular child. It is therefore fundamental that children participate in democratic political debate. Henaghan's close analysis of rights thinking is supplemented by an equally close look at the practical utility, implementation and enforcement of rights for children. He concludes with Michael's words that when rights for children prevail 'it will redound to the benefit not only of children, but of all of us' (200). Alderson too is inspired by Michael's breadth of vision in these respects and highlights not only theories of human rights but also the importance of the field of 'childhood studies' in understanding the meaning and effects of the UN Convention on the Rights of the Child. Echoing Michael's commitment to interdisciplinarity, she argues that ethnographic work, historical work, work in psychology and work with the most disadvantaged children, such as children of war or asylum, for example, can only enrich our interpretations of children's rights.

Laura Lundy, Elizabeth Welty, Natasha Blanchet-Cohen, Dympna Devine, Kylie Smith and Beth Blue Swadener offer a reply to one of Michael's critiques of the Convention on the Rights of the Child – how different the Convention would have been if children had participated in its drafting. As a testament to the importance of listening to children both in terms of respecting their rights and in enriching legal analysis, the authors talked with children in five national contexts, asking them for their views on Article 29 of the Convention, which deals with the aims of education. Their findings are astonishing, showing that children's inputs are significantly different in content, style and interpretation when compared with what adults have articulated for them. One insight that this participatory exercise shows us is that children felt that education should be more respectful of minorities, and should encourage children to be kind and considerate towards others.

Bernadette Saunders also draws upon narratives in her chapter on the corporal punishment of children. In making the case that their rights demand that we must listen to children, she reminds us of Michael's passionate campaign against this form of violence against children. She outlines the 'limited but promising progress towards full abolition of corporal punishment' (244) before she draws attention to social science research, the bulk of which suggests that 'corporal punishment does not achieve positive outcomes for children; the child's physical and mental health, cognitive and behavioural development and relationships with significant others may be adversely affected immediately and permanently' (250). Saunders then examines the language that is used when talking about corporal punishment; 'adultist' phrases like 'loving smack' or 'toddler taming' are euphemisms she says which demean children and contribute to their oppression. They must be contrasted with children's own candid, moving, often painful and usually insightful statements about their feelings and the effects of being struck by a loved one.

The papers in Part III reflect Roger Cotterrell's understanding of law as 'a practice of regulation to serve social needs and social values'. While all areas of law fall within this understanding, here, contributors are concerned with regulation as compulsion, as the state's direct, coercive regulation of behaviour through the criminal justice or child protection system. Robert Reiner re-visits a 'rare foray' (273) by Michael into criminology, *Law and Order in 1984*, in which Michael fulminated against the

Thatcher government's assault on civil liberties in the name of crime control and law and order. Reiner regards Michael's as a 'landmark analysis' (*ibid*), which is 'important as a state-of-the-art representation of liberal and Left thinking about law and order in the early 1980s' (*ibid*). However, looking back now, Reiner comments that the law and order arms race has exceeded Michael's worst imaginings, and he analyses the reasons for the entrenchment of what Michael hoped was a transient phase in British politics. Meanwhile, Heather Keating focuses in on one particular aspect of the law and order arms race, the low age of criminal responsibility for children, exacerbated through the abolition of *doli incapax*. In this focus, she combines two of Michael's chief concerns: civil liberties and children's rights; indeed her entry point is to draw on Michael's sustained emphasis on the inconsistency between refusing to give children rights on the one hand and holding them criminally responsible on the other. Keating joins a chorus of voices who find UK law in relation to children's criminal responsibility both morally and intellectually indefensible: she regards the law as unjustifiable in terms of what we know about children's development, in terms of a liberal conception of autonomy and responsibility, and in terms of how we treat children elsewhere in the law. She places a particular focus on the implications for children's criminal responsibility of extending the criminal law further into the field of anti-social behaviour.

Helen Reece reviews Michael's pioneering contribution to the legal literature on domestic violence, including his ambivalence regarding criminal law's response to it. She reminds us that Michael's intervention in 1979 was the first by a lawyer to bring to light not only the phenomenon of domestic violence, but its gendered nature and the feminist inspired explanations for it. She draws upon contemporary research to assess critically Michael's claims and eventually comes back to Michael's conundrum: if law is part of the problem, one of the props upholding male dominance, how can it also be the solution to the problem? Reece's explanation of Michael's ambivalence about the role that criminal law can have, either as protector of women or as solver of the problem of domestic violence against them, illustrates the complexity of law's coercive expression of social needs and values: criminal law's incursion into the 'private' sphere of the home may be as welcome as its message that violence in the home is unacceptable, yet its pro-arrest policy may make matters worse for the victim or more abstractedly disempower all victims.

Peter Alldridge's contribution also illustrates the symbiotic relationship between criminal law and social needs and values. Here, the social values in question are those in the sporting and betting world. Alldridge examines instances when the criminal law becomes involved in prosecuting betting scams, cheating, match fixing or corruption in sport and instances when such transgressions are left to the sport's self regulation. Cricket, he says, claims a unique 'spirit', a nobility that supplements the positive rules by which the game is played and which is invoked as moral justification for its self-governance. It also, he says, acts as an impediment to dealing appropriately with corruption. Alldridge's review of criminal law's intervention in cricket and other sporting scams shows that the values or 'spirit' assumed to infuse cricket affects criminal law's treatment of corruption in it: 'the person who is trying to win the game by cheating is in a different position from the person who is trying to fix the game so as to win money by gambling, even though both fall within scope of the criminal prohibition, because at least s/he is trying to "play the game"' (331).

Judith Masson examines the role of the state in safeguarding another social value: protecting children from 'significant harm' attributable to the care they receive in their homes. It is clear that the state has an important role here, yet Masson rethinks the grounds for its intervention to place children into its care while she revisits some assertions that Michael made in 1983 in his book *The Rights and Wrongs of Children*. Back then, Michael claimed that children have a right to be in care, if their parents did not uphold their rights. Describing a number of law reforms since the 1980s, focusing on the 1989 Children Act and the changes it introduced to the care system, Masson argues that while in principle Michael's approach has been adopted by parliament, in practice lack of funding and a presumption that children are better off living with their biological families led local authorities not to place children in care (349-350). Masson therefore suggests that policy should change in a way that will strike a different balance between Michael's position and the inclination to leave children with their families, by bolstering placement of children with relative carers.

In Part IV we offer a number of papers that illustrate law's influence on the most intimate and personal aspects of our lives. The decisions we take about who we will share our lives with, about reproduction, and about how we will care for our children and our elders are subject to normative influences, sometimes directly, from legal doctrine, and sometimes in more subtle ways. Felicity Kaganas and Christine Piper review, in the light of the observations Michael made in *The Rights and Wrongs of Children*, some key reforms in English family and child law, particularly reforms around a child's contact with both parents post separation, the welfare principle, and government's efforts to reduce the volume of litigation. Kaganas and Piper argue that the reforms, and the new presumption in the Children and Families Act 2014 in particular, will not achieve the aims that reformers claim they are designed to achieve. Referring to Michael's observation that change may lead to unintended or 'unproclaimed' consequences, they suggest there is no evidence that the presumption will promote co-operative parenting; that fathers' rights groups will be mollified by the change; that the use of law to send out 'messages' will ensure that those messages are heard or understood; or that law can be successfully used to educate the public. Moreover, they suggest, with the proliferation of bodies tasked with this education, there may well be a proliferation of norms being transmitted.

Ghislaine Lanteigne looked to both legal doctrine and legal practice to explore law's influence on child care decisions. She interviewed English lawyers who practice in the area of international relocation about parents' often irreconcilable differences concerning children's care in the context of relocation. Comparing her interview findings to findings from similar studies in England, Canada and other common law jurisdictions, Lanteigne focuses on how the 'best interests of the child' are taken into account in relocation cases. While litigation is often the least favorable way to solve relocation disputes and although alternatives to litigation are discussed with parents, their emotional turmoil and the binary outcome to relocation disputes reduces the possibility that these alternative processes are chosen. The difficulty is that once the course of litigation is chosen, lawyers observe that its demands can drain the parents' emotional and financial resources, damage their co-parenting capabilities post-litigation and open the possibility for the child to be co-opted into the dispute.

Amel Alghrani, Danielle Griffiths and Margaret Brazier take another piece by Michael as their springboard: "Is Surrogacy Exploitative" (1999). They suggest that his argument, that the regulation of surrogacy in general and the ban on commercial surrogacy in particular were not working, is as timely now as it was then. If anything, they suggest, time has proved Michael right, with problems that were emerging at the end of the century becoming entrenched. Surrogacy, he and they are clear, is here to stay and indeed is expanding and taking on an international dimension. After carefully laying out the social and legal background, Alghrani *et al* make a number of considered proposals for reform, which they suggest necessitate a new Surrogacy Act. One particular change that they follow Michael in calling for is the removal of the ban on commercial surrogacy, so that surrogates would be allowed to receive a 'moderate fee'. Dismissing the reasons given for such a ban, they argue that payment would make surrogacy arrangements more secure and sustainable for all parties.

Jo Bridgeman's chapter addresses one of Michael's significant contributions to medical ethics, which was his suggestion to establish an independent review process for decisions taken by parents about their children's medical care, and to recognise a right of the child to have 'reasonable parents' in this context. Bridgeman analyses key cases from the 1980s to late 2010, where English courts reviewed parents' decisions to sterilise their child. Bridgeman claims that using children's welfare or best interests as a guiding principle in deciding this matter is 'insufficient'. She argues that the courts' application of the welfare test gives sufficient consideration neither to parental concerns, nor to the fact that parents bear primary responsibility for the care of their children (461-463). Instead, Bridgeman would prefer law to see 'responsible parents' who respect their child as a separate individual, and who recognise that fulfilling their responsibilities also means pursuing the support of professionals. This 'responsible parent' will also realise that some decisions about a child's future, including healthcare decisions, will be scrutinised by an independent body who will make decisions according to a set of clear and comprehensive principles.

Jonathan Herring examines another aspect of the parent-child relationship: parental abuse. He begins by acknowledging Michael's pioneering role in exploring and exposing violence against women and children. He treats this as a launch pad to his discussion of child-to-parent abuse, a form of violence that is currently less explored and exposed than others. Herring provides a thorough account of the dimensions of this recently discovered phenomenon, and is particularly illuminating on the reasons that law and society find this an especially difficult type of abuse to recognise and respond to: 'parental abuse challenges some of the basic legal and social assumptions about the nature of childhood and parenthood' (484) and about the relationship between parents and children. He concludes with what some might think an uncommon acknowledgment for a lawyer: that there is no panacea and piecemeal solutions may work best.

Finally in this part, Andrew Gilbert takes inspiration from Michael's 1985 inaugural lecture, *Towards a Critical Theory of Family Law*, but takes this theory in an unusual direction by analysing the relationship between British conservatism and family law, an extremely under-explored relationship, as he points out. After careful exploration of the elements of conservatism as a political philosophy, Gilbert examines the extent to which they were present in Conservative MPs' contributions to the recent debate on same-sex marriage. He found that conservative arguments were more easily deployed against than for same-sex marriage and interestingly, on the basis of these statements, that most Conservative MPs are probably not 'true' conservatives.

Part V of the collection reveals not only the international reach of Michael's influence, but also his longstanding dedication to studying law's meaning and implications for people, wherever in the world they may be. Just as people do, concepts like best interests, rights and equality cross international borders, even if their meanings may take on the different nuances of time and place. The implications of that mobility and internationalism are important for families and for understanding the concepts themselves. In the first two papers in this part, our contributors examine the development locally of potentially universal legal concepts. Sanford Katz gives us a review of the most significant developments in US family law in what many consider to be a period of vast social upheaval and normative uncertainty, the second half of the 20th century. He reviews, among other reforms in this period, increasing juridical acceptance of gender equality and non-traditional living arrangements and tensions between parents' and children's rights in family living in the United States. He notes interestingly that during this time, 'the laws regulating family life began reflecting reality, rather than trying to mould families into outmoded archetypes' (519). Here we see the legitimacy of changing laws, about gender equality, ante nuptial and cohabitation agreements for example, derived precisely from that social change, which parallel in many ways similar reforms in England and Wales.

Meda Couzens also illustrates the way in which domestic context develops and gives meaning to universal concepts. The best interests of the child, a concept familiar to most jurisdictions, has a paramountcy in South Africa that surpasses that in many. South Africa's constitution (s. 28(2)) states that 'A child's best interests are of paramount importance in every matter concerning the child.' Couzens' comprehensive review of the South African case law illustrates the way in which this section has become a 'self standing right' in South Africa. The implications of this conclusion are potentially transformative for children; there is a difference as Couzens suggests, between treating best interests as a constitutional standard and treating it as a tool for child protection and family law adjudication. Even though more clarity is needed in the meaning of and use to which best interests can be put normatively, she argues 'the Court [has] created various positive obligations for the state, which, arguably, could not have been created by relying exclusively on other constitutional rights which the children enjoy' (521).

The next three papers in Part V assess a state's domestic legislation against that state's obligations under international and regional law and raise issues about the effects on men, women and children of compatibility or incompatibility. In the first,

Jane Stoll looks into donor offspring's right to information about genetic origins in Sweden, analysing the compatibility of Swedish legislation, which grants offspring some ability to trace their biological origins, with Sweden's international obligations under the UN Convention on the Rights of the Child and the European Convention on Human Rights. The law in Sweden enables children with sufficient maturity the right to obtain information about their genetic origins. However, Stoll asks whether this law is applicable in an era of domestic and cross-border surrogacy arrangements, since currently, the child may not have access to information about the surrogate mother. She therefore suggests that if the same logic applies, then upholding these children's best interests requires acknowledging their right to information as well.

Maria Federica Moscati's chapter explores children's access to justice in Italy, focusing on two elements: civil procedures and the criminal justice system. Moscati reviews the complex web of legislation that regulates children's relationships with the law, and compares it to Italy's obligations under the UN Convention on the Rights of the Child and the European Convention on Human Rights. She argues that while some progress in meeting international standards has been made in recent years, there are a number of conceptual barriers, primarily lack of respect for children's agency and autonomy, that limit children's ability to participate in proceedings that affect their life and their future. The chapter provides some interesting empirical data about Naples' prosecution authorities' policy regarding juveniles involved in organised crimes, which illuminates the many obstacles to the realisation of children's rights in the juvenile justice system in Italy.

Coby de Graaf queries the extent to which administrative justice in the Netherlands is compatible with the UN Convention on the Rights of the Child. By analysing 1,028 administrative, juvenile, immigration and family law cases from 2002 to 2011, De Graaf shows that while the legislation itself may lag behind Dutch international obligations, the courts often utilise the UN Convention on the Rights of the Child. This judicial tendency is most common in lower courts (the district court) and is less visible in the appeal court or Supreme Court, but demonstrates the gulf that can exist between the 'law' that comes from the legislature and the law in practice. Indeed, De Graaf claims that the Courts interpret Article 3 of the Convention and the best interests principle as having a direct effect on domestic law and policy, despite the fact that there is no specific law that mandates it.

The final two papers in this part look specifically at aspects of international family law. Sir Mathew Thorpe's contribution reflects his perspective as a former Lord Justice of the Court of Appeal of England and Wales, Deputy Head of Family Justice, Head of International Justice and longstanding member of the International Society of Family Law. He reviews the development of what we might call 'international family law' over the last 20 years; that which he calls the law aimed at meeting 'the challenge of the increasing mobility of people and the complexity of legal and practical problems created by cross cultural and cross border relationship breakdown' (603). While Sir Mathew sees many successes in meeting those challenges, including increasing judicial communication and collaboration and the development of 'global or regional law covering inter-country adoption of children, child protection, fortified provisions to combat abduction and reciprocal enforcement of maintenance orders' (604), there remain in his view, areas in which further work is required, particularly where differences in legal tradition, culture or belief are perceived as irreconcilable.

Rhona Schuz also examines international family law. She puts on record Michael's refusal to participate in the drafting of the Hague Convention on the Civil Aspects of Child Abduction 1980 on the basis that it was anti-women and anti-children. Looking at the operation of the Convention from the vantage point of the present day, she finds that Michael's assessment was justified, borne out by the interpretation of the Hague Convention, which she argues tends to look at abduction from the point of view of the left-behind parent rather than from the child's perspective, risking treating children as a means to an end, not an end in themselves. Still, she sees signs of hope in some cross-national developments in the case law, which she believes could be built upon, even without substantive reform of the Convention itself.

We conclude the collection with 2 papers in Part VI. The first is Michael's own further reflections on interdisciplinarity and children's rights. He highlights the ways in which lawyers' thinking about children's rights has been enriched by contributions from childhood studies and sociology more broadly. As a result of those contributions we as legal professionals look at children and childhood differently from the way we did 20 years ago. He calls for those concerned with children's rights now to approach questions such as 'what is a child?', or 'what rights?', or to think about the tension between the universal and the particular, differently. The sociology of childhood can only help us understand what children's rights might mean. As Michael states: 'those of us who espouse children's rights have a vision of a better world for children and through this, a better world for all of us. This requires us to acquire a better understanding of the lives of children, of what is important to them, how they perceive and construct their social worlds.' (647).

The second is a paper by Carrie-Menkel-Meadow entitled when she delivered it at the colloquium: 'Michael Freeman – A Renaissance Man'. In her written contribution, here, Menkel-Meadow rounds out the overall theme of the colloquium and this collection. Her personal reflections about her academic and social encounters over the years with Michael speak not only to his breadth of expertise, but to his generosity of intellect and spirit. Menkel-Meadow highlights Michael's constant thinking about 'law and …' in legally pluralistic ways, most importantly, as law and humanity. We hope there is something of interest here to all students and scholars of 'law and humanity', or as we have called it, 'Law and Michael Freeman'.

The editors are grateful to all those who assisted in the production of this volume, in particular Lea Raible, Inga Thiemann, Adele Cameron and Ruth Eldon who provided invaluable editorial assistance and Lindy Melman and Bea Timmer and all at Brill Nijhoff for their encouragement and support of this project from its inception. Finally, all proceeds from the sale of this book will go to UNICEF, Michael's choice of charity.

I

Law and Stories: Culture, Religion and Philosophy

Professing Jurisprudence

Roger Cotterrell
Anniversary Professor of Legal Theory, Queen Mary, University of London, UK[1]

Introduction

The first occasion on which Michael Freeman and I spent much time together was a two-week summer school in social science research methods at Churchill College, Cambridge, in July 1972. The course had been organised specifically for law teachers and it was one of several initiatives around that time reflecting a growing recognition in Britain that legal studies needed to open up to new possibilities and interdisciplinary perspectives. Certainly it encouraged my growing interest in socio-legal studies and Michael soon showed his interdisciplinary commitments by publishing the pioneering socio-legal text *The Legal Structure* in 1974. At around that time I moved to a lectureship in London and, ever since, we have been University of London colleagues regularly linked by various projects.

Another link is that we have both taught, throughout much of our careers, the subject called, in anglophone law schools, *jurisprudence*. We have professed a subject whose identity, purpose and scope is sporadically contested but, more often now, merely left unexamined. Perhaps because of a deep uncertainty about its nature, which has made it hard to defend intellectually, jurisprudence has increasingly, over the past few decades, been treated as having been incorporated or redefined into something with a different name – legal philosophy. Legal philosophy, as that term is now understood in Anglo-American scholarship, designates a field of theory often seen as having higher intellectual status than that which jurisprudence possessed before its incorporation or redefinition. Legal philosophy presents itself as having a clear identity and strong intellectual underpinnings located in philosophy. Its methods, choice of problems, forms of argument and criteria of relevance are seen as validated by philosophy as an academic discipline; legal philosophy is the branch of philosophy that takes law as its object.

1 I am grateful to Maks Del Mar and David Schiff for comments on a draft of this chapter, to David Nelken for invaluable discussion of related issues, and to Michael Freeman for many years of valued colleagueship which I seek to celebrate here.

A. Diduck, N. Peleg, H. Reece (eds.), Law in Society: Reflections on Children, Family, Culture and Philosophy
Copyright 2015 Koninklijke Brill NV. Printed in The Netherlands. ISBN 978-90-04-26148-8. pp. 15-30.

Indeed, the tendency among many self-identified anglophone legal philosophers has been to view jurisprudence, insofar as it is *not* legal philosophy in this contemporary sense, as unworthy of serious scholarly attention. And it is true that jurisprudence often seems to be a disconnected package of insights about law drawn with little discrimination from 'non-legal' academic disciplines in the humanities and social sciences and from lawyers' theoretical speculations on their own legal professional knowledge and practice. In the past it seemed important for legal philosophers to attack jurisprudence's 'syncretism of methods' (Kelsen, 1989: 1), the unsystematic package of approaches that characterised it in its primitive (pre-philosophical) state. Today, these attacks are usually considered unnecessary. Legal philosophers see the battle for intellectual rigour as won as far as they are concerned. Contemporary anglophone legal philosophy tends its furrow, unconcerned with the nature of jurisprudence insofar as this could be something different from what legal philosophers do;[2] jurisprudence might be acceptable as the name for a pedagogic package to broaden the minds of undergraduate law students, but this would not validate it as a serious field of academic research.

This chapter's purpose is to defend jurisprudence as something more than a pedagogic package and as an enterprise distinct from legal philosophy. It argues that, however undisciplined (in academic terms) and philosophically inept its literature may often have been, it is properly seen as an important body of thought about law that aims at exploring, aiding and developing the *prudentia* of jurists. A dictionary search reveals that *prudentia* can mean acquaintance, knowledge, sagacity, prudence, discretion and foresight, which will serve as a provisional set of meanings here: one to attach to an ideal juristic understanding of law. On this basis, jurisprudence is not an academic field, certainly not a modern academic discipline. It is, at best, a patchwork of insights related to the idea (and ideal) of law as a practice of regulation to serve social needs and social values, as these are recognised in particular times and places. So jurisprudence, on this view, is an exploratory enterprise aimed at serving an ongoing, ever-changing juristic practice. It is not aimed at finding ultimate truth about law's nature, or timeless, 'essential' or 'necessary' characteristics of the legal.

What may be timeless is the *task* for which jurisprudence, seen in this way, should provide enlightenment: the task of making organised social regulation a valuable practice, rooted and effective in the specific contexts and historical conditions in which it exists but also aimed at serving demands for justice and security through regulation as these perennial values are understood in their time and place, and as they might be further clarified and reconciled as legal ideals. Jurisprudence, in this view, is aimed at informing those who are enduringly (usually professionally) concerned with the well-being of the idea of law as a practice in this sense, equipping them with the means of promoting that well-being (itself a matter for interpretation). For the purposes of discussion here such people with such concerns can conveniently

2 Thus the *Oxford Handbook of Jurisprudence & Philosophy of Law* (Coleman and Shapiro, 2002) treats its subject as legal philosophy and makes no reference to jurisprudence as a field.

be called 'jurists' (cf. Cotterrell, 2013) and the aim here is to defend jurisprudence as a contemporary enterprise of gathering knowledge to assist them.

Bricolage Jurisprudence and Its Enemies

How could such an idea of jurisprudence be unpacked? Alongside Michael Freeman's path-breaking writings on children's rights, family law and related fields, a very notable scholarly contribution has been his editing and enriching, over four decades, of successive editions of *Lloyd's Introduction to Jurisprudence*, the textbook used by generations of students in many countries. The book primarily serves 'pedagogic' jurisprudence – it relies on educational justifications which, as noted earlier, this chapter aims to go beyond[3] – but in doing so it defends a vision of jurisprudence that clearly rejects the claim that this should be equated with, reduced to or reformed as legal philosophy. The approach adopted could be called theoretical 'bricolage'[4] – a bit of this, a bit of that, with each different theory or set of ideas given a hearing; never defined *ab initio* as outside the agenda of debate; not required to show its pre-validated ticket of entry into the 'province of jurisprudence' as 'an exclusive field of inquiry' (cf. Halpin, 2011: 184). The hallmark of the approach is open-minded curiosity as to what could be inspiring, what might show law in a new, perhaps surprising light.

Dennis Lloyd (1965: xvi) stated in presenting his textbook that he wrote 'as a lawyer and not as a philosopher'. Clearly he did not regard this as a fatal flaw, but it raised the issue of how the jurisprudential project should be related to the legal philosophical one. He contented himself with rejecting (as early as 1959) what he saw as excessive claims for linguistic philosophy as a route to legal enlightenment (Lloyd, 1965: xvi-xvii). As an undergraduate law student I listened to Lloyd's lectures and used the second (1965) edition of his book. His exploratory approach continued a jurisprudential tradition that was not oriented towards defending itself in modern academic disciplinary terms. As he made clear, his reference points were law (as an immensely important social, political and moral idea) and lawyers, and not the specific disciplinary orientations of any of the humanities or social sciences. The implication was that jurisprudence did not need the credentials of these disciplines to support its own validity. But, as I gradually discovered, this was certainly not the only acceptable (or even necessarily the most important) way to approach law theoretically, because law is not just something to be studied for juristic purposes. Defending a kind of bricolage jurisprudence á la Lloyd was entirely compatible with championing, for example, legal philosophy (in collaboration with moral and political philosophy) and legal sociology as powerful enterprises aimed at the theoretical study of law and legal phenomena for mainly non-juristic purposes (but which might produce much juristically valuable knowledge along the way).

'Open-minded curiosity' is not enough to justify jurisprudence. Open-mindedness and curiosity can lead in many directions and surely towards the plethora of ap-

3 I have discussed the specific value of pedagogic jurisprudence in Cotterrell, 2000.

4 On bricolage in jurisprudence, see Hull, 1997: 8-13.

proaches to legal scholarship existing today, which have often seemed to leave jurisprudence as a backwater. In part it is because of a failure to demarcate and defend jurisprudence with sufficient clarity as a project that a need was felt to replace it with an academically rigorous legal philosophy – one validated by philosophy as a profession. Despite this, many scholars have insisted on the non-equivalence of jurisprudence and legal philosophy, but usually in ways that put jurisprudence in a position of relative weakness.

For Julius Stone (1968: 16), jurisprudence is 'the lawyer's extraversion' – but how far this turning outwards should go, what it is a turning outwards from, and what is to be gained by this were not adequately explained. Stone was clear that most jurisprudential problems were different from those of philosophy (1968: 8) but not about what linked those problems into a coherent enterprise. William Twining (2002: 3), also refusing to equate jurisprudence with legal philosophy, defines it as 'the general or theoretical part of law as a discipline'. But this begs the question of the nature and boundaries of law as a discipline, and what is still needed is a unifying aim for the jurisprudential project.[5] Twining once listed at least five distinct functions that jurisprudence may perform for the discipline of law (1979: 575). These can be summarised as integrating it, facilitating its relations with other disciplines, philosophising about law's nature and functions, 'middle order' theorising about law as a practice, and exploring the intellectual history of legal scholarship.[6] On Twining's view legal philosophy is part of jurisprudence. But what the whole adds up to is a set of tasks without any very clear relationship between them; jurisprudence is thus described but not systematically justified.

A popular contemporary jurisprudence text takes a different approach: 'Jurisprudential questions, while "theoretical", are the sorts of questions about "the nature of law" to which any lawyer or judge might be expected to provide a reasonably intelligent answer ...' (Penner et al., 2002: 4). This has the virtue of linking jurisprudence not to any particular disciplinary protocols or academic field but to law as a diverse, ever-changing range of practices. It comes closest to the argument this chapter will make, but more needs to be said about the kind of contribution jurisprudence can make to these practices. And must *every* lawyer be expected to have answers to jurisprudence's questions?

By contrast, legal philosophers are often very clear. 'Jurisprudence,' writes Brian Leiter, is 'the study of philosophical problems about law' and 'distinctively *philosophical* problems ... define the discipline of jurisprudence' (Leiter, 2007: 84, 137, emphasis in original). These problems are given by a certain understanding of the nature of philosophy. Beyond this, it seems, there is no worthwhile legal theory and jurisprudents – for example, critical legal theorists, feminist legal theorists, the anti-positivist Lon Fuller, postmodernists, critical race theorists, and economic analysts of law – 'as opposed to legal philosophers', have purveyed 'so many half-baked ideas' (Leiter, 2007:

5 There is a similar problem in treating jurisprudence as, 'the epistemological basis of legal knowledge' (Tur, 1978: 158) when the *scope* of legal knowledge remains to be clarified.

6 For a broader but perhaps more diffuse listing see also Twining, 2009: 9-10.

100-101). But, as will appear, this 'philosophical view' of jurisprudence (Twining, 1979: 574) has had its costs.

The following sections of this chapter sketch characteristics of the dominant outlook (rather than the substance) of contemporary Anglo-American legal philosophy, focusing initially on its positivist core and then considering it more broadly. I argue that these characteristics disable it from standing in for jurisprudence as the *prudentia* of jurists, and have made it largely unconcerned to try to do so. One consequence has been to make the juristic value of much legal philosophy controversial, and even denied altogether in some quarters. In the legal world, it seems that the question of what legal philosophy has to offer is now rarely answered. From such sceptical views of current legal philosophy (based here mainly on a collation of critiques from within the ranks of legal philosophers themselves), the chapter goes on to ask what jurisprudence's special function might be and why this research field needs no specific justification from any of the particular academic disciplines that contribute to it.

Observing Contemporary Legal Positivism

Generalisation is risky but sometimes required to attempt to gain some overall perspective on an intellectual field, a sense of its shape and orientations, and an insight into the directions of its development. So it is necessary to try to identify here some general dominant characteristics of legal philosophy despite the variety of work it encompasses. Within it, what is often seen as its central part, around which much of the rest is organised or engages, can be called contemporary legal positivism (hereafter CLP).

This enterprise of description and analysis of the conceptual structures of law is unified most obviously by its adherents' recognition of H. L. A. Hart's *The Concept of Law* as its originating text. CLP has been said to stand 'as victorious as any research programme in post-World War II philosophy' (Leiter, 2007: 2). Its founding proposition, as formulated by John Gardner (2001: 199), is that in any legal system, 'whether a given norm is legally valid, and hence whether it forms part of the law of that system, depends on its sources, not on its merits'. This proposition is held to differentiate CLP from what it understands as opposing projects in legal philosophy associated with natural law theory. Thus, natural law thought is treated by CLP as a theoretical 'other' against which it asserts its identity. The consequence of accepting CLP's founding proposition is that conceptual inquiries about law can be conducted in a way that largely excludes any substantive moral or political concerns.

Indeed, it is tempting to see CLP as defined mainly by what it excludes from consideration. Gardner (2001: 223-4) has been explicit about this, noting that CLP's founding proposition addresses only the issue of law's *validity*; other philosophical questions about law exist beyond this but are not specific to CLP and hence not part of its unifying project of exploring the implications of its central proposition. This entails a commitment to the idea that what counts as law in any society is determined by the existence of certain social facts (Leiter, 2007: 122). Interpretation of CLP's founding proposition has produced two opposed factions, now termed 'exclusive' (or hard) and 'inclusive' (or soft) positivism: the former claiming that what determines legal validity *cannot* include purely moral criteria, the latter asserting that, while some (or many) legal systems might in reality exhibit moral criteria of validity, a legal system not relying on any such moral criteria *could* be envisaged (and, therefore, law is still analytically separable from morality). A huge literature now explores the ramifications of these and related claims. The focus of attention is thus on developing a rigorous concept of law based on a correct interpretation of CLP's founding proposition.

This chapter is not concerned with CLP's debates around these matters but only with what, from a juristic point of view, appears as their remarkable *narrowness*. While, as Gardner insists, they occupy only a part of legal philosophy, the intensity, intricacy and assumed crucial importance of arguments around them divert attention from other philosophical issues about law. Many theorists (e.g. Halpin, 2011: 200; Schauer, 2011; Priel, 2011; Dyzenhaus, 2000; Twining, 1979: 558) have noted (and regretted) the narrowing of the concerns of positivist legal theory over time from Jeremy Bentham, to John Austin, to Hart, and on to Hart's current CLP successors. Early legal positivism, treating law as 'posited' from identifiable political sources rather than produced through revelation, nature or speculative reasoning on the human condition, might be seen as providing a liberating basis for many theoretical enquiries about law's role in relation to morality and politics. But gradually, 'the needs of a detached, descriptive jurisprudence were ... relentlessly separated from the world of political theory, in which so many contestable conceptions of human nature strove endlessly with one another. This separation was not simply a dogma, open to debate, but a determination of the field of inquiry itself' (Coyle, 2013: 401-2). Tightening philosophical protocols, internalised throughout CLP, have encouraged and justified this narrowing, transmuting the enterprise of jurisprudence into a confined arena of debate, policed not by criteria of social or legal significance but by canons of technical sophistication in argument.

Legal philosophers outside the CLP camp, and some within it, have remarked on this situation. Ronald Dworkin (2006: 213) claims that CLP risks 'intellectual insularity', that it understands legal philosophy as 'distinct not only from the actual practice of law, but also from the academic study of substantive and procedural fields of law', from 'normative political philosophy' and from 'sociology of law or legal anthropology. ... It is, in short, a discipline that can be pursued on its own with neither background experience nor training in or even familiarity with any literature or research beyond its narrow world and few disciples. The analogy to scholastic theology is... tempting'.

More restrained complaints are widespread. On one view, the legal positivist tradition has produced 'exclusivity and disengagement' through its particular conceptual and definitional focus, but 'the frailty of the endeavour which rests a restrictive understanding of law on a single insight is obvious to everyone' except those pursuing it (Halpin, 2011: 200-1). The narrowing of English positivist legal philosophy has left it only 'a shrinking audience within the academy'; it fails 'to communicate its ideas to those outside its own caste' (Richard Cosgrove, quoted in Duxbury, 1997: 1996).

Anglophone legal philosophy has become a 'small, hermetic – and rather incestuous – universe' (Leiter, 2007: 2).

For some critics, the real indictment is that CLP has lost touch with the practice of law and its social and political contexts. To counter this, it is necessary to discard the idea,

> that the deepest questions confronting the doctrinal lawyer must await the 'solution' of prior philosophical problems. A different viewpoint must prevail: one must begin from the lawyer's perspective, the administration of justice at the concrete level…' (Coyle, 2013: 418).

The natural lawyer John Finnis, whose work has often been seen in the past by CLP scholars as compatible with (because distinguishable from) their projects, has recently passionately condemned Hart's CLP legacy for its complacency, blindness or narrowness of outlook, leading to its refusal to address what Finnis sees as vital and urgent political and moral issues surrounding law in contemporary society (Finnis, 2009: 180-5).

An answer to these criticisms might be that, even if they point to limitations of CLP's projects, they do not invalidate them on their own terms. At worst they might indicate the *irrelevance* of these projects as seen from certain viewpoints (see e.g. Dyzenhaus, 2000: 715). Other criticisms, however, bite at CLP projects themselves. Brian Leiter (2007: 1-2) has argued that CLP's view that philosophy requires a 'method of conceptual analysis via appeal to folk intuitions (as manifest, for example in ordinary language)' has been undermined by the 'naturalistic' revolution in anglophone philosophy from the 1960s. While CLP has recently been concerned with debates on method, these have been 'idiosyncratic and narrow' and divorced from wider debates in philosophy that fundamentally challenge the epistemic viability of conceptual analysis and of reliance on intuitions. But, in Leiter's view, CLP has usually unquestioningly assumed this viability of both matters as fundamental to its practice (Leiter, 2007: 164-75).

The kind of 'self-validating' conceptual analysis that has been central to CLP has also been challenged by Finnis on the ground, essentially, that conceptual analysis presupposes a choice (not a discovery) of concepts (such as a concept of law) and any such choice depends on the *purposes* for which concepts are sought. Hence CLP's projects of conceptual inquiry about law require an elaboration of these purposes, and therefore require the opening of CLP to matters (including moral or political matters) outside its self-imposed analytical remit (Finnis, 2001: ch. 1; Finnis, 2009: 163-6; cf. Endicott, 2001; Gardner, 2007). Efforts to go a little way towards this 'opening', while holding to CLP's fundamental tenets, seem to lead to much complexity.[7] Otherwise, CLP sometimes attracts criticism for making assumptions about the nature of law's social and political contexts (see e.g. Coyle, 2013; Twining, 1979: 564) that it does not

---

7 See e.g. Raz, 1994: 326-40 (on the place of moral reasoning in, about and through law); Dickson, 2001 (on 'indirectly evaluative' theory).

see as controversial because of its lack of concern to study these contexts in an empirical and comparative manner. The issue becomes how far CLP, accepting the validity of its narrow project, is based on firm foundations in pursuing it.

The value of CLP to any idea of jurisprudence as a broad, open inquiry is also put in doubt by criticisms of its typical modes of argument. Andrew Halpin (2011: 180-5) has discussed three ways of arranging argument that are relevant here. One is 'axiomatic disengagement' in which the acceptance of a certain theoretical approach to a defined subject-matter eventually makes meaningful communication with other theoretical approaches impossible. Another is the promotion of a particular 'insight' (such as CLP's founding proposition) so extensively that it is held actually to *define* the relevant field of inquiry; non-acceptance of the relevant insight or failure to see its full significance produces exclusion from the field of argument. The third approach, 'splitting the subject-matter', assigns opposing views to different categories of inquiry (so that they need not engage with each other). Halpin's example of this last approach is Hart's claim that his work and that of Dworkin represent entirely separate projects. What is important for the purposes of this chapter is that these three approaches (which Halpin sees as having helped to shape CLP) are all ways of *excluding argumentative engagement*, rather than encouraging the challenge of different perspectives.

An outward-looking, curious, exploratory jurisprudence would not be served by the approaches Halpin identifies, which limit 'external' engagement and exploration beyond pre-defined fields. As regards the debates that *do* take place with critics, or even sometimes 'internally' within CLP, what can be observed is their frequent intensity and aggressiveness. As one commentator notes, 'positivists and their critics have extracted innumerable technical satisfactions from their exploration of the weaknesses of each other's positions' (Coyle, 2013: 404). How far does this amount to *point-scoring* rather than constructive inquiry; to what Edward Shils (1985: 168) describes as the sharp-shooter approach of 'those who regard intellectual activity not as the extension of understanding but a game in which the prizes go for rigour and elegance of formulation and proof, and for proving the other fellow wrong'?[8] This style, often associated with certain kinds of lawyers' debates, may carry across to the kind of philosophy that finds a home in some law schools.

As Shils claims, intellectual sharp-shooting is not always the best way to understanding: 'Discoveries are not made in this way, least of all self-discoveries and the discoveries of the self in one's fellow-man' (Shils, 1985: 168). But the language of much debate around CLP does evoke the sharp-shooter image.[9] Indeed, the image has been

---

8 See also Collini, 2006: 113 (on H. L. A. Hart's philosophical environment): 'Seeing things in the form of "propositions", and then conducting a stiff philosophy tutorial on their clarity and coherence, could indeed dispose of a lot of fuzzy thinking, though it was perhaps less well adapted to doing justice to matters of deep human interest that could not without loss be formulated in a series of neat "propositions"'.

9 Describing opposing ideas as 'demolished', 'dismissed', 'happily defunct', 'ridiculous', 'absurd', 'asinine', 'preposterous', 'spectacularly wrong-headed', 'silly' and 'a joke', to take a few examples. See Kramer, 2011: 116; Leiter, 2007: 4, 20, 59, 100-1, 174; Leiter, 2004: 176; Gardner, 2001: 225.

explicitly invoked recently by one weary protagonist in a long debate around CLP's view of legality, seeing its culmination as the final showdown of a 'High Noon' encounter (Simmonds, 2011). But the irony only emphasises the destructive setting of debate.

Why Legal Philosophy is Not Jurisprudence

If contemporary anglophone legal philosophy is viewed beyond its positivist core, the problems for its jurisprudential utility appear differently. It contains a vast diversity of projects. Definitional limitations on its scope can be fixed only by reference to philosophy as its parent discipline and to some kind of concern with law as its focus. In earlier times when philosophy was less professionally compartmentalised in the academy it was easy to treat legal philosophy and jurisprudence as synonyms because both could indicate a research field unified only by a focus on speculation around law. What made problems 'philosophical' could remain a matter of little concern. In principle, nothing stopped jurists from declaring any of their general musings on law to be legal philosophy. Today, with legal philosophy's identity fixed by its relationship to philosophy as an academic field, matters are different.

This introduces a new criterion for assessing the worth of legal theoretical inquiries on the basis of whether or not they are 'philosophically interesting' (cf. Twining, 1979: 569-70). And ideas that could be of juristic interest – because relevant for a general understanding of legal practice or experience – are sometimes dismissed as 'a philosophical mess' (cf. Leiter, 2007: 60). Indeed, legal philosophical issues can, it seems, be pursued irrespective of any reference to law's actual settings. For example, on one view, 'the' concept of law can be elaborated philosophically in terms of law's 'essential' qualities whether or not these qualities exist in any particular social conditions; if the evidence of conditions reveals that the regulatory forms do not conform to the philosophical concept of law, it is not the concept that needs adjusting; the conclusion should rather be that in those conditions there is no law (see Raz, 2009a: 25, 91-2). What is philosophically essential is not governed by what contingently exists.

There are several problems here as seen from any jurisprudential viewpoint concerned with the idea (and ideal) of law as a practice of regulation to serve social needs and social values, as these are recognised in particular times and places. To philosophise about law irrespective of experience in particular times and places may be to show limited concern for juristic relevance. Legal philosophy mainly seeks universal truths rather than knowledge rooted in the particularities of social context,[10] and it is

10 See e.g. Raz, 2009b: 104, describing what he sees as 'the difference between legal philosophy and sociology of law. The latter is concerned with the contingent and with the particular, the former with the necessary and the universal.' As used by legal philosophers, however, this way of characterising the distinction implies misleadingly that sociology of law (unlike legal philosophy) is not concerned with or does not provide general legal theory. In fact, the key issue is: what is the object to be theorised? Is it law as experienced in particular kinds of society or civilization, or law as some kind of pure form detached from social context?

sometimes assumed that obtaining the latter would require 'life-consuming empirical studies' and 'a mountain of data' (Dworkin, 2006: 166-7). So, when legal philosophers refer to 'sociological' considerations they usually mean claims that can be made about the relevance of social conditions without actually studying these conditions. A famous instance is Hart's claim in *The Concept of Law* to be engaged in a project of 'descriptive sociology' (1994: vi). This means, for him, mainly speculation on how people actually use language – but without any empirical inquiry about this, any examination of its sociological significance, or any recognition of possible social variation in language use.

However, what usually insulates legal philosophy from systematical empirical inquiries is ultimately not the purported difficulty of the latter but a conviction that empirical research is uninteresting as compared with efforts to discover context-free truth or to conceptualise what is essential in law, these efforts being guided by intuitions as to what is philosophically significant, or what are reliable foundations for inquiry.

This chapter's concern is not to debate whether a philosophical search for truth, the universal or the essential in law (or in anything else) is appropriate as a philosophical project. The issue is whether it is appropriate as a *juristic project* and whether any effort at finding knowledge of the legal world that has timeless validity can be conducted without the kinds of empirical inquiries that philosophers regard as uninteresting or practically impossible. Can one speculate about timeless or essential characteristics of law without studying the variety of forms that social regulation can take, as well as the variety of social and historical contexts that influence the ways in which theoretical issues are formulated and how far these are seen as important and meaningful as juristic concerns?

If jurisprudence is understood as juristic knowledge focused on promoting the well-being of the idea of law as a socially valuable practice of regulation, this knowledge must represent regulatory practices in their time and place, reflecting the variability of socio-legal conditions. Certainly, jurisprudence, understood in this way, has no need to abolish from its range of interest broad speculations in moral and political philosophy; it can surely find much inspiration in efforts to portray values and ideals of law as capable of transcending particular cultural contexts. But these wide horizons of theory need juristically to be judged against and explicitly related to local circumstances. Any pretention to timelessness and universality needs to be discounted against empirical socio-legal study of the circumstances in which juristic tasks have to be performed.

From such a juristic outlook, theoretical resources appear as a continuum, involving different levels of generality, different scale and scope. But they are unified by an overarching project of serving the theoretical needs of juristic practice in its time and place, broadening this practice while keeping it rooted in changing experience; encouraging critical imagination in it by an open search for comparative and philosophically ambitious insights about legal doctrine and about the contexts in which it is created, interpreted, debated and applied.

Leaving aside contemporary legal positivism, the main juristic problem with those parts of the contemporary legal philosophical enterprise that are integrated with moral and political philosophy is not narrowness, but perhaps its opposite – the expansive ambition of the effort to find ultimate truth about some aspect of human experience. It might be said that many philosophical projects involve no more than working out the results of rigorous reasoning from certain accepted premises. Nevertheless, the product is often *systems* of thought – for example, theories of social justice, of liberalism as a value system, of democracy, or of the moral good – which claim or assume universal validity in relation to the matters they address. No doubt such philosophical systems are of interest for jurisprudence, but they are not normally directed to juristic purposes. This is certainly so if juristic tasks require a tempering of logic with (socio-legal) experience, a pragmatic, provisional managing of deep conflicts of values and understandings, and the pursuit of legal ideals only with awareness of law's operational limits in particular conditions.

Relations between legal philosophy and empirical socio-legal inquiry are certainly matters for debate. Leiter (2007: 4, 176), assuming a context of positivist legal philosophy, insists that philosophy must be 'continuous with empirical science', proceeding 'in tandem' with it 'as a reflective attempt at synoptic clarity about the state of empirical knowledge'; in other words, philosophy's task is to organise intellectually what empirical study reports as existing. The naturalistic critique entails that positivist descriptive legal philosophy depends for its validity on finding foundations in empirical inquiries about law. That must surely mean finding them especially in the related enterprises of comparative law and sociology of law: the former insofar as it reveals the empirical variability of law's doctrinal and institutional forms, the latter insofar as it studies legal practices, institutions and experience systematically and empirically as social phenomena. In some ways, Finnis' challenge to conceptual inquiry, noted earlier, is even more fundamental because it denies the possibility of separating CLP's projects from legal philosophy in a larger sense, integrated with moral and political philosophy. And behind everything is the problem of the role of intuitions in determining what counts as important as a starting point for inquiry. Perhaps a key to progress is to insist that intuitions be made explicit, and justified. Such a protocol would be almost guaranteed to widen the scope of intellectual discussion.

It is possible to interpret such contemporary critiques as nudging legal philosophy in the direction of a receptiveness to an indefinite range of types of knowledge about law as an idea, a set of practices and institutions, and a field of social experience: *broadening* it (into wider moral and political concerns) and *deepening* it (to assess socio-legal conditions). A legal philosophy changing in these ways would come closer to the orientation that this chapter has associated with jurisprudence. For the moment, however, these kinds of critique remain only at the edges of the contemporary anglophone legal philosophical enterprise. So, this enterprise does not provide the range of knowledge and insight to serve fully the theoretical *prudentia* of jurists. Legal philosophy's protocols divide, limit and insulate it from an outward-looking curiosity about the whole range of theoretical issues that might be raised in relation to law, and about the relevance of empirical and comparative inquiries about law seen as a matter of juristic practice and social experience, varying with time and place.

Current legal philosophy's focus is not on juristic experience in all its practical complexity, ethical ambiguity and contextual specificity, but on abstract problems defined by philosophical interest. Its dominant positivist approaches avoid or marginalise important moral and political dilemmas that surround the practice and experience of law. Its typical focus on the timeless, the universal or the necessary blinds it to social variation revealed by empirical studies of law in society and the resources of socio-legal theory. Its tendency to see its concerns as relatively independent of those of lawyers in practice and academic lawyers in general (see Gardner, 2001: 203; Leiter, 2004: 178. Cf. Coyle, 2013: 415; and Twining, 1979: 562) isolates it from many everyday juristic concerns.[11] But jurisprudence, I shall suggest, has to find its unity and purpose in its recognition of the way that these matters together make up the theoretical universe of the jurist.

Jurisprudence and Jurists

The structured character of legal philosophy today presents a striking contrast to bricolage jurisprudence represented by books such as *Lloyd's Introduction*. Lacking firm methodological commitments, this jurisprudence has collected, magpie-like, insights from anywhere they can be found – including, for example, English analytical jurisprudence, Scandinavian legal realism, many kinds of American and continental European theory, moral and political philosophy, economic analysis, Marxism, feminism, the comparative speculations of historical jurisprudence, and the legal anthropology of stateless societies. Linguistic limitations often confine jurisprudence's practical reach but no disciplinary protocols do so. And it has the freedom to draw on everything that legal philosophy has to offer, but it is a 'philosophical mess' (cf. Leiter, 2007: 60). What can unify it?

It is not enough to defend it in the way that pedagogic jurisprudence is often defended: as important for the 'liberal education' of lawyers. One might ask why lawyers need a liberal education, what that is, and why jurisprudence (rather than other subjects of study) is needed to provide it. Also, for reasons suggested earlier, it is not enough to advocate the lawyer's 'extraversion' (a close relation of the liberal legal education argument). Nor is it enough to state all the varied things jurisprudence might encompass in a checklist. Something has to hold all this together, but what that is cannot be the theoretical or methodological protocols of an academic discipline.

11 This situation might be altered if the study of legal interpretation and reasoning was more central in current legal philosophy. See Halpin, 2011: 197-8. That it is not (despite important contributions by legal philosophers) may reflect the difficulty of addressing such matters convincingly without assessing the relevance of various moral, political or other evaluative criteria that are avoided in the dominant positivist approaches to conceptual analysis. Similarly, in its dominant forms, contemporary legal philosophy has resisted studying the processes of legislation and administrative lawmaking. See Dyzenhaus, 2000: 719-21.

Jurisprudence is not an application to law of the disciplinary protocols of philosophy, sociology, economics or anthropology – to list only the most obvious contenders. Its orientation is not a *focusing down* from one or more of these disciplines to the special topic of 'law'. It has to be a *projection up* from law as practice and experience into any realms of theory that can support that practice or make sense of that experience.

It is easy to suggest how this shifts the focus of theoretical questions from a 'legal philosophical' orientation to a juristic one. For example, instead of asking abstractly, 'Is there a general obligation to obey the law?' one might ask how law can best be made fit to attract a sense of obligation from those who serve it professionally and those who appeal to it or are addressed by it as citizens. Instead of asking, 'What is the nature of law as a system of rules?', one can ask how rules operate (and should operate) in lawyers' practice and citizens' experience of law. Instead of asking, 'Does the concept of legality entail moral commitments?', one might ask what moral significance legality should be expected to have, and how that might be achieved in specific socio-legal conditions. Instead of asking generally, 'Is unjust law still law?', one might consider how far law can be just and what 'just' can mean: what should be understood in practice and in a particular time and place by the idea of law's 'flourishing', and how can such flourishing be promoted? Instead of asking how legal philosophy affects the world (e.g. whether legal positivism has promoted liberty or tyranny), one should ask jurisprudential questions: What in juristic practice has promoted quiescence in the face of tendencies to authoritarianism in particular societies and what could help to counter such tendencies?

From this perspective it is easy to see why some of the legal theory most often disparaged in legal philosophy is sometimes seen as among the most enlightening jurisprudentially. Clear examples are the work of Lon Fuller and Karl Llewellyn. Very different theorists, they were nevertheless indisputably jurists rather than philosophers, and their focus was on law as a practice and, indeed, a craft. As one writer suggests, jurisprudence for them was 'the love and pursuit of a sort of lawyer's wisdom' (Soosay, 2011: 32). For Llewellyn, its problems arise from the need for society, through its legal specialists, to fulfil what he called the 'law-jobs' – practical tasks of dispute-processing, fixing lines of authority, social co-ordination, 'smoothing friction' with 'vision and sense', and integrating all the dimensions of legal work (Llewellyn and Hoebel, 1941: 290-3; Llewellyn, 2008: 322). For Fuller (2001), these problems are about subjecting conduct to the governance of rules, involving the promotion of core social values to be expressed through the practice and in the experience of law.

What a philosophical mess all this produces! The idea of law as a craft may be *incompatible* with the idea of law as embodying any philosophically coherent system of thought. At one level, the juristic issues are about ensuring the efficiency of the tools of law for the social tasks to which it is to be directed, understanding the technical character and limits of those tools; at another the issues are about aspirations to elaborate and promote ultimate social values through law, and, indeed, to understand and assess the practice and experience of law in terms of those values. So, jurisprudence is concerned with asking about the juristic significance and meaning of such values. In one aspect, therefore, it points towards a need to clarify the nature of legal ideas as lawyers (and non-lawyers) understand these; in another it points towards exploring what the philosopher F. S. C. Northrop (1959) called the complexity of legal and ethical experience (a matter for which both philosophy and the social sciences are needed). In yet another aspect it involves exploring how juristic responsibilities relate to basic values (such as justice and security) associated with law, and to the prevailing ideologies of the society in which the jurist works (Cotterrell, 2013).

The essential point is that, however wide these jurisprudential inquiries become, they start from and must relate back to conditions of legal practice and experience in their particular time and place. This is why jurisprudence is unlikely to become a fully cross-cultural academic discipline, or a pursuit of universal knowledge. For that to happen, juristic experience would itself have to become uniform – perhaps in some future era of genuinely global law. Juristic practice would have to become a universal enterprise, crossing all national and cultural borders. How far it already has some limited characteristics of this universality depends on how its nature is understood. Perhaps it makes sense to distinguish a role for the jurist distinct from other legally-focused roles. The jurist's role might be seen as entailing a wider vision than that which many practising lawyers require for their everyday work, a longer and broader focus than that typically needed by legislators and law reformers, and a less case-focused, more systematic perspective than that of most judges; so, perhaps it might be possible to suggest elements of a flexible, context-sensitive juristic idea of law that can cross frontiers (Cotterrell, 2013). Yet any juristic perspective focused on such an idea needs to be rooted in narrower professional (lawyers', legislators', judges', etc.) and popular (citizens') perspectives on law.

The broader the jurist's vision the more universal the knowledge required to support it; and so, the more comprehensive the reach of jurisprudence should be. Its theoretical bricolage, its package of insights selected for their potential juristic relevance, can be unified only by the particular vision of the juristic role that the package supports. But the ideal of wide-ranging intellectual curiosity, which may be jurisprudence's most attractive feature, should surely be encouraged and extended. By that means it might help to promote a more universalistic – or at least more broadly comparative – understanding of the juristic role without denying its grounding in specific socio-legal contexts.

The aim of this chapter has been, partly, to celebrate the general idea of bricolage jurisprudence. Yet this tradition of jurisprudence has value only if its justifications and purposes are fully elaborated. This is rarely done in the pedagogic contexts where bricolage jurisprudence finds its main audiences. I have sought to make a case that jurisprudence is intellectually justified not through any validation from the methods and theories of any distinct contemporary academic discipline but by its potential for informing the *prudentia* of the jurist, centred on the craft-skills (and, one might hope, wisdom) involved in making sense of the entire complexity of law as ideal, practice and experience in its time and place. The nature of this juristic enterprise surely needs further clarification and it should be the explicit focus and unifying rationale of pedagogic jurisprudence today.

References

Coleman, J. and Shapiro, S. (eds), *Oxford Handbook of Jurisprudence and Philosophy of Law* (Oxford: Oxford University Press, 2002).

Collini, S., "A Life of H.L.A. Hart: The Nightmare and the Noble Dream", *Modern Law Review* 2006 69(1), 108-14.

Cotterrell, R., "Pandora's Box: Jurisprudence in Legal Education", *International Journal of the Legal Profession* 2000 7(3), 179-87.

Cotterrell, R., "The Role of the Jurist: Reflections around Radbruch", *Ratio Juris* 2013 26(4), 510-22.

Coyle, S., "Legality and the Liberal Order", *Modern Law Review* 2013 76(2), 401-18.

Dickson, J., *Evaluation and Legal Theory* (Oxford: Hart, 2001).

Duxbury, N., "The Narrowing of English Jurisprudence", *Michigan Law Review* 1997 95(6), 1990-2004.

Dworkin, R., *Justice in Robes* (Cambridge, MA: Harvard University Press, 2006).

Dyzenhaus, D., "Positivism's Stagnant Research Programme", *Oxford Journal of Legal Studies* 2000 20(4), 703-22.

Endicott, T. A. O., "How to Speak the Truth", *American Journal of Jurisprudence* 2001 46, 229-48.

Finnis, J., *Natural Law and Natural Rights* (Oxford: Clarendon, 2001).

Finnis, J., "H. L. A. Hart: A Twentieth-Century Oxford Political Philosopher: Reflections by a Former Student and Colleague", *American Journal of Jurisprudence* 2009 54, 161-85.

Fuller, L. L., *The Principles of Social Order: Selected Essays* (2nd edn) (Oxford: Hart, 2001).

Freeman, M. D. A., *The Legal Structure* (London: Longmans, 1974).

Gardner, J., "Legal Positivism: 5½ Myths", *American Journal of Jurisprudence* 2001 46, 199-227.

Gardner, J., "Nearly Natural Law", *American Journal of Jurisprudence* 2007 52, 1-23.

Halpin, A., "Austin's Methodology: His Bequest to Jurisprudence?", *Cambridge Law Journal* 2011 70(1), 175-202.

Hart, H. L. A., *The Concept of Law* (2nd edn) (Oxford: Oxford University Press, 1994).

Hull, N. E. H., *Roscoe Pound and Karl Llewellyn: Searching for an American Jurisprudence* (Chicago: University of Chicago Press, 1997).

Kelsen, H., *Pure Theory of Law* (Gloucester, Mass: Peter Smith, 1989).

Kramer, M. H., "For the Record: A Final Reply to N. E. Simmonds", *American Journal of Jurisprudence* 2011 56, 115-33.

Leiter, B., "The End of Empire: Dworkin and Jurisprudence in the 21st Century", *Rutgers Law Journal* 2004 36(1), 165-81.

Leiter, B., *Naturalizing Jurisprudence: Essays on American Legal Realism and Naturalism in Legal Philosophy* (Oxford: Oxford University Press, 2007).

Llewellyn, K. N., *Jurisprudence: Realism in Theory and Practice* (New Brunswick, NJ: Transaction, 2008).

Llewellyn, K. N. and Hoebel, E. A., *The Cheyenne Way: Conflict and Case Law in Primitive Jurisprudence* (Norman, OK: University of Oklahoma Press, 1941).

Lloyd, D., *Introduction to Jurisprudence with Selected Texts* (2nd edn) (London: Stevens and Sons, 1965).

Northrop, F. S. C., *The Complexity of Legal and Ethical Experience* (Boston: Little, Brown, 1959).

Penner, J., Schiff, D. and Nobles, R. (eds), *Jurisprudence and Legal Theory: Commentary and Materials* (Oxford: Oxford University Press, 2002).

Priel, D., *Towards Classical Legal Positivism*. Osgoode CLPE Research Paper No. 20/2011. Available at SSRN: http://ssrn.com/abstract=1886517 or http://dx.doi.org/10.2139/ssrn.1886517.

Raz, J., *Ethics in the Public Domain: Essays in the Morality of Law and Politics* (Oxford: Clarendon, 1994).

Raz, J., *Between Authority and Interpretation: On the Theory of Law and Practical Reason* (Oxford: Oxford University Press, 2009a)

Raz, J., *The Authority of Law: Essays on Law and Morality* (2nd edn) (Oxford: Oxford University Press, 2009b).

Schauer, F., "Positivism before Hart", *Canadian Journal of Law and Jurisprudence* 2011 24(2), 455-71.

Shils, E., "On the Eve: A Prospect in Retrospect", in M. Bulmer (ed), Essays *on the History of British Sociological Research* (Cambridge: Cambridge University Press, 1985).

Simmonds, N. E., "Kramer's High Noon", *American Journal of Jurisprudence* 2011 56, 135-50.

Soosay, S., "Rediscovering Fuller and Llewellyn: Law as Custom and Process", in M. Del Mar (ed), *New Waves in Philosophy of Law* (London: Palgrave Macmillan, 2011).

Stone, J., *Legal System and Lawyers' Reasonings* (Sydney: Maitland Publications, 1968).

Tur, R. H. S., "What is Jurisprudence?", *Philosophical Quarterly* 1978 28(2), 149-61.

Twining, W., "Academic Law and Legal Philosophy: The Significance of Herbert Hart", *Law Quarterly Review* 1979 95(4), 557-80.

Twining, W., *The Great Juristic Bazaar: Jurists' Texts and Lawyers' Stories* (Aldershot: Dartmouth, 2002).

Twining, W., *General Jurisprudence: Understanding Law from a Global Perspective* (Cambridge: Cambridge University Press, 2009).

Laws, Values, Cultures

John Eekelaar
University of Oxford, UK

Over many years Michael Freeman has been the most famous advocate of children's rights the academic legal community in this country has produced. His influence in that area has been immense. However (and this is also well known) his interests, and influence, go well beyond that important topic. One of them is the relationship between moral principles (in which I include rights) and cultural practice. I do not know, but it could be that this was a natural consequence of his interest in children's rights, because the very notion that children have rights immediately confronts social practice, which often, perhaps usually, fails to recognise such rights. The problem is compounded when the idea of children's rights is 'internationalised' and forms part of international human rights discourse. How can one justify holding communities to obligations regarding their behaviour towards their children which are inconsistent with their own beliefs?

It is probably rash of me to attempt to summarise what I believe may be Michael's position in these matters, but I have to try, at least in order to provide a baseline against which I can measure my own thoughts about them. In 1997 Michael (Freeman, 1997) made it very clear that he rejected 'relativism' of the kind that holds that values are synonymous with the social practices of groups, so that there is no standpoint outside such practices according to which they could be evaluated. As he put it then: 'The argument for any practice must be more than that the practice exists.'[1] He re-iterated this position in 2011 (Freeman, 2011: 16), approving the statement of Philip Alston that culture must not be given the status of a 'meta-norm' that 'trumps rights'.

But Michael equally rejected what he called 'monism', a view which holds that a single set of values applies, or should apply, because they would be accepted by all reasonable people, everywhere. It is sometimes a little difficult to know what is being rejected here. If it is an empirical claim that there are at least some values that are held by everyone, or perhaps by most people in all communities, then it is of course subject (at least in theory) to empirical proof. It seems that, even if it were empirically true, it would cover only a narrow range of activities (Michael gives the example

1 Freeman (1997: 139). See also Freeman (1998: 297); Freeman (2007: 26).

A. Diduck, N. Peleg, H. Reece (eds.), Law in Society: Reflections on Children, Family, Culture and Philosophy
 ISBN 978-90-04-26148-8. pp. 31-44.

of the wrongness of executing people for crimes committed while they are children: Freeman (2011: 17) and he would want children's rights to extend beyond that: for example, to safeguard against female genital mutilation and corporal punishment. But there is an even stronger reason to reject such an empirical claim, and that is that if one were to anchor moral values in empirical behaviour one would be conceding the basis of relativism in holding that values are only to be found in what people actually do, and the only universal values (if any) are found in what people universally do (if anything falls under this description). There may be good grounds for rejecting this, but it is probably not what 'monists' believe.

The claim being rejected is, therefore, I think one that holds that there are universal values which *should* bind everyone, irrespective of their actual beliefs or practices. Whether there are such values has long been debated in connection with human rights and Michael has himself contributed to that debate. In reviewing theories of human rights in 1994 (Freeman, 1994), Michael concluded that there were in fact no uncontested philosophical foundations for human rights. That was certainly true then, and is also true now. So how could there be universal values that everyone should follow? If there were, they would be grounded in one or other of these contested bases (I am assuming that the bases do not always yield the same concrete rights), so that would mean that one perspective would be foisted on everyone else, which would be difficult to defend, especially against those on whom they were foisted.

Yet Michael, like most of us, wants to uphold human rights, especially children's rights. The solution is found in 'pluralism'. In Michael's account, this appears to *accept* that the values people have derive from their socialisation, so that, for example, a belief in children's rights reflects the values of a 'community of judgment' (Freeman, 2002: 346). I am a little uncertain what a 'community of judgment' is, because it could simply be a description of a gathering of individuals who happen to share the same values, so that one could not say that the values emerged from the community, but rather that the community arose from the shared values. In fact, Michael's later discussion, when he asks, 'what is meant by community?', suggests a different meaning. For example, he considers whether the community may be the whole world, or the 'west' (Freeman, 2002: 348). From the context, it seems that communities are seen in the usual sense as referring to social or political groups. Therefore Michael argues that the way to achieve greater universalisation of 'community-grown' values, like children's rights, is through dialogue between communities, seriously engaging 'local perspectives', and in awareness of the shortcomings of one's own community (he here refers to UK treatment of refugee children) (Freeman, 2002: 351).

The distinguished writer on human rights, Abdullah An-Naim (1994), has also urged 'cross-cultural dialogue' as a means by which religious or customary laws might adapt to human rights norms. Of course such dialogue is valuable and should be encouraged. However, it is surely necessary to go further than merely to encourage debate. What should the terms of the debate be? Would each party simply describe their own culture to the others in the hope that, with greater knowledge and perhaps certain misperceptions dispelled, the others might begin to see each party's culture in more favourable terms? Is it to be an attempt to find common ground, so that ideas or practices that seemed foreign appear now to be closer? There is no doubt that these are important objectives and could be valuable outcomes. But it is not clear how far they would go in bringing about cultural change and, in particular, in extending acceptance of the 'rights' which Michael, and others, hold to be important.

I would suggest that, to obtain a fuller understanding of what may be involved in doing that, we should consider another point which Michael makes in these articles I have cited. He asks why some people, 'judge in opposition to their communities' (Freeman, 2002: 348)? I do not think Michael quite answers this important question, though he observes that such rebellions (if I may call them that) have 'long been the route to progress' (Freeman, 2002: 349). I think it is worth reflecting a little about such 'rebellions'. At the risk of over-generalisation (which I am prepared to take) I think they have often, dare I say even always, arisen from bringing into wider consciousness the fact that some practice, or community characteristic, is causing harm to individual human beings. These individuals may be many (slaves, women, children), or relatively few (members of minority groups) and the harms various, but the point is that a practice held to be morally justified as being one of the defining characteristics of a community is now undermined by a counterclaim based on a different moral basis: the well-being of individual people. The meaning and assessment of 'well-being' is discussed later.

The 'debate' in the 1960s between Herbert Hart and Patrick Devlin over the criminalisation of homosexuality, which the generation represented by Michael and myself confronted early in our careers, can be considered a classic case of this juxtaposition of 'moralities' and, in some way, stands for countless other cases of the emergence of an internal judgment against a community. Lord Devlin summed up his argument against the recommendation of the Wolfenden Report that homosexual acts in private should no longer be criminal offences in this way (Devlin, 1965: 13):

> Societies disintegrate from within more frequently than they are broken up by external pressures. There is disintegration when no common morality is observed and history shows that the loosening of moral bonds is often the first stage of disintegration, so that society is justified in taking the same steps to preserve its moral code as it does to preserve its government ... the suppression of vice is as much the law's business as the suppression of subversive activities.

Hart (1963: 21-22), on the other hand, focused on the effects of punishing individuals for such behaviour, and the suffering such punishment, or its threat, caused. Whether or how that could be justified is the basis of what he called the 'critical' morality by which a society's actual morality should be scrutinised. It is not my purpose to revive the extensive discussions about the merits of these positions: such as whether Devlin was simply putting the dilemma of the democratic legislature and the many nuances of the idea of 'harm' (see Cane, 2006). Rather, I would draw attention to the *structure* of the arguments used. Devlin puts the character of 'society' as a whole at the centre of his argument. I would call this a 'societal argument'. Hart, however, focuses on the well-being of individuals. Of course you could say that the well-being of individuals is implicated in Devlin's proposition. But the nature of that well-being is not articulated, let alone critically examined. The terms of his argument are all about the nature of the community.

This structure of debate on social issues recurs constantly. A typical example occurred when the former Archbishop of Canterbury, Lord Carey, proclaimed to a rally associated with the Conservative Party Conference in 2012, in connection with government proposals to allow 'gay marriage': 'Why does it feel to us that our cultural homeland and identity is being plundered?'[2] This clearly refers to the character and shape of a society, which he is defending against claims that they damage certain individual interests. Many of the arguments against the introduction of gay marriage had this structure (see Eekelaar, 2014). I do not suggest that the character and shape of a society are not important matters. But I do suggest that they cannot reasonably be seen as ends in themselves, to be sustained for no other reason than that they are there. Or, at least, if that position were to be maintained, any form of critique of the society from within would be impossible. There would be impasse: debate would be futile. If meaningful communication is to occur, there must at least be readiness to measure the *value* of the character and shape of the society and this can only be done by reference to how they affect the well-being of actual individuals.

People may, of course, differ over how that measuring is done, and over its results. For example, in a discussion on infant life preservation legislation in the National Association for the Promotion of Social Science in 1874, one Whateley Cooke Taylor made it very clear how he weighed individual well-being against the shape and character of society when he said:

> I would rather see an even higher rate of infant mortality prevailing than has ever yet been proved against the factory district or elsewhere ... than intrude one iota further on the sanctity of the domestic hearth and the decent seclusion of private life. That unit, the family, is the unit upon which a Constitutional government has been raised which is the admiration and envy of mankind.[3]

I am sure we can all think of many other examples, both historical and contemporary, from the male Victorian judges proclaiming that a child's welfare, indeed, the family's welfare, demanded maintenance of the authority of the husband, to the shooting of a schoolgirl by the Taliban in the cause of maintaining a social structure that denies women education. But without being prepared to view the social structure against its effects on individual well-being, 'progress', as Michael may have put it, would not be possible.

Now it seems to me that exactly the same considerations apply with regard to dialogue between communities. There is no point simply comparing the character and

---

2 *The Independent*, 9 October 2012.

3 *Transactions of the National Association for the Promotion of Social Science* (1874: 574-5) cited in Pinchbeck and Hewitt (1973: 359).

shape of communities. The terms of the dialogue must direct attention to the effects of such character and shape on the well-being of individuals within them.

This is a complex matter and I will revert to it, but I need first to look at a related matter, because that will allow me to reach a more complete conclusion.

The State and Minority Legal Orders

In a collection of essays on the subject of diversity and the law edited by Mavis Maclean and myself, I summarised strategies that might guide a state (I was thinking, of course, of the United Kingdom) in how its legal system could best respond to the fact that there were a number of communities within it which had their own 'legal orders' covering matters of family law (Eekelaar, 2013). I had developed these typologies from an analysis of the historical interaction between the law and families in England and Wales (Eekelaar, 2010; Eekelaar, 2012), and emphasised that these were not meant as 'socio-legal descriptions of any particular historic or contemporary system, and that any real system is likely to reflect features from each of them'.

One strategy followed the model of those jurisdictions that attached a 'personal' law to members of specific religious or community groups, enforceable by institutions controlled by the group; another was for the state to decline to give any recognition to the group's separate norms, but itself to prescribe and enforce the norms to operate within the group, and a third was to allow group members full use of their norms and institutions and to accord legal consequences to actions taken accordingly but only in so far as they corresponded with what I called the 'general law' of the state. So a marriage entered into according to a group's practices could be recognised, but it had to comply with the state's general norms regarding marriage and the legally recognised consequences would be those of the general law. Agreements and transfers of property according to the minority orders' norms would be given legal effect insofar as they complied with the general law. This would not, of course, prevent the minority from applying the consequences of its own norms to the marriage.

My preference was for the third strategy. The second was dismissed as potentially leading to totalitarian structures, though more benign versions would see the state seeking to apply the law of minority orders through its own institutions. While there could be attraction in this approach, I worried that giving state institutions such jurisdiction could raise many practical problems, for example, in selection of judicial personnel, which could undermine its legitimacy in the eyes of community members, and make culturally insensitive decisions. The first strategy would also raise practical problems regarding which community authorities were to be accorded the authorised status; there was a danger of great complexity. In the modern world, the nation-state assumes obligations towards all citizens (and indeed others) within its jurisdiction and the state would have difficulty in ensuring that it was maintaining its obligations to ensure human rights standards were applied to all its citizens. While people would not necessarily be permanently locked into their personal law, it seemed that such a strategy would make it difficult for members to move outside that regime should they wish to.

I called the third strategy 'cultural voluntarism' because it was based on the use of minority norms by group members on a voluntary basis. Since it recognises the importance of such use as a matter of self-identity, such use would not be forbidden, indeed it would be respected and encouraged, unless serious legal breaches (such as child protection issues) were involved. They could have legally recognised consequences if consistent with the general law. The strategy has been endorsed and developed by Maleiha Malik (2012) in a British Academy Policy Report which emphasises its pragmatic nature. Thus policy would decide, on a case by case basis, whether some minority practices should be forbidden (this is called 'severance') and others could be incorporated within state norms (a form of 'mainstreaming'). The decision by Baker J.[4] to give effect to an agreement reached through non-binding arbitration by a Beth Din (which he had encouraged the parties to undertake having been satisfied that it operated within accepted principles of English law) is a perfect illustration of this strategy.

Of course the merits of such a strategy are open to debate. Although I used the models as Weberian 'ideal-types' from which I suggested certain implications may be drawn, the process can properly be used as a springboard for further discussion about the strength or otherwise of those implications and the possible advantages of other approaches. In the same collection of essays, Prakash Shah did this, taking issue, for example, with the concerns I expressed about 'personal law' systems (Shah, 2013). In particular, he wrote that I presented an inaccurate version of the Ottomon 'millet' system, saying that there was cross-over of norms between the various jurisdictions and that individuals, too, could move between them. Shah does not believe that non-homogeneity within minority orders should be a problem, and wonders why human rights norms, 'based as they are on European Christian and liberal tradition', should 'out-trump' other community traditions. There are various other criticisms, but the general thrust seems to be that the models are not grounded in socio-legal reality so most, or even all, of the concerns I mentioned would not be realised.

Evidence of the kind mentioned by Shah is important in assessing how various strategies might work out if applied in this jurisdiction, and it is possible that I was unduly concerned on some aspects. This can all be the topic of useful debate involving assessment of evidence and exercise of judgment based on that evidence about the effects of particular institutional changes. But there is another aspect of Shah's response which I need to confront directly, and it brings me back to the issues raised at the beginning of this paper.

Liberal Imperialism?

The fundamental objection Shah seems to have with my paper, and which brought forth withering condemnation, is set out in these terms (Shah, 2013: 49):

---

4 *AI v. MT* [2013] EWHC 100.

> Eekelaar presumes, without saying so openly, that his audience accepts a liberal perspective, and that the minority subjects about whom he speaks are amenable to their legal issues being confined to that liberal ethical framework, even if they may not share it. This lack of an explicit acknowledgment implies that liberal values are above contestation and self-evidently universal; as such we are not required to assess their reasonableness in plural contexts. Still less, one assumes, should those liberal values be brought into juxtaposition with the ethics found in other, specifically non-Western, traditions, a position which Parekh (2011) has recently argued to be typical of the failure of liberals to engage in intercultural dialogue.
>
> Eekelaar accepts the liberal legal order the way it is. It seems also that we are asked to accept that there are no real problems in subsuming a variety of different communities under an overarching legal order with its liberal presuppositions, and that we need not problematise the potentially violent, oppressive, or absurd consequences of applying such a framework to non-liberal communities, that is, communities that do not operate from within a liberal ethical framework.

Shah twists the knife in a footnote (Shah, 2013: 49) that says:

> This sort of non-questioning in light of globalising and pluralistic realities, and a consequent denial of the intellectual heritage of others, switches off many brilliant students, acts as a block to deeper investigation and is thus a massive blow to intellectual life.

This is indeed a massive charge to make on the basis of a short paper that in fact seeks to support people who follow their cultural and religious traditions but in such a way that is intended to promote cultural fluidity, so that people have maximum opportunity to move within and between cultures. If this can have 'potentially violent, oppressive and absurd' consequences, and is a 'massive blow to intellectual life', I do indeed need to re-examine and, if necessary, retract the entire intellectual foundation on which it rests.

What, then, is that foundation? I think it comprises two parts. One is to do with constitutional structure, and the other, more fundamental, is philosophical. The constitutional point has nothing to do with liberalism, but is possibly based on democratic principle as manifested in the modern nation state. It is that whenever the state exercises, or authorises the exercise of, power within a territory subject to its jurisdiction, it is ultimately responsible for the way that power is exercised. It exercises that responsibility through its laws, or executive acts lawfully carried out. The state is answerable to the electorate in the way it discharges that responsibility.

I appreciate that this puts the matter starkly, and there are difficulties in how the electorate in fact holds the state to account, and that there are external constraints, including commitment to international instruments, that affect the state's scope for action. But the basic structure holds good. This can be illustrated by the following thought experiment. Suppose that French law applied not just in France, but was recognised by British courts as governing all transactions between British citizens of French origin taking place in Britain. The transaction need have no connection with

France. Suppose further that French lawmakers were entirely free of any influence from British institutions. Suppose this law was enforced in Britain either by legally authorised tribunals or within British courts by specialist French judges. No matter how virtuous the French norms might be, they would be outside the control of the British state. In my view, to accept such a system would be an abdication of responsibility by the state for its citizens. That would not follow if the law gave effect to transactions its citizens chose to make under this French law if doing this complied with the general law, as proposed by cultural voluntarism. Some might disagree with this position. There might be some intermediate positions which reach a reasonable balance. There could be debate. But surely not on the grounds that 'potentially violent, oppressive and absurd' consequences are at stake.

The more contentious issues probably lie at the philosophical level. There is, writes Shah, a 'lack of an explicit acknowledgment' on my part that my audience 'accepts a liberal perspective' and that this 'implies that liberal values are above contestation and self-evidently universal'. The reason there is no such acknowledgment is that I do *not* suppose that everyone reading my chapter accepts a liberal perspective, or that liberal values are beyond contestation. Indeed, it would be absurd to do so. I do, however, advance a *position*, and naturally hope that I may persuade others of it. But so, of course, does Shah, and anyone else engaged in debate. I am not even sure that my position is properly described as 'liberal'. I have preferred to say, and did so in my chapter, that at most, it is based on a commitment to an 'open society'; that is, one 'in which people believe they can make their own decisions for themselves, freed from the belief that their futures are determined by the past' and where 'the claims of the group, or its dominant members, to special knowledge about facts or that they have access to a more highly valued morality will never be allowed to go unchallenged' (see Eekelaar, 2007: 8-9). I understand that there will be some who cannot accept this, at least, not openly, and constructive debate could be very difficult as a consequence. However, if such debate is to be had at all we must at least believe that its participants are willing to accept at least some level of evaluation of their own community practices and capacity to adapt or change.

I therefore think, and hope, that Shah's real objection is not that I believe that no one would, or could, contest my position, but is to the position itself. I think this must be so in view of the terms in which he characterises that position, and his objection to it. Shah states several times that what he calls this liberal position is 'Eurocentric', and that it 'was brought forth within Western culture's now-occluded Christian religious structures' (Shah, 2012: 50); that 'human rights and liberal values emanate from the Western Christian religious tradition', and he describes human rights as being 'based as they are on the European Christian and liberal tradition' (Shah, 2012: 52). The objection is that this fails to engage with 'non-liberal communities, that is, communities that do not operate from within a liberal ethical framework' (Shah, 2012: 49).

This constructs my position in purely 'cultural' terms, associated with Christianity or, at least, 'western' Christianity. As such, Shah implies, it is foreign to non-Christian, non-western communities, whose members, presumably, because of their religion or culture, cannot be expected to find anything in it of any merit whatsoever. To do so would possibly be tantamount to accepting some form of imperialist domination.

I hope this is not a caricature of the objection and to misrepresent Shah in the same way as I believe he mistakenly criticises me. But why else make the cultural and religious sources of the position relevant, let alone so important? The unfortunate consequence is that constructive dialogue becomes almost impossible because it is conceived of as a confrontation between cultures, rather than, as it might have been, as a debate about ideas which can have value in any cultural context.

A Critical Morality

I revert here to the question posed by Michael to which I referred earlier: why do some people 'judge in opposition to their communities?' (Freeman, 2002: 348). It is certainly true that western societies have experienced strong traditions of dissent. This is one difficulty with Shah's identification of what he calls 'liberalism' with the western Christian tradition. I have no wish to enter the complexities of the history of ideas, but I think many of the thinkers of what Jonathan Israel (2010) called the 'radical enlightenment', which he described as bringing about a 'revolution of the mind', and from whom much so-called 'liberal' thinking originates, would be astonished to be described as drawing on religious tradition, as indeed would the fathers of the church at that time against whom they directed their intellectual fire-power (see Pagden, 2013: ch. 3). And in view of the history of imperialism, various nationalisms and communism, it is hard to attribute a dominant role to anything like 'liberalism' during the last two centuries of European history. Indeed, there is a vigorous debate today not only between the churches and liberal secularists, but also between people who are attracted to communitarian ways of thinking and those of a more individualist persuasion.

But Shah might reply that it is the very presence of this conflict between what we may call for simplicity 'liberal' and 'non-liberal' ideas that is a hallmark of western culture, as opposed to others, where 'non-liberal' ideas are more established or, perhaps, where there is a more stable synthesis between these ideas. I do not claim sufficient knowledge about world societies to assess whether this would be an accurate characterisation of non-western societies. But surely Shah is not claiming that non-western societies are or should be free from internal debate, that their social arrangements are everywhere uncontested, and that they should not develop a critical morality. In fact, Amartya Sen, who has drawn inspiration from both eastern and western philosophies, in discussing the role of ideas about freedom in western and 'Asian' societies, has frequently stressed that 'there is very little empirical basis' for holding that belief in individual liberty is a significant classificatory device separating the 'west' from the 'east' (Sen, 2009: 228).

Universal Rights?

Martha Nussbaum has recently rightly emphasised the extent to which identification with a culture or religion can be of the first importance to many, perhaps most, people, and this is why individual rights to make such identification are so important (Nussbaum, 2012). But a fuller picture would need to recognise that cultures and religions are also social power structures. To defend a culture or group is very often to defend a dominant section within it. In my view, the language of rights is the common rhetoric of a critical morality and the way in which claims for individual well-being are made against power structures within communities. I do not say that that is *all* that the language of rights covers. Communities, even nations, claim rights, usually against other communities or nations, but also to exercise power over their individual members. But if they have power, the claim of a right to exercise it, though important, is less significant than the claim to a right by someone without power – for to do that is to seek to limit the power of those who have it, or even to re-distribute such power.

But how can we say that rights are universal? In grappling with theories of human rights in 1994, Michael rejected essentialist theories, and drew on Ronald Dworkin in concluding that 'the deep foundations of human rights are found in the principles of equal concern and respect for human persons' (Freeman, 1994: 514). I have also rejected essentialist theories of human rights (the most recent being that of James Griffin (2009)), and argued that the basis of human rights is social recognition of actual or potential claims individuals make to outcomes reflecting their own evaluation of their well-being to which they believe they are entitled simply because they are human (with the important consequence that *all* humans must be similarly entitled) (Eekelaar, 2011). This looks as if this is giving priority to individual autonomy, about which Farrah Ahmed has recently written so well (Ahmed, 2010; Ahmed, 2012), and may be another reason why Shah might have thought I was attempting to create a 'liberal' hegemony. However, I am not sure that it is the same thing as autonomy because individuals may see their well-being as being advanced by having certain restrictions on their autonomy, whereas one could hardly see one's autonomy being advanced by restricting it. It is closer to what Amartya Sen (2009) calls the 'capability approach', according to which the yardstick for assessment is judged 'by a person's capability to do things he or she has reason to value'. That is essentially a measure of well-being. Sen (2009: 244) adds that 'capabilities are seen primarily as attributes of people, not of collectivities, such as communities'. That does not, however, ignore the significance of social influences on individuals.

Paying attention to such claims does not, of course, mean that they should all be realised. Many matters are relevant to deciding whether they should be realised, including the moral or cultural system in which they are made, and their weight (which refers to the significance of the matter to the claimant, since well-being is primarily to be assessed according to the viewpoint of the individual concerned).[5] Sen (2009:

5 I discuss this in Eekelaar (2007: especially at 133-140, 148-155; 177-178). For a more detailed consideration of human rights, see Eekelaar (2011).

232) writes of the 'capability approach' that, while it 'does point to the central relevance of the inequality of capabilities in the assessment of social disparities, it does not, on its own, propose any specific formula for policy decisions'. The same is true with respect to consideration of claims of rights. These are matters on which there can be dialogue and discussion, both within and across cultures. But such dialogue and discussion can only usefully proceed if it is accepted that the matters under discussion are individuals' assessments of their own well-being, their significance to the individuals concerned, and how they are to be weighed against the interests of other members of the community (often those in positions of power) and the nature of the community itself.

How these matters are balanced can be very difficult, but these difficulties are found in whatever culture they are discussed. Different cultures will reach different conclusions. A culture, and even the individuals within it, may perceive a practice thought to be harmful in a different society to be harmful to no one. It is, after all, only natural for people to believe that their social practices benefit members of the society and therefore to dismiss their questioning with scant examination. What is important is to allow serious discussion of the bases and strength of these beliefs. Do we really know what individuals think about the practices that affect them and what their consequences are? What are the constraints upon ascertaining these matters? To say that cultural practice prevails without any consideration of its effects cannot be accepted if dialogue is to take place. It is equivalent to shutting down such discussion.

It may be that the way I expressed this position in my chapter is the underlying reason for the hostility of Shah's response. In discussing whether a person's right to cultural identity implies a right to the perpetuation of a cultural group, I wrote (2013: 27-29) that, while culture is important to individual well-being and individuals have rights to manifest religious beliefs and engage in their culture, nevertheless '(and the distinction is important) none of that demands that any *particular* culture and belief system is *entitled, as of right, to continue* in perpetuity.' As regards cultural voluntarism, I observed (Eekelaar, 2013: 30):

> While it upholds the right of individuals to practise their culture, and should not attempt to undermine a culture through denigration or humiliation of its members, whether it supports a culture may depend on contingent judgements of its value: it need not consider all of them as being worth promoting or beyond criticism. It is legitimate (indeed important) for the state to encourage openness and toleration within the community, but that does not require it to sustain cultural practices into the future for no reason other than that people practise them today or to defer to attempts by contemporaries to compel subsequent generations to act in the same way as they do.

I concluded by observing that throughout history cultures, which seemed to their members indispensable and indestructible, have evolved, adapted and frequently disappeared. Their successors seemed none the worse, creating new cultures in their turn. This can be unsettling, but it is both true and important to remember, otherwise we are in danger of becoming so enamoured of the way we do things now that we fail to imagine that future generations will do things very differently, and try to obstruct these processes of change for no reason other than that they involve change to the way things are presently organised. This may have elicited Shah's comment that 'it looks as though Eekelaar regards culture as not worth defending' (Shah, 2012: 58). I do not think that can be reasonably spelt out from what I wrote. However, I did strongly express the view, as I have done before,[6] that I believe that the value of any community, or community practice, is contingent on their effect on the well-being of the community's constituent members, and that a community does not, or should not, have a right to perpetuate itself simply because it now exists.

Conclusion

Where does all this leave us with regard to the issues raised by Michael that I described at the beginning of this paper? As so often, I find myself coming to very similar conclusions to those he reaches, though our routes may be a little different. Neither of us accepts relativism, or believes that culture should be afforded a status that prevails over rights. In spite of Shah's strictures, I do not believe, any more than Michael does, that culture is not important, nor that 'western' cultural values are held universally, or should be imposed universally. But here I would develop the position from that which I understand Michael to have advanced. I would argue that the process of evaluating cultural practices by reference to individual well-being, as described above, should not be identified as a 'western cultural practice'. It may well have occurred in the west, often fitfully and usually against strong opposition, but I find it hard to believe that it cannot have occurred in other societies. In any case, it has been used *as a critique of* western cultural practice, and is therefore available for use as a critique of all cultural practices. I go further, and suggest that the cross-cultural dialogue that Michael and others have called for cannot usefully occur on any other basis.

In the case of children's rights, it means that the dialogue will focus on the effects of cultural and other practices on children's well-being. Of course it is natural that people will be inclined to think that their social arrangements enhance, or even define, the well-being of their children. However, it cannot be assumed that such arrangements will benefit all children in all circumstances. Such arrangements should always be subject to scrutiny, paying careful (but not conclusive) attention to children's perceptions of their well-being. Of course, the process does not guarantee that there will always be agreed outcomes. But without the process, existing social arrangements and practices would simply be self-justifying structures and the opportunity for expanding sensitivity through discussion, use of evidence and hearing affected parties, would be lost.

6 See Eekelaar (2007: especially at 164-168; 177-81); Eekelaar (2011).

References

Ahmed, F., "Personal Autonomy and the Option of Religious Law", *International Journal of Law, Policy and the Family* 2010 24(2), 222-244.

Ahmed, F., "Religious Norms in Family Law; Implications for Group and Personal Autonomy", in M. Maclean and J. Eekelaar (eds), *Managing Family Justice in Diverse Societies* (Oxford: Hart Publishing, 2012) ch. 2.

An-Naim, A.A., "State Responsibility under International Human Rights Law to Change Religious and Customary Laws", in R. J. Cook (ed), *Human Rights of Women: National and International Perspectives* (Philadelphia: University of Pennsylvania Press, 1994).

Cane, P., "Taking Law Seriously: Starting Points of the Hart/Devlin Debate", *Journal of Ethics* 2006 10(1-2), 21-51.

Devlin, P., *The Enforcement of Morals* (Oxford: Oxford University Press, 1965).

Eekelaar, J., *Family Law and Personal Life* (Oxford: Oxford University Press, 2007).

Eekelaar, J., "From Multiculturalism to Cultural Voluntarism: A Family-based Approach", *The Political Quarterly* 2010 81(3), 344-355.

Eekelaar, J., "Naturalism or Pragmatism? Towards an Expansive View of Human Rights", *Journal of Human Rights* 2011 10(2), 230-242.

Eekelaar, J., "Self-Restraint: Social Norms, Individualism and the Family", *Theoretical Inquiries in Law* 2012b 13(1), Article 3. Available at: http://www.bepress.com/til/default/vol13/iss1/art3.

Eekelaar, J., "Law and Community Practices", in M. Maclean and J. Eekelaar (eds), *Managing Family Justice in Diverse Societies* (Oxford: Hart Publishing, 2013) ch. 1.

Eekelaar, J., "The Road to Same-Sex Marriage in England", *International Journal of Law, Policy and the Family* 2014 28(1), 1-25.

Freeman, M., "Philosophical Foundations of Human Rights", *Human Rights Quarterly* 1994 16(3), 491-514.

Freeman, M., "Children's Rights and Cultural Pluralism", in M. Freeman, *The Moral Status of Children: Essays on the Rights of the Child* (The Hague: Martinus Nijhoff, Kluwer Law International, 1997).

Freeman, M., "Cultural Pluralism and the Rights of the Child", in J. M. Eekelaar and T. Nhlapo (eds), *The Changing Family: Family Forms and Family Law* (Oxford: Hart Publishing, 1998).

Freeman, M., "Human Rights, children's rights and judgment: some thoughts on reconciling universality and pluralism", *International Journal of Children's Rights* 2002 10(4), 345-354.

Freeman, M., "Article 3: the Best Interests of the Child", in A. Ale, J. Van de Lanette, E. Verhalle, F. Ang, E. Berghmans and M. Verheyde (eds), *Commentary on the United Nations Convention on the Rights of the Child* (Leiden: Martinus Nijhoff, 2007).

Freeman, M., "Culture, Childhood, Rights", *The Family in Law Review* 2011 5, 15-20.

Griffin, J., *On Human Rights* (Oxford: Oxford University Press, 2009).

Hart, H.L.A., *Law, Liberty and Morality* (Stanford: Stanford University Press, 1963).

Israel, J., *A Revolution of the Mind: Radical Enlightenment and the Intellectual Origins of Modern Democracy* (Princeton: Princeton University Press, 2010).

Malik, M., *Minority Legal Orders in the UK* (London: The British Academy, 2012).

Pagden, A., *The Enlightenment and why it still matters* (Oxford: Oxford University Press, 2013).

Pinchbeck, I. and M. Hewitt, *Children in English Society*, vol. 2 (London: Routledge & Kegan Paul, 1973).

Nussbaum, M., *The New Religious Intolerance: Overcoming the politics of fear in an anxious age* (Cambridge, Mass.: The Belknap Press of Harvard University Press, 2012).

Sen, A., *The Idea of Justice* (Cambridge, Mass.: The Belknap Press of Harvard University Press, 2009).

Shah, P., "Shadow Boxing with Community Practices: A Response to Eekelaar", in M. Maclean and J. Eekelaar (eds)., *Managing Family Justice in Diverse Societies* (Oxford: Hart Publishing, 2013) ch. 3.

Philosophy of Law: Secular and Religious (With Some Reference to Jewish Family Law)

Bernard S. Jackson
Liverpool Hope University, UK

It was a pleasure to participate in the UCL colloquium on 'Law and Michael Freeman' (a truly global oral *Festschrift*) in tribute to a friend, colleague and collaborator[1] for more decades than either of us might wish to recall.

Over the years, our interests have overlapped significantly in jurisprudence, family law and law and religion (especially Jewish law). In what follows I offer a reflection on the interaction of these three areas, in the light of a number of recent controversies.

1. The Application of Positivist Jurisprudential Models to Religious Law[2]

Secular jurisprudence, particularly in the positivist tradition, has paid relatively little attention to the phenomenon of religious law, but both the exceptions and the silences can prove instructive.

For Austin (see now Freeman and Mindus, 2013), 'divine law' fell within the genus of law 'properly so called' ('A law, in the most general and comprehensive acceptation in which the term, in its literal meaning, is employed, may be said to be a rule laid down for the guidance of an intelligent being by an intelligent being having power over him' (Austin, 1954:10)), since God was conceived as an intelligent being with power over humanity. Indeed, Austin was quite explicit on this: 'Of laws properly so called, some are set by God to his human creatures, others are set by men to men' (Ibid: 122. *Cf.* 'The divine laws and positive laws are laws properly so called', ibid: 1). Divine law failed, however, the test of the narrower species of 'positive law', not being 'set by *political* superiors to *political* inferiors' and failing the test of sovereignty:

1 Not least in his 30-year involvement as Vice-Chairman (to Lord Lloyd of Hampstead's shadow chairmanship), then Chairman of the Jewish Law Publication Fund, which initiated and supported a series of significant scholarly books on Jewish law.

2 See further, Jackson, 2002:75-83.

A. Diduck, N. Peleg, H. Reece (eds.), Law in Society: Reflections on Children, Family, Culture and Philosophy
 Printed in The Netherlands. ISBN 978-90-04-26148-8. pp. 45-62.

> If a *determinate* human superior, *not* in a habit of obedience to a like superior, receive *habitual* obedience from the *bulk* of a given society, that determinate superior is sovereign in that society, and the society (including the superior) is a society political and independent (Austin, 1954:194).

The test, notwithstanding its fuzzy edges, is widely regarded as reflecting Austin's commitment to philosophical (empiricist) positivism, designed to construct a jurisprudence which could stand up to scientific scrutiny.

Kelsen also accepted the possibility of a "religious norm system" which did not, however, pass his test for positive law. Such a system would have a *Grundnorm*: "The basic norm of a religious norm system says that one ought to behave as God and the authorities instituted by Him command" (Kelsen, 1946:115), where the source of authority was not the *fact* (real or supposed) of divine command but rather "the tacitly presupposed norm that one ought to obey the commands of God" (Kelsen, 1967:193-94). Kelsen's radical separation of fact and norm allowed him to avoid any empirical questions about the actual existence of either God or divine command. Nor did the *Grundnorm* depend on conscious acceptance by either the community or its officials, or even conscious knowledge of it on their part. It was, in his view, a logical presupposition of which they might be wholly unaware, but which provided the logical basis of their *experience* of legal validity (applying the Husserlian understanding of Kelsen's *Grundnorm*) (Kelsen, 1967: 202; Jackson, 1985: 238-234; 1996: 111-112, 127).[3] However, such a system of religious law would not be a system of *positive* law, since the latter must use socially immanent rather than transcendental sanctions, i.e. "those that according to the faith of the individuals subjected to the order originate from a superhuman authority", which Kelsen appears to understand (only) in terms of "punishment by a superhuman authority", an example of which is given as "the illness or death of the sinner or punishment in another world" (Kelsen, 1947: 20-21). Kelsen does not appear to envisage a religious legal system in which authority is delegated to human agencies to apply socially immanent sanctions. To the extent that religious legal systems do so, they would appear to fulfil his definition of positive law. Of course, he would apply here the same argument which he uses in relation to the position of a Marxist within a capitalist legal system.[4] The subject within a religious legal system

---

3 Smith, 2011, says: "Logic studies objective ideas, including propositions, which in turn make up objective theories as in the sciences. Psychology would, by contrast, study subjective ideas, the concrete contents (occurrences) of mental activities in particular minds at a given time. Husserl was after both, within a single discipline ... For Husserl, then, phenomenology integrates a kind of psychology with a kind of logic. It develops a descriptive or analytic psychology in that it describes and analyses types of subjective mental activity or experience, in short, acts of consciousness. Yet it develops a kind of logic – a theory of meaning (today we say logical semantics) – in that it describes and analyzes objective contents of consciousness..."

4 "A Communist may, indeed, not admit that there is an essential difference between an organization of gangsters and a capitalistic legal order which he considers as the means of ruthless exploitation. For he does not presuppose – as do those who interpret the coer-

who rejects the *Grundnorm* on ideological (here, atheist) grounds simply does not experience that normative system as legally valid.

Hart does not, to my knowledge, address the issue of religious law directly,[5] but the focus of his version of positivism – different from that of both Austin and Kelsen – is relevant to the analysis of religious systems. His conception of a legal system, characterised by the union of primary and secondary rules, is designed to provide certainty – a Rule of Law in which individuals may make informed choices as to their course of action, knowing in advance their legal consequences. This is the point of the so-called "demonstrability thesis", in which the secondary rule of recognition provides a "conclusive affirmative indication" (Hart, 1994: 94) of the existence or not of a valid legal rule, and this is why, in his account of legal interpretation, he describes cases falling within the "penumbra of uncertainty" as representing a "crisis of communication" (1994: 126-27) – the exceptional case where the legal system has to resort to a Rule of Men rather than a Rule of Law. Of course, for Hart, this is a function of "legal systems" as opposed to the mere "set of separate standards" characteristic of "primitive" or "simple" societies (1994: 92).[6] Like Kelsen's theory, Hart's account does not exclude religious law *a priori*; all will depend on how the religious system works.

In his reply to Dworkin's critique, Hart found it necessary to make some concessions on the "demonstrability" thesis (Hart, 1994: 251-52; Jackson, 1996: 207-09). Dworkin's claim that the law consists of principles as well as rules (a version of which Hart accepted) was designed to rid the legal system of gaps[7] (and in this sense to advance Hart's "informed choice"' agenda) but at the cost of abandoning the 'conclusive affirmative indication' based on the intelligibility of ordinary (legal) language in favour of an expert, rational intelligibility revealed by (or to?) a Hercules, a "lawyer of *superhuman* skill, learning, patience and acumen" (1978:105, emphasis supplied).

2. The Application of Jurisprudential Models to Jewish Law

It is not surprising that visions of a complete and coherent legal system, whether the product of a hierarchy of formal rules or of substantive rationality, have proved attractive to modern Orthodox students of Jewish law. Thus the late Menahem Elon, a

---

cive order in question as an objectively valid normative order – the basic norm. He does not deny that the capitalistic normative order is the law of the State. What he denies is that this coercive order, the law of the State, is objectively valid," see Kelsen, 1965:1143-44, quoted in Freeman, 1994: 308-09 and Jackson, 1996: 112. On the non-inevitability (psychologically) of attitudes which presuppose a Basic Norm, cf. Kelsen, 1991: 256 (ch.59 §iC).

5 On the nature of his Jewish background, see Lacey, 2004: ch.1.

6 Interestingly, this view is denied by Silberg, 1973:51, who claims that Jewish law, being a system of religious law, "does not define norms for deciding the law, but norms of behaviour" – thus apparently reducing Jewish law (in Hartian terms) to a system of primary rules only. He also denies (at 57) that there is any recognised competence to effect change in Jewish law.

7 For a semiotic analysis of the debate between Hart and Dworkin on the presence or absence of "logical spaces" in the legal system, see Jackson, 1985:193-203; 1996:200-205.

Jewish law scholar and Deputy President of the Israel Supreme Court, sought in what is the leading modern account of the Jewish legal system to invoke a version of the "sources" theory (Elon, 1994, especially vol.1), applying a hierarchy of sources model based on a "basic norm" (though he invokes primarily Salmond rather than Kelsen). His motivation was practical: it formed part of the political argument to make "Jewish law" (using the term *mishpat ivri*[8] rather than the traditional *halakhah,* often translated the "way (of life)"[9]) an acceptable basis of the law of the State of Israel – a project which failed, though religious law remains entrenched in areas of family law (Freeman, 2002), a legacy of the Ottoman Turkish millet system (which granted legal autonomy to the institutions of recognised religious community in matters of "personal status").

There are, however, major conceptual problems involved in such a strategy. Radical change (from rules regarded as having "biblical" status) is virtually excluded in Jewish law: there can be revolution against divine law; indeed in recent centuries (partly in reaction against progressive forms of Judaism), Orthodoxy has proved increasingly reluctant to make *any* changes in *halakhah,* as we shall see from a particular problem in the Jewish law of divorce. Elon himself had to accept a significant qualification: in a religious system based on revelation, the Constitution is unamendable.[10] Moreover, there is an acute ideological problem at the very foundation of the application of Jewish religious law within the State of Israel. The State, whose own legal system is secular, in that ultimate authority belongs to a democratically elected legislature (the Knesset), may delegate certain powers to religious courts (Jewish, Muslim and Christian), but that itself delegitimises those courts in the eyes of some religious circles, who claim that the ultimate authority is divine, and therefore should operate through religious institutions rather than through the State. It is the religion, they would claim, which should define the powers of the State, rather than vice versa. This is a fundamental issue for "law and religion" issues everywhere, and may be regarded as defining the distinction between theocracy and democracy.

But this is not the only conceptual problem. The history of Jewish law shows that charismatic rather than rational sources have played an important role from biblical times. It is striking that a series of instructions to judges (Jackson, 2006: 412-18)[11] fails to mention written sources of law: rather, they tell the judges to avoid partiality and corruption and apply their intuitive sense of justice (in the context, no doubt, of orally transmitted custom). Their authority was charismatic. Thus, the 9th century B.C.E. King Jehoshaphat of Judah charges his judges to avoid partiality and corruption and assures them that "(God) is *with you* in giving judgement" (2 *Chronicles* 19:6),

8 On the "Mishpat Ivri" movement (though using positivist models other than that of Hart), see Jackson, 2012:§2.1.

9 Perhaps better (and polysemically) the "direction".

10 For Elon, the constitution is the *Torah*; as for the ground of the constitution: "we leave jurisprudence and pass into the sphere of faith" (Elon, 1994: I.233).

11 Perhaps the most famous is that of *Deuteronomy* 16:18, where the judges are commanded to pursue a "righteous judgment" (*tsedek tsedek tirdof*). On Deut. 16 and the (different) use of written law in Deut. 17, see Jackson, 2002a:37-38.

rather than their referring to written sources (Jackson, 2006: 412-14). This survived in a residual power (explicit in Talmudic sources but increasingly submerged since then) for the judge to depart from the strict law when intuitions of justice demanded it. Ben-Menahem (1991) has studied some 30 cases recorded in the Babylonian Talmud where it is said that the rabbinic judge decided the case "not in accordance with the *Halakhah*".[12] Indeed, the *halakhah* is regarded as a minimum standard, and the judges are expected to go beyond it, wherever possible, in pursuit of justice. Thus, the Talmud quotes R. Johanan as saying (*Baba Mezia* 30b): "Jerusalem was destroyed only because they gave judgements therein accordance with *Torah* law… Were they then to have judged in accordance with untrained arbitrators? – But say thus: because they based their judgements [strictly] upon Torah law, and did not go beyond the requirements of the law. "

It is, perhaps, this issue that has prompted other students of Jewish law to incorporate Dworkinian "principles"', in order to account for both the development of the law and its substantive justice (Lamm and Kirschenbaum, 1979).[13] But it has been recently and persuasively argued that such a strategy takes just one aspect of Dworkin's theory (legal principles), and one not unique to Dworkin, out of its overall theoretical context and that the latter includes elements, notably its theory of mistakes, which are radically incompatible with the workings of Jewish law (Ben-Menahem, 2013).

Moreover, unlike the assumptions of modern secular jurisprudence (Hart, here, providing a particularly clear instance), the history and workings of Jewish law show that it is conceived to operate primarily in the private rather than the public sphere. Dispute resolution appears originally to have proceeded without third party adjudication (going to court was conceived as risking shame: *Proverbs* 25:7-9). The earliest rules of biblical law – the "*Mishpatim*" of *Exodus* 21:1-22:16 – appear to have evoked "typical" cases, where custom provided "self-executing" solutions designed largely to *avoid* the need for third party adjudication (Jackson, 2000: 82-87; 2006: 29-35, 389-95 *et passim*). Nor should the proceedings of the rabbinic law court be viewed in the same light to those of its secular counterparts. The very fact that the rabbinic court is *not* conceived as a public forum, that its proceedings are *not* reported, and traditionally there was no hierarchy of courts to sustain an appellate system, reflects the perception that the Rabbinic court often sees itself as engaged in a private activity of moral/religious persuasion and that its function is primarily to secure justice (in the sense of that which is conceived to be moral according to the tenets of the religion) in the particular situation faced by the parties.

Indeed, the role and responsibility of the *dayan* (rabbinic judge) is fundamentally different from that of his secular counterpart, in that the rabbinic judge owes both a

---

12 See also, more broadly, Ben-Menahem 1996, concluding, at 434f., that "we are justified in doubting the sufficiency of the modern, Western concept of law for the purposes of describing the *halakhah*."

13 In his last book, *Religion without God,* Dworkin explored the relation between religion (in general) and objective value (with a chapter on religious freedom, including the constitutional challenges it presents). He has a section (2013: 38-43) on Spinoza.

civil responsibility to the litigants and a religious accountability to God. The latter, in particular, has proved an obstacle to what is seen as taking risks in legal decision-making.[14]

3. "Rules of Recognition" in Jewish Law

Legislative authority in (Orthodox) Jewish law has always been limited by the sovereignty of the laws in the Pentateuch (*Torah*) and since the destruction of the Second Temple in 70 C.E., Jewish law has lacked anything resembling a central legislature, so that even the capacity to enact changes in non-Pentateuchal, "Rabbinic" *halakhah* has been geographically dispersed and often temporally limited. Nor does the *halakhah* endorse any strong theory of binding precedent: indeed, until recent times, decisions of rabbinic courts have not been published. The basic "source" of authority has long been the opinions of the leading rabbinic jurists (the *posqim*), often advising the courts rather than making decisions themselves. But who counts as having that status, and what happens when the *posqim* disagree?

The most basic "secondary rule" in Jewish law is that of majority decision (*rov*). But this itself is subject to a major controversy: does it apply only to the *posqim* of the current generation or does it extend to cross-generational disputes, where the participants had no opportunity for dialogue (Abel, 2008: Sec. 1)? In the course of a five-year research project (The Agunah Research Unit – ARU) I directed at Manchester on the vexed, practical problem of the "chained wife" (*agunah*) whose husband refuses to co-operate with the court in granting his wife a divorce (a *get*), thereby preventing her remarriage, and rendering any subsequent relationship she may enter adulterous and the children thereof "illegitimate" (*mamzerim*), we discovered that both this and other important aspects of the Jewish "rules of recognition" were themselves subject to significant controversy. Thus, as regards majority decision:

> Some authorities maintain that *rov* is *min ha-Torah* only when the argument was amongst contemporaries debating face to face but in the case of divergent opinions amongst authorities who never met together in debate, whether due to historical or geographical constraints, there is doubt if the majority rule applies by Torah Law (Abel, 2008: Section I, noting also the arguments of Rabbi Ovadya Yosef (former Sephardi Chief Rabbi of the State of Israel and a leading *poseq*) who maintains that in any *mahloqet* where the disputants are *in absentia* of each other, the situation remains one of doubt).

---

14 Here, a theological issue of trust in God also arises: do the religious judges really trust God with judging their own performance? In the context of the divorce problem discussed in the next section, should they make a sincere attempt to help the woman (within the boundaries of Jewish law), or should they "play safe" (cf. defensive medicine) just because others take a different view? Do they assume that God also adjudicates on a "play safe" basis? Some influential rabbinic voices have been raised recently against the predominant "play safe" attitude, arguing that the judges have a responsibility to risk their own eternal souls in pursuit of justice. See further, Jackson, 2012:§3.5.

An alternative to seeking a cross-generational majority is the rule that, as amongst post-talmudic authorities, later opinions are followed in preference to earlier ones (*hilkheta kebatra'ei*), on the assumption that the later authorities took the earlier ones into account. But this is qualified (by Rema), in the case where earlier sources are discovered, of which the later authorities were unaware (Shulhan Arukh Hoshen Mishpat 25:3 and Rema.[15] See Jackson, 2011: 61-62.) That leaves the contemporary judge with discretion *not* to follow the later authority on the grounds that his decision might have been different had he been aware of this (newly discovered) earlier authority. The criteria for the latter are stated in some detail in the 20th century *Enzyklopedia Talmudit*. One of my colleagues in the Agunah Research Unit analysed this statement, and found eight different areas of ambiguity in it (Abel, 2008: 8-10; Jackson, 2011:62-64.)

The Talmud is the Supreme authority (where it has anything to say), but what when new manuscripts are discovered which prompt reconsideration of what the Talmud (or indeed later sources) actually says? Does this itself fall under Rema's qualification to *hilkheta kebatra'ei*? One issue is whether the husband can be coerced by the court to give a bill of divorce where the woman says (and is believed to be sincere in saying) that she cannot stand to be near him any longer. In the early middle ages, various authorities said the court can and should coerce in such circumstances. Then, a 12th century French authority, Rabbenu Tam, rejected this, partly on the grounds that coercion of the husband was not found in the Talmud (see further, Jackson, 2011: 159-77.) In the last century, a Talmudic manuscript was discovered in the Cairo Geniza which had one Talmudic sage saying that in these circumstances "he is forced", against the traditional text which said: "she is not forced (back into marital compliance)". There is no clear rule in such cases of textual doubt, though there is considerable reluctance to reconsider the text of the Talmud, partly on providential grounds (see further, Jackson, 2012: §3.3 (last paragraph)): the traditional text, even if not historically accurate, is the one God intended to be used (but what of the counter providential argument?).

In all this, there is an underlying question: whose opinion counts? There is no official designation. It has become common to speak of the "*gedoley hador*" ("great ones of the generation"). And while there is often a considerable consensus as to which rabbinic scholars fall into this category, this may well differ amongst different Jewish communities. In an age of globalisation and mass communications, this represents a growing problem.

In the light of all this, Hart would surely not have regarded Jewish law as a "legal system". It manifestly fails anything like the demonstrability test (even in the form in which Hart watered it down, in response to Dworkin's critique).

A vital part of the ARU's approach was to capitalise on the very systemic features of the *halakhah* which render it "ineffective" in traditional positivist terms. For this

---

15 The Shulhan Arukh is a 16th century "Code" of Jewish law by the Sephardi scholar, R. Joseph Karo, and is traditionally printed with the glosses of Rema (R. Moses Isserles, 1520-72) (reflecting Ashkenazi practice).

is, indeed, an issue which the halakhic system has addressed, by developing rules regarding issues of legal (as well as factual) "doubt": a single doubt (*safeq*) may be used to permit behaviour prohibited by rabbinic law; a double doubt (*sfeq sfeqa*) may be used to permit behaviour prohibited even by Torah law (Jackson, 2011:55-59.) That does not provide the judge with *mandatory* guidance as to what to do in such cases; rather, it provides him with a discretion – to permit what otherwise would be prohibited. For sure, different authorities may decide differently how to exercise such discretion, but they cannot claim that a different decision to their own is outside the parameters of *halakhah*.[16] The ARU sought to use this doctrine of doubt in proposing a technical solution to the problem of the *agunah*, although its application, at least initially, would depend on rabbinic courts applying the discretion which, we argue, our analysis would gives them (Jackson, 2011: 282-85).

In the absence of any universally accepted central rabbinic authority, different rabbinic courts will exercise such a discretion in different ways. Some may even deny that the discretion exists. Is there an objectively correct answer to this question? Despite the continuing endorsement by some influential rabbinic voices of a positivist-inspired objectivity,[17] the better answer – and one, I would maintain, itself supported by Jewish tradition – is that the *halakhah* is based at least as much on the concept of trust as on that of truth.[18] And that applies equally, of course, to those performing speech acts different from adjudication in relation to *halakhic* matters, whether it be the advocacy of reform proposals or describing current practice to different communities of enquirers.

4. Semiotics, Truth and Trust

I now revert to legal theory. The semiotic approach, which I have advocated (Jackson, 1985; 1988; 1995; 1996) and which Michael admitted at one stage to the canon of Lloyd's *Introduction* (Freeman, 1994, in ch.14), has a particular advantage in this context. In advancing a universal model of sense construction, it provides a neutral ground for the comparison of the secular and religious, as indeed for the analysis of fact and law. Let me indicate very briefly how this might be applied in the present context.

For semiotics, "is" and "ought" are simply different modalities applied to behaviour patterns (whose sense is constructed in narrative terms). When we affirm the modality of "is", we are making a truth claim; when we affirm the modality of "ought", we are making a validity claim (just as when we go to an art gallery and affirm the beauty of a painting, we are making an aesthetic claim).[19]

---

16 Or, in our context, that the children of a woman's second union, when the first was dissolved on the basis of a double doubt, are illegitimate.

17 On the position of Rabbi J.D. Bleich, see Sprung, 2013.

18 Whether the attribute of "truth" may be attached to legal propositions is discussed, in the secular context, by Pintore, 1996/2000.

19 In this context, we may note that the *halakhic* "dogmatics of doubt" apply equally to factual or legal doubts. See Jackson, 2011:56, 60-70.

But what is it that induces us to make such claims and to regard them as making sense? Here, we may take the model of fact construction in the courtroom (Jackson, 1996: chs.10-12) as indicative of the more general process. Even a very moderate secular sceptic of the legal process will readily accept that truth is frequently constructed in the courtroom by *whom* we believe, not *what* we believe. (*Cf.* Landowski, 1989: 203 distinguishing *croire* in relation to *ce que dit* and *celui qui dit.*) A major factor is witness credibility, which is a function not only (often, not primarily) of what the witness says, but rather of the credibility (trustworthiness) of his/her speech behaviour. We may use semiotic resources to understand how this sense of trustworthiness is created (see Jackson, 1996: 408 on the relationship between speech style and perceived trustworthiness; 412-23, on the construction of the trustworthiness of expert witnesses in court).

Landowski has provided a conceptual account, indicating the roles of both the "deep structures of signification" (*structures élémentaires de la signification*) (Landowski, 1989: 204) and the "stereotypes" which, in any particular social context, manifest such structures (Landowski, 1989: 215-17). The particular social context of his study is electoral politics; he notes, in particular, that the senders of messages thereby constitute themselves as subjects of a new task, that of engaging in a *faire persuasif* (Landowski, 1989: 206, including the "auto-referential" transmission of messages about the speaker's own competence). I have proposed a similar structure, in less technical terms, which I call the narrativisation of pragmatics (Jackson, 1988: 33-36, 112-29, for examples of the narrativisation of pragmatics in the context of criminal trials): we deploy internalised (and socially constructed) narrative patterns of persuasive speech in assessing the credibility of the speech behaviour before us. Thus, two witnesses telling exactly the same story can prompt quite different reactions: hence, lawyers' judgments that some witnesses are "good", others not. In short, the semantics of evidence are mediated through the pragmatic of witnessing.

Can we really exclude such an analysis from our account of legal reasoning? I think not. And in this context, the seemingly counter-intuitive conclusion that Jewish law is based ultimately on what authorities we trust, rather than which opinions are objectively correct, may not appear so bizarre after all, and may need to be taken into account even in secular, rational (apparently non-charismatic) legal systems.

We should not, moreover, assume a universal conception of "truth". Steven Schwarzschild (Schwarzschild, 1973:1414; see further, Jackson, 2012a: 2001-02) writes: "In Judaism truth is primarily an ethical notion: it describes not what is but what ought to be," citing the association of truth with ethical notions in the Bible[20] and rabbinic literature.[21] Hermann Cohen (1904: ch.1) designates the normative unity of cognition and ethics as "the fundamental law of truth". And Martin Buber is said to

20 Peace (*Zechariah* 8:16), righteousness (*Malachi* 2:6ff.), grace (*Genesis* 24:27, 49), justice (*Zechariah* 7:9), and even salvation (*Psalms* 25:4ff.).

21 *Mishnah Avot* 1:18, "The world rests on three things – truth, justice, and peace."

identify faith (*emunah*[22]) with truth (*emet*), here conceived as interpersonal trust (Schwarzschild 1973:1415. See Buber, 1951:7-12. On Buber's non-referential conception of truth, and its relation to the I-Thou relationship, see Levinas, 1967:141-44). And such conceptions derive support from classical rabbinic sources. Thus, we read in a famous passage of the Talmud (*Erubin* 13b):

> R. Abba stated in the name of Samuel: For three years there was a dispute between Beth (the House of) Shammai and Beth Hillel, the former asserting, "The *halakhah* is in agreement with our views" and the latter contending, "The *halakhah* is in agreement with our views". Then a *bath kol* (heavenly voice) issued announcing, "These and these [the utterances of both] are the words of the living God, but the *halakhah* is in agreement with the rulings of Beth Hillel".
>
> Since, however, "both are the words of the living God" what was it that entitled Beth Hillel to have the *halakhah* fixed in agreement with their rulings? – Because they were kindly and modest, they studied their own rulings and those of Beth Shammai, and were even so [humble] as to mention the action of Beth Shammai before theirs.

The passage is remarkable in a number of respects. First, it accepts the legitimacy of intervention by a "heavenly voice" (thus, direct divine revelation as a source of law), despite the fact that such intervention is explicitly rejected in another well-known Talmudic passage.[23] Second, it claims that contradictory positions may simultaneously represent "the words of the living God", contrary to conventional human conceptions of the nature of truth (and objectivity).[24] Third, it indicates a "pragmatic" (in the linguistic sense) criterion for the "pragmatic" (i.e. practical) resolution of the conflict: the School of Hillel merit greater trust because of their superior (in Habermasian terms) conversational ethics.

---

22 The attribute of *emunah* is frequently attributed to God in Jewish liturgy. In context, it clearly refers to human perception of God's trustworthiness, rather than to human adherence to any abstract truth-claim. Does this sell out any "hard" conception of truth? In the theological context, the believer may very reasonably say: "My belief that X is true is based on my faith in the truthfulness/trustworthiness of my source of information (God), which is far more reliable than any attempt I might make at independent confirmation."

23 Babylonian Talmud, *Baba Mezia* 59b, where a heavenly voice validates the opinion of R. Eliezer (who had earlier performed miracles to demonstrate his authority), but is rejected by R. Joshua in favour of majority decision (supported by a biblical proof-text). For literature, see Jackson, 2012a:2003 n.16.

24 Indeed, Jewish theology also makes special claims for the properties of the *language* of the Bible: not only do the Rabbis claim for it a superhuman level of discursive coherence – as may be seen in the operation of several of the rabbinic "hermeneutic rules" (*middot*) for interpreting the biblical text; it also claims a capacity to address different audiences at different levels – at one extreme (seen above) in the capacity to transcend the law of non-contradiction; on the other, to be written in a form accessible to the general public: Babylonian Talmud, *Keritot* 11a: *dibrah torah kilshon bnei adam* (R. Ishmael). See further, Jackson, 2012a:2002.

The tension between truth and trust is also reflected in a story told of the relations between two leading 19th century rabbinic authorities:

> R. Hayyim of Brisk had a query regarding a practical matter. He decided to turn to the leading authority of these times, R. Isaac Elhanan of Kovno [Kaunas]. He wrote: "These are the facts and this is the question; I beg you to reply in a single line – 'fit' or 'unfit', 'Guilty' or 'not Guilty', without giving your reasons. " When R. Hayyim was asked why he had done so, he replied "... decisions of R. Isaac Elhanan are binding because he is the *Posek* of our generation, and he will let me know his decision. But in scholarship and analysis my ways are different from his and if he gave his reasons I might see a flaw in it and have doubts about his decision. So, it is better if I do not know his reasons" (Elon, 1980:89-90, n.52. At Jackson, 2012a: 206-07, I associate this with a "procedural" approach to truth).

R. Hayyim was prepared to trust the decision of R. Isaac Elhanan even though he might disagree with his reasoning. Unlike many modern positivists, he does not see legal decisions as nothing more than the outcome of explicit legal reasoning (on the relationship between decision-making and justification, see Jackson, 1996: 233-36). Here, deference was paid to personal status or reputation, in preference to argumentation, to attributes of the énonciateur rather than the content of the énoncé.

5. The Interaction of Secular and Religious Law

The conceptual and epistemological issues raised in the foregoing analysis are also relevant to ongoing controversies regarding the interaction between secular and religious law, issues which have also attracted Michael Freeman's active involvement.

Michael's interest in the *agunah* problem long predates my own. In the 1990s he advised Chief Rabbi Immanuel Jakobovits on a clause which was enacted as s. 9(3-4) of the Family Law Act 1996, allowing[25] the court to delay making a decree nisi of civil divorce absolute where (though expressed in indirect language) a religious remarriage would not be possible because of the withholding of a *get*. However, this whole Part of the Act, though it passed all its legislative stages, was never been brought into effect for reasons unrelated to the *get* problem. Later, a similar provision was enacted *and* brought into effect (separately from any general divorce law reform) in the Divorce (Religious Marriages) Act 2002, a private member's Bill sponsored by Andrew Dismore M.P. Of course, despite the clear humanitarian objective of assisting women caught in an intolerable situation, the involvement of secular law in religious marriage is controversial, from both secular and religious viewpoints, and Michael has

25 The order "may be made only if the court is satisfied that in all the circumstances of the case it is just and reasonable to do so." A stronger version, in which withholding the civil decree absolute would have been mandatory, had been proposed in 1990 by the late Dayan B. Berkovits (in his private capacity): see Berkovits, 1990:143-46. See further, Jackson, 2004:72 for such legislation in New York and South Africa.

subsequently changed his mind on the matter (Freeman, 2001: 367-68; 2002a): he now regards the *agunah* problem as an internal Jewish one, which it is the responsibility of the rabbinic authorities to resolve. With this, I firmly agree and would add that resort to secular law is necessarily a "parochial" solution; the problem is one which affects Jewish communities globally, but separate intervention is needed in each civil jurisdiction (as indeed has already been the case in England and Scotland) (Family Law (Scotland) Act 2006, s. 15). Moreover, even such "benign" intervention by secular law in Jewish law is regarded by some as problematic from the viewpoint of Jewish law[26] and raises the theoretical issues discussed by the Archbishop of Canterbury in his February 2008 lecture on "Civil and Religious Law in England: a Religious Perspective", at the Royal Courts of Justice (http://rowanwilliams.archbishopofcanterbury.org/articles.php/1137/. For a discussion, see Jackson, 2009).

Archbishop Williams' stated purpose was "to tease out some of the broader issues around the rights of religious groups within a secular state, with a few thoughts about what might be entailed in crafting a just and constructive relationship between Islamic law and the statutory law of the United Kingdom". To this end, he drew upon Ayelet Shachar's (2001) concept of "transformative accommodation", according to which (in the Archbishop's words):

> both jurisdictional stakeholders may need to examine the way they operate; a communal/religious *nomos*, to borrow Shachar's vocabulary, has to think through the risks of alienating its people by inflexible or over-restrictive applications of traditional law, and a universalist Enlightenment system has to weigh the possible consequences of ghettoising and effectively disenfranchising a minority, at real cost to overall social cohesion and creativity. Hence "*transformative* accommodation": both jurisdictional parties may be changed by their encounter over time, and we avoid the sterility of mutually exclusive monopolies.

In short, "transformative accommodation" implies a willingness on both sides to contemplate internal change (resulting in part from mutual influence), in competing for the loyalty of subjects who are simultaneously members of both civic and religious communities (see Jackson, 2009: 142-44, 145-46).

In effect, this means that both secular law and religious traditions have to consider what, in their own systems, is negotiable, and what is not. But such negotiations are not straightforward. The practical issues to be negotiated may invoke quite different values and associations for the two cultures, including many of the philosophical and ideological issues raised in this chapter. Nor can the tension between truth and trust be excluded.[27] Thus, in the context of divorce, it seems clear that for Orthodox Jews,

---

26 See p. 57 below on Mishnah Gittin, 9:8.

27 A factor underlying the politicisation of the issue in Ontario in 2005-2006, in relation to Muslim arbitration. See further, Jackson, 2009:20.

the divorce procedure itself is non-negotiable;[28] financial "ancillary" matters are in principle negotiable (see broadly, Jackson, 2009: 5-6, 13), and issues of custody are borderline. As for the divorce itself, non-Jewish courts are not here trusted to make such decisions, but their coercive role is accepted, provided that it is for the purpose of ensuring that the coerced husband, "Do[es] what the Israelites say to you" (Mishnah Gittin, 9:8). We may detect a converse issue of trust in the English family law principle that the jurisdiction of the family court is not to be ousted.

Similar issues arise in matters ancillary to divorce. In the UK, the major rabbinical courts (the London Beth Din and the Manchester Beth Din) require the parties to sign a deed of binding arbitration before formally entertaining any case, but in disputes on matters ancillary to divorce they recognise that such a deed would violate the principle against ouster of the jurisdiction of the family courts. In practice, however, they may informally advise (or mediate between) couples who seek their assistance, resulting in an agreed position being presented to the civil court.[29] In the recent (and somewhat unusual) case of *AI* v *MT* ([2013] EWHC 100 (Fam)), Baker J took a step towards formalisation of such practices, in accepting a form of *non-binding* arbitration[30] before a New York rabbinical authority,[31] thereby preserving the principle of non-ouster.

One might argue that, technically, the case arose before Mr Justice Baker in the context of abduction proceedings under the Hague convention,[32] rather than divorce proceedings and that this should not be viewed as setting a precedent in favour of non-binding arbitrations in custody matters by religious tribunals in the UK. Nevertheless, the decision has been welcomed in some Jewish circles. Personally, I have some reservations about the practical application of a multi-cultural approach to the "best interests" of children (despite Baker J's reliance on a dictum of Baroness Hale (*In Re J* [2006] 1 AC 18, paras. 37-38, cited by Baker J at para. 29) and indeed about

28 On the *humra shel eshet ish* (special severity regarding the status of a married woman), see Jackson, 2011: 47-55. This is reflected also in the jurisdictional position in Israel, where marriage and divorce are within the exclusive jurisdiction of the rabbinical courts, while "ancillary matters" are subject to "concurrent jurisdiction": see the Rabbinical Courts Jurisdiction (Marriage and Divorce) Law 1953, ss. 1-3. This is also the reason why the French rabbinical proposal of 1887/1907 to solve the *agunah* problem by a clause in the marriage contract recognising a civil divorce was firmly rejected: Jackson, 2011:100-103.

29 I am grateful to Dr. Tamara Tolley for making available to me the results of her, as yet, unpublished socio-legal research on this point (Tolley, 2013) and for correspondence on the 2013 case.

30 The actual agreement, as quoted by Baker J in para.11 was for "binding arbitration" (as between the parties and in the eyes of the rabbinical authority), though subject to the supervisory jurisdiction of the secular court.

31 Baker J refers to it in the judgment as the Beth Din of New York for ease of reference. It appears to have been an arbitration by Rabbi Geldzehler in New York in a religious tribunal whose exact status is not entirely clear. For further information, see Tolley: 2013.

32 Note Baker J's distinction between such proceedings and the court's inherent jurisdiction at para. 28.

the basis on which Baker J was willing to trust the New York arbitral body.[33] If there is no universally "true" understanding of "best interests" (which, in any event, is highly situation-dependent), surely it becomes all the more important to make a professionally informed judgment on the trustworthiness of the body to which, in effect, the decision is being delegated – even if it is subject to review. Perhaps it will be argued that such caution is based on irrational factors and that when one looks at the substance of the issues, such as the "best interests of the child", we may at least start from the presumption that there is a common, multicultural understanding. But I hesitate. In traditional Orthodox *halakhah*, preference is still given to the father once the child has reached six years old, on the grounds that only the father is capable of advancing the child's religious education beyond that level,[34] although in practice there has been a strong reaction against this in modern times.[35]

The problem extends beyond family law in the strict sense. In the *JFS* case (*R (on the application of E) (Respondent)* v *Governing Body of JFS and the Admissions Appeal Panel of JFS (Appellants) and others* [2009] UKSC 15, see further, Jackson, 2012b: 83-91) the Supreme Court ruled that the school's admission policy, giving preference to "halakhically Jewish" children as understood by the Chief Rabbi as the school's religious authority, i.e. children born to a Jewish mother or converted according to Orthodox *halakhah*, violated the Race Relations Act and constituted discrimination "on the grounds of ... ethnic origins". In this case the child's mother had been converted to Judaism (before the birth of the child) under non-Orthodox auspices not recognised by the Chief Rabbi. The child was therefore excluded because of the status of his mother, but the school (and the minority in the Supreme Court) argued

---

33 For Baker J's own account of this, see paras. 13-14. The closest to a statement he received regarding the substantive approach to be applied was: "In conjunction with Halacha the best interests of the children are the primary consideration in resolving cases like this." (para. 14). The problem is that there is no single, authoritative view of the *halakhah* in this area, as indicated by some of the material quoted by Baker J in para.13.

34 Babylonian Talmud Ketubbot 65b. Rabbi Y. Breitowitz (also a law professor at the University of Maryland and a well-regarded author on the interaction of Jewish and secular (US) law: see Breitowitz, 1993) writes in "Jewish Law and Child Custody", http://judaiclaw.org/Questions_Answers_010.html: "The Talmud, Ketubot 65b, lays down a number of rules concerning the adjudication of custody disputes :1) children below six are to be placed with the mother although the father continues to be liable for their support; 2) boys above the age of six are to be placed with their fathers; 3) girls above the age of six are to be placed with their mothers. Despite the seemingly-absolute nature of these directives, halachic authorities are unanimous in regarding them at most as rebuttable presumptions or guidelines to be superseded or ignored when their application would be inconsistent with the child's welfare. *De facto*, therefore, Jewish law does regard welfare of the child as the primary factor for consideration. This, however, does not mean that the halachic standard is identical to that employed under secular law. This divergence may stem from two distinct factors ...' (discussing further the evidence needed to rebut the talmudic presumption, and differing standards for the determination of fitness).

35 Dr. Tolley (2013), in stressing this point, suggests that it may itself represent an example of "accommodation".

that this was itself the consequence of following the Chief Rabbi's understanding of a *religious* rule defining what was a valid conversion. The issue then became one of statutory interpretation: what was meant by "on the grounds of". The majority held that the *grounds* were racial (in the ethnic sense) even though the *motive* for applying those grounds was religious.

Are we to say that the case fell within the penumbra of uncertainty of the meaning here of "grounds", or that Hercules could show that the majority gave the best possible solution? Or do we have to say that the issue was really one of whether the school authorities and their religious advisor were to be trusted in the matter?

In fact, it is arguable that this *was* an issue on which the Jewish authorities could have "accommodated" their policy in such a way as to avoid suspicion of discrimination. The issue here, in terms of Jewish law, was not comparable to that relating to the status of a married woman (as in the *agunah* issue). There is no prohibition on educating halakhically Jewish students alongside non-halakhically Jewish students. Indeed, the educational ideology of the school is that of *kiruv*, the desire to bring children from non- or semi-observant homes closer to Orthodox standards of observance. In pursuit of this goal, the school admitted without demur halakhically Jewish children from completely irreligious homes. The child they excluded in this case was a far better prospect for *kiruv* than many of those they admitted.

The effect of the decision has in fact been to force them to "accommodate" in this way: the admission criteria are now based on (somewhat minimal) tests of religious practice, rather than the status of the child's mother. It need hardly be said that had the issue been eligibility for (Orthodox religious) marriage, no accommodation would have been possible.

References

Abel, Y., "Halakhah – Majority, Seniority, Finality and Consensus", Section I (Working Papers of the Agunah Research Unit, June 2008, no.7, available at http://www.mucjs.org/publications.htm).

Austin, J., *The Province of Jurisprudence Determined* (London: Weidenfeld and Nicolson, 1954).

Ben-Menahem, H., *Judicial Deviation in Talmudic Law* (Chur etc.: Harwood Academic Publishers, 1991).

Ben-Menahem, H., "The Judicial Process and the Nature of Jewish Law", in *An Introduction to the History and Sources of Jewish Law*, ed. N. Hecht, B. S. Jackson, D. Piattelli, S. M. Passamaneck and A.M. Rabello (Oxford: The Clarendon Press, 1996), 421-437.

Ben-Menahem, H., "Dworkin and Jewish Law", Paper prepared for the 16th World Congress of Jewish Studies (WUJS), Jerusalem 2013.

Berkovits, B., "*Get* and *Talaq* in English Law: Reflections on Law and Policy", in *Islamic Family Law*, ed. Chibli Mallat and Jane Connors (London: Graham & Trotman, 1990), 119-146.

Breitowitz, Y., *Between Civil and Religious Law – The Plight of the Agunah in American Society* (Westport Conn.: Greenwood Press, 1993).

Buber, M., *Two Types of Faith* (London: Routledge & Paul, 1951).

Cohen, H., *Ethik des reinen Willens* (Berlin: B. Cassirer, 1904).

Dworkin, R., *Taking Rights Seriously* (London: Duckworth, 1978).

Dworkin, R., *Religion without God* (Cambridge Mass and London: Harvard University Press, 2013).

Elon, M., "More about Research into Jewish Law", in *Modern Research in Jewish Law,* ed. B. S. Jackson (Leiden: E. J. Brill, 1980), 66-111.

Elon, M., *Jewish Law, History, Sources, Principles*, trld. B. Auerbach and M. J. Sykes (Philadelphia: Jewish Publication Society, 1994, 4 vols.).

Freeman, M. D. A., *Lloyd's Introduction to Jurisprudence* (London: Sweet & Maxwell, 1994, 6th ed.).

Freeman, M. D. A., "Is the Jewish *get* Any Business of the State?", in *Law and Religion. Current Legal Issues Volume 4*, ed. R. O'Dair and A. Lewis (Oxford: University Press, 2001), 365-83.

Freeman, M. D. A., ed., *Jewish Family Law in the State of Israel* (Binghamton: Global Publications, 2002).

Freeman, M. D. A., "The Law on Get and Why it Disappoints", 2002a, http://www.agunotcampaign.org.uk/civil_law.htm.

Freeman, M. D. A. and Mindus, P., eds., *The Legacy of John Austin's Jurisprudence* (Berlin: Springer, 2013).

Hart, H. L. A., *The Concept of Law* (Oxford: Clarendon Press: 1994, 2nd ed.).

Jackson, B. S., *Semiotics and Legal Theory* (London: Routledge & Kegan Paul, 1985; paperback ed. 1987, reprinted Liverpool: Deborah Charles Publications, 1997).

Jackson, B. S., *Law, Fact and Narrative Coherence* (Merseyside: Deborah Charles Publications, 1988).

Jackson, B. S., *Making Sense in Law. Linguistic, Psychological and Semiotic Perspectives* (Liverpool: Deborah Charles Publications, 1995).

Jackson, B. S., *Making Sense in Jurisprudence* (Liverpool: Deborah Charles Publications, 1996).

Jackson, B. S., *Studies in the Semiotics of Biblical Law* (Sheffield: Sheffield Academic Press, 2000).

Jackson, B. S., "*Mishpat Ivri, Halakhah* and Legal Philosophy: *Agunah* and the Theory of 'Legal Sources'", *JSIJ - Jewish Studies, an Internet Journal* 1 (2002), 69-107, at http://www.biu.ac.il/JS/JSIJ/jsij1.html.

Jackson, B. S., "Judaism as a Religious Legal System", in *Religion and Tradition. Comparative Studies in Religious Law,* ed. A. Huxley (London: RoutledgeCurzon, 2002a), 34-48.

Jackson, B. S., "*Agunah* and the Problem of Authority: Directions for Future Research", *Melilah* 2004/1, pp.1-78, available from http://www.manchesterjewishstudies.org/publications/.

Jackson, B. S., *Wisdom-Laws: A Study of the Mishpatim of Exodus 21:1-22:16* (Oxford: Oxford University Press, 2006).

Jackson, B. S., "'Transformative Accommodation' and Religious Law', *Ecclesiastical Law Journal* 11 (2009), 131-53.

Jackson, B.S., *Agunah: The Manchester Analysis* (Liverpool: Deborah Charles Publications, 2011).

Jackson, B. S., "Constructing a Theory of Halakhah" (2012, available from the Resources page of the Jewish Law Association web site, http://www.jewishlawassociation.org).

Jackson, B. S., "Some Preliminary Observations on Truth and Argumentation in the Jewish Legal Tradition", in *Standing Tall: Hommages à Csaba Varga*, ed. Bjarne Melkevek (Budapest: Pázmány Press, 2012a), 199-207.

Jackson, B. S., "Jewish Law and State Law: 'Transformative Accommodation' and the JFS case in England", in *The Fordham Conference Volume*, ed. D.B. Sinclair and L. Rabinovich (Liverpool: The Jewish Law Association, 2012b; Jewish Law Association Studies XXIII), 76-92.

Jackson, B. S., "Trust in(g) Eric", in *As interações sensíveis: Ensaios de sociossemiótica a partir da obra de Eric Landowski*, ed. A.C. de Oliveira (São Paulo: Editions Estação das Letras e Cores e Editora CPS, 2013), 81-100.

Kelsen, H., *General Theory of Law and State*, trld. A. Wedberg (Cambridge Mass.: Harvard University Press, 1946).

Kelsen, H., "Professor Stone and the Pure Theory of Law", *Stanford Law Review* 17 (1965), 1130-57.

Kelsen, H., *The Pure Theory of Law,* trld. M. Knight (Berkeley and Los Angeles: University of California Press, l967).

Kelsen, H., *General Theory of Norms*, trld M. Hartney (Oxford: The Clarendon Press, 1991).

Lacey, N., *A Life of H. L. A. Hart, The Nightmare and the Noble Dream* (Oxford: University Press, 2004).

Lamm, N. and Kirschenbaum, A., "Freedom and Constraint in the Jewish Juridical Process", *Cardozo Law Review* 1 (1979), 99-133.

Landowski, E., *La Société Réfléchie* (Paris: Le Seuil, 1989).

Levinas, E., "Martin Buber and the Theory of Knowledge", in *The Philosophy of Martin Buber*, ed. P.A. Schilpp (London: Cambridge UP, 1967), 133-50.

Pintore, A., *Il Diritto Senza Verità* (Torino: Giappichelli, 1996), translated as *Law without Truth* (Liverpool: Deborah Charles Publications, 2000).

Schwarzschild, S. S., "Truth", *Encyclopedia Judaica* (Jerusalem: Keter, 1973), XV.1414-15.

Shachar, A., *Multicultural Jurisdictions: Cultural Differences and Women's Rights* (Cambridge: Cambridge University Press, 2001).

Silberg, M., *Talmudic Law and the Modern State,* trld. B. Z. Bokser (New York: Burning Bush Press, 1973).

Smith, D. W., "Phenomenology", *The Stanford Encyclopedia of Philosophy* (*Fall 2011 Edition*), Edward N. Zalta (ed.): http://plato.stanford.edu/archives/fall2011/entries/phenomenology

Sprung, Y., "How Does Halakha Work? (R. J. D. Bleich)", 2013, http://thinkjudaism.wordpress.com/2013/08/13/how-does-halakha-work-r-j-d-bleich/

Tolley, T., "When binding is not binding and when not binding, binds: An analysis of the procedural route of 'non-binding arbitration' in AI v MT", *Child and Family Law Quarterly* 25/4 (2013), 484-501.

Rules of Forgiveness and the Role of Narratives in Talmudic Law

David Nelken
Distinguished Professor of Sociology, University of Macerata, Italy; Professor of Comparative and Transnational Law in Context, Dickson Poon School of Law, Kings College

I am very pleased to contribute to this Festschrift for Michael Freeman. As with many of the other contributors to this volume we go back a long way. Indeed, Michael and I went to the same grammar school – although he was sufficiently older that our paths did not cross. I also spent a period (1984-1990) teaching with him at UCL, though again, Michael held down such a disproportionate load of teaching and writing that I felt reluctant to bother him too much. We have only really begun to collaborate properly very recently, during the last two years when we edited a journal together.[1] But if I took less advantage of his friendship and wisdom than I might have done, this did not stop him more than once showing me kindness, and I also had the opportunity to enjoy his and Vivien's famous hospitality.

The school we both went to was a Jewish one (the Hasmonean). And not least among Michael's many achievements must be counted his important role in seeking to reform aspects of the Jewish law of divorce. So I thought it might be a good idea to offer a short paper that starts from a Talmudic[2] discussion but, that, hopefully, also speaks to wider (or narrower?) matters of academic interest. The text in question includes a number of stories that illustrate the difficulties of asking for and giving forgiveness. It touches not only on issues in the sociology of law and criminology (my main areas of interest) but also legal philosophy; law and literature; law and religion; family law; and criminal justice. As Michael has made important contributions in all

1 *The International Journal of Law in Context* (Cambridge University Press), jointly edited together with Carrie Menkel-Meadow.

2 The Talmud is the fundamental text of Rabbinic Judaism. It records around 500 years of free-ranging discussions of the Mishnaic Code (itself derived from the written and unwritten Bible) which were eventually written down and redacted, mainly in Aramaic, c.500 CE. It has been commented on ever since (and turned back into codes!) and (to a greater or lesser extent) still guides the life of religious Jews. (See, e.g. Steinsaltz, 1976; Fonrobert and Jaffee, 2007) It is not only the fundamental source of legal authority, but its study is also seen as the supreme commandment that leads to all others – an attempt through the analysis of revelation to get on the Divine wavelength. See Fishbane, 2008. For evidence of a revival in Talmud study, see Kremer, 2013.

A. Diduck, N. Peleg, H. Reece (eds.), Law in Society: Reflections on Children, Family, Culture and Philosophy
 ISBN 978-90-04-26148-8. pp. 63-81.

these areas – amongst others – it thus allows me to pay homage to Michael's polymathic abilities.[3]

I shall first set out the relevant Talmudic texts. I then go on to discuss the contemporary interpretations provided by Emanuel Levinas[4] and Moshe Halbertal.[5] Levinas' reflections come from a lecture called, 'Toward the other' (Levinas, 1990a). It was presented in a colloquium on forgiveness held in October 1963, which was concerned with the problem of how to build normal relations with Germans and with Germany, so soon after the Holocaust/Shoah. Halbertal's paper, on the other hand, was published more recently, in the *Jewish Review of Books* (Halbertal, 2011). In Talmudic style I will also offer some further interpretation of their interpretations. In the next section of the paper I use this debate so as to examine the relationship between rules and narrative in Talmudic law, focusing on the way stories can supplement the use of rules. The claim, put forward especially by Halbertal, that the Talmudic authors were here trying to tell us something about the limits of reliance on rules for leading the good life, may be of special interest given that we are talking about a religious sensibility long seen in the Christian world as a particularly 'legalistic' one.[6] I end by suggesting some of the possible implications of these texts for thinking about the role of forgiveness in domestic and international forums of criminal justice.

---

3 As shown, for example, in the incredible range of topics he has written about and taught, his long-running editorship of successive editions of his wide-ranging *Lloyd's Introduction to Jurisprudence*, and his editorship of the ambitious, interdisciplinary *Current Legal Issues* series.

4 Emanuel Levinas was a famous existential philosopher and Jewish educationalist. See, e.g. Hand, 1989; Hand, 2009.

5 Moshe Halbertal is Professor of Law, NYU and Professor of Hebrew Thought at the Hebrew University Jerusalem. See, e.g. Halbertal and Margalit, 1992; Halbertal, 1997. Halbertal was a leading member of the Hartman institute – a modern orthodox centre seeking to apply Jewish law taking account of modern sensibilities. See especially Hartman, 2011.

6 The term 'Pharisaic' is regularly used in public discussions in contemporary Italy to signify sticking to the rules in such a way as to stifle the spirit of the law. For example, under the headline THE PHARISEES OF ALDO MORO AVENUE, (the headquarters of the Regional Government of Emilia Romagna), an editorialist in *La Repubblica,* a major national Italian newspaper, wrote recently '"We have respected the laws". This is the refrain that the Regional Councillors repeat every time. By now the political class only knows how to repeat this (excuse)'. (My translation). The easy use of this trope is particularly interesting in that *La Repubblica* is a notoriously anti-clerical newspaper. (*La Repubblica,* 15 November 2013).

On the many meanings of the polemical term 'legalism', see Jackson, 1979; Yinger, 2008.

יום הכפורים פרק שמיני יומא פז

בצבו נפשה לקטלא נפיק וצבו ביתיה לית הוא עביד וריקן לביתיה אזיל ולואי שהוא ביאה כיציאה וכי הוי חוי אמבוהא אבתריה אמר אם יעלה לשמים שיאו וראשו לעב יגיע כגללו לנצח יאבד רואיו יאמרו איו רב זוטרא כי הוו מכתפי ליה בשבתא דריגלא הוה אמר כי לא לעולם חסן ואם נזר לדור ודור שאת פני רשע לא טוב לא טוב להם לרשעים שנושאין להם פנים בעולם הזה לא טוב לו לאחאב (א) שנשאו לו פנים בעוה"ז שנאמר יען כי נכנע (אחאב מלפני) לא אביא הרעה בימיו להטות צדיק במשפט טוב להם לצדיקים שאין נושאין להם פנים בעוה"ז טוב לו למשה שלא נשאו לו פנים בעוה"ז שנאמר יען לא האמנתם בי להקדישני הא אילו האמנתם בי עדיין לא הגיע זמנכם ליפטר מן העולם אשריהם לצדיקים לא דיין שהן זוכין אלא שמזכין לבניהם ולבני בניהם עד סוף כל הדורות שכמה בנים היו לו לאהרן שראויין לישרף כנדב ואביהוא שנאמר הנותרים אלא שעמד להם זכות אביהם אוי להם לרשעים לא דיין שמחייבין עצמן אלא שמחייבין לבניהם ולבני בניהם עד סוף כל הדורות הרבה בנים היו לו לכנען שראויין ליסמך כטבי עבדו של רבן גמליאל אלא שחובת אביהם גרמה להן כל המזכה את הרבים אין חטא בא על ידו וכל המחטיא את הרבים כמעט אין מספיקין בידו לעשות תשובה כל המזכה את הרבים אין חטא בא על ידו מ"ט כדי שלא יהא הוא בגיהנם ותלמידיו בגן עדן שנאמר כי לא תעזוב נפשי לשאול לא תתן חסידך לראות שחת וכל המחטיא את הרבים אין מספיקין בידו לעשות תשובה שלא יהא הוא בגן עדן ותלמידיו בגיהנם שנאמר אדם עשק בדם נפש עד בור ינוס אל יתמכו בו: האומר ארחטא ואשוב ארחטא ואשוב: למה לי למימר ארחטא ואשוב תרי זימני כדרב הונא אמר רב דאמר רב הונא אמר רב כיון שעבר אדם עבירה ושנה בה הותרה לו הותרה לו סלקא דעתך אלא נעשית לו כהיתר: ארחטא ויום הכפורים מכפר אין יום הכפורים מכפר: לימא מתני' דלא כרבי דתניא רבי אומר על כל עבירות שבתורה בין עשה תשובה בין לא עשה תשובה יוה"כ מכפר אפילו תימא רבי אגב שאני: עבירות שבין אדם למקום וכו': רמי ליה רב יוסף בר חבו לרבי אבהו (ג) עבירות שבין אדם לחבירו אין יוה"כ מכפר והא כתיב אם יחטא איש לאיש ופללו אלהים מאן אלהים דיינא אי הכי אימא סיפא ואם לה' יחטא איש מי יתפלל לו הכי קאמר אם יחטא איש לאיש ופללו אלהים ימחול לו ואם לה' יחטא איש מי יתפלל בעדו תשובה ומעשים טובים אמר ר' יצחק כל המקניט את חבירו אפילו בדברים צריך לפייסו שנאמר בני אם ערבת לרעך תקעת לזר כפיך נוקשת באמרי פיך עשה זאת אפוא בני והנצל כי באת בכף רעך לך התרפס ורהב רעיך אם ממון (ג) יש בידך התר לו פסת יד ואם לאו הרבה עליו ריעים (ואמר) רב חסדא וצריך לפייסו בשלש שורות של שלשה בני אדם שנאמר ישור על אנשים ויאמר חטאתי וישר העויתי ולא שוה לי (ואמר) ר' יוסי בר חנינא כל המבקש מטו מחבירו אל יבקש ממנו יותר משלש פעמים שנאמר אנא שא נא ועתה שא נא ואם מת מביא עשרה בני אדם ומעמידן על קברו ואומר חטאתי לה' אלהי ישראל ולפלוני שחבלתי בו ר' ירמיה הוה ליה מילתא לר' אבא בהדיה אזל (ז) איתיב ארשא דר' אבא בהדי דשדיא אמתיה מיא מטא זריפי דמיא ארישא אמר עשאוני כאשפה קרא אנפשיה מאשפות ירים אביון שמע ר' אבא ונפיק לאפיה אמר ליה השתא צריכנא למיפק מדעתך דכתיב לך התרפס ורהב רעיך ר' זירא כי הוה ליה מילתא בהדי איניש הוה חליף ותני לקמיה וממציא ליה כי היכי דניתי וניפוק ליה מדעתיה רב הוה ליה מילתא בהדי ההוא טבחא לא אתא לקמיה במעלי יומא דכפורי אמר איהו איזיל אנא לפיוסי ליה פגע ביה רב הונא אמר ליה להיכא קא אזיל מר אמר ליה לפיוסי לפלניא אמר אזיל (*) אבא למיקטל נפשא אזל וקם עילויה הוה יתיב וקא פלי רישא דלי עיניה וחזייה אמר ליה אבא את זיל לית לי מילתא בהדך בהדי דקא פלי רישא אישתמיט גרמא ומחייה בקועיה וקטליה רב הוה פסיק סדרא קמיה דרבי עייל ארתא

Raba and the Butcher: A Talmudic Text about Forgiveness

The following is an abbreviated translation of the introductory text and four stories (or vignettes) about forgiveness[7] that are found in the Talmud (Masechet Yomah 87a).[8]

> For transgressions committed by man against his fellowman the Day of Atonement procures no atonement…[9] Rav [i.e. Rabbi] Isaac said: 'Whosoever offends against his neighbour, even if he does it only through words, must pacify him …' Rav Hisda said: 'He should endeavour to pacify him through three groups of three people each…'[10] Rav Jose ben Hanina said: 'One who asks pardon of his neighbour need do so no more than three times…'
>
> (*Story 1*) Rav. Abba had a complaint against Rav Jeremiah. He [Rav Jeremiah] went and sat down at the door of Rav Abba and, as the maid poured out (soiled) water, some drops fell upon his head. Then he said: They have made a dung- heap of me, and he cited this passage about himself: He raiseth up the poor out of the dust[11]… When Abba heard that verse he came out towards him, saying: Now, I must come forth to appease you, as it is written: 'Go, humble thyself and urge thy neighbour.'
>
> (*Story 2*) When Rav Zera had any complaint against any man, he would repeatedly pass by him, showing himself to him, so that he might come forth to [pacify] him.
>
> (*Story 3*) Raba [also read as Rav] once had a complaint against a certain butcher, and when on the eve of the Day of Atonement he [the butcher] did not come to him [to seek forgiveness]… He said: 'I shall go to him to appease him'. Rav Huna met him and asked: 'Where are you going, Sir?' 'To pacify so-and-so', he replied. He said (or he thought): 'Abba [Raba] is about to cause that person's death'.[12] He [Raba] went there and remained standing before him [the butcher], who was sitting and chopping an (animal's) head. He raised

---

7 It is important to stress that these texts are only some of the many materials relevant to forgiveness found in Jewish law and lore. Note that I have left out here the otherwise all-important biblical or other proof texts brought in support of each legal statement.

8 The numbering of the stories is mine –we will be concentrating on the third story, which is the one that has attracted most attention.

9 God's forgiveness, however extensive, only encompasses those sins that man commits directly against Him, 'bein adam la-Makom'; those in which an injury is caused to one's fellow man, 'bein adam le-haver', are not forgiven until the injured party has himself forgiven the perpetrator. Hence the obligation of seeking forgiveness from those one may have wronged on the eve of the Day of Atonement, without which proper atonement cannot be made.

10 In Jewish law, doing something three times establishes a pattern of behaviour. If one has refused reconciliation three times, then it is considered that they are set in their refusal and no more attempts would help.

11 Me'Ashpot Yarim (a play on his name, Yirmiyah).

12 As he knew that the butcher was a hard man and would not take advantage of Raba's offer of forgiveness.

his eyes and saw him [Raba], then said: 'You are Abba [another name for Raba]. Go away. I [will] have nothing to do with you.' Whilst he was chopping the head,[13] a bone flew off, struck his throat, and killed him [the butcher].

(*Story 4*) Once Raba was expounding portions of the Torah before the Rabbis, and there entered Rav Hiyya, whereupon Raba started again from the beginning. When Bar Kappara came in, he started again from the beginning. As Rav Simeon, the son of Ravvi entered, he started again from the beginning. But when Rav Hanina Ben Hama entered, he said: 'How often shall I start again?' And he did not go over it again.

Rav Hanina took that amiss. Raba went to him on 13 eves of the Day of Atonement, but he would not be pacified. But how could he do so? Did not Rav Jose ben Hanina say: 'One who asks pardon of his neighbour need not do so more than three times?' – It is different with Raba.[14] But how could Rav Hanina act so [unforgivingly]? ... Rav Hanina had seen in a dream that Raba was being hanged on a palm tree, and since the tradition is that one who in a dream is hanged on a palm tree will become head [of an Academy] he concluded that authority will be given to him, and so he would not be pacified, to the end that he departed to teach Torah in Babylon.[15]

Commentary

What do these somewhat cryptic stories set out to teach us? How, if at all, are they interconnected? The answer is a matter of ongoing interpretation. But a number of points seem clear enough. The stories include two examples of offenders seeking forgiveness and two giving it. The first two cases involve success in asking for and receiving forgiveness, the latter two are (apparently) stories of failure. These last two cases are also the ones where there is an evident power-difference, between Raba and the butcher,[16] and between Raba and the head designate of his Academy. But matters become more difficult if we ask whether the stories represent a logical progression of some sort. Both Levinas and Halbertal think they do. Halbertal tells us that, 'The ordering of these stories is not chronological; it's conceptual' (Halbertal, 2011: 34).[17] On the other hand, there are also differences between these commentators. Halbertal,

13 Some commentators see the animal's head as serving for the butcher as a surrogate for Raba's head.

14 He is someone who 'goes beyond' what is legally required.

15 He interpreted the dream to mean that he would die soon, to make place for Raba rather than himself become head of the Academy. In order to allow for another interpretation, with less fatal results to himself, he refused to become reconciled to Raba, forcing the latter to go to Babylon, where in accord with that dream Raba did become the head of the School of Sura.

16 We learn elsewhere in the Talmud that Raba was in control of the marketplace and the butcher had been called out for bad behaviour (butchers were regularly suspected of manipulating weights and measures).

17 He deduces this from the fact that the Talmud records that 'Raba lived before, not after, Rav Zera'. For Professor Jacob Neusner, who has also written extensively about the rela-

unlike Levinas, sees the stories as (intentionally?) teaching us the limits of rules. Although both authors concentrate on the third of the stories, Levinas also discusses the last story, which Halbertal does not.

For Levinas, Raba's action follows on from the previous story of Rav Zerah and has to do with doing everything possible to make forgiveness come about. Raba forgets his pride to the extent of going right up to the offender to give him the chance to repent. But the butcher is locked in his world – he has cut himself off from the chance of repentance. But if, in the third story, it was the butcher who was not ready to ask for forgiveness, in the one following it is Raba who is in difficulty. Levinas tells us that he is unhappy with a superficial reading of the story. How could Rav Hanina refuse to forgive so as to further his ambitions? He offers us a better explanation (1990),[18] and suggests that Raba's rudeness was revelatory to Rav Hanina of Raba's (Freudian) unconscious ambition to replace him as head of the Academy. Because Raba himself did not recognise his own motives, it was impossible to forgive him.

For Halbertal, by contrast, the stories tell us even more than this. They 'build up to teach us about the requisites of forgiveness, prerequisites that cannot be legislated but only intuited, the stories are telling something vital about rules and their limits' (Halbertal, 2011: 34). Their significance can be captured through the concept of the threshold. 'In the first incident', he says, 'R. Jeremiah, who has come to ask forgiveness from Rav Abba, is seated at the threshold, probably finding it difficult to enter, fearing that Rav Abba will rebuff him, or worse, that his appearance will renew the injury. But the humiliation he suffers at the hands of the maidservant reverses the situation; now, having been sprayed with dirty water, he is Rav Abba's victim. His ironic recitation of the verse brought Rav Abba out to ask his pardon, and, he says, the threshold (both literal and figurative) was crossed' (*ibid*: 34).

'The story', argues Halbertal, 'seems intended to point out a serious problem with trying to institutionalizing the requirement that forgiveness be requested. One can formulate rules that dictate how to ask for forgiveness, but these rules can only come into play when an encounter between the injurer and injured is possible. This requires a kind of preliminary appeasement. The narrative thus demonstrates the limitations of the law as it appears before us. One might say it places the law itself at the threshold. Every request for forgiveness is preceded by some forgiveness that makes the request possible.' (*ibid*: 34).

In the next story, Rav Zera's actions, which are presented as worthy of emulation, 'creates the conditions in which it will be possible for the injurer to approach him. The injured party extends the forgiveness that precedes forgiveness without any assurance that the injurer will in fact be remorseful and request his pardon.'(*ibid*: 34). Importantly, 'this act of grace does not obviate the remorse that must precede full reconciliation; it only makes it possible. Nor is it, apparently, legally required. The

---

tionship of Halacha and Aggada, the Talmud should not be seen as attempting to offer reliable history. See, e.g. Neusner, 2004.

18 Levinas says that he came up with this solution 'with the help of a young Jewish poet called Mrs Satlan' (1990: 24).

passage presents us with an exemplary story that expresses the greatness of grace without making it a binding norm' (*ibid*: 34).[19]

'The third story shows why Rav Zera's practice was an act of pure grace that cannot be turned into law. The story tells of Rav (i.e. Raba) who, on the eve of Yom Kippur, was awaiting the arrival of the butcher who had injured him. When the butcher does not come, Rav decides to go to him. At first blush, Rav's action seems quite similar to Rav Zera's. Knowing that Yom Kippur will not expiate the butcher's sin unless he appeases his fellow, Rav decides to waive his honour and go to the butcher himself. In fact, he does more than cross the threshold from the injured party's side to that of the injurer; he also crosses class lines. There is a vast class divide between Rav, the leading scholar of his generation, and the lowly butcher. Moreover, the timing of the story—the eve of Yom Kippur, the last minute for doing what needs to be done to make atonement possible—marks a threshold in time' (Halbertal, 2011: 34).

How far do Levinas and Halbertal disagree about the reasons the Talmud is offering for Raba's failure with the butcher?[20] Certainly, Levinas too admits that Raba's personality played a part in what happened. He describes him as someone who is 'so sensitive and so dangerous', and speaks of 'the enormity of the responsibility which Raba took upon himself in his premature confidence in the humanity of 'the other' (Levinas, 1990a: 23). As he puts it, 'purity can kill', what he calls Raba's 'excessive moral sensitivity' is the proximate cause of the butcher's death (*ibid*: 24). We could also perhaps add that, in his interpretation of the fourth story, Levinas again represents Raba as someone out of touch with his deeper motivations. But he still seems nearer than Halbertal to those mainstream commentators who do not blame Raba at all, seeing what happened as no more than the outcome of his best efforts to make peace. They assume that the butcher is risking death and punishment in this world and the next world by not asking for his forgiveness. Raba can therefore only help and not harm him by giving him a last chance to repent.[21] For Halbertal, by contrast, there

19 My King's colleague Irit Samet comments on this, 'I guess that what cannot be demanded by the law is to physically create the conditions for reconciliation. But what can be demanded is "not to burn all the bridges" within your own psyche, by brooding on the insult so as to close yourself to the possibility of forgiveness. Although creating a space for dialogue with the offender, or retaining such space, is not really necessary for forgiveness. I can think of cases where it is the *complete* cut off from the offender that leads to forgiveness, at least in the sense that your level of interest in the other is so low, that you don't entertain any wishes about him any more – that God will punish him, that you will be able to take revenge etc. In the sense you have forgiven him, you don't care about his sin any more at all.' (personal communication, 14/11/2013).

20 It is common to find even diametrically conflicting interpretations amongst the major commentators, even when it comes to some of the behaviour of the most respected (but sometimes also the least admired) figures in the bible stories, going back to early Midrash interpretations and through the medieval to the modern period. A classic example is the debate over the exact nature of King David's sin in sending the husband of Bathsheba to be killed at the battlefront.

21 Since the text does not actually say who was to blame in the original dispute, another, less plausible if not entirely impossible, reading would have it that Raba himself feared

is definitely a suggestion of emotional clumsiness in Raba's not understanding that forgiveness has its thresholds and that the butcher was totally unprepared for his approach. Hence it would have been better not to try.

Both these interpretations have some support in the texts. In favour of Levinas's approach we can bring a statement found in an earlier page of this section of the Talmud where we learn how careful Raba is said to be of their sensitivities in his dealings with butchers. In a discussion of those sins that cause a desecration of God's name such that the Day of Atonement can not atone for them, without it also being necessary for the offender to die, Raba's chosen example is 'he who gets his meat from the butcher and does not pay him at once.' This is seen as a desecration because 'he would learn from my bad example to treat debts dishonestly by delaying and ultimately ignoring them'. On the other hand, in support of Halbertal's interpretation, we have the warning given by Rav Huna (acting as the chorus in the third story) to Raba of the likely consequences of his actions.[22]

But more than the question of what blame, if any, to attribute to Raba, what is important for Halbertal is the reason for his failure with the butcher. For him,

> The first story ... shows the way in which there has to be a partial reconciliation before the full reconciliation, a forgiveness before the forgiveness. As a result of that limitation, the second story suggests a secondary, even saintly, norm, in which the injured person makes an effort to enable the crossing of the threshold by insinuating himself into the presence of the injurer. The third story then shows that solution to be limited, since the outcome of the intrusion could be a further injury. It may not be as drastic or seemingly supernatural as the butcher's tragic end, but a request for forgiveness can turn into a further insult all too easily (Halbertal, 2011: 34).

Halbertal concludes: 'The Talmud pointedly does not go on to formulate further legislation to resolve this issue' (*ibid:* 34). (He also points out that Maimonides does not in fact codify any requirements for copying the behaviour described in these stories. So what does this tell us about the general relationship between rules and narrative in the Talmud?

The Role of Narratives in the Talmud

Habertal asks,

> Would it be possible to use a further norm to structure the question of how to make the first step? Can one mark with any degree of generality the distinction between a delicate or indirect meeting and an accusatory intrusion? (*ibid*: 34)

---

he might have been at fault and was seeking to sort the matter out for his own sake.

22 Of course it is just possible to say that Rav Huna himself was mistaken, not understanding that what Raba was doing was the right thing- even if the butcher died as a result.

He answers,

> The law as a process of generalized rulemaking here reaches its limit. Requesting forgiveness ultimately requires tact, sound judgment, and a profound and precise analysis of one's own motives.' (*ibid*: 34)

More generally, his comments raise the question of the relationship between rules and narrative. To explore the normative implications of these stories we might want to locate them in the part of the Talmud known as Aggada – the passages in which we find not only stories (sometimes fantastical ones), but also philosophical and ethical sayings, health advice and folklore more generally (see Heinemann, 1986; Encyclopedia Judaica, 2008). Could this disagreement between Levinas and Halbertal be linked to their views about the relationship between rules and stories in the Talmud? Levinas does not spell out his general approach in this lesson. But elsewhere in other lectures he explains his preference for discussing texts from the Aggada in his 'Nine lessons' as a deliberate way of avoiding Halachic discussions with legal relevance, where he feels unworthy to tread. Nonetheless Levinas does, albeit in a loose way, draw out some implications from these stories for actual practice. Arguing that, 'whilst we can forgive the Germans it is not possible to forgive all Germans' – he points to the moral of the Raba and the butcher story for the then controversial case of Martin Heidegger, the pre-eminent philosopher who never publically expressed regret for his ambiguous role as Rector at Freiburg and partial fellow traveller with the Nazi party (Levinas, 1990a: 25).[23]

Halbertal, on the other hand, sees the third story as aiming to show the difficulty faced by rules in providing generalisable guidance of how to act in such circumstances. The message is that what he describes as the need for 'tact, judgement and self understanding' (Halbertal, 2011: 34) – or what we might perhaps also call 'emotional intelligence', can never be just a matter of rule-following. He insists, as we have seen, that the lack of codification of these stories confirms his reading that it is impossible to 'institutionalise', as a matter of hard and fast rules, how to achieve 'pre-forgiveness' before attempting forgiveness (*ibid*: 34), even if stories do help the understanding of standards and contribute to shaping that ability to follow rules wisely

According to the Jerusalem Talmud, in general, 'Aggada cannot be used in determining Halacha' (Jerusalem Talmud, Peah 11:6). The wider, and in some ways, 'wilder', materials categorisable as Aggada are also less tightly monitored than the Halachic parts. This is especially true with reference to their chains of authoritative transmis-

23 Disillusion with Heidegger also played some part in Levinas' own move from existential philosopher to more central concern in life and work with Jewish tradition and practice. The Heidegger affair exploded in 1987 with the publication of a book by Victor Farias on the subject. More recently the publication of Heidegger's war diaries has provided unequivocal evidence of his negative feelings towards Jews.

sion or the links to scriptural proof sources.[24] For Jeffrey Rubenstein, a leading scholar of Talmudic narratives, 'stories do not generally provide simple conclusions. They provide the sages a way to ponder the tensions inherent in their culture, not an easy means of resolving them' (Rubenstein, 1999: 3).[25] On the other hand, the demarcation line between Halacha and Aggada is not always clear cut, and not least because the passages attributed to each are interspersed and not labelled as such.[26] Assuming that these vignettes belong (only) to the Aggada therefore begs the question, especially if the only way to demarcate its boundaries is to define it, with unhelpful circularity, as all the material that does not determine the practical observances demanded by Halacha.

In practice, stories are placed by the redactors at points in the Talmud sections where they are in fact highly relevant to the Halachic discussion, and cross- reference is not uncommon. In our case the Talmud itself interrogates the last story in which Raba is forced to leave the country by asking why he kept trying thirteen times to find forgiveness (the *Halachic* answer being, that where one's teacher is concerned, one just has to keep on trying).[27] The same is true of its effort, on the other hand, to provide an answer as to how Rav Hanina could have refused to forgive after being asked so many times. Its highly unusual and specific account of the reasons could be said to demonstrate the need felt to show that this behaviour was an exception to the rule, one motivated by overriding life and death concerns.

But for those working within the Talmudic tradition, the way we classify the stories is perhaps less important than taking to heart the point that we need to learn *how* to live by rules (or sometimes even without rules) (for a Catholic-inspired approach to these matters, see Bankowski, 2001), rather than just establish what the rules should be.[28] As the Talmud itself teaches, it is perfectly possible to be *'Naval bir'shuth*

---

24 The Talmud records that certain rabbis were considered experts in Aggada, but there are also mentions of scholars being criticised for spending their time on this rather than on examining the tougher and more recondite aspects of legal doctrines (what would nowadays be called 'black- letter law').

25 Rubinstein tells us that the Talmudic stories reflect the Sassanian Persian cultural background, that they work as closed units and were intended for elites who understood subtleties. Having something in common with literary devices like *chria* or *exemplum*, anecdotes about deeds and sayings of wise men, they are often closer to myth than their Hellenic counterparts.

26 Estimates of what part of the Talmud counts as Aggada range from 10 per cent to 25 per cent of its contents. It should also be remembered, however, that, even in its Halachic part, the Talmud seems to defy codification. As Patrick Glenn rightly points out, truth is approached via commentary rather than codifications (Glenn, 2007). Each codification in Jewish history, not least that authored by Maimonides, was soon submerged by commentary that relied on and led back to the Talmud.

27 Maimonides, *Laws of Repentance*, (Mishneh Torah) 2: 9-10. Given that elsewhere he defines one's teacher as anyone from whom one has learned anything, this enlarges the implications considerably.

28 As Rubenstein tells us, the Stammaim, the final redactors of the Talmud, sought a combination of legal acumen and virtuous character. The legal *sugyot* (sections of discussion)

ha'torah', i.e. to behave abominably even whilst apparently keeping to the rules and so staying within the boundaries of the law.[29] And the periodic rises of Ethical revival (Mussar) movements, in both medieval and modern periods, testify to the recurrent need for education in psychological awareness of motives and behaviour to supplement the predominant focus on Halachic study.

Alternatively the behaviour described in these stories could also be read as showing leading Rabbis feeling obliged to meet a requirement of going beyond the legal minimum (*'lifnim b'shurath ha'din*) so as to climb the ethical heights (see Kirschenbaum, 1991).[30]

> Aggada is a refinement of Halacha: thus, whereas the latter, being a code applicable to all men at all times, must base itself on the capabilities of mankind in general, the former is free to suggest a greater degree of Godliness that might be applicable only to a chosen few (http://www.headcoverings-by-devorah.com/Aggadah_Halachah.htm).

Many contemporary thinkers have also stressed the significance of Aggadic material, irrespective of its contribution to rule making. For Rabbi Abraham Joshua Heschel,[31] Aggada plays an essential corrective role with respect to Halacha (Heschel, 1955) (exactly in the way that Halbertal has sought to show for these stories). For him, Halacha represents the strength to shape one's life according to a fixed pattern; it is a form-giving force. Aggada is the expression of man's ceaseless striving that often defies all limitations. Halacha is the rationalisation and schematisation of living; it defines, specifies, sets measure and limit, placing life into an exact system. Aggada deals with man's ineffable relations to God, to other men, and to the world. Halacha deals with details, with each commandment separately; Aggada deals with the whole of life, with the totality of religious life. Halacha deals with the law; Aggada, with the meaning of the law. Halacha deals with subjects that can be expressed literally; Aggada introduces us to a realm that lies beyond the range of expression. Halacha teaches us how to perform common acts; Aggada tells us how to participate in the eternal drama. Halacha gives us knowledge; Aggada gives us aspiration. To reduce Judaism to law, to Halacha, is to dim its light, to pervert its essence and to kill its spirit. We have a legacy of Aggada together with a system of Halacha, and although, because of a variety of reasons, that legacy was frequently overlooked and Aggada became subservient to Halacha, Halacha is ultimately dependent upon Aggada. Halacha, the rationalisation of living, is not only forced to employ elements which are themselves unreasoned, its ultimate authority depends upon Aggadah. Heschel sees Halacha as akin to Regularity (*Keva*). He sees Aggada as akin to spontaneity – or mindfulness

---

teach how to think like a sage, the narrative how to be one (Rubenstein, 1999).

29 This can be compared to the difference between law and equity in the common law.

30 As my friend Professor Roger Cotterrell pointed out to me, this is very similar to Lon Fuller's contrast between the 'morality of duty' and the 'morality of aspiration'.

31 Heschel was an important (and now iconic) Conservative Jewish leader from a famous Hassidic lineage who also played a role in the early civil rights movement.

(*Kavanah*). He explains that generally the pole of regularity is stronger than that of spontaneity and therefore we must take care, as there is a 'perpetual risk of our observance and worship becoming mere habit, a mechanical performance' (Heschel, 2007).

Another contemporary thinker, Rabbi Nathan Lopez Cardozo,[32] for his part, agrees that Aggada 'prevents mechanical observance by freeing man's inner spirit'. Aggada's role is to show why there are any rules at all.

> Aggada – from the Aramaic root, ngd, 'to flow' – is the part of the Torah that deals with the whole of life, rather than the laws in accordance with which it should be lived. ... It is the aspiration of man, whereas Halacha is the consummation...While there is no other option but to follow Halacha, Aggada's paths are suggestions and offer voluntary choices to each individual... it does not purport to possess or present the 'truth', although, as in the case of Halacha, there is often a consensus of the majority of the Sages. Rather, Aggada was cultivated so as to allow the unseen to enter the visible world and was formulated to give man the ability to go beyond the realms of the definable, perceivable, and demonstrable. It answers man's need to understand the reasons for the actions demanded of him and assures him that there is purpose to what he does (Cardozo, 1998: 168).

On the other hand, it is important to note that, even if these Talmudic stories suggest limits to the successful regulation of forgiveness, this has not discouraged Jewish law from continuing to develop rule-based systems for dealing with the complex issues that this social practice involves. Do you still need to ask forgiveness if you know that the other person has already forgiven you? (The answer is yes.) What if you spoke badly about someone but no one believed it. Do you still have to tell the victim? (No.) What if the person you bad-mouth doesn't know what was said about him or her. Do you still have to tell them the details when apologising? (Rabbi Israel Salanter, a leader of Jewish ethical movement in the 19th century, again says no, you will only upset them by doing so). What if you feel the other person is angry with you for no good reason? (Answer, you still have to appease them unless they are being clearly irrational. Note, this would seem to require very careful assessment.) As important, and touching on our stories, there are rules that specify those cases in which a person is allowed not to forgive, for example if the offender still has not admitted what is owed, or if the victim fears that the episode will be repeated, or if forgiveness is being withheld to reform the offender's future conduct.[33]

For its part, as Halbertal shows us, Halacha demonstrates an awareness of the truths revealed by these narratives. He tells us 'the clear intent is to make the request for forgiveness a social fact. A single, casual encounter involving only the injurer and the injured will not suffice' (Halbertal, 2011: 34). The institution of involving the com-

---

32 Rabbi Cardozo is a contemporary creative thinker within the Orthodox Jewish world, and Dean of the Cardozo Academy in Jerusalem.

33 http://www.thehalachacenter.org/at_a_glance/5771_yom_kippur.php. (The Center for the study and practice of monetary Halacha). In this list there is no reference to Rabbi Hanina's exceptional reasons for not forgiving Raba.

munity by taking three friends with us, when we ask for forgiveness, could well be viewed as the solution found to avoiding the dangers highlighted in these stories (the risk of going it alone).[34] But no rules can tell us when we should nonetheless try to go out of our way to help someone who needs forgiveness. Halbertal (*ibid*) calls this 'grace'; making rules about this would be going too far (and, as he explains, it would lead to infinite regress). As the stories also show us, the outcomes of attempts to forgive or to be forgiven are in any case not entirely in our hands (in one case being fortunate enough to have the contents of a bedpan thrown over you, and in another two cases encountering death or at least the risk of it). The main advice to be given about undertaking such hazardous missions is to recognise the dangers.

Drawing out the Implications

What, if anything, can legal scholars take away from this brief glimpse of texts that date back almost 2,000 years and whose main purpose is to contribute to unfolding a given tradition for the members of a specific faith-community? One line of research might be to look into the variety of ways stories and law interact in different systems of law, both old and new.[35] In particular, we could search for the current secular equivalents of law (Halacha) and stories (Aggada)? Is the latter to be found in biographies of great judges and lawyers (or the 'little judge' as hero, in France or Italy)? In the media and the Internet? In Civics lessons? (Or in all of the above?)

Another line of enquiry concerns the way that narratives can be displaced by expertise. Both purportedly secular as well as religious legal systems nowadays in-

34 Maimonides says that the first approach should be made by the offender alone. But most other authorities turn the issue between the parties into a community matter from the outset. I do not know why the Talmud does not comment on the lack of three friends in the stories themselves, but this certainly would seem to support Maimonides' view.

35 Much of the existing research concerns the somewhat different questions of what makes trial evidence convincing, or the way narratives can provide a basis for creating or distinguishing legal rulings. See Jackson, 1998; Nelken, 1994. The applied story-telling conference held in 2013 in London's City University included as themes: discussions of story structure and their application in law. The legislative process and storytelling, policy arguments as a form of narrative reasoning, statutory analysis, intersections with elements of narrative theory, empirical research into the role of storytelling in the lawyering process, the roles of different characters involved in legal actions, the ethical limits of using storytelling in the lawyering process, the relationship and use of metaphors in the language of specific areas of law, exploration of the use of narrative or metaphor in judicial opinions, comparative storytelling models across different legal systems and different classes of clients, and applications of story techniques borrowed from other writing genres.
But the writings of those concerned with the relationship between law and literature are perhaps more pertinent here. On the distinction between law in literature and law as literature, see eg. Nelken, 1996; Bruner, 2002; Ball, 2000.

creasingly reach out for scientific expertise for guidance and for legitimation.[36] Some Jewish religious counsellors on the Internet segue seamlessly from citing religious requirements to quoting the recommendations of social scientists. For example, an answer provided under the rubric of 'Ask the expert: apologizing',[37] begins by citing the major Halachic source, the Shulchan Aruch,[38] but moves on quickly to recommending the advice of Professor Everett L. Worthington Jr. of Virginia Commonwealth University, a psychologist who studies forgiveness and writes about what makes a good and effective apology. We are told that Worthington uses the term 'Confess' as a handy acronym to help people remember all the steps of a meaningful request for forgiveness.[39] Significantly, for our purposes, the 'Expert' then adds, basing himself on the teachings of Professor Worthington – rather than the Talmudic stories we have been discussing – 'Another thing to remember is that the person you're apologizing to might not be ready to accept your apology', noting that some people may need more time others and some may never be willing to forgive.[40]

Yet another response to these texts would be to use them to question the line between what is conventionally seen as the secular and the religious. Robert Cover, for example, in a celebrated piece in the *Harvard Law Review* (Cover, 1983; see also Minow et al, 1995), focused on what he called the 'jurisgenerative' qualities of religious communities and groups in civil society. He explained that living in a Nomos provides an integrated world of obligation and reality from which the rest of the world is perceived. For him, stories help create a normative universe, seeing law as a bridge to a vision of alternative world transformation of conditions of social life (Cover, 1983). Significantly, some have sought to show that what Cover has to say about Nomos and Narrative is rooted in his understanding of the interplay between Halacha and Aggada (Stone, 1993; Levine, 1998). Cover's examples were often drawn from minority religious groups but he sought to draw more general lessons. Other writers too have underlined other ways in which supposedly secular law also involves the unfolding of a tradition and the respecting of its constraints (see e.g. White, 1985, 1989, 1994).

36 http://www.spiritualcompetency.com/scrcQuiz.aspx?courseID=58. But religious sources are also drawn on by scientific texts. The Jewish approach to forgiveness can be found incorporated into the clinical practice of psychologists. See, e.g. Balkin et al., 2009.

37 http://www.myjewishlearning.com/ask_the_expert/at/Ask_the_Expert-Forgiveness.shtml. See also McCullough *et al.*, 2000.

38 Literally, 'The laid out table', the authoritative code complied by Rav Joseph Caro, taken to be binding by traditional Jews since the early modern period.

39 C = Confess without excuse. Be specific about what you're sorry for … O = Offer an apology that gets across the idea that you're sorry, and that you don't want to do it again; N = Note the other person's pain. Acknowledge that your actions were hurtful; F = Forever value. Explain that you value your relationship; E = Equalize. Offer retribution. Ask how you can make it up to the person. S = Say 'never again'. Promise that you won't do it again (and mean it); S = Seek forgiveness. Ask the other person directly, "Can you forgive me". (http://www.myjewishlearning.com/ask_the_expert/at/Ask_the_Expert-Forgiveness.shtml.

40 At this point 'the expert' then returns to citing the authorities of Maimonides and the Shulchan Aruch.

Finally, we could ask if insights drawn from ancient religious sources might be helpful for building better systems of criminal justice (bearing in mind, of course, that every religious tradition contains numerous points of view). As far as domestic criminal justice is concerned, it is often said that the need to curb and institutionalise vengeance is the starting point of law itself (Posner, 2009; Ferrajoli, 2009; Nelken, 1993). Religious legal systems, including the Talmud, also have much to say about apparently more modern sounding issues of retribution, restitution, deterrence or recidivism. According to mainstream interpretations of Jewish law, for example, compensation would not obviate the need for seeking forgiveness, the definition of true repentance is in the ability to resist offending faced with the same temptation, and using restitution schemes as a way of rehabilitating offenders rather than helping victims would be frowned on.

Where it comes to international criminal justice, the connection is even closer. It is essential to try and appreciate the 'internal' perspective of different religious communities to gaining forgiveness as failure to do so itself can create misunderstanding and conflict. What is meant by forgiveness is already a bone of contention between some members of Jewish and Christian faith communities. Christian writers present Jesus as a model for giving unconditioned forgiveness, as against what is seen as a vengeful Old Testament Divinity. Some Jewish writers, on the other hand, insist on the dangers of this approach for fallible human beings, as well as the drawbacks of delegating confession and absolution to religious intermediaries.[41] Similarly, differences in the understanding of forgiveness in Jewish and Muslim traditions could have implications for any future reconciliation between Israelis and Palestinians, which would therefore be likely to take a different form than the South African Truth and Reconciliation Commission.[42] Indeed some Jewish commentators on that Commission, whilst not questioning the importance of seeking and conceding forgiveness, note that reconciliation should not always be made to depend on forgiveness and forgiveness does not always require reconciliation.[43]

---

41 As opposed to the accusation that the Old Testament is a God of vengeance comes the reply that Christians forgive too easily! 'The principle that *Mechila* (forgiveness) ought to be granted only if deserved is the great Jewish "No" to easy forgiveness. It is core to the Jewish view of forgiveness, just as desisting from sin is core to the Jewish view of repentance. Without good grounds, the offended person should not forgo the indebtedness of the sinner; otherwise, the sinner may never truly repent and evil will be perpetuated. And, conversely, if there are good grounds to waive the debt or relinquish the claim, the offended person is morally bound to do so. This is the great Jewish "Yes" to the possibility of repentance for every sinner.' http://www.crosscurrents.org/blumenthal.htm. Rabbi Blumenthal is a professor at Emory University in the USA engaged in Jewish-Catholic dialogue.

42 This was certainly influenced by Christian ideas (and it is significant that its chairman, Archbishop Tutu, insisted on wearing the cloth).

43 Professor Schimmel, for example, tells us that, 'In South Africa's approach to reconciliation the emphasis was placed more on forgiveness than on justice, reflecting the country's Christian ethos. I don't believe a Muslim-Jewish Truth and Reconciliation Commission would have followed the South African model. They would have prioritized issues

For some writers, however, it is inappropriate to try to apply the approach to forgiveness found in religious legal systems as a model for secular ones. Only a legal system based on divine sanctions is at ease with an ethic starting from obligation rather than rights (Cover, 1987). Such a system is able to ask more of people and it can also provide more incentives. Forgiveness to one's fellowman wins forgiveness from Heaven (Stone, 1993). A religious approach also views forgiveness as something that is needed by all, not just those labelled criminal offenders.[44]

On the other hand, it could be argued that secular systems already build in religious ideas but that this is not always positive. As Foucault emphasises, confession plays a crucial role in any legal system but this usually means that the offender is thereby being made to legitimatise the system far more than if he or she ends up being punished whilst declaring him or herself innocent (Foucault, 2014)[45]. Moreover, when the state tries to institutionalise processes of forgiveness, this is often under the threat of more severe criminal justice penalties for those not wishing to go down this path. Indeed, there is a case for saying that it would be better to try and overcome religious ways of thinking. The recognition of a distinction between the public and the private, and religion and morality and the ability to treat anti-social behaviour as crime rather than sin –should be considered to be a conquest (or at the least a necessity) of modernity because of social complexity and the need to live in multicultural polities. In fact some websites on forgiveness pointedly try to explain how this can be achieved 'without being religious'.[46]

These doubts would seem to apply all the more to the role of religious readings in inter-community relations. Sometimes feeling in possession of the truth can lead to expecting higher standards of one's own group in relation to others. When underlining the importance of the Jewish requirement to be ready to forgive, Maimonides insists that not to forgive is to behave in a cruel way that he describes as characteristic of hard-heartened Pagans. Levinas (1990a: 25-29) ends his readings of the above Talmudic stories on forgiveness by giving us his comments on the source of Maimonides' ethnocentric claim. It derives from the story, found in 2 Samuel 21, that has to do with what happened when the gentile tribe of Gibeonites demanded retaliation against the family of King Saul for their loss of livelihood after the death of the priests of Nob, to whom they had been in service. King David agreed to put to death seven royal princes to satisfy their thirst for revenge and left their bodies exposed for months on a rock. But, as a consequence, the Gibeonites were not allowed to unite

---

of justice, been less inclined to grant amnesty to a perpetrator of horrific crimes, and placed greater emphasis on the feelings of the victims' families and their need for justice to be served.' (Schimmel, 2004).)

44 But this (in any event controversial) contrast between the secular and religious is much less clear-cut in non-Western social and legal systems, both because legal systems may be less secularised and because obligations to family and the community may in any case play a larger role.

45 Is the butcher – the anti-hero of the story – therefore an example of what Foucault terms 'resistance' to power? See also Brooks, 2000; Taylor, 2009.

46 http://www.wikihow.com/Forgive-Someone-Without-Using-Religion

with the Jewish people. Levinas (1990a) explains that David broke all Biblical rules in killing these innocent children and profaning the divine image of God by not burying them immediately. As he phrases it, the princes died a horrible death, so that these strangers would not be able say they had been injured by the Hebrew King. Whatever moderns would and should feel about such 'reasons of state', what is significant for Levinas, is the way that Maimonides draws from the story the lesson that being Jewish and insisting on vengeance are incompatible.

But, more often, apologetics and apology go ill together. Communities are even more successful in denying the harm that they have caused to others than individuals are (Cohen, 2000). When dealing with those of other faiths and loyalties, it is much harder to institutionalise reciprocal forgiveness than when dealing with people who share the same faith, (constructed) history and sense of destiny. In fact, religious traditions are often used to fuel animosities[47] and (his) stories are told to keep these ancient enmities alive.

The Talmudic stories teach us that no rules (whether legal or social scientific) can provide *guarantees* of successful outcomes for those trying to institutionalise forgiveness in either domestic or international settings (Nelken, 2014). But Rabbinic literature also shows us that we can, if we want to, find warrant in religious traditions for the task of seeking and giving even inter-communal forgiveness. Maimonides finds no place in his Code of Law for the Raba and the Butcher story, but this is not because he underplays the nobility of granting forgiveness. His textual source of why people need to grant each other forgiveness is in fact actually an inter-communal one. It comes from the Biblical story of Abraham praying to God for forgiveness for Avimelech, the ruler of Gerar. This ruler and his household had been struck with illness for having abducted Abraham's wife Sarah (having been told she was his sister). But Abraham showed no hesitation in appealing to God on his behalf- and this is taken as the right model of behaviour and the source of the requirement to forgive. At the same time, the Jewish approach to forgiveness, as represented by the Talmud, includes the postulate that the offender must also be willing to make amends to deserve forgiveness. What the stories we have been discussing show us is how far leading figures are willing to go in order to make it possible to forgive and to be forgiven. Certainly, the disastrous consequences of Raba's efforts to forgive warn us that great tact is needed. But, if the search to give forgiveness can itself *sometimes* cause harm, the Talmud also shows us that Rav Zerah's efforts to make peace were successful and are worth emulating. As the tradition would say, 'may their example be for a blessing'.

47 'Insofar as religious concepts are valued by the antagonists, and particularly by their leaders, I think they can be helpful in supporting political, economic, or diplomatic initiatives in a peace process, but these concepts alone are not likely to resolve ethnic or national conflicts ... At present, however, I think religion is serving more of a destructive than a constructive role in political conflicts.' (Schimmel, 2004).

References

Balkin, R. S., Freeman, S. J. and Lyman, S. R. "Forgiveness, Reconciliation, and *Mechila*: Integrating the Jewish Concept of Forgiveness Into Clinical Practice", *Counseling and Values* 2009 53, 153-160.

Ball, M. S., *Called by Stories: Biblical Sagas and Their Challenge for Law*, (Durham: Duke University Press, 2000).

Bankowski, Z., *Living lawfully, love in law and law in love* (Dordecht: Kluwer, 2001).

Brooks, P., *Troubling Confessions: Speaking Guilt in Law and Literature* (Chicago: University of Chicago Press, 2000).

Bruner, J., *Making stories: Law Literature, Life*, (Cambridge: Harvard University Press, 2002).

Cardozo, N. L., *The written and oral Torah: a comprehensive introduction* (Lanham: Rowman and Littlefield, 1998).

Cohen, S., *States of Denial* (Cambridge: Polity, 2000).

Cover, R., "Supreme Court 1982 Term Foreword: Nomos and Narrative", *Harvard Law Review* 1983 97, 4-68.

Cover, R. M., "Obligation: a Jewish jurisprudence of the social order", *Journal of Law and Religion* 1987 5(1), 65-74.

Encyclopedia Judaica http://www.jewishvirtuallibrary.org/jsource/judaica/ejud_0002_0001_0_00525.html (2008).

Farias, V., *Heidegger and Nazism* French translation (Lagrasse: Verdier, 1987).

Ferrajoli, L., *Diritto e Ragione: Teoria del Garantismo Penale* (10th edn) (Rome: Laterza, 2009).

Fishbane, M., *Sacred Attunement* (Chicago: University of Chicago, 2008).

Fonrobert, C. F. and M. S. Jaffee, eds. *The Cambridge Companion to the Talmud and Rabbinic literature* (Cambridge: Cambridge University Press, 2007).

Foucault, M., *Wrong-Doing, Truth-Telling: The Function of Avowal in Justice* (Chicago: University of Chicago Press, 2014).

Glenn, P., *Legal Traditions of the World* (Oxford: OUP, 2007).

Hand, S. (ed), *A Levinas Reader* (Chichester: Wiley, 1989).

Hand, S., *Critical thinkers, Emanuel Levinas* (New York: Routledge, 2009).

Halbertal, M., and Margalit, A., *Idolatry* (Cambridge: Harvard University Press, 1992).

Halbertal, M., *People of the Book: Canon, Meaning, Authority* (Cambridge: Harvard University Press, 1997).

Halbertal, M. "At the Threshold of *Forgiveness:* A Study of Law and Narrative in the Talmud", *Jewish Review of Books* 2011 7, 33-34.

Hartman, D., *The God who hates lies: Confronting and rethinking Jewish tradition* (Woodstock: Jewish Lights Publishing, 2011).

Heinemann, J., "The Nature of the Aggada" in G. H. Hartman and S. Budick (eds), *Midrash and Literature*, (New Haven: Yale University Press, 1986).

Heschel, A. J., *God in Search of Man* (New York: Farrar, Strauss and Giroux, 1955).

Heschel, A. J., http://curiousjew.blogspot.it/2007/03/aggada-vs-halakha.html.

Jackson, B., "Legalism", *Journal of Jewish Studies* 1979 30, 1-22.

Jackson, B., *Law, Fact and Narrative coherence* (Liverpool: Deborah Charles,1988).
Kirschenbaum, A., *Equity in Jewish Law: Beyond Equity: Halakhic Aspirationism in Jewish Civil Law,* (Brooklyn: KTAV Publishing House, 1991).
Kremer, J., "The Talmud: Why has a Jewish law book become so popular?" BBC News Magazine, 8 November 2013 http://www.bbc.co.uk/news/magazine-24367959
Levinas, E. (trans. A. Aronowicz), *Nine Talmudic Readings* (Bloomington: Indiana University Press, 1990a).
Levinas, E. (trans. S. Hand), *Difficult Freedom: Essays on Judaism* (Baltimore: Johns Hopkins University Press, 1990b).
Levine, S. J., "Halacha and Aggada: Translating Robert Cover's Nomos and Narrative", *Utah Law Review* 1998 4, 465 – 495.
McCullough, M. E., Pargament, K. I. and Thorese, C. E. (eds), *Forgiveness: Theory, Research, and Practice* (New York: Guilford Press, 2000).
Minow, M., Ryan, M. and Sarat, A. (eds), *Narrative, Violence and the Law: Essays of Robert Cover* (Ann Arbor: University of Michigan Press, 1995).
Nelken, D., "Le giustificazioni della pena ed i diritti dell'imputato" in L. Gianformaggio (ed), *Le Ragioni del Garantismo* (Torino: Giappicheli, 1993).
Nelken, D. "Rules and Stories: Comment on Jackson", in B. S. Jackson (ed), *Legal Semiotics and the Sociology of Law* (Oñati, IISL, *Oñati Proceedings Series*, 1994).
Nelken, D., (ed), *Law as Communication* (London: Dartmouth, 1996).
Nelken, D., "Afterword: The Politics of International Criminal Justice', in W. De Lint (ed), *Crime and Justice in International Society* (London: Willan, 2014).
Neusner, J., *The Idea of History in Rabbinic Judaism* (Leiden: E. J. Brill, 2004).
Posner, R., *Law and literature* (2nd edn) (Cambridge: Harvard University Press, 2009).
Rubinstein, J., *Talmudic Stories: Narrative Art, Composition and Culture* (Baltimore: John Hopkins University Press, 1999).
Schimmel, S. "How CAN I Forgive? A Conversation with Solomon Schimmel", originally published in *Reform Judaism* magazine (Fall, 2004). http://www.shalomboston.com/LinkClick.aspx?fileticket=qffIVtofkJw%3D&tabid=93&mid=48
Steinsaltz, A., *The Essential Talmud* (New York: Basic Books, 1976).
Stone, S. L., "In pursuit of the counter text", *Harvard Law Review* 1993 106, 813–876.
Taylor, C., *The Culture of Confession from Augustine to Foucault: A Genealogy of the Confessing Animal* (New York: Routledge, 2009).
White, J. B., *The Legal Imagination* (Chicago: University of Chicago Press, 1985).
White, J. B., *Heracles Bow: Essays on the Rhetoric and Poetics of the law* (Madison: University of Wisconsin Press, 1989).
White, J. B., *Justice as Translation* (Chicago: University of Chicago Press, 1994).
Yinger, K., "Defining Legalism", *Andrews University Seminary Studies* 2008 46, 91-108.

The People's Choice: Law in Culture and Society

Lawrence M. Friedman[1]
Marion Rice Kirkwood Professor, Stanford Law School, USA

The law and society movement has already produced a huge literature. The movement is complex and somewhat unruly: a big umbrella, or maybe a big circus tent, a three-ring or multi-ring circus, with its brilliant trapeze artists and lion-tamers (and hopefully very little in the way of clowns and freak shows). What I mean to do in this essay is to look at a small subfield: the relationship between law and popular culture. This is a fairly new area of research. The literature is not large, but is expanding (See eg, Freeman, 2005; Macaulay, 1987; Friedman, 1989.)[2] This literature concerns, for example, the way law and the image of law percolate into movies, novels, plays, television shows, songs, graphic arts, magazines, and the like.

A movie, book, or television show can deal directly with law or legal institutions; or touch on these indirectly. The famous movie, *Twelve Angry Men* (1957), is directly and explicitly about a legal institution, the jury. The main characters in the American television series, 'L. A. Law', which was quite popular (it ran from 1986 to 1994), were members of a law firm; the programme was directly concerned with their lives and careers. Quite a few movies are courtroom dramas, or feature a trial, the police, prison life, or some other aspect of the legal order. In addition, many movies – and also books, magazines and shows – may have a legal subtheme, or turn on an issue from an area or field of law, even though not strictly speaking 'about' law. *Kramer v. Kramer* (1979) dealt with divorce; George Clooney's movie, *The Descendants* (2011), concerned property rights and land trusts in Hawaii; in such movies, the 'law' is obviously part of the background or the setting.

---

1 I want to thank William Havemann for help with the research on this article. This article is written in honor of Michael Freeman, who has himself contributed greatly to the subject of the article.

2 With regard to law and the movies, see, for example, Bergman and Asimow, 1996; Asimow, 2001; Machura and Robson, 2001. In their introduction, Machura and Robson print a list of 'selected writings on law and film: a chronology.' (*ibid*: 3-6). On TV, see Robson and Silbey, 2012; Rapping, 2003. There are also a goodly number of essays which analyse and interpret particular books or movies. See, for example, Conley, 1996; Asimow, 2007; Davies, 2012.

A. Diduck, N. Peleg, H. Reece (eds.), Law in Society: Reflections on Children, Family, Culture and Philosophy
 ISBN 978-90-04-26148-8. pp. 83-99.

In many ways, 'popular culture' is not easy to define. Where does it begin and end? Is it the same as *mass* culture? A slasher movie is definitely popular culture; but what about a film version of *Hamlet*? Is opera high culture; while operetta and 'Show Boat' are popular culture? Where would we put a Noel Coward play? And wasn't Shakespeare popular culture in his day? Not to mention opera in Italy in 1850? And how to classify Gilbert and Sullivan? *My Fair Lady*? John Grisham is popular culture; Dickens is high culture; but wasn't Dickens enormously popular? What about *Uncle Tom's Cabin*? Perhaps it is best not to draw lines; popular culture could be simply defined to mean movies, plays and so on, which are genuinely popular, whether or not they are arguably high culture as well. David Papke defines popular culture as 'the body of cultural commodities and experiences produced by the culture industry for mass audiences' (Papke, 2007: 127). This is perhaps a bit narrow. We do, however, care about actual popularity; we can safely ignore, for example, 12-tone music, and *Finnegan's Wake*, not for any doctrinaire reason, but because these two noble enterprises have so few customers. It does not matter whether there is 'law' in *Finnegan's Wake* (and who on earth could tell), because almost nobody reads this book and its impact on society is bound to be small.

In any event, the study of law and popular culture is, potentially at least, a vast and an important field. Law, in modern societies, is ubiquitous; it is hard to separate it from other aspects of life, and of culture. In this essay, however, I want to make a few points, mostly about the United States, though they have, I hope, a wider significance.

First, that popular culture *distorts* the reality of the legal system. Second, that its vast power has invited, in the past at least, a movement to control and monitor popular culture. Third, that the line between 'news' and 'entertainment', in popular culture, has eroded. Fourth, that the impact of popular culture on the legal system, and on legal culture, is complex, probably powerful, but difficult to measure. The impact may be benign or harmful, depending on the circumstances.

The Fun-House Mirror

'Law' permeates popular culture to an extraordinary degree, and in the most obvious sense. But popular culture does not give its customers an accurate picture of the way the legal system works. The image of law and legal institutions in popular culture is like a person's image in a fun-house mirror. It is a systematic distortion of reality. The living law, as any lawyer knows, is often dull, workaday drone law. The distortion is pervasive. It is, perhaps, most obvious with regard to criminal justice. A big murder trial is exciting; a plea bargaining session is not (except to the defendant, one supposes). O. J. Simpson had an audience of millions (on this case, see Schuetz and Lilley, 1999; Hunt, 1999). The huge trial in 2012, between Apple and Samsung, was arguably vastly more important than the trial of O. J. Simpson; billions of dollars were at stake; but it hardly made a dent on popular consciousness. Further, if you judged only by television and the movies, you would never know that most lawyers have nothing to do with criminal justice.[3] Our adversary system may or may not produce a high grade of justice; but it is capable of putting on a terrific show (Machura and Ulbrich, 2001: 123). Indeed, Michael Asimow has argued that the 'dominance of the American adversarial ideology owes a lot to its glorification in television and film' (Asimow, 2005: 636-637). It is 'vastly more entertaining for spectators' than the 'inquisitorial system (in which lawyers have relatively little to do', and which consists in large part of shuffling pieces of paper (Asimow, 2006-2007, 668).

Taming the Beast

The law has also come down rather heavily on popular culture, or at least some aspects of it. In the past, many God-fearing citizens looked on popular culture as potentially dangerous: a threat to the moral health of society. Hence a search for engines of control, including censorship.

This was particularly true of the movies. The film industry sprang up, essentially, at the beginning of the 20th century. Movies soon became enormously popular everywhere. Too popular, in fact, for many people who worried about traditional values. Masses of people poured into dark theaters, watching vivid, lifelike images on the screen: this could corrupt the morals of the audience, especially young people. This was the rather shrill theme of a prominent book, published in 1933, about the impact of movies, with their 'morbid preoccupation' with sex and crime. Delinquents 'who come to grief' often 'trace their plight to the movies'. Young people get ideas about 'easy money'. Movies also teach young people how to 'look big' – and even how to commit crimes (Forman, 1933: 35, 41, 200-201).

As early as 1907, the city of Chicago enacted a censorship ordinance (on censorship, see Couvares, 1996; Grieveson, 2004a; Couvares, 1996). The police were given power to ban 'obscene or immoral' movies. The supreme court of Illinois upheld the ordinance. Some social classes, said the court, needed special 'protection against the evil influence of obscene and immoral representations', by virtue of their 'age, education, and situation in life' (*Block v. City of Chicago*, 87 N. E. 1011 (1909)). Ohio had a state board of censors; it was authorised to approve only movies that were 'moral, educational, or amusing and harmless'. The United States Supreme Court upheld this law against challenge in 1915 (*Mutual Film Co. v. Industrial Commission of Ohio*, 236 U.S. 230 (1915)). Freedom of speech, said the Court, did not apply to 'shows and spectacles'. The 'exhibition of moving pictures is a business, pure and simple.' Movies were vivid and entertaining, but also 'capable of evil'; and the evil was all the greater 'because of their attractiveness and manner of exhibition'. The case gave a green light to censorship; censorship boards flourished in the 1920s in such places as Dallas and Houston, Birmingham, and Palo Alto, California (Grieveson, 2004a: 212).

---

3 This is not true only of the United States and the United Kingdom. Machura and Ulbrich report that crime shows are ubiquitous in Germany; German defendants and lay assessors express surprise to learn that 'procedure in German courts was so different from what watching television had led them to expect'. (Machura and Ulbrich, 2001: 117).

Movie censorship was an extreme case of a broader principle: control of popular culture to prevent moral infection of the masses. There was widespread censorship of books, as well. Every American state had a law against pornography.[4] The label of obscenity was often attached to works in a way that would strike us today, on the whole, as absurdly extreme. The famous Watch and Ward Society, in Boston, put pressure on bookstores not to display or sell books that were, in the Society's view, obscene (Miller, 2010). Not even the classics – Rabelais, for example – were safe. In England, theater was under the guidance (if that is the word) of the Lord Chamberlain. A play like George Bernard Shaw's *Mrs. Warren's Profession* (1893), which dealt with a taboo subject, ran into serious trouble on both sides of the Atlantic. In Boston, the mayor could halt unsuitable plays; he relied on the advice of a man named John M. Casey, a former kettle-drummer for the Boston Symphony, who lost an arm in an accident and was given a job in City Hall. In 1929, a play called *Fiesta* (notable for a parrot who swore in Spanish), fell under the ban, along with so serious a drama as Eugene O'Neill's *Strange Interlude* (Miller, 2010: 119-121).

Censorship was aided and abetted by pressure groups – the Catholic Church very notably (Couvares, 1996). The American industry developed a deathly fear of a national censorship system. To avoid this, the industry elected self-censorship: the famous Hollywood Code, which dates from 1930. The Code announced a duty to produce 'correct entertainment' – entertainment which would uplift the nation. No movie should 'lower the moral standards of those who see it'. There were elaborate and detailed rules about what could and could not be shown. Nudity was taboo. No condoning or glorifying adultery. Even married people had to sleep in twin beds. No movie was supposed to deride or ridicule religion. In crime movies, the wicked had to be punished. A Production Code Administration (1934) enforced the Code.[5] The general policy of the Code was clear: movies were to give off messages of sexual restraint, religiosity and traditional morality (see, on the Code, Leff and Simmons, 1990).

There was, in general, no prior censorship of books and newspapers; but they could run afoul of rigid laws against obscenity after publication. To sum up: for many members of the elite, popular culture seemed at least potentially dangerous. The state – and respectable society – had both the right and the duty to protect the public from improper material. Popular culture was supposed to enlighten the masses; to spread correct and moral ideas; and to support these ideas through image and example. Anything else was subject to rigid control.

Today, the culture has changed radically. As far as the movies are concerned, basically anything goes (see Strub, 2013). The Production Code is gone. Sex is no longer

4 For example, Cal. Penal Code 1872, sec. 311 (3), which made it a crime to sell or exhibit 'any obscene or indecent writing ... or obscene or indecent picture'; or to sing 'any lewd or obscene song ... in any public place', sec. 311 (5).

5 The PCA, to be sure, had no actual power to ban a movie. It requested changes and deletions in movies, and negotiated with film-makers and studios. This is in no way to deny its power. Local pressure groups who protested against offensive movies were also effective. See Wittern-Keller, 2008: 6-7.

taboo. Crime sometimes pays. In a way, the message of the Code has been turned on its head. Adultery, interracial sex, same-sex love – these are ubiquitous in the movies. Television is a bit more puritanical – at least in prime-time hours, when the kids might be watching. You can, at least in theory, keep kids out of X-rated movies. But nobody stands at the door to enforce rules on TV. Parents have the power; but do they use it? Despite federal rules and other restraints, teenagers who watch TV, which almost all of them do, will see show after show discussing or showing subjects that were once taboo: contraception, abortion, same-sex relations, adultery, cohabitation, masturbation.

Moreover, movies (and TV, to a degree), can now freely violate all of the other rules of the Code. They can be critical of religion, for example. In *Burstyn v. Wilson* (343 U.S.495 (1952)) the United States Supreme Court overturned the ban on 'The Miracle', a movie that had been labelled sacrilegious. Movies are free to show some form of religion – or the FBI, or the CIA – as corrupt, incompetent, or downright evil. Victorian morality has lost its power over popular culture. Cynicism and distrust of institutions is no longer banned. Movies now can and do show judges who are venal and weak. One movie, in fact, featured a judge presiding over a murder – but the judge, not the defendant, had actually committed the murder (Papke, 2007: 140-141).[6]

Popular culture, then, is free to voice cynicism and distrust; and often does. Movies rarely exalt or even justify due process, procedural safeguards, or defendants' rights in general. In one popular movie, *The Star Chamber* (1983), a group of Los Angeles judges, in the course of their day jobs, felt obliged to let vicious and guilty scum go free, because of niggling and irrelevant points of criminal procedure or evidence. No problem: the judges meet quietly at night, retry these cases and sentence the scum to death. They hire hitmen to carry out these sentences.[7] Movie heroes, in general, have licence to violate the formal rules of criminal justice, in the interests of public safety – and to make sure bad guys get what they deserve.

Does all this contribute to cynicism, distrust of authority and opposition to civil liberties? Perhaps. On the other hand, Susan Bandes argues, rather, that the 'standard cop show... reflects and reaffirms a deeply ingrained, reassuring view of the world' (Bandes, 2011: 435). Bad guys get caught, and justice of a sort is done. Still, this may be 'reassuring' about the world, but not about due process. Some commentators – Elayne Rapping is one – feel that media portrayal of crime and criminal justice drives a 'right-wing political agenda', and fosters 'increasingly punitive legal policies' (Rapping, 2003: 107). Of course, 'popular culture' is a big tent; you can find exceptions and counter-examples to any generalisation. Crime shows usually cast a favourable light on detectives, forensic experts and police. But not on the law itself.

In one important regard, however, popular culture is on the side of the (liberal) angels. Popular culture today on the whole sends a message of racial brotherhood. In television and the movies, black Americans were essentially invisible before the civil

6 The movie in question is *Suspect* (1987).

7 The scheme collapses at the end of the movie and there is a plot twist; but the central point remains.

rights era. In 1912, Congress enacted the so-called Sims Act, which made it a crime to ship prize-fighting movies across state lines (37 U.S. Stats. Ch. 263, p. 240 (act of 31 July 1912)). The official excuse was to protect the 'more advanced States' that outlaws 'pugilism', a 'degrading' and 'brutalizing' sport. But one particular film was the real impetus for the Act: it showed Jack Johnson, the African-American boxer, pummeling a white contender (Grieveson, 2004a: 132-133; Grieveson, 2004b: 169). In the movies, African-Americans appeared as maids and servants, or as outrageous stereotypes, like Stepin Fetchit,[8] or occasionally – and this was about as good as it got – dancing or singing a song. Radio and TV were no better.[9] As late as 1954, the same year as the school segregation case, CBS broadcast a version of Mark Twain's 'Huckleberry Finn' in which the key black character, Jim, was completely omitted (Burns, 2010: 206).

The media reflected society, of course: even baseball and the Metropolitan Opera were restricted to white players and singers. That silent classic, 'Birth of a Nation', glorified the Ku Klux Klan.[10] Any role in movies for non-whites that even hinted at social equality was poison in the southern states. Racism in the northern states was more subtle, less brutal, with some islands of tolerance; but on the whole, white supremacy reigned there too. But as white supremacy crumbled, the media followed along. Perhaps the media helped it crumble: TV covered the civil rights struggle in great detail. TV showed the whole country the violence and cruelty of white supremacy, beefy rednecks cursing and abusing black protesters who were dignified and stoical, mobs trying to keep small black children from schools that had been only for whites. All this, on front pages, and beamed directly into homes on TV, may have had a political and cultural impact.[11]

In 1967, 'Guess Who's Coming to Dinner', burst onto the screen: in this movie, a young white woman brings home her new fiancé, a black doctor, played by Sidney Poitier. The movie was a success, apparently even in the south. Much has happened since them. The role of race in the media is still subject to debate. Some blacks were shocked or uneasy at 'Precious', a 2009 movie, which showed a violent and dysfunctional black family (*New York Times*, 2009). In general, however, minorities are everywhere in the media today. The public is used to seeing black people (and Asians) in TV shows, as detectives, lovers, heroes, villains and just plain human beings. Racism, of course, is far from dead. In TV, however, and in the movies, it is pretty close to dead.

---

8 Stepin Fetchit was a black movie actor, notorious for portraying black characters as lazy, superstitious, and fearful.

9 On Jack Benny's immensely popular radio programme, which ran from 1932 to 1948, and later on television, 'Rochester' (Eddie Anderson) was a featured character; and portrayed on the whole extremely sympathetically. But the role was the role of a servant: clever, but still a servant.

10 Ironically, this movie had problems with the censors in a number of places, because it was felt it was likely to foment trouble between the races. The Ohio censors, who were supposed to license only 'harmless' movies, decided this movie was not in fact harmless (Grieveson, 2004a: 193-194).

11 During this period, television was 'a new and powerful medium' that forced people 'to confront social issues in the comforts of their own home' (West, 2004: 312).

The menu of characters is more human and more balanced: it includes indigenous people, Hispanics, gay people, Pakistanis and ethnic minorities. Women, too, in general, are shown in more complex and less gendered ways – as business-people, police officers and so on. In the United Kingdom, black and East Asian men and women figure prominently on TV. Black actors appear in commercials; there are black sports announcers, anchors and news commentators. The taboo against interracial love and sex has broken down almost totally. And black actors in Shakespearean plays are no longer an oddity (Harewood, 2013). In general, today, the media reflect a pluralistic and tolerant ethos; they might even strengthen this ethos – just as in the past, they reflected and promoted the dark prejudices of the majority.

All the News That Fits

'Popular culture', however one defines it, is clearly distinct from the popular *reporting* of legal events: that is, 'news' about law, which the media convey to the public. The two are, to be sure, closely related. Particularly so, because, in our culture, the line between news and entertainment, between the real and the fictional, has become more and more indistinct. 'News' nowadays has to be interesting and entertaining; if not, it loses its audience. Newspapers and magazines without readers go out of business. News programmes with poor ratings get dropped or reworked; the 'prevailing criteria' for judging the success of these programmes are the ratings (Bogart, 1980: 209, 213). News reports are 'shows' just as much as the sitcoms and cop shows. News, of course, is supposed to be true, factual, a slice of life; but it would be naïve to take this literally. 'News' in the media passes through its own fun-house mirror. 'News' is not what really happened (ignoring the vexed question of what that might mean); but what the media *say* has happened; and how they say it.

In both fiction and news, law is everywhere. Almost every piece of domestic news in the papers, or on TV news programmes, touches on some aspect of the legal system – courts, the President, Congress, police, jails, regulations. Some stories are explicitly *about* the legal system; in the others, some 'legal' aspect will inevitably pop up.[12] The same is equally true of fiction, including novels, movies, and plays.

---

12 I took, as I was writing this, as an example, the front section of the *New York Times*, for Wednesday, 3 October 2012. There are six stories on the front page. All but one had a legal angle. One story told how a Pennsylvania judge blocked a 'key component' of a state law. A second story was about an upcoming presidential debate between President Obama and Mitt Romney. A third story concerned landmark preservation laws in Arizona (and the threat to a house by Frank Lloyd Wright). Two foreign policy stories concerned issues and actions which, whether plainly stated or not, are rooted in or controlled by law.
What was true of the front page was also true of domestic news in the rest of the newspaper. For example, one story (p. A18) recounted a 'scathing report' criticising 'regional intelligence-gathering offices known as "fusion centers"' which were financed by the Department of Homeland Security 'and created jointly with state and local law enforcement agencies'. The business section of the paper showed the same general tendency: one

Usually, when we talk about 'law' or the 'legal system', we refer to a discrete and concrete sub-system in society, made up of statutes, courts, judges, lawyers, prisons, police and the like. But, in addition, we include such concepts as property, marriage, ownership which are legal concepts, as well as fundamental ideas in society. It would not be too much of a stretch to say that every social role – parent and child, husband and wife, worker and boss – is either a legal construct, or else colored and influenced by 'law' in some broad, and yet realistic, sense.

In a way, no aspect of life in society can escape from 'law' in the broadest sense. Marriage, naturally, is a legal status; but when a couple decides to live together, and *not* marry, this too becomes (in a sense) a legal status. The shadow of the law colours and defines the relationship. Under the law, certain rights are only for married people. Hence these rules, which flow from the legal status of marriage, also define, by implication if nothing else, the legal status of non-marriage. In short, you can hardly write a paragraph in a newspaper or magazine, or write a novel or present a television show, without 'law' somehow creeping in. Law is, in a way, the very structure of society, the skeleton, the framework; nothing would hold together without it.

The great civil law codes, like the Napoleonic Code, or the *Buergerliches Gesetzbuch*, were, in theory 'gapless'; that is, all questions, situations and behaviours were either covered by the code, or were (by implication) left to private ordering. The common law, sprawling, hard to define, hard to pin down, never looked gapless and never even claimed to be gapless in the sense of the civil law codes. And yet, in a real sense, the system *is* gapless; and indeed, it has to be. In a society structured the way ours is structured, every act, every role, every behaviour, is either defined by law, or defined by the fact that law – formal law or living law – simply leaves it alone. Behaviour is either regulated or unregulated. These are two sides of a single coin. Thus, in modern societies at least, law is everywhere and everything; indeed, these societies are *defined* by law. 'Law' itself, of course, flows out of social norms and social forces. But these express themselves, necessarily, through 'law'.

'Law' is present, then, both in news, the presentation of 'facts', and in fiction. But news', of course, is not just 'facts'. 'News' is distorted; and in the same direction as movies, novels, or TV shows. The media, after all, 'mediate'; they 'interpose filters between the audience and the events on which they report' (Bogart, 1980: 222). Criminal justice, and in particular, sensational crimes and sensational trials, have an important place in the news (see Fox and Van Siuckel, 2001). And the media decide, in a way, what to make of these crimes and trials, what to put on the front page or the evening news, and how to colour or slant the events they report. In one sense, the media simply give the public what it wants; but the media also help shape what the public wants, or thinks it wants.

Mass market newspapers in the United States began to appear in the first half of the 19th century. They thrived on crime and gore – on such juicy stories as the murder of Helen Jewett, and the trial of young Robinson, who was accused of kill-

---

story, for example, deals with the way the Federal Trade Commission relates to social media sites.

ing her (on this trial, see Cohen, 1998; Tucher, 1994. Despite strong evidence against him, Robinson was acquitted.) Throughout the 19th century, there were many crimes and trials that made headlines: in the 1850s, the trial of Congressman Daniel Sickles, for murdering his wife's lover (see Brandt, 1991; Swanberg, 1956); at the end of the Civil War, trials that came out of the Lincoln assassination; later, the trial of Charles Guiteau, who killed President Garfield (Rosenberg, 1968); and at the end of the century, the trial of Lizzie Borden. Lizzie (allegedly) took an ax and smashed in the skulls of her father and stepmother. Her sensational trial has entered American folklore (see Robertson, 1996). And on into the 20th century: the lurid trial of Harry K. Thaw, for killing Stanford White, a prominent architect; in the 1950s, the political trial of the Rosenbergs for giving away atomic secrets; and the trial of Dr. Sam Sheppard, accused of killing his pregnant wife; and then, in more recent times, very notably, the trial of O.J. Simpson. Millions, perhaps billions, of people watched the Simpson trial on TV (see Friedman, 2011).

These trials mesmerise the public. They give the (false) impression of the primacy of criminal law; and within criminal law, the primacy of big jury trials. They also convey two powerful ideas which, in a sense, contradict each other. The public gets the impression that the system of criminal justice is exceptionally careful and rigorous. Everybody seems to play by elaborate rules. Jury selection is slow and laborious. Canons of evidence are scrupulously observed. The judge, an impartial umpire, makes sure both sides observe the rules of the game.

Yet at the same time, the public may get quite a different impression: that criminal justice is a bag of tricks, a game, a charade; that money can buy the right outcome; that cunning lawyers who know the ropes can play the system for all it's worth. After all, O. J. Simpson got off, even though most (white) people felt he was absolutely guilty.

The media downplay or ignore most other fields of law.[13] There is a certain amount of attention to tort law or, to be more specific, personal injury law. Here, too, there is massive distortion. A study that appeared in 1999 surveyed newspaper coverage of 361 cases in which someone sued a car or truck company for products liability. The manufacturer won about three quarters of these cases; they lost only 92. And only 16 cases produced punitive damages. The media ignored most decisions; they tended to cover mostly cases where the manufacturer *lost*. They reported only nine verdicts in favour of the defence, but 38 verdicts for plaintiffs, and ten of the 16 cases of punitive damages (Garber and Bower, 1999). A reader might think plaintiffs usually win these cases; which was not actually true. And this kind of coverage feeds into the idea that the tort system has gone totally amok, and that frivolous, if not fraudulent, claims clog the courts, damaging both the economy and the American soul.

William Haltom and Michael McCann (2004) tell the tale of a lawsuit brought by one Judith Haimes. Haimes claimed that a dye, injected before she took a CAT scan, produced awful headaches that put an end to her psychic practice. A jury was told to

---

13 To be sure, the business sections of the press, and business news on radio and television, pay some attention to banking, government regulation of business and similar topics. But, of course, fewer people read or watch these.

ignore this particular claim; still, the jury, for whatever reason, awarded her a substantial verdict. But the judge set this verdict aside and ordered a new trial. In the end she got absolutely nothing. No matter: the story entered the unreal world of urban legends. Judith became known as the woman who asked for a million dollars, because she lost her psychic powers. Her story was repeated endlessly, as evidence of the crazy and broken system of tort law. The fact that she recovered nothing somehow never got reported. Even more notorious was the huge to-do (systematically misreported) about the hot-coffee lawsuit against McDonald's. A group called 'Consumer Freedom.com' ran an ad about a 'fat guy' who sued restaurants – 'the food was too cheap so he ate too much'; the ad showed a huge, fat, hairy and naked belly. The point was 'the erosion of personal responsibility and common sense' (Haltom and McCann, 2004: 180).

You do not have to be a conspiracy theorist to be suspicious about what tort reform advocates are up to. The 'liability explosion' of the 20th century produced both winners and losers. Quite a few business interests are among the losers; and they are fighting back. The Center for Consumer Freedom, which ran the ad about the fat guy who sued restaurants, inveighs against the 'nanny state'; the tobacco industry, along with restaurant, food and hotel groups, seems to be funding this Center. The Center invokes themes of 'personal responsibility', sneers at government regulation, and helps spread the word that tort law is a madhouse. The United States Chamber of Commerce also crusades against 'frivolous lawsuits', citing 'the man suing a cruise line after burning his feet on a sunny deck', and the 'mother claiming hearing loss from the screaming at a Justin Bieber Concert' (Krauss, 2012).[14] The appeal is to American individualists – and there are millions of these – who are deeply suspicious of government and whose stable of villains includes greedy and crooked lawyers and whiny, dependent, money-mad litigants.

'News' plays a role in the tort reform movement and provides ammunition for a harsh regime of criminal justice. But we do not know how influential the media are; and they are also not totally one-sided. 'News' may have played a role in the mushroom growth of tort liability in the 20th century. Investigative reporting, and the huge publicity that follows disasters, like the famous Triangle Shirtwaist Fire (on this celebrated disaster, see, for example, Greenwald, 2005), or the sinking of the Titanic, put pressure on the system to change. Even coverage of criminal justice is not totally one-sided. When a man on death row goes free because of the results of DNA testing, the newspapers pay attention. This might be at least a minor factor in the decline of the death penalty. Executions are fewer today than in the recent past; some statutes – Illinois, New Mexico, Connecticut, and Maryland – have abolished the death penalty; and juries in the remaining states are condemning fewer people to death (New York Times, 2013).

---

14 The story focuses on a commercial using 'Blitz USA, a bankrupt Oklahoma gasoline can manufacturer' to make its point. Blitz went out of business because of high legal costs from lawsuits. But the ad makes 'no mention of the dozens of casualties linked to explosions while people used the cans in recent years'.

The public is, in a way, a sleeping giant. And a rather passive giant. And perhaps an easily manipulated giant. Still, in an open society, the potential power of public opinion is enormous. This power usually lies dormant. People watch TV, shop, go about their lives. The World Series or the World Cup catches their fancy; politics or public affairs bores them. Yet a rich, ripe scandal can rouse people from their torpor. There are many historical examples: the first federal food and drug law (1906), for example. Reformers had tried, for years, to get Congress to move; with no results. Then Upton Sinclair published *The Jungle*, his novel about a family of Lithuanian immigrants. Young Jurgis Rudkus found work in a meat-packing plant in Chicago. The book describes, in gruesome detail, the horrific conditions in the plant: tubercular pork offered for sale, factory rats killed by poison and ground up for sausage; and, worst of all, an account of workmen who fell into vats and ended up processed into lard. A firestorm of national outrage forced Congress to pass laws on meat inspection – and a pure food law as well.[15] Ralph Nader wrote *Unsafe at Any Speed*, in 1965. The Corvair, manufactured by General Motors, was dangerous, he claimed. The publicity, and the clumsy attempts of General Motors to silence him, helped persuade Congress to pass laws on automotive safety.[16]

In all these cases, popular uproar had a real impact on the lawmaking process. The media played a role. But the results were not revolutionary; instead, they followed the norms and values of society. Upton Sinclair hoped The Jungle would promote socialism. But the book helped consumers; it did nothing for workers. He had aimed, he said, at the public's heart; and hit them, instead, in the stomach (quoted in Macaulay *et al.*, 2007: 215).

The Impact of Popular Culture

Does the coverage of law in popular culture *impact* the law? The fate of *The Jungle* suggests that it does; but in a complicated way. 'News' can arouse the sleeping giant; but only in terms of the climate of existing opinion.[17] Studies do suggest that 'people's opinions are influenced by long-repeated, consistent themes in pop culture'; and that people who watch a lot of television believe 'in a meaner world – more crime, more drugs, more prostitutes – than people who do not'. Also, that 'heavy' watchers

---

15 A second scandal erupted in the 1930s. The sulfa drugs, the first practical antibiotics, were sold as pills. One company began to market the drugs in liquid form – as an 'elixir'. The elixir turned out to be a deadly poison. The FDA pulled the drug off the market. But a number of people, including children, had died. As a result of the ensuing scandal, the FDA was strengthened; under the new law, passed in 1938, no new drug could be marketed at all, without testing, and without prior approval from the FDA. (See Carpenter, 2010: 85-113).

16 The company was forced to admit that it had tried to find dirt on Nader (see New York Times, 1966).

17 And much depends on how much coverage there is; and what the public gets out of it. For example, violent crime is declining in the 21st century; but the public does not seem aware of this (see Beale, 2006).

of crime shows are 'more favorably disposed toward capital punishment than light watchers' (Asimow, 2006-2007: 671). But this research is about public opinion. What about behaviour? Do violent video games (for example) lead to violent behavior? One recent study said, yes: 'exposure to violent video games' was 'significantly related to higher levels of aggressive behavior' (Anderson *et al.*, 2010). But perhaps kids who are attracted to violent video games were apt to be aggressive to begin with. The studies are mostly experimental – lab studies; and mostly they measure short-term effects. To claim that violent video games lead to more violence – more assaults, murders, and rapes – goes beyond the available evidence.[18] An exhaustive survey on a related question – whether the flood of violence in the media has an effect on aggressive behavior – found that the evidence failed to support any such conclusion (Freedman, 2002).

There is heavy emphasis on sex and sexuality in the media today. A study published in 2008, by the RAND Corporation, suggested sex in the media correlated with rising teenage pregnancy. Adolescents exposed to a lot of sex on television were more likely to get pregnant, or make somebody pregnant, than those that watched less of this material (Chandra *et al.*, 2008). A team of economists claimed that soap opera fans in Brazil had fewer babies than other women. It is hardly likely that they were too busy watching TV to have sex; more likely, they watched shows about prosperous, attractive families, who produced few children and made up their minds to do the same (Ferrara *et al.*, 2012).

With regard to crime shows on TV, there is the so-called 'CSI Effect'.[19] People see programmes about the wonders of forensic techniques – hair follicles, fancy chemical tests, fibers and the like; all this bedazzles them; juries thus come to expect big science from the prosecution; and when it fails to appear, they simply acquit. One study of jurors, in Michigan, did find that jurors expected 'some scientific evidence' in major criminal cases, like murder or rape (Shelton et al, 2006; see also Robbers, 2008). Yet another analyst decided that the evidence failed to support any such effect (Tyler, 2006). Tyler speculates that prosecutors, 'when they lose cases, flail about for some explanation as to why the jury could have been so dumb or so wrong' and thus come up with the 'CSI effect' (*ibid*: 1078).

Are juries less likely to convict – Tom Tyler thinks so – because they 'increasingly lack trust in the legal authorities' and studies in fact do show this decline in trust (Tyler, 2006: 1050). In movie after movie, and TV show after TV show, we see corrupt and incompetent authorities; or even authorities that are sinister and evil; people who will stop at nothing and who do not play by the rules.[20] Yet CSI, and other pro-

---

18 The Supreme Court, in 2011, struck down a California law which outlawed the sale or rental of 'violent video games' to minors which might appeal to a 'deviant or morbid interest' among these minors. This was a violation of freedom of speech. See *Brown v. Entertainment Merchants Association* 131 S. Ct. 2729 (2011).

19 CSI is Crime Scene Investigation, an extremely popular programme, which began in 2000, on the (fictional) work of forensic investigators.

20 But some TV programmes try to make people think well of the armed forces; "Profiles from the Front Line", on the war in Afghanistan, had a clearly 'pro-military' stance (McMurria, 2009: 179, 192).

grammes, show dedicated detectives and technicians doing brilliant forensic work. The police can be shown as bumbling fools – the Keystone Cops; or as hapless, witless or just plain wrong; or as virtuous and brave. It is hard to know whether one sort of image outbalances the other. The modern rules – or no-rules – allow any or all of these images, unlike the old rules which, as we saw, insisted on showing law and order always in a positive light.

The media today, we argued, support a regime of racial tolerance. Do they have an impact on attitudes toward war and peace, national security and the like? The American TV show, *24*, glorified, or at least excused, torture. But *Homeland*, a popular and much praised programme, has been at least implicitly critical of drone warfare. In short, the impact of popular culture on attitudes and behaviour is elusive; too many variables interact with each other. In any event, watching TV is in a way 'an active process'; viewers have their own filters, which bend the messages they receive. And, of course, a TV watcher can always change channels if the message does not suit (Podlas, 2012: 105-106).

Irreality TV

Crime may dominate prime time TV; but it is much less salient in the daytime hours. Daytime TV in the United States is the domain of talk shows, cartoon and soap operas. It is also the domain of 'judge' shows – Judge Judy is the most famous of these (see Friedman, 2012; Terzic, 2012; Kohm, 2006).[21] These are imitation courts, with imitation judges, who decide small-scale civil cases. A parade of little people whine and complain about ex-boyfriends or girlfriends who owe money or who smashed up the car, landlords and roommates who borrowed things and refuse to give them back; divorced fathers wrangle over visitation rights, divorced mothers resist them and so on. Judge Judy decides quickly (the 'cases' have to fit the time-slot, with room for commercials). She scolds and rants and harangues the litigants, who stand there sheepishly and take it. No lawyers appear in these 'courts'; nobody cites cases or statutes. Judge Judy's 'law' is what Max Weber called 'khadi' justice:[22] It is based on common sense and common norms. Judge Judy's court, like everything else on TV, is a funhouse mirror; real small-claims court do not work this way.

Judge Judy has an audience of millions, and many imitators, including some in other countries (for example, Venezuela and Chile) (Friedman and Nuñez. forthcoming). Why is this show so popular? One reason is Judge Judy herself. She is a consummate show-woman; we love watching her castigate people who do wrong, or who act as helpless doormats. But people also like Judge Judy's brand of justice: it is swift and

21 Kohm (2006) thinks Judge Judy fosters 'neoliberal notions of governance and individual self-responsibility', a conclusion I find questionable.

22 Max Weber used the term 'khadi' (an Arabic word) to refer to a judge who does not render a decision legalistically but in terms of popular norms in each individual case. (Rheinstein, 1954: xlvii).

efficient. There is no nonsense, no technicality; she always reaches closure and she knows how to make decisions that satisfy the audience, if not the litigants.

Judge Judy's closest relative, in a way, is reality TV; and her show is, in fact, reality TV with a legal twist. It is one more example of how entertainment, in the broadest sense, pervades both the media and the culture. In a sense, reality TV is not new; real people have long appeared on TV, in quiz shows, for example, or on programmes like *Queen for a Day* (Watts, 2009: 301). In the late 20th century, the genre blossomed (if that is the word), and TV is now drenched with examples of this rather dubious art form. Reality shows are cheap; that makes them attractive to networks and cable stations. Do they have an impact on attitudes or behaviour?[23] This is as difficult to say as it is for crime shows and the like. We pointed out that, in the media, news and entertainment – fact and fiction – have tended to merge. 'Reality' TV is another example. The people on reality TV are ordinary people; but they have stepped into the entertainment world, blurring the line between their 'ordinary' life and their life on screen.

A Concluding Word

Popular culture is an important subject in general; and also in relation to the legal order. It reflects and also influences social norms. What is true of popular culture is also true of 'news'; and of high culture as well. In this brief essay, I have suggested, first, that the relationship of law and popular culture has evolved over time (no surprise) and in ways that parallel changes in general culture. Second, that 'news' has become a part of popular culture, a part of the entertainment world. In the broadest sense, 'law' is everywhere in society, so that it pervades both news and popular culture. 'News', however, has become a part of popular culture, a part of the entertainment world. Just as the line between 'law' and the non-legal sector is difficult to draw, so too is the line between fact and fiction, between '"news" about law' and the 'law' that appears in a dramatic show. How images of law in popular culture affect the actual legal system remains, however, an open question.

References

Anderson, C. A., Shibuya, A., Ihori, N., Swing, E. L., Bushman, B. J., Sakamoto, A., Rothstein, H. R. and Saleem, M. "Violent Video Game Effects on Aggression, Empathy, and Prosocial Behavior in Eastern and Western Countries: A Meta-Analytic Review", *Psychological Bulletin* 2010 136, 151-173.

---

23 For example *Sister Wives*, was a programme about a rather self-satisfied and dim-witted polygamist and his harem of wives and children. The people on *Sister Wives* actually believe in polygamy; and they seem almost aggressively ordinary; and, besides, quite law-abiding in every way but one. This, perhaps, might lead people to wonder why polygamy should be a crime. And the polygamist, Kody Brown, in fact won a smashing legal victory in late 2013, when a Utah federal court struck down the local statute aimed at polygamists. See Grossman and Friedman, 2013.

Asimow, M., "Embodiment of Evil: Law Firms in the Movies", *UCLA Law Review* 2001 48, 1339-1392.

Asimow, M., "Popular Culture and the American Adversarial Ideology", in M. Freeman (ed), *Law and Popular Culture* (Oxford: OUP, 2005).

Asimow, M., "Popular Culture and the Adversary System", *Loyola of Los Angeles Law Review* 2006-2007 40, 653 -686.

Asimow, M., "*12 Angry Men*: A Revisionist View", *Chicago-Kent Law Review* 2007 82, 711-716.

Bandes, S. A., "And All the Pieces Matter: Thoughts on *The Wire* and the Criminal Justice System", *Ohio State J. of Criminal Law* 2011 8, 435-446.

Beale, S. S., "The News Media's Influence on Criminal Justice Policy: How Market-Driven News Promotes Punitiveness", *William and Mary Law Review* 2006 48, 397-482.

Bergman, P. and Asimow, M., *Reel Justice: The Courtroom Goes to the Movies* (Kansas City: Andrews and McMeel, 1996).

Bogart, L., "Television News as Entertainment", in P. H. Tannenbaum (ed), *The Entertainment Functions of Television* (Hillsdale: Lawrence Erlbaum Assoc., 1980).

Brandt, N., *The Congressman Who Got Away With Murder* (Syracuse: Syracuse University Press, 1991).

Burns, E., *Invasion of the Mind Snatchers: Television's Conquest of America in the Fifties* (Philadelphia: Temple University Press, 2010).

Carpenter, D., *Reputation and Power: Organizational Image and Pharmaceutical Regulation at the FDA* (Princeton: Princeton University Press, 2010).

Chandra, A., Martino, S. C., Collins, R. L., Elliot, M. N., Berry, S. H., Kanouse, D. E. and Miu, A. "Does Watching Sex on Television Predict Teen Pregnancy? Findings From a National Longitudinal Survey of Youth", *Pediatrics* 2008 122, 1047-1054.

Cohen, P. C., *The Murder of Helen Jewett* (New York: Vintage Books, 1998).

Conley, T., "The Laws of the Game: Jean Renoir, La Regle du Jeu", in J. Denvir (ed), *Legal Reelism: Movies as Legal Texts* (Urbana: University of Illinois Press, 1996).

Couvares, F. G. (ed), *Movie Censorship and American Culture* (Boston: University of Massachusetts Press, 1996).

Davies, S., "From Maycomb to Nuremberg: cinematic visions of law, legal actors, and American ways", *International J. of Law in Context* 2012 8, 449-468.

Ferrara, E., Chong, A. and Duryea, S., "Soap Operas and Fertility: Evidence from Brazil", *American Economic Journal of Applied Economics* 2012 44, 1-31.

Forman, H. J., *Our Movie Made Children* (New York: Macmillan, 1933).

Fox, R. L. and Van Siuckel, *Tabloid Justice: Criminal Justice in an Age of Media Frenzy* (Boulder: Lynne Rienner 2001).

Freedman, J. L., *Media Violence and its Effect on Aggression: Assessing the Scientific Evidence* (Toronto: University of Toronto Press, 2002).

Freeman, M. (ed), *Law and Popular Culture* (Oxford: Oxford University Press, 2005).

Friedman, L. M., "Law, Lawyers, and Popular Culture", *Yale Law Journal* 1989 98, 1579-1606.

Friedman, L. M., "Front Page: Notes on the Nature and Significance of Headline Trials", *St. Louis University Law Journal* 2011 55, 1243-1284.

Friedman, L. M., "Judge Judy's Justice", *Berkeley J. of Entertainment and Sports Law* 2012 1, 125-133.

Friedman, L. M. and Nuñez, A. C., "Popular Legal Culture: Television Judges", text available with the author, Stanford Law School.

Garber, S. and Bower, "Newspaper Coverage of Automotive Product Liability Verdicts", *Law and Society Review* 1999 33, 93-122.

Greenwald, R. A., *The Triangle Fire, the Protocols of Peace, and Industrial Democracy in Progressive Era New York* (Philadelphia: Temple University Press, 2005).

Grieveson, L., *Policing Cinema: Movies and Censorship in Early Twentieth-Century America* (Oakland: University of California Press, 2004).

Grieveson, L., "Fighting Films: Race, Morality, and the Governing of Cinema, 1912-1915", in L. Grieveson and P. Kraemer (eds), *The Silent Film Reader* (London: Routledge, 2004).

Grossman, J. and Friedman "Kody's Big Score in Challenge to Polygamy Law", *Justia's Verdict* 2013 Sept. 27.

Harewood, D., "David Harewood on Black Theatre: Who Says We Can't Do Chekhov?", *The Guardian*, 17 July 2013

Hunt, D. M., *O.J. Simpson Facts and Fictions: News Rituals in the Construction of Reality* (Cambridge: Cambridge University Press, 1999).

Krauss, C., "Two Sides of Product Liability", *New York Times*, 5 October 2012, B1.

Leff L. J. and Simmons, *The Dame in the Kimono: Hollywood, Censorship, and the Production Code from the 1920's to the 1960's* (New York: Grove Weidenfeld, 1990).

Macaulay, S., "Images of Law in Everyday Life: The Lessons of School, Entertainment, and Spectator Sports," *Law and Society Review* 1987 21, 185-218.

Macaulay, S., Friedman, L. M. and Mertz, E., *Law in Action: A Socio-Legal Reader* (St Paul: Foundation Press, 2007).

Machura, S. and Ulbrich, S., "Law in Film: Globalizing the Hollywood Courtroom Drama", in S. Machura and P. Robson (eds), *Law and Film* (Chichester: Wiley, 2001).

Machura, S. and Robson, P. (eds), *Law and Film* (Chichester: Wiley, 2001).

McCann, M. and Haltom, W., *Distorting the Law: Politics, Media, and the Litigation Crisis* (Chicago: University of Chicago Press, 2004).

McMurria, J., "Global TV Realities: International Markets, Geopolitics, and the Transcultural Contexts of Reality TV", in S. Murray and L. Ouellette (eds), *Reality TV: Remaking Television Culture* (2nd edn) (New York: New York University Press, 2009).

Miller, N., *Banned in Boston: The Watch and Ward Society's Crusade against Books, Burlesque, and the Social Evil* (Boston: Beacon Press, 2010).

New York Times, 10 March 1966, "G.M. Acknowledges Investigating Critic".

New York Times, 20 November 2009, "To Blacks, Precious is 'Demeaned' or 'Angelic'".

New York Times, 20 December 2013.

Papke, D. R., "From Flat to Round: Changing Portrayals of the Judge in American Popular Culture", *J. of the Legal Profession* 2007 31, 127-152.

Podlas, K., "Testing Television: Studying and Understanding the Impact of Television's Depictions of Law and Justice", in P. Robson and J. Silbey (eds), *Law and Justice on the Small Screen* (Oxford: Hart Publishing, 2012).

Rapping, E., *Law and Justice As Seen on TV* (New York: NYU Press, 2003).

Rheinstein, M. (ed), *Max Weber on Law in Economy and Society* (Cambridge: Harvard University Press, 1954).

Robbers, M. L. P., "Blinded by Science: The Social Construction of Reality in Forensic Television Shows and its Effect on Criminal Jury Trials", *Criminal Justice Policy Review* 2008 19, 84-102.

Robertson, C., "Representing 'Miss Lizzie': Cultural Convictions in the Trial of Lizzie Borden", *Yale J. of Law and the Humanities* 1996 8, 351-416.

Rosenberg, C., *The Trial of the Assassin Guiteau* (Chicago: University of Chicago Press, 1968).

Schuetz J. and Lilley, (eds), *The O. J. Simpson Trials: Rhetoric, Media, and the Law* (Carbondale: Southern Illinois University Press, 1999).

Shelton, D. E., Kim, and Barak, G., "A Study of Juror Expectations and Demands Concerning Scientific Evidence: Does the '*CSI* Effect' Exist?" *Vanderbilt Journal of Entertainment & Technology Law* 2006 9, 331-368.

Steven, A. and Kohm, S. A., "The People's Law versus Judge Judy Justice: Two Models of Law in American Reality-Based Courtroom TV", *Law and Society Review* 2006 40, 693-728.

Strub, W., *Obscenity Rules: Roth v. United States and the Long Struggle over Sexual Expression* (Lawrence: University Press of Kansas, 2013).

Swanberg, W. A., *Sickles the Incredible* (New York: Charles Scribner's Sons, 1956).

Terzic, M., "Judge Judy: Construction of Justice with an Attitude", in P. Robson and J. Silbey (eds), *Law and Justice on the Small Screen* (Oxford: Hart Publishing, 2012).

Tucher, A., *Froth and Scum: Truth, Goodness, Beauty and the Ax Murder in America's First Mass Medium* (Chapel Hill: University of North Carolina Press, 1994).

Tyler, T. R., "Viewing CSI and the Threshold of Guilt: Managing Truth in Reality and Fiction", *Yale Law Journal* 2006 115: 1050-1085.

Watts, A., "Melancholy, Merit, and Merchandise: The Postwar Audience Participation Show", in S. Murray and L. Ouellette (eds), *Reality TV: Remaking Television Culture* (2nd edn) (New York: New York University Press, 2009).

West, L. V., "Awakening the Moral Consciousness: On the Numbing of the Conscience of a Nation", *No. Car. L. Rev.* 2004 83, 289-322.

Wittern-Keller, L., *Freedom of the Screen: Legal Challenges to State Film Censorship, 1915-1981* (Lexington: University of Kentucky Press, 2008).

'A Child's Mind as a Blank Book': Myth, Childhood, and the Corporation

Anne McGillivray[1]
Professor of Law, University of Manitoba, retired

I think of a child's mind as a blank book. During the first years of his life, much will be written on the pages. The quality of that writing will affect his life profoundly.
Walt Disney (n.d., Giroux 1999: 17)

Disneyland: a space of the regeneration of the imaginary as waste-treatment plants are [where] the dreams, the phantasms, the historical, fairylike, legendary imaginary of children... is a waste product, the first great toxic excrement of a hyperreal civilization.
Jean Baudrillard (1981: 14)

Children's Reading and Children's Thinking are the rock-bottom base on which this country will rise. Or not rise... books for children have a greater potential for good, or evil, than any other form of literature on earth.
Dr. Seuss (1960: 11)

Children's literature... is not like myth. It is myth. Children's literature is not a source of information about social structures of subjectivity [but] the very site of their emergence. Children's literature is not a series of texts about the law. It is a source of law.
Desmond Manderson (2003: 9)

---

1 This paper is for Michael Freeman, friend and mentor, who grasps at straws. He does not desperately clutch at them, or construct specious arguments from them, or overburden camels with last ones. He uses them to tell early which way a wind blows. Telling the winds has made him a pioneer in many fields of legal study, not least the promise and profundity of children's rights. My University of Manitoba colleagues Evaristus Oshenebo and John Pozios gave me insight into reforming the corporate conscience. The Legal Research Institute lent support. An early version of this paper was given at the Vulnerability and the Human Condition Initiative & Feminism and Legal Theory Project Workshop, 'Corporate Rights versus Children's Interests', University of British Columbia, 19 and 20 October 2012.

A. Diduck, N. Peleg, H. Reece (eds.), Law in Society: Reflections on Children, Family, Culture and Philosophy
Copyright 2015 Koninklijke Brill NV. Printed in The Netherlands. ISBN 978-90-04-26148-8. pp. 101-124.

Introduction

Walt Disney, master of marketing, saw in the child a blankness, an empty book to be filled, an innocence to be manipulated, in the cause of his corporate vision. Dr. Seuss, master of the sideways moral, saw stories for children as the most potent of all forms of literature (McGillivray, 2014). Awakened to the power of story by WWII and the US bombing of Japan (Nel, 2001), off to new start with his fable *Horton Hears a Who!* (1954), Seuss knew that 'the new generations must grow up to be more intelligent than ours'. The Seussian child sees things that others do not and opposes arbitrary and unjust authoritarianism. For Desmond Manderson (2003: 9), stories are the legal texts of childhood.

> For if childhood is a province of myth, and if myth itself is to be understood as central to the origin of our understanding of society and law, then the mythological elements of children's stories ought themselves to be regarded as an essential site for the emergence of particular understandings of law (*ibid*, 7).

The Child in literature for children is a child of the Enlightenment, born of Locke and Rousseau whose philosophies propelled a profound shift in how we see childhood and how we govern children. In the New Childhood of the late 17th century, the child came under tutorial surveillance, depictions of the family in art and philosophy centred around children, and childhood became explicitly about itself. Throughout the 19th and 20th centuries, the state sought to shape the child in the production of citizenship. Through the school, the family, and the clinic, by manipulating images of the family and activating parental guilt and desire, children were to be made fit subjects of law. Myth and law were once contiguous. The child to whom a vast body of stories in a multiplicity of media is directed is the Child at the heart of myth. Here she may appear as Wisdom, Mediator, Messenger, or protagonist. The mythic element of stories for children brings law into the child's shaping of her self and empowers her to cope with the complexities of the everyday. As tales of origin and return, betrayal and reconciliation, justice and love, stories constitute the legal texts of childhood.

Beneath childhood now flows a current more powerful than any state or storyteller. This is the power of the corporation, whose reach into childhood combines story-telling as ad-myth with the knowledges of the clinic. Governing childhood over the past two centuries was located in the family, the school, and the regulatory state, informed by the psy sciences. The primary locus is now the corporation. Children are no longer shaped in the production of citizenship but in the production of consumption. 'To convert (a state body) into an independent commercial company' is to corporatise (Shorter Oxford, 1993). Childhood is corporatised. It is a new New Childhood in which myth is deeply attenuated and, with it, the child's power over her childhood, over who she is and will be, in an inverse ratio to the enhancement of her power as consumer. Her dreams are corporate dreams. Her childhood is an exploitable commodity. The unsurpassed learning powers of children – their minds no blank book but books informed by the rich and complex cultural and genetic heritage of the human species, fully primed for knowledge – is now turned to profit margins and corporate hegemony.

Part 1 introduces the New Childhood and the new literature in which a mythic aspect emerged, becoming central to constituting the child as legal subject. Part 2 considers children's media consumption and 'kid-marketing' to show how deeply the child's psyche is penetrated by corporate tales. Childhood innocence is central to corporate strategies, as Part 3 suggests. Part 4 asks how corporations might be made to act responsibly in their uses of childhood and suggests two paths of resistance – the old powers of the state and the family; new resistance within the corporate structure in shareholder and stakeholder rights and the social-benefit corporation. Part 5 suggests a third path, a paradigm shift from the rights-bearing corporation to the rights-bearing child.

1. A New Literature for the New Child – Constituting the Legal Subject

The prolonged childhood unique to our species has left us, of 27 known hominins, 'the last apes standing' (Walter, 2013a). We are here because we evolved an extended childhood. 'Human children are the most voracious learners planet Earth has ever seen, and they are that way because their brains are still rapidly developing after birth' (Walter, 2013b). 'Neoteny, and the childhood it spawned, not only extended the time during which we grow up but ensured that we spent it developing not inside the safety of the womb but outside in the wide, convoluted, and unpredictable world.' Our lives, cultures, and continuation 'depend on the child in us, the part that loves to meander and play, go down blind alleys, wonder why and fancy the impossible'. The plasticity of the human brain, retained until early adulthood, is responsible for children's unparalleled powers of learning and our lifelong curiosity. How we see childhood is shaped by society. Childhood is not an anthropological norm or random by-product of law or policy aimed elsewhere, but an idea, a conception, a sentiment, in which the child is a screen for the infinite projection of adult desires (McGillivray, 2013).

Under Roman law and revived in the common law, children unless abandoned were owned absolutely by the father whose power over the *familias* made childhood the essence of the private (McGillivray, 2012b). In the long journey from Roman to modern law, governing childhood became a matter of trust. The child is no longer *res* or chattel but a rights-bearer in the fiduciary care of the parent and, preemptively, the state (McGillivray, 2004, 2012b). The journey from *res* to rights was propelled by the New Childhood (Ariès, 1962; Stone, 1982, Steward 1995). Philippe Ariès (1962: 125) argues that 'in medieval society the idea of childhood did not exist'. Childhood as *conception* grew from the 18th-century upper-class fashion for child-coddling, the tutorial surveillance of their children (*ibid*: 369 *et seq.*), and the individuation of affect. From this emerged a desire, a nostalgia for childhood in which the child remedies our own mortality. Children were no longer miniature adults to be moved from infancy to community by seven, the end of *infantia*. Childhood was now a bounded life stage, explicitly about itself. This 'new' childhood is what we mean by childhood (*ibid.*). Images of the New Child were celebrated and promulgated by the artists of Georgian England (Steward, 1995).

With the New Child came a new literature intended to socialise and entertain. Children's literature, Jacqueline Rose (1992: 8) explains, 'first became an independent commercial venture in England in the mid- to late-eighteenth century, at a time when the conceptualization of childhood was dominated by the philosophical writings of Locke and Rousseau'. This image of the child 'has never completely severed its links with a philosophy which sets up the child as a pure point of origin in relation to language, sexuality and the state'. As pure point of origin, the child has access to a lost world or primitive state denied to the socially-contaminated adult, a state which the child then restores to the adult (Rose, 1992: 10). Constructed on Rousseau's concept of innocence, the child of children's literature is 'the one the category itself sets in place, the one which it needs to believe is there for its own purposes'. If childhood preserves 'an older form of culture', then 'this same form of culture is infantilized'. Here 'children's fiction has a set of long-established links with the colonialism which identified the new world with the infantile state of man. Along the lines of what is almost semantic slippage, the child is assumed to have some special relation to a world which – in our eyes at least – was only born when we found it' (*ibid*: 50). The child is 'asked to retrieve a lost state of nature' (*ibid*: 47). If so, Rose argues, J.S. Barrie's Peter Pan (and see Dixon, 1977 on race and colonialism in books for children) are rightly suspect. It may be that no story-teller can escape this critique. But there is more.

The child in stories for children and the child for whom the stories are imagined is a child of the Enlightenment, the age of reason, rights and the individual and a child of the Romantic, the age of the recovery of the fantastic and the mythical in which childhood innocence masked cruelty and exploitation. Thus essayist Charles Lamb (1823: 108), could 'throw the halo of poetry' around the misery of child sweeps (Mayhew, 1851: 339-83). It was the age of *The Golden Bough* and *The Mabinogian*, Tennyson's Arthurian cycle, the collecting of folk fairy tales by Andrew Lang and the Brothers Grimm, and Charles Kingsley's Rabelaisian *The Water-Babies* (1863) which pulled elements of Celtic myth and Christian moralising, biology and Darwinian evolution, race caricature and notions of progress into the tale of the redemption of a sweep's boy. The excesses of abuse excused by the Romantic vision of Enlightenment notions of childhood innocence (discussed in Part 3, below) were slowly corrected by legislative reform (McGillivray, 2004, 2012; Freeman, 1983). The ban on child sweeps was effected in 1864. The desire of children for their own stories continued. The stream of myth as fantasy for children begun in *The Water-Babies* flows through the works of George MacDonald, J.R.R. Tolkein, C.S. Lewis and Ursula K. LeGuin, among many others (Swinfen, 1984; Egoff, 1988). Why should these stories matter?

In stories for children, the child protagonist encounters law in its mythic infancy, its fears, challenges, pathways, and reconciliations always the same and always different. For Carl Jung (1969a: 161), the Child of story is 'the preconscious, childhood aspect of the collective psyche... an image of "a mediator, bringer of healing, that is, one who makes whole"' (*ibid*: 164), the symbol of 'the strongest, the most ineluctable urge in every being, namely the urge to realize itself' (*ibid*: 170). There is a 'striking paradox' – 'the child is on the one hand delivered helpless into the power of terrible enemies and in continual danger of extinction, while on the other he possesses powers far exceeding those of ordinary humanity'. The child may be seen as 'insignificant, "unknown", "a mere child"' but he 'is also divine... endowed with superior powers and, despite all dangers, will unexpectedly pull through'. The tension lies not just in the tests and terrors of the journey but in the return (McGillivray, 2012). When secondary worlds intrude into the everyday, laws collide in complex and instructional ways. How should the child reconcile the competing normative orders of her mythic and everyday worlds? The child reader engages with the child protagonist in resolving mythic tensions, helping her to reconcile the competing normative orders of her own world. She becomes a critical legal pluralist, finding that 'knowledge is a process of creating and maintaining myths about realities' and legal knowledge 'is the project of creating and maintaining self-understandings' (Kleinhans, 1997: 39). As incipient subject of law and as a child preparing for that subjectivity, she is and will remain a subject of a plurality of normative orders. In navigating these orders or worlds, she becomes a law-inventing, law-subverting genitrix of normativity.

The child protagonist is invested by character or encounter with the power of myth. Following the tale through its mysteries, dangers and revelations, the child reader is invested with that mythic power. The tale may take her to the labyrinth, a mythic motif which resonates through children's stories (McGillivray, 2012). At the labyrinth's heart is hidden 'a monster or a metamorphosed god, or a secret that is the revelation of one's own being' (Rodriguez-Monegal, 1973). A 'place of paradox', the labyrinth fixes movement from form to contemplation, multiplicity to unity, within to without 'according to a symbolic progression' (*ibid.*). An ancient symbol of transformation, it is Jung's metaphor of the psyche, 'a state of imperfect transformation... the state of someone who, in his wanderings among the mazes of his psychic transformation comes upon a secret happiness which reconciles him to his apparent loneliness' (Jung, 1969b: para. 623; McGillivray, 2012: 10). The loneliness of transformation is nowhere more felt than in the child's neurologically-twisted journey through adolescence (Giedd, 2008; Johnson *et al.*, 2009). In stories, the labyrinth is manifest in forests and rivers, mines and caverns, night cities and cities underground, attics and cellars in ancient houses, or mazes of hedge or stone. Its transformative power is imposed on the everyday, its twisted paths and tests of reason and courage reflecting in unsettling ways the competing normative orders and conflicting rules of the child's ordinary world. The submerged geography of childhood through which Jung's labyrinth runs is Freud's unconscious, the site of the emergence of sexuality. The child's return from the labyrinth signals her incipient maturity and legal subjectivity (McGillivray, 2012).

'If we hope to live not just from moment to moment, but in true consciousness of our existence,' Bruno Bettelheim (1977: 3) writes, 'then our greatest need and most difficult achievement is to find meaning in our lives... the most difficult task in raising a child is helping him find meaning'. For Bettelheim, the meaning is a Grimm and Freudian one in which Snow White leads children through the Oedipal crisis and the cruelty of stepmothers is understood. Children's literature 'fails to stimulate those resources he needs most in order to cope with his difficult inner problems' and most is 'so shallow in substance that little of significance can be gained' (*ibid*: 4). Only the 'folk fairy tale' will do (*ibid:* 5). Seuss (1960) would disagree, as would Tolkein (McGillivray, 2014). Writing on the fairy-tale, Tolkein (1966: 52) explains that these

> are not in normal English usage stories about fairies or elves, but stories about Fairy, that is Faërie, the realm or state in which fairies have their being. *Faërie* contains many things besides elves and fays, and besides dwarfs, witches, trolls, giants or dragons: it holds the seas, the sun, the moon, the sky; and the earth and all the things that are in it ... the *adventures* of men in the Perilous Realm or upon its shadowy marches.

A fairy-tale is a 'sub-creation', a secondary world with rules and laws giving it the 'inner consistency of reality' (*ibid*: 88). As for Bettelheim's rejection of shallow modernity, 'the Cauldron of Story has always been boiling, and to it have constantly been added new bits, dainty and undainty' (*ibid*: 52). With Tolkein, Lewis (2000: 527-28) links fantasy with myth:

> The Fantastic or Mythical... can give us experiences we never have had and thus, instead of 'commenting on life', can add to it.

The structures of Harry Potter's wizard and Muggle worlds each mirror the other, as do the complexities of children's lives in both worlds (Jutras, 2001: 45). So it is in law, where 'architectural continuity is manifested in the fact that similar tensions or polarities are part of the structure of normative orders at each layer, from the brief encounter to the large-scale human interaction' and 'the mundane and very small' should come within law's gaze' (*ibid*: 64).

The mythic element in stories for children does more than prepare children as future legal subjects. It forms the stuff by which they make their childhood. 'There is nothing mysterious about myth,' Manderson (2003: 9) asserts. 'It shines in the most mundane of environments: a bedroom at night, on a parent's knee or under the covers, by a study light or the glimmer of a torch, silently or out loud, read or off by heart. These everyday contexts should not distract us from the significance of its function in the lives of children.' Myth in its original sense of 'narratives *about* the gods' is 'sustained by their constant echoes *in* the everyday' (*ibid*: 4). This is not the forced didacticism and moral foreclosure which feeds much of children's story-telling. Rather these stories engage the child on a different, deeper, more difficult level. It is not by prescription but by narrative, by 'a complex web of association, memory, history', that we are constituted as legal subjects (Manderson, 2003: 23). As myth 'is sustained by its echo in the everyday', so the everyday sustains myth, a relationship begun in early childhood (*ibid*: 4). The narrative strands woven by stories lie deep within us, deeply felt because first encountered in childhood. If law is derived from myth, if myth sustains law, and if childhood is a province of myth, then stories for children are 'the fusion of law and literature' (*ibid*: 18), holding 'the key to the constitutive myths and narratives that begin to organize our relationships to law' (*ibid*: 15). The journey begins in *infan-*

tia, a state without (legal) speech in which the child is in law *innocentia* and progresses toward *doli capax*, the understanding of evil which is the onset of legal subjectivity. To know evil is to be expelled from the garden of innocence. Myth takes the child safely through the gates.

Stories map the landscape of childhood, naming the places of love and fear, transgression and reconciliation, the loci of myth. Myth helps us to make sense of where we come from, who we are, and how we conduct ourselves in our relations with one another and with the natural world. In original cultures throughout the world and our own past, myth and law are contiguous. Myth contains the origin of law and the idea of law, establishing 'the limits of the world, of what can be meant and done' and 'transcends these limits in its relation to the sacred' (Fitzpatrick, 1992: 16). At its core is the Messenger, a trickster, magician, or child who locates and mediates 'the profane, mortal world within the sacred' and connects us to 'ultimate origins and ultimate identity, with the source and foundational force of all that is'. A Messenger travels between worlds to bring knowledge to the people. They resist, he suffers, Wisdom mediates, opposites are reconciled. Thrice-Great Hermes returns from heaven with the message, 'the below is as the above, and the above as the below' (Roob, 2001: 8). Horton the elephant hears a voice on a speck of dust and returns with the message: 'A person's a person, no matter how small' (Seuss, 1954; McGillivray, 2014). Both are myth, the first the paradigm of gnosticism revered by alchemists, the second an amiable elephant beloved of children. Hermes calls up the spark of divine Wisdom depicted as a Child. Horton calls up the Who-child Jo-Jo whose YOPP! 'put it over' to prove the existence of the invisible Whos to the doubting Nools.

The emergence of childhood resonated far beyond the world of children. It redefined the private, reconditioned motherhood, and fueled the enormous complex of therapeutic disciplines, Michel Foucault's (1977) strange sciences whose power to set the conditions of normality derives from the study of deviance. As stories map the child's inner self, so the psychometrics of childhood map the microstages of physical, emotional, social and intellectual development. The tutelage of the psy experts is all around us, in advice columns, tv shows, pamphlets, magazines, self-therapy and childcare books, in schools, clinics, and offices and in the discourse of juvenile and family courts. Their expertise – Foucault's *surveillance* and Nikolas Rose's (1989: 208) therapies of freedom – is installed within us in 'the unceasing reflexive gaze of our own psychologically educated self-scrutiny'. It is a self-surveillance in which 'we evaluate ourselves according to the criteria provided for us by others' and 'adjust ourselves by means of the techniques propounded by the experts of the soul' (*ibid*: 10). By the activation of 'guilt, anxiety, envy, and disappointment', we rear the child desired by the state. 'Childhood is the most intensively governed sector of personal existence' (*ibid*: 123). If governing the self was once between man and god, the great project of civilizing childhood shifted the locus of self-governance from the confessional to the clinic. The therapeutic expertise of multitudinous psy sciences fuelled child labour, schooling, health and family law reforms, shaping parental aspirations from the 19th century to the present ((Donzelot, 1979; Rose, 1989).

This expertise is now in the hands of corporations. Using psy science tools, technologies, and knowledges, corporations manipulate innocence to engage parental aspirations and assuage guilt by safely shaping children's desires. 'Normal' is the right toys, foods and goods. 'Deviant' is to be wrong or without. While children's books and serials of past centuries carried advertisements, corporate messages now infiltrate every part of the child's world. This tale begins with Mr. Potato-Head.

2. Meet Mr. Potato-Head – the Child, the Media, and the Market

Hasbro's Mr. Potato-Head was an assortment of plastic features – mouths, noses, ears, eyes, hands, feet, eyeglasses, hats – to be stuck into a potato provided by the mother. He debuted on television in 1952 in the first ad targeted at children in the first 30-second spot (Kelly, 2012). Children were told to tell their moms to buy Mr. Potato-Head, the 'pester power' that would become a staple of the kid-marketing lexicon (*Washington Post*, 1979). Corporate marketing has gone far beyond this primitive but effective sales tool. Childhood is no longer clinically split into the normal and the deviant, its mapped microstages no longer of interest only to clinicians, schools, juvenile courts and parents. The demographics of childhood now are split, splintered and realigned into a multitude of demographies for the design and marketing of consumer products. Psy tools are embedded in the media consumed by children.

Corporations address children through direct and indirect media for an average of seven hours 38 minutes a day or ten hours 45 minutes of multi-tasked media content. For 21 per cent of children, media consumes 16 hours of each day (Harris, 2012). Average use in 2004 was six hours 21 minutes, rising to seven hours 38 minutes in 2010 (Kaiser, 2010). 'Tweens' on average use media 8.4 hours a day and teens 12.6 hours (Harris, 2012). Teens average 3.6 hours per day online, 2.9 hours with television, 1.6 hours playing video games and 1.6 hours listening to an MP3 player (Harris, 2012). The study followed 5,077 US youth aged 8-24 in August 2011. The post-2005 proliferation of portable devices enables 99 per cent of Grades 4 to 11 Canadian children to access the Internet outside school, enabling constant and virtually unsupervised online access according to a 2013 survey of 5,436 children (MediaSmarts, 2014a, 2014b). Children search for information (sports, entertainment, health, relationships, sexuality), play online games and universally engage in social networking. One in six has gone offline to avoid harassment. Although Facebook bans under-13s, one in three Grade 5 students has an account. One in three of all children sleep with their cell phone. In 2005, two of three children had rules against meeting people encountered online, declining to one in two in 2013. For adolescents, rules and supervision are rare.

Corporate messages received through digital media are repeated in the streets, the stores, the schools and the child's social group. Games, films, spin-off toys, toys that spin off films, ads, music and the machines through which they are delivered, themselves symbols of status, of cuteness and coolness, are made by and for the benefit of corporations. The pedagogical power of the old New Childhood – the wise parent tutored by Locke, the intimate tutoring envisaged by Rousseau, the public school system instituted in the 19th century to give all children an equal start in the social complex – is now in corporate hands. 'The overall conclusion from research of all types is that media is a powerful tool and a powerful teacher' (Warburton, 2012: 9). Civilizing childhood is a for-profit enterprise. If childhood is the historically specific outcome of technologies governing the subjectivity of citizens (Rose, 1989), a new expertise armed with a rich arsenal of technologies has emerged.

The massive complex of corporations whose power derives from psy knowledge of the child and the child-parent consumer dyad uses the expertise of the psy sciences to manipulate desire.

> With the help of well-paid researchers and psychologists, advertisers now have access to in-depth knowledge about children's developmental, emotional and social needs at different ages. Using research that analyzes children's behaviour, fantasy lives, artwork, even their dreams, companies are able to craft sophisticated marketing strategies to reach young people' (MediaSmarts, n.d.).

Mental health clinicians wrote a public letter in 1999 asking the American Psychological Association to declare it unethical for psychologists to be involved in advertising to children. In 2004, the Association recommended that it 'undertake efforts to help psychologists weigh the potential ethical challenges involved in professional efforts to more effectively advertise to children, particularly those children who are too young to comprehend the persuasive intent of television commercials' (*ibid*). But infants of six months form mental images of corporate logos and mascots. Brand loyalty is established by the age of two. 'The current generation of children has been recognised as the most brand conscious ever' (Valkenburg and Buijzen, 2005: 466). Television exposure 'has consequences for the brand recognition of even the youngest children' (*ibid.*). Kid-marketing after Mr. Potato-Head targeted children six and older. Accelerated by the world-wide success of *The Teletubbies*, marketing to infants became 'a rapidly growing trend'. Psy experts working for corporate marketers keep their secrets: 'Probably due to the success of recent entertainment programs designed for toddlers, advertisers have become even more aware of the accessibility and susceptibility of the youngest target groups. They have undoubtedly gathered valuable information about cognitive, affective, and behavioral advertising effects on young children' but 'research findings are, in most cases, not accessible to academics and policy makers' (*ibid.*).

The lexicon of kid marketing is set. 'Buzz marketing' targets children through social media, viral videos and the cool kid factor. Children spy on children for ad agencies, sport new products, and message websites with tips and questions on what's hot or not. 'Behavioural targeting' uses personal information provided by children on entering internet sites to aim personalised ads back at them. Children are not children but 'demographics'. Kid-marketer Ted Mininni (2011) advises that, as 'Tweens and teens are increasingly creating their own content online, influencing a wider circle of their peers as they do', their engagement 'on all communication platforms, especially social media, is a "must".' Corporations who 'make the effort to connect with these groups in new, inventive ways will reap significant rewards. These demographics and their friends can become true brand devotees'. Rose's (1989) parental guilt is activated through children's two-pronged pester power – 'persistence nagging' and 'importance nagging' – which shapes parental spending in the amount of $US 500 billion a year. What parents agree to buy for children is augmented by those children whose own purchasing power amounts to $21.4 billion yearly (Minninni, 2011). Adult choice is conditioned by childhood. What young adults consume is conditioned by childhood branding. The total spent by those under the age of 25 will exceed $211 billion in 2012 (Harris, 2012). Children's troubador Raffi (Cavoukian, 2013) warns of cyber-bullying, media addiction, privacy violation, exploitation, the dark side of social media. Even so, it seems unfair that children are made responsible for preventing harms little understood and beyond their control.

'Each normal family will fulfil its political obligations best at the very moment it conscientiously strives to realize its most private dreams' (Rose, 1989: 5). The political is now the corporate. The technologies of the experts of the corporation are aimed not in the installation of citizenship to create a governable state but in the installation of consumerism to create profit. Deviance is not knowing what is cool or hot in brands and products. Private dreams are the lock of guilt and hope activated by the right product key. Little girls are not princesses but Disney princesses endlessly co-opted from the vast store of open-copyright fairy-tales to tie fantasy to dollars. Mattel's bottom line is more modest than Disney's but Barbie's once-erotic bosom still points at girls as it has done since 1959. If Barbie develops a social conscience about bullying, the message is still about buying Barbie. Gender-bending provocateurs Sponge-Bob and Dora are artfully crafted to fit the parameters of parental tolerance while occupying the place once reserved for small children's transgressive exploration of social and geographic spaces. On-line games track the ages, aspirations, affinities, pets, parents and product preferences of their child players. Play is work. Work is consumption. Children's dreams are the dreams of corporations. Fantasy is dead, long live Disney.

Parents are integral to corporate dreams of childhood. 'To be truly successful, brands will have to deliver on their promises and communicate those promises on multiple platforms for kids and their parents. And that means engaging the modern family on its own terms, (Mininni, 2011). Mininni continues:

> Do partner with parents. They need and want reassurances... Especially if the brand offers an opportunity to bring the entire family together. Hint: family game nights and activities have reappeared since the economic downturn. How can marketers capitalize on that?

The terms of engagement of the modern family include education: 'Do engage them by playing to their sense of adventure and their imaginations. Do get the point across simply and succinctly. Do engage them with activities that teach, educate or encourage creativity.' They include respect for children: 'Don't talk down to the kid's demographic you want to appeal to. Speak in their language. Better yet: show them in inventive ways. Remember: kids see themselves as more mature than they actually are.' They include telling the truth: 'Do make certain your messages are truthful and authentic. Kids can spot a phony from a mile away; that will turn them off to the brand for good. Hint: they'll take their friends with them away from the brand.' There is a nod to innocence: 'Do emphasize safety and wholesomeness' but only 'if these are central to the brand.'

This weird brew of psy science and corporate manipulation draws heavily on Enlightenment notions of innocence. If parents trust corporate promises to protect children's 'safety and wholesomeness', they are more likely to embrace corporate care. Innocence was key to the old New Childhood and it is key to the new corporate one.

3. Innocence in the New Childhoods

'Imagine,' Joel Bakan (2011: 50) proposes, 'that the "new curriculum" of childhood was an actual school curriculum.' The comparison is apt. The New Childhood of the 17th and 18th centuries began in a tutorial regime taking the child out of the community into the school-room and centering the family around the child. Now, for the equivalent of every school day, children sit before screens to learn that males are brutally violent, females are sex objects, 'identity, self-worth, happiness, and good fortune are defined by what people buy and own', and adults are good only for getting you what you want (*ibid.*). 'Violence is fun, lying, stealing, revenge and greed are fun; isn't it fun to kill more people each day in a video game?' observes James McNeal, guru-founder of children's marketing (*ibid.*). Children skimp schoolwork and are fat, unhealthy, and sleep-deprived, 'endangering themselves through over-consumption'. John Locke (1692) similarly describes the coddled children of the New Childhood three centuries ago.

Childhood innocence is a potent Enlightenment myth. Reflecting Avicenna's *tabula rasa*, Locke (1690: 2:1:2, para 2) writes, 'Let us then suppose the mind to be, as we say, white paper, void of all characters, without any ideas: How comes it to be furnished?' Rousseau (1762) warns against 'wanting to give innocence the knowledge of good and evil' (*ibid*: 96) and advocates a 'prolonged innocence' which, by preserving the child's 'nascent sensibility', lets 'the first seeds of humanity' to be sown (*ibid*: 220). Innocence was deployed in 19th century Romanticism poetically to cloak a multitude of harms to children and, conversely, to propel state and charitable reform of the conditions of childhood. Although innocence now is synonymous with protecting children from explicit sexuality, bad words and strangers, it is as central to the new New Childhood as to the old.

In his study of Disney, the *sine qua non* of children's marketers, Henry Giroux (1999: 4) takes the Gramscian view of popular culture as a site of public pedagogy (Mayo, 2009: 257). As education 'presupposes a particular view of citizenship, culture, and society', it is never innocent', yet 'it is this very appeal to innocence, bleached of any semblance of politics, that has become a defining feature of Disney culture and pedagogy' (Giroux, 1999: 31). Its 'attachment to the appeal of innocence' lets Disney 'reaffirm its commitment to children's pleasure' and sentimentalise innocence even as it commodifies it. Innocence is no longer historically or contextually constructed. It is 'an atemporal, apolitical, and atheoretical space where children share a common bond free of the problems and conflicts of adult society' under the benign eye of a 'corporate parent who safeguards this protective space for children by supplying the fantasies that nourish it'. Innocence invokes 'commitment to middle-class family values' and justifies corporate expansion into such noncommercial spheres as public schools. The rhetoric 'represents more than the staged authenticity of the corporate swindle; it also works strategically to celebrate innocence over politics and other forms of critical knowledge' (*ibid*: 23-24). Associated 'with a sentimentalized notion of childhood fantasy', innocence functions 'as the principle concept of moral regulation and as part of a politics of historical erasure'. Presented 'as the deepest truth', it 'becomes the ideological and educational vehicle through which Disney promotes conservative ideas and values as... normative' (*ibid*: 34). The dissonance between Disney's corporate culture as 'paragon of virtue and childlike innocence' and its 'cut-throat commercial ethos' (*ibid*: 25) is striking. By producing 'the meanings, desires, and dreams' that seduce us into the Disney world-view, the corporation 'has a political stake in creating a particular moral order favourable to its commercial interests' (*ibid*: 35; Giroux, 2000). Jean Beaudrillard (1981: 14) is blunt. Disneyland is 'a space of the regeneration of the imaginary as waste-treatment plants are... one must recycle waste, and the dreams, the phantasms, the historical, fairylike, legendary imaginary of children and adults is a waste product, the first great toxic excrement of a hyper-real civilization.'

Children cannot protect themselves from cleverly-constructed messages backed by billions of advertising dollars. These messages do far more than sell toys. They sell a corporate vision and a corporation-friendly politic. Their stories erase children's creativity and sense of myth. 'We're forcing the brain in the wrong direction, killing all creativity and fantasy,' pre-eminent children's brand-builder Martin Lindstrom concludes (Bakan, 2011: 52). 'Kids were once creative directors in neighborhood fantasies. No more. These days, kids rarely leave their bedrooms.' Their schools have moved beyond logos and product placement to a corporate hand in education. Where Disney sponsors schools, it is hard to tell where charity ends and marketing begins (Giroux, 1999). Corporations offer pizza for reading, dollars for soup labels, class trips, product samples, computer labs, smart-screens. There is no way to say no. The corporate reach goes beyond children's psyches, deep into their bodies. From toxins in fetuses and breast milk to non-nutritive food and infant formula (Durkovic, 2013; Moorhead, 2007), from the re-shaping of children's bodies through obesity, inactivity and eating disorders to the destruction of their environment, only some of the damage is known. 'We are conducting a vast toxicological experiment in which the research animals are our children' (Landrigan, 2001).

The corporation was invented to secure the personal assets of its owners. To separate personal from business assets, the corporation became a natural entity, a person vested with rights (Bakan, 2004). Corporations are people too. Presidential candidate Mitt Romney (*Washington Post*, 2012) told a heckler, 'Corporations are people, my friend... of course they are. Everything corporations earn ultimately goes to the people.' Senatorial candidate Elizabeth Warren disagreed (Berman, 2012): 'Corporations are not people. People have hearts, they have kids... they live, they love, and they die...

we don't run this country for corporations, we run it for people.' If so, why does the combined wealth of the poorer half of the world's population equal the combined wealth of the world's richest 85 people (Weardon, 2014)? A veil of protective statutes and judgments covers the corporate face, to be pierced only in exceptional circumstances. The corporation's sole duty is to its shareholders. Its directors' duty is to the best interests of the corporation, requiring a constant complex calculus of the damage-to-profits ratio in which legal compliance and consumer injury are part of the cost-benefit analysis. Detecting corporate wrong-doing in remoter parts of the planet and more subtle arenas of human and environmental health is at best difficult. Prosecution is compromised by nearly unreachable standards of causation and proof. Statutory remedies are notoriously unsuccessful (Bakan, 2011). There is nothing human about the corporation except its status as rights-bearer. It has no body to be punished. It has no duties commensurate with its rights. It is abstracted from the web of respect and interdependence marked out by the rights and commensurate duties defining human relationships (McGillivray, 1994). Without duties, without relationships, the corporation is an idiot, alone and self-defining. In its reach, power, and wealth it is bigger than states, parents and children. It gives – communication, housing, foodstuff, fun-stuff, things we need or not, stories – and it takes away.

The Borg in reverse, corporations are an invading force of artificial entities vested with human characteristics bearing rights without duties, sociopaths void of conscience, unable to die a natural death (StarTrek TNG, 1987-1994). The Borg is a single entity, a hive-mind embodied in captive humanoids retrofitted with bio-mechanical devices to connect cognition. Its sole purpose is to achieve perfection by assimilating every humanoid in the galaxy, absorbing all biological, intellectual, and technological knowledges and attributes. A successful sociopath, the Borg lacks emotion but learns from its mistakes. The economic and political power of the corporation enables a multi-tentacled reach into politics, governments, nations, the press, and the laboratory, skewing, vitiating or obliterating scientific findings contrary to its interests. Much of what we understand about the world, from global warming to how vitamins work, is not based on empirical study but on corporate sponsorship, bribery and spin. In breadth and penetration, the corporate reach is unprecedented in the history of the world. Resistance is futile.

Corporations are 'programmed to put their missions of creating wealth for their owners above everything else, and to view anything and everything – nature, human beings, children, the planet – as opportunities to exploit for profit' (Bakan, 2011: 11). Can the corporate conscience be reformed? Can the Borg hive-mind be directed to a purpose other than increasing its resources by exploiting others? If it is trapped by law in a sociopathic enterprise, resistance is futile. As Bakan (2004) observes, you may as well ask a shark to be nice to fish or a fox to go vegetarian. Even so, two paths of resistance emerge from the status quo, from without and within the corporation.

4. Resistance, Reform and the Responsible Corporation

External to the corporation are the old powers of parent and state. A benign remnant of the old law of *pater potestas*, the fiduciary duty of parents confers on them the correlative rights to assert and protect children's rights (McGillivray, 2012b). *Parens patriae*, the state's power and duty to protect children as its most vulnerable citizens, is exercised primarily but not exclusively through legislation (McGillivray, 2004). Internal to the corporation are the powers of stakeholders and shareholders and new corporate models combining profit-making with doing good.

As fiduciaries, parents must act in the child's best interests. Parents ought to be the natural enemies of corporations (Linn, 2009). Positioning parents in resistance is underway. Success is unlikely. Effective resistance needs hard information. Corporations misrepresent, obfuscate, appropriate and sometimes invent scientific evidence while selling innocence and promising safety. More subtly, product marketing centres children's gratification in parental dreams. Love is giving. Giving gets love. Parents learn to desire the instant gratification of instantly gratifying the child's desire. Desire becomes a spinning cycle of product awareness to desire to acquisition. Ads show children how to get parental approval for stuff and give parents easy access to it. Clever minds produce clever consumables whose allure is brilliantly exaggerated by other clever minds devising ad-tales in which wise, calm, beautiful children perfectly manipulate consumables in repetitive enactments of singular or familial pleasure. Hot cool stuff rolls endlessly off assembly lines, to be etched in entertaining electrons. The reach is dual: the child's psyche and parental aspiration. In the corporate dream, children raise parents. Parents are poorly positioned for rebellion.

The *parens patriae* power of the state implies a duty to restrain corporate activity which threatens children. No right is absolute. All rights can be limited by law where necessary to protect public safety and the rights of others. This says much and little. Corporations may be beyond state regulation. Many corporate economies outstrip national economies, many operate far beyond the level of nation-states, and transnational ones are beyond state regulation (Nolan, 2013). As employers, suppliers, developers and taxpayers are desired, corporations are courted by governments, their transgressions forgiven, barely punished, or undetected. Evaristus Oshenebo (2009: 216) finds 'an intriguing paradox' in empowering civil society to enforce corporate regulation. Civil society 'is capable of creating norms and values that are independent of, and insulated from, both the state and the corporation' but legalising these norms threatens not just corporate power but government power. He writes of the exploitation of weak regulatory power over multinational corporations in African extractive industries, but his question is universally relevant: 'Is it reasonable to expect that governments, knowing the constraining influence of civil society groups on state action, would empower them to a degree that they can effectively counterbalance the power of corporations? This question is significant because, unfortunately, the interests of governments and business seem to be coalescing with every passing day' (*ibid.*). Even so, 'it would be myopic for governments to shy away from empowering civil groups simply because such empowerment may whittle down corporate and governmental power in certain respects'. Empowering civil society will 'enhance the capacity, responsiveness, and effectiveness of public regulatory agencies and, by extension, that of the government itself' (*ibid*: 217). Where children are affected, empowerment is a *parens patriae* duty.

Can corporations themselves do good? The second path of resistance lies within. Corporations have a duty to protect human rights (United Nations, 2011: Principle 11). Corporations 'should avoid infringing on the human rights of others and should address adverse human rights impacts with which they are involved'. As Justine Nolan (2013: 27) explains, this 'global standard of expected conduct for all business enterprises wherever they operate... exists independently of States' abilities and/or willingness to fulfil their own human rights obligations'. Corporations may be more receptive to human rights policies than before but

> the limited mechanisms for enforcing such policies remain largely embedded in soft law, that unless hardened, will have a very limited effect in preventing future violations of human rights by corporations' (*ibid.*).

For-profit corporations can engage in philanthropy for tax and public relations purposes and own charitable entities. Charitable corporations can operate for-profit enterprises directly related to the founding purpose of the charity, a rule heavily and literally enforced. There is little room for movement either way. The flexible business form of the co-operative, the original hybrid of the charitable and the profitable, invites further investigation (McGillivray, 1992). Parents as stakeholders – those in the private sector who, whether or not they trade with the corporation, are or may be affected by its acts – are weakly situated, although inroads have been made. Parents as corporate shareholders are slightly better situated (Oshionebo, 2012). Even so, our evolution has made us prefer our own children in allocating our resources. Increasing these resources is why parents invest. This tends to defeat goodwill toward the children of unknown others. It also may blind us to the longer-term well-being of our own.

Corporations must profit their shareholders. Doing good must maximise profits. Operating a business corporation for a social purpose raises legal questions about the fiduciary duty of directors to shareholders. The US 'Revlon rule' requires that shareholder interest in maximising financial return be paramount over stakeholder interests. Recent decisions of the Supreme Court of Canada suggest that directors' duties include consideration of the interests of stakeholders in decision-making. In 2004, the court ruled that directors may take the interests of stakeholders into consideration provided that they do not disregard the interests of a particular stakeholder group (*Peoples Department Stores Inc. (Trustee of)* v. *Wise*, [2004] 3 S.C.R. 461). Directors owe fiduciary obligations to the corporation whose interests are not to be confused with the interests of creditors, shareholders, or any other stakeholder. In 2008, the Canadian Supreme Court rejected the Revlon duty to maximise shareholder value in change-of-control transactions, in favour of a duty to treat all stakeholders fairly (*BCE Inc. v. 1976 Debentureholders*, [2008] 3 S.C.R. 560). This, the court said, is commensurate with 'the corporation's duties as a responsible citizen'. Compared with US jurisprudence, Canadian jurisprudence makes it easier for for-profit corporations to achieve social goals. On the other hand, shareholder proposals are generally less restricted in the US than in Canada (Oshionebo, 2012).

Shareholder proposals promoting corporate social responsibility hold some promise (Oshionebo, 2012). The transnational corporation Enbridge Inc., for example, adopted a shareholder proposal for 'Voluntary Principles on Security and Human Rights' and Shell Canada adopted a shareholder proposal to implement environmental and human rights policies in developing countries. But, however well-supported, shareholder proposals do not bind management. Their function is to shame the corporation. Regulatory barriers and a culture of shareholder passivity further reduce their use and effectiveness. Even under reformed federal legislation in Canada, a proposal can be barred if it 'clearly appears that the proposal does not relate in a significant way to the business or affairs of the corporation' (Oshionebo, 2012: 635). This may rule out shareholder proposals based on human rights and, of course, children's rights.

Whatever possibilities for doing good are extant in the corporation, there is a movement toward business-worthy alternatives with fewer legal strictures. The social enterprise corporation is a statutory hybrid of the charitable and the profitable, combining corporate powers and profit-motive with the freedom to focus on social goals (Robson Hall, 2011). The social enterprise – 'social purpose', 'double bottom-line' (financial, social), 'triple bottom-line' (financial, social, environmental) – is a quasi-philanthropic corporation which reinvests profit into the community while 'growing' its business. It takes a variety of statutory forms. The low-profit limited-liability company or L3C is in place in several US states. The benefit corporation enables for-profit corporations to pursue a social mission, freeing directors to make decisions that embrace both profit and social benefit. Benefit corporations may be for-profit, not-for-profit, and not-for-loss, limited-liability and community-interest. B Corps operate with 'higher standards of corporate purpose, accountability, and transparency' under the protection of traditional corporations (B Corporation, 2012). 'The old models of traditional for-profits and charities no longer are sufficient tools for meeting these challenges. The future is far more likely to be dominated by businesses that are tracking more than their financial bottom line, and nonprofits that see enterprise as a fundamental part of large-scale social change' (Fruchterman, 2011: 47). B Corps certified by the non-profit B Lab as meeting 'rigorous standards of social and environmental performance, accountability, and transparency' use business 'to solve social and environmental problems'. Certified B Corps exist in 15 countries including Britain and the US, but not Canada.

Corporate powers, Disney-persuasive powers and the freedom to exploit enjoyed by transnational corporations with vast supply-side businesses suggest that parent and state duties to children, shareholder and stakeholder powers, and the social enterprise corporation, cannot compete with the hugely-scaled traditional corporation. For Oshenebo (2009), effective corporate regulation requires a pluralistic approach involving state agencies, corporations, NGOs and community associations. For Nolan (2014), the coming-together of all sources of resistance in 'soft law' – 'the interplay between national and international law and state and non-state actors' – could establish 'both a legal and quasi-legal basis and mechanism for holding corporations accountable for human rights violations'. Hard or soft, where do we find the collective will to prefer children's rights over corporate ones? How much do children matter? Resistance is futile, intones the Borg. Without a new paradigm of resistance, without a new understanding which renders belief in what went before impossible to sustain, corporate reform is an uncertain and prolonged endeavour. This new paradigm is the rights-bearing child.

5. Taking Myth and Children's Rights Very Seriously – in Conclusion

The New Childhood was the creation of philosophers, artists and writers, followed by the psy clinicians whose knowledge informed childhood's reformers. The new New Childhood is the creature of corporations and corporate media wielding the suasive powers of the psy sciences to sell products and exploiting notions of innocence to brand children from infancy. Lévi-Strauss (1955: 430) argues that, unlike poetry in translation,

> the mythical value of the myth is preserved even through the worst translation... functioning on an especially high level where meaning succeeds practically at 'taking off' from the linguistic ground on which it keeps on rolling.

But in corporate stories filling the spaces between corporate ads – those half-minute or 12- or 20-minute tv tales – questions are answered before they can be asked and myth is so deeply attenuated that all meaning is fractured. This is Rolande Barthes's (1970: 107) 'myth, today... produced from commercial and political words and images' where 'there never is any contradiction, conflict, or split between the meaning and the form'. It has 'an imperative, buttonholing character... directly springing from contingency... it is I whom it has come to seek. It is turned towards me, I am subjected to its intentional force, it summons me' (*ibid*: 123). It is 'poverty-stricken. It does not know how to proliferate; being produced on order and for a temporally limited prospect... It lacks a major faculty, that of fabulizing' (*ibid*: 148). Myth in corporate retelling is ad-myth. It is no-myth.

Jean Beaudrillard (1981: 87) goes further:

> All original cultural forms, all determined languages are absorbed in advertising because it has no depth, it is instantaneous and instantaneously forgotten. Triumph of superficial form, of the smallest common denominator of all signification, degree zero of meaning... This unarticulated, instantaneous form, without a past, without a future, without the possibility of metamorphosis, has power over all the others.

'Children's fiction draws in the child, it secures, places and frames the child,' Jacqueline Rose (1984: 2) writes. It is 'something of a soliciting, a chase, even a seduction'. The solicitation, chase and seduction of childhood by corporations, though, is a seismic shift in which consumption and conformity replace mystery, subversion and revelation. Corporations tell the stories which let children make their childhoods. They control the everyday world to which children return. The places where questions happen are foreclosed. The secret garden of childhood is drying up.

There is a third power, as firmly rooted in law as the powers of the state and the corporation, and instinct with myth. Its possibilities are not well understood. It is seen as a threat. This power is the child as rights-bearer (McGillivray, 1994, 2014). Taking children's rights very seriously (cf. Freeman, 1992) offers the only real opposition to the corporate grip on childhood. Regardless of whether a state has ratified the United Nations Convention on the Rights of the Child (1989), the rights it enumerates and the protocols developed under it represent, at an appropriate level of generality, the rights inherent or expressed in almost all legal systems. Are children's rights the paradigm that might tame corporate power? States must abolish 'traditional practices prejudicial to the health of children' under Art. 24. The corporation has been with us since Roman times. In its modern statutory form, it originated in 1844. Much of what it is and does may well be among the 'traditional practices' prejudicial to children's health. Legal argument for retaining and expanding corporate powers is framed as tradition – this is what X-Corp must be permitted to do because this is what corporations have always done. Corporations are artificial entities powered by law. What law gives, law can take away. Traditional practices of corporations harm children and violate their rights.

The child has all human rights from birth, under Art. 1. The child has the right to freedom of information under Art. 17 and to protection from all violence including mental violence under Art. 19. Under Art. 3, she has the right to have her best interests be made a paramount consideration in everything affecting her. She has the right to survival and development under Art. 6. and to the highest attainable standard of health, to 'adequate nutritious foods and clean drinking-water, taking into consideration the dangers and risks of environmental pollution' under Art. 24. This limits corporate power over food production, safety and nutrition, corporate representation of the nature of its products, environmental toxins and the promotion of pharmaceuticals. Under Arts. 28 and 29, the child has the right to an education that will develop her full potential and is science-based and rights-based. This education instals citizenship, not consumerism. Corporate pedagogy aims at precisely the opposite.

The child has the right to rest, play, age-appropriate recreation and cultural participation under Art. 31. Corporations control most of children's recreation and leisure. Are video-gaming, web-crawling, Facebook and television-watching 'cultural participation'? If so, we have much to answer for. The child has the right to access media offering information from diverse sources and to media promoting the full spectrum of health, under Art. 17. Being sold bad food, unneeded goods, violence and sexism, dangerous pharmaceuticals and, the ultimate product, the corporation's brand and its self-serving politics of innocence, is an extreme violation of these rights. The child has the right to protection from economic exploitation under Art. 35 and from 'all other forms of exploitation prejudicial to any aspects of the child's welfare' under Art. 36. Commercial exploitation is as bad as any other kind of exploitation. Corporations exploit children's credulity, creativity, imagination, fears, desires, love, loyalty, parents and resources, and their rights to information, education, play, voice and health. They plunder their planet and their futures. The scale of this intervention into childhood is unprecedented. Corporations govern childhood. If greed is going out of style, it needs a push.

Seuss's Horton transgresses Noolian law to save the minuscule Whos but, huge as he is, his success depends on the participation of the tiny Who-Child Jo-Jo. Of Seuss's subversive *The Cat in the Hat* ('one of the Cold War's most potent unguided missiles') written three years later, Louis Menand (2002) writes,

> But that was then, a long time gone. Now we have something different: we have 'anything goes' without the spirit. 'Transgression', "subversion', 'deconstruction' are praise words bestowed as solemnly as 'structure' and 'order' once were, little gold stars awarded to rappers and television comics.

Disabled from the public engagement and critical citizenship needed to challenge rights violations, without the right to be heard, there is little left to children but consumption. 'A million cats cavort frantically for our attention. Even the fish has been co-opted (though what choice did he have?). "Enjoy!" cries the fish. "Consume!"' And so children do. The unmitigated pursuit of profit causes immeasurable damage to the 'other' children who produce our endless supply of cheap branded goods. It damages the child consumers of these goods. The stakes are at an all-time high.

The mythic element of children's stories informed the New Child with an inventive, transgressive, engaged citizenship. The new New Child forged in corporate boardrooms is branded and consuming. Ad-myth does not inform childhood. It sells things to children. It is empty and demanding. The child has the right to express her views freely in all matters concerning her, under Art. 12. From the legislature to the courtroom to the boardroom, children are to be heard and their rights made a paramount consideration. If this were so in matters of corporate regulation, conduct and governance, childhood could not belong to corporations. We recall Jung's Child who, 'delivered helpless into the power of terrible enemies and in continual danger of extinction', is found to possess 'powers far exceeding those of ordinary humanity'. She who has survived the labyrinth will have little difficulty in the corporate boardroom. Her power as a child to question, to shame, to solve problems and to compel right behaviour is the stuff of myth deriving from tales forged in eons of human evolution. Our long childhood is the product of seven million years of evolutionary experience in being *hominin* and a million years in being *sapiens*. It inheres in the structure of the stories we tell our children. Without that myth, without the mythic child, there is no childhood but the corporate one of endless consumption, or exclusion from it.

Postscript

Children once found meaning in the mythic elements of stories. Corporate consumerism now informs most of what children see and read. Loss of myth as loss of meaning is now associated with a steeply-rising population of children who harm themselves. Health-care admission of adolescents with suicidal thoughts who cut their arms, thighs and bellies with razor blades and protractors or burn or bruise themselves by banging fists into walls has risen by two to five times across Canada in the past decade (Canadian Press, 2014). Doctors offer explanations ranging from existential crisis to social media. Self-harm 'is a way of kind of giving the body a whole different set of inputs that allows them not to feel so awful inside'. Self-harm or 'cutting' was once a symptom of depression but self-harming children now 'go from pretty average, functioning kids to suddenly they can't cope. They can't manage. They're depressed. They're presenting to emergency departments, hopeless.' Many meet no mental disorder criteria. 'Instead, they seem to be suffering an existential crisis... "I'm empty, I don't know who I am, I don't know where I'm going, I don't have any grounding and I don't know how to manage my negative feelings."' Many live affluent lives with supportive parents and experience few 'adverse events'. A break-up or bad grades or a death 'completely throws them'. Self-harm is becoming 'almost a fad'. Many self-harming children belong to Facebook self-harm groups and post their injuries. 'Personally,' one doctor said, 'I would love to see that access to social media was significantly restricted until adulthood.'

References

Ariès, P., *Centuries of Childhood* tr. R. Baldick (London: Jonathan Cape, 1962).

B Corporation. 'B Lab Home Page' (2013) at http://bcorporation.net/.

Bakan, J., *The Corporation: The Pathological Pursuit of Profit and Power* (New York: Free Press, 2004).

Bakan, J., *Childhood Under Siege: How Big Business Targets Children* (New York: Simon and Shuster, 2011).

Barthes, R., *Mythologies* tr. Annette Lavers (New York: Farrar, Straus and Giroux, 1970).

Baudrillard, J., *Simulacra and Simulation* (orig. pub. Éditions Galilée, 1981) at fields.ace.ed.ac.uk/.../uploads/.../Baudrillard-Jean-Simulacra-And-Simula...?

Berman, A., 'Elizabeth Warren to Romney: "Corporations Are Not People"' in *The Nation*, 5 September 2012 at http://www.thenation.com/blog/169773/elizabeth-warren-romney-corporations-are-not-people.

Bettelheim, B., *The Uses of Enchantment: The meaning and importance of fairy tales* (New York: Vintage Books, 1977).

Canadian Press, 'Canadian hospitals stretched as self-harming teens seek help: Emergency rooms across the country seeing spike in teens with self-inflicted injuries' 15 March 2014 at http://www.cbc.ca/news/canada/canadian-hospitals-stretched-as-self-harming-teens-seek-help-1.2574316

Cavoukian, R., *#lightwebdarkweb: Three reasons to reform social media be4 it re-forms us* (Homeland Press, 1913).

Donzelot, J., *The policing of families* (New York: Pantheon, 1979).

Durkovic, L., 'Nestle Kills Babies: An Inside Look at the 1970s Baby Formula Scandal', *Ethics in the News*, 18 September 2013 at http://www.ethicsinthenews.com/nestle-kills-babies-an-inside-look-at-the-1970-baby-formula-scandal/

Egoff, S., *Worlds Within: Children's Fantasy from the Middle Ages to Today* (Chicago, London: The American Library Association, 1988).

Fitzpatrick, P., *The Mythology of Modern Law* (London: Routledge, 1992).

Foucault, M., *Discipline and Punish: The Birth of the Prison*, tr. A. Sheridan (London: Allen Lane, 1977).

Freeman, M., *The Rights and Wrongs of Children* (London: F. Pinter, 1983).

Freeman, M., "Taking Children's Rights More Seriously", *International Journal of Law, Policy, and the Family* 1992 6(1), 52-71.

Fruchterman, J., "For Love or Lucre", *Stanford Social Innovation Review* Spring 2011, 42-47.

Giedd, J. N., "The Teen Brain: insights from neuroimaging", *Journal of Adolescent Health* 2008 42(4), 335-343.

Giroux, H., *The Mouse that Roared: Disney and the end of innocence* (Lanham: Rowmans and Littlefield, 1999).

Giroux, H., *Stealing Innocence: Youth, Corporate Power and the Politics of Culture* (Basingstoke: Palgrave Macmillan, 2000).

Harris Poll YouthPulse. 'Daily media use among children and teens up dramatically from 5 years ago' 10 January 2010, Kaiser Family Foundation at http://www.kff.org/entmedia/entmedia012010nr.cfm.

Harris Poll at http://www.harrisinteractive.com/NewsRoom/PressReleases/tabid/446/ctl/ReadCustom%20Default/mid/1506/ArticleId/896/Default.aspx.

Jenkins, H., 'No Matter How Small: The Democratic Imagination of Dr. Seuss' in H. Jenkins, T. McPherson and J. Shattuc (eds), *Hop on Pop: The Politics and Pleasures of Popular Culture* (Durham, NC: Duke University Press, 2002).

Johnson, S., Blum, R. J. and Giedd, J. N., "Adolescent Maturity and the Brain: The Promise and Pitfalls of Neuroscience Research", *Journal of Adolescent Health* 2009 45(3), 216-221.

Jung, C., *The Archetypes and the Collective Unconscious* (2nd edn) tr. R.F.C. Hull, *The Collected Works of C.G. Jung* (vol 9, pt 1) (Princeton, NJ: Princeton University Press, 1969a).

Jung, C., *Mysterium conionctionis*, tr. R.F.C. Hull, *The Collected Works of C.G. Jung* (vol 14) (Princeton, NJ: Princeton University Press, 1969b).

Jutras, D., "The Legal Dimensions of Everyday Life", *Canadian Journal of Law & Society* 2001 16, 45.

Kelly, J., "Is Mr. Potato Head to blame for 'pester power' ads?" *BBC News Magazine*, 30 April 2012 at http://www.bbc.co.uk/news/magazine-17871107.

Kleinhans, M. and Macdonald, R., "What is a Critical Legal Pluralism?", *Canadian Journal of Law & Society* 1997 12, 25-46.

Lamb, C., "The Praise of Chimney Sweepers" (1823) in E. V. Lucas (ed), *Essays of Elia, First Series. The Works of Charles and Mary Lamb* (New York: Putnam, 1903; Rpt. New York: AMS Press, 1968).

Landrigan, P., 'Trade Secrets'. Moyers Report, 27 March 2001. Transcript at http://www.pbs.org/tradesecrets/transcript.html.

Linn, S., "Honoring Children in Dishonorable Times: Reclaiming Childhood from Commercialized Media Culture" in R. Cavoukian and S. Olfman (eds), *Child Honoring: How to Turn This World Around* (Westport CT, London: Praeger, 2009).

Locke, J., *An Essay Concerning Human Understanding* (1690) at http://oregonstate.edu/instruct/phl302/texts/locke/locke1/Essay_contents.html.

Locke, J., *Some Thoughts Concerning Education* (1692) at http://www.fordham.edu/halsall/mod/1692locke-education.asp.

Manderson, D., "From Hunger to Love: Myths of the source, interpretation, and constitution of law in children's literature" *Law & Literature* 2003 15, 87.

Mayhew, H., *London Labour and the London Poor: A Cyclopaedia of the condition and earnings of those that will work, those that cannot work, and those that will not work* (vol 2) (London: Griffen, Bohn, 1851)

McGillivray, A., *Co-operatives in Principle and Practice* (Saskatoon SK: Centre for the Study of Co-operatives, 1992).

McGillivray, A., "Why Children Do Have Equal Rights: In Reply to Laura Purdy", *International Journal of Children's Rights* 1994 2, 243-258

McGillivray, A. with Ish. D. J., "Governing Childhood" in McGillivray, A. (ed), *Governing Childhood* (Aldershot: Dartmouth, 1997a).

McGillivray, A., "Therapies of Freedom" in McGillivray, A. (ed), *Governing Childhood* (Aldershot: Dartmouth, 1997b).

McGillivray, A., "Childhood in the Shadow of Parens Patriae" in S. Ross, H. Goelman and S. Marshall (eds), *Multiple Lenses, Multiple Images: Perspectives on the child across time, space and disciplines* (Toronto: University of Toronto Press, 2004).

McGillivray, A., "A State of Imperfect Transformation: Law, myth and the feminine in Outside Over There, Labyrinth and Pan's Labyrinth" in M.D.A. Freeman (ed), *Law and Childhood Studies* (Oxford: Oxford University Press, 2012a).

McGillivray, A., "Children's Rights, Paternal Power and Fiduciary Duty: From Roman Law to the Supreme Court of Canada", *International Journal of Children's Rights* (2012b) 18, 21-54.

McGillivray, A., "The Long-Awaited: Past Futures of Children's Rights", *International Journal of Children's Rights* 2013 21(2) 1-24.

McGillivray, A., "Horton Hears a Twerp: Myth, law and children's rights in *Horton Hears a Who!*", *New York Law School Law Review* 2014.

MediaSmarts. "How Marketers Target Kids" at http://mediasmarts.ca/marketing-consumerism/how-marketers-target-kids.

MediaSmarts. *Young Canadians in a Wired World, Phase III: Life Online*, 22 January 2014a at http://mediasmarts.ca//ycww.

MediaSmarts. *Young Canadians in a Wired World, Phase III: Online Privacy, Online Publicity*, 19 February 2014b at http://mediasmarts.ca/research-policy.

Menand, L., "Cat People: What Dr. Seuss really taught us", *The New Yorker*, 23 December 2001 at http://www.newyorker.com/archive/2002/12/23/021223crat_atlarge?currentPage=all.

Mininni, T., "Marketing to Kids While Partnering with Parents", *Bolt*, May 2011 at http://www.designforceinc.com/marketing-to-kids.

Moorhead, J., "Milking It", *The Guardian*, Tuesday 15 May 2007 at http://www.theguardian.com/business/2007/may/15/medicineandhealth.lifeandhealth.

Nel, P. "'Said a Bird in the Midst of a Blitz …" : How World War II Created Dr. Seuss' (2013) 34/2 Mosaic 65-85.

Nolan, J., "The Corporate Responsibility to Respect Human Rights: Soft Law or Not Law?" in S. Deva and D. Bilchitz (eds), *Human Rights Obligations of Business: Beyond the*

Corporate Responsibility to Respect? (Cambridge: Cambridge University Press, 2013).

Oshionebo, E., "Shareholder Proposals and the Passivity of Shareholders in Canada: Electronic Forums to the Rescue?", *Queen's Law Journal* 2012 37, 623-662.

Robson Hall (University of Manitoba Faculty of Law) and The Winnipeg Foundation, "Law, Philanthropy, and Social Enterprise: New Direction or Distraction?" Symposium, Hotel Fort Garry, Winnipeg, 21 September 2011.

Rodriguez-Monegal, E., "Symbols in Borges' Work", *Modern Fiction Studies* 1973 19.

Roob, A., *Alchemy and Mysticism: The Hermetic Museum* (Koln: Taschen, 2001).

Rose, J., *The Case of Peter Pan or The Impossibility of Children's Fiction* (rev edn) (London: 1984, 1992).

Rose, N., *Governing the Soul: The Shaping of the Private Self* (London: Routledge, 1989).

Rucker, P., "Mitt Romney says 'corporations are people' at Iowa State Fair", *The Washington Post*, 11 August 2011 at http://www.washingtonpost.com/politics/mitt-romney-says-corporations-are-people/2011/08/11/gIQABwZ38I_story.html.

Seuss, Dr., *Horton Hears a Who!* (New York: Random House, 1954).

Seuss, Dr., "Writing for Children: A Mission – Brat Books on the March", *Los Angeles Times*, 27 November 27 1960, 11 (cited in Pease, D. E., *Theodore Seuss Geissel: Lives and Legacies* (Oxford: Oxford University Press, 2010).

Shorter Oxford English Dictionary (5th edn) (Oxford: Oxford University Press, 2002).

StarTrek TNG 1987-1994.

Stone, L., *The Family, Sex and Marriage in England 1500-1800* (Abridged edn) (Harmondsworth: Penguin, 1982)

Swinfen, A., *In Defence of Fantasy: A Study of the Genre in English and American Literature since 1945* (London: Routledge, 1984).

Tolkien, J., "On Fairy Stories" in J. Tolkien, *The Tolkien Reader* (New York: Ballantyne, 1966).

United Nations General Assembly, Convention on the Rights of the Child, 20 November 1989, United Nations, Treaty Series, vol. 1577.

United Nations Human Rights Council, "Guiding Principles on Business and Human Rights: Implementing the United Nations 'Protect, Respect and Remedy' Framework: Report of the Special Representative of the Secretary-General on the Issue of Human Rights and Transnational Corporations and Other Business Enterprises [2008]" 21 March 2011, A/HRC/17/31.

Valkenburg, P. and Buijzen, M., "Identifying determinants of young children's brand awareness: Television, parents, and peers", *Applied Developmental Psychology* 2005 26, 456–468.

Walter, C., *Last Ape Standing: The Seven-Million-Year Story of How and Why We Survived.* (New York: Walker, 2013a).

Walter, C., "Why Are We the Last Apes Standing? How childhood let modern humans conquer the planet" in *Slate*, 29 January 2013b at http://www.slate.com/articles/health_and_science/science/2013/01/evolution_of_childhood_prolonged_development_helped_homo_sapiens_succeed.html.

Warburton, W., "Growing Up Fast and Furious in a Media Saturated World" in W. Warburton and D. Braustein (eds), *Growing Up Fast and Furious: Reviewing the impacts of violent and sexualized media on children* (Sydney, AU: Federation Press 2012).

Washington Post, February 1979 cited in Phrasefinder at http://www.phrases.org.uk/meanings/pester-power.html.

Wearden, G., "Oxfam: 85 richest people as wealthy as poorest half of the world", *The Guardian*, 20 January 2014 at http://www.theguardian.com/business/2014/jan/20/oxfam-85-richest-people-half-of-the-world.

II

Law and Rights

Taking Children's Rights Seriously: The Need for a Multilingual Approach*

John Tobin
Melbourne Law School

Children's rights must be taken seriously. For over 25 years, Michael Freeman has combined passion and academic rigour to defend this position. In a ground-breaking paper published in 1987 (299), he chastised the renowned legal theorist Ronald Dworkin for failing to mention children in his much lauded text, *Taking Rights Seriously* (1977). Since then Freeman has continued to advance a moral and political defence of children's rights which is grounded in the concepts of dignity, respect and agency, rather than the alternative conception of children as mere victims who are vulnerable and in need of protection (1992; 2000; 2007; 2010). For Freeman, rights are a discourse of entitlement rather than discretion. They demand accountability rather than charity and a genuine commitment to prioritise and empower, rather than ignore, demean or devalue children. His commitment to the cause has been unwavering. Indeed few scholars, if any, have done as much over such a sustained period both to advance and to defend the case for children's rights.

But Freeman himself would be the first to concede that his appeal for children's rights to be taken seriously has not persuaded everyone. Certainly there have been significant achievements, not least of which is the fact that all states apart from the USA, Somalia and South Sudan have ratified the *UN Convention on the Rights of the Child* ('*CRC*'). Moreover, children's rights are now a regular feature in new constitutions (Tobin, 2005), often demand attention in court proceedings (Sloth Nielsen, 2008; Fortin, 2004; Tobin, 2009) and are increasingly used as a research paradigm by scholars (Pounder, 2008; Whitzman, Worthington and Mizrachi, 2010; Reynaert, 2009). The CRC itself is having an impact on domestic legislation (Lundy et al, 2013), it is increasingly common for states to appoint national children's commissioners (Sedletzki, 2012) and even the UN Human Rights Council has an annual resolution on children's rights. Meanwhile, the UN Security Council has also developed a comprehensive system to

* Special thanks to the anonymous referee for his/her thoughtful comments on an earlier draft of this chapter and to Elliot Luke for his assistance in preparing this chapter which was prepared as part of the Australian Research Council Discovery Grant, 'Children's Rights: From Theory to Practice' DP12014.

A. Diduck, N. Peleg, H. Reece (eds.), Law in Society: Reflections on Children, Family, Culture and Philosophy
 ISBN 978-90-04-26148-8. pp. 127-140.

monitor children's rights in armed conflict (UN Security Council Resolutions 1882, 1888 and 1998 and 2068). A cursory glance at the daily newspapers, however, reveals the constant violations of children's rights that occur in every society and the failure of decision makers to conceive of solutions to the problems confronting children in terms of their rights. Ideas about children's well-being, welfare and protection, equity and the new discourse on the policy block, justice reinvestment, are more likely to be mentioned in discussions about issues concerning children than their rights. Given this crowded space, how then can children's rights be taken seriously?

This chapter does not seek to answer this question in its entirety. Space, and the deficit in my wisdom, preclude such a task. Instead, it seeks to promote a discussion with respect to one piece of the puzzle that I have previously identified as an obstacle in the struggle to take children's rights seriously, namely, the potential for disciplinary resistance (2011: 85). By this, I mean that there are numerous disciplines – public health, education, urban planning, even economics - that have already developed their own discourses and methodologies regarding how best to improve children's lives. This presents a challenge for those of us who, like Freeman, are seeking to persuade these disciplines to take children's rights seriously. Why should they relinquish or compromise their own discourses for the protection and/or empowerment of children in favour of an abstract and legalistic concept such as rights?

In response to this dilemma, two central arguments are advanced. First, there is a need for the children's rights movement to maintain a high level of reflective practice in which the limitations of rights discourse and its potential for colonisation are constantly acknowledged. Second, any strategy that seeks to engage other disciplines in the agenda to take children's rights seriously must be informed by sociological insights about behavioural change. In practical terms, this requires the children's rights movement to adjust the prism through which it views issues concerning children in a way that acknowledges the perspective of other disciplines. It must then develop strategies by which to persuade these disciplines of the relevance and benefit of incorporating a rights-based perspective into their work. The aim must be to create a complementary rather than competitive approach to improving children's lives, in which children's rights and alternative disciplinary perspectives are each treated seriously.

I The Need for Reflective Practice

One of the greatest ostensible achievements of the CRC has arguably given risen to one of the greatest weaknesses of the children's right movement. Rarely will an advocate for children's rights not rely on the fact that the CRC has been ratified by 193 States. It is an understandable strategy. States parties to the CRC have voluntarily ratified this treaty and in doing so accepted an obligation, which is binding under international law, to perform their obligations in good faith (*Vienna Convention on the Law of Treaties*, art 26). This legalism is then combined with the moralism derived from the purported universality of human rights to create a double-barrelled assault on any disciplinary perspective that would challenge the relevance of children's rights. The result is that children's rights risk becoming an 'ideological fortress' (Cantwell, 2004: 1) where there is little need to justify the idea of rights for children because law and the universality of rights are considered to have done the hard work of elevating this idea to the high moral ground.

It is in this context that David Kennedy's warning about the colonising effects of human rights becomes relevant because of the potential for children's rights to be seen as occupying the 'field of emancipatory possibility' (Kennedy, 2002: 18). The commitment to the children's rights agenda may be understandable given the precarious state in which so many of the world's children live, but if the discourse is invoked to silence, marginalise, overlook or simply ignore other disciplinary perspectives on how to secure the needs and interests of children, disciplinary resistance and scepticism become predictable. How then should the risk of over-reliance on the legal and moral justifications for children's rights be managed?

As a minimum, any commitment to children's rights should be accompanied by reflective practice. This demands some introspection and critique on the part of those who advocate children's rights in order to recognise not only the transformative potential of this discourse, but also its dangers and limitations (Reynaert, 2012). This requires an acknowledgement of the risk that an evangelical commitment to children's rights may effectively silence and overlook other transformative discourses. Beyond this, however, there is a range of other dilemmas that cannot be overlooked and which can be broadly categorised as conceptual, normative and strategic dilemmas.

(a) The Conceptual Dilemma

The conceptual foundations of children's rights still remain relatively under-theorised (Dixon and Nassbaum, 2012; Guggenheim, 2005: ix). The idea that children should have rights may be blindingly obvious for those who believe in children's rights, but this faith is far from universal. There remains a legitimate question as to whether theory really matters when the urgent needs of children require tangible measures rather than mere theoretical reflections. However, as Freeman has declared, to evade this conceptual question is to 'demonstrate a lack of intellectual responsibility' (1994: 493). Thus, it is hardly surprising that much of his work, along with that of scholars such as Archard (2004) and Eekelaar (1986, 2008), has been dedicated to providing the normative foundation for the idea of children's rights. But Freeman himself would probably acknowledge that this project remains incomplete and that more work is required to meet the challenge of advancing the most 'intellectually compelling case' to justify the idea of children's rights (Sen, 2004: 317).

A comprehensive discussion of the conceptual foundations and moral justification for children's rights is beyond the scope of this paper (Archard, 2004; Eekelaar, 2008; Tobin, 2013), however, it is important to stress that dignity and the idea that children have equal moral value simply by virtue of being human (Archard, 2004: 218; McCrudden, 2008: 679; Habermas, 2010: 474) assume a central role in enabling the idea of children as rights bearers. When viewed from this perspective, rights become the means by which to realise the dignity of every child.

(b) The Normative Dilemma

For many, human rights are seen as being excessively legal, confrontational, abstract and incapable of reconciling cultural tensions and conflicting interests. Proponents of children's rights must be able both to acknowledge and to address these normative concerns. Take, for example, the resolution of a conflict between competing interests. There is an accepted methodology within human rights law which provides that, subject to a few exceptions such as the prohibition against torture, the rights of a child can be subject to interference, provided there are reasonable grounds for doing so (Tobin, 2012: 180-84; Siracusa Principles). The assessment of reasonableness requires consideration of whether it sought to achieve a legitimate aim or pressing social need (which includes the interests of other persons) and whether the measures to achieve the aim were proportionate. In turn, the assessment of proportionality requires consideration of whether there was a rational connection between the aim sought and the measure employed to achieve this aim. Where this is the case, a further question arises as to whether an alternative, less intrusive measure was reasonably available.

Thus, the discourse of children's rights has at its disposal a well-established methodology for resolving conflicts between rights. There remains, however, a tendency by advocates to sometimes overlook this methodology and label any act or omission that causes ostensible harm to children a violation of their rights. This approach serves only to create the impression that children's rights are an 'unfeasibly demanding' (Archard, 2004: 62) agenda, which is insensitive to, and incapable of, accommodating the rights and interests of others.

(c) The Strategic Dilemma

The third characteristic of a reflective approach to children's rights concerns an examination of the strategic measures used to implement this discourse. The traditional strategy for demanding compliance with children's rights has been to rely heavily on the fact that the CRC has been ratified by 193 states. This appeal to international law is not even sufficient to compel states, let alone other disciplinary perspectives, to engage with the idea of children's rights. A more sophisticated model of behavioural change is required, and in this respect, the work of Derek Jenks and Ryan Goodman, who use sociological research to reveal insights about the implementation of human rights treaties, is particularly useful (Jenks and Goodman, 2004, 2008).

According to Jenks and Goodman, implementation of human rights treaties occurs via the processes of coercion, persuasion and acculturation (Goodman and Jinks, 2005, 2008). Coercion occurs where a material incentive, whether a cost or benefit, catalyses change. The reality is that this option is particularly weak with respect to children's rights as there are few, if any, coercive mechanisms, which create the type of incentive that would lead states or indeed other disciplines to embrace children's rights. Acculturation essentially reflects peer pressure, where the embrace of a discourse such as children's rights is motivated by a desire to adopt an approach that is consistent with the emerging or dominant use of rights within a particular discipline.

There is certainly evidence of acculturation with respect to children's rights. Indeed, King has declared that 'children's rights have ... become perhaps the dominant programme within a social system which makes sense of the adult/child relationship' (2004: 275). It is debatable whether the status of children's rights has yet reached this status. Within areas such as development, however, there is certainly evidence to suggest that the acculturation of children's rights has occurred and continues to occur, at least among NGOs working in this area (Tobin, 2011: 62-64).

For Goodman and Jinks, acculturation is considered to be an important process by which the intentions of human rights treaties such as the CRC can be translated into practice (2008). However, acculturation is not without risks (Mushkat, 2008), which stem from the fact that this process is not necessarily the result of the complete internalisation of the values underpinning a particular treaty, such as the CRC. This creates a risk that engagement with children's rights is not just superficial but also subject to manipulation. This first fear was borne out in the UNICEF study of the effectiveness of a rights-based approach to its programming and policies (2012). The study revealed that there were variations in the degree of conceptual understanding of its staff with respect to the core principles of a rights-based approach (UNICEF, 2012: 39-40). In such circumstances, there is a risk that children's rights will become no more than a rhetorical vessel into which the subjective preferences and values of a policy maker may be poured.

Thus, while acculturation may play a facilitative role in raising awareness of children's rights, there is need for a more enduring strategy that will lead to deeper engagement with children's rights. This will require the adherents of alternative disciplines to be persuaded to internalise and validate the values that underpin children's rights. But how can persuasion be achieved? The answer is by framing the justification for children's rights in a way that resonates with the relevant discipline (Goodman and Jinks, 2004: 636). The predicament here is that the dominant *frames* used by children's rights advocates – international law and its purported universalism – are of limited utility when seeking to persuade adherents of disciplines such as public health, urban planning, education or economics.

So herein lies the challenge. If children's rights are to be taken seriously, advocates must treat seriously the underlying principles and values of those disciplines that are vital to the effective implementation of children's rights. Scholars such as Freeman have long argued for the need to adopt a multidisciplinary approach to children's rights (2012). This is a practical approach. Law and morality are limited in the extent to which they can guide states with respect to the *practical measures* required to achieve, for example, the right to the highest attainable standard of health, the right to an adequate standard of living or the right to survival and development. The contributions and insights of non-legal disciplines are critical in this regard. Yet it is insufficient for advocates of children's rights to be merely multidisciplinary: they must also be multilingual if they are to understand how best to translate the values that animate the idea of children's rights into a discourse which resonates with, and persuades, other disciplines. They must understand the language of other disciplines, whether welfare, equity, well-being, active citizenship or justice reinvestment, and develop strategies to frame the idea of children's rights in the vernaculars of these alternative discourses.

This strategy is not without risks. The very idea that children's rights should be translated into a different discourse could be seen to threaten the purported universality of rights. This risk is heightened where attempts are made to persuade disciplines such as economics, which is founded upon instrumentalist justifications for rights. This approach might even be considered heretical, given the orthodox stance that children's rights are inherent, inalienable and beyond utilitarian considerations. However, as Galit Sarfarty revealed in her anthropological study of the World Bank and its engagement with human rights, an insistence on the legal and moral justifications for human rights has proved fatal to their embrace within an institution dominated by economists (2009). Thus an appeal to the high moral ground may leave children's rights marooned and at the margins of decision-making by bodies that prioritise other considerations.

As a consequence, children's rights advocates must learn to speak more than one language. Importantly, multilingualism need not, and indeed must not, equate with complete abandonment of the fundamental principles that underpin the notion of children's rights. On the contrary, the intention must be to persuade other disciplines of the value of these principles so that they are internalised by these disciplines. The process of framing is therefore the means by which to gain intellectual access to alternative disciplines so as to enter a dialogue regarding the value and merit of internalising children's rights for a particular discipline. Rather than seeing other disciplines in oppositional or adversarial terms that must be 'converted' to the cause of children's rights, the challenge is to proceed on the basis of interdisciplinary respect and to create a dialogue in which the complementarity of discourses is explored and highlighted (Seymour and Pincus, 2008). By way of example, in the next section I demonstrate this approach in the context of contentious medical procedures and the relationship between the discourse of medical ethics and children's rights.

II Exploring Multilingualism – Medical Ethics and Children's Rights

It is generally accepted that there are four basic principles of medical ethics: autonomy, beneficence, non-maleficence and justice (Beauchamp and Childress, 2013). These principles are used to guide medical practitioners and bioethicists in evaluating the risks and benefits associated with medical procedures. The temptation when examining contentious medical procedures from a human rights perspective is to replace these four principles with references to human rights standards. However, medical practitioners and bioethicists would be understandably reluctant to abandon their commitment to principles which have long been held within their interpretative community. Indeed, there is every prospect that they would resist interference from human rights outsiders. This creates the potential for a parallel discussion in which bioethicists and medical practitioners use one discourse to evaluate a procedure, while human rights advocates draw upon another.

Of course multiple perspectives should be adopted with respect to all social and policy issues, including medical procedures, but the most effective conversations usually occur when the various perspectives are *listening* to each other rather than seeking to dominate. Moreover, they are even more effective when each attempts to *understand* the others – a prospect that is enhanced when proponents of the various perspectives are multilingual, that is, capable of understanding and speaking the language of alternative perspectives. What then might such a conversation between bioethicists and medical practitioners on the one hand, and children's rights advocates on the other, look like?

The following table illustrates that the core principles of medical ethics are closely aligned with, if not mirrored by, the fundamental principles underlying children's rights.

Principles of Medical Ethics	**Relationship to Human Rights**
Autonomy	
This principle presumes that all persons are autonomous and therefore free to consent to or refuse any medical procedure. Where a child lacks capacity to understand a medical procedure, medical professionals and the child's parents must be guided by what is in the best interests of the child.	The autonomy of an individual is a foundational principle of human rights (Griffin, 2008) and finds expression in the catalogue of rights that prevent interference with a child's rights to private life, family life, freedom of expression and freedom of association (CRC arts 13, 25 and 16). As with medical ethics, if a child lacks the capacity to consent to or refuse medical treatment, the best interests of the child must guide the child's parents and medical professionals (CRC, arts 3 and 18).
Beneficence	
This principle demands that a medical procedure must be intended to benefit a patient and that health care providers develop and maintain skills and knowledge necessary for the health of a patient.	Human rights include a right to the highest attainable standard of health (CRC art 24). This imposes an obligation to take all reasonable steps, subject to available resources, to provide health care to children of the highest quality, which includes a requirement to ensure effective training of medical professionals (Tobin, 2012, 172-173).

Principles of Medical Ethics	Relationship to Human Rights
Non- Maleficence This principle is a corollary of the beneficence principle and requires that medical professionals should do no harm to patients.	Human rights has a number of standards which protect children against harm, including the protection against violence, abuse, neglect and the protection against torture, cruel, inhuman and degrading treatment (CRC arts 19 & 37).
Justice The principle captures the idea that the benefit of health care should be enjoyed equally within society. This principle has been the subject of significant discussion (Daniels, 2008; Denier, 2007; Ruger, 2010; Segall, 2010). It is sufficient to note here that it requires a consideration of how to distribute scarce resources equitably and balance competing health needs.	Although there is no express right to justice, human rights are essentially a model which aims to achieve a particular vision of justice. It provides that every child must enjoy his or her right to health without discrimination on the basis of gender, religion, political belief or any other status (CRC arts 2 & 24). Human rights also recognise the reality of resource constraints and offer a model by which to ensure the equitable allocation of resources (Tobin, 235-38).

Although the table above simplifies some rather complex issues, it still demonstrates the significant complementarity of the discourses. Indeed, the overlap between the principles of medical ethics and children's rights is so great that a bioethicist or medical practitioner might be justified in asking if a discussion of children's rights can in fact bring any value to an evaluation of medical procedures involving children. The standard response is that states have an international legal obligation to protect children's rights. Of itself, however, this is not particularly persuasive given that international law offers limited mechanisms by which to enforce children's rights.

A more nuanced response might be that a rights-based approach adds value to the application of medical ethics in at least two ways: one conceptual, the other strategic. With respect to the conceptual benefit, children's rights provide clarity with respect to the meaning and content of the principles that underpin medical ethics. Take, for example, the best interests principle, which is relevant when a child lacks autonomy. Historically, the indeterminacy of this principle has often allowed it be used as a 'proxy' for the interests of others (Van Krieken, 2005: 39). In contrast, a rights based approach provides guidance with respect to the determination of a child's best interests by demanding that a child's best interests be informed by a consideration of the other rights under the CRC (CRC Committee, 2013: para 51). As such, it offers a decision-making framework for medical practitioners within which the rights-based analysis informs the substantive content of the principles that inform medical ethics.

The strategic benefit offered to medical ethics by a rights-based approach can be measured on several fronts. First, human rights demands that states take active measures to secure the right to the highest attainable standard of health progressively. This obligation not only complements the principles of beneficence and justice, but also demands an extended commitment to health. In other words, it rejects the status quo and enables bioethicists and medical professionals to demand that states take continuing measures to improve health. Second, unlike medical ethics which seeks to impose obligations on medical professionals, human rights law imposes obligations on states to allocate the necessary resources to secure the right to health progressively. Moreover, it holds states accountable for their failure to do so and such creates various requirements, such as states' obligation to submit reports to the Committee on the Rights of the Child, to monitor compliance. Thus, strategic benefits for bioethicists and medical professionals flow from the discourse of children's rights, which will enable them to demand more from states with respect to resource allocation for children's health and to hold states accountable where they fail to fulfil their obligations.

It remains important to stress that the benefits flowing from an interdisciplinary dialogue between medical ethics and children's rights are not unidirectional. On the contrary, children's rights advocates also stand to benefit from engagement with the knowledge and wisdom of medical ethicists. Consider, for example, the issue of resource allocation. Although some progress has been made in this area, most child rights advocates would concede that their discourse offers limited insights into how best to allocate scarce resources. In contrast, there is a considerable volume of literature within medical ethics dedicated to this issue, from which children's rights advocates would benefit.

Moreover, there is a risk that children's rights advocates might view this discourse with an 'aura of virtue' (Heydon, 2013: 10), which overlooks the substantive content of the relevant human rights principles. In such circumstances, medical ethicists and medical practitioners may offer a more circumspect perspective, which is less clouded by passion and more grounded in evidence. An example of the complementary nature of the relationship between human rights and medical professionals can be seen in elements of the recent Australian Senate inquiry (2013) into the coercive and involuntary sterilisation of women and girls with an intellectual disability ('*Senate Report*').

The following is the author's summary of the key arguments made in the submissions of several medical associations to the Senate Inquiry, alongside a summary of the principles required for a substantive rights-based analysis of this issue.

Key submissions of medical associations (e.g. *Royal Australasian College of Physicians; Royal Australian and New Zealand College of Obstetricians and Gynaecologists*)
Women and girls with an intellectual disability are entitled to respect for their dignity, which demands respect for their sexual autonomy and presumed capacity to enjoy their sexual and reproductive health. Supported decision-making, including access to sexual and reproductive health education and parental support, ought to be preferred. There remains the possibility, however, that substituted decision-making may be necessary in the rare circumstances in which a woman or girl lacks, and will never gain, the capacity

to regulate her own sexual and reproductive health. In such circumstances, the principles of medical necessity and the best interests of the patient may justify involuntary sterilisation, strictly as a measure of last resort where the procedure is necessary to secure the health of a woman or girl with a profound intellectual disability.

Key principles to be adopted under a substantive rights-based analysis
Every woman and girl with an intellectual disability is entitled to enjoy her rights without discrimination. States must take active measures to enable such women and girls to enjoy their rights, which supports a presumption in favour of supported decision-making. It is recognised, however, that in some cases the additional support provided to women, or the additional time allowed for a girl, to develop capacity may be insufficient to enable these women and girls to exercise their sexual and reproductive rights autonomously. In these rare circumstances, substituted decision-making will be permissible. Any interference with the woman or girl's sexual and reproductive rights, however, must be reasonable. It will only be reasonable where: the aim of the interference is legitimate; evidence supports the need for the interference; and there are no other measures reasonably available to achieve the aim. In practical terms, this will only occur in limited circumstances where the alternatives to sterilisation, such as long-term contraception, are incompatible with the woman or girl's overall health. This may occur where, for example, long-term contraception would be incompatible with medication being taken to address epilepsy (Tobin and Luke: 2013).

This substantive rights approach to involuntary sterilisation, which involves an inquiry into the reasonableness of interference with a right, is closely aligned with, and indeed heavily informed by, medical ethics. Indeed, it is medical evidence which reveals that long-term contraception is not always the appropriate means to regulate a woman or girl's menstrual cycle or reproductive capacity. Involuntary sterilisation may actually be necessary, albeit as a measure of last resort, to secure the woman or girl's right to the highest attainable standard of health.

This is at odds with the position advanced by certain human rights bodies and advocates, who maintain that involuntary sterilisation must be absolutely prohibited. (Human Rights Council, 2011: para 86.39; the Committee on the Rights of the Child, 2007: para 60, 2011: para 23; the Special Rapporteur on Torture, 2008: para 38; Committee on the Rights of Persons with Disabilities, 2013: paras 39-40; Amnesty International Australia, 2013). Their position, however, is often premised upon an incomplete application of the rights to equality and non-discrimination. These rights do not demand identical treatment of girls and women with an intellectual disability, but actually permit differential treatment, provided it is reasonable (Human Rights Committee, 1989: 13). Thus it is insufficient to argue that the involuntary sterilisation of women and girls with an intellectual disability must be prohibited simply because this is a violation of their rights to equality and non-discrimination. Such a procedure will clearly *interfere* with these rights, but under a substantive rights approach the next question is whether this interference can be *justified* as being *reasonable*. Importantly, when assessing reasonableness, appeals to human rights standards or the high moral ground alone are insufficient, as this assessment will require a consideration of the actual evidence. When viewed from this perspective, the discourses of medical ethics and children's rights are closely aligned. Moreover, this case study highlights the need for children's rights advocates to be 'multilingual'. They must not only be able to understand and engage with the language of medical practitioners and bioethicists, but they must also understand how to use and interpret the principles used and evidence generated by other disciplines in order to determine both the appropriate measures to protect children's rights and the circumstances in which any interference with these rights will be justified.

Conclusion – the Need for More Multilingual Entrepreneurs

The paper started with an affirmation of Freeman's appeal for children's rights to be taken seriously. If children's rights advocates expect other disciplines to do this then they too must treat children's rights seriously. This requires a level of reflection and introspection regarding the conceptual, normative and strategic dilemmas confronting the children's rights movement. It may be easy to exalt the fact that 193 states have ratified the CRC and assume the high moral ground on this basis. However, this is not an effective strategy to persuade other disciplines, which have their own conceptions of justice, as to the merits of rights discourse. Something more is required if Freeman's appeal is to be answered.

The American human rights academic and activist Peter Rosenblum has spoken of the need for human rights advocates to become entrepreneurial and to mine the text of treaties in search of creative arguments to deliver just outcomes for clients (2002: 305). This is certainly a skill required by all children's rights advocates. It remains, however, a legal skill, and something more is required if children's rights are to be taken seriously outside the field of law. This must include multilingualism, which is defined in this paper as the capacity to understand the alternative disciplinary perspectives that are relevant to the realisation of children's rights, and to frame the principles, which underpin children's rights in ways that resonate with those disciplines.

This strategy is not without risks. The shift to instrumentalism that will be required to persuade economists may, for example, marginalise ideas about dignity, while a shift to the language of equity, which is commonly used in public health, may marginalise the importance of accountability, which is so fundamental to human rights. These risks are certainly real. However, they are inevitable if the children's rights movement is to engage with other disciplines and develop a more collaborative understanding of children's rights, which has the capacity to transform policy and practice relating to children across all disciplines. It is an ambitious agenda but, if it is realised, there is the possibility that Michael Freeman's call to take children's rights seriously might one day actually come to fruition.

References

Amnesty International Australia, *Submission to the Committee Inquiry into the Involuntary or Coerced Sterilisation of People with Disabilities in Australia* (7 March 2013).

Archard, D., *Children: Rights and Childhood* (London: Routledge, 2004).

Beauchamp, T. L. A and Childress, J. F., *Principles of Biomedical Ethics* (Oxford: Oxford University Press, 2009).

Cantwell, N., "Is the Rights Based Approach the Right Approach?", Paper to the Defence for Children International, International Symposium 25th Anniversary (Geneva, 22 November 2004, copy on file with author).

Committee on the Rights of the Child, *General Comment No. 13: The Right of the Child to Freedom from All Forms of Violence*, UN Doc CRC/C/GC/13 (18 April 2011).

Committee on the Rights of the Child, *General Comment No. 9: The Rights of Children with Disabilities*, UN Doc CRC/C/GC/9 (27 February 2007).

Committee on the Rights of Persons with Disabilities, *Concluding Observations on the Initial Report of Australia*, UN Doc CRPD/C/AUS/CO/1 (21 October 2013).

Daniels, N., *Just Health: Meeting Health Needs Fairly* (Cambridge: Cambridge University Press, 2008).

Denier, Y., *Efficiency, Justice and Care: Philosophical Reflections on Scarcity in Health Care* (Dordrecht: Springer, 2007).

Dixon, R. and Nussbaum, M., "Children's Rights and a Capabilities Approach: The Question of Special Priority", *Cornell Law Review* 2012 97(3), 549-593.

Dworkin, R., *Taking Rights Seriously* (Harvard: Harvard University Press, 1977).

Eekelaar, J., *Family Law And Private Life* (Oxford: Oxford University Press, 2006).

Eekelaar, J., "The Importance of Thinking that Children have Rights", *International Journal of Family Law* 1992 6(1), 221-235.

Fortin, J., "Children's Rights: Are the Courts Now Taking Them More Seriously?", *King's College Law Review* 2004 15(2), 253-272.

Freeman, M. (ed), *Law and Childhood Studies* (Oxford: Oxford University Press, 2012).

Freeman, M., "The Human Rights of Children", *Current Legal Problems* 2010 63(1), 1-44.

Freeman, M., "Why it Remains Important to Take Children's Rights Seriously", *International Journal of Children's Rights* 2007 15(1), 5-23.

Freeman, M., "The Future of Children's Rights", *Children and Society* 2000 14(4), 277-293.

Freeman, M., "The Philosophical Foundations of Human Rights", *Human Rights Quarterly* 1994 16(2), 491-514.

Freeman, M., "Taking Children's Rights More Seriously", *International Journal of Law and the Family* 1992 6(1), 55-71.

Freeman, M., "Taking Children's Rights Seriously", *Children and Society* 1987 1(4), 299-319.

Goodman, R. and Jinks, D., "Incomplete Internalization and Compliance with Human Rights Law", *European Journal of International Law* 2008 19(4), 725-748.

Goodman, R. and Jinks, D., "How to Influence States: Socialization and International Human Rights Law", *Duke Law Journal* 2004 54(3), 621-704.

Griffin, J., *On Human Rights* (Oxford: Oxford University Press, 2009).

Habermas, J., "The Concept of Human Dignity and the Realistic Utopia of Human Rights", *Metaphilosophy* 2010 41(4), 465-480.

Heydon, J., "Are Bills of Rights Necessary in Common Law Systems?" 2013 (lecture delivered at Oxford Law School, 23 January 2013, copy on file with author).

Human Rights Committee, *General Comment No 18: Non-Discrimination*, 37th sess (1989).

Human Rights Council, *Report of the Working Group on the Universal Periodic Review: Australia*, UN Doc A/HRC/17/10 (24 March 2011).

Kennedy, D., "The International Human Rights Movement: Part of the Problem?", *Harvard Human Rights Journal* 2002 15(1), 101-126.

King, M., "The Child, Childhood and Children's Rights within Sociology", *King's Law Journal* 2004 15(2), 273-300.

Lundy, L., Kilkelly, U., Byrne, B., and Kang, J., *The United Nations Convention on the Rights of the Child: A Study of the Legal Implementation in 12 Countries* (Unicef, 2012).

Nowak, M., *Promotion and Protection of all Human Rights, Civil, Political, Economic, Social and Cultural Rights, Including the Right to Development: Report of the Special Rapporteur on Torture and Other Cruel, Inhuman Or Degrading Treatment Or Punishment*, UN Doc A/HRC/7/3 (2008).

McCrudden, C., "Human Dignity and the Judicial Interpretation of Human Rights", *European Journal of International Law* 2008 19(4), 655-724.

Mushkat, R., "Incomplete Internalisation and Compliance with Human Rights Law: A Reply to Ryan Goodman and Derek Jinks", *European Journal of International Law*, 2008 20(2), 437-442.

People with Disability Australia, *Senate Standing Committee on Community Affairs: Inquiry into the Involuntary or Coerced Sterilisation of People with Disabilities in Australia Submission* (March 2013).

Pounder L., "Never Mind Human Rights, Let's Save the Children", *Australian Indigenous Law Review* 2008 12(2), 2-21.

Reynaert, D., Bouverne-de-Bie, M., and Vandevelde, S., "A Review of Children's Rights Literature since the adoption of the United Nations Convention on the Rights of the Child", *Childhood* 2009 16(4), 518-524.

Reynaert, D., Bouverne-de-Bie, M., and Vandevelde, S., "Between 'Believers' and 'Opponents': Critical Discussions on Children's Rights", *International Journal of Children's Rights* 2012 20(1), 155-168.

Rosenblum, P., "Teaching Human Rights: Ambivalent Activism, Multiple Discourses and Lingering Dilemmas", *Harvard Human Rights Journal* 2002 15(1), 301-316.

Royal Australian and New Zealand College of Obstetricians and Gynaecologists, *Submission to the Inquiry into the Involuntary or Coerced Sterilisation of People with Disabilities in Australia* (20 February 2013).

Royal Australian College of Physicians, *Submission to the Senate Inquiry into the Involuntary or Coerced Sterilisation of People with Disabilities in Australia* (5 February 2013).

Ruger, J., *Health and Social Justice* (Oxford: Oxford University Press, 2010).

Sarfaty, G., "Why culture matters in international institutions: the marginality of human rights at the World Bank", *American Journal of International Law,* 2009 103(4), 647-683.

Segall, S., *Health, Luck and Justice* (Princeton: Princeton University Press, 2010).

Sen, A., "Elements of a Theory of Human Rights", *Philosophy and Public Affairs* 2004 32(4), 315-356.

Senate Community Affairs References Committee, Parliament of Australia, *Involuntary or Coerced Sterilisation of People with Disabilities in Australia* (Canberra: Australian Parliament, 2013).

Seymour, D. and Pincus J., "Human Rights and Economics: The Conceptual Basis for their Complementarity", *Development Policy Review* 2008 26(4), 387-405.

Sloth-Neilsen, J. and Mezmur, B. D., "2 + 2 = 5: Exploring the Domestication of the CRC in South African Jurisprudence (2002-2006)", *International Journal of Children's Rights* 2008 16(1), 1-28.

The Siracusa Principles on the Limitation and Derogation Provisions in the International Covenant on Civil and Political Rights, UN Doc E/CN.4/1985/4 (28 September 1984).

Tobin, J. and Luke, E., "The Involuntary, Non Therapeutic Sterilisation of Women and Girls with an Intellectual Disability: Can it Ever Be Justified?", *Victoria University Law and Justice Journal* 2013 3(1), 27-46.

Tobin, J., "Justifying Children's Rights", *International Journal of Children's Rights* 2013 21(3), 395-441.

Tobin, J., *The Right to Health in International Law* (Oxford: Oxford University Press, 2012).

Tobin, J., "Judging the Judges: Are they Adopting the Rights Approach in Matters Involving Children?", *Melbourne University Law Review* 2009 33(2), 579-625.

Tobin, J., "Increasingly Seen and Heard: The Constitutional Recognition of Children's Rights", *South African Journal of Human Rights* 2005 21(1), 86-126.

UNICEF, *Global Evaluation of the Application of the Human Rights Based Approach to UNICEF Programming* (New York: UNICEF, 2012).

UN Security Council Resolution 2068, UN Doc S/RES/2068 (2012).

UN Security Council Resolution 1998, UN Doc. S/RES/1998 (2011).

UN Security Council Resolution 1882, UN Doc. S/RES/1882 (2009).

UN Security Council Resolution 1888, UN Doc. S/RES/1888 (2009).

Van Krieken, R., "The Best Interests of the Child and Parental Separation: On the Civilizing of Parents", *Modern Law Review* 2005 68(1), 25-48.

Whitzman, C., Worthington, M. and Mizrachi, D. "The Journey and the Destination Matter: Child-Friendly Cities and Children's Right to the City", *Built Environment* 2010 36(4), 474-486.

The Jurisprudence of Making Decisions Affecting Children: An Argument to Prefer Duty to Children's Rights and Welfare

Lucinda Ferguson*
University of Oxford, UK

1. Introduction

Writing in 2000, Michael Freeman argued that, whilst much had been achieved for children in the 20th century, it had not been the century of the child (2000: 553-554). He expressed the hope that the next century would turn out otherwise (*ibid*: 555). In this chapter, I explore the extent to which we are now able to realise this ambition in relation to decision-making affecting children. The need for some measure of state regulation of decision-making about children is beyond doubt. Not all children can make significant decisions for themselves, and we cannot assume that families will always be intact or agree sufficiently to make such decisions for children. This is the case even if we assume that 'families' generally make decisions in their children's 'best interests'.[1] The issue then arises as to the shape of this regulation. The legal decision-making framework employed is critical because it determines both the scope of decisions that can be made without state scrutiny or supervision and the weight that can be placed on particular factors they can take into account, such as religious or cultural concerns.

* I began thinking about what the debate over the legal regulation of children might learn from virtue ethics whilst I was Assistant Professor of Law at the University of Alberta, and am grateful to former colleagues for the lively discussion. I discussed ideas in this chapter in particular at the International Academy for the study of the Jurisprudence of the Family's fifth international symposium at Cardozo Law School, Yeshiva University (10-11 June 2013) and the Law and Michael Freeman Colloquium at University College London's Faculty of Laws (1-2 July 2013); I thank participants for their feedback.

1 This assumption, which underpins the current law and the child protection threshold for intervention, is itself open to debate insofar as it arises from the acquisition of legal parental status at birth. Dwyer, for example, argues that additional hurdles should be imposed on all parents seeking to acquire legal recognition of the parent-child connection: see Dwyer (2006: ch 8.I).

A. Diduck, N. Peleg, H. Reece (eds.), Law in Society: Reflections on Children, Family, Culture and Philosophy
Copyright 2015 Koninklijke Brill NV. Printed in The Netherlands. ISBN 978-90-04-26148-8. pp. 141-189.

In order to make this a century of the child, I suggest that we need to reach a common understanding of the reasons why it is important to regard children as a 'special case',[2] whether this is implemented by thinking of children as rights-holders,[3] by prioritising children through a 'best interests' or welfare perspective, or by focusing on the duties adults owe to children. These three types of approach should be taken together for this purpose because, I argue, they are simply tools – language descriptors, ways of framing individual considerations, processes and frameworks – for working with the same substantive content. Once we have agreed upon the reasons why it is important to treat children as a special case, we need to assess which of these three ways of interacting with the substantive content of decisions affecting children makes achieving these aims most likely. It is the substantive outcome for affected children that holds critical importance. Which approach we prefer or emphasise (where multiple approaches co-exist in any particular context) should thus depend on how well it guides decision-makers towards or makes more likely better outcomes for affected children.

After briefly outlining why current conceptions of children's rights cannot meet this test, I explain why a welfare or 'best interests' approach[4] is no better suited towards achieving this end.[5] The remainder of the chapter explores the potential for a duty-based approach. I argue that duty can have three roles: as a tool to give specificity and resolve conflicts in current rights- and welfare-based decision-making; as a theoretical framework, focused on the decision-maker; and as part of the justification for adopting a virtue-inspired understanding of the aim for legal decision-making affecting children – to enable children to flourish on their own terms. I conclude by exploring the practical implications of a duty-based argument and discuss three key examples, namely the Court of Appeal's decision in *Re A (Conjoined Twins: Surgical Separation)* [2001] 1 Fam 147, the United Nations' Convention on the Rights of the Child (20 November 1989, 1577 U.N.T.S. 3 [UNCRC]) and private law disputes concerning children.

---

2 For my argument to this effect, see section 2, below.

3 Freeman's (2007b) articulation of such reasons in the context of a rights-based approach is both classic and compelling. For the purpose of my argument, the will and interest theories of rights are taken together as 'rights-based' approaches insofar as they are both ways of trying to articulate what it means to say that children have children's rights. This is not to suggest that the differences between the theories are irrelevant, just that they both, even in modified form, fail to present a coherent vision of children's rights, as I have argued elsewhere: Ferguson (2013).

4 For present purposes, 'best interests' and the 'welfare principle' may be treated as interchangeable. This view has been endorsed judicially. See, for example, *Re A (Male Sterilisation)* [2000] 1 FLR 549, Thorpe LJ.: 560, cited with approval: *Portsmouth NHS Trust v. Wyatt* [2005] 1 FLR 21, Hedley J: [26]; *Re A (Conjoined Twins: Surgical Separation)* [2001] 1 Fam 147, Walker LJ: 242H. Only where I use 'welfare' or 'welfare-based approach' to reference the framework for decision-making is it interchangeable with the 'welfare principle'; otherwise, it may also refer to individual competing considerations operating within a different framework.

5 This includes the rejection of a relational welfare approach, such as that argued for by Herring (2005) and Herring and Foster (2012).

2. Children as a 'Special Case'

In this section, I outline what it means to see children as a 'special case' and present an account of the justification for approaching the legal regulation of children on the basis that they are a special case.

'Special Case' Defined

Seeing children as a 'special case' means prioritising children's interests over those of other parties as recognition of children's unique position in society. This prioritisation can take two forms, namely providing children with additional legal protection over that not available to others and, when there is a conflict between children's interests and other parties' interests, prioritising children's interests in the resolution of the dispute.

The s. 1 Children Act 1989 'welfare principle' assumes children are a special case. Viewing the child's 'best interests' as the only lens through which to problematise complex factual circumstances entails a prior decision that the importance of the context for the child merits determining the issue with the impact on the child as the sole concern. Competing counter-arguments have necessarily already been dismissed except to the extent that they can be expressed in terms of the child's 'best interests'. As expressed in terms of the oft-cited dicta of Lord MacDermott in *J v. C* [1970] AC 668, the 'welfare principle':

> connote[s] a process whereby when all the relevant facts, relationships, claims and wishes of the parents, risks, choices and other circumstances are taken into account and weighed, the course to be followed will be that which is most in the interests of the child's welfare (710H-711A).

This holds true even to the extent that the welfare assessment is contextualised rather than, as is often argued, atomistic (see section 4, below).

In relation to rights-based arguments, the idea of seeing children as a special case is evident in the contrast I draw between 'rights for children' and 'children's rights'. The former comprise fundamental human rights that apply equally to all individuals, children and adults alike; thus, 'rights for children' do not treat children as a special case. 'Children's rights', however, employs the language of rights to recognise children as a special case; for children's rights, it is critical that the rights-holder is a child (Ferguson, 2013: section 2).[6] For this reason, re-evaluating the value of children's rights

---

6 Freeman (2006: 89; 2007b: 7) disagrees, seeing children's rights as human rights or, in the terminology used here, seeing 'children's rights' as identical with 'rights for children'. The theoretical basis of 'human rights' is itself now subject to much discussion. Citing Raz, Waldron notes that 'analytically, the whole field is a bit of a mess. The question is not: What does the 'human' in 'human rights' *really mean?* The question is: what is the more convenient and illuminating use to make of the term in this context?' (2013: 21,

leaves the role for fundamental human rights unaffected. This is significant given that, in practical terms, fundamental human rights have achieved much for children.

It is interesting to ask how we might conceptualise rights protected by the European Convention on Human Rights (ECHR) in this regard. Children are only rarely explicitly mentioned in Convention Articles. A purposive reading of Articles 1 and 14 together, however, means that they are seen as possessing ECHR rights just as adults; children thus have 'rights for children' under the ECHR. In this sense, the ECHR does not on its face see children as a special case. However, it is important to distinguish between 'no conflict' and 'conflict' scenarios as, in its application by the European Court on Human Rights ([ECtHR]) and domestic courts, the ECHR may be employed in a way that assumes children are a special case, whose interests are to be prioritised over those of others.

In a 'no conflict' scenario, the only ECHR rights at stake are those of the affected child or children. In relation to the physical punishment of children, for example, the ECtHR's decision in *A v. UK* (*Human Rights: Punishment of a Child*) [1998] 2 FLR 959 employed Article 3 of the ECHR to provide greater protection to children than that recognised under domestic law, which the UK government itself conceded ([19]). The requirement that the ill-treatment reach a minimum level of severity in order to fall within the scope of Article 3 ([20]) applies to children and adults alike, though the Court does specifically refer to the entitlement of 'children and other vulnerable individuals, in particular …' to state protection from serious violations of personal integrity ([22]). Yet, this is insufficient to suggest the prioritisation of children's interests, particularly when taken together with the ECtHR's interpretation of Art. 3, which views some physical punishment of children as permissible. But this is not to say 'rights for children' cannot trigger improvements for children's position in society. Prior to the hearing, the UK government undertook to reform the law ([33]). In addition to featuring prominently in the debate over the ultimate shape of s. 58 of the Children Act 2004, those in favour of both absolute prohibition and the compromise position ultimately enacted in s. 58 drew on aspects of the ECtHR's reasoning in relation to Article 3 generally and in *A v. UK* in particular (*Hansard*, 2004).

In a 'conflict' scenario, however, the child's ECHR rights compete against either other rights of others or other rights of their own. If the latter, there is a sense in which the conflict is illusory as, properly understood, only one of the child's rights would extend to resolve the issue in question. If the former, and the child's rights are seen as having priority, these rights might be best conceptualised as having acquired the status of 'children's rights' rather than remaining 'rights for children'. For that to be the case, however, children's rights would need to be preferred as the presumptive starting-point, rather than only in the outcome of the balancing exercise.

---

emphasis in original). Thus, we should not be surprised at the difficulties of providing a coherent theoretical account of children's rights, with its additional complicating aspect of claiming to focus on the child as rights-holder in a particular child-centred way. Indeed, this may be impossible.

Rather than clearly evolving over time, the ECtHR's reasoning is currently best understood as inconsistent on this point. In *Johansen v. Norway* (1997) 23 EHRR 33, the Court suggested that 'the Court will attach particular importance to the best interests of the child, which, depending on their nature and seriousness, may override those of the parent' ([78]). By contrast, in its later decision in *Yousef v. The Netherlands* (2003) 36 EHRR 20, the Court expressed the relationship differently, reasoning that 'in judicial decisions where the rights under art 8 of parents and those of a child are at stake, the child's rights must be the paramount consideration. If any balancing of interests is necessary, the interests of the child must prevail' ([73]). In *Neulinger v. Switzerland* (2012) 54 EHRR 31, the ECtHR characterised children's interests as being 'the primary consideration', though referred to the Preamble of the Hague Convention on the Civil Aspects of International Child Abduction (25 October 1980) in which children's interests are described as being of 'paramount importance' ([134]). Most recently, in *YC v. United Kingdom* (2012) 55 EHRR 33, the Court stressed that 'the best interests of the child are paramount' when considering termination of familial ties via adoption ([134]).

Taking the case law together, it may be that the Court is coming to distinguish more clearly between a stronger prioritisation in the public law context compared with more significant balancing in the private law context; as yet, the Court has not explicitly articulated this view. The distinction between the stronger and weaker views of the role for children's interests is not just one of extent, but also of kind. The *Johansen* reasoning prioritises children in terms of their welfare in the process of the balancing exercise; in this way, it treats children as having 'rights for children' only. The *Yousef* court, however, prioritises the child's rights as a starting-point, and presumptively in any balancing exercise, inferring that they should be seen as having 'children's rights'. Even this view of the reasoning in *Yousef* must be approached with caution, however, because the Court does not frame its consideration of child-oriented concerns in terms of rights alone, but also adopts the language of interests. Yet the distinction between the two approaches is important because only the latter, *Yousef*, perspective views children as a special case. If we do not accept there is sufficient justification for seeing children as a special case, we have reason to prefer an ECHR approach, more precisely a version of the ECHR approach that prioritises children only in the outcome, after the weighing of 'rights for children' against other competing rights claims.

The Justification for Recognising Children as a 'Special Case'

Can we justify the assumption within the s. 1 Children Act 1989 'welfare principle' and the perspective inconsistently adopted by the ECtHR on conflicts between ECHR rights that children are a special case? There has been a shift in the academic literature away from an assumption that a consensus for prioritising children meant that there was no need to explore justifications (Reece, 1996: 270).[7] Some more recent writings question and challenge the nature and extent of the preference for children's interests. Gilmore and Bainham, for example, argue that '[i]t is certainly open to question whether children's interests should always be given priority' (2013: 326).

There are two significant theoretical objections to treating children as a special case: first, that childhood is a social construct, hence incapable of comprising a justifiable class of individuals whose interests ought to be prioritised over those of others; second, that there is a strong argument from equality that all individuals' interests should be given equal consideration and existing arguments to justify derogation from such equal consideration are inadequate.

The first concern recognises that, if the distinction between childhood and adulthood is artificial, it cannot support a theoretically sound argument for privileging children. Whilst the existence and embracing of an artificial – socially constructed – distinction highlights a societal choice to value the content of that construct, it does not of itself give a reason to value that content. The response lies in distinguishing between the definition of childhood and the underlying concept. At the core, childhood as a concept may justify being treated as a special case even if its definitional representation for legal purposes is constructed.[8] If the construction is based on proxies for the conceptual content of childhood, it is itself justifiable. If it is arbitrary, either because the intended proxy is not or is no longer accurate or because the definitional boundary has been drawn based only on other concerns, such as administrative efficiency, that lack of justification does not of itself undermine the normative value of the conceptual core; it might suggest, of course, that reform to the definition is required in order for it more faithfully to serve as a proxy for the underlying concept.

Age is a critical example of the definitional construction. There are both general definitions of childhood based on age and specific age-based rules for particular contexts. Section 105(1) of the Children Act 1989 contains the latter and defines a 'child' as 'a person under the age of eighteen', excepting Schedule 1 financial relief for children.

---

7 Dwyer suggests otherwise, arguing that, historically, children have been seen as inferior in social and moral status (2011: 1). Writing in the context of US law, he extends this to the 'best interests' principle, suggesting it governs rarely and that, when it does, it frequently masks the predominance of adult interests (2011: 191). In respect of the domestic position in England and Wales, however, his characterisation represents a minority perspective.

8 Tobin draws a similar distinction in relation to the UNCRC. He reasons that 'a further issue exists as to whether the concept of childhood can actually be justified. The point to stress here is that although the outer boundaries of the concept remain socially constructed and flexible under international law, there remains agreement among states as to the concept of childhood (2013: 400-401). Elsewhere, however, Tobin appears to suggest that the socially constructed aspect of childhood is part of its justification, contending that the 'empirically grounded and socially constructed' conception of childhood 'provides the foundation for the "special" human rights that are granted to children under international law' (*ibid*: 396). Taking his two remarks together, it is not clear whether he would agree with my suggestion that the socially constructed aspect of childhood does not perform a normative function, though it may – as a proxy for conceptual aspects – reflect one.

If the age of 18 represents a sufficiently close proxy for the conceptual idea of childhood, it is justifiable; if not, it might require reform, either generally or in particular contexts, but that does not undermine the conceptual basis of childhood. I return to the concept of childhood below, as that is what underpins the special case of children's interests.

The second theoretical concern is an argument from equality. In writing about the moral status of children, Brennan and Noggle argue for the 'equal consideration thesis', namely that '[c]hildren are entitled to the same moral consideration as adults' (1997: 2). Yet, as they recognise, equal consideration does not mean identical outcomes: '[T]wo people can receive equal moral *consideration* without having exactly the same package of moral rights and duties' (1997: 2; emphasis in original). In her criticism of the 'welfare principle' in English law, Reece argues that there is a 'fallacy .... [of] equat[ing] priority with protection' (1996: 277). Once we recognise this, she argues, we can see that decisions, which in the outcome give more weight to one party's interests than those of others, may have given equal weight to all parties' interests in the process by which that outcome was reached (1996: 278-279; cf. Dwyer (2011: 12)). Two issues arise from this observation: First, is it unjustifiable to do other than give equal weight to all parties' interests? Second, does treating children as a special case require us to give unequal consideration to their interests or might it be compatible with equal consideration of all parties' interests? My answer to the latter means that there is no need to consider the former.[9] Dwyer notes:

> Because equal moral consideration can produce unequal treatment and unequal moral consideration can allow for equal legal protection, it is often difficult to determine when decision makers are systematically treating one group as occupying a lower moral status than another, or are instead treating them as moral equals (2011: 14).

For that reason, we need to be cautious in concluding that our approach does not demonstrate equal consideration. As Brennan and Noggle explain

> a certain moral status attaches generally to all persons, including children. To deny this would be to claim either that persons do not derive moral status from their status as

9 By contrast, Dwyer (2011) presents a case for prioritising children's interests in the sense of giving them unequal – greater – consideration compared to the consideration given to the interests of others. He does not use the socially constructed class of children to delineate those whose interests are to be preferred, but instead argues for placing greater moral weight on the characteristics of youthfulness, which are typically possessed by children. In arguing against the 'egalitarian impulse of modern liberalism' (143), however, a key contention is that unequal consideration ought to at least 'shake us loose finally from traditional assumptions of children's inferiority' (143). In other words, excessive correction in theory should lead to moderate, justifiable correction in practice. Given this aim is based on a current regime that views children as inferior, this argument may not be directly applicable to the English context where excessive correction via unequal consideration in theory may lead to unjustifiable, unequal outcomes in practice.

> persons, or that children are not persons. Because neither of these claims is particularly plausible, it does not seem plausible to deny the Equal Consideration Thesis (1997: 2).

Indeed, I suggest that we do not need to have unequal consideration for children's interests in order to see them as a special case. We do not need to confine prioritisation to application to the facts, but can prioritise children's interests in a way that does not fall foul of this equality concern. If we elevate children's interests within the guiding legal principles and concepts – treat them as a special case – this need not entail unequal consideration. Equal consideration relates to moral regard.

Children's unique circumstances, such as their special vulnerability, may require the adaptation of legal principles particular to children or in a way that presumes children's interests are weightier. As this occurs at the legal stage, not in the application to the facts, this treats children as a special case. Yet this adaptation is grounded in the contextualisation of equal moral regard, and does not evidence unequal moral regard.

Recent academic proposals for law reform generally do not treat children as a special case in the way that I suggest is envisaged by the 'welfare principle' and 'children's rights'. Eekelaar argues for a 'least detrimental alternative' approach to the process of decision-making in contexts currently governed by the welfare principle. When discussing his qualifications to this approach, he distinguishes between children's interests being 'privileged' and children's interests being 'given priority' (Eekelaar, 2002: 244). As a result, an outcome can be adopted that is *not* the least detrimental alternative for the child if it is much less damaging for the affected parent or parents than the alternative, which would have enhanced the child's interests to a larger extent at great expense to the parent or parents (244). The child's position is privileged to the extent that no solution that actively diminishes the child's interests can be chosen unless all options would do so (244). Eekelaar does not believe it necessary to see children as a special case in order to explain this privileging. In respect of children's rights in particular, he suggests that they:

> should be seen as a species of people's rights .... In themselves, these rights are no different from adults' rights. Due allowance being made for issues of competence and children's special vulnerability, they should be respected just like adults' rights should be; certainly no less, but also no more (249).

Whilst it is possible to privilege children's interests in the application to the facts and not see them as a special case, I would argue that even this privileging in the weighing of competing interests is hard to justify if we do not see children as a special case. On Eekelaar's account, it is not the particular facts of the case that lead to more weight being placed on the child's interests in the outcome, but rather a principle to be applied to situations of detriment for children. The distinction he draws between privileging and prioritising the child's interests is one between allowing the weighing at all and not. Choudhry and Fenwick similarly argue for a 'parallel analysis' approach (2005: 481) that starts by seeing children's and adults' interests 'on a presumptively equal footing' (2005: 471, 479). Making use of Eekelaar's language, they suggest that children's interests would be 'privileged within the processes of reasoning' (2005: 485). Whilst the distinction between 'privileging' and 'prioritising' is thus an important one, I suggest its significance relates only to the *extent* to which children are seen as a special case, rather than, as Eekelaar's reference to children's rights as people's rights implies, to whether they are a special case *at all*.

At this point, it is important to distinguish the two ways in which we prioritise children's interests: first, by providing children with additional legal protection to that available to others; second, by prioritising children's interests in conflicts with other parties' interests. The compatibility with equal consideration is most straightforward where children are being afforded additional recognition of rights and interests in law. For example, we recognise that all individuals are vulnerable and are equally concerned about the vulnerability of all, but there are certain contexts in which the child's vulnerability is greater than that of adults. Article 24 of the UNCRC provides a helpful illustration. It recognises the child's interest in healthcare. Adults and children alike have an interest in access to the 'highest attainable standard of health and to the facilities for the treatment of illness and rehabilitation of health' (para. 1). Yet children are particularly vulnerable to the imposition on them of 'traditional practices prejudicial to ... health' (para. 3), so their interests are specifically recognised in this regard. Recognition of this additional right to protection is not because we have less consideration for adults, but because children are less able to protect themselves against such infringement. In this sense, *additional* protection is a way of implementing *equal* consideration.

Compatibility with equal consideration is more difficult where children's interests are being prioritised in conflicts with other parties' interests. The 'welfare principle' might be best seen as a framework for decision-making that prioritises children's interests in conflicts with those of others. It does not fall foul of the equal consideration concern, however, because equal consideration conceptually precedes the 'welfare principle'. Just as with additional legal protection, we approach children's and others' interests on the basis that they are of equal value. Where the context implicates children's interests more than adults', children's interests need to be prioritised. As a result of this recognition of the need to prioritise, the 'welfare principle' is applied to these contexts. This is why the 'welfare principle' does not apply to all situations affecting children; if it did, it would be harder to justify because that would imply there could have been no earlier point at which all parties' interests were regarded equally. Thus, its limited scope is a strength, rather than weakness as Reece suggests (1996: 281, 285).

The foregoing makes clear that what becomes critical are the factors that, when approached with equal consideration for all parties' interests, necessitate prioritising children's interests. These factors can be identified within the concept of childhood. I consider one here: the vulnerability of children,[10] by which I mean the lack

10 There may be other aspects of the concept of childhood that have a similar impact on the translation of equal consideration into the legal recognition and regulation of children's interests.

of capacity, means and opportunity for children to protect their own interests. This idea is reflected in the UNCRC's Preamble reference to the 'United Nations ha[ving] proclaimed that childhood is entitled to special care and assistance', which Tobin contends is justified by 'empirical reality' (2013: 401). Whilst vulnerability can be empirically demonstrated, what is critical is that we are entitled to assume that vulnerability for 'children' as a class, rather than relying on the premise that every child – every member of that class – is vulnerable in a way and to an extent that they require additional protection.

Herring acknowledges a role for vulnerability, but does not see it as capable of justifying treating children as a special case. He contends that '[t]he law in its treatment of children based on vulnerability exaggerates the vulnerability of children and exaggerates the capacity of adults' (2012: 250). Beyond suggesting that everyone is vulnerable (2012: 253, 257), he draws on the interdependency of caring relationships to conclude that 'it is wrong to regard [children] as especially vulnerable' (2012: 262). I disagree; whilst we can redefine vulnerability to include the complex ways in which particular groups of adults, and adults in general, are also vulnerable, that does not eliminate the unique vulnerability of children. Indeed, Reece notes – in the course of her argument against treating children as a special case – that '[i]t is self-evident that, as a general rule, children need more protection than adults' (1996: 277). In fact, it is that need for greater protection that she believes has confused academics into assuming children's interests need to receive unequal consideration from adults'.

Equal consideration of everyone's interests also explicitly allows for consideration of adults' vulnerability. As a factor approached with equal consideration to determine the correct legal approach to regulating children, however, children's vulnerability is distinctive. The inability of young children to make decisions about whether or not to consent to medical treatment or to avoid being taken to a contact session illustrates the distinctive nature and extent of their vulnerability as a class. The extent of these children's vulnerability includes the degree of capacity for autonomous decision-making that particular children might have; the distinctive nature of that vulnerability lies in recognising children's intended and actual increasing capacities and children's significant and intimate dependence on adults for large measures of their well-being. When equal consideration of all parties' interests is applied to the concept of childhood, we are entitled to assume that the unique character of the vulnerability is possessed by all children. As a consequence, we are justified in adopting a legal approach that prioritises children's interests. Which legal approach best recognises this priority becomes the key issue.

3. Three Approaches to Treating Children as a 'Special Case', Criteria for Preferring One Approach, and the Rejection of 'Children's Rights'

Three Approaches – Three Ways to Organise the Same Content Considerations

As concepts, children's rights, welfare and duties owed to children all enable us to treat children as a special case and prioritise their interests. As I have argued elsewhere (Ferguson, 2013: section 6), these approaches do not exist discretely. This is an important point as it allows us to see the potential for concepts other than children's rights to give effect to the reasons for thinking that children have children's rights. Self-evidently, these three concepts are distinctive language descriptors. Yet when each is employed as a framework and/or used to articulate individual considerations within a broader framework for decision-making about children, they work with the same substantive content.

For example, all three concepts incorporate consideration of the child's autonomy. Within a welfare framework, the nature and extent of the child's developing capacities for decision-making is a factor specifically referenced in the welfare checklist in s. 1(3) of the Children Act 1989. In the children's rights context, it serves as the basis of the child's right to express their views in matters affecting them contained in Article 12(1) of the UNCRC. If we focus on duties owed to children, Article 12(1) takes on a different character with the emphasis on the requirement that states assure that right to capable children. Article 12(2), which seeks to secure the implementation of the state's duty to assure the child's right to be heard, is similarly framed in terms of duty – that of the state to provide the child with the opportunity to be heard in judicial and administrative proceedings affecting them.

This overlap in content is inevitable, as the concepts of children's rights, welfare and duty seek to capture deeper moral concerns that are inherent within children's unique position in society. Further, there is also significant overlap in the way that these concepts articulate the framework for decision-making and individual considerations to be included in the analysis. In situations involving a conflict of rights, typically parents' rights and children's rights, a rights-based framework cannot determine outcomes without drawing on welfare-based reasoning. In relation to the application of the ECHR, for example, this is evident in the role given to Article 8(2) in determining residence and contact disputes in which the parties rely on their Article 8(1) rights.[11] Duties are also intrinsic to the successful implementation of children's rights as evident in the previous reference to Article 12 of the UNCRC. Reference to

11 As I discuss in section 2, above, the ECtHR's jurisprudence is inconsistent in terms of how welfare is employed to weigh children's rights and interests in the balance. Cf. *Hokkanen v. Finland* (1994) 19 EHRR 139; *Johansen v. Norway* (1996) 23 EHRR 33; *Yousef v. Netherlands* [2002] 3 FCR 577 (ECtHR); *Kearns v. France* [2008] 1 FLR 888 (ECtHR). Fortin (2009: 70-71) also provides a neat discussion of the interpretive point.

children's rights has also been used to ascribe a particular role for the child's autonomy within the welfare-based framework of the Children Act,[12] though the same outcome has also been achieved without invocation of the language of rights.[13]

With a rights-based framework, the interplay with other concepts is inevitable; a welfare-based framework need not specifically integrate rights. The need for domestic compatibility with the ECHR may mean implicit reference to rights under the current law and duty-based reasoning remains a necessary part of implementation. This co-mingling between concepts (in both working with the same substantive content and being integrated together into decision-making frameworks) highlights that we cannot assume that the reasons for viewing children through the lens of children's rights are specific to that concept. In fact, they may be better seen as reasons for treating children as a special case more generally. The three concepts of children's rights, welfare and duty compete only in the sense of emphasis. Once we have decided which of the reasons for seeing children as a special case are important to us, we have reason for preferring one form of conceptual emphasis.

Reasons to Prefer One Conceptual Approach

The justification for treating children as a special case affects the criteria according to which we should evaluate the various competing approaches to the legal recognition of children's interests and regulating of decision-making about children. These criteria need to reflect the way in which children are a special case.

Elsewhere (Ferguson, 2013), I have argued that there are three types of criteria according to which we can evaluate the success or failure of a particular approach to prioritising children's interests. These comprise the expressive aspect of employing a particular concept or conceptual framework, the process of decision-making required by that conceptual approach and the extent to which, if at all, that conceptual approach impacts on outcomes reached. Whilst the rights and children's rights literature I discuss (2013) treats the three types of reason as separable, I suggest that the first two types of criteria – expressive and procedural – are contingent on the value of the third – the impact on substantive outcomes. As a result, it is the potential for ensuring a better outcome from the child's perspective that should determine which approach or approaches we prefer.

These criteria also embrace the justification for treating children as a special case. When the language of rights is employed, the expressive aspects highlight the equal consideration to children and adults; use of the 'welfare principle' and children's rights, however, makes clear that applying such equal consideration to the conceptual content of childhood may lead to differential outcomes. Outcome-oriented reasons for preferring one approach to another are grounded in the conceptual core of childhood to which equal consideration has been applied. The extent to which the

---

12 See, for example: *Gillick v. West Norfolk and Wisbech Area Health Authority* [1986] AC 112; *Mabon v. Mabon* [2005] EWCA Civ 634 [Mabon].

13 *Re R (A Child)* [2009] EWCA Civ 445 [*Re R*].

outcome satisfactorily recognises children's vulnerability, for example, is taken into account here. Process-oriented criteria can be distilled either into expressive aspects which, depending on the particular procedural feature, highlight equal consideration or the conceptual aspects of childhood, or into the potential to impact on outcomes, hence draw on the factors within childhood that require equal consideration to lead to differential outcomes.

The Rejection of Children's Rights as the Preferred Approach

Before examining in detail the potential for a welfare-based approach to regulating decision-making affecting children, I briefly outline my argument, made at greater length elsewhere (Ferguson, 2013), as to why children's rights cannot successfully withstand evaluation against my three criteria.

In this context, the expressive aspect refers to the value of the language of children's rights, more particularly, that usually the language of children's rights recognises the dignity of children, a key aspect of Freeman's (2007b: 7) argument as to the value of children's rights.[14] The procedural aspect refers to the way that decisions are reached, whether in relation to the framework used and/or the content given to that the framework. The idea is that reasoning in terms of children's rights in at least one of these two senses is preferable to reasoning any other way. I suggest that these two types of reason depend on the third, final type of reason: that thinking of children in terms of children's rights improves outcomes for children.[15] Without better outcomes or the likelihood of better outcomes, the signalling and process value of thinking of children in terms of children's rights loses its normative force.[16]

What we might mean by 'better' or 'improved' outcomes is open to question, yet we cannot escape the need for normative judgment.[17] For the purpose of my argument, I understand this to have two components. First, this is a necessarily child-centred evaluation. In other words, whether the outcome is better than the outcome that would have been attained under an alternative approach falls to be assessed from the child's perspective. Second, the child's perspective entails maximising opportunities for that child's future subject to limits imposed by the child themselves directly com-

14 But that dignity explanation does not save it from being contingent upon improved outcomes.

15 Freeman (2007b) does not categorise arguments as I do, seeing each as a powerful argument in favour of thinking of children as rights-holders.

16 Indeed, Baroness Hale (2013: 13), speaking extra-judicially, comments that:

> the family judiciary, and the family justice council, have taken the view that, even though children may be encouraged to come to court and see where their futures will be decided, this is more in the nature of a public relations exercise – reassuring the child that she is seen as a real person and enabling her to learn more about what goes on in court – rather than an exercise in helping the judge to make the right decision.

17 For broader discussion about the inevitability of normative judgments in legal reasoning, see Singer (2013: especially 8, 11).

mensurate with their developing autonomy. The broad idea here is not controversial,[18] though the firm requirement directly to reflect the child's capacity might be to the extent that it places more weight on autonomy than leading accounts of children's rights (Eekelaar, 1992, 1994, 1998; Freeman, 1983, chs 2-3)[19] and 'best interests'.[20] As autonomy is being taken seriously, a high threshold for capacity is applied.[21] But, once satisfied, the child's decision is to be respected. Focusing on maximising opportunities for the child's future also ensures a strong focus on empirical evidence about what contextual circumstances benefit children, in what ways, and to what extent when compared with alternatives. This practical enquiry is critical once we accept that the choice between children's rights, welfare, and duties is, in actuality, an assessment of the correct emphasis to take to the substantive considerations that underpin decision-making that affects children.

I argue that there is no good evidence that children's rights, at least as currently understood, and as expressed as the content of a decision-making exercise, the framework within which decisions regulating children are made, or both, *necessarily* leads to better outcomes for children (Ferguson, 2013: sections 4-5). In fact, there is no evidence that children's rights *necessarily* even render more likely better outcomes for children. There are some cases, such as the Court of Appeal's decision in *Mabon*,[22] in which the court itself suggests that it would or might have reached a different decision without the additional role for children's rights within the welfare-based framework where exercises of autonomy are at stake. But it is not clear that there was anything in the reference to rights that made that difference; the content ascribed to it might have, but that was not a necessary consequence of using the term 'children's rights'. It is not possible to make the reference to children's rights truly child-centred in the way that a theory of children's rights would require. This means that any improved outcome has in fact come through a misunderstanding that there exists a phenomenon called 'children's rights' that requires a particular outcome. The recent Court of Appeal decision in *Re R* makes this clear; the court here employed a welfare-based

18 In the sense that the child's wishes and feelings are specifically referenced in s. 1(3)(a) of the welfare checklist in the Children Act 1989 and Article 12 of the UNCRC, as well as featuring as a key element of the leading theories of children's rights such as Eekelaar's (1992, 1994, 1998) 'working principle', which includes 'autonomy interests' as one of children's three types of interests.

19 Freeman (1997b: 38) sets the limit as follows: 'The question we would want to ask ourselves is: what sort of action or conduct would we wish, as children, to be shielded against on the assumption that we would want to mature to a rationally autonomous adulthood and be capable of deciding on our own system of ends as free and rational beings?'

20 Article 12 of the UNCRC, for example, has never been interpreted as requiring that a child's autonomous decision be determinative.

21 For discussion of what considerations this might include, see Ferguson (2005: Part 4).

22 Indirect evidence can also be garnered from cases decided outside of the s. 1 Children 1989 context, such as *Re Roddy* [2003] EWHC 2927 (Fam).

approach to achieve the same respect for autonomy and an improved outcome in that child-centred sense.[23]

In the absence of evidence that a children's rights perspective makes better outcomes more likely, it is prudent to ask if we can gain benefits in relation to one or more of the three aspects of recognising children as a special case by instead emphasising either of the other conceptual approaches. The reasons some would like to think of children in terms of children's rights are important, but the present understanding of the concept of children's rights is unable to attain these goals. In this way, the force of Freeman's arguments in favour of taking children's rights seriously might be better interpreted as both justification for seeing children as a special case and a call to explore non-rights based alternative approaches to enable the aims of seeing children as a special case to be more readily fulfilled. Arguments in favour of a welfare-based approach also focus on similar expressive and procedural benefits.[24] This further illustrates the value of understanding the three competing conceptual approaches for seeing children as a special case as simply three ways for placing normative emphasis on the same substantive content.

4. Difficulties with Welfare as the Preferred Approach

In English law, many decisions that affect children are made within a 'best interests' framework under the 'welfare principle' set out in s. 1 of the Children Act 1989. If a welfare-based approach were to be emphasised, it would entail either integrating the 'welfare principle' with the approach taken in other contexts in which s. 1 does not apply[25] or developing a coherent account that justifies emphasising welfare in some contexts and children's rights and duties in others.

---

23 The majority in the Supreme Court of Canada's decision in *AC v. Manitoba* (*Director of Child and Family Services*) 2009 SCC 30 presented an approach to respect for children's autonomy within a welfare-based framework that appears to go further than the rights-within-welfare reasoning in *Gillick*. Justice Abella explains how '[t]he "best interests" standard operates as a sliding scale of scrutiny, with the adolescent's views becoming increasingly determinative depending on his or her ability to exercise mature, independent judgment' ([22]).

24 See, for example, Herring (2005: 168), who stresses the symbolic message it sends to use the welfare principle; the impact its use can have on the procedure adopted by the court; the significance of the language adopted.

25 Excluded contexts include the decision whether to order genetic testing in a paternity dispute. Yet, the child's 'best interests' provides the basis upon which the court may decline to hear such an application: s. 55A(5), Family Law Act 1986. Ward L.J.'s comment in *Re H* (*Paternity: Blood Test*) [1996] 2 FLR 65 that, 'every child has the right to know the truth unless his welfare justifies the cover up' (82) reflects the current general approach well. Our conceptual understanding of 'welfare' is critical to how we approach legal decision-making in such cases, especially because there is no guidance beyond the language of welfare and 'best interests' such as that offered in s. 1 Children Act 1989 to aid us in its interpretation and application.

The current welfare-based approach is not without its critics.[26] I argue that there are two types of criticism against welfare-based approaches: on the one hand, those that should be seen as related to the *conception* of 'best interests' currently embodied in the s. 1 Children Act 1989 'welfare principle'; and on the other, those that are better seen as deeper, *conceptual* reservations about a welfare-based approach. These different types of concern are blended together in the existing literature but there are two reasons it is important to keep them distinct. First, it might be that only the former, but not also the latter, are capable of being remedied. Second, in specifically focusing on conceptual concerns, we can test the value of exploring alternative actual and potential welfare-oriented accounts other than the current conception of the 'welfare principle'.

Generally, the response to criticisms of 'best interests' and the 'welfare principle' is either to advocate for a move to regulating children in terms of children's rights[27] or, less commonly, to argue that the suggested defects of the 'welfare principle' can be remedied through modification of the principle itself.[28] The first response, and arguments for shifting to a rights-based approach, generally assume that welfare and rights are conceptually discrete. At first glance, there are certain differences between the s. 1 Children Act 1989 conception of welfare and the ECHR conception of a rights-based approach, particularly: the absence of an explicit balancing exercise under s. 1; the starting-point to the analysis; and whether the prioritisation of children's rights or interests depends on their nature and seriousness.[29] However, as discussed above, these differences do not prevent both approaches from reaching the same outcome. This is because, at the conceptual level, it is a 'contradiction in terms' (Fortin, 2009: 26) to see rights and welfare as 'diametrically opposed' (*ibid*: 25, discussing the role for the child's wishes in both approaches). Fortin explains:

> The rights contained in the European Convention are formulations, albeit sometimes in awkward phraseology, of aspects of the good life, not the bad and should be interpreted in a way that enhances a person's life. Admittedly, a person may suffer a deficit in well-being if his or her rights are displaced by those of another, but no concept of rights can prevent the occurrence nor can the courts always balance the rights of one person against another in ideal fashion. Developing this notion, and adopting an interest theory

26 In relation to the 'welfare principle' in s. 1 Children Act 1989, as well as more theoretical concerns, see, for example, Reece (1996). In relation to 'best interests' in Article 3 UNCRC see, for example, Freeman (1997a, 2007a, 2011).

27 Choudhry and Fenwick (2005), for example, ground their argument in the context of the current law rather than the broader conceptual debate. They argue for a shift from a s. 1 Children Act 1989 framework to one based squarely in ECHR rights. Reece (1996) argues for the replacement of the s. 1 Children Act 1989 exercise with a framework that balances the interests of the affected parties. Eekelaar (2002) proposes moving to a similar balancing approach, but one which privileges children's interests within the balancing exercise.

28 Herring (1999, 2005), for example, proposes shifting to a 'relationship-based' welfare model, discussed below.

29 For discussion of the differences in approach, see Choudhry and Fenwick (2005).

> of rights as a basis for the proposition that children are rights holders, it follows that a child's welfare cannot be inconsistent with his rights (Fortin, as cited in *ibid*: 26).

If the fundamental distinction is one of emphasis rather than discreteness, the first response should nevertheless be rejected because, as I have outlined above, there is no coherent case to be made that regulating children in terms of children's rights either improves or makes more likely improved outcomes. It remains to reject the second response. This requires a brief exploration of the criticisms levelled at welfare-based approaches, in order to assess whether the best way forward is in fact to emphasise a modified welfare-based approach to legal regulation affecting children.

Criticisms of the Current Conception

Perhaps (somewhat ironically) the criticism that has attracted most academic support is that the s. 1 'welfare principle' is too focused on the particular child before the court. Critics are not suggesting that the principle is too child-centred – surely, that is precisely what we would want – but merely that other parties' interests are unjustifiably significantly or entirely excluded from affecting the outcome achieved. This is most commonly expressed as a charge that the principle is too 'individualistic' (e.g. Herring, 1999)[30] or 'atomistic' (e.g. Herring and Foster, 2012: 491). This represents a criticism of the current conception, rather than a conceptual concern, because there is nothing within the idea of a welfare-based approach that requires the exclusion of other parties' interests in this way. All individuals necessarily exist within a context.[31]

An overlapping substantive concern is that the principle takes too narrow a view of the child's welfare, which would include insufficient consideration of the significance of particular adult relationships for the child's welfare. The issue is to what extent and in what manner the decision-making framework accommodates the child's context. On its terms, the language of s. 1 and the limited reference to the child's parents and caregivers (s. 1(3)(f), Children Act 1989) invites the 'atomistic' critique. In practice, what this would mean is that:

> if one option would slightly improve the child's welfare but would have a disastrous effect on the parents, while the other option would slightly harm the child's welfare but would be greatly beneficial to the parents, under the paramountcy principle the former option should be taken (Reece, 1996: 275).

30 He argues that, under the current law, '[t]he child and his or her welfare are viewed without regard for the welfare of the rest of his or her family, friends and community. The claims of the other members of the family and of the community are only relevant to the extent they directly affect the child's welfare' (unpaginated).

31 I have discussed this in relation to a different legal issue: Ferguson (2012, especially section 6).

But how often does that actually occur in practice? Would the child's interests really be read so narrowly? It is certainly true that s. 1 need not be interpreted so narrowly. The child's s. 1(3)(b) 'emotional needs', for example, might readily accommodate significant attention to the parents' well-being. Lord Justice Munby made clear this potential breadth of contextual understanding in his analysis in *Re G (Children)* [2012] EWCA Civ 1233. In his reflective, philosophically-rich judgment, Munby L.J. proposed that:

> evaluating a child's best interests involves a welfare appraisal in the widest sense, taking into account, where appropriate, a wide range of ethical, social, moral, religious, cultural, emotional and welfare considerations. Everything that conduces to a child's welfare and happiness or relates to the child's development and present and future life as a human being, including the child's familial, educational and social environment, and the child's social, cultural, ethnic and religious community is potentially relevant and has, where appropriate, to be taken into account. The judge must adopt a holistic approach ([27]).

He proceeded to discuss the significance of the child's relationships:

> The well-being of a child cannot be assessed in isolation. Human beings live within a network of relationships.... Our characters and understandings of ourselves from the earliest days are charted by reference to our relationships with others. It is only by considering the child's network of relationships that their well-being can be properly considered. So a child's relationships, both within and without the family, are always relevant to the child's interests; often they will be determinative ([30]).

Yet, there are natural limits to this contextual approach. It remains child-centred or, rather, it remains an attempt to be child-centred. There is a distinct contextual approach that does not require altruism on the part of the child. Children's interests, interpreted contextually, are intended to take precedence over those of others. As such, we are on a slippery slope if we consider that that includes the child being required to be altruistic, making 'sacrifices' for the benefit of others in the family.[32]

We might get to the same outcome in a different way where we can read the child's interests sufficiently broadly to mean that it is genuinely[33] better for them in the longer term or in some larger understanding of immediate benefit. But there is a child-centred dividing line between being able to describe an outcome as in the child's 'best

32 As argued for by Herring (2005); Herring and Foster (2012).

33 In setting out the 'main virtue' of the 'welfare principle,' Eekelaar explains that 'it would be inconsistent with the welfare principle to make a decision that is *overtly* justified by reference to the way the outcome benefited some *other* interest or interests' (2002: 240; emphasis in original). To the extent that there is a difference, my reference to the genuineness of the benefit to the child is intended to signal that it a substantive, not semantic requirement.

interests', broadly read, and describing it as an 'altruistic' 'sacrifice' on their part.[34] Objecting to this dividing line as it applies to how one thinks about the child's context is actually an objection to children as a special case, rather than to welfare-based approaches. Seeing children as a special case, through any of the three currently-available concepts, necessarily entails children's interests taking precedence over parents' interests though, on my account, also necessarily incorporates parents' interests as part of the contextual analysis of the child's position. This is precisely why Reece, who believes that children are not a special case (1996: 276), highlights this concern as part of her argument that the 'welfare principle' is 'regressive' (1996: 302).

More weight should be placed on empirically-grounded arguments about the apparently individualistic or relationally skewed nature of s. 1 determinations. Critical voices suggest both mothers' and fathers' interests are unjustifiably overlooked: Choudhry and Fenwick contend that the 'welfare principle' has 'paradoxically gradually elevated the mother's rights above those of the father' (2005: 458); elsewhere, Choudhry *et al* reason that s. 1's 'focus on the child in isolation from those caring for him' (2010: 8) creates a risk of concealing the burdens of caregiving, so that fathers' rights groups can strengthen their arguments for residence and contact by putting them in terms of welfare. In addition, Reece argues that a policy of 'supporting normality *per se*' (1996: 293) has resulted in gay and lesbian parents being treated unfairly in the application of s. 1.

Does the co-existence of these apparently contradictory concerns undermine the weight to be attached to any of them individually? If the 'welfare principle' is being criticised from all sides in terms of the outcomes reached, perhaps that suggests that the question asked may be impossible of uncontroversial resolution, or at least that no particular decision can satisfy everyone. However, as suggested below, even if controversial decisions are inevitable, these critical perspectives may be unnecessarily exacerbated by the process within which the 'welfare principle' operates. Further, one might conclude that the potential for diminishing a large range of parties' interests suggests that the 'welfare principle' is simply 'unfair' in practice (e.g. Eekelaar, 2002: 238).

This last substantive concern is allied to criticisms that focus on the process by which these decisions are reached: that the principle leaves too much discretion for the decision-maker (e.g. Fortin, 2006: 314), which can lead to lazy reasoning (e.g. Eekelaar, 2002: 248) and over-reliance on expert evidence (e.g. Eekelaar, 2002: 248); that there is insufficient transparency in the reasoning (e.g. Eekelaar, 2002: 237; Choudhry and Fenwick, 2005: 471); and that the principle operates as a 'smokescreen' (Reece, 1996: 296) for the underlying basis of the decision made, including subjective decision-making (e.g. Reece, 1996: 273) and judicial bias (e.g. Herring, 2005: 161-162;

34 Elster criticises the 'best interests' standard for failing sufficiently to accommodate parents' rights and interests, but acknowledges that, were the approach modified to have more regard to the parents' position, children would need special protection in any balancing between parents' and children's interests (as summarised and discussed in Breen, 2002: 59, 61-62).

Reece, 1996: 273). To the extent that these process concerns have weight, they reinforce the potential for substantive exclusion of other parties' interests.[35]

Rather than focusing on these process concerns individually, we might simply view them as a consequence of or enabled by[36] the uncertainty of the 'welfare principle' in practice. If these conception-based concerns were the real problem with the 'welfare principle', however, further specifying the s. 1 principle in one or more various ways might straightforwardly remedy them and introduce a more certain approach to determining what was best. We might, for example, take seriously Munby L.J.'s articulation of the 'welfare principle', discussed above, which would require judges to articulate their understanding of the significance of a wide range of considerations extending beyond those on the s. 1(3) checklist. Or we might make the application of the s. 1(3) checklist mandatory in all circumstances[37] or require judges to explicitly work through each and every subsection of the checklist in every case, as Baker J. demonstrates in his judgment in *CW v. NT and another* [2011] EWHC 33: [58-71].[38] Given that these appear to be straightforward remedies, it is important to ask why we have not further specified the s. 1 principle. This is particularly because, as Dwyer notes, 'we should be suspicious of arguments for abandoning the best-interests test that give no serious consideration to the possibility of improving its implementation' (2006: 239).

Arguably, the critical difficulty is that greater concretisation requires consensus about how to interpret empirical evidence about what is 'best' for children of various competing alternatives. The benefits assumed to stem from applying the checklist, benefits which would be extended if the checklist were made mandatory in every case and every item on the checklist required to be explicitly considered, depend on

35 These process concerns are particularly troubling if they make negotiation more difficult, litigation more likely, and resolution more costly. There is no evidence for increased costs or litigation as a result of the current conception of a welfare-based approach to decision-making about children. Further, as Herring notes, 'the legal principles are relatively clear' in relation to residence and contact disputes (2005: 163). Those 'bargaining in the shadow of' the much-criticised 'welfare principle' arguably have no more need to litigate than if the principle were in fact a set of rules.

36 The 'smokescreen' charge provides a good example here, suggesting that only certain types of considerations are appropriate, and that the uncertainty of the 'welfare principle' has enabled it to be used as a smokescreen.

37 The checklist currently applies only in the circumstances specified in s. 1(4) of the Act. That said, the court in *Dawson v. Wearmouth* [1997] 2 FLR 629 (EWCA) suggested that the judge hearing an application not covered by s. 1(3) would 'invariably have regard to the considerations identified in s. 1(3) in his search for welfare as the paramount consideration even if under no specific statutory duty to do so' (635). This indicates that this particular reform might be of little consequence in practice.

38 However, in *B v. B (Residence Order: Reasons for Decisions)* [1997] 2 FLR 602 (EWCA), Holman J. agreed that it was 'not always necessary or appropriate for a judge laboriously to go, item by item, through the checklist' but also suggested that 'the checklist does represent an extremely useful and important discipline in ensuring that all relevant factors in a case are considered and balanced' (607-608). Setting aside the potential excess administrative burden of applying a strict interpretation of the checklist in every case, what is the basis of this balancing exercise?

a common understanding of how to both assess each item and weigh them against each other, possibly via an implicit hierarchy of considerations. When Baroness Hale in *Re G (Children) (Residence: Same Sex Partner)* [2006] UKHL 43 outlines the role of the checklist in difficult cases, she assumes that systematic application would have avoided the particular outcome reached below ([39]) and that the checklist and other considerations would have been factored in 'so as to ensure that no particular feature of the case is given more weight than it should properly bear' ([40]).

Yet, the unresolved debate over which parties' interests can be said to be unjustifiably neglected in applying s. 1 reveals the current lack of consensus, a problem that becomes self-reinforcing. Failure to work towards agreement on beneficial outcomes for children undermines the current conception of 'best interests'; the weak conception suggests individualised justice in a way that denies the need for research into generalised or categorised benefits and detriments of particular outcomes. Yet, without that research, we should be careful to trust that decision-makers dispensing individualised justice have appropriately considered and weighed *all* of the right, and *only* the right, factual circumstances.

In addition, specificity requires consensus about the nature of the debate. Van Krieken suggests that, in relation to residence and contact disputes at least, the 'best interests' standard is really about governing disputes between parents, yet:

> the belief [is] apparently built into the development of Western family law that it fulfils this function more effectively when such a recognition is never made explicit, and the focus remains on the best interests standard as a proxy or code for that function (2005: 45).

If this is correct, and the dispute is essentially one between parents, we could not straightforwardly incorporate that into a more detailed child-focused 'best interests' assessment. The current 'best interests' discretion adds an extra layer to the analysis, which avoids the need to confront this issue directly. Further, even if we could specify resolution of that dispute between parents, how could the same, more specific test also apply to situations which are much more readily seen as truly child-focused? This is especially acute in the debate over whether to grant a s. 8 specific issue order that authorises medical treatment against the wishes of the child and/or parents. This analysis makes clear that it is not uncertainty itself that is the difficulty for the 'welfare principle', but rather the failure to recognise that the concept is normative all the way down. Those normative choices need to be specifically addressed in order to justify any particular conception of a welfare-based approach.

Inherent, Conceptual Concerns

There are two significant conceptual concerns to address: first, that the 'welfare principle' is indeterminate (e.g. Reece, 1996: 271, also citing Mnookin; Freeman, 2007a: 2; Todres, 1998: 174, citing Parker), a charge which has received significant attention in the literature; second, that the 'welfare principle' is insufficiently or not at all child-centred, an argument that, surprisingly, has received very little attention.

The indeterminacy argument is sometimes blended with discussion of the principle's uncertainty. Herring, for example, discusses 'complaints of indeterminacy' under the heading of 'uncertainty' (2005: 161).[39] Yet it is important to keep the two charges distinct because only the former is of itself terminal to the viability of the 'welfare principle'. If the principle is indeterminate, it is impossible to determine its concept and it should be abandoned. If it is merely uncertain, however, it is simply difficult, but not impossible, to give content to the concept. An uncertain 'welfare principle' is one that is under-determined. Freeman suggests otherwise, arguing that, whilst the concept itself is indeterminate, one might articulate a particular conception at any one time (2011: 19-20). Similarly, Choudhry *et al* cite a practical response to indeterminacy, noting that court decisions are actually more predictable than often assumed (2010: 7). But, whether set out in precise detail or vague outline, articulating a workable conception in such circumstances only presents the chimera of justifiability because the more specified conception nevertheless lacks a normative basis. A more certain approach without normative underpinning can only be seen as arbitrary.

Is the 'welfare principle' conceptually indeterminate? I argue it is, and that the underlying values needed to give content to particular conceptions of the principle are not inherent within the principle itself. Reece discusses the value-laden nature of the principle (1996: 272) but also comments that 'while everybody agrees that children's welfare should be paramount, nobody knows what children's welfare demands' (1996: 271, citing Cretney).[40] If the principle were truly value-laden, how could it also be indeterminate? Underlying values might suggest a basis for shaping a particular conception. However, this is not the case for the conceptually thin 'welfare principle', given content by inherently incommensurable, yet competing, fundamental values.

In her analysis, Breen argues that the 'best interests' standard 'may be regarded as being a weave of social and legal traditions in addition to being an interpretive tool in the analysis of these social and legal traditions' (2002: 87). The potential for its underlying values to make the principle determinate depends on social consensus over how to reconcile and weight those values. Weakening consensus has made indeterminacy a more significant problem (van Krieken, 2005: 32). As the principle is normative all the way down, this problem extends to the underlying substantive content and our understanding of why children are a special case, hence how to realise that through children's rights, welfare or duty.

---

39 Similarly, Choudhry *et al* discuss the 'unpredictable' application of the principle under the heading of 'indeterminacy' (2010: 7).

40 The inability to answer this question also underpins a related criticism, namely that the 'welfare principle' asks an unrealistic question as it is often impossible to make the order that is best for the child (Herring, 2013: 447).
Yet, there is arguably real value in asking what is best, and then implementing as best as we can on the facts. Indeed, when we ask what is best, we may already be thinking in terms of implementable solutions, namely what is best all things considered, rather than what is best ideally. For discussion of this, see Dwyer (2006: 213).

The second important conceptual concern is that the 'welfare principle' is either insufficiently or not at all child-centred. This is not an argument that the principle does not sufficiently focus on the child; rather that it does not, and cannot, govern decision-making affecting children from the child's own perspective. This might seem counter-intuitive to the extent that the child's position is the sole consideration under the 'welfare principle'. Yet the outcome of the welfare exercise is determined externally to the child. At best, the outcome is based on the decision-making adult's reflective and researched estimation as to what is 'best' for the child; at worst, the outcome is based on the adult's assumptions as to what is best, regardless of the particular interests – including the developing autonomy – of the child before them. Yet the danger in the 'welfare principle' is not unique: as I have argued elsewhere (Ferguson, 2013), we also have no theoretically coherent way of expressing a children's rights approach in child-centred terms.

Further, the problem is not just that the 'welfare principle' is not child-centred but that, as with current theories of children's rights, this external aspect of assessing the child's position is not made explicit. It is for this reason that the conceptual indeterminacy and uncertainty in practice are significant concerns. Whilst suggesting throughout that the outcome is truly 'best' for the child because it focuses exclusively on the child, they allow outcomes to be dictated by excessive weight placed on other parties' interests and/or on only particular externally-preferenced interests of the child, hidden from scrutiny by the smokescreen of 'best interests'.

Yet, reform that presented the 'welfare principle' as a non-child-centred approach would be an insufficient remedy. The framework would remain one layer removed from the critical decision-making exercise. Under an explicitly non-child-centred approach, the parties would argue for their external view as to what outcome would be best for the child, thereby implicitly acknowledging that their view may be influenced by other factors such as what is best for them personally. Giving that role to external non-child-centred factors, however, would make the use of the terminology of 'best interests' and the 'welfare principle' counter-intuitive. In addition, these arguments then have to be weighed and translated into a single outcome by a decision-maker. How that decision-maker approaches these arguments is the most critical part of making decisions affecting children. Neither the 'welfare principle' nor children's rights provide inherent child-oriented limits of interpretation and application. A duty-based approach focuses directly on this decision-maker, which provides good reason to consider whether a duty-based approach might be a preferable way to structure our analysis of substantive concerns affecting decision-making about children.

5. The Potential for a Duty-Based Approach: The Decision-Maker, Virtue and Flourishing

Three Roles for Duty

I argue that there are three potential roles for a duty-based approach. Individually, or in combination, each is valuable in enabling us to provide the correct emphasis to substantive concerns that underpin decision-making about children. First, duty can be used as a tool, a mechanism, to be applied within the current law to determine how to resolve apparent conflicts of rights and children's rights; to help apply rights and children's rights in practice;[41] or to help give certain content and specificity to the welfare exercise. If we cannot determine what 'best interests' means in any particular case – which its indeterminacy makes a real issue – we can ask what a virtuous decision-maker would understand it to require on the facts.

Second, a duty-based approach constitutes a theoretical framework of itself, squarely focused on the decision-maker and the correlative outcomes for the child that a 'judicial parent' would expect to accrue to that child. There is no need for the additional layer of children's rights or welfare when a duty-based approach is understood in its fullest sense. Given that each approach addresses the same content (hence why rights-based decisions usually reach the same outcome as welfare-based decisions), this makes sense. Preferring duty is thus about preferring this particular way of framing and weighting the content. As individuals making decisions affecting children, parents would be bound by the same duties as judges. The governing legal regime would proceed on the assumption that parents made decisions bound by the duty-based framework, unless or until challenged or otherwise held subject to judicial or administrative intervention.

Third, the duty concept provides the purpose of the exercise of a duty-based framework. The nature of the decision-maker's duty is conceptually linked to a specific understanding of outcomes for children through a virtue ethics perspective. In that domain, the virtuous decision-maker strives to enable the subject of their decisions to flourish on their own – the subject's own – terms.[42] We will need to consider and approve of this purported inherent connection between duty and flourishing; if we do, virtue ethics may then assist us in our attempt to establish a framework for decision-making that *necessarily* leads to better outcomes for children.

O'Neill (1998) provides the leading philosophical argument for preferring an obligation- to a rights-based approach[43] when considering ethical issues affecting chil-

---

41 In his discussion of the changing role for human rights, Raz stresses the importance of the task of 'establish[ing] a case for holding others to be under a duty to secure, at least to some degree or in some ways, the right-holders' enjoyment of the rights' (2010: 43). He explains that '[t]he value of the right to its possessor is its ground. It is that value which justifies holding others to be duty-bound to secure or at least not interfere with the right-holder's enjoyment of the right, and it is only when such duties exist that the right exists. It exists because it gives rise to such duties' (2010: 36). Thus, even for rights theorists such as Raz, duty is fundamental and critical to the existence and application of rights.

42 In this way, my duty-based approach avoids the apparent conflict between current and future-oriented interests, which Freeman (2007a: 3) considers as a difficulty in relation to 'best interests' within the terms of Article 3, UNCRC. Under my duty-based approach, what is required for flourishing at any current moment is necessarily viewed through a future-oriented lens: one cannot flourish in terms of short-term benefits alone. The two apparent types of interest are thereby integrated without any conflict.

43 O'Neill does not distinguish between 'rights' and 'children's rights' but uses both terms in her discussion. She does, however, distinguish between children's 'positive rights' and

dren's lives. These arguments relate to all three of the ways in which duty may add to our understanding of how legally to regulate children in a way that leads to better outcomes. She reasons:

> When we take rights as fundamental in ethical issues in children's lives we ... get an indirect, partial and blurred picture. ... If a clearer, more direct and more complete view of ethical aspects of children's lives is available, we have good reason to prefer it (O'Neill, 1998: 445).

O'Neill explains how imperfect obligations occupy an ethical space outside of that within which (perfect) obligations correspond with rights (*ibid*: 449-451). For that reason, '[i]f we think imperfect obligations important,' she suggests, 'we cannot see a choice between obligation-based and rights-based theories as mere choice of perspective' (*ibid*: 451-452).

I agree that there are difficulties with children's rights, but disagree that, once we recognise these concerns, the selection of perspectives on the underlying substantive content cannot remain a choice. In fact, I suggest that preferring children's rights represents a choice to reject particular considerations *ab initio* as important and worthy of influencing outcomes in relation to any future individual decisions. Whether that part of the substantive background on which certain duties draw is dismissed at the outset or distinguished at the end, it is nevertheless accounted for on both perspectives. It is then a question as to how significant we consider those substantive concerns to be.

In addition, it is O'Neill's distinction between imperfect and perfect obligations (*ibid*: 447-448) that underpins her argument for the need to shift to an obligation-based approach. On her view, no one has a right to the former being performed (*ibid*: 463) yet, as they are important to the ethical aspects of children's lives, it is critical to include them in our ethical scheme. Focusing on obligations directly does that, though she explicitly takes no view on the legal enforceability of imperfect obligations (*ibid*: 458). However, as I see imperfect and perfect obligations as simply part of the obligations landscape that constitutes the choice to prefer duty over children's rights or welfare, I am not bound to agree with O'Neill that there are a cluster of obligations for which no right to performance exists.[44]

---

children's 'fundamental rights' (1998: 445-446, 448): the latter seems to be similar to my view of children's 'rights' *qua* fundamental human rights, though the former does not correspond to my use of 'children's rights' (Ferguson, 2013). In that sense, O'Neill is not concerned, as I am, with the significance of the fact that it happens to be a child that is the rights-holder.

44 To comment on this briefly, I have some difficulty with O'Neill's distinction (*supra*, note 36) between perfect and imperfect obligations insofar as she sees universal obligations owed to all children as perfect, yet sees obligations potentially owed to all children – she names the obligation to be kind and considerate in dealing with children – as imperfect because they could not be discharged if owed to all. The criterion of universality for one of the two types of perfect obligation – the other type is grounded in special relationships between the parties – does not of itself require capacity for implementation

Critically, I have a different aim to O'Neill in turning to duty. We both consider children's rights (or, for O'Neill, rights more generally) might not be the best way to regulate children's lives. Whereas O'Neill focuses on the idea of obligation as a larger ethical concept to capture the full range of ways in which we want children to be provided for, I focus on the moment at which a decision has to be made between differing outcomes and consider the value of the duty concept in relation to the assigned decision-maker's task.

Virtue, Duty and the Decision-Making Exercise

The conceptual link between duty and the aim of enabling children's flourishing lies in understanding the decision-maker's role in terms that draw on insight from virtue ethics. Virtue ethics is a term of art to describe the third branch of normative ethics, which emphasises virtues or moral character.[45] As Hursthouse explains, this means that it is not capable of precise definition (1999: 4-5).[46] Cimino suggests that '[t]he very idea of 'virtue' seems intuitively too lofty, too vague, too ambitious, and too indeterminate for law' (2009: 281). But that criticism is to misunderstand the purpose of virtue ethics and to overlook its current state of development.[47] It is not aimed at establishing rules and rigid decision-making procedures (Hursthouse, 1999: 18),[48] but enabling individuals with particular character features (*ibid*: 12) to employ those aspects of their character to guide their decision-making, exercising practical wisdom.[49] Hursthouse, for example, proposes that '[a]n action is right if it is what a

---

without more. O'Neill recognises that 'no act description can be fully determinate' (1998: note 2). If implementation without more were required, it is not clear which obligations would straightforwardly qualify and which would not; the line between the two types is ambiguous. Yet, without placing weight on determinacy, it is not clear how O'Neill can distinguish between perfect and imperfect obligations, as her examples of the latter are also universal in their phrasing (1998: 448 – care; 450 – kindness and consideration), though she suggests that they could not be owed to everyone. It is not clear why such obligations could not be owed to all, with performance required based on interactions with others. Relying on the presence or absence of a corresponding right presents only circular reasoning. As Coady (1992: 45) argues, it is not clear why one cannot have a right to something such as kindness and consideration.

45 This revival began with Anscombe (1958).

46 Kochan concludes that 'there is no single virtue ethics' (2014: 316). MacIntyre, however, argues that we can give a unifying core definition to virtue, which brings together earlier accounts, though the definition is necessarily complex (1985: 186, 191).

47 Unlike deontology and consequentialism, 'virtue ethics in its modern development is still in its infancy. It should not therefore be shackled by preconceived ideas about its progeniture and nature' (Swanton, 2003: 5).

48 Cimino explains that, within virtue ethics, we focus on 'making choices about courses of action based on what acts will best help each actor become her best self (or 'flourish'), not to follow rules' (2009: 289).

49 Practical wisdom is an Aristotelian concept; itself both an intellectual and moral virtue, it is also a master virtue that enables an individual to use the other virtues to guide action. See Aristotle (1992, trans. Ross, D.: Book VI chapter 5).

virtuous agent would characteristically (i.e. acting in character) do in the circumstances' (1998: 22). Similar arguments are made within virtue jurisprudence[50] about legal decision-making and the justifiability of legal decisions. Cimino explains that '[v]irtue jurisprudence [is] … much less about virtue as a substantive *source* of law than it is about a method of reasoning *about* law' (2009: 299, emphasis in original). Whilst much attention in the developing literature focuses on judging (e.g. Solum, 2003; Duff, 2003), this also naturally supports focus on process.

I propose that a particular decision-making process should be employed. This is not the kind of codification that is troubling to advocates of virtue ethics such as Hursthouse (1999: 56-57), as there is no suggestion of a particular ranking of underlying substantive factors. As a neo-Aristotelian approach, the rightness of the chosen outcome of the decision-making exercise is not derived from the process used and the individual decision-maker, but exists 'as in some measure independent of agent evaluations' (Slote, 1995: 84); the virtuous decision-maker perceives which is the right decision because it is the right thing to do (*ibid*: 83).

The first requirement is that the full range of substantive factors is taken into account by the decision-maker. In particular, the goal that the child will be better enabled to flourish on their own terms necessitates incorporating empirical evidence as to which factual situations benefit children and in what ways. What do we know, for example, about outcomes for children whose parents separate when they are young and raise their children through court-ordered shared parenting arrangements? How does that compare to outcomes for similarly-placed children who reside principally with one parent? This should also encourage more research into children's lives and lived experience.

Second, the decision-maker must be transparent in the way that the decision is reached, which entails detailing the reasoning employed in examining and evaluating the underlying substantive issues, as well as the reasons for the weighting ultimately reached. This process enables duty to fulfil the guiding role I suggested for it, above, as well as constitutes the content of its proposed framework role. In relation to the former, for example, conflicting legal rights claimed by parents and children may be included as factors in the presumed-virtuous decision-maker's flourishing-oriented analysis and, viewed through that aim, be more readily reconciled or weighted.

50 The nature of the relationship between virtue ethics and virtue jurisprudence is not uncontested. Farrelly and Solum comment that '[t]he connection … certainly does not rise to the level of entailment' (2008: 6). The directness or otherwise of this relationship is outside the scope of my discussion as I am drawing on insights from virtue theory, rather than claiming to apply a particular instantiation thereof, whether in virtue ethics or virtue jurisprudence.

These two requirements embody and enable the exercise of the virtues of justice[51] and practical wisdom.[52] Decision-makers are enabled to exercise particularised judgment based on the facts and empirical evidence about outcomes for children. This fits with the way that the 'best interests' exercise is conceived within s. 1 of the Children Act 1989, giving discretion to the decision-maker to determine what is best for the particular child as long as particular considerations – the s. 1(3) welfare 'checklist' – are taken into account.

The need to incorporate empirical research goes further than s. 1 and provides one restriction on the type of decision that can be reached: a decision-maker will be prevented from preferring a possible outcome when empirical evidence indicates an alternative outcome would be more likely to enable the child to flourish on their own terms. Of course, flourishing is not to be understood as simply physical health, so the decision-maker might prefer an alternative outcome where they take the view that they would enable to flourish in a broader sense. Viewing the judge's need for solid expert and empirical evidence as critical to making good decisions also has consequences for the place of other actors in the court process. It suggests a particular role for expert witnesses as part of the necessary foundations for the virtuous judge's decision-making. As evinced in the Children and Families Act 2014, the place of expert witnesses and evidence for court is currently in flux in both the public law and private law contexts. Whilst legislative and practice reform suggests a reduced role for experts, a duty-based approach highlights the need to be cautious about the extent to which we limit the potential for courts to draw on external expertise. A virtuous decision-maker, of course, would also have regard to delays for children, so might be better placed to strike the right balance than legislated confinement.

In the case of irresolvable dilemmas (Hursthouse, 1999: 63), decision-makers may reach different conclusions and yet have still acted well (ibid: 68-71) because their character underpins their reasoning. This focus on the decision-maker directly makes it more likely that they explicitly treat these dilemmas as such and explore their resolution, which is important for the child's sense that their situation has been treated justly and fairly. In her virtue jurisprudence exposition of the good character traits of

51 There is debate over how to understand 'justice' as a virtue. Solum, for example, explores two possibilities, 'justice as fairness' and 'justice as lawfulness,' preferring the latter (2008: 174-180). This debate goes beyond the scope of my argument, though my duty-based approach reduces freedom for the private and emphasises the public aspects of justice, as under a lawfulness conception.

52 In terms of Aristotle's understanding of the virtue of justice, my requirements relate to 'universal justice' rather than 'particular justice' (Aristotle, 1992: Book V). Swanton discusses the 'virtues of practice,' which are to be employed in making decisions: '[T]he aim is to get things right by acting in an overall virtuous way in integrating constraints on solutions to problems' (2003: 253). She envisages three types of virtue: focus, creative solution-oriented thinking; and dialogue. She elucidates personal features and aspects of how virtuous decision-makers should make decisions, whereas my procedural requirements focus on the public aspects of decision-making and enable inclusion of all decision-makers, regardless of their personal virtue.

judges, Sherry explains that it is not the decision-maker's personal character that is critical, but their judicial character (2008: 91). My virtue-inspired account goes further and treats decision-makers and third parties interacting with children as if they possess these features in their character, even though it is possible that they may not. Assuming decision-makers are virtuous, they are under a duty to take into account empirical evidence, reason transparently and provide an account of their reasoning. These requirements make it more likely that they will reach the better outcomes that a virtuous decision-maker would reach.

Fulfilling the requirements of exercising virtue makes the decision reached more justifiable.[53] Being virtuous enables the decision-maker to flourish as practical wisdom is acquired through practice; it is in everyone's interest that they are treated as if they are virtuous.[54] As Foot argues, '[i]t seems clear that virtues are, in some general way, beneficial. Human beings do not get on well without them' (1978: 2).[55] For the virtuous decision-maker, these requirements frame their decision-making but impose no restrictions on the process they would otherwise employ. I consider how this duty-based approach might be applied in particular cases in section 6, below.

Duty and the Aim of Flourishing

The aim of my duty-based approach directly flows from its virtue-inspired process. Virtues are character traits that a person needs in order to flourish (Hursthouse, 1998: 23) and constitutive of flourishing (Hursthouse, 1999: 136). In this way, the child flourishing on their own terms becomes the necessary aim of a virtue-inspired approach. Flourishing means living a 'good human life,' which 'is a life of human excellence, and

---

53 Amaya makes a similar argument in respect of the 'connoisseurship' model of legal reasoning, arguing that positing a normative ideal of virtuous decision-making best explains legal justification (2013: 51-66, especially 58, 65).

54 There is debate over the implications of the view that being virtuous enables the possessor to flourish, but this is outside the scope of this discussion. Does it 'provide a motivating reason ... for being virtuous ... in accordance with the standard list of virtues'? Or might it provide a means for 'critical reflection on the standard list'? (Hursthouse, 1999: 170 *et seq.*)

55 As Foot notes, this may be more obvious for some virtues, such as courage, temperance and wisdom, than others. Charity and justice, she notes, require sacrifice, yet generally still benefit the possessor (1978: 3). MacIntyre's understanding of the concept of virtue also supports this view:

> Every practice requires a certain kind of relationship between those who participate in it. Now the virtues are those goods by reference to which, whether we like it or not, we define our relationships to those other people with whom we share the kind of purposes and standards which inform practices. (1985: 191)

The decision-maker reluctant to explain their reasoning in the detailed and transparent terms required by my duty-based approach, for example, would nevertheless do so as they understood that that was their contribution to the decisions that needed to be made, was expected of them by others affected by those decisions, and helped define their role within that group of affected individuals as one who treated others justly.

we treat people well when we help them to become more excellent humans' (Keller, 2013: 102). Whichever understanding of decision-making capacity one adopts, only some children are sufficiently autonomous to be treated as adults; children's flourishing is thus best seen as empirically-driven. This underpins the requirement to focus on the individual child, the need to avoid rule-based decision-making and to base decisions on empirical evidence and research regarding outcomes for children. We might also see the approach to flourishing in virtue ethics as empirically-driven. Foot, for example, reasons that

> [t]o determine what is goodness and what defect of character, disposition, and choice, we must consider what human good is and how human beings live: in other words, what kind of a living thing a human being is. (2001: 51)

Natural goodness requires an in-depth understanding of outcomes for individuals and empirical evidence on what makes it more likely that someone will develop into such a person.

Does this understanding of flourishing capture all that we might hope for children's potential future lives? For example, might one argue that there is no place for appreciation for, or a devotion to, the arts or music? Within virtue ethics, this is a subject of debate: to what extent does flourishing consist of both moral and non-moral virtues? (Swanton, 2003: 84). How should the two be weighed against each other? Flourishing requires a balance between different virtues and recognition that individuals 'may fail to flourish because of factors virtuous *forgone*, such as physical and mental health, contentment and lack of stress' (Swanton, 2003: 88, emphasis in original). Paying attention to empirical evidence as to what makes and has the most potential to make children 'deeply happy' (Foot, 2001: 88)[56] creates space for balancing such competing concerns. It also enables us to see how the child's short-term preferences and interests may be reconciled against their long-term interests in a way that removes any apparent conflict between the two. When the short-term is read in light of the longer-term goal of enabling and maximising flourishing, any conflict between the two dissipates. We might see this as akin to integrating the child's wishes through the lens of psychosocial maturity (discussed: Ferguson, 2005: Part 4).

Such an empirically-driven, but virtue-oriented, aspect encourages us to be explicitly evaluative. This can only be a positive, given the criticism that the 'welfare principle' currently operates as a 'smokescreen' in practice, as discussed in section 4, above. This approach also meshes well with s. 1, acting to direct the weighing of various considerations within the s. 1(3) checklist and to ensure that 'best interests' is understood in broad terms. In writing about the value of persons, Keller reasons that:

> it is possible that a single story about the value of persons could incorporate the importance of welfare, flourishing, and autonomy. Perhaps, for example, a concern with a

56 This does not refer to happiness in the sense of contentedness, but rather in a non-superficial sense, which entails the basics of good living such as friendship, family and work.

> person's flourishing, properly understood, will turn out to include within it both concern for her best interests and respect for her autonomy (2013: 103-104).

It is this potential for flourishing and its natural connection to a duty-based approach that marks it out as capturing more of the relevant substantive content underpinning decision-making about children and more readily enabling the particularisation of such content than either children's rights or welfare.

Reasons to Prefer Duty

Aside from the theoretical appeal of my virtue-based approach, there are other strong reasons to prefer my duty account in comparison to the two predominant alternatives of children's rights and welfare when considering which framework should be adopted. The value of these arguments is contingent on their potential to increase the likelihood of improved outcomes for children.

First, looking initially to the decision-maker, not the child, more readily enables prioritisation of the child's position than adopting an ostensibly child-centred approach. Both children's rights and welfare are propounded as the latter yet, as discussed above, they are theoretically incapable of being so. Inaccurately presenting the two alternative accounts as child-centred means less scrutiny is applied to the decision-making process and outcome than if the approach were explicitly non-child-centred. This makes it easier to reach decisions that prefer interests of others or a subjective view of the best outcome for children with insufficient scrutiny thereof. This may seem counter-intuitive, but we should recall that, as O'Neill argues, a significant part of the reason for the prominence of children's rights as an approach is historical (1998), rather than conceptual or based in substantive improvements achieved for children. Further, the welfare approach was in its origins itself focused on the decision-maker: the 'best interests' principle grew out of the Court of Chancery's *parens patriae* jurisdiction which, as van Krieken explains, focuses on the judicial decision-maker, acting as parent (2005: 27).

Freeman argues that an obligations argument 'places parents, not children, centre stage' (2007b: 10), yet this is only true at first glance. The initial focus on the decision-maker within a duty-based approach, whether parents (as Freeman notes) or others, immediately turns to the child about whom the decision must be made, and the need for transparent, evidence-based reasoning about the best outcome for that child. As Keller argues

> [a]s a parent, you will show special concern for your child's welfare, but you are also likely to have a separate special concern for her flourishing. Much of what we do as parents is directed towards making our children good and virtuous people. We teach them to care about others and tell the truth, and we encourage them to develop their minds and cultivate their talents. We may believe that a virtuous child will grow into a happy adult or that in bringing up good children we are bringing up children who will be better off, but, for many of us, the concern with a child's flourishing cannot be straightforwardly

> reduced to a concern with her welfare. It makes perfect sense to want your child to be a good person, even if you doubt that being a good person is the best strategy for achieving happiness. (2013: 104)

Flourishing is a natural concern for decision-makers, particularly parents, and focusing on them as decision-maker makes it more likely it will be achieved.

Second, a duty-based account more readily enables particularisation to the individual child. Bainham criticises both the 'welfare principle' and rights for their indeterminacy, arguing that best interests are 'dependent, ultimately, on determination by judges' (2002: unpaginated) and children's UNCRC rights are 'meaningless until their content is judicially determined and applied' (2002: unpaginated). Rather than requiring translation from either the conceptual expression of individual rights or the ideal understanding of 'best interests', the decision-maker acting under duty exercises practical wisdom,[57] as discussed above. This is empirically-driven and focuses on the circumstances of the individual child affected to determine what, on the particular facts, will most enable that child to flourish. In this sense, it also sees the child as a contextualised subject,[58] which requires, enables, and justifies the incorporation of other parties' interests in a necessarily limited capacity. As I explain elsewhere, a contextualised analysis 'remains focused on the child as a subject throughout, rather than on the predicates that comprise their [...] backgrounds' (Ferguson, 2014: 74). The nature of this contextualised focus ensures that my duty-based account is not vulnerable to the charge of excessive individualism made against the 'best interests' standard, discussed above, regardless of the extent to which one accepts the validity of this criticism.

Third, a duty-based approach reduces the potential for the reasoning to be vague, insufficiently articulated, or act as a 'smokescreen' for the actual rationale. With the focus squarely on the decision-maker, the empirical orientation of both the process of reasoning – practical reasoning – and the goal to be attained – flourishing – means the decision-maker is more likely to provide detailed reasoning that justifies the decision reached. This benefits both affected parties and broader society. In addition to increasing the decision's legitimacy, more detailed, fact-oriented reasoning helps the affected child and other relevant parties understand the decision reached. Greater articulation of the reasoning also increases the likelihood of the reasoning being transparent. These are key advantages compared with children's rights and welfare frameworks.

Fourth, and relatedly, in the public gaze of more detailed, transparent reasoning, the judge's explicit consideration of all relevant concerns is more likely to result in a

---

57 Amaya, citing Wallace, explains how practical reason involves focusing on situation-specific reasons for action, rather than applying general principles or rules (2013: 64). These situation-specific reasons are necessarily grounded in the particular facts, here the child's factual circumstances.

58 Cimino describes practical wisdom as embodying 'contextualism' when contrasted with deontology and consequentialism (2009: 282).

better balance being struck between competing concerns. Take a child's refusal of critical medical treatment as an example. Being required to explain the decision to apply a cognitive-only capacity test or the choice to draw on evidence concerning other aspects of capacity, such as psychosocial development, should make the decision reached more likely to reflect the child's true capacity and more legitimate in the eyes of the child and other interested parties. This represents an improvement upon the current position, which includes assumptions about both what the child must understand in order to be permitted to refuse,[59] and how capacity to consent is related to capacity to refuse.[60]

Fifth, in considering all relevant factors as part of a duty-based approach, the decision-maker is more likely to draw on the relevant empirical evidence, hence reach more empirically-grounded judgments. Could we not achieve the same openness and detailed, empirically-grounded reasoning within the s. 1(1) Children Act 1989 exercise or in the application of rights-based arguments to particular facts?[61] There is precedent, of course, for courts explicitly exploring the empirical research and how it relates to the question of law they are being asked to resolve. A well-known example is the Court of Appeal's examination of pertinent research findings regarding contact and domestic violence in its decision in *Re L, V, M, and H* [2000] EWCA Civ 194 in relation to a s. 8 Children Act 1989 contact dispute. Whilst the social science literature was considered, however, it is unclear that it was correctly assessed (cf. Gilmore, 2008) or weighed. No particular hierarchy of or methodology for weighing competing considerations can be derived from the s. 1 exercise itself.

---

59 *Re E (A Minor) (Wardship: Medical Treatment)* [1992] 2 FCR 219 (EWHC) provides a good example. As I explain elsewhere (Ferguson, 2013: note 15 and corresponding main text), a 15-year-old was adjudged cognitively capable of refusing critical medical treatment for leukaemia, but held to lack the capacity overall to refuse based on other matters that had not been tested on the facts. Mr Justice Ward reasoned that 'in my judgment A does not have a full understanding of the whole implication of what the refusal of that treatment involves' (224). Yet, this absence of 'full understanding' was based on an assumed inability to understand the impact of the full process of dying, particularly seeing his family's distress (224) and the particular details of the pain and fear that he would suffer as he died – the frightening struggle for breath, of which neither the treating physician nor Ward J. had informed him (224).

60 There was no differentiation in the leading case of *Gillick*; the facts were concerned solely with consent. Yet more recent cases such as *Re R (A Minor) (Wardship: Consent to Treatment)* [1991] 4 All ER 177 (EWCA) and *Re W (A Minor) (Medical Treatment: Court's Jurisdiction)* [1992] 2 FCR 785 (EWCA) were decided on the basis that such a distinction exists. This is now the subject of a reinvigorated debate. Gilmore and Herring (2011, 2012) seek partially to justify this distinction, supported by a parallel argument in ethics, though without consideration of empirical evidence about the nature of decision-making capacity. Cave and Wallbank (2012) suggest that the asserted potential distinction between the capacity required to make decisions about particular treatment and to refuse all treatment is not so straightforward, and argue for a contextual approach to all medical decision-making.

61 Thanks to an anonymous reviewer for posing this reply.

This is what makes the virtue-inspired approach particularly powerful. It guides decision-makers in how to weigh competing considerations without unjustifiably restricting the discretionary exercise, namely by asking them to weigh factors against each other as regards their ability to attain the normatively rich aim of the child's flourishing. Simply mandating that decision-makers explain their application of s. 1 does not achieve this, yet going further to focus on substantive matters immediately imposes an unjustifiable gloss on the legislation.

More generally, the centrality of the informed decision-maker to the duty-based approach emphasises that what matters is not so much which language descriptor for ethical considerations we employ – children's rights, welfare, or duty – to mediate state regulation of children, but whether we have the tools to enable the decision-maker to determine which outcome or range of outcomes really is best for any particular child or children. This encourages us more fully to develop our body of knowledge concerning the content of 'better' or 'best' outcomes for children in empirical terms. Whilst a children's rights or welfare-oriented perspective can accommodate this consideration of empirical research, neither approach of itself makes it central to justifiable decision-making in the way that immediate focus on the decision-maker does.

Sixth, a duty-based approach removes an unnecessary layer of complexity from the process of reasoning. At first glance, it might seem to add a further layer given that it does not focus directly on the child, but first on the decision-maker.[62] Yet the reverse is true. As O'Neill explains, '[t]hose who urge respect for children's rights must address not children but those whose action may affect children' (1998: 462; see also 463). If we focus directly on the child, as children's rights and welfare do, we need to add in an additional layer of reasoning in order to translate into implementation via adult action any conclusions on of what is best for the child or how to balance various competing rights claims. Under a duty-based approach, the decision-maker is invariably the adult actor concerned, so that this additional step is unnecessary. This applies to my fifth point: whilst we can make consideration of the empirical research and what we know about good outcomes for children part of the requirements of the s. 1 Children Act 1989 welfare exercise carried out by a judge, that nevertheless requires an additional stage of reasoning to be realised. As that additional stage comprises the judge's actions, why not focus directly on the judge?

Further, given that we cannot even focus directly on the child in a child-centred way under children's rights or welfare, that first layer of reasoning itself involves unnecessary confusion through presenting non-child-centred interests and concerns in child-centred terms. In the absence of any additional reason to use children's rights or welfare as a framework, there is no rationale for introducing this additional complexity to making decisions affecting children.

Seventh, focusing directly on the decision-maker in this way is also proactive, not reactive. A duty-based approach imposes positive obligations on those making decisions affecting children to do so virtuously and to take positive steps to benefit the

62 Thanks to Helen Reece for raising this argument.

child. By contrast, children's rights and welfare are reactive approaches. Until particular children's rights or conceptions of welfare have been translated into duties imposed on adults, neither children's rights nor welfare themselves require any action. Only when there is an assertion by a rights-holder or a dispute over what is in a particular child's 'best interests' are the approaches applied and translated into duties to act.

6. Current and Potential Roles for Duty in Practice

In this section, I explore how a duty-based approach underpins aspects of the current law, as well as how it might work if incorporated into new areas. The selected examples serve to highlight its potential to fulfil the three roles outlined above, namely, as a tool for enabling the resolution of conflicts of interest in difficult cases where children's rights and/or welfare-based reasoning runs out; as a theoretical framework itself; and as the foundation of a virtue-led normative approach to the legal regulation of children that necessarily has flourishing as its goal.

Re A (Children) (Conjoined Twins: Surgical Separation) (2001)[63]

Re A is a well-known, difficult case in which a hospital applied to court for a declaration that it could lawfully separate conjoined twin girls without their parents' consent. The parents' refusal was based at least in part on their devout Roman Catholic beliefs. If the parents' wishes were respected and the operation was not carried out, both girls would die within a few months. If the court authorised the separation, it would lead to the certain death of the weaker twin, Mary, but provide the possibility of a relatively normal life to the other, Jodie. As I have explained elsewhere (Ferguson, 2013: 203), the Court of Appeal employs interwoven rights- and welfare-based reasoning in reaching their conclusion to uphold the order of the court below, which authorised the operation to separate the twins. Blended rights- and welfare-based reasoning is necessary, and even the different blend in each judgment perhaps unsurprising, because neither approach can accurately characterise the nature of the conflict on the facts.

Whilst rights can be weighed against each other, the nature of the rights at stake here cannot, at least without risking artificial construction of the content of particular rights. Thus, Ward L.J. discusses the right to life, based on the understanding that 'each life has inherent value in itself and ... is equal for all of us' (*Re A*: 186H; cf. 187H-188A). For that reason, the right to life is both central to the case and incapable of resolving the conflict. Lord Justice Walker, however, considers that not separating the twins 'would be to deprive them of the bodily integrity and human dignity which is the right of each of them' (*Re A*: 258D). Yet, he makes this point to explain why, in addition to it being in Jodie's best interests, it would also be in Mary's best interests to separate them. Lord Justice Walker's interpretation of the right to life, however, might

63 Thanks to an anonymous reviewer for suggesting discussion of this decision.

well be argued to be 'illusory' in its application to Mary, as Ward L.J. himself contends (*Re A*: 184C). Whilst Brooke L.J. argues that separation would respect the sanctity of life of each, he does not phrase this in terms of the right to life (*Re A*: 240E). As Brooke L.J. concurs with Ward L.J.'s view that separation is preferable because Jodie's best interests outweigh Mary's (*Re A*: 205D), his comments about separation supporting each twin's sanctity of life are unable to be weighed in the balance of interests and become merely an additional buttressing reason for separation. Rights are not determinative either alone or within a welfare-based framework.

The s. 1 Children Act 1989 'welfare principle' contemplates the individual child before the court, rather than the sum of balancing one child's 'best interests' against those of another. The welfare-based approach thus does not of itself accommodate conflicts between the interests of particular children. Whilst Walker L.J. recognises that there are cases in which courts have balanced different children's 'best interests' (*Re A*: 242H-243C), he also notes that these cases did not involve the right to life. Unless one adopts Brooke L.J.'s artificial interpretation of the right to life, its equal, inherent value disrupts the potential to see the twins' interests as capable of being weighed against each other. For that reason, Walker L.J. finds himself required to reach the artificial conclusion that it is in the 'best interests' of each that they be separated when, as Ward L.J. explains, it is clearly not in Mary's' best interests' to be separated as '[i]t denies her inherent right to life' with 'no countervailing advantage for her at all' (*Re A*: 190D).

Lord Justice Ward resolves the case by balancing each twin's interests against the other's, however, and concludes that Jodie's interests outweigh Mary's (*Re A*: 192F-G); as noted, Brooke L.J. agrees with this approach. Yet the balancing cannot come from the 'welfare principle' itself, but must be externally constructed. It is a mistake to treat this resolution as part of the 'best interests' analysis since, whilst it is a pragmatic solution, the s. 1 evaluation of what is 'best' for a particular child contemplates its implementation and does not envisage subsequent counter-balancing. In that way, it is distinct from the 'double proportionality' approach more straightforwardly employed in respect of ECHR rights arguments in relation to which the rights at stake admit of justifiable infringement. Resolving the case by balancing the interests of one twin against those of the other is just as artificial as suggesting that the 'best interests' of each supports separation. Neither rights nor welfare, taken alone or together, are able to accommodate the nature of the conflict here.

A duty-based approach may enable us to cut the Gordian knot and both recognise and resolve the conflict in a less artificial way. In preferring Jodie's interests to Mary's, Ward L.J. reasons in terms of duty:

> If the duty of the court is to make a decision which puts Jodie's interests paramount and that decision would be contrary to the paramount interests of Mary, then, for my part, I do not see how the court can reconcile the impossibility of properly fulfilling each duty by simply declining to decide the very matter before it. That would be a total abdication of the duty which is imposed upon us. Given the conflict of duty, I can see no other way of dealing with it than by choosing the lesser of the two evils and so finding the least

> detrimental alternative. A balance has to be struck somehow and I cannot flinch from undertaking that evaluation, horrendously difficult though it is (192F-G).

Viewed in context, Ward L.J.'s balancing of one twin's 'best interests' against the other's is better seen not as part of a broader welfare assessment – akin to the relationship between 'double proportionality' and individual rights – but as a distinct role for a duty-based approach being exercised by a virtuous decision-maker. Drawing on Ward L.J.'s reference to the duties at stake, the conflict might be better represented as a conflict in the duties owed to each child than as a conflict between each of the twin's 'best interests'. Understanding the conflict in duty-based terms enables balancing in a way that neither a welfare nor rights perspective does: not only is the court under a larger duty to resolve cases referred to them (*Re A*, Ward LJ: 174C), but the conflicting duties are to enable each child to flourish on her own terms. Hard though it is, it is less artificial to recognise that the only circumstance in which either twin's chances for flourishing are increased is via separation, which increases Jodie's potential to flourish. This is the evaluation which we 'cannot flinch from undertaking', reasoned more transparently than the smokescreen judgment that separation either is in the best interests or respects the right to life of each twin.

In addition, approaching either the resolution of conflicting 'best interests' determinations or the exercise as a whole through the lens of duty clarifies the role for other decision-makers involved, particularly the parents and the treating doctors and hospital. Lord Justice Ward comments:

> It would, nevertheless, have been a perfectly acceptable response for the hospital to bow to the weight of the parental wish however fundamentally the medical team disagreed with it. Other medical teams may well have accepted the parents' decision. Had [the treating hospital] done so, there could not have been the slightest criticism of them for letting nature take its course in accordance with the parents' wishes (173G-H).

Yet this would not be supported by a duty-based approach. If Ward L.J. is correct that the court must not flinch from its duty to decide this case, and if exercise of that duty requires preferring Jodie's interests to Mary's, can he also be correct that the treating doctors and hospital did not have a duty to intervene? This is a critical issue because of Ward L.J.'s further comment that, if the medical team chose to respect the parents' refusal, they would not need to refer the case to court:

> [W]hilst I would not go so far as to endorse a faint suggestion made in the course of the hearing that, in fulfilment of that duty of care, the hospital were under a further *duty* to refer this impasse [between the medical team and the parents] to the court, there can be no doubt whatever that the hospital are entitled in their discretion to seek the court's ruling. In this case I entertain no doubt whatever that they were justified in doing so (173H-174A; emphasis in original).

If there is a right answer for the court and there is a duty to intervene and protect Jodie from harm and inevitable death, might the medical team not also be under that same duty?[64] Or might the medical team at least be under a duty to subject to judicial scrutiny any decision not to intervene?

Parents are under a duty to seek medical advice – not to do so would constitute neglect: s. 1, Children and Young Persons Act 1933 – and then consent to or refuse medical treatment. Medical practitioners and parents work in partnership; the authority, and responsibility, for the final decision rests with the parents. Where both agree on intervention, as is most commonly the case, they can proceed without independent legal review. If parents refuse to consent to recommended treatment, their decision-making is subject to the court's independent review (*Re A*, Ward L.J.: 178F-179A).

In his *dicta*, but not on the facts, Ward L.J. envisages the situation in which both the parents and the medical team agree on non-intervention. At common law, courts have recognised circumstances in which medical practitioners have authority to decide not to intervene (*Re J* (*A Minor*) (*Wardship: Medical Treatment*) [1991] Fam 33 (EWCA); *Re J* (*A Minor*) (*Child in Care: Medical Treatment*) [1993] Fam 15 (EWCA); *NHS Trust v. MB* [2006] EWHC 507 (Fam); *Re A*, Walker L.J.: 248H). Professional guidance similarly recognises a limited number of situations in which it may be justifiable to withhold or withdraw treatment (Royal College of Paediatrics and Child Health, 2004: 10-11). These are situations in which intervention is in some sense futile. However, this authority is in fact rooted in duty. As Lord Donaldson explains in *Re J* (1993), requiring the medical practitioner 'to adopt a course of treatment which in the bona fide clinical judgment of the practitioner concerned is contra-indicated as not being in the best interests of the patient' would be requiring them 'to act contrary to the fundamental duty which he owes to his patient' (26H-27A).

Recognising that the authority to choose not to intervene is based in the duty owed to the individual patient suggests that Ward L.J. may have erred in his representation of the medical team's freedom not to treat. As he recognises elsewhere (192F-G), there is a conflict of duties owed to each twin precisely because it is only Mary's medical situation that is futile, not Jodie's. The duty owed to Jodie is one to intervene and operate. Given that duty, it is not at all clear why there could be no criticism of the medical team if they had opted not to intervene, and possibly also not sought court authorisation not to intervene.

What if the medical practitioner grounded their judgment not strictly on physical well-being, but on broader ethical concerns? There is judicial authority that ethically-grounded concerns can justify a medical practitioner's decision not to treat (*Re B* (2006), Holman J. at [24]). But the recognised duty to intervene should have already accommodated such ethical concerns to the extent they are relevant. A duty-based approach calls into question the assumption, noted by Morris (2009: 355, citing

---

64 Bridgeman (2007: 93) disagrees. Citing Ward L.J.'s comments (173G-H, above), she suggests that there is a range of views as to what is in the 'best interests' of a child, including each of the twins, such that a reasonable refusal by the parents, as the medical team, will discharge their duty to the child.

Holman J. in *NHS Trust v. MB* (2006): [24]), that medical practitioners, and not the courts, are equipped to consider these ethical aspects. In its immediate focus on the decision-maker, rather than the outcome prior to translation back into obligations on the decision-maker, a duty-based approach better represents the contributions of each actor to attaining the best outcome. It enables us to explicitly recognise the contributions of each – parents, medical team, and court – to assessing the best outcome based on their own unique perspectives.

Lord Justice Ward explains that '[t]his court is a court of law, not morals, and our task has been to find, and our duty is then to apply, the relevant principles of law to the situation before us' (*Re A*: 155E). By contrast, focusing directly on the outcome to be achieved, the child's 'best interests', assumes each actor can approach the determination of the preferred outcome objectively, equally able to take into account the full range of considerations, without exploring the detail of how that translates into their practical reasoning – their duty to decide in practice. As Ward L.J.'s comments show, that is not the case.

A duty-based perspective removes the conflict and emphasises the partnership between different actors' assessments of the way forward. There is no longer an assumption of conflicting accounts of what is best for the child, but rather a view that each is contributing, via exercise of their duty, to a larger discussion of which outcome will enable the child to flourish on their own terms. It also becomes easier to explain why decision-makers might reach differing views – because the duty to make the decision that most enables flourishing embraces the distinctive competencies of each actor. Thus, where parents and the medical team reach different conclusions on the preferred outcome, as here, we need not see their views as conflicting, but rather multiple, partial perspectives on flourishing, with the independent review of the court available to provide a fuller perspective. In the end, rather than a conflict between different decision-makers' perspectives, we are simply left with the conflict between duties owed to each twin. This has the benefit of more closely corresponding to the conflict of duties owed by the medical team in criminal law (cf. *Re A*, Ward L.J.: 201G, 202H-203D; Walker L.J.: 255G).

Of course, all of this remains a criticism of one particular legal construction of the medical team's duties here; best practice and good practice may well be different, and it is important not to overlook that.

The United Nations' Convention on the Rights of the Child

The speed and extent of the ratification of the UNCRC is often seen as evidence of the importance of children's rights; Freeman, for example, cites it as 'the best-known example' of 'political initiatives' in 'the case for children's rights' (2007b: 19-20). Whilst it might seem somewhat counter-intuitive, the Convention itself provides strong support for regulating children's lives through a direct focus on the decision-maker. There are two aspects to consider here: first, the language and concepts employed in the Convention; second, the existing approach to domestic incorporation.

There are a large number of Articles, expressed in duty-based terms, that prescribe what 'States Parties shall [do]' for the children within their jurisdiction. For example, consider Article 11, paragraph 1, which requires signatories to 'take measures to combat the illicit transfer and non-return of children abroad' or Article 19, paragraph 1, which mandates that 'States Parties shall take all appropriate legislative, administrative, social and educational measures to protect the child from all forms of physical or mental violence'. There is no mention of rights; the language of duty alone is used as the most effective means to convey the underlying relationship between the child and desired outcome. This is not unusual phrasing for a United Nations' Convention,[65] but it is significant as it highlights the role already being played by duty-oriented reasoning in improving outcomes for children. Adopting a virtue-inspired approach to the duty owed also helps concretise an otherwise uncertain obligation; the goal of flourishing enables us to determine a natural limit to the measures required.

In addition to Articles expressed exclusively in terms of obligation, other Articles blend rights- and duty-based reasoning, with the latter emphasised as a means to implement the former. Article 12, paragraph 1, for example, states that 'States Parties shall assure to the child who is capable of forming his or her own views the right to express those views freely in all matters affecting the child'. This highlights the existing role for duty as a means for concretising and giving effect to children's rights. Duty similarly interacts with welfare-based reasoning in Article 3, which is one of the four guiding principles of the Convention and secures the child's 'best interests' as 'a primary consideration'. Paragraph 2 thus begins that 'States Parties undertake to ensure the child such protection and care as is necessary for his or her well-being'.

Implementation of the UNCRC is also expressed in terms of particular duties and obligations, regardless whether the Article is expressed in rights-based terms, as demonstrated in UNICEF's UNCRC *Implementation Handbook* (Hodgkin and Newell, 2007). For each Article, the authors provide detailed guidance from a number of sources, particularly the Committee on the Rights of the Child, on the interpretation of the provision in question, concluding with a checklist of general and specific measures to which State action needs to be held. It is not unusual to employ duty-based reasoning and obligations in this way, to implement broader aims. However, for a number of Articles this involves translating our aims from the language of rights into duties.

Arguments for better implementation are often couched in terms of stronger duties, as well as greater weight to be placed on, and a greater respect for, the content of these duties. Speaking extra-judicially, Baroness Hale, for example, critically compares the duty s. 11(2) of the Children Act 2004 imposes on various public bodies and

65 See, for example, the United Nations' Convention on the Rights of Persons with Disabilities (UN General Assembly, A/61/611), which, as Bartlett explains, is centred on 'the re-articulation of rights found in other treaties in ways that will make those rights meaningful to people with disabilities' (2012: 752-753). Yet, as the UNCRC, it also expresses the relationship between persons with disabilities and the goals to be achieved in a mixture of rights-based reasoning and obligations, including Articles, such as Article 11, worded solely in terms of the duty imposed on signatory states.

actors to 'make arrangements for ensuring that their functions are discharged', 'having regard to the need to safeguard and promote the welfare of children' to s. 1 of the Rights of Children and Young People (Wales) Measure 2011, which imposes a duty on Welsh Ministers to 'have due regard to the requirements of Part I of the Convention' (2013: 18-20). As Baroness Hale explains, the Welsh duty 'goes much further than the English duty, because it covers the whole range of government activity and the broad sweep of the Convention rights' (2013: 20).

The potential for improved outcomes for children in Wales is thus a product of an enhanced duty. We might wonder if governments would be more responsive to the demands of the Convention if no translation from the language of children's rights to duty were involved, and their performance were straightforwardly measured against the extent to which they fulfilled their duties. Might thinking directly in terms of duties resonate more with governments in terms of the obligations they owe children? Yet what of the argument, standardly raised in the theoretical context that, without corresponding perfect rights in every case, individual children would not be able to challenge in court the failure by state actors to fulfil their duties? Does this not create difficulties for a duty-based approach to regulating children's lives?[66] As a strict matter of theory, that seems correct. Yet the expression of children's fundamental interests as duties, not rights, in the Convention, and the translation at the implementation stage of those expressed as rights into duties reveals that children's fundamental interests are not readily capable of expression solely in terms of rights. This concern thus rests on overlooking the significant difficulties of articulating the delicately complex nature of flourishing in terms of children's rights.

Private Law Disputes Concerning Children

Lord Justice Munby's reasoning in *Re G* suggests the potential to focus more on the decision-maker within the current welfare-based framework, so that duty and virtue might operate in the first sense discussed above, as an aid to application of the current law, giving certain content and specificity to the welfare exercise. The decision concerned a private dispute between the estranged parents of five children, framed in terms of a specific issue order and residence order under s. 8 of the Children Act 1989.

At the time of the appeal, the three girls were 11, 8 and 5 years old, and the two boys, 9 and 3 years old. The parents had both been members of the ultra-Orthodox Chassidic Jewish community. After separation, however, the mother had become more moderate, though still self-identified as an Orthodox Jew. The dispute was over the education of the children although, as Munby L.J. noted, this was in effect over the rules by which one lives for the ultra-Orthodox father ([4]). The mother wanted the children to receive a more liberal Jewish education, in order to maximise the children's, particularly the girls', career and life opportunities ([54]). The father was concerned that the children's relationship with their grandparents and other rela-

66 Thanks to Jim Dwyer for raising this point.

tives would be detrimentally affected by being educated outside of the community, particularly when taken with a more liberal home life. That was also set against the negative outcome for the relationship with the mother if they persisted in the ultra-Orthodox lifestyle, which would implicitly criticise the mother's more liberal choices. Lord Justice Munby was quite clear that the court was addressing the issue solely because the parents had specifically put the issue before the court ([91-92]).

In articulating how to give content to welfare, Munby L.J. focuses on the decision-maker and asks:

> [w]hat in our society today, looking to the approach of parents generally in 2012, is the task of the ordinary reasonable parent? What is the task of a judge, acting as a 'judicial reasonable parent' and approaching things by reference to the views of reasonable parents on the proper treatment and methods of bringing up children? What are their aims and objectives? ...
>
> In the conditions of current society there are, as it seems to me, three answers to this question. First, we must recognise that equality of opportunity is a fundamental value of our society: equality as between different communities, social groupings and creeds, and equality as between men and women, boys and girls. Second, we foster, encourage and facilitate aspiration: both aspiration as a virtue in itself and, to the extent that it is practical and reasonable, the child's own aspirations. Far too many lives in our community are blighted, even today, by lack of aspiration. Third, our objective must be to bring the child to adulthood in such a way that the child is best equipped both to decide what kind of life they want to lead – what kind of person they want to be – and to give effect so far as practicable to their aspirations. Put shortly, our objective must be to maximise the child's opportunities in every sphere of life as they enter adulthood. And the corollary of this, where the decision has been devolved to a 'judicial parent', is that the judge must be cautious about approving a regime which may have the effect of foreclosing or unduly limiting the child's ability to make such decisions in future ([79-80]).

By concentrating directly on the judge's role, Munby L.J. employs duty-based reasoning to determine the best outcome on the facts. Cutting through the difficulty of giving content to the 'best interests' of the child, the judge is instead asked to reflect explicitly on their own views, assumed to be those of a judicial parent. Lord Justice Munby carefully reviews the expert report from CAFCASS, and concludes that, on the particular facts, the children's opportunities would be maximised by attending the more liberal schools proposed by the mother.

This focus on the duties of the decision-maker is particularly valuable in *Re G* because it enables the court to resolve a conflict in relation to which both parties' competing views are acceptable. In this sense, the duty-based perspective acted as the mechanism to resolve an extremely difficult 'best interests' question. The decision in *Re G* also highlights the potential for the duty-based approach to act as a mechanism for resolving disagreements grounded in cultural norms and practices. In addition to the judge being treated as a virtuous decision-maker, both parents should be treated as 'ideal' parents, such that the outcome for the child reflects the decision that 'ideal' parents would have made. Obviously, seeing the parents as virtuous decision-makers is a construct, and what it really means is that the child is entitled to be treated in such a manner as if all her interactions were 'ideal'. In this way, the duty-based approach has real potential to remove the conflict between the parents that exists when we posit the debate through the prism of rights, or the uncertainty as to whose perspective on the child's 'best interests' should count when we posit the debate through the prism of the welfare principle.

Under the duty-based approach, both parents are constructed as virtuous, thus each must make any necessary sacrifices in order to achieve the preferred outcome for children. However, there is also a real sense in which these are not real sacrifices. As Foot explains, 'there is a way in which a loving parent does not really separate *his or her good* from the good of the children' (2001: 102, emphasis in original). Yet, parents should also take into account both self-oriented and other-oriented concerns (Swanton, 2003: 244, 295) so that they are not excessively self-sacrificing. Parents' flourishing is thus inherently and complexly related to children's flourishing.

Herring and Foster propose the opposite implication of this connection between flourishing and sacrifice, contending that 'there will be circumstances in which it is in the child's/the incapacitous adult's best interests/welfare to act towards a third part in a way in which, viewed objectively, seems altruistic' (2012: 482). Elsewhere, Herring suggests that 'there will be occasions on which children will be required to make sacrifices as part of a beneficial on-going relationship' (2005: 166). But their argument overlooks what fundamentally underpins and connects all three conceptual approaches to regulating children's lives – children's rights, welfare, and duty. These approaches are premised on the view that children are a special case. Only if we abandon that view can we explain parental or judicial decisions that require children to make sacrifices as part of their relationships with their families. In drawing on virtue ethics to conceptualise flourishing as the aim of any particular approach, whether duty or welfare, we must be careful not to lose sight of the consensus to prioritise children's position.

Clearly, there will be difficult cases, as exemplified within the current law. However, this approach enables us more readily to justify to the parties involved why a father might need to be treated as if he accepts that shared residence is not best for his children, or why a recalcitrant mother, despite her hostilities, would need to agree to a schedule of increasing contact as time went on, as any virtuous parent would. As the complex reasoning in *Re G* also illustrates, the advantages of a duty-based approach may not make it any easier, only more predisposed to determine the outcome most likely to enable the particular child to flourish.

7. Conclusion

Farrelly and Solum argue that 'contemporary normative legal theory, despite its vibrancy and sophistication, is stuck in certain recurring patterns of irresolvable argument' (2008: 6). In particular, they cite the treatment over time of the antimonies of rights and consequentialism, as well as realism and formalism as support (2008: 4-5).

In this chapter, I have sought to break the stranglehold of the rights-welfare binary on thinking about how to regulate children's lives. I have contended that children's rights, welfare and duty are all simply tools for working with the same substantive content affecting outcomes for children.

This perspective is evident in recent developments in other areas of family law, notably the replacement of residence orders and contact orders in s. 8(1) of the Children Act 1989 with child arrangements orders set out in s. 12 of the Children and Families Act 2014.[67] Whilst the change in language is intended to 'encourage[e] parents to focus on their child's needs rather than what they see as their own 'rights'' (Department for Education, 2013: 13), there is also a sense in which the reform highlights the priority of outcomes over language. With the shift to a single type of order, the court and disputing parties negotiating outside of court are directed to focus exclusively on the best outcome on the facts, without being distracted by perceived status-oriented concerns about the language used to describe their involvement with the child, sustained by the bifurcation into residence and contact. It remains to be seen, however, whether that will be sustainable given the potential for s. 11's introduction of a presumption of involvement of each parent in the child's life – via a new s. 1(2A) of the Children Act 1989 – to give rise to the impression of a 'right' to involvement. The accompanying s. 1(2B) explicit disavowal of a particular starting-point for division of time to recognise involvement also highlights the centrality of the decision-maker, whether the virtuous judge, mediator, or parents, to reaching the best outcome.

There are three ways in which duty can contribute to this landscape: as a tool to give specificity and resolve conflicts in current rights- and welfare-based decision-making; as a theoretical framework of itself, focused on the decision-maker; and as the basis for anchoring a virtue-led view of the aim for legal decision-making affecting children – to enable children to flourish on their own terms.

As a framework, I have argued that a duty-based approach has a number of distinct benefits. First, it openly acknowledges the impossibility of a truly child-centred approach, which enables us to ensure that child-oriented reasoning cannot be used as a smokescreen for other parties' interests or the decision-maker's personal preferences. Instead, the decision-maker needs to ask which outcome is more likely to lead to the child's flourishing. Recognition that we cannot be genuinely child-centred thus makes it more likely that the child's interests are at the centre. Second, as a contextualised approach, it is more readily particularised to the individual child's circumstances. Third, there is reduced scope for vagueness; this is achieved through both the context-oriented role for empirical evidence and the focus on the decision-maker and their process of reasoning. Fourth, the greater likelihood of transparent reasoning in turn increases the likelihood of a better balance being struck between competing considerations. Fifth, it emphasises the justifiable and necessary place of empirical research and expert evidence on outcomes. Sixth, it removes an unnecessary layer of reasoning by focusing on those individuals who need to implement outcomes for children. Finally, it suggests a proactive attitude to improving children's circumstances,

67 Thanks to an anonymous reviewer for raising this point.

compared with the reactive children's rights and welfare-oriented perspectives. As a result, my virtue-inspired account better enables us to implement the concern and respect for children upon which thinking in terms of children's rights or welfare is justified.

Giving the keynote address at the Association of Lawyers for Children Annual Conference in November 2012, Ryder J., as he then was, suggested a new role for judges, particularly in the public law context. Noting that the welfare principle was 'arguably too subjective' (2012: 4), he proceeded to suggest that there was a need to adopt 'an investigative rather than an adversarial system of justice' (2012: 6). Within this new approach, judges would have a more active role in determining the issues for discussion and the evidence needed to reach decisions (2012: 7). Mr Justice Ryder characterised this as a shift 'into the problem solving arena ... [that will] move judges from the Hartian fount of authority, the Zeus who applies fixed rules to Dworkin's Hercules' (2012: 8), a decision-maker who will distil principles out of legal policy (2012: 8). This investigative, evidence-based role for the judiciary fits my duty-based approach. It remains to be seen to what extent, if at all, this will be reflected in the single Family Court reforms, which are now in the hands of Sir James Munby, President of the Family Division. Even if one disputes my framework argument, the fact that a duty-based approach can work within rights-, welfare-, or rights-and-welfare-based approaches, and be used as a tool for implementation, offers a more modest, and theoretically sound, option for reform.

Whilst Freeman may well not agree with my turn to focus on duty, it is in his clear, cogent articulation of the on-going very real reasons in favour of thinking of children in terms of rights that the basis of a non-rights-based approach is born. In this way, his arguments in favour of a rights-based approach unite rights advocates and sceptics: if Freeman is right about all the reasons children's rights matter, whilst children's rights are unable to achieve these reasons, sceptics are left with no choice but to look for a non-rights based methodology for achieving the aims of children's rights. In that way, Freeman's continued call to action was not merely preaching to the choir, but providing a much-needed challenge to sceptics to strive toward the same goal: improved outcomes for children. At the very least, whether my duty-based argument convinces or not, it follows in Freeman's tradition of 'keep[ing the debate] alive and healthy' (2007b: 19).

References

Amaya, A. "The Role of Virtue in Legal Justification", in A. Amaya and H. Hock Lai (eds), *Law, Virtue and Justice* (Oxford: Hart Publishing, 2013).

Anscombe, G.E. "Modern Moral Philosophy", *Philosophy* 1958, 33(124), 1-19.

Aristotle, *Nicomachean Ethics*, trans. D. Ross (Oxford; Oxford University Press, 1992).

Bainham, A. "Can We Protect Children and Protect their Rights?", *Family Law* 2002, 32(April), 279-89.

Bartlett, P. "The United Nations Convention on the Rights of Persons with Disabilities and Mental Health Law", *Modern Law Review* 2012, 75(5), 752-778.

Breen, C., *The Standard of the Best Interests of the Child: A Western Tradition in International and Comparative Law* (The Hague, Netherlands: Martinus Nijhoff, 2002).

Brennan, S. and Noggle, R. "The Moral Status of Children: Children's Rights, Parents' Rights, and Family Justice", *Social Theory and Practice* 1997, 23(1), 1-26.

Bridgeman, J., *Parental Responsibility, Young Children and Healthcare Law* (Cambridge: Cambridge University Press, 2007).

Cave, E. and Wallbank, J. "'Minors' Capacity to Refuse Treatment: A Reply to Gilmore and Herring", *Medical Law Review* 2012, 20(3), 423-449.

Choudhry, S. and Fenwick, H. "Taking the Rights of Parents and Children Seriously: Confronting the Welfare Principle under the Human Rights Act", *Oxford Journal of Legal Studies* 2005, 25(3), 453-492.

Choudhry, S., Herring, J. and Wallbank, J. "Welfare, Rights, Care and Gender in Family Law" in J. Wallbank, S. Choudhry, and J. Herring (eds), *Rights, Gender, and Family Law* (Abingdon, UK: Routledge, 2010).

Cimino, C. F. "Private Law, Public Consequences, and Virtue Jurisprudence", *University of Pittsburgh Law Review* 2009, 71(2), 279-312.

Coady, C. A. J. "Theory, Rights, and Children: A Comment on O'Neill and Campbell", *International Journal of Law and the Family* 1992, 6(1), 43-51.

Department for Education, Cm 8540: *Children and Families Bill 2013: Contextual Information and Responses to Pre-Legislative Scrutiny* (London: HMSO, 2013).

Duff, R. A. "The Limits of Virtue Jurisprudence", *Metaphilosophy* 2003, 34(1-2), 214-224.

Dwyer, J. G., *The Relationship Rights of Children* (Cambridge: Cambridge University Press, 2006).

Dwyer, J. G., *Moral Status and Human Life: The Case for Children's Superiority* (Cambridge: Cambridge University Press, 2011).

Eekelaar, J. "The importance of thinking that children have rights", *International Journal of Law, Policy and the Family* 1992, 6(1), 221-235.

Eekelaar, J. "The interests of the child and the child"s wishes: The role of dynamic self-determinism", *International Journal of Law, Policy and the Family* 1994, 8(1), 42-61.

Eekelaar, J. "Children's rights: From battle cry to working principle", in J. Pousson-Petit (ed), *Liber Amicorum Marie-Thérèse Meulders-Klein: Droit Comparé Des Personnes Et De La Famille* (Brussels: Bruylant, 1998).

Eekelaar, J. "Beyond the Welfare Principle", *Child and Family Law Quarterly* 2002, 14(3), 237-250.

Farrelly, C. and Solum, L. B. "An Introduction to Aretaic Theories of Law" in C. Farrelly and L. B. Solum (eds), *Virtue Jurisprudence* (New York, NY: Palgrave Macmillan, 2008).

Ferguson, L., *The End of an Age: Beyond Age-Based Legal Regulation of Minors' Entitlement to Participate in and Make Health Care Treatment Decisions* (Ottawa: Law Commission of Canada, 2005), online: <http://papers.ssrn.com/sol3/papers.cfm?abstract_id=998227> (accessed 12 August 2013).

Ferguson, L. "'Families in all their Subversive Variety': Over-Representation, the Ethnic Child Protection Penalty, and Responding to Diversity whilst Protecting Children", *Studies in Law, Politics, and Society* 2014, 63, 43-87.

Ferguson, L. "Not Merely Rights for Children but Children's Rights: The Theory Gap and the Assumption of the Importance of Children's Rights", *International Journal of Children's Rights* 2013, 21(2), 177-208.

Foot, P. "Virtues and Vices", in P. Foot, *Virtues and Vices and Other Essays in Moral Philosophy* (Berkeley: University of California Press, 1978).

Foot, P., *Natural Goodness* (Oxford, UK: Oxford University Press, 2001).

Fortin, J. "Accommodating Children's Rights in a Post Human Rights Act Era", *Modern Law Review* 2006, 69(3), 299-326.

Fortin, J., *Children's Rights and the Developing Law*, 3rd ed (Cambridge: Cambridge University Press, 2009).

Freeman, M., *The Rights and Wrongs of Children* (London: Pinter, 1983).

Freeman, M. "The Best Interests of the Child? Is *The Best Interests of the Child* in the Best Interests of Children?", *International Journal of Law, Policy and the Family* 1997a, 11(3), 360-388.

Freeman, M., *The Moral Status of Children: Essays on the Rights of the Child* (Netherlands: Brill, 1997b).

Freeman, M. "The End of the Century of the Child?", *Current Legal Problems* 2000, 58(1), 505-558.

Freeman, M. "What's Right with Rights for Children?", *International Journal of Law in Context* 2006, 2(1), 89-98.

Freeman, M., *A Commentary on the United Nations Convention on the Rights of the Child, Volume 3: Article 3 – The Best Interests of the Child* (The Hague: Martinus Nijhoff, 2007a).

Freeman, M. "Why It Remains Important to Take Children's Rights Seriously", *International Journal of Children's Rights* 2007b, 15(1), 5-23.

Freeman, M. "Culture, Childhood and Rights", *The Family in Law* 2011, 5(1), 15-33.

Gilmore, S. "Disputing contact: challenging some assumptions", *Child and Family Law Quarterly* 2008, 20(3), 285-311.

Gilmore, S. and Herring, J. "'No' is the hardest word: Consent and children's autonomy", *Child and Family Law Quarterly* 2011, 23(1), 3-25.

Gilmore, S. and Herring, J. "Children's refusal of treatment: the debate continues", *Family Law* 2012, 42(August), 973-978.

Hale, B., "Who's Afraid of Children's Rights?", Inaugural Lecture for the Wales Observatory on Human Rights of Children and Young People (14 June 2013), online: <http://www.swansea.ac.uk/media/Baroness%20Hale%20Lecture%20-%20Wales%20Observatory_UNICEF%20lecture%20-%202013.pdf> (accessed: 15 July 2013).

Hansard, HL Deb vol XXX 663 col 518-527 (5 July 2004), available: <http://www.publications.parliament.uk/pa/ld200304/ldhansrd/vo040705/text/40705-04.htm> (accessed 10 July 2013).

Herring, J. "The Human Rights Act and the Welfare Principle in Family Law: Conflicting or Complementary?", *Child and Family Law Quarterly* 1999, 11(3), 223-235.

Herring, J. "Farewell Welfare?", *Journal of Social Welfare and Family Law* 2005, 27(2), 159-171.

Herring, J. "Vulnerability, Children and the Law", in M. Freeman (ed), *Law and Childhood Studies: Current Legal Issues Vol. 14* (Oxford: Oxford University Press, 2012).

Herring, J., *Family Law*, 6th ed (Harlow: Pearson, 2013).

Herring, J. and Foster, C. "Welfare means relationality, virtue and altruism", *Legal Studies*, 2012, 32(3), 480-498.

Hodgkin, R. and Newell, P., *Implementation Handbook for the Convention on the Rights of the Child*, fully revised 3rd ed (UNICEF, 2007), online: <http://www.unicef.org/publications/index_43110.html> (accessed 12 August 2013).

Hursthouse, R. "Normative Virtue Ethics", in R. Crisp (ed), *How Should One Live? Essays on the Virtues* (Oxford: Oxford University Press, 1998).

Hursthouse, R., *On Virtue Ethics* (Oxford: Oxford University Press, 1999).

Keller, S., *Partiality* (Oxford: Princeton University Press, 2013).

Kochan, D.J. "The Mask of Virtue: Theories of Aretaic Legislation in a Public Choice Perspective", *Saint Louis University Journal* 2014, 58, 295-354.

MacIntyre, A., *After Virtue* (London: Duckworth, 1985).

Morris, A. "Selective Treatment of Irreversibly Impaired Infants", *Medical Law Review* 2009, 17(3), 347-376.

O"Neill, O. "Children's Rights and Children"s Lives", *Ethics* 1998, 98(3), 445-463.

Raz, J. "Human Rights in the Emerging World Order", *Transnational Legal Theory* 2010, 1(1), 31-47.

Reece, H. "The Paramountcy Principle: Consensus or Construct?", *Current Legal Problems* 1996, 49(1), 267-304.

Royal College of Paediatrics and Child Health, *Withholding or Withdrawing Life Sustaining Treatment in Children: A Framework for Practice*, 2nd ed (RCPCH, 2004), online: <http://www.gmc-uk.org/Witholding.pdf_40818793.pdf> (accessed 12 January 2014).

Ryder, E., Association of Lawyers for Children: Annual Conference Keynote Speech *<www.alc.org.uk/uploads/Keynote_speech_16_Nov_123.pdf>* (2012) (accessed 12 August 2013).

Sherry, S. "Judges of Character", in C. Farrelly and L. B. Solum (eds), *Virtue Jurisprudence* (New York: Palgrave Macmillan, 2008).

Singer, J. W. "Normative Methods for Lawyers", *UCLA Law Review* 2009, 56(4), 899-982.

Slote, M. "Agent-Based Virtue Ethics", *Midwest Studies in Philosophy* 1995, 20(1), 83-101.

Solum, L. B. "Virtue Jurisprudence: A Virtue-Centred Theory of Judging", *Metaphilosophy* 2003, 34(1/2), 178-213.

Solum, L.B. "Natural Justice", in C. Farrelly and L.B. Solum (eds), *Virtue Jurisprudence* (New York: Palgrave Macmillan, 2008).

Swanton, C., *Virtue Ethics: A Pluralistic View* (Oxford: Oxford University Press, 2013).

Tobin, J. "Justifying Children"s Rights", *International Journal of Children's Rights*, 2013, 21(3), 395-441.
Todres, J. "Emerging Limitations on the Rights of the Child: The UN Convention on the Rights of the Child and its Early Case Law", *Columbia Human Rights Law Review* 1998, 30(1), 159-200.
Van Krieken, R. "The 'Best Interests of the Child' and Parental Separation: on the 'Civilizing of Parents'", *Modern Law Review* 2005, 68(1), 25-48.
Waldron, J., "Human Rights: A Critique of the Raz/Rawls Approach", *NYU Public Law and Legal Theory Research Paper Series*, Working Paper No 13-32 (2013), online: <http://papers.ssrn.com/sol3/papers.cfm?abstract_id=2272745> (accessed 12 August 2013).

Michael Freeman's Contribution to Childhood Rights

Mark Henaghan
Professor and Dean of Law, University of Otago Faculty of Law*

1. Introduction

Michael Freeman has made an immense contribution to the field of children's rights throughout his career. His theory of children's rights, first proposed in his work *The Rights and Wrongs of Children* (1983), has stood the test of time because of its emphasis that children's rights must be grounded in a contemporary understanding of children and their development, within the confines of what is achievable within existing political structures. It is an approach based on realism, which places importance on the social context of children who influence (and are influenced by) others through their relationships.

This chapter will analyse the fundamental tenets of Freeman's theory of children's rights, and will discuss why children's rights are important and how such rights can be implemented. It will demonstrate that Freeman's theory is a radical one that if fully adopted would lead to a more diverse, open and inclusive society.

2. Freeman's Theory in Context

From an early stage Freeman was concerned about the trite nature of children's rights discourse, observing that he had been 'struck by the intemperate nature of some of the proposals and by the lack of a coherent structure' (*ibid*: i). A major hurdle faced by proponents of children's rights was the implications of HLA Hart's 'will theory' of rights which identifies rights holders *only* by virtue of their ability to enforce or waive the right in question (Freeman, 1995: 52). This would deny rights to those lacking competence to make decisions (such as disabled children) or those in respect of whom no enforcement mechanisms are accessible.[1] An early response to this position

1 In fact, Scottish legal philosopher Neil MacCormick relied on the children's rights paradigm as a test-case in demonstrating how impoverished will theory actually is and in proposing an 'interest theory' of rights (MacCormick, 1982: 154). He argues that will theory 'puts the cart before the horse' in insisting on there being a means to remedy a right

A. Diduck, N. Peleg, H. Reece (eds.), Law in Society: Reflections on Children, Family, Culture and Philosophy
 Printed in The Netherlands. ISBN 978-90-04-26148-8. pp. 191-202.

came from the 'liberationists' such as Holt, Farson, and Cohen (and more recently Harris and Franklin) who propounded the equal treatment of children and adults, arguing that 'even young children are capable of competent thought and of making informed choices, (see Fortin, 2003: 6). While these claims served as an impetus for the development of the movement, they were radical and according to Freeman – who distinguished himself from the liberationists as early as 1983 – they were 'politically naïve, philosophically faulty and plainly ignoring psychological evidence' (Freeman, 1983: 2, 3. See also Holt, 1975 and Friedenberg, 1971). Instead, he takes a middle position that while rights *can* be justified on the basis of a child's incapacity or immaturity, they should simultaneously be brought 'to a capacity where they are able to take full responsibility as free, rational agents for their own system of needs' (Freeman, *ibid*: 57, cited in Fortin, 2003: 6).

In fact, this theoretical tension between protecting children and giving them the autonomy to make their own decisions – a dichotomy framed as the distinction between 'protecting children and protecting their rights' (Farson, 1978: 165 cited in Freeman, 1983: 5) – is at the core of Freeman's theory of children's rights, which is distinct in proposing a *continuum* encompassing both positions. Freeman's theory is one of liberal paternalism,[2] under which interventions into the lives of others would be permissible to protect them against 'irrational' actions (Freeman, 1992: 38). Critically, he champions the primacy of children's rights, which he justifies – in response to criticism from those such as Martin Guggenheim who argue the children's rights discourse undermines the interests of others, such as parents (Guggenheim, 2005)[3] – in the following terms:

---

before one can accept the existence of that right (Fortin, 2003: 14). Instead, he posits that rights exist *regardless* of the obligor's performance (for instance, if a parent defaults on their right to care for their child, the child still has the right). For more, see Picton Howell, 2010). Picton Howell characterises Freeman as an advocate of MacCormick's 'interest theory' of rights (*ibid*: 6). Interestingly, Freeman has also observed that 'many references to children's rights turn out on inspection to be aspirations for the accomplishment of particular social or moral goals' (1983: 37, cited in Fortin, 2003: 13).

2 Freeman himself notes the ideological similarity of his position to John Eekelaar's theory of 'dynamic self-determinism', the goal of which is 'to bring a child to the threshold of adulthood with the maximum opportunities to form and pursue life-goals which reflect as closely as possible an autonomous choice' (Eekelaar, 1994: 53 in Freeman, 2011: 17-18). He also notes Jane Fortin's comments that '[t]here are respectable jurisprudential arguments for maintaining that a commitment to the concept of children's rights does not prevent interventions to stop children making dangerous short-term choices, thereby protecting their potential for long-term autonomy' (Fortin, 2004: 259 cited in Freeman, *ibid*: 18).

3 While Guggenheim is clear that he is against improper use of the 'children's rights' rhetoric rather than the movement himself, he is a vocal advocate for the parental rights doctrine as 'the only way to constrain government from over-intrusion into the family, (26); and contends that the transfer of power from parents (who are best able to serve their children's interests) to the state (who must rely on the 'best interests' doctrine) creates a chaotic situation for all parties.

> Children are especially vulnerable. They have fewer resources – material, psychological, relational – upon which to call in situations of adversity [...] For too long they have been regarded as objects of concern (sometimes, worse, as objects), rather than as persons, and even today they remain voiceless, even invisible, and it matters not that the dispute is about them (Freeman, 2011: 18).

III. Freeman's Theory of Children's Rights

Having established that Freeman's theory of children's rights is one of liberal paternalism grounded in the reality of the particular child's life (Freeman, 1983: 4), several features in particular merit closer attention.

a. *A Realistic Conception of Childhood*

At the core of Freeman's theory of children's rights is the necessity for society to provide 'a childhood for every child' (Gerzon, 1973, cited in Freeman, 1983: 3). Within this, he observes that the very notion of childhood is constructed by adults who 'impose their conceptions of childishness on beings whom they consider to be children (Freeman, *ibid*: 7).[4] Freeman notes for instance that in Dickens' time, girls could be married and in control of households by the time they were 13 or 14 (*ibid*: 10),[5] and young children worked for a living; whereas today we expect them to learn and play. Freeman argues that this emergence of childhood as a concept is due in part to the growth of capitalism and the nascent bourgeoisie, as the increased complexities of life demanded education and training. The result was that children no longer regulated themselves, but instead were 'trained out of [their] childish ways into normal and rational perfection of regulated manhood, (Coveny, 1967: 40 cited in Freeman, *ibid*: 11). Ultimately, Freeman posits that children are fundamentally distinct from adults, with different needs, claims, and interests (*ibid*: 12; see also Kellmer-Pringle, 1980). A central feature of this difference is their dependence on adults, which is the corollary of the human state of continuing development and maturity (ibid: 120).[6] In addition, the vast literature on child development, and neuroscientific studies, demonstrate that younger children think in a different way than older children and differently from adults (*ibid*: 12 citing Piaget, 1926; and for a more recent theory, see Siegler, 1996. See also Freeman, 1998). Any workable theory of children's rights must

---

4 Freeman also discusses the work of Phillippe Ariès, who argues the concept of childhood is a modern invention. Ariès is careful to distinguish childhood from affection for children: '[the idea of childhood] corresponds to an awareness of the particular nature of childhood, that particular nature which distinguishes the child from the adult, (Ariès, 1962: 28 cited in Freeman, 1983: 8).

5 Freeman notes Aries' comment that even in the 17th century 'by the age of ten, girls were already little women' (Ariès, 1962: 332).

6 Freeman cites Nicholas Tucker's observation that 'man is born very much unfinished, (Tucker, 1977: 31).

therefore accommodate this; recognising and accepting the reality rather than the ideal of children.

b. Primary Principles

Freeman's conception of children's rights, based as it is on modern theories of child development, is not only realistic but also – crucially – allows for each child's personality to emerge and be given full expression. He propounds the need for 'a fine balance, so that the personality and autonomy of children are recognised and they are not abandoned to their rights' (Freeman, 1983: i).[7] At the core of this balance are a number of social principles, such as the right to equal concern and respect. While this does not amount to equal treatment, it requires society to give the interests, competency and capacity of children the same concern and respect as those of adults when making decisions. Freeman emphasises flexibility over certainty, and as such any application of rights depends on the child and context, not a mechanical application (*ibid*: 4). This avoids the stark approach of treating children as one block of society who should not be afforded consideration until they can understand the world as adults do, under which their interests would be ignored until they are able to participate in political life. Freeman's theory places their interests firmly on the political agenda, and ensures the dignity and personality of each child is considered in each situation.

Freeman's theory is therefore not only realistic but is also radical in that it provides a basis for the most precious of all human goods: the freedom to develop one's own being and personality. It enables a society to constantly renew and adapt itself, as each new child brings his or her own unique personality and character to the common weel. His theory is antithetical to the position that children are simply a means to society's ends who must be moulded in certain ways to meet society's expectations. Such a pre-determined life stifles the diversity of human nature, which is so vital for survival. Freeman's theory, if adopted, would eliminate many of the psychological and emotional problems caused by controlling children and imposing society's expectations on them, rather than accepting children for who they are.

c. The Ultimate Goal

The goal of Freeman's theory is to allow children to develop rational independence (*ibid*). As this cannot be achieved at a young age without abandoning children to their rights, Freeman would impose duties on parents to prepare their children for eventual independence. As such, he frames the test for achieving this goal as follows:

---

7 An example of abandoning children to their rights would be to permit a young child to decide their own diet, which would likely lead to health problems. Alternatively, when designing a playground for young children, to ignore the needs of three and four year olds (for whom the playground is intended) would make the playground unfit for its purpose.

> We must ask ourselves the question: from what actions and decisions would we wish, as children, to be protected, on the assumption that we would in due course desire to be rationally autonomous, capable of planning our lives and deciding on our own system or ends as rational beings? (*ibid*)

From this premise, the application of children's rights would center not on age, but on the activity in question and indeed the particular child.[8] For instance, a child who has grown up on a farm may be able to ride a pony at a young age, while others of the same age, who lack the same experience with animals, would require closer supervision. Another example is that the freedom of children to walk to school alone may differ between small towns with little traffic and large cities where there are high volumes of traffic. Therefore, social structures created by adults determine what children can and cannot do of their own accord. Equally however, external socio-economic and cultural realities create environments where it may be impossible for children to thrive, such as where children are born into poverty.

This is the real rub of children's rights: how are we to determine from which actions or activities children must be protected, and to whom should this determination fall? Ultimately, where there is disagreement within a society over where the line is to be drawn, it must be resolved through the process of public debate and dialogue (Waldron, 1999). A classic example of this is the smacking debate, which sharply divides members of society into two factions: those arguing children must be protected from physical discipline, and those (often parents) who defend what they consider to be a 'right' to use this form of discipline in order to establish boundaries.[9] At the heart of this debate is the robust sentiment that governments should not control how parents raise their children (Naylor and Saunders, 2009). However, the regulation of contentious issues is precisely a matter the democratic process should – and does – resolve. It is in this way that society will evolve in harmony with the prevailing morals and social mores of the day.

Freeman's position would require a general shift in social attitudes, because children – excluded as they are from the political process – could not effect change alone. This demonstrates that at its heart, Freeman's theory is essentially political in nature. Its aim is that, once children's rights are accepted as a feature of the political landscape, account will be taken of children's interests in the setting of policy at a governmental level. This would make governments accountable to children's interests and would impose a check on their power. Those who oppose children's rights argue that children should *not* be given the right to express views on matters that affect them,[10] not only because it will render them self-centered, but because they funda-

8 In fact, Freeman expressly warns against the use of 'unhelpful' rigid age stereotypes (*ibid*).

9 For more on the New Zealand context, see Austin, 2010; Page, 2011; Hornibrook, 2008; and Ahdar and Allan, 2001).

10 A right enshrined, for instance, in Art 12 of the United Nations Convention on the Rights of the Child 1989.

mentally lack the wisdom and experience to give meaningful views that should carry any weight (see Guggenheim, 2005). However, empirical research demonstrates that children whose views are taken into account are more satisfied with the outcomes, even if their views are not fully adopted (Parkinson and Cashmore, 2008). Whether the outcomes of such decisions are measurably better or not, the fact that those affected by a decision – as well as the decision-maker – are happy about it is a form of progress in itself. Further empirical evidence shows that inclusive societies, where wide ranges of people contribute to policy formation, function better in comparison to other societies (Acemoglu and Robinson, 2012).

IV. The Importance and Utility of a Children's Rights Framework

A conception of children's rights is essential to underpin the public debate furthering children's interests. Rights are 'valuable and distinctive moral commodities' (Wassterstrom, 1964: 629, cited in Freeman, 1983: 32), which not only give their holder dignity and confidence, but also provide a stake in the ground whereby redress is possible (Freeman, *ibid:* 33). Freeman argues that without rights 'children easily become victims' (Freeman, 1995: 54) because rights provide the moral justification for claims.[11] The establishment of a rights framework therefore ensures that attention is given to the interests at stake, and that actions or decisions are justified in view of which rights have priority.

However, there are several important limitations to the utility of such a framework. Because the emerging field of children's rights remains largely open to interpretation – Hillary Rodham describes it as 'a slogan in search of a definition' (Rodham, 1973, cited in Freeman, 1983: 34) – there is a risk it will 'backfire' by being taken either too far or not far enough (Freeman, *ibid*: 34). On the one hand, the liberationists' extreme case may be so naïve as to undermine the credibility of the whole argument in favour of children's rights. On the other hand, there is a danger that words alone will be mistaken for deeds. As Gross and Gross put it:

> The rights of children is an abstract, general, legalistic concept. It is an idea, an ideal, at best an affirmation of principle. It does not help children until it is put into practice. If it is ignored, obstructed, or perverted, it does no good; in fact, it may do harm, because many people will take the words for the act and think that because the words have been spoken the condition of children's lives has changed (Gross and Gross, 1977: 7, cited in Freeman, *ibid*: 33).

Rights are only effective in their implementation: as Freeman argues, 'rights without services are meaningless' (Paulsen, 1967, cited in Freeman, *ibid*: 33). Freeman's theory responds to this limitation by encouraging the phenomenon of children's rights to be regularly scrutinised and updated in order to best fit the contemporary society

---

11 Although it must be noted that rights are not foolproof, as in most cases a competing right can also be identified.

in which children live. For instance, although the United Nations Convention on the Rights of the Child contains a wide range of rights, it does not include the right to 'nourishment' both in the physical sense of food and the psychological sense of love and care. This is arguably the most basic need of all; there is a great deal of empirical evidence demonstrating that exposure to safe and healthy environments in the first three years of life is likely to have long term consequences in terms of the child's future academic achievement and their ability to contribute to society later in life.[12] Yet this right is perhaps so basic it is taken for granted and assumed to be present in all children's lives. Even in a country so rich in natural resources as New Zealand, around 25 per cent of children live in poverty (Craig *et al.*, 2013:14).[13] A framework of rights that recognises evolving circumstances would give substance to that most basic principle of a child's right to healthy food, and a healthy home; the implementation of which would lead to meaningful change for the next generation.

V. Enforcing Children's Rights in Practice

Martha Minow has argued that the failure of children's rights initiatives can be attributed, at least in part, to the fact that children lack both the right to vote and a lobbying group to speak on their behalf (Minow, 1995, cited in Dalrymple, 2006: 141). Freeman, an academic of action, believes theory is futile unless put into practice. He argues, as noted above, that children's rights should be firmly embedded in the policy-making process and identifies the importance of meaningful child advocacy. As he put it:

> If children's rights are to be more than a political slogan, then children must demand them and must be encouraged and educated to do so. Access to people, lawyers and others, with an expertise and a commitment will enable the young to develop the sort of claims consciousness which is a part of a rational autonomy (Freeman, 1983: 281).

a. Implementation

Freeman identifies implementation as the major hurdle for children's rights, particularly in the context of international legal instruments.[14] Without the ability to vote, children rely on adult support or existing institutional structures to represent

12 For more information about the long term effects of children's childhood experiences see generally Craig et al, 2013; the Children's Commission Expert Advisory Group on Solutions to Child Poverty, 2012; and the Dunedin Multidisciplinary Health & Development Research Unit.

13 Poverty is defined as 'deprivation of the material resources and income that is required for [children] to develop and thrive, leaving such children unable to enjoy their rights, achieve their full potential and participate as equal members of New Zealand society' (Children's Commission Expert Advisory Group on Solutions to Child Poverty, 2012: 2).

14 In the words of Thomas Hobbes, 'Covenants, without the Sword, are but Words and of no strength to secure a man at all' (Thomas Hobbes, *Leviathan Part II: Of Commonwealth* (1651) at Chapter XVII, p 85).

and strengthen their interests, without which they may be left off the policy agenda. However, consider the built-in implementation mechanism of the United Nations Convention on the Rights of the Child 1989 (Freeman, 2000: 289-90):[15] it is effectively toothless, as it relies on parties to respond to international pressure or opprobrium. Reports made to governments may not be implemented where there is insufficient political will or machinery, and the international treaty system lacks the resources to undertake a thorough investigation of individual State party compliance. For instance, New Zealand last appeared before the Committee in January 2011 where its combined third and fourth periodic review, submitted in 2008, was examined. The committee issued a number of concluding observations,[16] yet the UNCROC Monitoring Group issued a report in June 2012 observing the lack of formal steps taken to date by the New Zealand Government in response.[17]

To ensure effective implementation, Freeman propounds the need for a Cabinet Minister who is solely responsible for children's rights (Freeman, 2000: 280). While the democratic process means there would be no guarantee of success, this would at least ensure children and their interests are represented in the development and implementation of policy at the highest level. Nonetheless, Freeman is a realist and recognises that a strategy of moving forward on all fronts is needed for children's rights to be truly embedded into the fabric of a society. As such, he recognises the importance of grassroots networks (*ibid*: 280), as well as moves within international institutions such as proposals to establish a Permanent Bureau for Children with an attached International Code of Children's Rights in the Hague. To guard against such an institution becoming overbureaucratised and existing for its own ends rather than those of the children, the fundamental principle for such a Bureau must be that all its actions and decisions are based on thorough and accountable consultation with a wide range of children from a wide range of cultures and backgrounds.

---

15 The mechanism in this case effectively comprises a Committee on the Rights of the Child, established under Article 43 of the Convention, which considers reports submitted every five years by State parties to the Convention on their compliance. Other United Nations bodies (and in some cases non-governmental organisations or other specialized agencies) often participate in the consideration of reports, increasing the accountability of member States across the United Nations network.

16 These included the withdrawal of reservations to the Convention, the establishment of a permanent mechanism to ensure high-level and effective coordination of the Convention's implementation, and the taking of urgent measures to address disparities in access to services of Māori children and their families. See the New Zealand Human Rights Commission website (<www.hrc.co.nz>).

17 UNCROC Monitoring Group "Monitoring the Implementation of the United Nations Convention on the rights of the Child in New Zealand [Report 1: Implementation of UNCROC (Articles 4, 42 44)]" (June 2012) <www.occ.org.nz>. The Group, convened by the Children's Commissioner, includes members of UNICEF New Zealand, Save the Children New Zealand, Every Child Counts, and the Child Poverty Action Group. It meets quarterly to review the progress made on the implementation of the Convention.

b. *Advocacy*

The other key aspect to rights enforcement is the role played by children's rights advocates, who are on the front line of holding society accountable. The importance of advocacy is illustrated in particular by the case of the 'left-outs': Freeman observes that *even when* a society recognises children's rights, some children will nonetheless be left out when it comes to the implementation of their rights. Disabled children, gay children, street children and refugee children are cited as examples of children whose rights are more vulnerable (Freeman, *ibid*). These subgroups are minorities, often not visible in a society, frequently misunderstood in terms of their capabilities and needs, and sometimes even incorrectly seen as a burden to society.[18] Advocacy is critical in such cases, as without it children who would otherwise have no access to power, decision-making or influence risk becoming invisible, marginalised, and forgotten.

Advocacy is not easy. In the absence of any measure for what is 'morally right' (see Waldron, 1999), children's rights advocates must employ many techniques of persuasion, such as appeals to important values in society or consequential arguments as to the cost of inaction; and they must also set the best possible examples in their own practices. While the development of active advocacy may have been slow, it is 'undoubtedly an expanding field that is likely to lead to increased use of procedures by children and their representatives' (NGO Working Group, 2009). Already a number of non-governmental organisations act as advocates for children,[19] and children are on occasion independently legally represented in order that their views and positions can be recognised in court. An important instance of this was in *ZH (Tanzania) (FC) v Secretary of State for the Home Department*, where the United Kingdom Supreme Court considered the principle of the 'best interests of the child' ([2001] UKSC 4). This case concerned the proposed deportation of a Tanzanian woman, whose two children were British citizens (as was their father). The Supreme Court emphasised the importance of discovering the child's own views, and held that 'the important thing is that those conducting and deciding these cases should be alive to the point and prepared to ask the right questions' (*ibid*: para 36). Similarly, a recent best practice guide makes the following point:

> [The United Kingdom Supreme Court's] emphasis on listening to the child and taking their wishes and feelings properly into account may yet prove to be a more fundamental

---

18 For instance, Freeman notes that 'there is urgent need to review policing policies in relation to children on the streets – too many are treated as criminals or vagrants and punished accordingly, (Freeman, *ibid:* 285).

19 Examples include Amnesty International (www.amnesty.org), Oxfam (www.oxfam.org), Save the Children (www.savethechildren.org); see also Save the Children *Advocacy Matters: Helping children change their world (An International Save the Children Alliance guide to advocacy)* (2007) <www.savethechildren.org.uk>) and the Women's Refugee Commission (www.womensrefugeecommission.org). Local organisations also offer similar advocacy support, such as the Refugee and Migrant Forum East London (www.ramfel.org.uk).

> shift [...] it will require legal representatives, decision-makers and the courts to re-think their procedures where children's interests are affected, and to ensure that they have the skills and processes necessary for effective interaction with children in a way which provides child-friendly access to justice (Bolton *et al.*, 2012: 15).

Such comments are significant beyond their specific context of a court case or practitioners' manual: they demonstrate the shift in consciousness in favour of giving substance to children's rights, and they reflect the important dual roles played by policy-makers and advocates.

VI. Conclusion

Based on his pioneering and original work in *The Rights and Wrongs of Children*, Freeman has continued to write eloquently and strongly on children's rights. His core commitment to a theory rooted in liberal paternalism remains unchanged, although its application has widened in scope (see, for example, Freeman, 1997 and Freeman, 2005). His prime aim has always been to hold decision-makers accountable for how they work with children and protect their interests. He urges a conception of children's rights, which, far from being a static phenomenon, is constantly rethought in order to adapt to the changing world in which children live. Freeman's work is widely cited and has been hugely influential in inspiring a whole generation of children's rights advocates, of which I am privileged to be one. Ultimately, in Michael Freeman's words:

> The case for children's rights will prevail. We have to believe this because out of it will emerge a better world for children and this will redound to the benefit not only of children but of all of us (Freeman, 2011: 23).

References

Acemoglu, D., and Robinson, J. A., *Why Nations Fail: The Origins of Power, Prosperity, and Poverty* (New York: Crown Publishing Group, 2012).

Ahdar, R., and Allan, J., "Taking Smacking Seriously: The Case for Retaining the Legality of Parental Smacking in New Zealand", *New Zealand Law Review* 2001, 1-34.

Ariès, P., (trans. R. Baldick), *Centuries of Childhood* (London: Jonathan Cape, 1962).

Austin, G., "The amendment to section 59 of the Crimes Act 1961: A case study in the process of legislative change" (Master of Laws thesis, University of Waikato, 2010).

Bolton, S., Kaur, K., Luh, S. S., Peirce, J. and Yeo, C., *Working with refugee children: Current issues in best practice* (2nd edn) (London: Immigration Law Practitioners' Association, 2012).

Children's Commission Expert Advisory Group on Solutions to Child Poverty, *Solutions to Child Poverty in New Zealand: Evidence for Action* (Wellington: Children's Commissioner, December 2012).

Coveney, P., *The Image of Childhood* (Harmondsworth: Penguin, 1967).

Dalrymple, J.K., "Seeking Asylum Alone: Using the Best Interests of the Child Principle to Protect Unaccompanied Minors", *BC Third World Law Journal* 2006 26(1), 131-168.

Dunedin Multidisciplinary Health & Development Research Unit *Dunedin Multidisciplinary Health and Development Study* (<www.dunedinstudy.otago.ac.nz>).

Eekelaar, J., "The Interests of the Child and the Child's Wishes: The Role of Dynamic Self-Determinism", *International Journal of Law and the Family* 1994 8(1), 42-61.

Farson, R., *Birthrights* (Harmondsworth: Penguin, 1978).

Fortin, J., *Children's Rights and the Developing Law* (2nd edn) (Cambridge: Cambridge University Press, 2003).

Fortin J., "Children's Rights: Are the Courts Taking Them More Seriously?", *King's College Law Journal* 2004 15(2), 253-272.

Freeman, M. D. A., *The Rights and Wrongs of Children* (London: Frances Pinter, 1983).

Freeman, M., "The Limits of Children's Rights", in M. Freeman and P. Veerman (eds), *The Ideologies of Children's Rights* (Leiden: Brill Academic Publishers, 1992).

Freeman, M., "Taking Children's Rights More Seriously", in P. Alston, S. Parker, and J. Seymour (eds), *Children, Rights, and the Law* (Oxford: Clarendon Press, 1995).

Freeman, M., "Removing Rights from Adolescents", in M. Freeman (ed), *The Moral Status of Children* (The Hague: Kluwer Law International, 1997).

Freeman, M., "The Sociology of Childhood and Children's Rights", *International Journal of Children's Rights* 1998 6, 433-444.

Freeman, M., "The Future of Children's Rights", *Children & Society* 2000 14(4), 277-293.

Freeman, M., "Rethinking *Gillick*", *International Journal of Children's Rights* 2005 13, 201-217.

Freeman, M., "Why It Remains Important To Take Children's Rights Seriously", in M. D. A. Freeman (ed), *Children's Rights: Progress and Perspectives: Essays from the International Journal of Children's Rights* (Leiden: Martinus Nijhoff Publishers, 2011).

Friedenberg, E., (ed), *The Anti-American Generation* (New Brunswick: Transaction Publishers,1971).

Gerzon, M., *A Childhood For Every Child: The Politics of Parenthood* (New York: Outerbridge & Lazard, 1973).

Gross, B., and Gross, R. (eds), *The Children's Rights Movement* (New York: Anchor Books, 1977).

Guggenheim, M., *What's Wrong with Children's Rights?* (Cambridge Mass: Harvard University Press, 2007).

Holt, J., *Escape From Childhood* (Harmondsworth: Penguin, 1975).

Hornibrook, C., "Parental control and the child's right not to be hit" (Master of Laws thesis, University of Otago, 2008).

Kellmer-Pringle, M., *The Needs of Children* (2nd edn) (London: Hutchinson, 1980).

MacCormick, N., "Children's Rights: A Test-Case for Theories of Rights", in N. MacCormick (ed), *Legal Right and Social Democracy* (Oxford: Clarendon Press, 1984).

Minow, M., "What Ever Happened to Children's Rights?", *Minnesota Law Review* 1995 80(2), 267-298.

Naylor, B., and Saunders, B., "Whose Rights? Children, Parents and Discipline", *Alternative Law Journal* 2009 34(2), 80-85.

NGO Working Group on a Communications Procedure for the CRC Draft Briefing: Children's use of international and regional human rights complaint/communications procedures (January 2009) www.crin.org.

Craig, E., Reddington, A., Wicken, A., Oben, G. and Simpson, J., *Child Poverty Monitor 2013: Technical Report* (Dunedin: Child & Youth Epidemiology Service, University of Otago, December 2013).

Page, S., "Parents' perceptions of the s 59 Crimes Act debate and law change (the "Anti-Smacking Bill")" (Master of Arts thesis, Auckland University of Technology, 2011).

Parkinson, P. and Cashmore, J., *The Voice of a Child in Family Law Disputes* (New York: Oxford University Press, 2008).

Paulsen, M., "Child Abuse Reporting Laws: The Shape of the Legislation", *Colorado Law Review* 1967 67(1), 1-49.

Piaget, J., *The Language and Thought of the Child* (London: Routledge, 1926).

Picton Howell, Z., "Disabled Children's Rights – A theoretical approach", paper presented to ESCR Seminar Series: Researching the Lives of Disabled Children and Young People (Strathclyde University, 2010).

Rodham, H., "Children Under The Law", *Harvard Educational Review* 1973 43(4), 487-514.

Siegler, R.S., *Emerging Minds: The Process of Change in Children's Thinking* (New York: Oxford University Press, 1996).

Tucker, N., *What Is A Child?* (London: Fontana, 1977).

Waldron, J., *Law and Disagreement* (New York: Oxford University Press, 1999).

Wassterstrom, R. A., "Rights, Human Rights, and Racial Discrimination", *Journal of Philosophy* 1964 61(20), 628-641.

Michael Freeman's View of Children's Rights and Some Ideas Arising from His Views

Priscilla Alderson
Professor Emerita of Childhood Studies at the Institute of Education, University College London, UK

Introduction

I will begin with four examples that illustrate the range of research and activities concerning children's rights. They lead on to a discussion about Michael Freeman's contribution to the present richly complex and evolving international understanding of children's rights, in their immense variety of social and geographical contexts, and in related activities that cover 'all matters affecting the child' (UN, 1989). They involve both universal principles and also flexible, local interpretations and applications.

The theory and practice of children's rights are further developed through the complicated range of speakers and actors: children, young people and adults; specialists from many academic disciplines; professionals and policymakers in state, voluntary, commercial and international agencies; those who plan and provide services and those who use them. A few of Michael's crucial contributions to these debates and developing knowledge through his writing, lectures and editing will be reviewed.

Scholars and advocates from a range of disciplines and professions have analysed and conducted research related to the UNCRC. Some childhood specialists are very familiar with the law (for example, Judy Cashmore, Megan Gollop, Jane Fortin, Laura Lundy, Aoife Nolan, Nicola Taylor, Kay Tisdall, Carolyn Willow with colleagues at CRAE, Karen Winter and others). Yet there has not always been a clear grasp of the basically legal nature of the UNCRC and of rights. Children's rights are more than 'participation', or contingent social constructs. Michael's incisive legal approach to children's rights will be considered. It is grounded in his knowledge of international, statutory and common law, medical and family law, jurisprudence and the history of human rights, as well as his robust defences of children's rights. He combines academic and practical advocacy approaches to children's rights. I will mention some of his criticisms of UNCRC and his interest in actively furthering children's rights. In the final chapter in this volume Michael gives a more direct and detailed account of his views of children's rights, which are also further discussed in other chapters. I will simply review and comment on some of his main concerns, and then also add some ideas, which have been encouraged by his work, and with which I hope he would agree.

A. Diduck, N. Peleg, H. Reece (eds.), Law in Society: Reflections on Children, Family, Culture and Philosophy
 ISBN 978-90-04-26148-8. pp. 203-221.

Four Examples

The examples illustrate a little of the range of research about children's rights.

(1) Australian lawyers were interviewed about their work of defending Aboriginal families, whose children are removed by social workers. Indigenous children make up only three per cent of the population, but they are 24 per cent of children placed in care. In Queensland nearly half of all infants aged under one year placed in care are indigenous babies.

> 'Lawyer 1. Most parents whose children are removed have been removed themselves [as children from their families].
> Lawyer 2. So that's pain on top of pain...Five generations in some families now.'

The lawyers wanted the children's human rights and their history to be understood and respected by the social workers who tended to be young and inexperienced (Douglas and Walsh, 2013).

(2) Many thousands of young people each year are excluded from school. This sets them at higher risk of losing their school education and qualifications, and of engaging in unhealthy and criminal behaviours, with potentially very long-term adverse effects. Researchers have examined how school policies ignore children's rights, and how applying the United Nations 1989 Convention on the Rights of the Child (UNCRC) could inform and transform these school policies (Hemphill and Schneider, 2013).

(3) Children who work as domestic servants more or less fulltime – or very much overtime – are particularly hidden away from the public. They are therefore most vulnerable to abuse. Many are trafficked or coerced. Yet many others, wisely or not, decide to migrate and take on this domestic work, hoping to increase their family's income or at least not to be a burden to their parents.

All children work, at school, and usually at home, besides often having part-time employment. Therefore to make all work or specific types of work illegal for all children, or for children under certain ages, raises problems.

It can disrespect their valuable contributions to society and to their family.

- It can disrespect the fact that their employed work is often essential to pay for their food and schooling and other family expenses.
- It can remove vital legal protections from working children.
- It can increase the risks that children outside the law will be trafficked, concealed, exploited or abused.

If migrant young domestic workers are discovered in households in Britain, would it therefore be better to treat some of them as capable agents rather than as helpless victims? How might this respect their UNCRC rights, especially Articles 3 (best interests), 12 (right to express views), and 32 (protection from economic exploitation and hazardous work)? How could this connect to national and international law? Would these children and young people be better served if English law recognised the rights of certain minors to choose to migrate and to work in Britain? (Scullion, 2013).

(4) The UN Security Council works to maintain world peace and security and to prevent violations of human rights, by setting standards and influencing national and international law, though it does not make law. Whereas the Council respects adults primarily in terms of their human rights, the Council tends to favour the protection of children over all their other human rights.

This does not necessarily best promote the rights and freedoms, for example, of children affected by armed conflict: their rights to life, survival and development, to healthcare and education, to promotion of their best interests, to non-discrimination, to express their views and to be heard, as well as the decision of many to become child soldiers. It is paradoxical and self-defeating to exclude children from the Council's main concern and guiding priority with human rights.

Sarah Field documents the disadvantages for children of their exclusion from human rights, and concludes that the Security Council is insufficiently influenced by the UNCRC. Instead, it is driven by social conceptions of immature children and by biomedical models of children's vulnerability and reactions to adversity. However, the UNCRC, she argues, provides a framework:

> for negotiating the chaotic fusion of social conditioning, emotion and powerful interests that weave through political decision-making about children, in order to refocus on children's interdependent rights (Field, 2013: 160-161).

Understanding and Advocating Children's International Rights

The four examples will be familiar to readers of *The International Journal of Children's Rights* (IJCR). They all appear in a single issue (2013: 21(1)), illustrating the way examples from around the world and from every UNCRC article and concern are packed together. IJCR has played a key part in building up the living, international, widely interdisciplinary study and debate about children's rights, with close links to policy and practice. For 21 years the IJCR has consistently been doing the sterling work of negotiating 'the chaotic fusion of emotions, myths and powerful interests' (Field, 2013) that can both undermine but also promote children's rights. And the IJCR keeps redrawing everyone's attention to those specific rights.

As the founder-editor of the IJCR, Michael Freeman has immensely contributed to the present richly complex international understanding of children's rights. The IJCR does justice to these rights in their variety of social and geographical contexts, covering 'all matters affecting the child' (UN, 1989), in other words, every aspect of life, with examples from every part of the world.

Understanding of children's rights is further developed through a complicated range of speakers and actors. In its reports of research and activity with children, young people and adults, the IJCR publishes papers by specialists from many academic disciplines. The work of professionals and policymakers in state, voluntary, commercial and international agencies is reported and critically discussed along with the views of those who plan and provide services and those who use them. Work that unreservedly supports children's rights as well as cautious or sceptically critical work is published and reviewed. All help to promote debate leading towards greater knowledge and evolving awareness in Michael's edited books and the IJCR. The fat later volumes of the IJCR, compared with the thin earlier ones, show the great increase of interest and activity around children's rights, for which the IJCR can take some credit. The increase is also shown in the IJCR's rate of rejecting submitted papers, which has doubled from around 30 per cent to around 60 per cent today.

Besides the daunting demands of teaching, lecturing at many conferences, convening these annual colloquia on 15 different topics in relation to law, and editing the 15 books that report them, as well as editing other journals, Michael has published over 60 books, and many chapters and papers. He is a very involved editor of the IJCR, frequently reviewing the submitted papers and often writing the book reviews. His book reviews note errors frankly. For example, on a book that aims to present a critical philosophy of rights law, he commented: 'This is a noble ideal, but whether the book as a whole lives up to it may be doubted' (Freeman, 2013a). Michael's reviews also do the vital work, too rarely undertaken, of critiquing books, which attend mainly or only to adults and generally ignore children, and of showing how fully relevant these works are to children too (just one example is Freeman, 2013b). His reviews are usually encouraging as well as critical – unless the book opposes children's rights without convincing logic or evidence. There is his well-known demolition of Martin Guggenheim's (2005) book, *What's Wrong with Children's Rights?,* in the paper, *What's Right with Children's Rights?* (Freeman, 2006).

Academics generally aim to hold mixed, cautious and inquiring views about any topic they research, but many academics also attempt to sit on an imaginary neutral fence, such as trying to hover somewhere between being basically either pro- or anti-children's rights. 'Objectivity' involves the crucial values of being fair and open-minded, of striving to analyse and understand all relevant data impartially, and to work towards balanced conclusions with a certain detachment that avoids prejudice, bias, self-interest and premature judgments. However, 'objectivity' is sometimes hijacked also to mean 'value-free', as if no academic should have guiding values, or at least should not let these influence their work (see for example, Hammersley, 1995; Seale, 1999). (These authors do have values, but they count their 'liberal' views as neutral, in contrast to 'ideologies' such as feminism).

Steven Lukes (2008) and Andrew Sayer (2011) show at great length that relativist claims to be 'value-free' are illusions and deceptions, because values are central not only to researchers' own lives, but also to the topics and the people they are researching. Human life and relationships can only be understood in relation to inherent values such as honesty, respect, justice, equality and compassion, or their opposites. Michael's academic experience helps him to be objective, while his barrister training also helps him to be a strong advocate of children's rights, prepared to admit and explain his values of respect for them. He protests against corporal punishment

(Freeman, 1999) and supports children's viewpoints, critical of groundless complacence when 'smug satisfaction still oozes from the government' (Freeman, 2002: 97).

Childhood Studies and Children's Rights

Editing the IJCR and reading the submitted papers, both accepted and rejected, means that Michael probably knows more than anyone in the world about the whole current range of children's rights activity and research in law and policy, in anthropology, sociology, geography, psychology, social work, history, healthcare, education, economics, cultural and media studies, crime, youth studies, comparative and development studies, and other disciplines, as well as by NGOs in every continent. This involves some understanding of different theories and methods, technical terms and concepts in each discipline. His interest in different disciplines is shown in the 15 multi-disciplinary colloquia 'Law and –' he convened. The 14th colloquium, 'Law and Childhood Studies', was followed by a book of 30 chapters, which included Michael's comprehensive introduction and his review, 'Towards a Sociology of Children's Rights' (Freeman, 2012: 1-9, 29-38).

Michael is one of the few lawyers working, speaking and writing on adult and child rights and law, and also on childhood studies. He works to bridge the gaps between lawyers and social researchers, and to promote cross-disciplinary, critical debate. He commented:

> Each discipline can learn much from the other but I suggest the law has most need of Input... one employs research methodology, the other tests out ideas pragmatically from case to case (Freeman, 2012: 9).

The pragmatic legal testing can be greatly informed by the wealth of social research about children's diverse views and experiences, needs and interests, and by sensitive methods of communicating, which researchers have developed with children and young people. Karen Winter's book (2011) based on her PhD research reported her skilful new approaches to listening to children aged four to seven years, who had been severely neglected and abused. For example, Karen sat next to each child instead of opposite them, which could be potentially intimidating and overbearing. Able to avoid eye contact if they chose, while they talked the children decorated shoe boxes with art work and drawings. On the outside they showed the kind of person they were or felt they seemed to be, and on the inside they expressed their 'wishes and feelings', to which the 1989 Children Act requires professionals to listen. The children were able to control the pace and topics during the interviews; if they wished to avoid or delay answering a question, they could deflect it by saying, 'pass the glue', or by being absorbed in their art work.

Although the youngest children are at highest risk of severe and even lethal abuse, and although repeated public inquiries stress the urgent need for adults to listen to them, these children are still seldom heard. Most lawyers and social workers appear to believe that either these children cannot express their views, and/or they do not have views worth expressing. As Karen's supervisor, I was impressed that her young interviewees shared such profound views with her about their hard lives, which she reported and analysed so carefully. As one of her viva examiners, Michael showed his concern and respect for these very young children's views and rights and for Karen's important work on developing listening methods for professionals to use.

Childhood studies differ from the older and still dominant discipline of child development. Child development theory stems from bio-medical traditions, including the philosopher, doctor and educationalist John Locke in the 17th century up to today's medico-psychological experts (Hardyment, 1984). Children's gradual cognitive development mapped, for example, by Jean Piaget (1928) tends to be seen as a universal genetic unfolding that mirrors physical growth (Morss, 1990). Another medical influence is the emphasis in child psychology on identifying the abnormal or pathological, in the hope of providing preventions and remedies to such problems. However, if psychometrics treat children mainly in terms of pathologies and problems, which are given high scores, and dismiss 'normality' with a zero score, it is hard to respect children as competent agents (Oswell, 2013) or as citizens (Cockburn, 2013). And if young children are seen as pre-social, pre-moral, quite helpless becomings and not yet human beings, they can scarcely be entitled to human rights. This poses the great problem of how rights can genuinely be 'human' if they cannot apply to every human being from birth.

In contrast to child development theory, and like the UNCRC (1989), interdisciplinary childhood studies emerged much more recently. They were formally set out, theorised and researched from around the mid-1980s. For example, with colleagues Jens Qvorturp (1991) established in a cross-European survey that childhood is a universal social phenomenon. The numbers of children in Europe were falling, while numbers of older people were rising. Children featured ever less often in public and political concerns, and they were increasingly likely to live in poverty. Jens's warnings from over 20 years ago have been vindicated by the way current austerity policies especially hurt children and young people, when they cut state benefits and services in Britain (CRAE, 2013), as well as around Europe and the United States (Nadesan, 2010), and across the globe through International Monetary Fund restructuring (Klein, 2007; Harvey, 2012). The economic oppressions increase the urgent need to understand childhood through the perspectives of political and economic rights, rather than through the lens primarily of personal psychological development. The IJCR plays a vital part in mapping children's economic needs and rights around the world (among many examples see Nolan, 2013).

Childhood studies move on from developmental psychology's concern with immature, unstable, incomplete, dependent children, who slowly work up the genetically determined stages towards mature, stable, complete, independent adulthood. Instead we recognise that people of all ages, children and adults, can be competent and incompetent, foolish and wise.

In 1990, six tenets of interdisciplinary childhood studies were proposed by Allison James and Alan Prout (1990/1997). They held that:

- Childhood is understood as a social construction, not an inevitable biological state;
- It varies in time and place, and with class, gender and ethnicity – there is not one childhood but many;
- Children's lives are worthy of study in their own right;
- Children are active agents in their own lives and relationships, not simply passive subjects of social or biological structures and processes;
- Ethnography is a particularly useful method of studying children's views and behaviours through observations, interactions and interviews directly with them (not depending wholly on adults' reports);
- In a double hermeneutic, adults and children together construct children – as helpless victims with rescuing adults, or needy dependents with providing adults, as naughty deviants with disciplining adults, or as resourceful actors interacting with respectful adults.

There were, of course, precedents. Philippe Ariès (1962) showed how today's sheltered childhoods are partly a middle-class, post-feudal invention, and John Holt (1975) advocated far more respect for children's rights. Margaret Donaldson's (1978) research demonstrated that young children are much cleverer than Piaget supposed. Her book appeared in a remarkable series in the 1970s about babies' and young children's profound understanding and agency. Myra Bluebond-Langner (1979) recorded the insight and courage of young children who had cancer, while they tried to protect their parents from stress and grief. Michael Freeman started writing about children's rights in 1980 and his *Rights and Wrongs of Children* (Freeman, 1983) predates the UNCRC and is likely to have influenced its ten years of being slowly written and agreed. And the English *Gillick* case (*Gillick v West Norfolk & Wisbech A.H.A.* [1985] 3 All ER) partly exceeded the rights in the later UNCRC. The Convention, in article 12, only allows children to express views on matters that affect them according to their age and maturity, and states that adults should give 'due weight' to these views. That leaves adults with great power to determine whether, when or how to give this 'due weight'. The *Gillick* ruling, however, respects legal minors' right to be the main decision maker in certain personal matters. The UNCRC article 41 respects any national cases or laws, such as *Gillick*, 'which are more conducive to the realisation of the rights of the child' than the UNCRC is'.

These and other matters relating to law and children have been extensively analysed in Michael's many edited volumes. His work finely balances social science theories of childhood and children's lives with the more precise and abstract world of the law. Crucially, childhood studies pave the way for social researchers to respect children not only as agents but also as active rights holders, with legal rights such as '*Gillick* competence', and to see children as real, complicated human beings as well as the becomings that we all are at every age (for example, Alderson, 1993 on children's rights to give or withhold informed consent to major surgery).

Children's Rights, Dissent and Protest

The UNCRC rights are said to be indivisible and interdependent. Central to them all is a degree of freedom for rights holders as agents to choose, including their options to dissent and protest without fear of punishment or prejudice. Children's and adults' rights are, however, qualified by the demands of public law, order and morals – the common good. Free speech does not include the right to be racist, for example. Yet without freedoms, 'rights' might better be understood in terms of welfare, benefits, needs or interests. And these welfare aspects of children's entitlements, to basic protections and provisions to sustain their life and growth, are generally accepted – despite neoliberal policies to cut state benefits and services with little mention of how children are especially affected (Harvey, 2012; Klein, 2007; Nadesan, 2010).

Still, the main controversies around children's rights involve their freedoms: of information and expression, thought, conscience and religion, association and peaceful assembly and privacy (specifically in UNCRC articles 12 to 17). Michael has repeatedly criticised the views of those who would deny children's freedoms. They belong to two main groups that could broadly be called pro-rights liberals and anti-rights critics.

Pro-rights, paternalist liberals tend to believe that rights and freedoms are defined as the prerogative of rational adults, and that children can only risk harming themselves or others if they try to exercise them. If adults choose to harm themselves they may do so, but children must be protected. Liberals allege that all children are immature and unable either to know their best interests or to make rational choices. Liberals fear the threat to adults' freedoms and responsibilities, especially those of parents and teachers, if children's rights are respected (O'Neil, 1988; Brighouse, 2002) (see Freeman, 2006, 2011 and his other critical papers).

Some childhood researchers confuse traditional liberalism with ruthlessly individualistic and competitive neoliberalism. They then dismiss liberal rights as neoliberal ploys (for example, Wells, 2009). When the US and UK cite 'abuses of human rights' as grounds to oppress and invade other states, the accusations do indeed seem hypocritical. The US and UK also violate rights, when they too commit torture and hugely invasive public surveillance, hold secret trials, and deny entry to asylum seekers. Yet these travesties demonstrate how liberal rights, far from originating in neoliberal policies, challenge them.

Anti-rights arguments come from anthropologists on two main grounds. First, research should be value-free, impartial inquiry, and therefore should not be influenced by normative concerns about rights. I have considered this illusion of value-freedom earlier. And the notion and aim to be value-free could itself be seen as a moral ideology. The anthropologists' second objection is that universal rights are untenable in a world of vastly differing cultures, especially because they are social constructs based on Western norms. To support this claim, an extreme and unreal concept of rights may be advanced. For example, Jo Boyden (2004: 247) reports many practical difficulties in her valuable ethnographies with children in war zones. She then concludes, without referring to any rights treaties or literature, that human rights are normative assumptions, which 'clash with the way different societies organise themselves and think about infractions and justice'. In the 'Judeo-Christian' rights worldview:

> the individual human being exists as an autonomous entity in itself [*sic*]...In most other cultures, the individual cannot be isolated from the whole in this way, but forms an integral part of the natural, spiritual and social worlds. Persons are bound to social groups through a complex network of obligations and duties that are associated with their position in those groups: individuals have no claims that are independent, or outside, of these groups and the notion of rights is entirely foreign. [War and atrocities] may be understood as caused not by [individual or group] human agency...but by upheavals in the social, supernatural or natural worlds. (Boyden, 2004: 247)

These are untenable, extreme dichotomies. One set of children and adults is no more entirely isolated, than another set is entirely integrated. Human rights exist within relationships and are necessary because of them, to guard against abuse or neglect. One type of culture is not wholly concerned with autonomy and rights any more than others are entirely concerned with duties. If, as implied, non-Western societies run wholly on 'obligations and duties', their wars and terrible atrocities that Boyden researched would not occur. The UNCRC Preamble moves beyond the alleged individualism into social concepts of rights to equality and solidarity (fraternity) as well as liberty: 'recognition of the inherent dignity and of the equal and inalienable rights of all members of the human family is the foundation of freedom, justice and peace in the world'. Many 'westerners' are aware of their integral dependence on natural (physical, ecological), spiritual (religious, ethical, aesthetic) and social (plus political and economic) worlds; they acknowledge these deep, structural causes of armed conflict, such as over land, water or oil, besides individual causal agency.

To claim that 'the notion of rights is entirely foreign' could mean, as I found with school students I interviewed, that although they did not use the language of rights, they were centrally concerned with the bases of rights in justice and respect. Alternatively, the claim could mean the absence of any concept of oneself as partly a separate, needy individual whose integrity can be honoured or violated. That would entail children's and adults' indifference to being abused or exploited, starved, raped or tortured. It implies they would socially construct such experiences as meaningless, or as duties to be borne without protest for the good of the whole community.

Jo Boyden (2004: 247-8) is concerned that 'by framing war events in terms of human rights standards, researchers may neglect' the respondents' own perceptions and experiences. They may perceive children as victims to protect, instead of as 'conscious agents' with 'political consciousness and activism' and 'motives' to join in armed conflict. Unsurprisingly, the last few phrases (inadvertently) fall into the language of human rights, indispensible to any analysis of war. Jo Boyden makes a powerful case to respect the right of children to protest, apart from avoiding explicit rights language.

Since all children's rights are too often shrivelled into protection and provision, the following points are reminders about the crucial 'participation' freedoms. Human rights have been refined by philosophers and lawyers over centuries, and are enshrined in international treaties. Yet originally, pre-notions of rights slowly emerged through many centuries of protests and rebellions. The biblical story of Exodus, the so-called 'children of Israel's' escape from slavery in Egypt, may have been told in the sixth or eighth century BCE. Many or most of the migrants literally were children and young people, given the very short life-span then. The British Empire saw many mass protests by Muslims, Hindus and adherents of other faiths.

Moving to the 20th century, the longest running strike in Britain (1914-1939) was conducted by school children, in support of two teachers who were sacked for such enormities as lighting a fire in the damp school without permission – to dry the clothes of children who had walked three miles to school in the rain (Bertram, 1971). In Poland, child rights advocate Janusz Korczak fully shared with the children the democratic running of their orphanage in a Warsaw ghetto, with a parliament and a newspaper, and his final protest was to choose to share their death in the gas chambers in Treblinka. A student on our MA course on children's rights, Gabriel Eichsteller, submitted a version of his dissertation on Korczak to the IJCR. Michael responded that although he had been writing a paper for the journal about Korczak, one of his heroes, Gabriel's paper was better and he would publish that instead (Eichsteller, 2009). School and college students sparked the American civil rights movement in the 1960s by refusing to be served in blacks-only canteens (Red Card, 2013). And an estimated 20,000 school students in Soweto ignited the anti-apartheid movement in South Africa in 1976, when they protested against the introduction of Afrikaans as the medium of instruction in local schools. Between 170 to 700 school students are believed to have been killed, an indictment that no one knows all the names and numbers of those who perished (Ndlovu, 2010). Even today and contrary to UNCRC article 7, every year an estimated one third of births are not recorded, signifying that states do not treat these babies as citizens with rights, which states undertook to honour when they ratified the UNCRC and related treaties.

In the tradition of protest, this century has seen unprecedented gatherings by young people facing violent police and armies (Mason 2012). They are willing to die for 'our rights' – meaning other people's as well as their own rights – in extreme solidarity. They demonstrate how some, many or most children and young people understand justice in terms of human rights, and how to protest if they believe they have just cause. For example, Rene Silva Santos (2013) lives in one of the largest of the many favelas (slums) of Rio de Janeiro. Housing is crammed into tiers rising up the hills around the city, with open sewers and few if any public utilities or services. Dominated by drug cartels, the favelas are regularly raided by the police. Rene described how when he was 11 years old he started a community newspaper in 2005. 'No one heard the children and the people who live in the favela and we never went into the central city. I knew then that it was very important that we should be heard.' In November 2010, televisions reported a police raid with helicopters and armed vehicles searching for traffickers. The sloping hillsides exposed great tracts of the favelas to view.

> I started reporting on twitter, correcting the media reports. I couldn't believe it, my live tweets were on TV about what was happening. I already had 600 followers, and suddenly I had 10,000. Famous people were asking, 'Are you ok? We want to know your view? Is it true? How do you know?' I said, 'I live here, not like you journalists who cannot get in'.... Next day all the media wanted to interview me. I knew I had to show positive things about our favela and change people's minds... It's very important that we take part and fight for our rights and for democracy in Brazil. The youth on social media started the protests about the rise in bus fares [in June 2013]. (Santos, 2013)

Such examples illustrate how misleading arguments, that children cannot and should not understand and exercise their freedom rights, may serve adults' interests rather than children's. From 1990, many researchers hoped that the new paradigm of childhood studies would emancipate children away from child development theory and into mainstream 'adult' academic research and policy, practice and public debate. They hoped that childhood studies might advance children's rights, just as feminism and gender studies have advanced women's rights. Similarly, many people hoped that the UNCRC would remind everyone that children have human rights too, and that the Convention would increase practical and moral respect for all children in all areas of public and private life.

This has hardly happened. There have been some moves forward but many reversals. Developmental psychology continues to dominate professions such as paediatrics, teaching, social work and international development, as well as public opinion and policymaking. Psychology stresses protection of children and provision for them, but scarcely endorses their freedoms, as Boyden (2004) rightly criticised when she reported research in armed conflict zones. Too often, psychological attempts to explain problems that confront children involve implicitly or explicitly blaming children's ascribed, immature dependence or deviance. The effect can be to shrink massive economic problems down from international politics and into the personal failing of individual children or parents.

There are now fewer public and commercial spaces where young people are 'allowed' to meet one another. Painful mosquito alarms, which adults cannot hear, whine to drive young people and children away from shopping centres. Town centres are being privatised, with private police to move young people away – unless they are avidly shopping. The rural areas and pleasanter, greener, city areas where they once lived and played are being emptied of younger families, many of whom cannot afford the rising mortgages and rents (Harvey, 2012). Children and young people are generally more excluded than they were 20 years ago, let alone 120 years ago, off the streets and into spending longer hours in pre-schools and schools.

Many babies stay (or 'work') full-time ten-hour days in British nurseries (8.00 a.m. - 6.00 p.m. or more), longer than the eight-hour days that European laws allow the staff to work. And the shorter staff hours mean that babies have to cope with changing shifts and rotas so that they lack continuing care by the same group of adults through the day. Among numerous examples, in another very different aspect of children's rights, the great increase of children and young people in detention centres and prisons includes many very young parents whose own children are punished too. Young prisoners are likely to have been looked after (in care). They are often moved between prisons far from home, causing great distress. They tend to have poor literacy and numeracy skills, and to have housing, unemployment, addiction and mental health problems. Many have been sexually abused (Jacobson et al., 2010).

Researchers can inform public protests, and other work with and for children to benefit their daily lives, by documenting, analysing and explaining such experiences through a children's rights lens and through such channels as the IJCR, the Children's Rights Alliance for England's annual reports and website (CRAE, 2013; www.crae.org.uk), the Children's Rights Information Network (www.crin.org), and the Centre for Crime and Justice Studies (www.cimeandjustice.org.uk).

Theories of Children's Rights

Besides collecting and reporting data, the central task of research is to develop or reveal theories. Theories have three main meanings here: to help to clarify and define formerly blurred and confused concepts; to explain often underlying, hidden and misunderstood but powerful processes; to examine and connect outcomes to these processes.

Childhood studies are strong on certain theories, such as meanings and explanations about the child and childhood. For example, Jo Boyden (2004) challenged the dominant psychological theories of children as passive, traumatised victims of war. She showed how 100,000s of children are instead deliberate agents during warfare. She criticised the favoured research method of standardised psychometric questionnaires. Children are asked to select responses already determined by the researchers and their theories. These may yield only superficial, irrelevant or misleading data. Almost inevitably the outcomes replicate and confirm the theories and methods. These tend to miss children's real experiences and concerns, and their local contexts. More relevant and revealing research relies on more complex theories of children as conscious agents, who have concerns about their future as well as their past.

However, there is generally less clarity and insight in childhood studies in theories about rights. One common limitation is to reduce the whole range of human rights into UNCRC article 12, children's right to express views, or to 'participate' in 'decision making' (neither term is mentioned in the Convention) mainly in adult-organised agendas. Some researchers criticise the UNCRC, when faults actually lie in the many ways the Convention has been misunderstood or misapplied, misquoted or misinterpreted, or simply not read.

Whereas mainstream 'adult' law and policy tend to ignore children's rights, childhood researchers tend to pay little attention to rights and law. They often miss basic meanings and theories of rights: that these are legal, carefully worded, practical and potentially enforceable concepts, about specifically defined behaviours, which can at least partly be held to account in a court of law. Love is not a right because parents cannot be sued for not loving their child enough, for example, but parents can be held to account for neglect or abuse. Researchers who miss this basic theory, that rights are about law, risk inventing vague rights that would be quickly dismissed in a court of law: the 'right to a childhood', or 'the right to be properly researched'. The meaningless 'right to health' claim opens up rights to be ridiculed by critics. Try telling a child who is dying of cancer, 'don't worry, you have a right to health'. Instead, the carefully worded UNCRC (article 24) speaks of 'the highest attainable standard of health', and of international cooperation between richer and poorer states towards achieving this. On my above third point about theories, that they examine and connect outcomes to earlier processes, rights are not simply slogans or debates but goals to work towards.

A potentially useful project about 'citizenship from below' (Liebel, 2008: 32) involved African children in townships and African working children 'being able to confer rights on themselves'. This phrase ignores structural, political, historical and accountable aspects of rights. Which powerful groups would recognise or respect any invented, self-conferred rights of weak disadvantaged groups? 'Top down' pressure from the UN is so weak that separate pressure 'from below' is likely to be even less effective, unless these two work together.

The African children discussed and then 'formulated' and 'adopted' rights that were mainly 'orientated to the UNCRC', although they do not seem to have read the Convention. For example, the working children claimed: 'We should be allowed to play with our friends on Saturdays and Sundays' (Liebel, 2008: 40). The township children stated: 'All children have the right to demand health and medical care, without obtaining permission from their parents or mentors' (Liebel, 2008: 39-42).

The hope of these important aims being formally honoured by authorities could have been considerably strengthened if the children had had more informed legal help. This could have advised them about knowing which rights are already enshrined in the UNCRC and the African Charter (1990) and so are already ratified by their governments. Legal help could have furthered their understanding of how rights are general and quite sparsely worded principles, open to a great range of local interpretations. Then they could have seen how to build on the general and already ratified rights in order to explain and claim the specific further ways in which these needed to be interpreted and implemented. This would involve seeing the crucial importance of clear, specific wording.

A 'right to demand' healthcare does not mean much, since it requires no response. It is much weaker than: 'State parties shall strive to ensure that no child is deprived of his or her right of access to such health care services' (UNCRC article 24, 1). This can then be followed by the vital point that if parents and mentors deny such access, children should not therefore have to depend on their permission. The *Gillick* English case law applies in many of the 54 or so British Commonwealth countries, of which South Africa is one, so that in theory the children already have this right, on certain conditions.

The claim, 'We should be allowed to play with our friends on Saturdays and Sundays', slips from the rights language of entitlement down to the conditional language of permission, and sets unhelpful limits on the time and type of play. The phrase is more weak and limited than the UNCRC's unconditional, complementary and mutually reinforcing rights: to rest and leisure (article 31), freedom of association (article 15), freedom of expression in any medium (including play) (article 13), best interests (article 3), non-discrimination (article 2) and other powerful rights.

The examples illustrate how childhood researchers and advocates, as well as children and young people, need to know more about rights within legal frameworks and how these can serve children. More of Michael's interdisciplinary law↔childhood work is much needed. He has helped to clarify knotty problems of the relationship between international law, national statute and numerous common law cases, in Freeman (2007b), for example, a work that also addresses the minefields of how concepts of children's best interests can further their rights rather than undermining them, whether there can be international checklists, and how the world's resources can serve children's best interests.

Exploring New Areas

Unfortunately, research journals about childhood tend to expect empirical papers, with little space for new thinking, and to reject more wide-ranging reflective work. For example, the leading international journal *Childhood* refused to publish a review of a splendid book on *Education, Asylum and the "Non-citizen' Child: The Politics of Compassion and Belonging* (Pinson *et al.*, 2010), as outside their remit. The book reports English school children's successful campaigns to stop their asylum-seeking friends from being detained or deported. The authors extended their empirical work into theorising about the growing political awareness of children who challenge received ideas, including xenophobic views held by some of the adults in their lives as well as by the mass media and politicians. The children learned to look beyond prejudices and to relate to young asylum seekers in their school in terms of compassion, belonging and justice.

The book crucially questions the received wisdom: that uncivilised children are taught and socialised by adults into gradually becoming mature citizens. First, like many children and young people around the world who join in public protests, the children in the book could show political maturity and courage at an early age, from around six years, when they had relevant experience of injustice and suffering. Second, although some teachers and parents joined in the children's campaigns, adults cannot be counted on to teach the politics of compassion rather than the dominant neoliberal politics of self-interest and competition. Third, the authors identified political maturity with the children's awakening awareness of their need to question and protest against received and dominant views when these are unjust. This raises vital questions about citizenship education, and its present emphasis on *talking* about current systems. In contrast, in this book, children learned through directly *experiencing* and actively challenging dominant but unjust systems. The IJCR did publish a review of this book, and it accepts other papers rejected by journals, which seem to find them too unusual, or maybe too challenging, for their readers.

Michael is willing to publish a variety of formats from empirical research reports, to critical overviews, to analytical and sometimes provocative papers, which he also authors. He accepted my paper (Alderson, 2012), which was rejected by the editors of a special issue of a sociology journal on human rights. They chose detailed empirical studies instead. My paper hovered on the edges of mainstream sociology, childhood studies, history and ethics. It reflected on possible reasons for sociology's neglect of human rights – let alone of children's rights. The first stream on human rights was not convened at a British Sociological Association meeting until the 60th annual conference in 2011. Yet the BSA opened shortly after the European Convention on Human Rights was agreed in 1950, the Universal Declaration of Human Rights was agreed in 1948, and the Nuremberg Code on international medical research ethics was agreed in 1947. Research ethics is another topic that has been grossly neglected and even rejected by sociologists until recently. All three international quasi-legal documents were outcomes of the Nuremburg Trials following the Holocaust. The Holocaust, too, is almost entirely missing from sociology (Bauman, 2003). Yet human rights could count as a major social concern, and the Holocaust was a key social event of the twentieth century.

Like the book by Pinson *et al.* (2010), my paper considered whether rights are wholly taught to children by adults, or are learned through personal experience. It looked at how childhood studies, through research about the early origins of rights awareness among young children, might inform research about adults' rights. Years ago Michael argued for a shift in understanding children's rights, to move from rights of having to rights of being, from assessing (adult-orientated) capacities and competencies to respecting the rights of all children 'by virtue of being children' (Freeman, 1998: 442). Zygmunt Bauman (2003) questioned the assumption that rights have to be taught to antisocial children. That implies rights belong to culture but not also to human nature. Yet if rights are somehow against nature, what are their origins and relevance to our daily lives? The views of Emile Durkheim and Talcott Parsons assumed that educators must teach children a moral compliance that supplants their initial dysfunctional, amoral noncompliance. However, Bauman (2003: 173) saw dangers if compliance is seen as the sole moral option, when 'actions are evil because they are socially prohibited, rather than socially prohibited because they are evil'. Instead, he identified morality with those rare people who are brave enough to protest against injustice and cruelty, such as the Holocaust. Powerful feelings about compassion and sharing, respect and trust, justice, questioning and protest, all grounds for practical support for shared human rights, seem to exist in very early childhood. The feelings appear to be part of our authentic human nature, sometimes arising from embodied pain and fear, and not solely through synthetic instructions, although these early intuitions can be gradually refined and clarified through years of experience and education. I have explored these new areas, linked to Michael's phrase 'rights of being', in a book on childhood and realism, which centres on being (ontology) (Alderson, 2013).

Conclusion

Among other people, Michael has criticised the UNCRC and the UN Committee (such as in Freeman, 2007b) for omissions, for instance, under-attention to the most disadvantaged children, lack of children's own views, and the lack of enforcement procedures. Although he has called for a revised Convention, he agrees that would hardly be a realistic hope. It would not get the near universal ratification of the present version, largely achieved by the great efforts of an American, James Grant. Governments are now much more aware of what they have ratified, and how their reports to the UN Committee can embarrass them. The UN is now more torn by disputes than between 1979-1991 when the UNCRC was being written and ratified. There are new conflicts and angers, such as between religious sects, which seem likely to preclude future international consensus on any matter, let alone on children's rights. The US has less influence, and in any case it has not ratified the UNCRC, while no other major power seems interested in taking a lead to promote children's rights.

The best way forward would seem to be to promote ever more understanding of the meaning of the present UNCRC and its links to other UN Conventions, with the potential relevance of their broad terms to address longstanding problems, new problems, and old problems as they become newly visible, such as climate change, which especially affects the youngest generations. Research, practical action and debates among states, services, NGOs, and among adults and children generally (see Laura Lundy's chapter in this volume) could all help to expand the positive influence of the UNCRC. This would include increasing general understanding of the crucial importance of children's rights, and of the benefits as well as the barriers in efforts to implement them, with possible ways to overcome the barriers, thereby further developing much of Michael's work.

I will end by listing some of the essential qualities or powers of children's rights, which Michael identified in one of his papers (Freeman, 2007a), in the hope that everyone researching and working on children's rights will keep them in mind.

Children's Rights

- Respect children as subjects in their own right;
- Are inclusive;
- Are indivisible and interdependent;
- Cover the whole range of civil, political, social, economic and cultural life;
- Respect the dignity, integrity and humanity of every rights bearer;
- Respect children's competence and also their needs and interests;
- Address power, and the real, risky, often dangerous world, not an idealised one;
- 'Trump' all other considerations;
- Enable agency and effective decision making;
- Are advocacy tools and weapons;
- Make long-suppressed needs visible;
- Are entitlements, beyond the vagaries of whim or privilege;
- Are most necessary and potentially powerful when they seem to be absent and are violated because they demand remedies and, therefore, basic resources and changes;
- Support legitimate protests;
- Promote equity and emancipation;

- Offer internationally agreed, reasoned moral arguments and advocacy;
- Can justify and be the basis for positive action.

References

Alderson, P., *Children's Consent to Surgery* (Buckingham: Open University Press, 1993).

Alderson, P., "Young Children's Human Rights: a sociological analysis", *International Journal of Children's Rights* 2012 20(2), 177-198.

Alderson, P., *Childhoods Real and Imagined: An Introduction to Critical Realism and Childhood Studies, Volume 1* (London: Routledge, 2013).

African Charter on the Rights and Welfare of the Child (Organisation of African Unity, 1990).

Ariès, P., *Centuries of Childhood* (Harmondsworth: Penguin, 1962).

Bauman, Z., *Modernity and the Holocaust* (Cambridge: Polity, 2003).

Bertram, E., *The Burston School Strike* (London: Lawrence and Wishart, 1974).

Bluebond-Langner, M., *The Private Worlds of Dying Children* (Princeton NJ: Princeton University Press, 1978).

Boyden, J., "Anthropology Under Fire: Ethics, Researchers and Children in War", in J.

Boyden and J. de Berry (eds), *Children and Youth on the Front Line: Ethnography, Armed Conflict and Displacement* (Oxford: Berghahn Books, 2004).

Brighouse, H., "What Rights (if any) Do Children Have?" in D. Archard and C. Macleod (eds), *The Moral and Political Status of Children* (Oxford: Oxford University Press, 2002).

Cockburn, T., *Rethinking Children's Citizenship* (Basingstoke: Palgrave Macmillan, 2013).

Corsaro, W.A. and M-S. Honig (eds), *The Palgrave Handbook of Childhood Studies* (Basingstoke: Palgrave Macmillan, 2011).

Centre for Crime and Justice Studies: www.cimeandjustice.org.uk.

CRAE - Children's Rights Alliance for England: http://www.crae.org.uk.

Children's Rights Information Network: www.crin.org.

Donaldson, M., *Children's Minds* (Edinburgh: Fontana, 1978).

Douglas, H. and Walsh T., "Continuing the Stolen Generations: Child Protection Interventions and Indigenous People", *International Journal of Children's Rights* 2013 21(1), 59-87.

Eichsteller, G., "Janusz Korczak – His Legacy and its Relevance for Children's Rights Today", *International Journal of Children's Rights* 2009 17(3), 377-391.

Field, S., "United Nations Security Council Resolutions Concerning Children Affected by Armed Conflict: In Whose 'Best Interests'?", *International Journal of Children's Rights* 2013 21(1), 127-161.

Freeman, M., *The Rights and Wrongs of Children* (London: Frances Pinter, 1983).

Freeman, M., "The Sociology of Childhood and Children's Rights", *International Journal of Children's Rights* 1998 6(4), 433-44.

Freeman, M., "Children Are Unbeatable", *Children & Society* 1999 13, 130-141.

Freeman, M., "Children's Rights, Ten Years After Ratification", in B. Franklin (ed), *The New Handbook of Children's Rights* (London: Routledge, 2002).
Freeman, M., "What's Right with Children's Rights?", *International Journal of Law in Context* 2006 14(1), 89-98.
Freeman, M., "Why it Remains Important to Take Children's Rights Seriously", *International Journal of Children's Rights* 2007a 15(1), 5-23.
Freeman, M., "Article 3: The Best Interests of the Child" in A. Alen, J. Vande Lanotte, E. Verhellen, F. Ang, E. Berghmanns and M. Verheyde (eds), *A Commentary on the United Nations Convention on the Rights of The Child* (Leiden: Martinus Nijhoff, 2007b).
Freeman, M., "Children's Rights as Human Rights: Reading the UNCRC", in J. Qvortrup, W.
Freeman, M., "Towards a Sociology of Children's Rights", in M. Freeman (ed), *Law and Childhood Studies* (Oxford: Oxford University Press, 2012).
Freeman, M., "Review of Butler, C.", *The Movement, International Law and Opposition, International Journal of Children's Rights* 2013a 21(2), 390-392.
Freeman, M., "Review of Wolff, J.", *The Human Rights to Health, International Journal of Children's Rights* 2013b 21(2), 393-394.
Guggenheim, M., *What's Wrong with Children's Rights* (Cambridge MA: Harvard University Press, 2005).
Hammersley, M., *The Politics of Social Research* (London: Sage, 1995).
Hardyment, C., *Dream Babies: Child Care from Locke to Spock* (Oxford: Oxford University Press, 1984).
Harvey, D., *Rebel Cities: From the Right to the City to the Urban Revolution* (London: Verso, 2012).
Hemphill, S. and Schneider, S., "Excluding Students from School: A Re-examination from a Children's Rights Perspective", *International Journal of Children's Rights* 2013 21(1), 88-96.
Holt, J., *Escape from Childhood* (Harmondsworth: Penguin, 1975).
Jacobson, J., Bhardwa, B., Gyateng, T., Hunter, G. and Hough, M., *Punishing Disadvantage: A Profile of Children In Custody* (London: Prison Reform Trust, 2010).
James, A. and Prout, A. (eds), *Constructing and Reconstructing Childhood: Contemporary Issues in the Sociological Study of Childhood* (Abingdon: Routledge Falmer, 1990/1997).
Klein, N., *The Shock Doctrine* (London: Allen Lane, 2007).
Liebel, M., "Citizenship From Below", in A. Invernizzi and J. Williams (eds), *Children and Citizenship.* (London: Sage, 2008).
Lukes, S., *Moral Relativism.* (London: Profile, 2008).
Mason, P., *Why It's Kicking Off Everywhere: The New Global Revolution* (London: Verso, 2012).
Morss, J., *The Biologising of Childhood: Developmental Psychology and the Darwinian Myth* (Hillsdale NJ: Lawrence Erlbaum, 1990).
Nadesan, M., *Governing Childhood into the 21st Century: Biotechnologies of Childhood Management and Education* (New York: Palgrave Macmillan, 2010).

Ndlovu, S., "The Soweto Uprising", *The Road to Democracy in South Africa, Volume 2, 1970-1980* (Pretoria: South African Development Trust, 2010) http://www.sadet.co.za/docs/RTD/vol2/Volume%202%20-%20chapter%207.pdf, accessed 15 September 2013.

Nolan, A., "Economic and Social Rights, Budgets and the Convention on the Rights of the Child", *International Journal of Children's Rights* 2013 21(2), 248-277.

O'Neill, O., "Children's Rights and Children's Lives", *Ethics* 2011 98(3), 445-463.

Oswell, D., *The Agency of Children: From Family to Global Human Rights* (Cambridge: Cambridge University Press, 2013).

Piaget, J., *The Child's Conception of the World* (London: Routledge & Kegan Paul, 1928).

Pinson, H., Arnot, M., and Candappa, M., *Education, Asylum and The "Non-Citizen" Child: The Politics of Compassion and Belonging* (Basingstoke: Palgrave Macmillan, 2010).

Qvortrup, J., (ed), *Childhood as a Social Phenomenon.16 National Reports* (Vienna: European Centre, 1991).

Red Card: http://www.theredcard.ie/civil_rights.php accessed 15 September 2013.

Santos, R., Notes of his translated interview with Matthew Bannister (*Outlook, BBC World Service*, 30 September 2013).

Sayer, A., *Why Things Matter to People: Social Science, Values and Ethical Life* (Cambridge: Cambridge University Press, 2011).

Scullion, D., "Passive Victims or Empowered Actors: Accommodating the Needs of Child Domestic Workers", *International Journal of Children's Rights* 2013 21(1), 97-126.

Seale, C., *The Quality of Qualitative Research* (London: Sage, 1999).

United Nations, *Convention on the Rights of the Child* (New York: UN, 1989).

United Nations, *Universal Declaration of Human Rights* (New York: United Nations, 1948).

Wells, K., *Childhood in Global Perspective* (Cambridge: Polity, 2009).

Winter, K., *Building Relationships and Communicating with Young Children: A Practical Guide for Social Workers* (Abingdon and New York: Routledge, 2011).

What if Children Had Been Involved in Drafting the United Nations Convention on the Rights of the Child?

Laura Lundy and Elizabeth Welty
Queen's University Belfast

Beth Blue Swadener
Arizona State University

Natasha Blanchet-Cohen
Concordia University

Kylie Smith
University of Melbourne

Dympna Devine
University College Dublin

Introduction

Michael Freeman was the first scholar to identify and capture the paradox of children's lack of involvement in the drafting of the United Nations Convention on the Rights of the Child, observing that:

> *The 1989 Convention was not formulated by children. Nor did they have any real input into it. How different a convention in which the child's voice is heard would look is a matter of some controversy. There is, though, not a little irony in having a Convention which emphasises participatory rights (in Article 12) whilst foreclosing the participation of children in the formulation of the rights encoded.*
> *(Freeman, 2000: 282).*

In his first critical overview of the scope and limits of the UNCRC, the renowned advocate of children's rights shed light on what may at best be perceived as a somewhat naïve oversight and at worst as an example of international hypocrisy – the failure to consider children's views in the construction of the international treaty which guarantees their right to have their views given due weight in all matters affecting them. Van Bueren (2011) observed some attempts to consult with children in order to influence the content of the Convention, these were "ad hoc rather than structured and occasional rather than comprehensive" (p.118) Nonetheless she suggests that the majority of the children's suggestions on issues to be covered (such as the death penalty and prohibition of children's participation in armed conflict) were accepted by the drafters. However, these interventions around specific issues appear to have been coordinated by NGOs rather than the negotiating parties themselves: there is little evidence of any systematic efforts by states to consult the children in their jurisdictions directly on the content of the proposed Convention nor to involve them in the drafting process. Michael Freeman queries whether the Convention would look differently if children had been involved in its development and that question became the inspiration for the research project which forms the basis of this chapter. Taking

A. Diduck, N. Peleg, H. Reece (eds.), Law in Society: Reflections on Children, Family, Culture and Philosophy
 ISBN 978-90-04-26148-8. pp. 223-242.

up Michael Freeman's challenge, a team of international researchers working in five different national contexts undertook participatory research with groups of young children with a view to exploring whether and how the UNCRC might change if children had been involved in drafting it, focusing on one Article of the Convention – Article 29, which defines the aims of education – as an example. The key aim of the research was to show whether and how the UNCRC might read differently if children had been afforded meaningful opportunities to input their ideas into the text of the Convention. However, before describing how this was carried out and what emerged, it is arguable that there is one related issue which might also be a matter of controversy to some and must be addressed first, that is the question of whether children should in fact have been involved in drafting the UNCRC.

Should Children Have Been Involved in Drafting the UNCRC?

The answer to question of whether children should have been involved may appear straightforward in the light of the text of Article 12 which states:

> *States Parties shall assure to the child who is capable of forming his or her own views the right to express those views freely in all matters affecting the child, the views of the child being given due weight in accordance with the age and maturity of the child.*

In essence, for Article 12 to apply, all that needs to be asked is first whether the matter affects children and then if they are capable of forming and expressing a view on the issues. However, experience of over 20 years of implementation tells us that:

> *Children are often denied the right to be heard, even though it is obvious that the matter under consideration is affecting them and they are capable of expressing their own views with regard to this matter*
> *(UN Committee, 2009: 66).*

It is difficult to conceive of an argument that the UNCRC is not a matter that affects children, especially since it was clear from the drafting process that it would, as a minimum, apply (but not be limited to) any discussion related to their rights. However, an obvious starting point would have been to ask children themselves (Lundy, 2007). While it would not have been apparent to most of the world's children in the 1980s that the drafting process of an international human rights treaty with bespoke rights for children had been going on for more than a decade, a reasonable assumption is that, had they been provided with information as to its existence and import, many would have recognized its significance and may have been willing (keen even) to contribute their ideas for its construction. As will be discussed in this paper, this was in fact the response in the five different national contexts in which this research was carried out.

The second issue is whether children would have been capable of expressing a view on its content bearing in mind that the right to express views is not restricted by the child's age or maturity. (UN Convention, 1989; Lundy, 2007). This too has a relatively simple answer since there is a body of research that has focused specifically on the question of what rights children think they should have. It is noteworthy in this context that the earliest studies conducted by Gary Melton (1980, 1993), were written well in advance of the final draft of the UNCRC. Since then, there have been several studies that have demonstrated that children are both willing and able to give their views on the rights they think they should have (e.g. Taylor *et al.*, 2001; Teresevičienė and Jonynienė, 2001). Other research has shed light on how children understand specific rights contained in the UNCRC such as the right to participation (Morrow, 1999), to play (Davey and Lundy, 2011) and to education (Swadener *et al.*, 2013). While there is no published research until now that has engaged children in discussing the actual text of the Convention with a view to amending its content, the previous studies provide ample evidence that children are capable of not only articulating a list of rights that they think they should have in broad terms but also of defining what it means for them to be enjoyed fully.

If we accept that the UNCRC is a matter that affects children and that children are capable of expressing their views on its content, it might be thought that this should be enough to engage the application of Article 12. However, a possible (and typically legal) excuse in this instance is that Article 12 was not in fact in force until the adoption of the UNCRC by the UN General Assembly in November 1989, with the result there was no legally binding obligation to engage with children at all before then. Put simply, states did not have to comply with Article 12 as it was not yet in force. Moreover, Article 12 is unique – unlike many UNCRC rights, it has no equivalent in the other human rights instruments that apply to adults and children and which might otherwise have mandated or even prompted governments to consult with children. All human beings have a right to express their views but it is only children who enjoy the right to have them given due weight (Lundy, 2007). Nonetheless, given that the original version of Article 12 was under discussion from very early on in the drafting process, it is surprising that states parties did not spot the failure to engage with or attempt to resolve the lack of involvement of children.

The final possible 'get-out' clause is that the contracting parties to the UNCRC are in fact States Parties and that rights-holders are not therefore usually involved directly in any of these negotiations. There is therefore an argument that it was legitimate for public officials who were acting on behalf of elected politicians to determine the content of the Treaty without consultation with its proposed beneficiaries. That might, however, be more sustainable if those who appeared for the States Parties in the negotiations had a direct and democratic mandate to represent children. While the ability of any politician or public official to "represent" adults who may or may not have voted them into power is contested, there is a particular difficulty in assuming that it is the case in relation to children since, having had no vote in most instances, they are without any form of democratic representation in the drafting processes. In fact it is this voicelessness and relative imbalance of power, peculiar to children, that provides the underpinning rationale for Article 12. Nor can this be remedied by the contribution of adults working for children's lobbying groups, important and influential as that was in relation to the UNCRC, (see Cohen, 1990): current guidance from the Committee on Article 12 stresses that indirect representation on behalf of children through NGOs, for example, is not a substitute for direct engagement by government (UN Committee, 2009).

In conclusion, although Article 12 was not in force at the time the UNCRC was being drafted, its rationale, significance and potential scope were understood sufficiently to place at least a moral onus on the governments who were shaping its content to seek and give due weight to the views of children in their jurisdictions about its content. Nonetheless, as is so often the case, the final product, the UNCRC was made for rather than by children. Almost a quarter of a century later, at a time when the commitment to and understanding of the importance of Article 12 has been much advanced, not least through a dedicated General Comment of the Committee (2009), this study set out to first explore the consequences of the lack of the involvement of children on the UNCRC itself and then to reflect on the implications of that for the implementation of children's rights more generally.

Methodology and Methods

The key aim of the research project was to answer this paper's title question – would the UNCRC be different if children had been involved in drafting it? As should be the case, the question itself determined the methods and indeed the methodology. A fatal flaw would have been to repeat the original mistake. Answering the question demanded that research was conducted directly with children themselves (bearing in mind that twenty years ago many researchers might have thought it was acceptable to ask adults what their thoughts on that were!). Moreover, the research process itself needed to adopt a rights-based approach by engaging with children in ways that are in themselves respectful of Article 12 of the Convention (Lundy and McEvoy, 2012). This requirement, along with the desirability of getting the perspectives of children in more than one national context, then determined to a large extent the team of researchers who were invited to participate.

The lead author approached international colleagues who had experience of conducting participatory research with children and a sound knowledge of and interest in children's rights. This unashamedly opportunistic approach was universally welcomed by the invitees, not least for the fact that it allowed each participant to pay tribute to the contribution of Michael Freeman to children's rights scholarship. The result was that the study, although small, has a global spread (Australia (Smith); Canada (Blanchet-Cohen); Ireland (Devine); United Kingdom (Lundy and Welty); and United States (Swadener). Each member of the team had to apply locally for ethical clearance following the procedures relevant to their context; all children received parental consent to participate and agreed to be involved themselves, having been informed in child-accessible information sheets of the nature of the study and their right to participate or withdraw at anytime. This group is obviously *not* representative of the diverse nations that comprise the United Nations since the countries involved are all high-income, industrialised democracies and for the most part English speaking (the exception to the latter was Montreal). That said, the children involved – in total 45 across the five research sites – offered a broad spectrum of experience and perspectives within those confines. While they are all aged between 8 and 10 (a deliberate decision to focus on the youngest children with the necessary skills to read the actual text of the UNCRC), they include: a rural primary school beside a public housing estate in a village in Northern Ireland; immigrant children in Montreal; affluent children from a Dublin suburb; an inner city primary school between a public housing estate and an affluent area in Melbourne; and a Boys and Girls Club after-school program serving primarily low income children in Arizona. Each of these perspectives is entitled to be heard and this pilot study enables that. However, we are fully aware that an Article 12-compliant process would require engaging with diverse groups of children of different ages in all UN countries. As such, the intention in this study was not to demonstrate definitively how the UNCRC would be different but if it would in fact be different and, if so, the nature of some of the possible changes.

A second limitation of the study was that it was not possible in the timescale to work on every provision of the UNCRC. Article 29, which defines the aims of education, was chosen as a working example for several reasons: it reflects the main interests of the lead and co-researchers; previous research suggests that it is something that children have views on and like to talk about; it is one of the longest (and most detailed of the UNCRC provisions) and thus provided a degree of substance for discussion; and it was the subject of the Committee's first General Comment (UN Committee, 2001) giving us further scope to compare adult and children's perspectives on its meaning. Ideally we would have started the process by asking the children which rights they thought the UNCRC should contain and then which one they would like to work on but time did not allow for that. We did, however, ask children if they thought that the UNCRC should contain a right to education which included a statement about the aims of education before we embarked on discussing its content.

In order to ensure that there was a degree of consistency across the research sites a common set of methods was developed, allowing for flexibility so that the individual researchers could adapt and develop the materials to be relevant to the children participating. Common to all the research teams was an understanding that children would need assistance to understand the context and the issues. Thus, a methodological approach developed by Lundy and McEvoy (2012) which aims to assist children towards an '(in)formed view' was used when conducting the research with children. This approach is one feature of an overall children's rights-based to research and is based on the premise that children have the right to information (CRC, Article 13, 17) and adult guidance (Article 5) in the formation of their views, which they should then be assisted in expressing freely (Article 12) (Lundy, 2007). According to Lundy and McEvoy (2012: 3), a children's rights-compliant approach to research may in certain instances "require that children are assisted not only in expressing their views but also in forming them." As such, this approach uses deliberate strategies to assist children in the formation of their views as part of the research process. Lundy and McEvoy (2012: 4) explain the rationale for this approach, arguing further that:

> *Research is conducted on many issues which impact on children's lives, but to which children may not have given any consideration and therefore, understandably, are unlikely to have a predetermined or informed view.*

The focus of this study – children's views on the text of the UNCRC – is just such an issue: children are unlikely to have given this or indeed the aims of education much, if any, thought and this were entitled to assistance to think through the issues and come to their own views. Building capacity on the substantive research issues is intended to enable children to contribute more confidently to the research without leading them to pre-determined or as Cruddas (2007) describes it 'adulterated' perspectives.

In the first session, children were introduced generally to the UNCRC and how it was developed. In order to enable the children to understand that the Convention is in effect a politically negotiated agreement whose content is the product of compromises between states with very different and sometimes directly competing interests, the children in most sites participated in an interactive exercise where they represented four fictitious countries that had radically different perspectives on child labour. The process of negotiation (sometimes without reaching a collective agreement) was the focus of this exercise and enabled the children to see that the UNCRC itself was not a perfect articulation of an ideal state of childhood but could be what Tomasevski (2003) has described as the bare minimum to which governments have grudgingly agreed.

In the second session, we asked the children to contemplate two questions: 'Why do you think children should go to school?' and 'What should children learn at school?' While 'education' and 'school/ing' are not the same thing, it was easier for children of this age to understand the issues this way. The purpose of this research exercise was to elicit children's ideas, words and perspectives on what the aims of education should also be. We found it helpful to visualise the dimensions of these questions in concentric circles (see figure 2). In order to assist the children to form their views, we worked outwards from their own perspective, then that of their parents, their communities and then the other nations of the world. This encouraged the children to think beyond their own perspective to the broader aims of education in terms of both national and international interests.

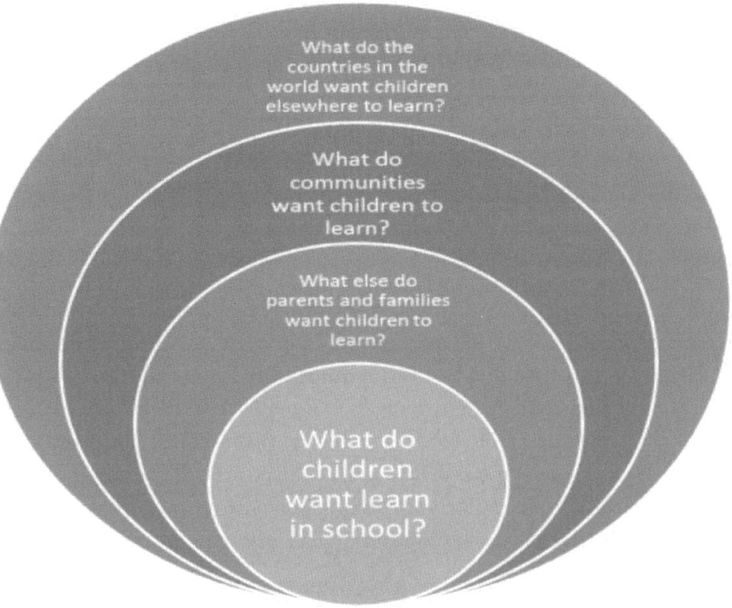

In the final session, we presented the focus groups with the text of Article 29. In most instances, children were given the actual text. In some, this was abbreviated slightly but with no loss of content. It was not appropriate to provide them with so-called "child-friendly" versions as these are often so truncated that there is fundamental loss of substance (a point to which we return at the end of the chapter). Children were reminded of their thoughts on the aims of education from the previous session and than asked: Do you agree with everything that is in Article 29? 'What do you think is missing?'; 'How would you change it?'. They went through each individual paragraph of the Article, discussing how the existing text of the UNCRC could be altered to represent their perspectives on the aims of education. Research teams took field notes and sessions were audio recorded. The transcripts from each site were shared and then analysed to identify common themes and discussed across the international research teams for verification and refining. The following sections summarise these findings in three categories: differences in content; differences in interpretation; and differences in style.

Would the UNCRC Have Been Different if Children Had Been Involved in Drafting It?

The main aim of this was study was to see how the UNCRC would have been different if children had been afforded an input into the drafting process. To achieve this, children's informed views on the aims of education were mapped against the actual final text of Article 29. This enabled the children and researchers to explore areas where the children's views aligned with or differed from the agreed adult text. What emerged was that the main differences in the adult and children's perspectives of the aims of education was not limited to content alone (which had been the starting point of the study). Rather, the differences that emerged were threefold: differences in content; differences in interpretation; and differences in style.

Differences in Content

Overall the children's expressed views on the aims of education matched up well with its actual content, although they made some important suggestions for amendments and identified some omissions. So for instance, all of the children readily accepted the content of Article 29 (d) which includes: *'the spirit of understanding, peace, tolerance, equality of sexes, and friendship among all peoples, ethnic, national and religious groups and persons of indigenous origin"*. Children across all the research sites agreed that education should help children get along peacefully with others having defined this to be one of the key aims of education in the following terms:

> *Learn respect, friendship and kindness.*
> (*Australia*)

> *Coperating with others and coming to an agriment* [*sic*].
> (*Ireland*)

> *To be calm... no wars, no violence.*
> (*USA*)

The children's focus on this is important and interesting showing their awareness of the link between education and peace, as well as the increased global realities of children, including war and conflict.

Children were also in agreement with the broad purposes of education in 29(a), albeit that they tended to define these very specifically in relation to actual topics they should learn at school (such as writing, etc). Their responses to the purpose of education especially with regards to Article 29(c) were also supportive of the need to respect children's own culture and language as well as other languages, particularly that of the country in which they were living. Interestingly, many of the children involved in the study sites were in a situation of minority which made them all the more aware of the importance of safe-guarding their right to their own culture. Comments include:

> *Speak in your language.*
> (*USA*)

> *Celebrate your own culture.*
> (*USA*)

To learn Irish.
(*Ireland*)

They should learn languages and maths, haoin +haoin = do.
(*Ireland*)

We need to learn a lot of language to communicate with many languages.
(*Canada*)

Interestingly, one of the things that did not appear at all in the children's original activity on defining the aims of education was that education should promote understanding of human rights (that is Article 29(b)). When asked why they hadn't thought of this initially, the Northern Irish group suggested that it was too obvious when the whole point of the activity was to define their human rights so that they hadn't thought about it. When asked if they agreed with it being included, they were unanimous about its importance and, once again, keen to discuss and list the types of rights that children should learn about.

There were, however, several objectives for education that the children identified that did not appear to their satisfaction in Article 29 itself. One of those was that education should aim to show children how to be caring and to care for others, a particularly strong theme with the group from Northern Ireland but mentioned elsewhere too. Examples include:

When we're adults we will have to care for our own children
(*N. Ireland*)

To help the needy. And know how to help people that are sick
(*N. Ireland*)

Learn how to be kind
(*Ireland*)

Learn to be good in your life.
(*Canada*)

This was not thought to be covered sufficiently by Article 29 (d) since it seemed to them to be aimed at people who were different from them such as people in other countries or from different cultures. For the children, the emphasis on 'tolerance' was not the same as encouraging children to be kind and considerate towards others generally.

A second prominent theme that children identified rapidly as something missing from the UNCRC was that school should prepare children to get a good job, enabling them to support themselves. They queried whether this was part of "preparation for a responsible life" but felt that it should be stated explicitly in the aims of education.

It is noteworthy that similar suggestions were made during the drafting process: several countries had flagged the desire for a more explicit description of how education should prepare children for economic sustainability. For example, Spain requested the following wording:

> *so that he will be capable, by himself and as a result of the training he has received, of coping with the necessities of life and will be a useful member of society.*
> *(taken from UN Doc, 1978-1989)*

Examples from the children about this were abundant from all research sites:

> *On va à l'ecole pour savoir lire et écrire. Si vous allez a l'ecole vous devez avoir un bon metier.*
> *(Canada)*

> *Own your own business*
> *(USA)*

> *Works and Learn for a job and to go to college (to learn specific things for preparing for a job, practical things such as paying taxes).*
> *(USA)*

> *To make money when u r older.*
> *(Ireland)*

> *Have a good education. To learn all the subjects before you graduate. Make good friends. Follow your dreams. Have a good career.*
> *(Australia)*

While children were not the only ones who saw this functional purpose of education as core, explicit references to it did not make it to the final text. Moreover, when the aims of education were further elaborated in the Committee's first general comment, the need to provide an education which would put children in a position to get a job or to be self-sustaining was not included. The closest statement to this is the somewhat indirect comment that:

> *the curriculum must be of direct relevance to the child's social, cultural, environmental and economic context and to his or her present and future needs and take full account of the child's evolving capacities, teaching methods should be tailored to the different needs of different children.*
> *(UN Committee, 2001)*

This difference in emphasis between the children we spoke to and the adult drafters and interpreters on this issue is interesting, however not surprising. For many children school is experienced as 'work' by them, especially when it comes to learning subjects and skills that they know are directly related to their future work as adults. From the perspective of adult drafters, the emphasis reflects wider tensions between an over prescriptive and human capital orientation to children's education versus one that embraces the whole person of the child (Devine and Luttrell, 2013). However, in the midst of a global recession and often for children who come from families who are struggling to cope, it is unsurprising that children in all research jurisdictions are concerned about 'making money' and getting a 'good job'.

With regards to their future preparedness, children from the USA and Australia identified specifically that their education should prepare them to be good leaders. Therefore according to these children, school should prepare children not just to be economically independent but to undertake leadership in the future:

> *They [children] could be a Prime Minister if they want. They [children] could be a good leader.*
> (*Australia*)

> *To be the president (you have to go to school to be president).*
> (*USA*)

> *They could also be a good leader.*
> (*Australia*)

Within the Australian context this might be explained by the fact that the research was conducted during a successful challenge by the government of the day to the Prime ministerial leadership and then campaigning for the 2013 Australian Federal election. Media saturation on leadership of and for Australia was therefore prevalent.

We also asked children if there was anything they did not agree with. As discussed above, children generally thought that everything that was included in Article 29 needed to be there, even when they had not thought of it themselves originally, with one interesting exception. One child in Ireland queried the universal nature of respecting all cultures:

> *How can you respect a civilisation like North Korea? Is the section suggesting we should respect societies such as Saudi Arabia or North Korea? That would be against a personal feeling on human rights. If so, I do not think that this makes sense.*
> (*Ireland*)

This child is bringing a critical analysis to the sweeping universality of the adopted statement, thus demonstrating the ability to critically engage with the content of the UNCRC. Had this child been part of the initial negotiations, it is likely that this provision would not have been worded in such an all-encompassing way.

Differences in Interpretation

As discussed above, children agreed with almost everything that Article 29 says. However, it was readily apparent in some of the discussions that children were interpreting aspects of it in different ways so that it matched their own views on the aims of education and that the children's understanding may or may not align with adults' views of the same. So for instance, children were keen to list all the topics that they should cover in education, including the traditional subjects like Mathematics, History, Geography as well as a significant emphasis on sport, art, music and "creativity" which is not always valued to the same extent in national curricula.

In the Dublin group, there was some discussion here also on how far the development in Article 29(a) should go (i.e. what was meant by the phrase 'to the fullest potential') Children queried:

> *should children be pushed to develop their talents?*
> *some people may not be as good as other people and it's only supposed to develop their skills and not make them the best ...*
> *there is loads of pressure to em to actually do ... what people are actually trying to make you good at ... say if you want to be able to sing or play football or hurling ... they should have a choice to which they want to do.*

There was also some discussion in the groups about what actually counts as a 'talent' in Article 29(a). One boy in Northern Ireland pointed out that his skill in video games was not recognised as a 'talent'

> *My best talent is playing MineCraft. I am really good at it and it requires lots of skill and creativity but adults think it is a waste of time.*
> (*Northern Ireland*)

In fact, children interviewed across all sites mentioned explicitly that their education should enable them to use technology adequately. One child suggested that it should be, in fact, a right *'to go on computer'.* The children's narrative highlights the double play between their wishes and desires – what they love - and what is considered practical and 'useful' in their learning. The dichotomy between children and adults in these views is not always clear cur but mirrors the broader tensions both children and adults (teachers and parents) struggle and negotiate over in a rapidly changing social (and technological) context as the school system tries to catch up with changing child and youth cultures. The fact that the UNCRC itself lags behind children's views in this is, however, not surprising when the date the Convention was drafted is considered. As Veerman (2010) points out:

> *Where the drafters of the Convention had only just stopped working on their typewriter and started to use a computer and had to pay for buying records, the new generation (the "dot com" generation) have already had computers available at kindergarten.*

Likewise, children in all sites suggested that education should develop respect for the natural environment. While environmental degradation is often a prominent issue for children (Blanchet-Cohen, 2008), there was very little discussion regarding the environment in the negotiations leading up to the final draft adopted by the General Assembly in 1989 albeit that this was remedied to some extent in General Comment no.1, (2001) which states:

> *For the development of respect for the natural environment and sustainable development with the socio-economic, sociocultural and demographic issues. Similarly, respect for the natural environment should be learnt by children at home, in school and within the community, encompass both the national and international problems, and actively involve children in local, regional or global environmental projects.*

The children's interpretation of Article 29(d) was, however, to some degree context-specific. All of the children mentioned the need to learn about the environment or pollution stating for example:

> *You shouldn't waste paper, because it comes from trees.*
> *(USA)*

> *Know that littering is wrong. And it hurts the planet you live in.*
> *(Dublin)*

However, children in Australia are seeing and living through natural disasters in different ways, for example: tsunamis, drought, floods, bush fires, and earthquakes etc. Traditionally, many of these natural disasters have occurred in rural areas. However large cities in Australia have endured floods and cities in neighbouring countries like Auckland, New Zealand, sustained devastating earthquakes have made an impact on children's lives and their understanding of the world. The Australia children were acutely aware of this and suggested that children:

> *[learn about] earth quakes and natural disasters.*
> *(Australia)*

These differences in interpretation and emphasis between children and adults as well as children in different contexts are potentially significant. Children and adults might well agree on a text to describe their rights in the UNCRC. However, as with all international human rights treaties, the breadth of the chosen phraseology enables those whose obligation it is to apply it (as well as those who claim rights) to hold sometimes very different opinions about what it means in practice. This is, in fact, a feature of human rights treaty drafting: provisions are deliberately worded very broadly so that the various parties agree to ratify them and then return to their home context and apply their own vision of that - a process sometimes referred to as "constructive ambiguity". In this instance, however, different "takes" on the meaning of substantive rights are crucially important. If we want to make rights "real" for children, there is a need to understand how they understand it in their own contexts since it is apparent that this will not always coincide with an adult vision of the same.

Differences in Style

Although children's views about the aims of education were often similar to the adult drafters, the way in which they expressed these rights was often very different. In particular, children were more likely to give examples of the things that they felt that children should be learning at school rather than broadly stated aims of education. The table below outlines some of the examples of suggestions the children made what children should learn in school, grouped within the existing Article 29 categories. (See table 1)

A	Develop the child's personality, talents, mind and bodies;	'Maths', 'Social Studies', 'Exercise', 'Healthy snacks' 'art' 'music'
B	Develop respect for human rights;	'No slavery', 'right to be free', 'should be able to choose your own religion'
C	Develop respect for the child's parents, their own culture and language and for cultures different from their own;	'Speak in your language', 'celebrate your own culture', 'Learn the history of your country', 'History of your family', 'Learn about the bible'
D	Prepare the child for responsible life and to learn about peace, tolerance, equality of boys and girls, and friendship among all peoples;	'To get a good job', 'to make friends', 'peaceful', 'learn manners', 'We want to get on with each other, no matter the skin'
E	Develop respect for the environment.	'Clean up environment', 'do not pollute', 'protect animals', 'if we don't clean it up – we won't have an environment – it will be bad'.

Table 1: Art. 29 in children's words

When children were shown the actual content of Article 29, all of them reported difficulty with some of the vocabulary used. In Montreal, children read and underlined all of the words they did not understand, including terms such as 'fundamental' and 'civilisations'. When these children were asked what was missing, they suggested that it needed to use images:

> *Photos are missing, so we could understand it well*
> *(Canada)*

The actual text of the UNCRC is displayed below, and as discussed above, children from all sites had difficulty understanding it on their own:

> Article 29 – actual text.
> 1. *States Parties agree that the education of the child shall be directed to:*
> (*a*) *The development of the child's personality, talents and mental and physical abilities to their fullest potential;*
> (*b*) *The development of respect for human rights and fundamental freedoms, and for the principles enshrined in the Charter of the United Nations;*
> (*c*) *The development of respect for the child's parents, his or her own cultural identity, language and values, for the national values of the country in which the child is living, the country from which he or she may originate, and for civilizations different from his or her own;*
> (*d*) *The preparation of the child for responsible life in a free society, in the spirit of understanding, peace, tolerance, equality of sexes, and friendship among all peoples, ethnic, national and religious groups and persons of indigenous origin;*
> (*e*) *The development of respect for the natural environment.*

Whilst there are various 'child friendly' variations of the UNCRC, we struggled to find one that was both accessible to children yet did not compromise its substance. Displayed below is a popular 'Child Friendly' variation of Art. 29:

> *Your education should help you use and develop your talents and abilities. It should also help you learn to live peacefully, protect the environment and respect other people.*

Whilst this variation is more accessible to children, it does not cover all of Article 29 (such as human rights education, respect for their own culture and the natural environment, etc.) and is therefore incomplete. The Belfast team (who were working with the youngest group of children) produced the adaptation below in an attempt to be both accessible and legally robust:

> The Government agrees that education should:
> - *Develop the child's personality, talents, mind and body*
> - *Develop respect for human rights*
> - *Develop respect for the child's parents, their own culture and language and for cultures different from their own;*
> - *Prepare the child for responsible life and to learn about peace, tolerance, equality of boys and girls, and friendship among all peoples*
> - *Develop respect for the environment*

This version could undoubtedly be improved upon with the input of children as the study participants still needed support to understand some aspect of this. What is apparent in the wake of the research is that the Convention was not only not drafted *by* children; it was not in fact drafted *for* use by children. While its primary target audience is States Parties, Article 42 requires that its provisions be made widely known to children and adults alike. It is therefore imperative to find ways of communicating its content without sacrificing its meaning: child friendly should not be a substitute for just plain wrong.

Child-friendly versions were not the only "translations" of the text to jeopardise children's ability to work with an accurate understanding of the UNCRC. In the discussion with children in Montreal, it became apparent that the French version of Article 29 was not consistent with the English one, and most disturbingly, the choice of words reflected a different conception of children's education. Three of the sub articles in the French version use the term 'inculquer', with translates into English as "inculcate." The term is however not equivalent to "develop" found in the official version. From the latin *inculcare*, there is a forceful and uni-directional connotation to 'inculquer' The New Oxford Dictionary defines inculcate as meaning "to instil by persistent instruction"; conveying a vision of the learner as an empty vessel to be filled, a vision inconsistent with the spirit of the UNCRC, which recognizes the active role of the learner (UN Committee, 2001). It is noteworthy that any direct or indirect reference for inculcate has been removed from UNICEF child-friendly version of Article 29. The notion of "develop" having been replaced by "helping you learn." Was this a translation mistake that reflected their dominant views on education? That could be the case because only in Article 29 is the word 'inculquer' used as a translation for develop. The discrepancy is stark reminder of how underpinning language are power discourses that reflect norms and context (Holzscheiter, 2011). If francophone children had been at least been consulted on the drafts, this official "mistake" could have been identified and possibly been avoided.

Conclusions and Implications

Would the content of the UNCRC be different if children had been involved in its drafting? It was likely that the answer to the question was always going to be "yes" but interesting that this study suggests that it would probably not be radically different, certainly in terms of its content. When children had time to explore their own views on the aims of education and then look at the actual text of Article 29, they agreed with most of what had been adopted over twenty years previously. This is in some senses a further endorsement of the legitimacy and relevance of the UNCRC itself – the adults appear to have got it right from children's perspectives, at least for the most part.

That said, if the adults had taken their responsibilities under Article 12 seriously during the drafting process, it is conceivable that there would have been some additions or changes in emphasis. In particular, the drafters might have agreed with the children in this study that education should aim to teach children to be caring or to prepare them to get a job. Moreover, in terms of other rights beyond Article 29, it might be anticipated that, had children been involved, they would not have squeezed the right to play in between culture and leisure in Article 31; that children with disabilities would have had more specific suggestions for Article 23; and that sexual orientation would have been included in the list of prohibited categories of discrimination in Article 2 if young gay and lesbians had had a say. It also seems very likely that the Convention would have been renamed. It may not have been limited to the rights of the 'child': young people would undoubtedly have advocated for the inclusion of a term which covered those under 18 who do not describe themselves or want to be described as children (Cantwell, 2011).

Does it matter that children's views were not incorporated in terms of the validity of the instrument itself? The answer to that is also probably not. The UNCRC is an imperfect political compromise whose many shortfalls were identified at the outset (Freeman, 2000). The broad wording of the provisions and the fact that they need to be interpreted and applied together means that they are "elastic" enough to cover most situations (Kilkelly and Lundy, 2006). The key then is in ensuring that it is interpreted and understood in a way that is respectful of children's views and opinions. An important opportunity to do that exists in the drafting of the General Comments which become authoritative statements of the meaning and application of particular rights or the rights of particular groups. While it is too late for General Comment no.1 on the Aims of Education, in recent General Comments such as the right to play and business (UN Committee, 2013a), and the impact of business on children's rights (UN Committee, 2013b) there has been a move to consult children and include their perspectives. While these appear to have been relatively limited in scale and facilitated by NGOs, they are a small step in the right direction. A goal would be to ensure that states parties (who have the primary responsibility under Article 12) undertake this work with children and enable their views to be fed directly into the drafting of all future General Comments.

This research adds to a growing body of literature that suggests that differences between child and adult views may not be as simplistic as once assumed. Other research has evidenced a sense of social justice, empathy and ethics in young children, in contrast to assumptions that they are egocentric and cannot take other's point of view until age five or six (MacNaughton and Smith, 2009, 2008). Indeed, children's sense of empathy and fairness are often quite striking, and were reflected in responses across all the settings in this study. For example, children not only expressed concerns about their own families, neighbourhoods, and personal well-being and future goals, but talked about saving the planet, poverty, animal rights, and a range of social issues. While children's examples were often clearly anchored in their lifeworlds and recent experiences, they were highly engaged with notions of universal rights and wanted to talk about these at some length (and depth). Their sensitivity to people and groups experiencing social and educational exclusion and what their futures might be was further evidence of the importance of giving their views due weight.

More generally, the failure to engage children in the drafting of the UNCRC and in its subsequent interpretation and communications raises important questions around inter-generational relations of power and status between adults and children and how the Convention itself reflects adult discourses of what is considered 'good' and of 'value' in children's childhoods. Our concern to identify both children's capacities to critique and constructively engage with the text of the Convention in a manner that is meaningful to them highlights the lacuna that exists currently in framing the Convention without reference to children's own (and multiple) voices. This is an important issue of principle not only with respect to the content of the UNCRC itself but also with respect to the realisation of children's rights in practice. Incorporating children's views is no less challenging than incorporating the views of the many adults who were involved in drafting and negotiating the convention. Yet it is only when children's voices – and discourses – are reflected in the text that the convention fully comes alive in both its potential and challenges.

In his Children and Society paper, Michael Freeman went on to state that "The next Convention cannot afford to ignore the views of children." (2000: 282) This is true for the reasons outlined at the start – once the UNCRC was adopted and ratified, the governments become under an obligation to seek and take children's views seriously in such activities. Nonetheless, subsequent United Nations treaty drafting processes (such as the United Nations Convention on the Rights of Persons with Disabilities (UN, 2008) and even Optional Protocol No. 3 on the UNCRC itself (UN, 2012) have proceeded to do the same. The same issues that undermine children's participation at local and national levels (the tension between ensuring meaningful involvement of a broad reach of children versus the time and resources to do it properly) appear to work against the meaningful participation of children in these international debates. Currently it is mainly NGOs who are taking the lead on this (Lundy *et al.*, 2012). However, it needs be seen as a responsibility of the main duty bearers – the states parties who are bound in law to implement Article 12. For those conversations to be meaningful, it is important that children and young people learn about their existing rights in language that they would use and understand. Experience in this project suggest that child-*authored* would be a key means to achieve so-called child-*friendly*.

References

Baker, J., Lynch, K., Cantillon, S. and Walsh, J., *Equality: From Theory to Action.* (Basingstoke: Palgrave MacMillan, 2004).

Blanchet-Cohen, N., Ragan, D. and Amsden, J., "Children becoming social actors: Using visual maps to understand children's views of environmental change.", *Children Youth and Environments* 2003 13(2), 278-299.

Cantwell, N., "Are Children's Rights still Human?" in A. Invernizzi (ed), *The Human Rights of Children: From Visions to Implementation.* (Aldershot: Ashgate Publishing, 2011).

Cheney, K. E., *Pillars of the nation: Child citizens and Ugandan national development* (Chicago: University of Chicago Press, 2007).

Cohen, C. P., "The Role of Nongovernmental Organizations in the Drafting of the Convention on the Rights of the Child.", *Human Rights Quarterly* 1990 12(1), 137-147.

Cruddas, L., "Engaged voices—dialogic interaction and the construction of shared social meanings.", *Educational Action Research* 2007 15(3), 479-488.

Davey, C. and Lundy, L., "Towards Greater Recognition of the Right to Play: An Analysis of Article 31 of the UNCRC", *Children and Society* 2011 19(1), 129-144.

Devine, D., "Children's citizenship and the structuring of adult/child relations in schools", *Childhood* 2002 9, 303

Devine, D. and Luttrell, W., "Children and value – education in neo-liberal times", *Children and Society* 2013 27(4), 241-244

Freeman, M., "The future of children's rights.", *Children and Society* 2000 14(4), 277-293.

James, A., *European Childhoods: Cultures.* Politics and Participation (New York: Palgrave Press, 2008).

Kjørholt, A. T., "Childhood as a Symbolic Space. Searching for Authentic Voices in the Era of Globalisation" in S. Aitken, K. Lund and A. T. Kjørholt (eds), *Global Childhoods. Globalization, Development and Young People* (Oxon: Routledge, 2007)

Kilkelly, U., Kilpatrick, R., Lundy, L., Moore, L., Scraton, P., Davey, C. and McAlister, S., *Children's Rights in Northern Ireland.* (Belfast: *Northern Ireland Commissioner for Children and Young People*, 2004).

Killkelly, U. and Lundy, L., "Children's Rights in Action: Using the UN Convention on the Rights of the Child as an Auditing Tool.", *Child and Family Law Quarterly* 2006 18, 331.

Liebel, M. (ed), *Children's rights from below: Cross-cultural perspectives* (New York: Palgrave Macmillan, 2012).

Lundy, L., "'Voice' is not enough: conceptualising Article 12 of the United Nations Convention on the Rights of the Child.", *British Educational Research Journal* 2007 33(6), 927-942.

Lundy, L., Kilkelly, U., Byrne, B. and Kang, J., *The UN Convention on the Rights of the Child: A Study of the Legal Implementation in 12 Countries.* (UK: UNICEF, 2012)

Lundy, L. and McEvoy, L., "Children's rights and research processes: Assisting children to (in) formed views", *Childhood* 2012 19(1), 129-144.

MacNaughton, G. and Smith, K., "Engaging ethically with young children: principles and practices for listening and responding with care." in G. MacNaughton, P. Hughes, & K. Smith (eds), *Young children as active citizens: principles, policies and pedagogies* (London: Cambridge Scholars Publishing, 2008).

MacNaughton, G. and Smith, K., "Children's Rights in Early Childhood." in M. J. Kehily (ed), *Introduction to Early Childhood Studies* (2nd edn) (Maidenhead: Open University Press, 2009).

Melton, G. B., "Children's concepts of their rights 1", *Journal of Clinical Child & Adolescent Psychology* 1980 9(3), 186-190.

Melton G. B. and Limber, S. P., "What Children's Rights Mean to children: Children's Own Views" in M. Freeman and P. Veerman (eds), *The Ideologies of Children's Rights* (Leiden: Martinus Nijhoff, 1993).

Morrow, V., "'We are people too': Children's and young people's perspectives on children's rights and decision-making in England", *The International Journal of Children's Rights* 1999 7, 49-170.

Rizvi, F., "Experiences of Cultural Diversity in the Context of an Emergent Transnationalism.", *European Educational Research Journal* 2011 10(2), 180-188.

Swadener, B., Lundy, L., Hobashi, J. and Blanchet-Cohen, N., *Children's Rights and Education, International Perspectives* (New York: Peter Lang Publishing, 2013).

Taylor, N., Smith, A. B. and Narin, K., "Rights Important to Young People: Secondary Students and Staff Perspectives.", *The International Journal of Child Rights* 2001 9, 137.

Teresevičienė M. and Jonynienė, Ž., "Students' Perceptions of their Rights in Lithuania School", Psychology International (2001) 22(2), 152–174.

Tomasevski, K., *Education denied: Costs and remedies* (London: Zed Books, 2003).

UN Committee on the Rights of the Child, *General Comment No. 1, The Aims of Education.* UN/CRC/GC/2001/1 (Geneva, United Nations, 2001).

UN Committee on the Rights of the Child, *General Comment No. 12, The right of the child to be heard.* CRC/C/GC/12 (Geneva, United Nations, 2009).

UN Committee on the Rights of the Child, *General Comment No. 17, The right of the child to rest, leisure, play, recreational activities, cultural life and the arts* (art. 31) CRC/C/GC/17 (Geneva, United Nations, 2013a).

UN Committee on the Rights of the Child, *General Comment No. 16, State obligations regarding the impact of the business sector on children's rights.* CRC/C/GC/16 (Geneva, United Nations, 2013b).

UN Doc E/CN.4/1324 (1978) Centre for Human Rights Legislative History of the Convention on the Rights of the Child. (Traveaux Preperatoire 1978-1989)

UN, *United Nations Convention on the Rights of the Child.* (Geneva, United Nations, 1989)

UN, *United Nations Convention on Persons with Disabilities.* (Geneva, United Nations, 2008).

Veerman, P. E., "*The ageing of the United Nations Convention on the Rights of the Child.*", *International Journal of Children's Rights* 2010 18(4), 585-618.

Ending Corporal Punishment in Childhood: Advancing Children's Rights to Dignity and Respectful Treatment

Bernadette J. Saunders
Monash University, Australia

Introduction

Children have long endured pain and humiliation at the hands of adults entrusted with their care and protection. On children's behalf, Michael Freeman has tirelessly contributed to the important pursuit of each child's human rights to dignity and respectful treatment. Michael's insights and wisdom are captured in his extraordinarily long list of oft-cited publications that for many decades have inspired people around the world. His very generous acknowledgment and selective encouragement of others' work are a feature of his writing, as are his astute sense of humour, and his tongue-in-cheek remarks, often used so effectively to powerfully communicate his message. When I first came across Michael's profound and inspirational writings I was in awe of his work and did not envisage the pleasure of meeting him. However, in 2008, Michael was the keynote speaker at the 17th Biennial Congress of the International Society for the Prevention of Child Abuse and Neglect (ISPCAN) in Hong Kong, and I was fortunate to be present at his eloquent and stirring paper. After his address, with much hesitation, and a lot of encouragement from a colleague, I introduced myself to him, and was delighted to learn that Michael is not only inspiring but generous with his time, helpful and supportive. Since then, opportunities to converse with him have been a very special privilege and I was especially delighted to be invited to present at the 2013 University College London colloquium, 'The Law and Michael Freeman', which honoured this much admired, respected and caring man, and his remarkable work.

In his keynote address in Hong Kong, Michael posed the question: 'Can we conquer child abuse if we don't outlaw the physical chastisement of children?' His answer, unsurprisingly, was a very clear, 'no'. Indeed, he concluded his paper by confidently asserting that the corporal punishment of children will be banned:

> ... in Asia as elsewhere. And when it does we will have nailed a further nail in the coffin of child abuse, and we will have advanced the status of children. (Freeman, 2008:11)

A. Diduck, N. Peleg, H. Reece (eds.), Law in Society: Reflections on Children, Family, Culture and Philosophy
Copyright 2015 Koninklijke Brill NV. Printed in The Netherlands. ISBN 978-90-04-26148-8. pp. 243-270.

This chapter extensively draws on Michael Freeman's work on children's rights and, in particular, the corporal punishment of children. It explores the limited but promising progress towards full abolition of corporal punishment; the historical and ongoing tolerance of corporal punishment in schools and by parents; the inspiring visions and example of some early children's rights advocates and, of particular significance, some children's perspectives gained from research on physical punishment in various parts of the world. Drawing on Michael's work, the chapter ends with some thoughts on how progress towards full recognition of children's human rights to dignity, and thus their right not to be corporally punished (see Freeman, 2010b), might be hastened.

Corporal Punishment, the United Nations Convention on the Rights of the Child (UNCRC), and Other Human Rights Treaties

Children's human rights are internationally recognised under the UNCRC (1989), and Article 24(1) of the International Covenant on Civil and Political Rights (ICCPR) which states that: 'Every child shall have, without any discrimination ... the right to such measures of protection as are required by his [sic] status as a minor, on the part of his family, society and the State'. However, it is disappointing that 'omnibus terms' within treaties may diminish the power of human rights law as only their broad interpretation will ensure children's rights to privacy, social and economic protection, and physical and mental health (Bitensky, 2006: 48). Article 19(1) of the UNCRC states that:

> States Parties shall take all appropriate legislative, administrative, social and educational measures to protect children from *all forms* of physical or mental violence, injury or abuse... Or... maltreatment... (emphases added)

It is notable that Article 19 'does not specifically refer to corporal punishment' (Freeman, 2010b: 220). Moreover, consensual definitions of 'abuse' and 'maltreatment' remains elusive. Indeed, Nolan draws on parental physical punishment case law to conclude that 'protections' thought to be inherent in the UNCRC 'can be undermined and even perverted by being subject to selective interpretation' (2011: 550). Given that 'we beat children in the name of discipline and pretend it is not violence' (Freeman, 2000c: 287; see also, Freeman, 2011a: 20), the imprecision of Article 19 of the Convention is troubling.

Fortunately, in recent years, the Committee on the Rights of the Child has defined 'corporal punishment' as 'any punishment in which physical force is used and intended to cause some degree of discomfort, *however light*' (2006: 4), and in General Comments, Nos. 8 and 13 (2006, 2011), the Committee has unambiguously stated that Article 19(1) of the Convention inarguably extends to the child's right not to be subjected to corporal punishment. This is undoubtedly a welcome and an influential interpretation of Article 19 but, as Nolan contends, assertions made by the Committee on the Rights of the Child are only '"soft" law'; less binding than the responsibilities tied to the treaty provisions (2011: 549). Freeman has long been critical of the Convention for, among other concerns, not explicitly protecting children from corporal punishment. Indeed, he espoused its improvement 'by giving it more "teeth"', by adding 'to the rights contained within in it', by weakening 'the emphasis on adult values', and by making children's rights 'more specific', such as rewriting Article 19 to give children 'the right not to be hit' (Freeman, 1997a: 72).

Other articles in the Convention also inexplicitly support the abolition of physical punishment. In particular, Freeman (1999) draws attention to both Article 37 which states that 'no child shall be subjected to... cruel, inhuman or degrading treatment or punishment', and Article 24(3) which states that 'States Parties shall take all effective and appropriate measures with a view to abolishing traditional practices prejudicial to the health of children'. Common sense arguments linking the tradition of physically punishing children with consequent poor physical and mental health are now well supported by increasing empirical research evidence (discussed in more detail below). Freeman (1999) further advises that the non-discrimination principle in Article 2, the best interests principle in Article 3, the participation principle in Article 12 and the emphasis on human dignity in Articles 28(2) and 39, may all be interpreted to support arguments for the child's right to freedom from all forms of violence, including physical punishment in all settings. Additionally, Peleg contends that Article 6, the child's right to development, and Article 27, the child's right to a standard of living that helps her or him to develop fully, may also be violated in contexts that permit children's corporal punishment (2011: 384).

Moreover, the legal prohibition of 'cruel, inhuman or degrading treatment', including children's physical punishment, has been encouraged by the UN Human Rights Committee (see, for example, Office of the High Commissioner for Human Rights, 1992, Article 7 'which relates not only to acts that cause physical pain but also to acts that cause mental suffering [and] must extend to corporal punishment ... as an educative or disciplinary measure ... [A]rticle 7 protects, in particular, children ...), the UN Committee against Torture (see, for example, its 2008 report on Australia's implementation of Article 16, which states that '[t]he State party should adopt and implement legislation banning corporal punishment at home and in public and private schools, detention centres, and all alternative care settings in all States and Territories', the UN Committee on Economic, Social and Cultural Rights (see, for example, EPOCH, 2013a excerpts from ESCR Committee reports on Denmark, Jamaica and Rwanda, in which full abolition of 'corporal punsihment of any kind' is recommended), the African Committee of Experts on the Rights and Welfare of the Child (see, for example, its 2012 report on Addis Ababa, Ethiopia, which identified and requested a response to 'shortcomings' including 'violence against children such as corporal punishment'), and the European Committee of Social Rights (EPOCH, 2013b excerpts from ECSR reports on France, Ireland, Italy, Slovenia, Czech Republic, Cyprus, and Belguim, in which it is noted that in these countries 'laws protecting children from corporal punishment are inadequate and therefore in breach of the European Social Charter').

Law, 'whatever its source', symbolises 'what is right and wrong' and it has 'the capacity to effect change'; international law may thus be a lever for education and 'social engineering' and it 'should not be discounted' (Freeman, 2000b: 511-12. See also

Freeman, 2010b and Bitensky, 2006) for more detailed discussion of human rights treaties that potentially afford children protection from all forms of inhumane and degrading treatment, including corporal punishment).

Limited Progress toward Abolition of Physical Punishment

To varying degrees, children depend on adults for their care and protection. Characteristically in a stage of becoming, this ought not detract from children's status as human beings and should not disallow them their human rights as 'people of today' (Janusz Korczak, in Joseph, 2007:19). Indeed, 'to take children's rights seriously requires us to take seriously both protection and recognition of autonomy' (Freeman, 1997b: 95), and '[d]ependency should not be a reason to be deprived of choice and respect' (Freeman, 1998: 440, 2011b :35). However, in many countries parents retain the right or, as Michael has nuanced, 'actually the freedom to hit' their children (Freeman, 2008: 2). Both receiving and observing corporal punishment instill fear and reinforces children's subjugation and low status; these experiences may deny 'their present autonomy' and threaten 'their capacity for future autonomy' (Freeman, 1992b: 66).

For too long, children have been punished for being children, and progress towards abolishing physical punishment, while promising, is much too slow. As at March 2014, with the exception of the United States, Somalia and South Sudan, 193 countries have ratified the UNCRC (1989) yet, following Sweden's lead in 1979, only 36 countries have since banned physical punishment in all locations, including the child's home. The numbers of states with full abolition are, however, steadily and promisingly increasing. Prior to the beginning of the 21st century, only eight countries had introduced a ban. Sweden was the first country in 1979, followed by Finland (1983), Norway (1987), Austria (1989), Cyprus (1994), Denmark (1997), and Croatia (1999). In 2000 Germany, Israel and Bulgaria introduced a ban, followed by Iceland (2003), the Ukraine (2004), Romania (2004), and Hungary (2005). In 2007, seven more countries took this significant step – Spain, the Netherlands, Togo, Portugal, and Venezuela. Also Uruguay, which was the first Latin American country, and New Zealand, which remains the only English-speaking country to do so (see Wood *et al.*, 2008 for a detailed account of strategies that led to this inspiring outcome). The Republic of Moldova, Liechtenstein, Luxembourg and Costa Rica banned corporal punishment in all settings in 2008 and, in 2010, Poland and Albania joined this special group. Four African countries, in addition to Togo, have recently adopted this enlightened stance – Kenya, Tunisia and the Republic of Congo in 2010, and South Sudan in 2011. In 2013, Honduras became the fourth Latin American country to ban physical punishment in all settings and, most recently, Macedonia introduced legislation to ban this degrading practice and Turkmenistan's ban (introduced in 2002) was officially confirmed (End All Corporal Punishment of Children (EPOCH), 2014). In these progressive countries the assault of a child can no longer be tolerated as 'simply a fact of childhood' (McGillivray, 1997a:211), nor can it be defended as a lawful, reasonable, or justifiable violation of a child's body even, and perhaps particularly, if misconstrued as discipline.

In 41 countries it remains lawful for children to be sentenced to caning, whipping or flogging (see the EPOCH website for updates on global progress towards abolition of corporal punishment). Over 70 countries still allow children's corporal punishment in schools (EPOCH, 2014). In Australian schools it is not prohibited in three states (see Barrett, 2012; Holzer and Lamont, 2010) and in the US, it is allowed in 19 states (see Farmer and Neier, 2008; Farmer and Neier, 2009 for disturbing reports on the corporal punishment of children, particularly children with disabilities, in US public schools). For reports on school punishment in some other parts of the world, see Khoury-Kassabri (2012) on Arab schools in Israel; Ayanniyi *et al.* (2011) on eye injuries in schools in Ilorin, Nigeria; Kim *et al.* (2000) on Chinese and Korean teachers' violent 'disciplinary' methods; Burton (2008) on South African corporal punishment in schools; Raj (2011) on physical discipline in India; Gwirayi (2011) who focuses on schools in Zimbabwe; Mweru (2010) who reports on schools in Kenya; and Nelson and colleagues (2009) who report on the persistence of corporal punishment in Thailand. Some children's perspectives on corporal punishment at school are also noted below.

A society's tolerance of physical punishment degrades and insults all children, whether they are victims or whether they simply belong to the group of people in society who may be treated in this way. Many years ago, Peter Newell, founder of the EPOCH organisation, felt the need to remind us that children are people too; entitled to dignity and to be treated with respect (Newell, 1989). Given enlightened responses toward other previously disempowered and victimised people, including women, condemning all forms of prejudicial treatment of children in all settings seems at very least a reasonable if not a civilised and well overdue step in the 21st century. While violence towards women in the home is now more readily condemned, hitting children as discipline may remain lawful and, as previously noted, may not be considered violence:

> ... there is powerful cultural reinforcement, through language, through legislation and through practice, that, in respect of children, physical punishment does not equate with violence, even where a directly comparable assault on an adult would constitute a criminal offence. However, it is not the action which differs when children, as opposed to adults, are being hit. It is the social attitude that accompanies it (Lansdown, 2000: 417).

Male and female children, children with and children without disabilities, occupy a separate, ambiguous status yet to be recognised as human (Scutt, 2009).

Limiting Rather Than Banning Physical Punishment

Freeman has argued that attempts to distinguish 'ordinary safe smacks and inhuman or degrading punishment' are 'morally bankrupt'; '[i]magine', he taunts, 'legislation which allowed husbands to smack their wives but withheld from them the power to use an implement!' (1999: 132). Incremental law reform or 'half measures', he contends, stunt necessary attitudinal change in contexts where laws have the power to foster moral behaviour even in relationships involving parents and children (1999: 132).

However, it appears that the community and the judiciary must limit violence before questioning its legitimacy (see Freeman, 1980).

Notably in Australia, Canada and the UK a number of absurd legislative limits or, as Anne McGillivray aptly describes them, 'a shifting geojurispudence of licit and illicit body contacts' now explicitly define rather than reject the legitimacy and inhumanity of violent parental responses to children (1997: 211). She notes the ludicrous attention given to 'instruments' and 'sites of punishment', 'reasons for punishment', 'who can administer punishment', 'degree of force', 'risk of harm' and 'susceptibility to punishment' (1997: 211). In the Australian state of New South Wales, a child may be legally hit as long as he or she is struck below the shoulders and the harm caused does not last for more than a short (undefined) period of time. In the UK, children may be hit as long as they are not visibly marked or bruised and in Canada, children may not be hit if they are younger than two and older than 12, on their head or with objects.

Moral arguments against lawful violence against children appear to be less powerful than arguments that uphold both adults' rights and children's subordinate status. It is particularly significant that when the defence of lawful correction is allowed in an assault trial it is more likely to be successful when the child is portrayed as '"difficult", "wilful" "undisciplined", "disobedient", "provoking", "obstinate', "hard to manage", "resistant" or "having behavioural problems"' (McGillivray, 1997: 220). In this context, demeaning attitudes towards children must be challenged, and parents and others responsible for children's care and protection must be persuaded to stop habitually 'hitting children because it is wrong ... as it is wrong to hit adults... The 21st century must consign it to history' (Freeman, 1999:139, 2000b: 54).

Early Children's Rights Advocates' Thoughts about Children and Childhood

In reference to the corporal punishment of children, Ellen Key, an early advocate of children's rights, commented over 100 years ago that, 'both soul and body are equally affected by this practice' (1909:135). Key in Sweden implored adults to 'respect the joys of the child, his tastes, work, and time, just as you would those of an adult' (1909: 173). 'Corporal punishment', she wrote, 'must be done away with not because it is painful but because it is profoundly immoral and hopelessly unsuitable' (1909: 167). Key, along with like-minded people such as Kate Douglas Wiggin in the United States (Wiggin, 1892) and Janusz Korczak in Poland (see Eichsteller, 2009; Jilek, 2011; Korczak and Joseph, 2007), empathised with, and appreciated, children as beings as well as becomings, as capable individuals with many and various special qualities who, like other people, learn through knowledge and experience, and as people with much to contribute in the present and with an entitlement to human rights. Indeed Jilek contends that both Key and Korczak:

> ... emancipate the child and apportion the same social value to childhood as to adulthood... [They] agree on the child's right to respect, and their work has similarity in terms of the arguments and concepts that they use: freedom, equality, self-determination, autonomy and the individuality of each child. (2011: 86)

Korczak observed that children 'love laughter, running about and playing tricks'. Children, in his view, should be allowed:

> ... to make mistakes and to joyfully strive for improvement [and they] have a right to be taken seriously and to be treated with tenderness and respect ... There are many terrible things in the world [he observed] but the worst is when a child is afraid of his father, mother or teacher. He fears them, instead of loving and trusting them. (Korczak in Joseph, 2007:19, 27, 55. Also cited in Freeman, 2010b: 213)

Ellen Key boldly contended that hitting children 'demoralizes and stupefies the educator, for it increases his thoughtlessness, not his patience, his brutality, not his intelligence' (1909: 139). Kate Wiggin similarly suggested that 'the rod of reason will have to replace the rod of birch' (1892: 19, also cited in Freeman, 1993:38 , 2000b: 514; 2004: xii;,2010b: 212) and Janusz Korczak, whose respect for children would not accommodate their corporal punishment, aptly afforded children the 'right to protest an injustice' (Eichsteller, 2009: 388). Kurzwell highlights the following extract as 'typical' of Korczak's writing as it portrays his persistent 'defense of children's rights' and it advocates a 'considerate attitude towards them' (1968: 26):

> Children are not fools: the fools among them are no more numerous than among adults. Frequently we wrap ourselves in a mantle of authority and hand out orders which lack understanding or consideration, and are sometimes even impossible to carry out. Many a time an intelligent child stands, taken aback and confused, before the foolish, offending and inconsiderate orders of the grownups. (Korczak, *Keizad Le'ehov Yeladim*, 40, cited in Kurzwell, 1968: 27)

As Michael Freeman often notes, Korczak fostered children's intelligence and abilities by working with them to establish children's parliaments, juries and newspapers. It is disappointing that, even in the 21st century, many of these early children's rights advocates' ideas remain visionary. Children may still be regarded and treated as 'not yet fully persons' (Freeman, 1983: 18). Indeed to illustrate this, Freeman surmised:

> If I asked you what percentage of people in your country favoured the smacking of children, you would almost certainly tell me the percentage of adults, because you wouldn't include children in 'people'. (2008: 9)

Children may be described as an 'out-group' subject to negative and unjust 'out-group biases' increasing their vulnerability to physical aggression and subsequent harm.

> ... out-group biases toward children may underlie widespread beliefs regarding the justification of aggression toward children and foster the double standard that says it is permissible to strike a child but illegal to do the same to an adult. (Risser *et al.*, 2011: 522)

Adults' power over children and indifference to each child's unique needs and perspectives continues to stunt many children's childhoods. Indeed Waksler (1991) has drawn an analogy between persistent, limiting perceptions of children and enlightened perceptions of tribal groups who were previously demeaned as 'child-like'. He suggests that children may only be 'child-like' in response to adults' stereotypical expectations of them:

> ... a stereotype that facilitates adult control and an adult assumption of superiority ... If the adult view of children as immature and ... partially developed is set aside, children emerge as full-fledged actors in the social world, drawing on the resources they possess to make sense of and act in the worlds that confront them. (1991: 235)

In contexts that undermine children's status and rights, progress towards bans on corporal punishment, even in schools, is characteristically resisted and is then slow and incremental. In a University College London newsletter, Michael Freeman is quoted as saying:

> I remember getting involved in a campaign called STOP in 1973. People at that time thought that those of us who were advocating the end of corporal punishment in schools were completely crazy and had not the slightest chance of being successful. (Mokal, 2003: 9)

It took another 26 years before corporal punishment was banned in all schools in England and Wales, but progress did occur thanks to Michael and other like-minded people.

More Recent Empirical Research on Physical Punishment's Effects and Effectiveness

The 'loving smack', as Michael has observed, is 'a classic oxymoron if ever there was one' (Freeman, 1999: 138). Children experience pain, distress and confusion when parents hit them and many parents express remorse and regret (Saunders and Goddard, 2010). Increasing empirical evidence confirms that corporal punishment does not achieve positive outcomes for children; the child's physical and mental health, cognitive and behavioural development and relationships with significant others may be adversely affected immediately and permanently (see, for example, Benjet and Kazdin, 2003; Durrant and Ensom, 2012; Gershoff, 2002; 2013; MacKenzie *et al.*, 2013; Straus and Pascall, 2009; Taylor *et al.*, 2010; Tomoda *et al.*, 2009). Moreover, the links between physical punishment and, often unintended, severe, even fatal, injury have been well established (see, for example, Nielssen *et al.*, 2009). If there is a line between physical punishment and abuse it is, as Freeman has aptly stated, 'at best fuzzy' (1994a: 21). 'A society which does not use physical violence as a means of correction is', he contends, 'far less likely to abuse its children' (2006: 240). The extent of harm potentially caused by this culturally entrenched and legally condoned response to children is alarming and lends significant support to calls for its full abolition. It is important to emphasise, however, that, from a moral and human rights perspective, the protection of children's rights ought not to be contingent upon proof that physical punishment is either harmful or ineffective (Durrant, 2011; Saunders and Goddard, 2010).

The Role of Language in the Continued Tolerance of Parental Physical Punishment, and Some More Recent Adults' Thoughts about Children

Parental physical punishment of children may be less common and less severe than in the past (Freeman, 2008) but it nevertheless continues to be a not uncommon practice, particularly in countries that have not introduced legislative prohibitions together with ongoing education and supports for parents and children (see Global Initiative, for recent European prevalence statistics). Where law and culture allow children to be hit, ideas that parents own their children and that the child is lesser than the adult persist and support this discriminatory behaviour.

Michael Freeman often notes Mia Kellmer-Pringle's hope that we will abandon the view that 'a baby completes a family, rather like a TV set or fridge... possessions over which [parents] may exercise exclusive rights' (1975: 69-70, cited in Freeman, 1979: 11, 2001: 187, 2008: 7). Other notable examples of this perception of children as objects and possessions are Green's reference to the child under one year old as a 'cuddly little article' (1984: 2), and Archard's observation that:

> While it is true that... a child cannot be owned by anyone, it is also true that very few other things can be owned either... [The parent] has rights over something, the child, which the non-parent lacks. But then again, the latter may have rights of ownership over other objects which the parent does not (1993, emphases added).

The Influence of Euphemistic and Demeaning Language

In the mid-1980s in Australia, when physical punishment had been banned in most Australian schools, medical doctor and parenting guru, Christopher Green, published the first edition of his popular book, *Toddler Taming – A Parent's Guide to (Surviving) the First Four Years*, in which he expressed the view that parents manage well in their child's first year 'but as soon as that negative, stubborn, self-centred terrorist toddler appears, many [parents] wonder what has hit them' (1984: 45). Given the words 'Toddler Taming' in his book's title, Green predictably highlighted situations in which he advised that it would be appropriate and effective to 'smack', or more precisely to hit, a child. It was thus not uncommon for naturally adventurous small children or 'toddlers', as Green referred to them, to be perplexed and distressed when parents, often with the support of family and friends, struck them, ostensibly as discipline. Fortunately, in the 1970s and beyond, some parents alternatively sought or received parenting advice from Penelope Leach's classic book, *Baby and Child: From Birth to*

Age Five (empathetically written, as stated on its back-cover, 'from the baby's point of view'). In this book Leach, a psychologist, observed that:

> ... today's careful slap can easily become next years' real spanking ... smacked children can never remember what they were smacked for. Pain and indignity make them so angry that they go away seething with anger rather than full of repentance. You cannot get his cooperation through blows. (1979: 440)

That a parent who loves and cares for a child may be motivated unnecessarily to hurt that child is particularly disturbing, perplexing and inconsistent and language, in combination with disparaging views of children, plays a powerful role in rationalising this inconsistency (also see Saunders and Goddard, 2001; Saunders, 2013). Among other euphemisms for violent responses to children, the words 'smack' and 'spank' are cleverly designed literally to soften the intent and the impact associated with hitting a child, and to carry with them a degree of acceptability. The meaning of the word 'smack', however, is unclear and precariously unreliable. It may mean 'a good open-handed slap ... around the legs, the bottom or ... face' and it may mean a forceful blow with or without an implement (Saunders and Goddard, 2010: 67, 68). Moreover, the reason for 'smacking' a child may be retributive, educative, habitual or cathartic (see Gough and Reavey, 1997). Indeed, language used in reference to children and to actions directed at children plays a significant part in the perpetuation of violence commonly perceived and justified as reasonable and acceptable. Encouraging the use of more appropriate and precise language may motivate desirable changes. For example, it seems likely that few parents would readily admit to lawfully assaulting their children.

Contrasting Adults' Views about Children and Their Place

In 1979, Sweden was the first country to recognise the child's right not to be physically punished. This was 'part of a strategy to create a new culture of childhood, one in which children are identified as persons as rights holders' (Freeman, 1999: 133). Indeed, the Swedish legislation, as amended in 1983, states that:

> Children are entitled to care, security and a good upbringing. They shall be treated with respect for their person and their distinctive character and may not be subject to corporal punishment or any other injurious or humiliating treatment. (Children and Parents Code, ch.6, 1)

In Sweden's child-friendly culture, positive statements about children are explicit, as evidenced in the 2013 visitor's guide to Stockholm:

> Stockholm is an accessible, safe and child-friendly city. There are many parks and playing grounds, museums and experiences for children of all ages. Many restaurants and coffee shops have high chairs and children's menus and public transport is easily ac-

> cessible even with prams. In Stockholm, children are allowed to be seen and heard. (Stockholm Visitors Board, 2013: 10)

This positive acknowledgement of children stands in stark contrast to some reported attitudes toward children in the English-speaking world. For example, Michael Freeman (2010a) expressed disgust upon reading a 2006 opinion piece in *The Guardian* newspaper entitled, 'Six Weeks of Suffering' (Bindel, 2006). The piece details adults' 'suffering' when 'kids', also described as 'undisciplined', 'spoilt', 'hysterical', 'noisy', 'little monsters', are on holidays instead of attending school. Children, Bindel contended, are an unwarranted imposition in adults' spaces, including streets, parks, restaurants and museums. She forthrightly criticises the Mayor of London at the time who commendably gave 'school children free bus travel' (Bindel, 2006, cited in Freeman, 2010: 1). Under the headline: 'The shame of Britain's intolerance of children', the UK organisation Barnados (2008) similarly raised concerns about adultist attitudes. Moreover, in response to Belkin's (2000) *New York Times Magazine* article, 'Your kids are their problem', describing people who advocate 'child-free zones', Qvortrup (2005: 1) observed that, in these people's opinion, parents should be obligated to restrict their children's presence to private spaces. '[P]ublic areas', they argue, are the 'domain and prerogative' only of adults as:

> ... children should neither be seen nor heard, and should enter the social arena only when they have matured ... children's intrusion into public areas is thought of in terms of a 'status offence' (2005: 1).

More recent examples of adultist attitudes include the introduction by two airlines – Singapore-based Scoot airlines and Malaysia's Air Asia – of child-free zones for adults who are willing to pay for this 'upgrade'. In a survey of 1,300 frequent flyers, children were reportedly considered 'the most irksome in-flight irritant' (Webb, 2013: 5). And, in India, Dutt's (2013) opinion piece on corporal punishment in schools draws further attention to adults' complicity in children's oppression:

> In our country, there is a profoundly influential social and policy discourse which has conveniently chosen to either ignore or make children's voices invisible from the public domain. There is no dearth of ceremonial holding of events such as children's parliament, or children's summits and so on, self-indulgently claiming to represent children's voices. However if we try to look for a more sincere and realistic presence of children's voices in the discussions on education and the general state of schools, in most cases we are sure to draw a blank... children's voices and well-being are not important enough concerns... According to the study titled 'Child Abuse in India-2007' commissioned by the Ministry of Women and Child Development, Government of India, 'every two out of three school children reported facing corporal punishment'.

Children's Perspectives on Physical Punishment in Their Childhoods

In Michael Freeman's aforementioned (2008) address to the ISPCAN audience in Hong Kong, he also posed the question, 'What do children think [about physical punishment]?' And he noted how infrequently children are consulted. 'Imagine' he suggested 'if we wanted to know opinions about domestic violence and we only asked men?' (Freeman, 2008: 4). He also remarked, as he has done in several of his publications, that among other limitations of UNCRC it gave us a definition of children's rights but it did so without 'any real input' from children – a future Convention, he contends, 'cannot afford to ignore the voice of children' (Freeman, 1992a: 5, 1992b: 69, 1998: 439, 2000c: 282, 2010a: 35).

The Convention, despite largely overlooking children's perspectives, nevertheless embraces Janusz Korczak's view of children's right to respect, as 'respect demands *protection*, calls for *provision* and requires *active participation*' (Eichsteller, 2009: 386). Article 12 of the Convention stipulates the child's right to 'freely' communicate his or her views 'in all matters affecting' him or her. And, as Freeman contends, such participation hinges upon 'dialogue', 'negotiation' and 'peaceful resolution of conflict' not resolution by physical force. The remainder of this paper thus focuses on children's voices in relation to both physical punishment and children's concept of self within environments that condone hitting them.

Adults have much to learn from children. Listening to children can enable adults to understand better the perspective of the individual child and to appreciate the nature of unique childhoods occurring within a socially constructed childhood (James and Prout, 1997; Jenks, 1996; Qvortrup *et al.,* 1994). In accord with Childhood Studies theorists, Henegan has written that children 'can only be understood by seeing the world through their eyes… the dignity of the child is respected by listening to their views' (2011: 40). Moreover, as Menkel-Meadow has observed, '[e]ach time we let in a new excluded group … each time we listen to a new way of knowing, we learn more about the limits of our current way of seeing' (1987: 52). Enabling children to communicate their first-hand perspectives is integral to understanding the nature and meaning of physical punishment yet children's knowledge and thoughts on this issue have only rarely been sought. Indeed Smith, amongst others, has noted a deficit in the literature on physical punishment even though 'children's understanding and experience of family discipline' is considered to 'mediate its effects' (2011: 29).

It is my hope that even the most committed proponents of lawful physical chastisement may reconsider their stance if they gain insight into children's experiences as victims and as witnesses to other children's physical punishment. Children articulate physical punishment's association with poor self esteem, feelings of powerlessness and vulnerability, physical and emotional pain, confusing and negative feelings about the adults whom they love and respect. Children also experience the swift resolution of conflict and the expression of negative emotion through physical power rather than by rational and constructive means.

In 1998, Caroline Willow and Tina Hyder in the UK talked about 'smacking' with 72 children aged between 4 and 8. Willow and Hyder invented Splodge, a story-book character. Splodge was curious about the world, and asked the children questions such as: 'Why do you think children get smacked? How does it feel to be smacked? How do adults act after they have given a smack? And, when you are big do you think you will smack children? Children described a 'smack' as a hit or a 'very hard hit'. Indeed, a child aged seven said that 'smacking' is 'parents trying to hit you, [but] instead of calling [it] a hit they call it a smack' (1998: 27). Children said they felt 'sad', 'hurt', 'grumpy', 'upset' and 'angry' (1998: 46-49). Seven year olds said a smack is 'painful and it sets a wrong example...' and '...you feel like you don't like your parents any more' (1998: 80, 47). Many children said parents feel sorry or regret hitting them (1998: 55).

Willow and Hyders' research was one of the first studies to clearly demonstrate that even very young children can reflect upon their experiences of physical punishment and eloquently express their feelings and opinions. Similar consultations with children around the world have followed, and each one has provided further evidence that children's observations are articulate, insightful, and empathetic. Children appear to have embraced these opportunities, and adults have been privileged to listen to what children have to say.

In qualitative research each child's voice conveys his or her unique experience and insight. When a number of children are consulted, common themes and notable differences tend to emerge. For example, children have alerted us to notable variations in the nature and severity of physical punishment that children in different cultures describe as normal and acceptable. 'Normal' punishment could mean being hit with a hand on the leg, beaten with implements, pinched, having your head pushed against a wall, or forced to kneel on sharp objects. Indeed, as Durrant (2011) has observed, some common punishments have not been included in empirical research designs that did not define 'normal' from the child's perspective. Despite some important differences, the consistent themes emanating from children's voices from many cultures around the world are striking.

The following six selected themes emerged from children's voices published in the limited number of refereed journal articles reporting on qualitative research that engaged children in discussion about physical punishment, a book (Saunders and Goddard, 2010), and in research reports, primarily stemming from research conducted for the International Save the Children Alliance.

Physical Punishment Hurts Children Physically and Can Escalate in Severity

Lawful physical chastisement allows adults responsible for children's care and protection to respond to children in ways that enhance their risk of accidental and unintended physical harm, along with other counter-productive impacts on children's positive development and potential. Children's size, dependency and powerlessness enhance their vulnerability. Children may be at heightened risk when in the care of adults who are affected by physical, emotional and/or economic stressors. Parents and other adults may also lack understanding of, be inconvenienced by, or be intolerant of, normal or challenging childhood behaviours. Abuse, as Freeman has cautioned, is a tag retrospectively assigned and, regrettably for vulnerable children, responsible adults 'who skate on thin ice cannot expect a sign to alert them to the exact point where the ice will cave in' (1994: 23). In this context, children may suffer the brunt of emotion-driven, uncontrolled physical responses that spiral, become more painful, and result in both short and long-term harm:

> ...if we've done it many times before, then they start to get more angrier and angrier, and harder punishment. (11yrs, New Zealand) (Dobbs *et al.,* 2006: 142)

> If someone's been bold, she'll slap them and...next time you do it, it will be ten times harder. (Ireland) (Nixon and Halpenny, 2010: 47)

Physical Punishment Arouses Negative Emotions

A key insight into the connection between physical punishment and abuse emerged from Mason and Falloon's (1999) consultation with some Australian children, aged between 11 and 17, who 'described abusive behaviour as that perpetuated by persons who use power to control those they consider as lesser'. Abuse, they said, is 'feeling let down by those with whom they are in an emotional relationship [and] discounted because of their age' (1999: 9). The context of 'physical punishment' was perceived to be an integral component of abuse in that adults are 'not allowed to smack anyone else but children' and a child 'can't do anything back' (Mason & Falloon, 1999: 11).

Children describe feeling heartbroken, resentful, emotionally torn, humiliated and worthless:

> It hurts you inside... because it breaks your heart. (6yrs, England) (Alexandrecu, *et al.*, 2005: 16)

> You feel anger and feel as though you have no self worth. (Scotland) (Alexandrecu, *et al.*, 2005: 15)

> I hate being kicked. I don't mind the pain but feel humiliated. (Pakistan) (Alexandrecu, *et al.*, 2005: 15)

> ... I wanted to run away, but... my brother would miss me too much. Then... I wanted to hug [mom]... I didn't know which one I should do. (6yrs, US) (Vittrup, 2004, cited in Buck *et al.,* 2007: 121)

Physical Punishment Creates Fear and Impedes Children's Optimal Development

Children tell us that being hit diminishes their confidence, enhances their insecurity and reduces their potential. This is particularly apparent in older children's reflections on corporal punishment in schools but even very young children may recognise that physical discipline can unreasonably curtail children's natural curiosity and yearning for new, developmentally enhancing experiences. Children may live in threatening rather than in safe environments in which reasonable expectations and appropriate limits are explained and negotiated:

> Teachers tell students that beating will make them learn... I just wait with fear... I cannot even communicate... I am worrying that he will beat me. I cannot learn that way. (17yrs, Kenya) (Alexandrecu *et al.*, 2005: 9)

> I could...not cope with my domestic responsibilities as well as all my homework... My teacher started to beat me really hard for not knowing the right answers... I decided to drop out of school. (14yrs, South Africa) (Alexandrecu, *et al.*, 2005: 31)

> With smacking...it makes you think you're doing wrong stuff. [Children] wanna explore but sometimes they do something wrong when they explore and... smacking sends something to their brain that makes them not to want to explore. (9yrs, Australia) (Saunders and Goddard, 2010: 154)

Physical Punishment Perpetuates Violence as a Means of Resolving Conflict

In contexts in which physical punishment is a lawful and accepted response to children only very severe physical responses will be easily described as violence or abuse. Physical punishment is more likely to be euphemistically described as 'smacking' or 'spanking'; words primarily reserved for violent responses to children that also serve to effectively condone and perpetuate its use (see Goddard and Saunders, 2010). In contrast, authoritative parental responses to children encourage the development of constructive personal interaction and similarly lead to intergenerational transmission but of positive rather than disrespectful discipline techniques (see, for example, Chen and Kaplan, 2001). Children suggest that there are better ways to encourage co-operation and reasonable compliance, and that adults must decide to adopt them if hitting children is to stop:

> When children grow up they keep what was done to them in mind and in the end they also do the same... (14yrs, Uganda) (Naker, 2005: 35)

> It's giving the message that it's okay to smack...It's just a big cycle...people are gunna get smacked until someone finally doesn't smack in your family. (12yrs, Australia) (Saunders and Goddard, 2010: 199)

> When I have children, I'll explain their mistakes to them, but if they don't behave I'll beat them gently on the bottom. (Child in Vietnam, Beazley *et al.*, 2005: 162)

Physical Punishment Diminishes Positive Relationships and Communication Channels

Physical punishment subjugates children and may impair relationships based on love and trust (see Gershoff, 2002). Children who are physically hurt as punishment or discipline may resent the adults who cause them pain and indignity. The behaviour that prompted a disciplinary response may be of little, or no, significance to a child overcome by anger, fear and confusion. Adults' regular use of physical punishment to curb common childhood behaviours that they deem to be unacceptable is testament to its futility. Children describe feeling unloved, sad, betrayed and bewildered when deliberately hurt by parents who have loved and cared for them:

> You feel that your parents don't love you if it's your parents smacking you because why would they smack you? (10yrs, Northern Ireland) (Horgan, 2002, cited on EPOCH website)

> ...you go off and cry...They've hurt my feeling for one. They've kind of let me down, 'cause I really trust...'cause they're taking care of me, and then as soon as you get hit, you think... they're...breaking your trust...and...then your heart just goes down and...you get very sad. (10yrs, Australia) (Saunders and Goddard, 2010: 154)

> I am very scared, puzzled and hurt. I was whipped by my mother, I begged her for forgiveness but she still beat me (Child in Vietnam) (Beazley *et al.*, 2005: 168)

Physical Punishment is Not Constructive; Children Prefer Reasoning

Mayall maintains that '[t]aking children seriously as people leads to shifts in thinking' (2000: 248). From the child's perspective, parents may make an unwise choice to resort to physical punishment rather than reasoning as a means of effective discipline. Children who have not been physically punished understand that children may need to be disciplined and that it is reasonable for adults to guide and sensibly limit some childhood behaviours by non-violent means: 'I've been brought up to sit down and talk' (12yrs, Australia) (Saunders and Goddard, 2010: 201). Indeed, children observe that disempowering and unconstructive rather than nurturing, insightful outcomes result from physical chastisement:

> Parents should help you understand; sometimes I don't know why I get a smack. (5yrs, New Zealand) (Dobbs, *et al.*, 2006: 151)

> [Spanking] doesn't show him how to do something better; it just shows that you have more power over him. (9yrs, United States) (Vittrup and Holden, 2010: 218)

> It's wrong to smack because it doesn't really help the child learn...It's not like saying, 'Don't do that again 'cause you could hurt yourself or you could burn yourself'...It's not telling them what to do... (9yrs, Australia) (Saunders and Goddard, 2010: 116)

> There are other ways to solve problems other than hitting and it doesn't do parents or children any good. (10yrs, Scotland) (Alexandrecu, *et al.*, 2005)

Children's Perceptions of Their Rights and Position in Society

Some children tell us that various forms of 'physical punishment' are reasonable and they express a resigned but limited acceptance. This may be for cultural reasons. It may also reflect children's social positioning and sense of self. A girl from Barbados appears resigned to some degree of inflicted physical pain in her life:

> Children in the school... need punishment but... I don't think (we) have to be flogged or spanked every time... there are many different ways to punish us... You and all people must remember kids have rights too. We are human beings like anybody else. (Anderson and Payne, 1994: 382)

And a Filipino child claims responsibility:

> At first I was angry but then I realised I was at fault and my parents just want me to be good. (Sanapo and Nakamura, 2010: 49)

A child in Ghana defends some corporal chastisement for wrong-doing:

> Physical punishment is not bad if the child is wrong but should not be done excessively. Beating the child all over mercilessly is not good. (Twum-Danso, 2013: 481)

In Cambodia, a child appears to approve of corporal punishment as the last resort:

> Teachers should ask for the reason first and then beat later or talk first and if students still didn't listen beat later. (Miles and Varon, 2005: 52)

An Ethiopian child recognises human fallibility but accords parents the right to use physical means to ensure obedience:

> I am a human being and naturally make a mistake. Humans do not always follow rules. So it is necessary to use the whip when they don't obey rules...parents have the right to physically punish their children. (Save the Children Sweden, 2007: 39)

And, in Ireland, a child effectively uses the word 'little' to minimise and justify physical punishment:

> It's better for the parents to give them a *little* slap... sometimes a *little* wrong can help them on the way. (Nixon and Halpenny, 2010: 48)

The following Australian children's voices represent a selection of themes arising in research involving 33 children aged between eight and 17 years old in the state of Victoria. The children participated in either in-depth interviews at home or focus groups in schools. These children's comments shed further light on how contexts that condone physical punishment impact children's perceptions of their rights and position in society, and their sense of self.

Children Know Their Place in Relation to Us Adults

People whose current importance and value to society are not well recognised are more vulnerable to disrespectful and degrading treatment. Historically considered to be parents' chattels, children's compliance with parents' demands has been enforced with little, if any, oversight or intrusion into family privacy. Indeed, clear parallels appear when comparing the once common treatment of women and other disempowered groups of people and some persistent attitudes and responses to children (see, for example, Saunders and Goddard, 2010). In this context, children describe division, diminished status, powerlessness and vulnerability:

> It's what keeps us apart, adults are more important than children. (10yrs, Saunders and Goddard, 2010: 230)

> Parents have a right to smack you...'cause you are their kids. (11yrs, Saunders and Goddard, 2010: 138)

> [There's] the control...over you...There is...helplessness...with being a child...I don't think it's appropriate for [my parents] to physically punish me any more...'cause I think I am becoming a bit of a person, not a child anymore. (13yrs Saunders and Goddard, 2010: 155, 134)

Children Are Sensitive to Inequality and Double Standards

Children are aware of being hurt and unfairly treated on the basis of their relative size, age, life experience, and status. Children also note adults' apparent lack of empathy. Indeed, when reflecting on parent/child relationships, children appear to more readily empathise with adults' feelings and motivations:

> You shouldn't smack people. You shouldn't smack children, 'cause it's hurting them. Treat others like you treat yourself. (8yrs, Saunders and Goddard, 2010: 223)

> ...last time the adults prob'ly got smacked was when they were a little kid and they wouldn't know what it felt like...if I went up and smacked them then they'd know but children don't normally go up to their parents and go, 'Stop behaving like that', and smack them. (12yrs, Saunders and Goddard, 2010: 159)

> ... if adults [have] physical contact with someone, like punching 'em, it's against the law... they could go to jail, they could be charged with assault. And that's exact same for smacking. But...if you're a kid, and it's in the house, it's okay because they're your kids. If you are a kid, it doesn't really matter...You barely have any say. (9yrs, Saunders and Goddard, 2010: 138)

Children Urged us to Respect Children and to Act Responsibly

Children observed that adults may demonstrate little, if any, respect toward children, yet hypocritically expect children to respect them. Children also observe that adults may engage in behaviours that may jeopardize children's current and future well-being:

> Children are our future so they have got to be important...Parents think hitting children is sort of their right...parents have gotta learn to respect children (13yrs, Saunders and Goddard, 2010: 222).

> ...because children are small and...can't fight back, [adults] shouldn't take advantage of them...[children] have rights too...adults are...there to teach their children, and if they do it the right way...[it] can be some of the happiest times of your life, but if treated badly it can wreck...your life. (12 yrs, Saunders and Goddard, 2008:11)

> I'd like to say to...the government, to the parents, this is not the way to discipline, by hitting a child...you can see a bruise but you can't see how it mentally affects someone and they'll carry that right through their childhood, right through their adulthood (12yrs, Saunders and Goddard, 2010: 231).

A Way Forward

Children's insights and wisdom draw attention to the 'limits of our current way of seeing' (Menkel-Meadow, 1987:52). Children are important people whose voices should be heard. It is 25 years since the UNCRC came into being yet children may still live in circumstances where they are too afraid to speak because they fear physical punishment.

> ... conventions, though important symbols, do not change anything. More, much more, is required if the conditions of children's lives are to improve, if they are to be regarded truly as persons rather than as social problems, burdens or pretty playthings... (Freeman, 1997a: 64)

An 8-year-old child perceived that adults do not 'have to smack because you can choose' (Saunders and Goddard, 2010). Since the 1960s, when Henry Kempe and his colleagues drew attention to the 'battered child syndrome' (1962), definitions of child abuse have evolved and extended, as have explanations for its occurrence.

Psychopathological and socio-environmental explanations shed some light on the problem but, as Freeman has long argued, 'the status of the child in culture' is surely pivotal:

> ... it becomes so much easier to understand the wrongs perpetrated against children in terms of a denial of their personality and integrity and in terms of the power which others exercise over them. Children's rights – or their absence – are very much a key to the understanding of abuse and neglect. Children without rights are by that very fact vulnerable (2000a: 3).

Children are harmed in numerous and cumulative ways in the guise of discipline yet corporal punishment is still not, without reservation, included in commonly accepted definitions of abuse - children's voices may still be silenced (Saunders and Goddard, 2010).

> If child abuse is to be tackled more successfully, there must be a new vision of childhood. A conception of childhood must be developed which acknowledges the personality and integrity of children... To protect children one must also protect their rights... Children must be seen as individuals, not merely as "assets" or even subsumed within a family and its interests (Freeman, 1994b: 93).

Together with law reform that incorporates the UNCRC (Freeman, 2010: 33), and explicitly condemns the physical punishment of children in any setting and to any degree, education campaigns are needed to change out-dated and disrespectful attitudes and responses to children. Recognising that '[support] for a child necessarily involves supporting the child's care-giver and vice versa' (Freeman, 2007: 16), the campaigns could be both hard-hitting and motivational. They could through words and pictures:

- inform parents about children's rights as set out in the Convention, and by the Committee on the Rights of the Child;
- provide parents with clear messages about the importance of their parental role and society's indebtedness to them for taking seriously their responsibility to nurture their children to their full potential;
- provide parents with information about normal childhood development, and demonstrate positive ways to interact with, and to set reasonable boundaries for, children;
- portray the immediate and possible impacts of corporal punishment and illustrate the risks that parents might be taking in response to their precious children;
- enable children to have a voice on this and other issues affecting them by 'giving them the vocabulary, debating with them, engaging, including...recognizing... that they have a part in the public arena' (Freeman, 2010: 29); and
- provide children with opportunities to talk about the impact of being hurt by parents on whom they depend, and whom they love, trust, and imitate.

Policies that include supports and programs for parents and children, and that demonstrate that the society values its children and their optimal development will bolster the impact of law reform and accompanying education campaigns. As Freeman has proposed, we need to appoint Children's Rights Ombudsmen, set up procedures by which children and child-focussed adults can 'make complaints and representations' to the UN Committee on the Rights of the Child, establish 'an international court (or tribunal) to hear complaints by children against their governments for breaches of the UNCRC', and either afford children the right to vote or set up respected Children's Parliaments (2010: 29, 39, 41, 43).

Conclusion

Children are perceptive, often refreshingly candid, people. Their comments are frequently insightful and pithy. An eight-year-old observed that:

> Since adults are older, they think they know most stuff but sometimes they don't...sometimes they're mistaken. (8yrs, Saunders and Goddard, 2010: 222)

And a 10-year-old child reflecting on adults hitting children surmised that rather than 'using their mind...they use action instead (Saunders and Goddard, 2010: 115).

Encouraging children to speak, and listening to what they say, enables us to 'see things in a different way' (16yrs, Saunders and Goddard, 2010: 233). Children's observations and astute remarks can bring us to our senses. We may even finally concede that 'you shouldn't hit people because there's a better way...than hurting someone (12yrs, Saunders and Goddard, 2010: 224). Children should no longer have to wait to be fully recognised as people with human rights to dignity and respectful treatment:

> ... nothing is a clearer statement of the position that children occupy in society, nor a clearer badge of childhood, than the fact that children are the only members of society who can be hit with impunity. There is probably no more significant step that could be taken to advance the status and protection of children than to outlaw the practice of physical punishment (Freeman, 1996: 100).

Michael Freeman's commitment to children's rights, evidenced in his writings, oral presentations and media work are, and will long continue to be, a wonderful source of inspiration and motivation to others who, like him, strive to make the world a better place for children.

References

Alexandrecu, G., Bhavani, Y. G., Derib, A., Habasch, R., Horno, P., Nilsson, M., Noueri, R., Pierre-Plateau, D., Sequeira, S. M., Soneson, U. and Stuckenbruck, D., *UN Study on Violence against Children*, (Stockholm: The International Save the Children Alliance, 2005). Available at: http://www.endcorporalpunishment.org/pages/pdfs/reports/Making%20it%20Happen.pdf Accessed 31.10.13

Anderson, S and Payne, M., "Corporal Punishment in Elementary Education: Views of Barbadian Schoolchildren", *Child Abuse & Neglect* 1994 18(4), 377-86.

Archard, D. *Children: Rights and Childhood* (London: Routledge, 1993).

Ayanniyi, A., Mahmoud, A., and Salman, M. "Observations of teachers in llorin, Nigeria on their practices of corporal punishment that are potentially injurious to their pupils eyes", *Annals of African Medicine* 2011 10 (2), 150. Barnados, "The shame of Britain's intolerance of children", 2008. Available at http://www.barnardos.org.uk/news/media_centre/press_releases.htm?ref=42088 Accessed 31.10.13

Barrett, R., "States refuse to buckle amid calls to ban cane". *The Australian,* 2012. Available at: *http://www.theaustralian.com.au/national-affairs/education/states-refuse-to-buckle-amid-calls-to-ban-cane/story-fn59nlz9-1226407027267.* Accessed 31.10.13

Beazley, H., Bessell, S., Ennew, J., and Waterson, R., *What Children Say: Results of comparative research on the physical and emotional punishment of children in Southeast Asia and the Pacific.* (Sweden: Save the Children, 2005). Available at: http://seap.savethechildren.se/Global/scs/SEAP/publication/publication%20pdf/Child%20Protection/What%20Children%20Say.pdf. Accessed 31.10.13

Belkin, L., "Your kids are their problem", *New York Times Magazine* July 2000.

Benjet, C and Kazdin, A., "Spanking Children: The Controversies, Findings and New Directions", *Clinical Psychology Review* 2003 23(2), 197-224.

Bindel, J., "Six Weeks of Suffering", *The Guardian,* 18th August 2006, 35.

Bitensky, S., *Corporal Punishment of Children: A Human Rights Violation* (Ardsley: Transnational Publishers, Inc, 2006).

Buck, M. J, Vittrup, B. and Holden, G. W., "'It makes me feel really sad:' The role of children's reactions to discipline in internalization", *Advances in Psychology Research* 2007 38, 117-38.

Burton, P., *Merchants, Skollies and Stones: Experiences of School Violence in South Africa,* (Cape Town Centre for Justice and Crime Prevention, 2008).

Chen, Z. and Kaplan, H., "Intergenerational Transmission of Constructive Parenting." *Journal of Marriage and the Family* 2001 63, 17-31.

Dobbs, T., Smith, A. and Taylor, N., "No, We Don't Get a Say Children Just Suffer the Consequences: Child Talk about Family Discipline", *The International Journal of Children's Rights* 2006 14, 137-56.

Durrant, J., "The Empirical Rationale for Eliminating Physical Punishment", in A. B. Smith and J. E. Durrant (eds), *Global Pathways to Abolishing Physical Punishment* (New York: Routledge, 2011).

Durrant, J and Ensom, R., "Physical punishment of children: lessons from 20 years of research", *Canadian Medical Association Journal* 2012 184(12), 1373-1339.

Dutt, Y., In corporal punishment we are all complicit. *The Hindu* January 14, 2013. Available at: http://www.thehindu.com/opinion/op-ed/in-corporal-punishment-we-are-all-complicit/article4304901.ece. Accessed 31.10.13

Eichsteller, G., "Janusz Korczak: his legacy and its relevance for children's rights today", *International Journal of Children's Rights* 2009 17(3), 377-91.

End All Corporal Punishment of Children. Available at: www.endcorporalpunishment.org Accessed 14.3.14

EPOCH, "Committee on Economic, Social and Cultural Rights recommends prohibition", 2013a. Available at http://www.endcorporalpunishment.org/pages/news/CESCR50.html Accessed 31.10.13

EPOCH , "Seven European states to face European Committee of Social Rights for not clearly prohibiting corporal punishment of children", 2013b. Available at http://www.endcorporalpunishment.org/pages/news/ESCRFeb13.html Accessed 31.10.13

Farmer, A. and Neier, A., *A Violent Education: Corporal Punishment of Children in US Public Schools*, (New York: Human Rights Watch, 2008).

Farmer, A. and Neier, A., *Impairing Education: Corporal Punishment of Students with Disabilities in US Public Schools*, (New York: Human Rights Watch & American Civil Liberties Union, 2009).

Freeman, M., "Childen's rights: some unanswered questions and unquestioned answers", *Poly Law Review* 1979 5, 9-18.

Freeman, M., "Violence against women: Does the legal system provide solutions or itself constitute the problem?", *Canadian Journal of Family Law* 1980 3, 377-401.

Freeman, M., *The Rights and Wrongs of Children* (London: Frances Pinter, 1983).

Freeman, M., "Introduction: Rights, Ideology and Children", in M. Freeman and P. Veerman (eds), *The Ideologies of Children's Rights* (Dordrecht: Klewer Academic Publishers, 1992a).

Freeman, M., "Taking Children's Rights More Seriously", *International Journal of Law & the Family* 1992b 6, 52-71.

Freeman, M., "Laws, Conventions and Rights", *Children & Society* 1993 7(1), 37-48.

Freeman, M. "Legislating for Child Abuse", in A Levy (ed), *Reforms on Child Abuse* (London: Hawksmere, 1994a).

Freeman, M., "Protecting Children on Both Sides of the Globe", *Adelaide Law Review* 1994b 16, 79-97.

Freeman, M., "The Convention: An English Perspective", in M. Freeman (ed), *Children's Rights: A Comparative Perspective* (Aldershot: Dartmouth, 1996).

Freeman, M., "Beyond Conventions - Towards Empowerment", in M. Freeman (ed), *The Moral Status of Children: Essays on the Rights of the Child* (The Hague, The Netherlands: Kluwer Law International, 1997a).

Freeman, M., "The Limits of Children's Rights", in M. Freeman (ed), *The Moral Status of Children: Essays on the Rights of the Child* (The Hague, The Netherlands: Kluwer Law International, 1997b).

Freeman, M., "The Sociology of Childhood and Children's Rights", *The International Journal of Children's Rights* 1998 6, 433-44.

Freeman, M., "Children are Unbeatable", *Children & Society* 1999 13, 130-41.

Freeman, M., "Child Abuse: The Search for a Solution", in M. Freeman (ed), *Overcoming Child Abuse: A Window on a World Problem* (Issues in Law and Society; Dartmouth: Aldershot, 2000a).

Freeman, M., "The End of the Century of the Child", in M. Freeman (ed), *Current Legal Problems* (Vol. 53) (Oxford: Oxford Univerisity Press, 2000b).

Freeman, M., "The Future of Children's Rights", *Children & Society* 2000c 14, 277-93.

Freeman, M., "The Child in Family Law", In J. Fionda (ed.), *Legal Concepts of Childhood* (Oxford: Hart Publishing, 2001)

Freeman, M., "Introduction", in Michael Freeman (ed), *Children's Rights: Volume 1* (Aldershot: Ashgate, 2004).

Freeman, M., "Why it remains important to take children's rights seriously", *International Journal of Children's Rights* 2007 15, 5-23.

Freeman, M., "Can we conquer child abuse if we don't outlaw physical chastisement of children?", *ISPCAN Congress, Hong Kong, 9 September* (Hong Kong, 2008).

Freeman, M., "The Human Rights of Children", *Current Legal Problems* 2010a 63, 1-44.

Freeman, M., "Upholding the Dignity and Best Interests of Children: International Law and the Corporal Punishment of Children", *Law & Contemporary Social Problems* 2010b 73, 211-51.

Freeman, M., "Culture, Childhood and Rights", *The Family in Law* 2011a 5(15), 15-33.

Freeman, M., "Towards a Sociology of Children's Rights", in M. Freeman (ed), *Law and Childhood Studies: Current Legal Issues* (Vol. 14) (Oxford: Oxford University Press, 2011b).

Freeman, M., "Spanking and Child Development: We Know Enough Now to Stop Hitting Our Children", *Child Development Perpectives* 2013 7(3), 133-37.

Gershoff, E., "Corporal Punishment by Parents and Associated Child Behaviors and Experience: A Meta-Analytic and Theoretical Review", *Psychological Bulletin* 2002 128(4), 539-79.

Global Initiative. *Prohibiting corporal punishment: achieving equal protection for children in EU member states: Progress Report 2013*, Global Initiative to End All Corporal Punishment of Children (2013). Available at: http://ipa-world.org/society-resources/code/images/10040ac-EU%20report%202013.pdf Accessed 31.10.13

Gough, B. and Reavey, P., "Parental Accounts Regarding the Physical Punishment of Children: Discourses of Dis/Empowerment", *Child Abuse & Neglect* 1997 21(5), 417-30.

Green, C., *Toddler Taming: A parent's guide to (surviving) the first four years* (Sydney & Auckland: Doubleday, 1984).

Gwirayi, P., "Functions served by corporal punishment: Adolescent perspectives", *Journal of Psychology in Africa* 2011 21(1), 121-24.

Heneghan, M., "Why Judges Need to Know and Understand Childhood Studies", in M. Freeman (ed), *Law and Childhood Studies: Current Legal Issues* (Vol. 14) (Oxford: Oxford University Press, 2011).

Holzer, P. and Lamont, A., "Corporal Punishment: Key Issues" *National Child Protection Clearinghouse Resource Sheet* (2010). Available at: http://www.aifs.gov.au/nch/pubs/sheets/rs19/rs19.html Accessed 31.10.13

Horgan. G., *It's a hit not a smack* (Northern Ireland: Save the Children, 2002).

International Covenant on Civil and Political Rights. Available at: http://www.ohchr.org/en/professionalinterest/pages/ccpr.aspx Accessed 10.1.14

James, A. and Prout, A., *Constructing and Reconstructing Childhood: Contemporary Issues in the Sociological Study of Childhood* (London: Falmer Press, 1997).

Jenks, C., *Childhood* (London: Routledge, 1996).

Jilek, D., "The Invisible Dialogue on the rights of the Child: Ellen Key and Janusz Korczak", *Czech Yearbook of Public & Private International Law* 2011 2, 85-93.

Kempe, C. H., Silverman, F. N., Steele, B. F., Droegemueller, W. and Silver, H. K., "The battered-child syndrome", *Journal of the American Medical Association* 1962 18(1), 105-12.

Key, E., *The Century of the Child* (New York and London: G. P. Putnam's Sons, The Knickerbocker Press, 1909).

Khoury-Kassabri, M., "The relationship between teacher self-efficacy and violence toward students as mediated by teacher's attitude", *Social Work Research* 2012 36(2), 127-39.

Kim, D. H., Kim, K. I. and Park, Y. C., "Children's experience of violence in China and Korea: A transcultural study", *Child Abuse & Neglect* 2000 24(9), 1163-73.

Korczak, J. and Joseph, S. (eds), *Janusz Korczak Loving Every Child: Wisdom for Parents* (North Carolina: Algonquin Books of Chapel Hill, 2007).

Kurzwell, Z., "Korckak's Edcuational Writings and the Image of the Child", *Journal of Jewish Education* 1968 38(1), 19-28.

Lansdown, G., "Children's Rights and Domestic Violence", *Child Abuse Review* 2000 9, 416-26.

Leach, P., *Baby and Child From Birth to Age Five* (London: Penguin, 1979).

MacKenzie, M. J., Nicklas, E., Waldfogel, J. and Brooks-Gunn, J., "Spanking and Child Development Across the First Decade of Life", *Pediatrics,* 2013 132(5), 1118-25.

Mason, J. and Falloon, M., "A Children's Perspective on Child Abuse", *Children Australia* 1999 24(3), 9-13.

Mayall, B., "The Sociology of Childhood in Relation to Children's Rights", *The International Journal of Children's Rights* 2000 8, 243-259.

McGillivray, A., "'He'll learn it on his body': Disciplining childhood in Canadian law", *International Journal of Children's Rights* 1997 5, 193-242.

Menkel-Meadow, C., "Excluded Voices: New Voices in the Legal Profession Making New Voices in the Law", *University of Miami Law Review* 1987 42(29), 29-53.

Miles, G. and Varon, S., *"Stop Violence Against Us!" A preliminary national research study into the prevalence and perceptions of Cambodian children to violence against children in Cambodia, Summary report,* (2005). Available at: http://www.justice-and-peace.org/PolicyAdvocacy/pahome2.5.nsf/allreports/959DoDDEB18DA9668825714D00250470/$file/StopViolenceAgainstUs!1_web.pdf Accessed 31.10.13

Mokal, R., "A Man for all Seasons: An Interview with Professor Michael Freeman", (London: Faculty of Laws, University College London, 2003).Mweru, M. "Why Are Kenyan Teachers Still Using Corporal Punishment Eight Years After a Ban on Corporal Punishment?", *Child Abuse Review* 2010 19, 248-58.

Naker, D., *Violence against Children: The Voices of Ugandan Children and Adults.* (Uganda: Raising Voices and Save the Children, 2005) Available at: http://raisingvoices.org/wp-content/uploads/2013/03/downloads/resources/violence_against_children.pdf Accessed 31.10.13

Nelson, L., Honrath, M., Lacci, L., and Menzano, K. "Corporal punishment of children in Thailand: An international illustration on the challenges of confronting the final frontier", *Children's Legal Rights Journal* 2009 29(2), 9-33.

Newell, P., *Children Are People Too: The Case Against Physical Punishment* (Society Today; London: Bedford Square, 1989).

Nielssen, O., Large, M., Westmore, B. and Lackersteen, S. "Child homicide in New South Wales from 1991 to 2005", *Medical Journal of Australia* 2009 190(1), 7-11.

Nixon, E. and Halpenny, A., "Children's Perspectives on Parenting Styles and Discipline: A Developmental Approach", *The National Children's Strategy Research Series* (Dublin: Office of the Minister for Children and Youth Affairs, 2010).

Nolan, A., "Litigating the Child's Right to a Life Free from Violence: Seeking the Prohibition of Parental Physiocal Punishment of children Through the Courts", in M. Freeman (ed), *Law and Childhood Studies: Current Legal Issues* (Vol. 14) (Oxford: Oxford University Press, 2011).

Office of the High Commissioner for Human Rights. "General Comment No. 20", Available at: http://www.unhchr.ch/tbs/doc.nsf/(Symbol)/6924291970754969c12563ed004c8ae5?Opendocument Accessed 31.10.13

Peleg, N., "Time to Grow Up: The UN Committee on the Rights of the Child's Jurispudence of the Right to Development", in M. Freeman (ed), *Law and Childhood Studies: Current Legal Issues* (Oxford: Oxford University Press, 2011).

Qvortrup, J., "Varieties of Childhood." in J. Qvortrup (ed), *Studies in Modern Childhood* (Hampshire and New York: Palgrave Macmillan, 2005).

Qvortrup, J., Bardy, M., Sgritta, G. and Wintersberger, H. (eds), *Childhood Matters* (Aldershot England: Avebury, 1994).

Raj, L., "Understanding Corporal Punishment in India", *Career Educator: An Interdisciplinary Education Journal* /Spring 2011, 3-18. Available at: http://www.academia.edu/773061/Understanding_Corporal_Punishment_in_India Accessed 31.10.13

Risser, H. J, Skowronski, J. J. and Crouch, J. L., "Implicit attitudes toward children may be unrelated to child abuse risk", *Child Abuse & Neglect* 2011 35, 514-23.

Sanapo, M. S. and Nakamura, Y., "Gender and Physical Punishment: The Filipino Children's Experience", *Child Abuse Review* 2010 20, 39-56.

Saunders, B. J., "Ending the physical punishment of children by parents in the English-speaking world: The contribution of language, tradition and law", *International Journal of Children's Rights* 2013 21, 278-304.

Saunders, B. J. and Goddard, C., "The Textual Abuse of Children in the English-speaking World: The Contribution of Language to the Denial of Children's Rights", *Childhood* 2001 8(4), 433-462.

Saunders, B. J. and Goddard, C., "Some Australian Children's Perceptions of Physical Punishment in Childhood", *Children & Society* 2008 22(6), 405-17.

Saunders, B. J. and Goddard, C., *Physical punishment in childhood: The rights of the child* (Chicester: John Wiley & Sons, 2010).

Save the Children Sweden. "Ending legalised violence against children", in Global Initiative to End All Corporal Punishment of Children (ed.), *All-Africa Special Report - A Contribution to the UN Secretary General's Study on Violence Against Children* (Stockholm: 2007).

Scutt, J., "Sparing Parents Pain or Spoiling the Child by the Rod: Human Rights Arguments against Corporal Punishment", *The University of Tasmania Law Review* 2009 28(1), 1-22.

Smith, A., "The theoretical rationale for eliminating physical punishment", in J. E. Durrant and A. B. Smith (eds), *Global Pathways to abolishing Physical Punishment* (New York: Routledge, 2011).

Stockholm Visitors Board. 'Guide 2013 Stockholm', Available at: http://shop.visitstockholm.com/pub_docs/files/Broschyrer/Stockholmsbroschyren/stockholm-guide2013_english.pdf Accessed 31.10.13

Straus, M. and Pascall, M. J., "Corporal punishment by mothers and development of children's cognitive ability: a longitudinal study of two nationally representative age cohorts", *Journal of Aggression, Maltreatment and Trauma* 2009 18, 459-83.

Taylor, C. A., Manganello, J. A., Lee, S. J. and Rice, J. C., "Mother's spanking of three-year old children and subsequent risk of children's aggressive behavior", *Pediatrics* 2010 125, 1057-65.

The African Committee of Experts on the Rights of the Child. "Report - Executive Council, Twenty-First Ordinary Session, 9 – 13 July, Addis Ababa, ETHIOPIA". Available at: http://www.peaceau.org/uploads/ex-cl-744-xxi-e.pdf Accessed 31.10.13

Tomoda, A., Suzuki, H., Rabi, K., Sheu, Y.S., Polcari, A. and Teicher, M., "Reduced pre-frontal cortical gray matter volume in young adults exposed to harsh corporal punishment", *Neuroimage* 2009 Supplement 2, 47, T66-T71.

Twum-Danso, A., "Children's perceptions of physical punishment in Ghana and the implications for children's rights", *Childhood* 2013 20, 4, 472-486.

UN Committee on the Rights of the Child, General Comment No. 8 (2006) "The right of the child to protection from corporal punishment and other cruel or degrading forms of punishment (articles 19, 28(2) and 37, inter alia)", Available at http://www.unhchr.ch/tbs/doc.nsf/(Symbol)/CRC.C.GC.8.En?OpenDocument Accessed 31.10.13

UN Committee on the Rights of the Child, General Comment No. 13 (2011) "Article 19: The right of the child to freedom from all forms of violence", 56th Session 17 February 2011, Available at: http://www.crin.org/docs/CRC.C.GC.13_en_AUV-1.pdf Accessed 31.10.13

United Nations Convention on the Rights of the Child G.A. Res.44/25, U.N. GAOR, 44th Sess., Supp. No. 49, U.N. Doc.A/44/49", (1989, November 20). Available at: http://www.unicef.org/crc/ Accessed 31.10.13

United Nations Committee against Torture. "Consideration of Reports Submitted by States Parties under Article 19 of the Convention". Available at: http://hrlibrary.ngo.ru/cat/observations/australia2008.pdf Accessed 31.10.13

Vittrup, B. and Holden, G. W., "Children's assessments of corporal punsihment and other disciplinary practices: the role of age, race, SES, and exposure to spanking", *Journal of Applied Developmental Psychology* 2010 31, 211-20.

Waksler, F. (ed), *Studying the Social Worlds of Children: Sociological Readings* (London: Falmer Press, 1991).

Webb, S., "Child-free no kidding." *The Sydney Morning Herald,* 31 August, 2013.

Wiggin, K. D., *Children's Rights: A Book of Nursery Logic* (Boston: Houghton, 1892).

Willow, C. and Hyder, T., *It Hurts You Inside: Children Talking About Smacking* (London: National Children's Bureau Enterprises, 1998).

Wood, B., Hassal, I. and Ludbrook, R., *Unreasonable force: New Zealand's journey towards banning the physical punishment of children* (Wellington: Save the Children, 2008).

III

Law and the Coercive State

Reflections on Michael Freeman's 'Law and Order in 1984'

Robert Reiner
London School of Economics and Political Science, UK

Personal Prologue

Michael Freeman and I (and David Nelken who also talks about this) went to the same Jewish secondary school in London, more than half a century ago now. Indeed Michael was my Prefect for some years (perhaps the source of my interest in the injustices of law and order?) I am grateful to Michael for support at various times in my career, but most of all for two invitations to give papers (in 1988 and 2005) in the Current Legal Problems series that he organised with such distinction at UCL for several decades. On both occasions I was completing research that the invitations gave me the opportunity to air for the first time. Helped greatly by the insightful and stimulating comments from Michael and others, both resulted eventually in books (on chief constables, and on law and order). This paper is a continued exploration of the themes of that law and order book, which was rooted in ideas stimulated by an earlier inspiring Current Legal Problems paper of Michael's that is the focus of this chapter. So thank you Michael.

Introduction

Some thirty years ago Michael Freeman made a rare foray into the fields of criminal justice and criminology. *Law and Order in 1984*, which he contributed to the Current Legal Problems lecture series and annual volumes (1984), was a stirring call to arms against what was then only beginning to be discussed as Thatcherism. I see it as a landmark analysis, well worth revisiting.

This is not because it foresaw the future accurately. For all his many talents, Michael Freeman isn't a contender to be Mystic Michael. The paper is important as a state-of-the-art representation of liberal and Left thinking about law and order in the early 1980s. But it now reads nostalgically as a memento of a by-gone age of comparative innocence. Inspired by Orwell's dystopian vision, it nonetheless failed to anticipate the enormity of the crime and control changes, and broader social transformations,

A. Diduck, N. Peleg, H. Reece (eds.), Law in Society: Reflections on Children, Family, Culture and Philosophy
 ISBN 978-90-04-26148-8. pp. 273-291.

that were to come. No analyses at the time provided any inkling of how profoundly the politics of crime and criminal justice were to change over the following decades.

Michael's paper is of importance, however, as more than a benchmark of how profound subsequent changes have been. The values and the analytic framework that underpin it remain beacons that can continue to inspire contemporary efforts to understand and critically assess the unsettling and in many ways mysterious challenges of the 21st century in criminal justice, crime and social order.

"Law and Order in 1984": A Summary

The paper provides an impressively knowledgeable and accurate analysis of the rise of law and order politics in Britain in the run-up to the 1979 Conservative victory, and during the early years of Thatcher government (for accounts of how this has developed since, see Reiner, 2007: Chap. 5; Downes and Morgan, 2012). Michael's analysis reflects meticulous scholarship: there are 10 pages of detailed footnotes supporting the arguments.

The paper probes the truncheon-rattling rhetoric of the '(then) New Right', and the Thatcher government's budget bonanzas for expenditure on policing and prisons, lavished at the same time as it culled social spending.

There is a particularly close critical analysis of the Police and Criminal Evidence Act 1984 (PACE), depicted as 'the cornerstone of contemporary "law and order" politics' (186). Michael Freeman was one of the first scholars to publish a book on PACE, so this was clearly a particular concern of his at the time (1985).

There is also perceptive and informative discussion of many of the Thatcher government's incursions into civil and political rights that had slowly expanded over the previous two centuries. These included restrictions on trade union powers; new public order legislation; expanded powers against terrorism; tougher penal policy; and transformation of policing towards more proactive social control, information-led surveillance and targeting (an issue of considerable contemporary debate that Michael's paper was one of the first to identify).

The analysis concluded that New Right law and order policies threatened civil liberties, and set us in the dystopian direction of Orwell's *1984*. The final plea was a rousing call to 'fight against current law and order policies' (220), in favour of more socially just ones, that paid at least equal attention to the crimes of the powerful as they did to the crimes of the powerless.

I will critically assess the core arguments of Michael's 'law and order in 1984' paper, suggesting where subsequent developments confirm or call into question his acute analysis. This evaluation benefits from the 20:20 vision of hindsight, and is not intended to minimise the profound scholarship and penetrating analysis of the 1984 paper. I will organize the assessment under the following heads:

1) Are the evolving political and popular attitudes to law and order best understood as moral panic, reasonable reaction to a crime and disorder explosion, both, or neither?

2) Has the 'functions of welfare' thesis (O'Connor, 1973; Gough, 1975, 1979; Offe, 1984), which plays a key part in the argument, now been (sadly) refuted?
3) Is PACE really a cornerstone of 'law and order' politics?
4) Was Thatcher's war against crime something of a 'phoney war'?
5) Is the 'New Policing' thesis in the paper now problematic, as intelligence-led policing (ILP) has become embedded and seen as virtuous, and the research agenda has shifted from sociology *of* policing to sociology *for* policing. It will be argued that policing is a necessary evil, and cannot fit the efficient detection model portrayed by its friends or foes. Control and policing are inevitably Janus-faced.
6) How does the mystery of the crime fall since the mid-1990s play into the changing politics of law and order? Is law and order still central to what is now usually labelled as the neoliberal project, kick-started by Thatcher?

Whilst in most of these respects the politics of law and order has developed in ways beyond the worst forebodings of Michael Freeman and other critical analysts in 1984, the analytic and moral kernel of his argument remains acutely relevant. It can be summed up by the slogan: 'no justice, no peace'. Tough law and order, in its infancy in 1984, cannot provide the security it promises. It may hold the lid down on the social, economic and cultural roots of the crime and disorder it feeds on. But ultimately security depends on wider pacification and civilizing processes, which mainly lie beyond the reach of criminal justice alone, and are framed more by political economy than policing.

1) *Keep Calm or Moral Panic?*

The paper begins by noting the late Geoff Pearson's brilliant application of moral panic theory: *Hooligan: A History of Respectable Fears* (1983). Pearson vividly demonstrated the perpetual recurrence of belief that we were 'going to hell in a handcart', that there was occurring an unprecedented threat of crime and disorder, largely stemming from the decaying morals of the young. Regardless of any evidence supporting or denying such apprehensions at particular times, respectable people through the centuries echoed similar fears and condemnation of youth. Moral panic, exaggerated spirals of self-reinforcing fright, was a generational phenomenon essentially attributable to senescence. As people grew older so too did their concerns about youthful deviance, decadence and disorder. Pearson's thesis does not entail that there are never periods in which crime and delinquency increase. But it offers a warning that such claims should not be taken at face value.

This is almost the only discussion of what is happening to crime and disorder, as opposed to criminal justice (there is a later acknowledgement of widespread public concern about crime, and a hint at what was to become 'Left Realism' with reference to Ian Taylor's pioneering 1981 book, *Law and Order: Arguments for Socialism*). Criminal justice policy, politics and practices are far from a straightforward, rational response to crime problems (Beckett (1997) shows how varying public concerns about crime are shaped by politicians' and mass media discourse, rather than by fluctuations in recorded crime). Nonetheless, there is a complex dialectical interaction between law breaking, law making, and law enforcement. Criminal justice cannot be analysed adequately without also considering trends in crime and disorder. Crime and criminal justice are both shaped by broader currents in political economy, social structure, and culture (Taylor, 1999; Garland, 2001; Matthews and Young, 2003; Reiner, 2007; Lacey, 2008).

Although by 1984 recorded crime had been rising inexorably for nearly 30 years, there is reason to suspect that this was in large part a recording phenomenon. The only longitudinal evidence about crime trends apart from the police recorded statistics, which were well known to be unreliable because of fluctuations in victim reporting and police recording practices (Reiner, 2007: Chap. 3), was the General Household Survey (GHS). During the 1970s the GHS regularly asked respondents about their experience of victimization by burglary. Between 1972 and 1983 recorded burglaries doubled, but victimisation increased by only 20% according to the surveys (Hough and Mayhew, 1985: 16). There was a considerable increase in the proportion of victims reporting burglaries to the police, and the reason is plain from the GHS. In 1972 the property stolen was insured in only 19% of burglaries, but by 1980 this had increased to 42% (Mayhew, Elliott and Dowds, 1989: 19-22). Burglary is of course only one crime amongst many, but it did account for about one fifth of all recorded crime in the 1970s, and was a significant concern fuelling the politicisation of law and order. It is important therefore that the first set of victimisation statistics, from the GHS in the 1970s, reinforced criminological scepticism about how much of the huge increase in recorded crime statistics was really due to increased offending.

But with the advent in the early 1980s of the regular British Crime Survey (now Crime Survey for England and Wales), it is clear that the next decade witnessed a veritable crime explosion (Reiner, 2007: Chap. 3). In addition, the 1980/81 riots, whilst not without precedent in British history, were without parallel for more than a century – and of course there was much more to come (the Miners' Strike is indicated in the final footnote of Michael Freeman's paper, but it was written before the recurrence of serious urban rioting in 1986 at Broadwater Farm and elsewhere).

The use of the moral panic concept to play down 'respectable fears', as Michael's paper does, was a common trope of what Ian Loader has called the 'Platonic Guardian' perspective, then dominant in left/liberal commentary (2006). Its crucial concern was not crime, but the criminal (in)justice/social control reaction to it. However, accepting the reality of what was a new scale of crime/disorder is quite compatible with the heart of Michael's analysis. The crime and disorder explosion, *and* the strong state, law and order reaction to it, were both shaped by the Thatcherite neoliberal economic policies that the paper condemned (Reiner, 2007). What is more problematic (for all criminologists) is how to understand the mystery of the post-1995 crime fall throughout the Western world, which absolutely nobody saw coming, and will be discussed later.

2) *Functions of Welfare?*

Michael's vigorous defence of the Welfare State against the Thatcher cuts was only partly on moral or humane grounds. Analytically his case rests on the argument (then influential on the Left (cf. O'Connor, 1973; Gough, 1975, 1979; Offe, 1984)), that rather than being a threat to capitalism, welfare had a central role in promoting 'capitalist stability'. This was primarily by offering legitimation of the inequalities and regular crises generated by capitalism, and defusing social tensions. Indeed, to some it was itself a form of social control, and hence a functional prerequisite of viable capitalism. On this basis it was assumed that the Thatcher-Reagan 'New Right' assault on welfare would be largely rhetorical, or ultimately reversed.

Would that were so! There have been huge shifts in public attitudes and in the parameters of debate on welfare (Pierson, 2006), permitting cuts in welfare on a scale unimaginable in 1984, largely facilitated by the acceptance of the fundamentals of neo-liberal economics by 'New' Labour and the Clinton (and Obama) Democrats. The post-2010 British Coalition government, in common with many others, has succeeded in portraying the financial and economic crisis since 2008 as caused by excessive state welfare expenditures. 'Austerity' has become the consensual, or at any rate dominant, solution, despite much evidence of its murderous social harms (Stuckler and Basu, 2013; Blyth, 2013; Mirowski, 2013; Xenakis and Cheliotis, 2013; Schafer and Streeck, 2013), with little effect on the stability or legitimacy of the neo-liberal hegemony.... At least, not yet!

3) *PACE and 'Law and Order'*

At the time of its passage the 1984 Police and Criminal Evidence Act (PACE) was widely seen (on all sides of a protracted and often ferocious debate) as advancing police power over suspect safeguards, despite the claim by the government that it rested upon the principle of a 'fundamental balance' between powers and safeguards, as advocated by the 1981 Royal Commission on Criminal Procedure (RCCP) Report from which PACE derived (Leigh, 1986; Reiner, 2010: 99-101, 205-207; Zander, 2012). On the one hand, the police were confident that the 'shopping list' of further powers sought by their representative associations had largely been achieved. On the other hand, civil liberties groups and most radicals were aghast that legislation that originated in Parliamentary concern about miscarriages of justice enhanced police powers considerably, subject only to safeguards that seemed at best paper thin. Many took to the streets under banners declaring 'Kill the Bill!' (pun intended no doubt). Michael Freeman's analysis succinctly and passionately articulates the critical case against PACE, and the apprehensions that it was a significant step towards authoritarian governance.

After only a few years, however, PACE came to be seen widely as having established a new regime of suspect protection against (gross) past abuse. An extensive programme of evaluative empirical research, mounted by the Home Office and academics, came to complex, mixed and somewhat conflicting results and interpretations, but generally found that PACE had achieved some measure of greater protection for suspects although more was needed (McConville, Sanders and Leng, 1991; Dixon, 1997; Brown, 1997; Reiner, 2010: Chap. 7). The research evaluations largely came to a halt in the mid-1990s, as the agenda shifted to a clear trajectory of enhanced powers without even token safeguards (Cape and Young, 2008; Reiner, 2010: 219-222). Nonetheless, PACE itself is now discussed as primarily having achieved an enhanced system of regulation of the exercise of police powers, through more clearly defined (albeit extended) powers and safeguards, a strategy succinctly summed up by Dixon as 'authorise and regulate' (2008).

The PACE safeguards worked better than expected by critics such as Michael Freeman. In general the judges exercised their discretion under the s78 exclusionary rule in tougher mode than anticipated. The symbolism of safeguards underpinned by statute was significant. Internal discipline and record keeping had greater effect than feared by critics. There was some significant penetration of the low visibility backstage areas of policing by tape (and subsequently video) recording, computerisation of the custody process and its records, a proliferation of external 'intruders' (solicitors, 'appropriate adults', lay station visitors, doctors, researchers, and a greater demographic diversity amongst the police themselves (more women, ethnic minorities, graduates etc.).

The impact of even the thinnest safeguards is shown by the contrast between the (much too great) ethnic disproportionality of the exercise of the s1 PACE stop and search power, with the far higher disparity with which 'suspicionless' stops and searches are conducted under s60 of the Criminal Justice and Public Order Act 1994, and s44 of the Terrorism Act 2000 (Shiner, 2013). Since the early 1990s, when a tougher 'law and order' approach became a new consensus between the main political parties, there has been a gradual pull-back of safeguards, an unbalanced increase of powers, and little research evaluating these trends. Michael's 1984 forebodings have been borne out, but not by PACE but rather by its undermining in a new climate of exaggerated fear and insecurity.

4) *Thatcher: A 'Phoney War' on Crime?*

During the late 1970s the Conservative opposition under Margaret Thatcher politicised law and order as a key weapon in their attacks on the Labour government, importing from the US the rabble-rousing rhetoric that the Republicans under Nixon had deployed against Johnson with deadly effect in the 1968 Presidential Election (Reiner, 2007: Chap. 5; Downes and Morgan, 2012). During the late 1970s, in the build-up to her election victory in 1979, Mrs Thatcher blamed the Labour government directly for rising crime and disorder, pledging a 'ring of steel' to protect people against lawlessness. She promised to boost the resources and powers of the police to prevent and clear up crime, and to sharply toughen penal policy, reversing the softness on crime that was attributed to Labour. The Tories' law and order campaign was greatly helped by the emergence of the police as a political lobby, backing up the Conservatives' agenda in a series of advertisements and speeches. The issue was a major factor in Thatcher's 1979 election victory, according to polls monitoring the shifts in public opinion.

Michael documented the politicisation of law and order by Thatcher in detail. He details many policies that appeared to be delivering on the campaign promises, notably the significant resource bonanza for the police, who were made a special case in the face of the general policy of cutbacks and fierce 'value for money' scrutiny in the public sector. PACE was interpreted in the same light as a straightforward boosting of police powers, although this isn't how it worked out in practice as seen earlier. The one area of criminal justice where the Thatcher governments really did deliver on their promised toughness was public order, where police powers were clearly expanded and policing tactics militarised, with highly controversial consequences (Jefferson, 1990; Waddington, 1994; Waddington and Wright, 2008).

By contrast with the post-1992 law and order consensus that emerged as 'New' Labour accepted the broad parameters of the 'New Right' settlement, Thatcher's war on crime was a 'phoney' one, rhetoric more than reality (Reiner, 2007: Chap. 5; Farrell and Hay, 2010). Her Home Secretaries tended to be liberal ones, notably Whitelaw and Hurd, and the policies more nuanced than the Attila the Hun soundbites at Tory Party Conferences. Thatcher's neoliberalism and the tough law and order she pledged were still resisted, mainly by the (divided) opposition parties, but also by the 'wets' in her Cabinets.

The real toughening of penal and policing policy began with the Blair v Howard criminal justice arms race of the 1990s, and was embedded by New Labour in office (Downes and Morgan, 2012). It was slightly attenuated with Cameron's 'hug a hoodie' attempts at detoxification of the 'nasty party' image in the late 2000s, but in office as the dominant party in the Coalition after 2010 the Conservatives are reverting to 'tough on crime' type (following a brief lull whilst Kenneth Clarke was Justice Minister).

5) A New Policing?

Michael's paper argues that a 'new policing' had developed under the New Right, which was aimed at social control rather than crime detection. 'Normally after a crime the police attempt to identify the offender' (214), but now, he claimed, they operate increasingly pre-emptively, by proactive surveillance, and targeting. This concern was expressed by a number of critical criminologists in the mid-1980s, who saw in such seemingly benign developments as community policing an insidious - because disguised - attempt to penetrate communities in order to gain information for more effective social control. In this view policing should be 'minimalist', restricted to the investigation of specific crimes by methods strictly defined and limited by law (Gordon, 1984; Kinsey, Lea and Young, 1986).

Developments since 1984 have in many ways confirmed this prediction. As a response to the huge rise in crime (itself in no small part a product of the growing inequality and social exclusion engendered by neo-liberalism), and the intensifying politics of fear and law and order, police have attempted to find innovative methods to boost their crime control performance. This has been interdependent with a shift in the agendas, perspectives and values underpinning research on policing. Increasingly academic research is *for* not *of* the police, governed by their organisational concerns rather than independent or critical analysis, and there has been a considerable expansion of official policing research by government agencies and by the police themselves (Reiner and Newburn, 2007). This is fired by the quest to find 'what works' in narrow terms of crime fighting. In part this is a response to the predicament of government crime control policies in the new political economy and culture of neoliberalism, which has eroded or abolished many past informal social controls, from stable employment and families to bus conductors and park-keepers. Policing and penality become the only games in town.

Central to the innovative strategies developed by researchers and adopted by police has been intelligence-led policing – ILP (Cope *et al*, 2001; Tilley, 2008; James, 2013). The essence of this was the realisation of the inevitable scarcity of police resources compared to the plethora of possible targets for crime and potential offenders. To enhance effectiveness in dealing with crime, it was necessary to get 'the grease to the squeak' in the words of a seminal Home Office study (Hough and Tilley, 1998), to concentrate policing resources to the locations and people (potential victims or offenders) most prone to crime. This has produced volumes of research evaluating tactics such as 'hot spots' policing, 'target-hardening' techniques of many kinds, and profiling and targeting of those identified as prolific offenders (Sherman, 1992; Sherman *et al*, 1997; Weisburd and Braga; 2006; Braga and Weisburd, 2010). These tactics are widely deemed to be success stories, and credited with a significant role in the crime fall of the last twenty years (which will be considered further below). In particular they are at the heart of the now legendary 'New York miracle' in which 'Compstat' – '*Comp*uter *Stat*istics' played a pivotal part (Weisburd *et al*, 2003; Moore, 2003; Zimring, 2012).

The wider ambitions of the ILP movement, to make it the basis of all policing, have never been realised, although some forces tried to implement a full ILP based system, and it has been influential in crime prevention and detection departments in all forces (James, 2013). There is no doubt that the analysis of crime and other data relevant to policing, and its impact on operations, have been qualitatively transformed, with some scholars suggesting the police are now better seen as information-brokers than law enforcers (Ericson and Haggerty, 1997).

In common with many other liberal analysts, Michael Freeman saw the beginnings of this process towards more proactive, intelligence-led policing as a new and sinister development, contrasting it with a minimalist law-governed focus on detecting crimes. The considerable expansion of criminal justice intervention based on predictions of what people might do, as distinct from crimes they have actually committed – memorably labelled by Lucia Zedner as 'pre-crime' – is a highly dubious departure from due process principles of the rule of law (Zedner, 2006, 2007; Ashworth and Zedner, 2012). This is compounded by the frequent malpractices associated with the police collection of information by unauthorised surveillance methods or undercover operations, as illustrated by recent revelations in Britain (Lewis and Evans, 2013).

These tactics of intelligence gathering have long histories of abuse, in all jurisdictions (Marx, 1989; Fijnaut and Marx, 1995).

However, the increasing prevalence of ILP methods in relation to crime detection and prevention are in many ways welcome. It is hard to prefer stupidity-led policing to intelligence-led smart policing. When used to improve the performance of the police in relation to the prevention and detection of unequivocal and consensually understood crimes, and if subject to adequate accountability (admittedly a big if in practice), ILP is not 'reactionary' (Sherman, 1993), and arguably compatible with the 'left realist' criminologists' plea for 'minimalist policing' (Kinsey, Lea and Young, 1985). Contrary to the claims both of its more enthusiastic promoters, and of those critics who bewail it as a sinister corruption of democratic policing, ILP is neither a panacea nor a poison, but a useful way of enhancing public protection to a limited extent.

Paradoxically, both fans and critics of what Michael dubbed the 'new policing' misrepresent the fundamental character of policing. They assume in effect the mass media 'cops and robbers' image of police as at least ideally and aspirationally effective detectives (the latest incarnation of which is the *CSI* model of policing as the appliance of science), which is at the heart of law and order ideology. However much it is governed by smart, scientific analysis of evidence, and however well managed, well resourced and well conducted investigations are, most crimes recorded by the police are simply not detectable (and most crimes are not recorded by the police). Volume property crime, the majority of recorded offences, seldom offers investigating detectives any clues at all. The minority of serious violent offences, notably murder, that preoccupy media and public attention, are mostly what detectives call 'self-solvers', with the identity of the perpetrator pretty clear from the outset and the skill of the detectives lying in constructing a legal case. The minority of 'whodunnits' are much more likely to be cleared up than property crimes, but this is more because as (usually bloody) contact crimes there is more likely to be evidence on which to base an investigation, rather than because of the greater resources or skills devoted to them (Innes, 2003, 2007; Maguire, 2008).

Contrary to the popular culture image of the police as primarily crime fighters (which also underlies Michael's critical account), empirical research and theoretical reflection upon it have suggested a rather different, more complex picture. Policing, research has shown, is mainly order-maintenance or peace-keeping. And in so far as they impact on crime, it is more in terms of prevention, than detection after the event (I have summarised the evidence in 2010: 139-147).

Two seminal papers (Bittner, 1974; Marenin, 1983) summarise the implications of empirical research for understanding the nature of policing. Bittner's highly influential analysis suggests that the uniting feature of policing tasks is that they all involve 'something that ought not to be happening and about which someone had better do something now!' (1974: 30). The reason the police are called to such emergency conflict situations is that they are 'equipped, entitled and required to deal with every exigency in which force may have to be used' (Bittner, 1974: 35). The distinctiveness of the police lies not in their performance of a specific social function, but in being the specialist repositories for the state's monopolisation of legitimate force in its territory. But the control attempted by the police is Janus faced: it delivers both 'parking tickets and class repression' (Marenin, 1983). Police simultaneously seek to reproduce both 'general' *and* 'particular' order – the conditions of existence of any viable social coexistence and the perpetuation of existing hierarchies of power and advantage (Marenin, op. cit.). Most police are 'good people' doing 'dirty work' (Hughes, 1961), that potentially and sometimes actually requires the wielding of legitimate (occasionally deadly) force. They are a necessary evil, not a forensically limited precision instrument for catching criminals.

6) *Mystery of the Crime Drop*

Michael Freeman argued that 'heavy policing can actually create crime' (214). This claim is in line with Lord Scarman's analysis of the Brixton disorders (1981), which argued that the riots were sparked by the heavy policing crackdown on street robbery (unfortunately called 'Operation Swamp'). Strict law enforcement, Scarman suggested, sometimes had to be subordinated to the requirements of preserving public tranquility, which was the greatest priority. This was a restatement of the policing principles outlined in the instructions to the first recruits to the new Metropolitan Police in 1829 by the founder of the British police, Sir Robert Peel, and the two Commissioners he appointed, Rowan and Mayne (Lentz and Chaires, 2007). Michael's analysis also draws on the critical criminology perspective of labelling theory. This showed how an unintended consequence of social control and criminal justice reactions was to exacerbate the behaviour they purport to reduce, by solidifying the deviant labels and identities that they are addressed against.

Certainly most criminologists have been sceptical about the possibility of reducing crime by tough policing, fearing instead that it could aggravate offending (some right wing criminologists were exceptions, who always believed in tough – and smart - policing and punishment, notably Wilson (1975)). Scepticism about police effectiveness in crime control was also the official consensus during the 1970s and 80s, when a substantial body of research seemed to show that 'nothing works' in terms of either policing or penal policy (Clarke and Hough, 1980, 1984; Martinson, 1974). This began to turn around in the early 1990s, when a renewed faith in the effectiveness of police (and penal policy) crime control was born again as part of the new tough (and smart) law and order consensus, as indicated in the previous section.

The new 'can do' mentality in criminal justice agencies appeared to be confirmed by an unanticipated and surprising turnaround: the substantial and continuing fall in both property and violent crime throughout the Western world, whether measured by police recorded data or crime surveys. Police and government spokespersons were quick to claim credit. 'Crime is down, blame the police!' boasted Bill Bratton about the celebrated crime drop in New York City whilst he was Chief of the NYPD (Bratton, 1998). Such claims were challenged by researchers early on (e.g. Bowling, 1999; Blumstein and Wallman, 2000; Karmen, 2000), who found that detailed analysis of the timing and spatial spread of the crime decline did not fit with the policy changes that were invoked as explanations (such as the much debated 'zero tolerance' attributed to the NYPD, or its Compstat programme). Later contributions have suggested that certain policing reforms (Zimring, 2007, 2012) or changes in police strength (Levitt, 2004) did contribute significantly, alongside other criminal justice and other social changes (e.g. according to Levitt the decriminalisation of abortion in the 1970s and the massive increase in imprisonment, or according to Rosenfeld and Messner (2009) economic variables such as rising consumer confidence).

A major defect of most of the debate about the crime drop is its domination by American criminologists looking only at the USA. When the perspective is expanded to take in the fact that the crime fall occurred throughout the Western world it becomes highly dubious to consider only policy changes in the USA (and *a fortiori* only in New York) as the explanations. The most plausible candidate for explaining the widespread drop is the so-called 'security hypothesis' (Farrell, Tseloni, Mailley, and Tilley, 2011). This argues that much more effective technological means of protecting property (especially cars and houses) became sufficiently widespread to account for most if not all the international decline in property crime, quantitatively the bulk of recorded offences.

Nonetheless the crime drop of the last two decades remains shrouded in deep mystery, for all the claims to have found an explanation. The 'security hypothesis' is a convincing account of the fall in property crime (and hence crime overall). But it doesn't really explain the substantial falls in homicide and serious violence. The security hypothesis authors suggest that the suppression of property crimes may have stopped youngsters graduating further into serious criminal careers including violence. But this is not a convincing explanation of the overall fall in violence, so much of which is domestic.

What is certain is that the problem of falling crime would have been unimaginable in the 1984 debates, which took place against a backdrop of massively rising crime rates. What all the explanations of the crime drop seem to accept is that the fall is not to do with an abatement of the deeper causes of criminal propensity ('criminality' as Currie (2000) called it), whether we look at the favoured grand narratives of the political right (post-60s permissiveness) or left (unemployment, inequality, consumerism). These root causes have flourished during the crime drop as they did during the earlier crime explosion. The explanations are in terms of a cutting-off of opportunities to commit crime (by a mix of smarter and tougher policing, penal incapacitation, target-hardening). The criminal justice lids have been kept on the bubbling cauldron of escalating social and economic tensions and insecurity with great success so far. In the process, criminology has become liddology, research on better lid design and deployment. A big question mark remains over how long this can be sustained. Has cultural accommodation to a new normal - of widening economic injustice and insecurity for the vast majority, the 99% - become so embedded that these factors no longer fuel criminogenic pressures? I suspect not: when the lids were temporarily lifted during the recent British riots, an explosion of looting and other property crime occurred. What is clearly required is deeper analytic engagement with the social causes of crime and disorder in the light of the economic crisis, and not only of authoritarian turns in criminal justice.

Conclusion: Law, Order and Neo-liberalism since 1984

When he wrote his 1984 paper, Michael Freeman, together with most other liberal and left commentators, implicitly saw the assaults (still largely rhetorical) on the post-war welfarist and Keynesian consensus by the 'New Right' as temporary challenges and aberrations. This was not only because their consequences for the mass of the population were harsh and unjust, provoking backlashes in the form of urban riots and industrial militancy. It was also because there were opposition parties who remained committed to reversing the basic thrust of the New Right (however remote their electoral prospects seemed to be). To many Left-liberals in the early 1980s the New Right's programme seemed to be a quixotic attempt to reverse a long march towards more inclusive civil, political and socio-economic citizenship (in the seminal language of Marshall (1950)), under a tacit slogan of 'back to the 1600s!' Moreover the 'functions of welfare' thesis suggested reassuringly that they violated the functional prerequisites of capitalist order. So moral, political, historical, cultural and theoretical political economy arguments gave comfort that the 'New Right' were only temporary residents of the seats of power. And impassioned papers assembling with scholarly meticulousness evidence of the violations of truth and justice by their misguided policies would help send them more speedily into the dustbin of history. And yet … under the more common contemporary label 'neo-liberalism' the strategies of the 1980s 'New Right' remain dominant.

Since the early 1990s, with the rise of 'New Labour' in Britain and other 'third ways' in other Western countries, neoliberalism has become an unchallenged hegemony. 'Law and order' discourse and policy formed a new consensus between the main political parties (Reiner, 2007: Chap. 5; Downes and Morgan, 2012). So too did attacks on welfare, labour organisations. The well deserved targets of Michael's 1984 critique had become entrenched as a newly dominant neoliberal orthodoxy.

The financial crisis and economic crash since 2007 would seem at least to call into question, if not utterly refute, the neo-liberal model, but a zombie neo-liberalism remains dominant in policy. This is one indication of a clear and present danger that democracy is being supplanted by plutocracy, the 'finest government money can buy', as Greg Palast put it (2004). There is mounting evidence that we are moving towards a plutocracy: government of the rich, by the rich, for the rich. The massive increase in inequality engendered by neo-liberalism since the late 1970s, reversing two centuries of slow movement towards greater social inclusion, threatens the democratic process in a variety of ways. The process is far more advanced and evident in the USA, where distinguished political scientists have for many years charted the increasing takeover of the political process by the power of capital (Jacobs and Skocpol, 2005; Wolin, 2008).

This trend towards plutocracy was hugely strengthened by a notorious 2009 US Supreme Court decision. As summarised in a devastating critique by the late Ronald Dworkin, 'Against the opposition of their four colleagues, five right-wing Supreme Court justices have now guaranteed that big corporations can spend unlimited funds on political advertising in any political election.... This appalling decision, in *Citizens*

United v. *Federal Election Commission*, was quickly denounced by President Obama as "devastating"; he said that it "strikes at our democracy itself." In his State of the Union speech of January 27, he said, "Last week, the Supreme Court reversed a century of law that I believe will open the floodgates for special interests—including foreign corporations—to spend without limit in our elections." He is right: the decision will further weaken the quality and fairness of our politics. The Court has given lobbyists, already much too powerful, a nuclear weapon' (2010).

The same processes are happening in Britain, although so far to a lesser extent, and less studied by academics (although radical journalists have assembled evidence of the march of plutocracy e.g. Monbiot (2001)). However, the growing conflicts about the role of political lobbying, and the revelations about the intimate inter-connections between the right-wing press, politicians and the police that produced the Leveson Enquiry (Leveson, 2013; Watson and Hickman, 2013), point in the same direction. All underline the threat posed to democracy (based on the principle one person, one vote) by the neo-liberal unshackling of corporations and markets (in which one pound carries one vote, so we are dominated by the mega-rich few, the 1% identified by the Occupy Movement (that flourished in many cities around the world in 2011-12 protesting the austerity policies implemented in the wake of the 2008 crash)), which increasingly renders the outcome of elections irrelevant because of the constraints on the actions of national governments. While government policy pursues the interest of the 1%, the 99% mostly accept that the blame should be cast on the underclass and outsiders.

Law and order implicitly has receded as an issue, playing little part in the 2010 General Election, compared to all other elections since 1979 (Downes and Morgan, 2012). This has created the political space for the Coalition to inflict massive cuts on the police (Brogden and Ellison, 2013) and the criminal justice system, and to pursue an increasingly blatant privatisation agenda. Tabloid headlines and political rhetoric still stoke a climate of fear about crime, fanned by media focus on spectacularly violent and horrific but extremely rare savage offences. Most people continue to state in surveys that they believe crime is rising – even though crime rates have been falling for two decades. Nonetheless, the far lower risk of victimisation (by volume property crime in particular) has taken some of the steam out of the law and order issue.

A persuasive line of analysis suggests that the attempt to free markets necessitates a 'strong state' to control the social consequences of crime and disorder (Polanyi, 1944/2001; Gamble, 1994). Certainly the potential for protest and riot remains, and there have been stirrings of resistance to the austerity agenda for (mis)handling the economic crisis in many parts of the world (Mason, 2012). Yet in view of the extreme social damage done to the mass of the population by the assaults of 'austerity' (as opposed to the alternative Keynesian remedies for economic crises) the puzzle is how little resistance there has been, even in Greece and other places that have experienced truly savage cuts in welfare with huge, indeed often life-threatening consequences for health (Stuckler and Basu, 2013; Blyth, 2013; Mirowski, 2013; Red Cross, 2013). The 'free' economy seems to be supported mainly by passive acquiescence rather than any need for overt strong state repression (though police powers, surveillance and anti-riot techniques have hardened yet further in the 21st century), especially but not only in the UK. This may be facilitated by a number of diversionary processes. To some extent the ills of 'austerity' and rampant inequality are turned inwards rather than outwards – increasing rates of stress related physical and mental disease, suicide and other symptoms of despair (Wilkinson and Pickett, 2009; Stuckler and Basu, op. cit.; Red Cross, op. cit.; Dorling, 2013). There is evidence of a displacement of anger and hate from the powerful authors of the plight of the mass of the population on to powerless and vulnerable scapegoats, such as ethnic minorities, migrants, welfare recipients, convicted street criminals (Xenakis and Cheliotis, 2013), processes that carry sinister echoes from the last Great Depression of the 1930s (Cheliotis, 2013).

Epilogue: Justice, justice You Shall Pursue

Michael's 1984 paper ended with a rousing call to demonstrate the true nature of the law and order threats to general security and well-being – which comes much more from the suites, not the streets. The distorted focus on the crimes of the poor, obscuring the vastly more harmful and heinous crimes and wrongs of the rich and powerful, has grown even greater since then (Hillyard *et al*, 2004; Coleman *et al*, 2009; Nelken, 2012; Green and Ward, 2012, 2013).

Michael Freeman's *1984* nightmare has become more deeply embedded, partly by morphing into *Brave New World* - Aldous Huxley partnered with George Orwell. Popular culture offers a seductive consumerist dream of have-it-all success (Hall, Winlow and Ancrum, 2008). You can enjoy Woodstock *and* Wall St., Sex *and* the City, Make Love *and* War *and* Loadsamoney, or at least buy a lottery ticket so that it could be you. Seduction, rather than repression, personal or political, is how the injustices so acutely criticised by Michael Freeman in 1984 are now perpetuated.

Understanding and challenging that is a tougher task than ever. But as Michael's final sentence in the 1984 paper said, 'Until we do (demonstrate the deception), justice will suffer, and so will we'.

Bibliography

Ashworth, A. and Zedner, L., "Prevention and Criminalization: Justifications and Limits", *New Criminal Law Review* 2012 15(4), 542-571.

Beckett, K., *Making Crime Pay* (New York: Oxford University Press, 1997).

Bittner, E., "Florence Nightingale in pursuit of Willie Sutton: A theory of the police", in H. Jacob (ed), *The Potential for Reform of Criminal Justice* (Los Angeles, CA: Sage, 1974).

Blumstein, A. and Wallman, J. (eds), *The Crime Drop in America* (Cambridge: Cambridge University Press, 2000).

Blyth, M., *Austerity: The History of a Dangerous Idea* (New York: Oxford University Press, 2013).

Bowling, B., "The Rise and Fall of New York Murder", *British Journal of Criminology* 1999 39(4), 531–554.

Braga, A. and Weisburd, D., *Policing Problem Places* (New York: Oxford University Press, 2010).

Bratton, W., "Crime is Down: Blame the Police", in N. Dennis (ed), *Zero Tolerance: Policing A Free Society* (2nd edn) (London: Institute of Economic Affairs, 1998).

Brogden, M. and Ellison, G., *Policing in an Age of Austerity: A Postcolonial Perspective* (London: Routledge, 2012).

Brown, D., *PACE Ten Years on: A Review of the Research* (London: Home Office, Home Office Research Study 155, 1997).

Cape, E. and Young, R. (eds), *Regulating Policing: The Police and Criminal Evidence Act 1984 – Past, Present and Future* (Oxford: Hart, 2008).

Cheliotis, L., "Neoliberal Capitalism and Middle-class Punitiveness: Bringing Erich Fromm's "Materialistic Psychoanalysis" to Penology", *Punishment and Society* 2013 15(3), 247-273.

Clarke, R. and Hough, M. (eds), *The Effectiveness of Policing* (Farnborough: Gower, 1980).

Clarke, R., and Hough, M., *Crime and Police Effectiveness* (London: Home Office Research Unit, 1984).

Coleman, R., Sim, J., Tombs, S. and Whyte, D. (eds), *State, Power, Crime* (London: Sage, 2009).

Cope, N., Innes, M. and Fielding, N., *Smart Policing? The Theory and Practice of Intelligence-Led Policing* (London: Home Office, 2001).

Currie, E., "Reflections on Crime and Criminology at the Millenium", *Western Criminology Review* 2000 2(1), 1-15.

Dixon, D., *Law in Policing* (Oxford: Oxford University Press, 1997).

Dixon, D., "Authorise and Regulate: A Comparative Perspective on the Rise and Fall of a Regulatory Strategy", in E. Cape and R. Young (eds), *Regulating Policing* (Oxford: Hart, 2008).

Dorling, D., *Unequal Health* (Bristol: Policy Press, 2013).

Downes, D. and Morgan, R., "Overtaking on the left? The politics of law and order in the "Big Society"", in M. Maguire, R. Morgan and R. Reiner (eds), *The Oxford Handbook of Criminology* (Oxford: Oxford University Press, 2012).

Dworkin, R., "The "Devastating" Decision", *New York Review of Books* 2010 February 25th.

Ericson, R. and Haggerty, K., *Policing Risk Society* (Oxford: Oxford University Press, 1997).

Evans, R. and Lewis, P., *Undercover: The True Story of Britain's Secret Police* (London: Faber, 2013).

Farrall, S. and Hay, C., "Not So Tough on Crime? Why Weren't the Thatcher Governments More Radical in Reforming the Criminal Justice System?", *British Journal of Criminology* 2010 50(4), 550-569.

Farrell, G., Tilley, N., Tseloni, A. and Mailley, J., "The crime drop and the security hypothesis", *Journal of Research in Crime and Delinquency* 2011 48(2), 147-175.

Fijnaut, C. and Marx, G. (eds), *Undercover in Comparative Perspective: Some Implications for Knowledge and Social Research* (The Hague: Kluwer, 1995).

Freeman, M., "Law and Order in 1984", *Current Legal Problems* 1984 37(1), 175-231.
Freeman, M., *The Police and Criminal Evidence Act 1984* (London: Sweet and Maxwell, 1985).
Gamble, A., *The Free Economy and the Strong State* (London: Macmillan, 1994).
Garland, D., *The Culture of Control* (Oxford: Oxford University Press, 2001).
Gordon, P., "Community Policing: Towards the Local Police State", *Critical Social Policy* 1984 10 (summer), 39–58.
Gough, I., "State Expenditure in Advanced Capitalism", *New Left Review* 1975 92, July-August.
Gough, I., *The Political Economy of the Welfare State* (London: Macmillan, 1979).
Green, P. and Ward, T., "State Crime: A Dialectical View", in M. Maguire, R. Morgan and R. Reiner (eds), *The Oxford Handbook of Criminology* (5th ed) (Oxford: Oxford University Press, 2012).
Green, P. and Ward, T., *State Crime* (London: Pluto, 2013).
Hall, S., Winlow, S. and Ancrum, C., *Criminal Identities and Consumer Culture* (Cullompton: Willan, 2008).
Hillyard, P., Pantazis, C., Tombs, S. and Gordon, D. (eds), *Beyond Criminology: Taking Harm Seriously* (London: Pluto, 2004).
Hough, M. and Mayhew, P., *Taking Account of Crime: Key Findings From the Second British Crime Survey* (London: Home Office, 1985).
Hough, M. and Tilley, N., *Getting the Grease to the Squeak: Research Lessons for Prevention,* Crime Prevention and Detection Series Paper 85 (London: Home Office, 1998).
Hughes, E., "Good People and Dirty Work", *Social Problems* 1961 10(1), 3-11.
Innes, M., *Investigating Murder: Detective Work and The Police Response to Criminal Homicide* (Oxford: Oxford University Press, 2003).
Innes, M., "Investigation and Major Crime Enquiries", in T. Newburn, T. Williamson and A. Wright (eds), *Handbook of Criminal Investigation* (Cullompton: Willan, 2007).
Jacobs, L. and Skocpol, T. (eds), *Inequality and American Democracy* (New York: Russell Sage, 2005).
James, A., *Examining Intelligence-Led Policing: developments in research, policy and practice* (London: Macmillan, 2013).
Jefferson, T., *The Case against Paramilitary Policing* (Milton Keynes: Open University Press, 1990).
Karmen, A., *New York Murder Mystery* (New York: New York University Press, 2000).
Kinsey, R., Lea, J. and Young, Y., *Losing the Fight Against Crime* (Oxford: Blackwell, 1986).
Lacey, N., *The Prisoners' Dilemma: Political Economy and Punishment in Contemporary Democracies* (Cambridge: Cambridge University Press, 2008).
Leigh, L., "Some Observations on the Parliamentary History of the Police and Criminal Evidence Act 1984", in C. Harlow (ed), *Public Law and Politics* (London: Sweet and Maxwell, 1986).

Lentz, S. and Chaires, R., "The invention of Peel's principles: A study of policing "text-book" history", *Journal of Criminal Justice* 2007 35(1), 69-79.
Leveson, Lord Justice, *The Report into the Culture, Practices and Ethics of the Press* (London: Stationery Office, 2012).
Levitt, S., "Understanding why crime fell in the 1990s: four factors that explain the decline and six that do not", *Journal of Economic Perspectives* 2004 18(1), 163–190.
Loader, I., "Fall of the "Platonic Guardians": Liberalism, Criminology and Political Responses to Crime in England and Wales", *British Journal of Criminology* 2006 46(4), 561-586.
Maguire, M., "Criminal Investigation and Crime Control", in T. Newburn (ed), *Handbook of Policing* (2nd ed) (Cullompton: Willan, 2008).
Marenin, O., "Parking Tickets and Class Repression: The Concept of Policing in Critical Theories of Criminal Justice", *Contemporary Crises* 1983 6(2), 241–266.
Marshall, T. H., *Citizenship and Social Class* (Cambridge: Cambridge University Press, 1950).
Martinson, R., "What Works? Questions and Answers about Prison Reform", *The Public Interest* 1974 10(1), 22-54.
Marx, G., *Undercover: Police Surveillance in America* (Berkeley, CA: University of California Press, 1989).
Mason, P., *Why It's Kicking Off Everywhere: The New Global Revolutions* (London: Verso, 2012).
Matthews, R. and Young, J. (eds), *The New Politics of Crime and Punishment* (Cullompton: Willan, 2003).
Mayhew, P., Elliott, D. and Dowds, L., *The 1988 British Crime Survey* (London: Home Office, 1989).
McConville, M., Sanders, A. and Leng, R., *The Case for the Prosecution: Police Suspects and the Construction of Criminality* (London: Routledge, 1991).
Mirowski, P., *Never Let A Good Crisis Go to Waste: How Neoliberalism Survived the Financial Breakdown* (London: Verso, 2013).
Monbiot, G., *Captive State: The Corporate Takeover of Britain* (London: Pan, 2001).
Moore, M., "Sizing Up Compstat: An Important Administrative Innovation in Policing", *Criminology and Public Policy* 2003 2(3), 469-494.
Nelken, D., "White Collar and Corporate Crime", in M. Maguire, R. Morgan and R. Reiner (eds), *The Oxford Handbook of Criminology* (5th ed) (Oxford: Oxford University Press, 2012).
O'Connor, J., *The Fiscal Crisis of the State* (New York: St Martins, 1973).
Offe, C., *Contradictions of the Welfare State* (Cambridge Mass.: MIT Press, 1984).
Palast, G., *The Best Democracy Money Can Buy* (New York: Plume, 2004).
Pearson, G., *Hooligan* (London: Macmillan, 1983).
Polanyi, K., *The Great Transformation* (Boston: Beacon, 1944/2001).
Red Cross, *Think Differently: Humanitarian Aspects of the Economic Crisis in Europe* (Geneva: International Federation of Red Cross and Red Crescent Societies, 2013).
Reiner, R., *Law and Order: An Honest Citizen's Guide to Crime and Control* (Cambridge: Polity, 2007).

Reiner, R., *The Politics of the Police* (4th ed) (Oxford: Oxford University Press, 2010).
Reiner, R. and Newburn, T., "Police Research", in R. King and E. Wincup (eds), *Doing Research on Crime and Justice* (2nd ed) (Oxford: Oxford University Press, 2007).
Rosenfeld, R. and Messner, S., "The crime drop in comparative perspective: the impact of the economy and imprisonment on American and European burglary rates", *British Journal of Sociology* 2009 60(3), 445-472.
Scarman, Lord, *The Scarman Report: The Brixton Disorders* (London: HMSO, Cmnd 8427, 1981).
Schafer, A. and Streeck, W. (eds), *Politics in the Age of Austerity* (Cambridge: Polity, 2013).
Sherman, L., "Attacking Crime: Police and Crime Control", in M. Tonry and N. Morris (eds), *Modern Policing* (Chicago: Chicago University Press, 1992).
Sherman, L., "Why Crime Control Is Not Reactionary", in D. Weisburd, C. Uchida, and L. Green (eds), *Police Innovation and Control of Police* (New York: SpringerVerlag, 1993).
Sherman, L., Gottfredson, D., Eck, J., Reuter, P. and Bushway, S., *What Works? What Doesn't? What's Promising?* (Washington, D. C.: Department of Justice, 1997).
Shiner, M., *Report on the use of section 60 of the Criminal Justice and Public Order Act 1994 by the police* (http://www.stop-watch.org/uploads/documents/Shiner_expertwitnessstatement_s60.pdf), accessed 17 November 2013.
Stuckler, D. and Basu, S., *The Body Economic: Why Austerity Kills* (London: Allen Lane, 2013).
Taylor, I., *Law and Order: Arguments for Socialism* (London: Macmillan, 1981).
Taylor, I., *Crime in Context: A Critical Criminology of Market Societies* (Cambridge: Polity Press, 1999).
Tilley, N., "Modern Approaches to Policing: Community, Problem-oriented and Intelligence-led", in T. Newburn (ed), *Handbook of Policing* (2nd ed) (Cullompton: Willan, 2008).
Waddington, P. A. J., *Liberty and Order: Public Order Policing in a Capital City* (London: UCL Press, 1994).
Waddington, P. A. J. and Wright, M., "Police Use of Force, Firearms and Riot-Control", in T. Newburn (ed), *Handbook of Policing* (2nd ed) (Cullompton: Willan, 2008).
Watson, T. and Hickman, M., *Dial M for Murdoch: News Corporation and the Corruption of Britain* (London: Allen Lane, 2013).
Weisburd, D. and Braga, A. (eds), *Police Innovation: Contrasting Perspectives* (Cambridge: Cambridge University Press, 2006).
Weisburd, D., Mastrofski, S., McNally, A., Greenspan, R. and Willis, J. "Reforming to Preserve: Compstat and Strategic Problem Solving in American Policing", *Criminology and Public Policy* 2003 2(3), 421-456.
Wilkinson, R. and Pickett, K., *The Spirit Level: Why Equality is Better for Everyone* (London: Penguin, 2009).
Wilson, J. Q., *Thinking about Crime* (New York: Vintage, 1975).
Wolin, S., *Democracy Inc.* (Princeton: Princeton University Press, 2008).

Xenakis, S. and Cheliotis, L., "Crime and Economic Downturn: The Complexity of Crime and Crime Politics in Greece since 2009", *British Journal of Criminology* 2013 53(5), 719-745.

Zander, M., *PACE (The Police and Criminal Evidence Act 1984): Past, Present and Future* (London: LSE Law, Society and Economy Working Papers, 2012).

Zedner, L., "Pre-crime and post-criminology?", *Theoretical Criminology* 2006 11(2), 261-281.

Zedner, L., "Preventive justice or pre-punishment? The case of control orders", *Current Legal Problems* 2007 60(1), 174-203.

Zimring, F., *The Great American Crime Decline* (New York: Oxford University Press, 2007).

Zimring, F., *The City That Became Safe: New York's Lessons for Urban Crime and its Control* (New York: Oxford University Press, 2011).

Children's Rights and Children's Criminal Responsibility

Heather Keating
University of Sussex, UK

In 1981 Michael Freeman asked the question 'whether and to what extent, children who do wrong should be treated differently from adult offenders?' (210). Some ten years later he urged us to take children's rights more seriously (1992); he reminded us again of the need to do so some 15 years later (2007) and in all three essays, rightly, he drew attention to the marked contrast between the reluctance to recognise children's rights and the willingness with which the responsibility of even very young children has been upheld by the criminal law of England and Wales.

Against the backdrop of current legislative initiatives, our current understanding of children's development and international conventions, and drawing upon Michael's scholarship, this chapter explores the appropriate yardstick by which to determine the fundamental question of how we treat children who do wrong.

Doing full justice to this question would require an exploration of the entirety of the youth justice system – from questions about the age of criminal responsibility to arrest and trial through to sentencing and the use of custody. This would be well beyond the scope of one chapter so the focus instead is upon a narrow but fundamentally important question: the age at which we hold children criminally responsible for their harmful behaviour, with one apparent diversion into the issue of anti-social behaviour. The reason for this is twofold.

First, currently before Parliament are two Bills: one is Lord Dholakia's private member's Bill to raise the age of criminal responsibility, the other is a government Bill, the Anti-Social Behaviour, Crime and Policing Bill, which, if passed in its current form, would substantially enlarge the range of behaviour which could lead children into conflict with the law. If one were to draw upon Oliver Wendell Holmes' statement that the important thing is, 'not so much where we stand, as in what direction we are moving' (1858) the best that could be said is that we are pulling in two directions – more realistically, the fear must be that we are moving towards increased responsibility rather than less. The second reason is closely allied to the first. One cannot ignore the issue of state responses to anti-social behaviour when considering the age of criminal responsibility because the impact of such measures upon children, as

A. Diduck, N. Peleg, H. Reece (eds.), Law in Society: Reflections on Children, Family, Culture and Philosophy
Copyright 2015 Koninklijke Brill NV. Printed in The Netherlands. ISBN 978-90-04-26148-8. pp. 293-308.

Michael has commented, may exceed even the shock waves which emanated from the case of the killing of James Bulger (2007: 11).

In exploring both the minimum age of criminal responsibility and the government's latest response to anti-social behaviour, this chapter subscribes to the view expressed so eloquently by Lord Dholakia:

> It cannot be right to deal with such young children in a criminal process based on ideas of culpability which assume a capacity for mature, adult-like decision-making. There is no other area of law – whether it is the age for buying a pet, the age for paid employment, the age of consent to sexual activity or the age for smoking and drinking – where we regard children as fully competent to take informed decisions until later in adolescence. The age of criminal responsibility is an anomalous exception. (*Hansard,* HL Deb, vol. 749, col. 477, 8 November 2013)

This chapter concludes that our law is currently intellectually indefensible both in terms of children's responsibility and children's rights and that while we should support the direction of travel of Lord Dholakia's Bill, the measures proposed in relation to anti-social behaviour require fundamental revision.

Responsibility and the Criminal Law: Where We Stand

Our system of criminal law is built upon the moral premise that it is legitimate to hold individuals answerable for their behaviour when they have both the capacity and choice to do otherwise (Hart, 1967). This concept of responsibility is two-dimensional: it consists of a cognitive element – an ability to understand both the law and the consequences of not acting in accordance with it - and a volitional element – an ability to control one's action (Hart, 1967).[1] In other words, criminal law addresses itself to the responsible subject. If someone lacks capacity or the ability to conform to the law, he or she cannot be said to be a responsible actor and should not be subject to criminal law sanctions. This would be true of very young children and thus most (although not all) jurisdictions have a fixed age below which children, as a category, are exempt from criminal liability.

The age of criminal responsibility in England and Wales is ten years old. This has been the case since 1963 (Children and Young Persons Act 1963, s.16, amending the Children and Young Persons Act 1933, s. 50) when it was raised from eight, having been as low as seven at common law. In Northern Ireland, the age of criminal responsibility is also ten whilst in Scotland, it is still eight. However, as a result of legislation in in Scotland in 2010, children cannot be prosecuted below the age of 12 although they may be the subject of a Children's Hearing (Criminal Justice and Licensing Act 2010, s. 38). Ireland increased the age of criminal responsibility to 12 in 2006 (Criminal Justice Act 2006, s. 52, amending the Children Act 2001). Ireland's reform is of particu-

---

1 The concept of responsibility underpinning criminal law is explored further in Keating (2007) and Keating (2008).

lar interest and will be explored in more detail later in this chapter. The average age at which criminal responsibility is imposed throughout Europe is 14, although some jurisdictions do not hold children responsible until they are older than this (for example, in Denmark, Finland, Norway and Sweden the age of criminal responsibility is 15).

Running alongside the fixed age of criminal responsibility was, however, for many hundreds of years, a further protective mechanism or 'benevolent safeguard' (Lord Lowry in *C* v *DPP* [1996] AC 1 at 33): the presumption of *doli incapax*. This required courts to establish that a child between the age of criminal responsibility and 14 knew that what he or she was doing was 'seriously wrong' and not merely 'naughty' (*Gorrie* (1919) 83 JP 136). There were significant problems with this test,[2] the most fundamental of which were first, that it appeared to equate *knowledge* of right and wrong with capacity: even a seven year-old child might have a basic grasp of this. An *understanding* of such concepts and the consequences their behaviour may have for themselves and others might be deemed a more appropriate starting point for moral responsibility. Even if an understanding of right and wrong were to be required, however, the second aspect of responsibility – an ability to control one's behaviour in accordance with the law – would still be absent.

Thus, as a yardstick of moral responsibility, the basis upon which the presumption operated was flawed but, unlike the categorical exemption provided by a minimum age, it was an important recognition that children develop at different rates. Paradoxically, at around the same time as greater insight into children's intellectual and psychological development was being gained – which highlights the very significant differences between the thought processes of, say, a ten-year-old child and those of an older adolescent (considered further below) – the presumption became seen as reflecting 'an outworn mode of thought' (Law Com, 1972: para. 11.21) and 'outdated and unprincipled' (*C* v *DPP* [1994] 3 WLR 888 at 896 per Laws J.).

It is difficult to know how many children were saved from prosecution, especially towards the end of the presumption's existence: the consultation and debate which preceded its abolition (by the Crime and Disorder Act 1998, s. 34)[3], as part of an approach which viewed children who offend as 'adults in everything but years'[4] was not, as the government acknowledged, based upon any empirical evidence about how the presumption had operated in practice (House of Commons, 1998). Some commentators have concluded that the presumption offered little by way of a safety net in practice (see, for example, Bandalli, 1998) but what we do know is that the numbers of children under 14 who were prosecuted for indictable offences increased by over 25 per cent in the year following abolition of the presumption and rose further thereafter

2 Considered in more detail in Keating (2007), 191-195.

3 Northern Ireland also abolished the presumption. Arguments that s. 34 abolished only the *presumption* of *doli incapax* and that it was still open to a child aged 10-14 years old to plead the defence of *doli incapax* were rejected by the House of Lords in *R* v *T* [2008] EWCA Crim 815.

4 An expression used by Michael Howard MP whilst Home Secretary and cited in Goldson 1997: 130).

(Bateman, 2013: 14).[5] This may very well be ascribed to the abolition of the presumption (Bateman, *ibid*), but it should be remembered that there were a number of other developments during this punitive era which may too have played a part.

In an era of 'no more excuses' – the title of the White Paper which preceded the Crime and Disorder Act 1998 (Home Office, 1997) – once aged ten, children are fully liable to prosecution. It is true that there are mechanisms to divert children from the courts, for example, via the 'new' system of youth cautions (introduced to replace reprimands and warnings by the Legal Aid, Sentencing and Punishment of Offenders Act 2012, s. 136, inserting ss. 66ZA and 66Zb into the Crime and Disorder Act 1998) and referral orders under the Criminal Evidence Act 1999. It is also the case that if the offence is not serious, children will be tried in the Youth Court and that if convicted, special sentencing provisions, which are dependent upon the age of the child, exist. But none of these measures alters the basic fact of criminal responsibility and it is still, regrettably, the case that a child who is charged with a serious offence faces trial in the Crown Court.[6]

The Direction in Which We are Moving?

Currently before Parliament, as noted above, is a private member's Bill (the Age of Criminal Responsibility Bill), the aim of which is to raise the age of criminal responsibility. This is not the first such attempt: over 40 years ago the Children and Young Persons Act 1969, which marked the zenith of the welfare approach to children in trouble, would have increased the age of criminal responsibility to 14. However, although this provision became law, following a change in government it was never implemented and was eventually repealed by the Criminal Justice Act 1991 (s. 72).

Lord Dholakia's private member's Bill received its second reading in November 2013. Whilst it is perhaps remarkable in the current climate that any parliamentary time was found for it, the debate in the House of Lords was also remarkably short (at just over an hour on a Friday afternoon). In introducing this very short Bill which had only one key clause and, at one level, a very modest aim, Lord Dholakia stated:

---

5 In its response to the Law Commission's consultation on *Unfitness to Plead* (2010), the All Party Parliamentary Group for Children reported that there had been an 87 per cent increase in convictions for 10-12 year olds since the abolition of the presumption (All Party Parliamentary Group for Children, p. 1).

6 As a result of the trial of Thompson and Venables, when the UK was found to be in breach of the children's Art. 6 rights (*V and T* v *United Kingdom* (2000) 30 EHRR 121), a practice direction was issued to reduce the formality of Crown Court procedures and to take the youth of such defendants into account (*Practice Note* (*Trial of Children and Young Persons: Procedure*) [2000] 2 All ER 285. However, the continued trial of very young children in the Crown Court is deeply troubling, as was noted by the appeal judge, Hughes L.J., following the trial of two boys aged 10 and 11 for attempted rape in *R* v *W and M* [2010] EWCA Crim 1926, [38]-[40].

> My Bill is designed to raise this country's unusually low age of criminal responsibility from 10 to 12. At present ... children are deemed criminally responsible from the age of 10. That means that children who are too young to attend secondary school can be prosecuted and receive a criminal record. ... The simple proposition [which the Bill] contains, if enacted would be an important step towards dealing with vulnerable, difficult and disturbed children in a way that befitted our civilised society. (*Hansard* HL Deb vol 749, col. 476, 479, 8 November 2013).

His Lordship supported his proposal by citing the conclusions drawn by a recent report on youth justice (*Hansard*: col. 477):

> There is now a significant body of research evidence that early adolescence (under 13-14 years of age) is a period of marked neurodevelopmental immaturity, during which children's capacity is not equivalent to that of an older adolescent or adult. Such findings cast doubt on the culpability and competency of early adolescents to participate in the criminal process. (Centre for Social Justice, 2012: 201).

The research evidence is indeed substantial: as Farmer (a clinical psychologist) states, 'over the last two decades considerable progress has been made in mapping the neuropsychological and social development of children and adolescents' (2011: 86). Having reviewed the research she concludes that 'children aged 10 and 11 are most definitely not competent to participate effectively in the legal system and have reduced culpability. Additionally ... they are likely to be especially vulnerable' (*ibid*: 91). She supports an initial increase to the age of 12 with a subsequent review to increase it further. The Royal College of Psychiatrists has also concluded that the age of criminal responsibility is too low (2006) and a recent report by the Royal Society, after examining the neuroscientific evidence, stated: 'it is clear that at the age of ten the brain is developmentally immature and continues to undergo important changes linked to regulating one's own behaviour' (2011: 14). Children aged ten not only may have difficulty thinking through the consequences of their behaviour (thereby lacking cognitive responsibility) but are also impressionable and suggestible and may thus be easily led (so may lack volitional responsibility).

Without taking any other considerations into account, such as welfare or autonomy rights (to be considered shortly), the case for reform would seem to be compelling – but not, it is clear, to successive governments. In its response to Lord Dholakia's Bill, Lord Ahmad articulated the view of the current administration:

> [There are] no plans to raise the age of criminal responsibility from 10 to 12. We believe that children aged 10 and above are able to differentiate between bad behaviour and serious wrongdoing and should therefore be accountable for their actions. When a young person has committed an offence, it is important that they understand that this is a serious matter and will be dealt with as such. The public must also have confidence in the youth justice system and know that offending will be dealt with effectively ... We are aware that offences committed by young people may have a devastating effect on both

> victims and the wider community, and it would be wrong to ignore this. The tragic case of Jamie Bulger ... immediately comes to mind in this context. (*Hansard*, HL Deb, vol. 749, col. 487-488, 8 November 2013).

Instead of a considered reflection upon the developmental evidence (which, it seems, it is legitimate for governments to ignore), we have the assertion of 'belief' that children are responsible together with a recollection of the killing by Thompson and Venables of James Bulger and the near moral panic which accompanied it: the shadow cast by that tragedy is long indeed. Lord Ahmad went on to argue that early identification may trigger positive intervention; no mention is made that early criminalisation may exacerbate a situation, or that the alternative to criminalisation is not doing nothing. In the face of this, one ought perhaps to be relieved that the government has not counter-argued for a reduction in the age of criminal responsibility so that even younger children can be helped to 'take responsibility for their actions' (*Hansard*, HL Deb, vol. 749, col. 489, 8 November 2013).[7] Such an argument was advanced in Northern Ireland (Driver, 2011) when the justice minister, David Ford, expressed his support for an increase in the age of criminal responsibility from 10 to 12 (Department of Justice Northern Ireland, 2011: 107).[8]

Given the opposition of the government, the chances of sufficient parliamentary time being found (especially in the House of Commons) to debate the Bill and of this small step in the right direction ever becoming law would appear to be very slight. One would need a small miracle for it to succeed.

Which brings us to the other Bill currently before Parliament: it is one which is more likely to become law and, as is now so commonplace with government Bills, tackles a wide range of issues.[9]

Anti-Social Behaviour: Where We Stand

Children's responsibility for their behaviour extends beyond that which amounts to a criminal offence: from the age of ten years old they may also be held accountable for anti-social behaviour.[10] There is no doubt that anti-social behaviour can wreck individuals' enjoyment of their lives and blight communities. Successive governments

7 The distinction between 'being' responsible and measures taken to 'make' children responsible is discussed in Keating, 2008.

8 Ford having accepted the findings of an independently commissioned report (DoJNI, 2011:107).

9 This Bill, which has been debated in both Houses of Parliament, has received a good deal of parliamentary time. However, concern has been expressed, given the size of the Bill and the range of subjects it encompasses, that it is being pushed through with insufficient time to debate it properly (see, for example, the speech of Lord Beecham, *Hansard*, HL Deb vol. 748, col. 1499, 29 October 2013).

10 There are also civil measures in relation to children under ten to deal with their anti-social behaviour or behaviour which would be criminal in a child aged ten or above: for example, child safety orders under the Crime and Disorder Act 1998, s. 11.

have been right to try to protect both individuals and communities from such damaging behaviour. There is, of course, a 'but': the measures taken must be proportionate and not lead either to abuse or exacerbation of the problem.

One key initiative has been the introduction of the anti-social behaviour order (the ASBO). This was introduced by the Crime and Disorder Act 1998 and was designed as a solution to a specific problem: to address the difficulties individuals faced in obtaining injunctions to stop anti-social behaviour. Instead of individuals trying to secure redress, the state would do so on their behalf. ASBOs are civil orders, breach of which is a criminal offence. They have been controversial from the outset. The threshold, against behaviour likely to cause harassment, alarm or distress (s. 1), has been regarded as low. The standard of proof was initially just one of the balance of probabilities.[11] They have been used disproportionately against children (as young as ten) and used inappropriately against children with underlying behavioural issues. The breach rate is very high, especially for children. Between 1999 and 2012, 23,078 ASBOs were issued: 37 per cent were against children, who accounted for over 40 per cent of all breaches (Ministry of Justice, 2013). Such children may then receive a custodial sentence for behaviour which was not criminal.

The Direction in Which We are Moving

One might have hoped, therefore, that the recent review (Home Office, 2012) leading to the Anti-social Behaviour, Crime and Policing Act would have addressed these difficulties. Instead, the review seems to have been motivated by a desire to streamline what is now a proliferation of measures along similar lines to ASBOs, together with a desire to make new provisions easier to obtain with tougher sanctions for breach (Liberty, 2013: para. 3). The proposal is for ASBOs to be replaced by IPNAs: injunctions to 'prevent nuisance and annoyance', which could be granted by a court 'whenever it is just and convenient to do so' (clause 1(2)). These injunctions would be civil orders, but unlike ASBOS, breach would not automatically be a criminal offence – instead the civil sanction of contempt of court would be used and the civil standard of proof would apply (following criticism, this has been made explicit in the latest version of the Bill: clause 1(2)). They would be available to deal with anti-social behaviour by those aged ten and above although a custodial sanction would not be available until the recipient of the injunction was 14 years old (considered further below)..

In its scrutiny of the Bill, the Human Rights Joint Committee accepted that 'preventative measures against anti-social behaviour are in principle a welcome fulfilment of the positive obligation on the state to protect people against having their rights interfered with by others' (2013: para. 11). However, it was highly critical of the substance of the proposals; some of these criticisms apply generally whilst others relate to the impact the provisions could have upon children. In terms of the former, concern focuses upon the low threshold against which the IPNA may be granted, the

---

11 In *R (on behalf of McCann)* v *Crown Court at Manchester* [2002] the House of Lords concluded that the criminal standard of beyond reasonable doubt had to apply to ASBOs.

width of the proposed provision and its subjectivity. The Joint Committee was of the view that the phrase 'conduct capable of causing nuisance and annoyance to any person' is not sufficiently precise to satisfy the requirement of legal certainty' (para. 26). Indeed, adding annoyance to nuisance adds little, if anything. Also troubling is the absence of a requirement that the behaviour is intended to annoy or be a nuisance. The potential width of this provision was illustrated by Lord Hope of Craighead in debate in the House of Lords when he gave the example of an ice-cream van plying its trade by playing chimes which disturbs the sleep of night shift workers. Such conduct was a nuisance to them (*Hansard*, HL Deb, vol. 748, col. 1518, 29 October 2013):[12] would it now be the basis for an IPNA? Indeed, how many of us can say that we have not conducted ourselves in a way that could cause someone (whose reaction may or may not be reasonable – this is not material under the proposed provision) nuisance and annoyance?[13]

A further general concern is that the injunction may be granted whenever it is 'just and convenient to do so'. This was criticised both by the Joint Committee and in debate. The Joint Committee took the view that this test 'is not compatible with the ECHR, because it is a considerably lower test than the requisite test of "necessary and proportionate"' (para. 37). Moreover, under clause 1(4)(b), the IPNA may, unlike the ASBO, contain positive requirements. The inclusion of positive requirements has the potential to be helpful (just as a referral order may act as a gateway to much needed assistance for a child) but not only may it not be experienced as such by the recipient but also there are few statutory limits to the requirements which may be made. Justice has called for there to be more limitations on the types of requirements which may be made so that the injunction remains proportionate and so as 'to avoid setting people up to fail' (2013: para. 19, 22).

Beyond these far-reaching general criticisms are those which pertain more specifically to children, not least of which is clause 17 which stipulates that the reporting restrictions which ordinarily apply in proceedings involving children (Children and Young Persons Act 1933, s. 49) would not apply to this legislation and that the court could consider naming any child in relation to whom an IPNA is granted. As has been commented, 'the naming and shaming of children is almost always counterproductive. It can seriously hinder a child's rehabilitation. In some cases people react by regarding this notoriety as a badge of honour. Then they try to live up to their reputation by increasingly extreme behaviour' (*Hansard*, HL Deb, vol. 748, col. 1512, 29 October 2013, per Lord Dholakia). Children would not get a criminal record but 'that protec-

---

12 *Raymond* v *Cook* (1958) 3 All ER 407.

13 The draft guidance for front-line professionals given to peers states that applications for IPNAs 'should *not* be used to stop reasonable, trivial or benign behaviours that have not caused, and are not likely to cause, harm to victims or communities'. But as Lord Rosser pointed out in debate, 'if one of the tests ... is that behaviours must have caused or be likely to cause harm ... then why does the Bill not refer to causing harm and clearly define it?'(*Hansard*, HL Deb, vol. 748, col. 1567, 29 October 2013).

tion is undermined by the fact that the courts may allow them to be named' (*Hansard*, HL Deb, vol. 748, col. 1560, 29 October 2013, per Lord Marks of Henley-on-Thames).[14]

Further concerns arise from the provisions relating to breach and sanctions for breach. The Impact Assessment for the Bill assumes a high breach rate of 40 per cent for IPNAs (*Hansard,* HL Deb, vol. 748, col. 1492, 29 October 2013, per Baroness Hamwee). Given what has been said about children's reduced capacity to exercise control over their behaviour, the fact that they disproportionately breach ASBOs and that positive as well as negative requirements may be included, it seems reasonable to conclude that children would also figure disproportionately in the breach figures for IPNAs – one does indeed have to wonder if they are being set up to fail.

If the IPNA is breached, the adult sanction of contempt of court would be replaced by measures such as curfews and supervision orders. If the child is 14 years old or above and the court considers that a supervision order is an insufficient sanction given the extent and severity of the behaviour, it would be possible to impose a detention centre order. It would need to be proved to the criminal standard of proof and custody could be for a maximum of three months (Clause 11: Schedule 2, clauses 1(5), (6), 14(2)). However, the Joint Committee has opposed this provision: the risk remains that a child could be imprisoned for conduct which was not criminal (2013, para. 15).[15]

In sum, as the Chief Executive of the Children's Society has commented, IPNAs 'radically widen the scope of the types of behaviour subject to anti-social behaviour measures … [They] will cover a huge range of normal childhood behaviour and could result in many more children being unnecessarily drawn into the criminal justice system' (Reed, 2013). Thus, the Joint Committee of Human Rights, Liberty, Justice, ACPO,[16] the Children's Society and the Children's Commissioner (OCCE, 2013) have been among the many organisations and individuals criticising the proposals. Yet the government believes it has got an appropriate balance in the Bill between the rights of the individual who may be issued with an injunction and the rights of the wider community (*Hansard*, HL Deb, vol. 748, col. 1484, 29 October 2013, per Lord Taylor of Holbeach).

---

14 Both Justice (2013, paras. 26-27) and the HRJC (2013, para. 15) have also condemned this clause.

15 Liberty was even more forthright in its criticism: 'These are punitive powers designed to impose coercive sanctions on a child who has not been found guilty of any offence. Child protection laws exist to protect children from harm, and criminal laws exist to prosecute law-breakers. There is no need for additional bespoke powers such as these' (2013, para. 29).

16 In evidence to MPs, ACPO warned that the new type of injunction against children has 'the potential to be used inappropriately' (Anti-Social Behaviour, Crime and Policing Bill: Written Evidence – Consolidated Version 2013: para. 10).

How Do Rights Fit In?

International Standards

The orthodox liberal philosophical concept of responsibility would appear to be open to being influenced by modern understandings of child development or at least to be compatible with it. And this is certainly also the case in so far as international human rights conventions are concerned. The United Nations Convention on the Rights of the Child (UNCRC) and the Beijing Rules do not set a minimum age of criminal responsibility because it is recognised that jurisdictions have systems of youth justice and social care which interact in different ways. However, there is consensus that the age of criminal responsibility should not be fixed at too low an age level (Art. 4(1) of the United Nations Standard Minimum Rules for the Administration of Justice: the Beijing Rules). Further, the official commentary to the Beijing Rules states: 'in general there is a close relationship between the notion of responsibility for delinquent and criminal behaviour and other social rights and responsibilities' (such as, for example, marital status or civil majority).

The UNCRC also exhorts governments to 'seek to promote the establishment of laws, procedures, authorities and institutions ... [to respond to children's harmful behaviour] without resorting to judicial proceedings' (Article 40(3)) and stipulates that in all actions concerning children, the best interests of the child 'shall be a primary consideration' (Article 4(1)). Unsurprisingly, therefore, England and Wales has been repeatedly criticised by the UNCR Committee in its reports (1995, 2002) for the low age at which it holds children criminally responsible and also in relation to the use of ASBOs against young children. In 2008 the Committee recommended that 'the State Party fully implement international standards of juvenile justice ... [and] raise the age of criminal responsibility' (2008: para. 78). It has stated that 'the age of 12 years [should be set as] the absolute minimum' (2007: para. 16) and urges governments to work towards increasing it further, suggesting an age range of 14-16 as appropriate (para. 30).

Insofar as ASBOs and IPNAs are concerned, the Joint Committee of Human Rights suggested (in addition to the concerns identified above) that the use of custody as a sanction for breach of an IPNA may not be compatible with Article 37 of the UNCRC which stipulates that custody should be reserved for the most serious crimes only. It also noted that the UNCR Committee had found that the imposition of ASBOs did not appear to be in the best interests of a child and that 'naming and shaming' was in direct conflict with a child's right to privacy (2013: paras. 16-19). The Joint Committee recommended that in order to comply with Art. 3, the Bill should be amended 'to include an express requirement that the courts must take into account the best interests of the child as a primary consideration when deciding whether to impose the following: any injunction; the terms of any prohibition or requirement; sanctions for breach; and when determining reporting of a child's case' (2013: para. 20). Regrettably, the government declined to take up this recommendation and has failed to conduct an analysis of the Bill against the UNCRC.

Despite the government's views, it is clear that at the international level, an increase in the age of criminal responsibility to at least 12 years old would be warmly supported. The remaining question is whether such a move would be consistent with a broader discourse of children's rights.

Children's Rights

What are the implications of the discussion so far if children are seen as rights holders? The key question here is whether recognising children's agency means that arguments that the age of criminal responsibility should be increased are misplaced and that concerns about the imposition of ASBOs and IPNAs need to be refocused?

It has been argued that the changes made by the Crime and Disorder Act 1998, including the abolition of the presumption of *doli incapax* and the introduction of anti-social behaviour orders, 'might represent a real shift in the way youth are regulated and governed. There may be a move away from a more paternalistic model of regulation that stresses the essential passivity of youth towards the cultivation of a more active subjectivity within young people who will be required to *take more* responsibility for their lives' (Vaughan, 2000: 348). In broadly similar vein, Hollingsworth has claimed that the 'conferral' of criminal responsibility is symbolically important because not to do so strikes at the identity of the actor: its conferral, even where a child 'lacks actual capacity, can be seen as giving effect to the child's autonomy rights' (2007: 196).[17] Finally, Cipriani has argued:

> Children's criminal responsibility is indeed an integral and necessary part of children's rights – a logical extension of the concept of children's evolving capacities insofar as it is an appropriate step in respecting children's progression from lesser to greater competence, which gradually prepares them for adult rights and responsibilities (2009: 34).

One might well respond that there are other, less potentially damaging, ways in which a child can be helped to prepare for adult life. But clearly, the 'conferral' of criminal responsibility *is* fundamentally symbolically important. Leaving aside that it currently has profound practical importance for children drawn within the criminal justice system, what does it symbolise within the context of rights? To answer this one should go back to Michael Freeman's seminal article, "Taking Children's Rights more Seriously":

> To respect a child's autonomy is to treat that child as a person and as a rights-holder ... But it is also clear that the exercising of a child's autonomy can have a deleterious impact on that child's life chances ... Without welfare rights being recognised, they will not be in a position to exercise autonomy ... [We need] to recognise that children, particularly

---

17 Although Hollingsworth does not defend the current age of criminal responsibility (2007).

> younger children, need nurture, care and protection. Children must not, as Hafen (1997) put it, be abandoned to their rights (1992: 65-66).

A law which holds children responsible at ten so that they can be tried in a court (or made subject to an IPNA) does just this. What is needed is a law which respects children's welfare rights as articulated by Michael, so that young children are protected until such time that the developmental evidence supports the ascription of responsibility. If this was in line with other jurisdictions and other stages at which the law confers rights and responsibilities, then so much the better.

The Direction in Which We Should Move

In 2010 an Independent Commission on Youth Crime and Anti-social Behaviour was not opposed to any increase in the minimum age of criminal responsibility but did not press for it. Instead, it concluded that a system based on prevention, restoration and integration would provide a more effective and humane response to children's harmful behaviour. However, whilst an 'effective and humane' approach might lead to improvements (such as increased emphasis upon diversion and restorative justice) in the youth justice system, it does not tackle the fundamental injustice of the current law.

The age of ten was set in 1963 without any clear or evidenced rationale (Farmer, 2011: 92). The Law Commission has similarly concluded that today it is 'not founded on any logical or principled basis' (LCCP, no. 197: para. 8.59; see also, Centre for Social Justice, 2012: 201).. Yet children are still being prosecuted for offences committed when they are of primary school age. The number of such children is not large: for example, in 2012, 262 children aged 10 and 11 were proceeded against at court (*Hansard*: HL Deb, vol. 749, col. 488, 8 November 2013),[18] but rather than concluding that it is thus a trivial issue, we should conclude that, despite rhetoric to the contrary (as was suggested with the potential reforms in Northern Ireland: Driver (2011)), 'anarchy' is unlikely to result from a change in the law. In fact, there is evidence that countries with higher minimum ages of criminal responsibility do not have higher rates of offending (MoJNI, 2011: 104).Taken together with the view of the UNCRC that 'a minimum age of criminal responsibility below the age of 12 years is considered by the Committee not to be internationally acceptable' (2007: para. 32), this constitutes a powerful case for raising the age of criminal responsibility. Thus, Lord Dholakia's Bill, which attempts to make England and Wales compliant with its minimum international obligations, should be warmly welcomed.

However, Lord Dholakia has stated in debate that when his Bill goes through Committee he would be prepared to consider a similar caveat to that which accom-

18 By way of contrast, 859 children aged 12 or over were proceeded against at court. However, these figures exclude children, for example, who receive a youth caution. In 2009/10, for example, while 396 10-11 year olds were convicted and sentenced in a court, a further 2,490 were subject to out of court disposals (Ministry of Justice, 2011: 21).

panied Ireland's reform.[19] In 2006 when Ireland increased the age of criminal responsibility from 10 to 12 it did so with a notable qualification: the age of criminal responsibility for murder, manslaughter, rape or aggravated sexual assault remained at ten (Criminal Justice Act 2001, s. 52(2) as amended).[20] The Centre for Social Justice has made a similar proposal: it recommended that in the short-term the age of criminal responsibility should be raised to 12 for all but the most serious offences (murder, attempted murder, rape, manslaughter and aggravated sexual assault) with a blanket increase to 12 as soon as it is feasible to do so (2012, 211).

There is no principled basis for such a qualification. Indeed, the Centre for Social Justice recognised the contradictions inherent in its proposal: that those children possibly most in need of help would be subject to the rigour of a criminal prosecution (*ibid*: 211). If this is the price which has to be paid to ensure that politicians, concerned with how the public or media will react, will support the reform, it is a very substantial concession. England and Wales would still not be fully compliant with even the absolute minimum advised by the UNCRC and, unless the law changes, we would still witness the invidious spectacle of 10 and 11 year-olds being tried in the Crown Court.[21]

Instead, the minimum age of criminal responsibility should be raised to 12 on the basis that children under this age should no longer be deemed responsible in law. Being preoccupied by this issue is not a 'red herring' as suggested by the Centre for Social Justice (2012: 210) but a fundamental principle of English criminal law. Then we should consider further increases based upon not only questions of capacity and control but also upon broader questions of policy. A civilised system of youth justice might conclude that a child of say 14 might have responsibility in the sense considered here and it still not be appropriate to invoke the criminal law in response to harmful behaviour, following the example of other jurisdictions which set a higher minimum age of criminal responsibility. However, the Centre of Social Justice is right to conclude that raising the age of criminal responsibility is not the only reform needed to improve the youth justice system (*ibid*): one such priority is to oppose the introduction of IPNAs as currently drafted.

Conclusion

Discussions concerning children's harmful behaviour can be emotive and often reveal highly polarised views (MoJNI, 2011: 106): this is true of both the age at which children should be criminally responsible and determining appropriate responses to

---

19 No date has yet been set for the Committee stage of this Bill.

20 It also abolished the presumption of *doli incapax*: Criminal Justice Act 2001, s. 52(3) as amended.

21 It is possible that some of these children would be saved from prosecution by the proposed changes to the test for fitness to plead (Law Com, 2010) but as has been commented, 'such an evasion of blameworthiness does not accurately reflect the position of this type of defendant' (Howard and Bowen, 2011: 389): the issue is more than one of competency to stand trial, important although this is, it is one of capacity to be subject to the criminal law.

anti-social behaviour. Government after government has increased the accountability of children for their harmful behaviour and, unless the opposition currently being expressed in the House of Lords is successful, this pattern will continue, with 'breathtakingly wide' provisions in relation to anti-social behaviour, (Liberty, 2013: para. 17) which have the potential to encroach upon normal childhood behaviour.

In relation to the age of criminal responsibility, the abolition of the presumption of *doli incapax* and the repeated assertion that children are 'responsible enough' at ten to stand trial in a criminal court can only be described as wilful political blindness in the face of an overwhelming argument for reform to the law, a law which has rightly been condemned as 'unsafe, unsatisfactory and harmful to wider society' (Centre for Social Justice, 2012: 210). It is indefensible that, reiterating Lord Dholakia's words, a child is criminally responsible at ten but is not deemed mature enough to buy a pet until he or she is aged 16.[22]

Instead of a political 'arms race' in being tough, what is needed is an approach to children's harmful behaviour, encompassing both criminal and anti-social behaviour, which is based upon principle and evidence. Considering what it means to be responsible and having regard to both welfare and autonomy rights provides us with a more principled yardstick upon which to make decisions which are both symbolically and practically so significant for children.

Postscript

Since writing this chapter, significant developments have occurred. The government's proposals in clause 1 of the Anti-social Behaviour, Crime and Policing Bill have been rejected by the House of Lords (*Hansard*, HL Deb, vol. 750, col. 1543, 8 January 2014) by 306 votes to 178. Despite arguing that the fears (highlighted in this chapter) which led to its defeat are unfounded, the government, in order to make progress with the Bill, accepted an amendment put forward by Lord Dear. In what is a very substantial concession, the injunction may only be imposed if alarm, harassment or distress is caused or is likely to be caused rather than the lower standard of nuisance or annoyance. There is an exception: where the individual's conduct relates to another person's occupation of residential premises, the nuisance or annoyance threshold is retained (*Hansard*, vol. 751, col. 981, 27 January 2014). After this, the Bill proceeded through its final stages and received Royal Assent on 13 March 2014. Sadly, as was anticipated, no further time was given to consideration of the Age of Criminal Responsibility Bill before the end of the parliamentary session and, thus, this opportunity for reform has been lost.

22 Indeed, the Animal Welfare Act 2006 raised the age from 12 to 16.

References

All Party Parliamentary Group for Children, *Response from the officers of the All Party Group for Children to the Law Commission's consultation on Unfitness to Plead* in *Unfitness to Plead: Consultation Responses* (London: Law Commission, 2013).

Anti-Social behaviour, Crime and Policing Bill: Written Evidence – Consolidated Version (London: TSO, 2013).

Bandalli, S., "Abolition of the presumption of *doli incapax* and the criminalisation of young children", *Howard Journal* 1998 37(2), 114-123.

Bateman, T., *Children in Conflict with the Law: An Overview of Trends and Developments* (National Association of Youth Justice Briefing) (NAYJ, 2013).

Centre for Social Justice, *Rules of Engagement: Changing the Heart of Youth Justice* (London: Centre for Social Justice, 2012).

Cipriani, D., *Children's Rights and the Minimum Age of Criminal Responsibility: A Global Perspective* (Farnham: Ashgate, 2009).

Department of Justice Northern Ireland, *A Review of the System of Youth Justice in Northern Ireland* (Belfast: DoJNI, 2011).

Driver, M., "Northern Ireland: Increasing criminal responsibility age to 12 will cause 'anarchy'", *The Solicitor,* 27 September 2011.

Goldson, B., "Children in Trouble: state responses to juvenile crime", in P. Scraton (ed), *Childhood in Crisis?* (London: UCL Press, 1997).

Goldson, B., "Counterblast: Difficult to Understand or Defend: A reasoned case for raising the age of criminal responsibility", *Howard Journal* 2009 48(5), 514-521.

Farmer, E., "The Age of Criminal Responsibility: developmental science and human rights perspectives", *Journal of Children's Services* 2011 6(2), 86-95.

Freeman, M., "The Rights of Children When they do Wrong", *British Journal of Criminology* 1981 21(3), 210-229.

Freeman, M., "Taking Children's Rights More Seriously", *International Journal of Law and the Family* 1992 6(1), 52-71.

Freeman, M., "Why it Remains Important to Take Children's Rights Seriously", *International Journal of Children's Rights* 2007 15(1), 5-23.

Hansard, HL Deb, vol. 748, 29 October 2013.

Hansard , HL Deb, vol. 749, 8 November 2013.

Hart, H. L. A., "Varieties of Responsibility", *Law Quarterly Review* 1967 83(3) 346-364.

Hollingsworth, K. "Responsibility and Rights: Children and their Parents in the Youth Justice System", *International Journal of Law, Policy and the Family* 2007 21(2), 190-219.

Holmes, O. W., *The Autocrat of the Breakfast Table* (Boston: Phillips, Sampson Co., 1858).

Home Office, *No More Excuses: A New Approach to Tackling Youth Crime in England and Wales,* Cm 3909 (London: Home Office, 1997).

Home Office, *Putting Victims First: More Effective Responses to Anti-Social Behaviour,* Cm. 8367 (London: Home Office, 2012).

House of Commons, *Standing Committee B on the Crime and Disorder Bill* (9th sitting) clause 31 (12 May 1994).

Human Rights Joint Committee, Legislative Scrutiny: Anti-Social Behaviour, Crime and Policing Bill (2013), www.publications.parliament.uk/pa/jt201314/jtselect/jrights/56/5606.htm (accessed 31/10/2013).

Independent Commission, *Time for a Fresh Start* (London: The Police Foundation/Nuffield Foundation, 2010).

Justice, *Anti-Social Behaviour, Crime and Policing Bill (House of Lords Second Reading)* (2013).

Keating, H., "The 'responsibility' of children in the criminal law", *Child and Family Law Quarterly* 2007 19(2), 183-203.

Keating, H., "Being Responsible, Becoming Responsible and Having Responsibility Thrust upon them" in J. Bridgeman, H. Keating and C. Lind (eds), *Responsibility, Law and the Family* (Farnham: Ashgate, 2008).

Law Commission, *Unfitness to Plead*, LCCP No. 197 (London: Law Commisson, 2010).

Liberty, Briefing on the Draft Anti-Social Behaviour Bill (London: Liberty, 2013).

Mason, R., "Children face court action for being "annoying" under new Asbo scheme", *The Telegraph,* 29 January 2013.

Ministry of Justice, *Youth Justice Statistics 2009/10 England and Wales: Youth Justice Youth Justice Board/Ministry of Justice Statistics Bulletin* (London: Ministry of Justice, 2011).

Ministry of Justice, *Anti-Social behaviour order Statistics: England and Wales 2012*
https://www.gov.uk/government/publications/anti-social-behaviour-order-statistics-england-and-wales-2012 (2013) (accessed 22 February 2014).

Office of Children's Commissioner of England, *A Child Rights Impact Assessment of the Anti-Social Behaviour, Crime and Policing Bill* (London: OCCE, 2013).

Reed, M. (Chief Executive of the Children's Society), "The New Anti-Social Behaviour Bill Risks Criminalising Children for Being Children", 19 June 2013 (http://www.huffingtonpost.co.uk/matthew-reed/anti-social-behaviour-bill_b_3415823.html) (accessed 20 June 2013).

Royal College of Psychiatrists, *Child Defendants,* Occasional Paper No 56 (2006).

Royal Society, *Neuroscience and the Law* RS Policy Document 05/11(London: The Royal Society, 2011).

UNCRC, *Eighth Session: Consideration of Reports submitted by State Parties-Concluding Observations: United Kingdom of Great Britain and Northern Ireland* (United Nations, 1995).

UNCRC, *Thirty-First Session: Consideration of Reports submitted by State Parties-Concluding Observations: United Kingdom of Great Britain and Northern Ireland* (United Nations, 2002).

UNCRC, *General Comment No 10: Children's Rights in Juvenile Justice* (United Nations, 2007).

UNCRC, *Forty-ninth Session: Consideration of Reports submitted by States Parties Under Article 44 of the convention – concluding Observations: United Kingdom of Great Britain and Northern Ireland* (United Nations, 2008).

Vaughan, B. "The Government of Youth: Disorder and Dependence", *Social and Legal Studies* 2000 9(3) 347-366.

Michael Freeman and Domestic Violence

Helen Reece
London School of Economics and Political Science

Introduction

The fields of scholarship in which Michael Freeman has pioneered are legion, as is admirably demonstrated by the breadth and depth of the chapters in this volume. One such field is domestic violence. In what follows, I aim to discuss Michael's contribution to our understanding of domestic violence. This is in one sense a hard task, not only because of the richness and subtlety of Michael's writing on this subject, but also because of how prolific he has been here as elsewhere (see e.g., Freeman, 1979a; Freeman, 1979b; Freeman, 1980; Freeman, 1981; Freeman, 1984a; Freeman, 1985a; Freeman, 1985b; Freeman, 1987; Freeman, 1989; Freeman, 2007: ch. 3; Freeman, 2008a). It is in another sense an easy task though, because Michael's writing is clear. He has important messages to communicate, and he communicates their importance. Specifically, in the preface to his monograph entitled *Violence in the Home* published in 1979 – probably his most important work on domestic violence and one that I will be drawing on throughout – he sets out the importance of his work in three reasons.

> First, it is the only book written on the subject by a lawyer and the first to discuss in depth legal responses to the problem. Secondly, it is the first book to attempt to integrate the problems of wife abuse and child abuse and to apply to each a relatively consistent theoretical framework. Thirdly, the book draws attention also to newer aspects of the problem (newer, that is, in surfacing to public attention): husband battering; 'granny bashing'; and violence between children are thus briefly considered (viii).

Systemic Nature of Domestic Violence

Michael suggests that his monograph is particularly important because he places domestic violence within a consistent theoretical framework, specifically feminism. This, I suggest, gives both the greatest and the most enduring importance to *Violence in the Home*.

A. Diduck, N. Peleg, H. Reece (eds.), Law in Society: Reflections on Children, Family, Culture and Philosophy

ISBN 978-90-04-26148-8. pp. 309-329.

Michael is unremitting in adopting a feminist explanation for this social phenomenon. In the preface to his monograph, Michael suggests as a general theme 'that the problems it discusses cannot be solved or ameliorated until they are properly understood' (viii; see also Freeman, 1980: 5), and this is indeed a general theme running through all Michael's scholarship. So how are we to understand the problem of domestic violence? 'Violence against women', he proclaims on the second page, 'is largely to be explained in terms of the subordinate position they occupy in society' (128). Michael examines the other contemporary explanations for domestic violence (136-141), acknowledging elements of truth within each one: 'Some battering husbands are undoubtedly psychopaths and many do have drink problems. Many also have been battered as children. These factors are important' (137; see also Freeman, 1980: 8). But he sets his face firmly against individualised explanations because 'seeing the problem in terms of the pathology of the men concerned (and sometimes the women as well) ... individualises a problem which is embedded in the social structure' (129): 'it seeks an exceptionalistic explanation of what is a universalistic problem' (Freeman, 1980: 8). Ultimately Michael 'sees violence as a necessary concomitant of women's generally oppressed position in the social structure' (142; see also Freeman, 1980: 14). The true causes of domestic violence, according to Michael, are 'deeply embedded in the consciousness, institutions and practices of a society committed to women's subordination' (1989: 18).

Michael did not invent this explanation, as he is at pains to remind us. For this, as for bringing the plight of battered women to public attention, credit is due to the then vibrant Women's Liberation Movement (1979b: 142). But what Michael does deserve credit for – no mean feat – is to have brought the Women's Liberation Movement explanation into the legal academy. At the time Michael was writing his monograph, as he tells us, the dominant explanation of domestic violence was well represented in the writings of Erin Pizzey (29), who favoured a pathological, exceptionalistic, explanation of wife battering (136-137; see also Freeman, 1980: 6).

It is hard to appreciate just how unpalatable an explanation based on women's subordination was to the 1970s legal academy. In the decades since, the feminist explanation for violence against women has become ubiquitous (Reece, 2011). I have evidenced elsewhere that this ubiquity occurred earlier than is commonly imagined, among constituencies that are generally assumed to have been unaffected by feminist discourse, specifically Conservative Parliamentarians deliberating over the 1997 Protection from Harassment Act (*ibid*). But this feminist infusion of legal discourse certainly does not stretch back as far as the 1970s; Michael writes in 1980 that 'the traditional personality-psychiatric approach ... has proved immensely influential and social and legal policies remain firmly under its spell' (6):

> As the development of the Women's Movement has been a primary factor in sensitising our consciences to the plight of the battered woman, it is hardly surprising that theories as to the aetiology of male violence towards women should have developed within the ideology of its liberation politics. Nor is it surprising that the views of militant feminists should have created so little interest amongst government department, the media or the

general public. To them Erin Pizzey and Chiswick epitomise the problem and her definitions and solutions have become public property. The National Women's Aid Federation with a definition of the problem which indicts society is accorded little or no attention; its views, its solutions are too unpalatable for society to stomach (Freeman, 1979b: 141-142).

Violence against Women

Arguably the most basic tenet of a feminist approach to domestic violence is that domestic violence is a highly gendered phenomenon, with men the main perpetrators and women the main victims (Radford *et al*, 1996; Melton and Belknap, 2003; Hunter, 2006; Kaganas, 2006). While Michael alerts us to the fact that *Violence in the Home* is unusual in drawing attention to then outlying manifestations of domestic violence with, *inter alia,* a chapter on 'battered husbands' (ch. 9), it is important to appreciate that his monograph leans acutely towards the problem of what he then described as battered wives. This is plain even from a word count: in a book consisting of ten chapters and 242 substantive pages, he includes one seven-page chapter on battered husbands. It is also clear from the way that he delineates domestic violence, with his first sentence on domestic violence: 'The second part of this book is about the problem of *women*' (127, emphasis added). In case we are still in doubt, he tells us explicitly that 'the real problem is the violence perpetrated against *women*' (127, emphasis added). Moreover, he is alive to the dangers of the research that he includes on battered husbands: he hopes that these findings 'will not divert attention from the problem of wife battering' (133). This is a stance that he maintained and indeed strengthened: in *Dealing with Domestic Violence* nearly a decade later, he writes more forcefully: 'There is violence against men as well, but as a problem it is insignificant and has been blown up to trivialise the real problem, which is violence against women' (1987: 104). He remains steadfast in his most recent book on domestic violence, namely his selection of some of the most influential writings on the subject entitled *Domestic Violence* and published in 2008, in the introduction to which he clarifies that domestic violence against men 'cannot be considered to be the major social problem' (xiv). According to Michael, 'it must be stressed that the social problem is domestic violence against women' (2008a: xvii).

For it to be legitimate to treat this social problem as gendered, its gendered nature must be an empirical reality. Most research does indeed support the view that women are the main victims and men the main perpetrators of domestic violence: notably, the 2001 British Crime Survey self-completion module on domestic violence found that one in five women and one in ten men had been victims of domestic violence since the age of 16 (Walby and Allen, 2004: i, 12), and four per cent of women compared with two per cent of men had been subject to domestic violence during the previous year (*ibid*: vi).

The 2001 British Crime Survey self-completion module claimed to provide 'the most reliable findings to date' (*ibid*: i) of the extent of domestic violence in England and Wales (ibid: i, 1). The confidential method of interviewing via a computer-assisted self-completion questionnaire facilitated disclosure (*ibid*: i, 1, 124), and the scale of the general British Crime Survey allowed the domestic violence module to draw on a large and nationally representative sample of approximately 20,000 men and women aged 16-59 (*ibid*: v). The module achieved a response rate of two-thirds (*ibid*: 118). Nevertheless, there are still a number of methodological problems associated with both the sampling and the interviewing (*ibid*: Appendix A; see further, Walby and Myhill, 2001; Reece, 2006: 774-775).

In an important and thorough review of these methodological issues with particular application to the 1996 self-completion module – a review which Michael includes in his 2008 anthology on domestic violence – Walby and Myhill conclude that the module is not specialised enough to facilitate maximum disclosure (2001: 519) and is accordingly likely to provide an underestimation of the extent of domestic violence (*ibid*). Whether or not they are right, an inaccurate estimation of the total extent of such violence would not be of direct concern at this point, because it would not affect the findings of gender asymmetry.

However, some other findings suggest that the phenomenon of domestic violence is equally likely to be women's violence against men, early examples of which Michael surveyed in his monograph (132-133). In connection with this apparent gender symmetry, in his chapter on battered husbands, Michael Freeman writes intriguingly: 'even if the incidence of husband battering is higher than that of wife battering, the latter remains the more serious problem' (227). After careful consideration of the evidence for violence against husbands, he sets out multiple reasons for this assertion. First, at least some violence perpetrated by wives might be in response to violence initiated by husbands. Secondly, male violence tends to be more extreme. Thirdly, violence against wives tends to recur more frequently. Fourthly, there are questions about which gender is more prone to under-report violence. Fifthly, pregnancy is a particularly dangerous period for battered wives, so there are implications for unborn children. Sixthly, men are stronger. Finally, wives may find it more difficult to escape (133).

This passage is remarkable in its prescience. Michael predicts the arguments against gender symmetry first explored in detail by the Dobashes in 1992 and latterly in 2004 in an important article which Michael includes in his 2008 anthology. There they suggest that those researchers who have found symmetry in domestic violence have primarily relied on the measurement of discrete acts. The usual scoring method is that it is only necessary for a man or woman to have committed one act to be classified as violent: this means that a woman who has committed one trivial act is equated with a man who has committed several serious acts of a different nature. These researchers most frequently use the Conflict Tactics Scales, which has been widely criticised for not taking into account the highly variable meanings, nature and outcomes of some of the acts on its list. Generally, these researchers' narrow 'act-based' approach to the definition and measurement of violence has led them to ignore the context, consequences, motivations, intentions and reactions that accompany the acts. In contrast, those researchers who have examined acts alongside their consequences, within the wider context of ongoing violent events and intimate relationships, have found that domestic violence is overwhelmingly an issue of male violence against women. Michael did not have the benefit of this work, of course, when writing his monograph. He reaches his conclusions on symmetry solely by drawing on the data and analysis of Straus, Gelles and Steinmetz, the originators of the survey evidence on battered husbands (see Freeman, 1979b: 150-151).

Later evidence confirms Michael's earlier instincts. The 2001 special module on inter-personal violence found more pronounced gender asymmetry when regard was paid to context and consequences: women were more likely to experience multiple attacks, severe injuries and serious disruption to their lives (Walby and Allen, 2004: v). With regard to multiple attacks, only 28 per cent of the women who had been subject to domestic violence in the previous year had experienced one incident, the mean number of incidents experienced being 20. In contrast, for men, the mean number of incidents was seven, with 47 per cent having experienced one incident (*ibid*: vi, 23). Moreover, women constituted the overwhelming majority of the most heavily abused group: among people subject to four or more incidents of domestic violence from the perpetrator of the worst incident, 89 per cent were women (*ibid*: vii, 25, 34). Accordingly, the report estimated that there had been 12.9 million incidents of domestic violence acts against women compared with 2.5 million against men in England and Wales during the previous year (*ibid*: vi, 22-23).

In relation to severity of injuries, during the worst incident of domestic violence experienced in the previous year, six per cent of women compared with one per cent of men sustained severe injuries (*ibid*: viii, also 33). Moreover, ten times as many women as men reported that they had experienced the potentially life-threatening form of violence of choking or attempted strangling (*ibid*: 19). Turning to the effects of the violence, 31 per cent of women compared with nine per cent of men experienced consequential mental or emotional problems (*ibid*: viii, also 33), and 11 per cent of women compared with one per cent of men reported having been frightened by threats since the age of 16 (*ibid*: 19). Michael was clearly correct that empirically measuring domestic violence is more complex than counting blows.

Violence against Wives

Michael delineates domestic violence more finely than just by gender. When he defines what he sees as the social problem in *Violence in the Home*, the sentence ends: 'the real problem is the violence perpetrated against women *in the domestic setting*' (127, emphasis added), and his first sentence on domestic violence in his monograph finishes: 'The second part of this book is about the problem of women physically ill-treated by the men *with whom they live*' (127, emphasis added). A further delineation is provided over the page in his definition, which clarifies that he is using the phrase 'with whom they live' in the common sense of 'living together': despite his inclusion in his monograph of a two=page section on the contemporarily outlying manifestation that he then called 'Granny bashing' (237-239), the main social phenomenon is for him partner violence.

There are a couple of provisos to put in place here. In 1979, Michael uses the contemporary label 'battered wife' in his chapter headings, definition and text. However, in his first paragraph on this subject in his monograph he clarifies: 'Nor is the problem confined to wives; the absence of a wedding ring is no safeguard against brutal assault, and women are battered by men with whom they cohabit' (127). A few lines later, Michael elaborates: 'If anything the plight of cohabitees is worse than wives.' His definition could not be clearer: 'For my purposes a battered wife is a wife *or cohabitee* who has suffered ... at the hands of her partner' (128, emphasis added). This stance will come as no surprise to anyone remotely familiar with Michael's work: not only has Michael always been at the forefront of progressive social trends – witness his espousal of same-sex marriage by 1999 – but when he wrote *Violence in the Home* he was already planning a path-breaking monograph devoted to the subject of cohabitation, *Cohabitation without Marriage*, published just four years later with Christina Lyon. By the time he wrote *Dealing with Domestic Violence* in 1987, he was using the terminology of 'battered women' rather than 'battered wife' (104), and in his 1985 inaugural, he confirms that the former is preferable as 'acknowledgment of the fact that absence of a wedding ring is no protection' (1985b: 169).

Later empirical research confirmed that Michael was right to draw no distinction between wives and cohabitants. It was not until the 1996 British Crime Survey included a self-completion module on inter-personal violence that there existed official United Kingdom evidence of the prevalence of domestic violence in different relationships: the module found that 54 per cent of all lifetime incidents of domestic violence involved a spouse or former spouse compared with 43 per cent that involved a partner or ex-partner, and 43 per cent of incidents in the last year involved a spouse or former spouse compared with 55 per cent that involved a partner or ex-partner (Mirrlees-Black, 1999: 44).

The second proviso is that Michael recognises that violence does not necessarily end with the demise of the cohabiting relationship (1979b: 127), a prescient recognition of the prevalence and significance of post-separation violence demonstrated by the 1996 self-completion module mentioned just above. While an unfortunate routing error in the computer programme meant that the module was unable to distinguish between violence involving spouses as opposed to ex-spouses, in relation to unmarried couples, the report found that for all lifetime incidents of domestic violence, 32 per cent involved a partner and 11 per cent an ex-partner, and for incidents in the last year, 45 per cent involved a partner and 10 per cent involved an ex-partner (Mirrlees-Black, 1999: 44). In 1992, Lord Donaldson recognised the importance of violence during the throes of relationship breakdown, stating: 'Very often the need for a non-molestation injunction buttressed by a power of arrest is greater when the parties have recently split up or the marriage has recently ended than it was during the earlier stages in the relationship' (*Duo v. Osborne* [1992] 1 WLR 611, 622; see also *Pidduck v. Molloy* [1992] 2 FLR 202, 206). In an important article, Humphreys and Thiara counsel that it is not always straightforward even to discern a clear point of separation in a violent relationship (2003: 198). Later evidence again confirms the correctness of Michael's 1970s stance.

The necessary legitimation for Michael's delineation of domestic violence as the protection of women in intimate domestic partnerships is once again empirical. The self-completion module statistics cited above bear out Michael's view that domestic violence occurs disproportionately in the couple relationship. This report included all intimate relationships within its scope (Mirrlees Black, 1999: 1) and, as is clear from the statistics cited above, the report found that 97 per cent of lifetime incidents and 98 per cent of incidents in the last year of domestic violence occurred between couples or former couples (*ibid*: 44).

We have already recognised the methodological criticisms of the self-completion modules on inter-personal violence: an inaccurate estimation of the total extent of such violence would not be of direct concern at this point either. This is because the reason for examining the data at this juncture has been to determine whether or not Michael was right in his suppositions about the distribution of domestic violence in diverse relationships rather than to determine the absolute amount of such violence. While it would be reasonable to assume that most of the methodological problems highlighted above would not affect the accuracy of the proportions of violence found in different relationships, there are a couple of methodological issues that could affect the proportions.

The first is the upper age limit of 59, which means that the module provides no information on the relationships in which violence against the elderly predominates. The second is the over-representation of partners and spouses among the people other than the interviewee who were present in the room and who participated in the interviews. Walby and Myhill hypothesise that while the number of partners actually involved in the interviews in the module was small, violent partners might be over-represented in this number and they further suggest that the presence of a violent partner or spouse in the room where the victim is being interviewed would be expected to reduce the reporting of such violence, particularly with regard to current violence, which is likely to be even more sensitive than lifetime violence (2001: 509). It would follow from their argument that this factor would lead the module to underestimate the proportion of violence between intimates committed by spouses and partners, making the high proportion found even more remarkable.

Current Feminist Framework

The strength of Michael's view that domestic violence is a systemic problem is apparent in his assertion that 'what is surprising is not that women are beaten by men with whom they live, but that more women are not battered' (1979b: 148). He explains and expands in his 1984 chapter:

> Violence by husbands against wives should not be seen as a breakdown in the social order, as orthodox interpretations perceive it, but as an affirmation of a particular sort of social order. Looked at in this way domestic violence is not dysfunctional; quite the reverse, it appears functional (52) … given the position of women in society the behaviour of violent husbands is rational, if extreme (72).

For Michael, violence is rational because it serves a purpose (1979b: 146):

> The purpose of male violence is to control women. It is the result of a macho ideology which supports the male's use of violence to maintain dominance over his mate. Women are battered because they are powerless and dependent (Freeman, 1980: 14; see also Freeman, 1979b: 142).

In these passages, Michael adopts and develops the contemporary Women's Liberation Movement explanation of domestic violence.

It is important to underscore the distinction between this formulation and the current feminist approach to domestic violence. In this formulation, violence is used to control; in the current formulation, violence *is* control. Current domestic violence research is commonly divided into two relatively distinct approaches, namely a family violence (FV) approach and a violence against women (VAW) approach (Dobash and Dobash, 1992; Dobash and Dobash, 2004), the latter being broadly associated with a feminist perspective (Melton and Belknap, 2003). VAW research conceptualises domestic violence as a form of domination and control, with physical violence characterised as merely one tactic embedded among many, all integral to a systematic pattern of power and control (Pence and Paymar, 1993; Johnson, 1995; Hanmer, 1996; Hearn, 1996a; Johnson and Ferraro, 2000; Piispa, 2002). VAW researchers have described this cluster of control tactics variously as a 'constellation of violence' (Dobash *et al*, 2000), a 'constellation of abuse' (Dobash and Dobash, 2004: 328), 'patriarchal terrorism' (Johnson, 1995: 284) and the 'power and control wheel' (Pence and Paymar, 1993: 3).

The 'constellation of violence' (or 'constellation of abuse') includes not only violent acts and injuries but also other forms of controlling and intimidating behaviour as integral and inseparable parts of the constellation (Dobash *et al*, 2000). Concretely, Dobash *et al* (*ibid*: 80) outline a detailed context for researching domestic violence in the form of a Controlling Behaviors Index that lists behaviours ranging from, 'Question her about her activities' to 'Try to provoke an argument' to 'Criticise her family/friends' (see also Brush, 1990; DeKeseredy, 2000; Gordon, 2000). 'Patriarchal terrorism' is similarly described as 'a form of terroristic control of wives by their husbands that involves the systematic use of not only violence, but economic subordination, threats, isolation, and other control tactics' (Johnson, 1995: 284). The power and control wheel, arguably the most influential depiction of the dynamics of domestic violence (Dempsey, 2006), likewise places power and control in the middle, abusive behaviours on the spokes, and physical and sexual violence around the edges (Pence and Paymar, 1993).

In the 1970s analysis, violence serves the purpose of patriarchy; currently, violence is equated with patriarchy (Liddle, 1989). The equation of these concepts helps to explain the significance attached to control tactics in the VAW approach to domestic violence, at the same time as the significance attached to control tactics usefully demonstrates the equation of the concepts. VAW researchers regard the cluster of control tactics as at least as harmful as acts of physical or sexual violence (see Dempsey, 2006;

Hunter, 2006; Stark, 2006). For VAW researchers, it is accordingly important not to become overly focused on physical or sexual acts that are seen as at most only part of an overall pattern of control (Breines and Gordon, 1983; Johnson, 1995). VAW researchers view control tactics as either a defining feature of, or at least a clear species of, domestic violence. According to Das Dasgupta (1999: 199), 'battering may or may not be established by actual acts of physical and/or sexual abuse. Coercing and terrorizing a victim are often accomplished by non-physical manipulations.' With regard to control tactics as the defining feature of domestic violence, 'battering' is defined by Hanmer (1996: 8) as 'behaviours designed to control, dominate and express authority and power' and by Das Dasgupta (1999: 200) similarly as 'acts that intimidate, isolate, and deny victims personal power and establish the abuser's control over them'. Hanmer (*ibid*: 8) stresses that women's particular definition of violence is 'being unable to avoid becoming involved in situations and, once involved, being unable to control the process and outcome', a definition that covers visual, verbal or physical behaviour (see also Piispa, 2002).

Turning to control tactics as a species of domestic violence, an instructive example is Ramazanoglu's account of the violence of academic life. Ramazanoglu explains that while violence is most often envisaged as physical assault, restraint or the use of force, a violent academic situation is 'not so much an experience of fisticuffs and flying chairs as one of ... sarcasm, raised voices, jokes, veiled insults or the patronising put-down ... techniques of subordination ... used by academic men ... for intimidating or silencing others... diminishing other human beings' (1987: 64), demonstrating that 'violence in academic life is part of the general need for men to control women'; violence is 'widely used in academic life for purposes of social control':

> Academics are verbally highly skilled and can use verbiage to confuse and intimidate others; they are also powerful users of the voice to convey sarcasm, to interrupt, to prevent interruption and to override counter-arguments ... These verbal forms of intimidation were not generally recognised as violent until this point was made by feminists.

The VAW approach to domestic violence represents a remarkable downplaying of the physical. This downplaying reaches its zenith when some VAW researchers choose not to count acts of physical or sexual violence as domestic violence unless they are accompanied by the appropriate cluster of control tactics. According to Das Dasgupta (1999: 199), the 'hasty attempt to equate men and women who have used physical force against intimate partners to batterers stems from the misinterpretation of the concept of battering itself.' The non-physical is treated as profoundly more important than the physical because it both sets the context for and determines the meaning of the physical.

This means that potentially empirically verifiable statements are turned into definitions. VAW researchers have made the relatively modest converse claims that control tactics are generally associated with men's physical and sexual violence against women and are not generally associated with women's violence against men (Dobash *et al*, 1992; Das Dasgupta, 1999; Yllö, 1993; Dobash and Dobash, 2004). Both of these assertions are empirically testable and some VAW researchers have indeed treated them as straightforwardly empirical (Dobash *et al*, 2000; Piispa, 2002). However, while the statement that domestic violence is associated with a wide cluster of control tactics is verifiable, the statement that domestic violence is not violence unless it is associated with a wider cluster of control tactics is definitional and therefore unchallengeable by empirical evidence.

Making the presence of control tactics an essential component of domestic violence becomes both more and less significant once we realise that employing control tactics just is what men do to women, and not what women do to men. Looking first at the idea that this is what men do to women, for some VAW researchers it is not a matter of empirically investigating whether or not a man questions his female partner's activities or criticises her friend and family: instead this just is what men do:

> Although there are occasionally some fine lines between ambiguities around different forms of touch – comfort, caress, cuddle, hugging – one usually knows when they are or could be selflessly loving, taking advantage of or exerting power in touch. Such culturally specific 'knowledge' of particular men is likely, however, to neglect the full weight of power relations between men, women and young people, especially in the family. For this reason it is unlikely, and probably impossible, for men to touch in a completely non-dominant, and thus potentially non-abusing, way, unless the whole relationship is without dominance. (Hearn, 1996a: 33; see also Ptacek, 1990: 139.)

It is impossible that 'the whole relationship is without dominance' because the 'social and psychological identity called "man" says and shows power relations. It is "*identical*"' (Hearn, 1996b: 101).

Conversely, because women do not use control tactics against men, when women do commit acts of physical or sexual violence against men, these acts do not count as domestic violence. Women's violence to men cannot be equated to men's violence against women (Brush, 1990: 57; Johnson and Sacco, 1995: 291; Nazroo, 1995: 489; Johnson, 1998: 57; Das Dasgupta, 1999: 212) because women's acts of violence against men just do not have the same meaning as men's acts of violence against women (Brush, 1990: 57; Johnson and Sacco, 1995: 291; Nazroo, 1995: 489; Melton and Belknap, 2003: 334). Das Dasgupta (2002: 1378) explains in more detail that 'although both genders use violence to achieve control, women try to secure short-term command over immediate situations, whereas men tend to establish widespread authority over a much longer period.' Importantly, these gendered meanings are irrespective of intention: 'even when such results are not consciously intended, historical, political and ideological components of society *confer* these consequences on men's and women's abusive behaviors' (*ibid*: 1378, emphasis added). Domestic violence is thus *defined* as what men do to women, not what women do to men (Hearn, 1996a: 29; see also Dempsey, 2006: 325, 328; Dempsey, 2007: 917, 918). This is a shame, not least because, as we have just seen, the feminist conclusion that women are the principal victims of domestic violence does not need ring-fencing: it withstands open empirical probing.

These are not charges that can be levelled at Michael's monograph, nor the contemporaneous Women's Liberation Movement analysis.

Writing in 2008, Michael quotes the 2005 Home Office definition of domestic violence that it is '[a]ny incident of threatening behaviour, violence or abuse (psychological, physical, sexual, financial or emotional) between adults who are or have been intimate partners or family members, regardless of gender or sexuality.' (This definition has recently been widened still further to include also any pattern of incidents of coercive or controlling behaviour between anyone aged 16 or over (Home Office, 2013).) Michael notes: 'The definition has widened considerably in thirty-five years. ... It was common to confine domestic violence to physical attacks: it is now accepted that "abuse" embraces a range of behaviours' (2008a: xiv). The absence of any critical commentary on this expansion can be taken to imply his approval (see also 2007: 60). It would be interesting to know whether Michael accepts current feminist interpretations of violence as expressions of power and control, and where he would place a limit on domestic violence definitions in his current thinking.

Material Dimension

Michael brings to the legal academy the 1970s Women's Liberation Movement explanation for domestic violence; but of course, he makes it his own, and I suggest that he gives particular emphasis to two dimensions of the feminist framework. The first is the material dimension, in which it is possible to find echoes of Michael's sensitivity towards Marxist explanations embodied in his work on Jurisprudence (2008b: ch 13) as well as the many years he spent teaching Law and Marxism as a special option on the Jurisprudence course in the UCL LLB. According to Michael, in explaining domestic violence, the potency of the purse is undeniable (1979b: 144). Michael returns to this theme in his inaugural, emphasising the significance of women's economic dependency in explaining women's subordination and thereby domestic violence against women (1985b: 174).

Empirical evidence bears out Michael's emphasis on economic dependency in explaining domestic violence. In Levinson's cross-cultural study, the strength with which economic inequality predicted wife beating led him to conclude that male control of wealth and property was the basic cause of wife beating. He defined male control of wealth and property as the combination of four factors – control of fruits of labour, inheritance, control of female wealth and ownership of the family dwelling – each of which was itself correlated with wife beating. However, he cautioned that male control of wealth and property as a cause of wife beating was mediated by both the degree of male authority in the household and the severity of divorce restrictions placed on women (1989: 73, 84). Levinson regarded his central conclusion as being that family violence did not occur in societies in which family life was 'characterized by cooperation, commitment, sharing and equality' (*ibid*: 104).

In concurrence with Levinson's conclusion, the 2001 special module on domestic violence found that women were more likely to be victims of domestic violence if they were unemployed (Walby and Allen, 2004: 78). Treating women's unemployment as one of three variables indicating economic dependence on their spouse with the other two being whether the woman had children under the age of five at home and whether her husband earned 75 per cent or more of the couple's income (Kalmuss and Strauss, 1976: 373), Kalmuss and Strauss found that the primary group of wives who endured severe violence were those who were the most economically dependent (*ibid*: 380; see also Levinson, 1989: 57-58). Farmer and Tiefenthaler analysed two sets of data: first, the Domestic Violence Experience in Nebraska, in which a sample of over 150 women generated from police calls were interviewed three times over a one-year period in 1986-87; secondly, the North Carolina Spouse Assault Replication Project, in which 340 women were interviewed between 1987 and 1989. They found that women with higher incomes experienced less domestic violence (1997: 348).

However, when Tauchen *et al* interviewed 125 women in California in 1982 and 1983 who had been physically abused by their male partners and whom they recruited through refuges, victim programmes and personal contacts, they found that for low income families, an increase in the man's income increased the violence but an increase in the woman's income had an insignificant effect, while for high income families in which the man provided most of the family income, any increase in income decreased the violence and for high income families in which the woman provided most of the family income, increases in her income and significant increases in his income increased the violence (1991: 492). Nevertheless, the preponderance of the evidence suggests a link between financial dependence and domestic violence.

With regard to women leaving a violent partner, women have been found to experience both material and ideological constraints (see Reece, 1996: 784-785). But in his monograph Michael pays particularly close attention to the importance of material constraints (158), representing a significant aspect of Michael's arguments against gender symmetry. In so doing, Michael draws on the explanation that Gelles provides in his important 1976 article, "Abused Wives: Why Do They Stay?". While Gelles recognises an ideological dimension, he evidences in particular the material dimension: when he interviewed members of 80 families in New Hampshire, 40 of which were selected from social services and police records and the other 40 of which were neighbouring families, he found that the variable that best distinguished abused wives who obtained assistance from those who remained with their husband was whether the wives were working. In his sample, 25 per cent of those wives who did not seek help were employed, compared with 50 per cent of the wives who called the police, went to a social service agency or were separated or divorced from their husbands (1976: 664). Gelles' explanation generally meets with Michael's approval, particularly in its material aspects; nevertheless Michael criticises Gelles for omitting to emphasise the importance of young children (see also Dobash and Dobash, 1980: 146, 156; Homer *et al*, 1985a: 90; Pahl, 1985: 37). Can we possibly hear echoes of Michael's experiences as a hands-on father with his own children, young at that time, in a passage that is sensitive to the burdens of childrearing (1979b: 159)?

Here too, evidence demonstrates that Michael is right that 'marital dependency traps women in abusive marriages' (Kalmuss and Straus, 1990: 370). It is true that when Okun studied data from a domestic violence project pertaining to 300 battered wives who had stayed in the refuge and 119 violent husbands who had received counseling between 1978 and 1981, he found that whether the women worked full-time, part-time or not at all and whether they were receiving welfare benefits or not made no statistically significant difference to whether they left their violent partner, either immediately or eventually (1986: 193; but cf. Kalmuss and Straus, 1990: 370). However, he also found that the greater the woman's economic resources were, relative to her partner's income, the more likely she was to end the relationship, so that battered women who were unambiguously the main breadwinners were twice as likely as the rest of the refuge sample to end the relationship immediately following violence (1986: 225, 231). The Dobashes found that the first financial hurdle for some women was finding the bus fare to leave the house (1980: 157; see also Martin, 1976: 84; Pagelow, 1981: 139).

Emphasising the material dimension in explaining domestic violence implies that there is more than pure empirical justification for honing in on violence against women in intimate domestic partner relationships. Once domestic violence is accepted as 'a necessary concomitant of women's generally oppressed position in the social structure' (Freeman, 1979b: 142), it is likely to be not only most frequent but also most significant at the focal point of women's subordination, namely women's role as homemaker and childcarer in the domestic sphere. The justification for focusing in on 'violence against wives' concerns the special unequal features of intimate domestic partnerships: isolation; unequal power; and, as particularly emphasised by Michael in his monograph, barriers to leaving the relationship including financial dependence. The significance of the social phenomenon rests partly in the context in which domestic violence occurs, that is, women's subordination (see further, Reece, 2006; Reece, 2009).

Legal Dimension

The dimension of the feminist framework on which Michael places the most emphasis is the law. Although visible in his monograph, Michael takes this point much further a few years later, making it the main theme of *Legal Ideologies, Patriarchal Precedents, and Domestic Violence* (1984a), as well as an important theme in his inaugural lecture (1985b). Michael begins the former with the puzzle that legal remedies had by then been developed, but there was still little indication that they were working. Michael poses the question whether this failure reflects 'the limits of effective legal action' or legal ambivalence towards this form of social deviance. He writes simply: 'Can the law provide solutions to the problems of violence against women when it constitutes part of that problem?' (51).

In suggesting that law is part of the problem, Michael first had to tackle what he describes as a 'pathological view of the law' (1985b: 158) as playing a very minor role in regulating family relationships, entering the picture only when things go wrong. Writing contemporaneously with Olsen (1985) and Smart (1984), and pulling in the same direction as they do, Michael suggests that this common view turns reality on its head: 'It is clear that not only does the law serve to reproduce social order, but it actually constitutes and defines that order' (1984a: 55; see further, 1985b: 158). But this is not straightforward because the relationship between law and society is symbiotic, with law diffracting as well as defining the social order: writing in 1989 about police failure to take domestic violence seriously, Michael cautions that the police 'only reflect in exaggerated form prevailing social attitudes' (20).

Secondly and relatedly, Michael has to challenge the idea of law as neutral or value-free. This is the major theme of his inaugural, in which he asserts clearly and forcefully that 'law needs to be socially located and that family law cannot be understood if it is assumed to operate neutrally, ahistorically or cocooned from indices of power' (1985b: 154). What we see here is the importance Michael places on law. Others in this volume have rightly emphasised the interdisciplinary strength of Michael's work, but we should not forget that for Michael law is no sidewind. As a legal academic, he is interested in the law, and by law he means not just law's material effects, but law as messenger, embodiment of ideology (see Freeman, 1989: 18).

What is the nature of the order that law constitutes and defines? For Michael, the legal system is nothing less than 'a prop of patriarchy, a cultural underpinning of male dominance' (1989: 32). He expands that 'the English legal system is permeated by ideological considerations that express the subordination of women to the patriarchy' (1984a: 52). He postulates that domestic violence cannot be eradicated through legal means 'so long as the law reflects an ideology supportive of the behaviour' (*ibid*: 51).

How does law underpin patriarchy? Michael suggests that this happens through law's accordance of a dependent role to women, and he flings this charge far and wide: 'The law in Britain relating to national insurance, pensions, supplementary benefit, sickness and unemployment benefit, family income supplement, and income tax are all based on stereotypical sex classifications that impute a dependent role to women' (*ibid*: 58; see also, 1979b: 144-145; 1980: 14). In the next section of his chapter, Michael is concerned to substantiate this charge, giving particulars in each and every domain. One domain that illustrated women's legal inferiority particularly starkly, and about which Michael was exercised perhaps above all else, was the marital rape exemption. Michael never writes about domestic violence without emphasising this iniquity (1979b: 46; 1980: 10, 15; 1984a: 71; 1985b: 170; 1987: 12-14; 1989: 19-20; 2007: 63-64; 2008a: xvi); moreover, he scorns the marital rape exemption in three articles devoted to the subject, namely, "Rape by a husband?" (1979a), "'But If You Can't Rape Your Wife, Who(m) Can You Rape?': The Marital Rape Exemption Re-examined" (1981) and "Doing His Best to Sustain the Sanctity of Marriage" (1985a). A society which retains the marital rape immunity', he remonstrates in 1989, 'does not take domestic violence seriously' (20).

I will not dwell on the details of the myriad ways in which Michael demonstrates that the legal system created and reinforced women's dependency, because the legal landscape has changed beyond measure, partly as a result of the human rights framework (Human Rights Act 1998). As is well known, Michael's most egregious illustration, the marital rape exemption, fell even prior to the human rights era, over-ruled by the House of Lords in 1991 (*R v. R* [1992] 1 AC 599) and abolished by statute in 1994 (Criminal Justice and Public Order Act). Michael does not frame specific indictments against the current legal system, but rather implies that the former legal order has left a stain; indeed, as early as 1984, he relies on the relevance of residue, remarking that: 'It is not necessary for husbands to have formal rights such as to chastise their wives. That they once had this right and exercised it is sufficient' (72). Note Michael's careful choice of the present perfect tense in 2007 and 2008: 'the law *has played* a part, perhaps a major part' (2007: 62; 2008a: xvi) in underpinning patriarchy (see further, Dempsey, 2007; Reece, 2011).

That law is patriarchal is, however, not the only reason that Michael believes the law is incapable of solving the problem of violence against women. In "Domestic Violence: The Limits of Effective Legal Action", Michael suggests that law reform can mask social reality and even obstruct real social change: legislation and litigation that tackle violence against women 'divert public consciousness away from the deeper roots of the problem' (1989: 18). Law obscures and obstructs by framing the issue in terms of individual rights. This legal drive accords with the general tendency to individualise the issue of domestic violence, embodied in particular in social and psychological discourse (*ibid*: 18). Michael concludes: 'The legal system cannot solve the problem of domestic violence because the problem cannot be solved by tackling known cases of violence and that is the only way the law can operate' (*ibid*: 32).

This does not mean that Michael believes we should eschew attempts at law reform. Indeed, Michael is highly critical of the historical tendency of the law not to intervene in the private sphere. In *Violence in the Home*, Michael first criticises the then nascent tendency to treat domestic violence therapeutically through the adoption of mediation and counselling approaches (191-193; see also 1989: 28), an important criticism that runs through Michael's scholarship (see Freeman, 1984b; Freeman, 1996). Michael then sets out his stall:

> My conclusion is that violence against a wife should be treated like violence against a stranger. Women should have the right to expect that men who assault them are treated as criminals whether those men are their husbands or not (193-194).

In his inaugural six years later, Michael clarifies that he is drawing on a classically feminist approach (see e.g., Olsen, 1985; Gavison, 1992; Smart, 1984) in intertwining scepticism towards the power of law to ameliorate domestic violence with hostility towards legal non-intervention:

> I have stressed earlier in this lecture that protection is a problematic notion. What I indicated was that the rhetoric of protection should not be mistaken for the real thing and that even the best-laid plans could sometimes backfire. But if women ... are dependents, all that non-intervention achieves is protection of the dominance of men against women ... (168).

Thirty years on, there are little more than traces left of an official stance of non-intervention in the private sphere (see e.g., Gillies, 2005); Michael grapples with the complexities of this sea-change in *Understanding Family Law*. In relation to third party powers to apply for civil orders (included in the Family Law Act 1996 but never implemented), Michael notes, 'dangers in adopting this approach', as 'it may disempower victims, so that private violence is replaced by a form of public paternalism' (67). Turning to the criminal law, Michael sees pro-arrest policy as a mixed blessing. On the one hand, it provides the victims with immediate protection, as well as breathing space if the assailant is remanded in custody. Moreover, 'it sends important messages to all that domestic violence is a serious crime which will not be tolerated' (80). On the other hand, it may make matters worse for the victim, by placing her in more danger as well as jeopardising her financial security. More abstractly, it can be questioned whether 'tough criminal justice responses empower the victim' (81). Concluding his discussion of criminal law responses, Michael expresses ambivalence towards the 'increasing shift in emphasis by policy-makers towards tackling domestic violence through the criminal justice system' (85). On the one hand, this emphasises that violence is criminal, whoever the victim is. 'On the other hand, there is a danger that resolution is taken away from victims and that her needs are subsumed in the state's imperative to punish the offender, with whom she may wish to have a continuing relationship' (*ibid*). This illustrates Michael's flexibility and openness when faced with changing context, at a later as well as earlier stage of his academic career.

So to what extent can law ameliorate domestic violence, in Michael's opinion? The answer is a little opaque in his work, but a few points are plain. First of all, throughout his writing, Michael is crystal clear that domestic violence cannot be eradicated through legal means, 'so long as the law reflects an ideology supportive of the behaviour' (1984a: 51). But as we have seen, it is a moot point the extent to which Michael believes the law can still be castigated as patriarchal.

Secondly, Michael certainly believes that legal solutions are important and worthwhile; his sustained concern with careful legal analysis bears testament to this point. When he wrote *Violence in the Home*, as he tells us, it was 'the only book written on the subject by a lawyer and the first to discuss in depth legal responses to the problem' (viii). It is worth underscoring Michael's pioneering role here too. Now the bookshelves groan with legal treatises on domestic violence (e.g., Bird, 2006; Burton, 2008): Michael's was first. In 1987, he followed this with a second legal first, in his next book-length treatment of domestic violence, *Dealing with Domestic Violence*, which was the first book entirely devoted to the law of domestic violence (vii). Nor has Michael tired of legal exposition: he gives a full account of current domestic violence law in chapter 3 of *Understanding Family Law*, which he published as recently as 2007.

Thirdly, Michael is plain that law cannot be the complete solution: 'The law is never going to conquer domestic violence', he writes in 2007, 'Only a cultural revolution will achieve that' (65). Perhaps he is most transparent in his conclusion to "Domestic Violence: The Limits of Effective Legal Action", where he clarifies that the legal system cannot solve domestic violence, but can contribute to a solution if legal actors appreciate that the problem is both systemic and caused by gendered power inequalities. While only a profound cultural revolution can rectify these inequalities, legal agents 'can and should participate in this cultural struggle for that work will ultimately prove more valuable than constructing and tinkering with new remedies or new techniques' (1989: 32).

Michael thus finds the ultimate solution to domestic violence in 'redefining the position of women in society and removing those factors which make women powerless against male violence' (1979b: 129-130; see also, Freeman, 1980: 14). While this goal has, of course, not yet been achieved, it is a fitting tribute to Michael not only to celebrate the richness of his understanding of domestic violence but also the part that his scholarship has played in moving us towards that worthy goal.

References

Bird, R., *Domestic Violence Law and Practice* (Bristol: Jordan Publishing, 2006).

Breines, W. and L. Gordon, "The New Scholarship on Family Violence", *Signs* 1983 8(3), 490-531.

Brush, L., "Violent Acts and Injurious Outcomes in Married Couples: Methodological Issues in the National Survey of Families and Households", *Gender and Society* 1990 4(1), 56-67.

Burton, M., *Legal Responses to Domestic Violence* (Abingdon: Routledge-Cavendish, 2008).

Coleman, D. and M. Straus, "Marital Power, Conflict, and Violence in a Nationally Representative Sample of American Couples" in M. Straus and R. Gelles (eds), *Physical Violence in American Families* (New Brunswick, NJ: Transaction Publishers, 1990).

Das Dasgupta, S., "Just Like Men? A Critical View of Violence by Women" in M. Shepard and E. Pence (eds), *Coordinating Community Responses to Domestic Violence: Lessons from Duluth and Beyond* (California: Sage Publications, 1999).

Das Dasgupta, S., "A Framework for Understanding Women's Use of Nonlethal Violence in Intimate Heterosexual Relationships", *Violence Against Women* 2002 8(11), 1364-1389.

DeKeseredy, W., "Current Controversies on Defining Nonlethal Violence against Women in Intimate Heterosexual Relationships: Empirical Implications", *Violence Against Women* 2000 6(7), 728-746.

Dempsey, M., "What Counts as Domestic Violence? A Conceptual Analysis", *William and Mary Journal of Women and the Law* 2006 12(2), 301-334.

Dempsey, M., "Toward a Feminist State: What does 'Effective' Prosecution of Domestic Violence Mean?", *Modern Law Review* 2007 70(6), 908-935.

Dobash, R. and R. Dobash, *Violence against Wives: A Case against the Patriarchy* (London: Open Books, 1980).

Dobash, R. and R. Dobash, *Women, Violence and Social Change* (London: Routledge, 1992).

Dobash, R., R. Dobash, M. Wilson and M. Daly, "The Myth of Sexual Symmetry in Marital Violence" , *Social Problems* 1992 39(1), 71-91.

Dobash, R., R. Dobash, K. Cavanagh and R. Lewis, *Changing Violent Men* (London: Sage Publications, 2000).

Dobash, R. and R. Dobash, "Women's Violence to Men in Intimate Relationships: Working on a Puzzle", *British Journal of Criminology* 2004 44(3), 324-349.

Evason, E., *Hidden Violence: A study of battered women in Northern Ireland* (Belfast: Farset Co-operative Press, 1982).

Farmer, A. and J. Tiefenthaler, "An Economic Analysis of Domestic Violence", *Review of Social Economy* 1997 55(3), 337-358.

Freeman, M., "Rape by a husband?", *New Law Journal* 1979a, 332-333.

Freeman, M., *Violence in the Home* (Farnborough: Saxon House, 1979b).

Freeman, M., "Violence in the family", *South African Journal of Criminal Law and Criminology* 1980 4(1), 5-16.

Freeman, M., "'But If You Can't Rape Your Wife, Who(m) Can You Rape?': The Marital Rape Exemption Re-examined", *Family Law Quarterly* 1981 15(1), 1-29.

Freeman, M. and C. Lyon, *Cohabitation without Marriage: An Essay in Law and Social Policy* (Aldershot: Gower, 1983).

Freeman, M., "Legal ideologies, patriarchal precedents, and domestic violence", in M. Freeman (ed), *The State, the Law, and the Family: Critical Perspectives* (London: Tavistock Publications, 1984a).

Freeman, M., "Questioning the Delegalization Movement in Family Law: Do We Really Want a Family Court?", in J. Eekelaar and S. Katz (eds), *The Resolution of Family Conflict* (Toronto: Butterworths, 1984b).

Freeman, M., "Doing his Best to Sustain the Sanctity of Marriage", in N. Johnson (ed), *Marital Violence* (London: Routledge and Kegan Paul, 1985a).

Freeman, M., "Towards a Critical Theory of Family Law", *Current Legal Problems* 1985b 38, 153-185.

Freeman, M., *Dealing with Domestic Violence* (Bicester: CCH Editions Limited, 1987).

Freeman, M., "Domestic Violence: The Limits of Effective Legal Action", *Cambrian Law Review* 1989 20(1), 17-37.

Freeman, M., "Down with informalism: Law and lawyers in family dispute resolutions", *Family Law Journal* 1996 2(3), 67-71.

Freeman, M., "Not Such a Queer Idea: Is There a Case for Same Sex Marriages?", *Journal of Applied Philosophy* 1999 16(1), 1-17.

Freeman, M., *Understanding Family Law* (London: Sweet and Maxwell, 2007).

Freeman, M., (ed), *Domestic Violence* (Farnham: Ashgate, 2008a).

Freeman, M., *Lloyd's Introduction to Jurisprudence* (London: Sweet and Maxwell, 2008b).

Gavison, R., "Feminism and the Public / Private Distinction", *Stanford Law Review* 1992 45(1), 1-45.

Gelles, R., "Abused Wives: Why Do They Stay?", *Journal of Marriage and the Family* 1976 38(4), 659-668.

Gillies, V., "Meeting parents' needs? Discourses of 'support' and 'inclusion' in family policy", *Critical Social Policy* 2005 25(1), 70-90.

Gordon, M., "Definitional Issues in Violence against Women: Surveillance and Research from a Violence Research Perspective", *Violence Against Women* 2000 6(7), 747-783.

Hanmer, J., "Women and Violence: Commonalities and Diversities", in B. Fawcett, B. Featherstone, J. Hearn and C. Toft (eds), *Violence and Gender Relations: Theories and Interventions* (London: Sage Publications, 1996).

Hearn, J., "Men's Violence to Known Women: Historical, Everyday and Theoretical Constructions by Men", in B. Fawcett, B. Featherstone, J. Hearn and C. Toft (eds), *Violence and Gender Relations: Theories and Interventions* (London: Sage Publications, 1996a).

Hearn, J., "Men's Violence to Known Women: Men's Accounts and Men's Policy Developments", in B. Fawcett, B. Featherstone, J. Hearn and C. Toft (eds), *Violence and Gender Relations: Theories and Interventions* (London: Sage Publications, 1996b).

Home Office, *Circular: new government domestic violence and abuse definition*, available at https://www.gov.uk/government/publications/new-government-domestic-violence-and-abuse-definition (2013).

Homer, M., A. Leonard and P. Taylor, "The burden of dependency" in N. Johnson (ed), *Marital Violence* (London: Routledge and Kegan Paul, 1985a).

Homer, M., A. Leonard and P. Taylor, "Personal Relationships: Help and Hindrance" in N. Johnson (ed), *Marital Violence* (London: Routledge and Kegan Paul, 1985b).

Humphreys, C. and R. Thiara, "Neither justice nor protection: women's experiences of post-separation violence", *Journal of Social Welfare and Family Law* 2003 25(3), 195-214.

Hunter, R., "Narratives of Domestic Violence", *Sydney Law Review* 2006 28(4), 733-776.

Kalmuss, D. and M. Straus, "Wife's Marital Dependency and Wife Abuse" in M. Straus and R. Gelles (eds), *Physical Violence in American Families* (New Brunswick, NJ: Transaction Publishers, 1990).

Johnson, H. and V. Sacco, "Researching Violence against Women: Statistics Canada's National Survey", *Canadian Journal of Criminology* 1995 37(3), 281-304.

Johnson, H., "Rethinking Survey Research on Violence against Women", in R. Dobash and R. Dobash, R. (eds), *Rethinking Violence Against Women* (California: Sage Publications, 1998).

Johnson, M., "Patriarchal Terrorism and Common Couple Violence: Two Forms of Violence Against Women", *Journal of Marriage and the Family* 1995 57(2), 283-294.

Johnson, M. and K. Ferraro, "Research on Domestic Violence in the 1990s: Making Distinctions", *Journal of Marriage and the Family* 2000 62(4), 948-963.

Kaganas, F., "Domestic violence, men's groups and the equivalence argument" in A. Diduck and K. O'Donovan (eds), *Feminist Perspectives on Family Law* (Oxford: Routledge-Cavendish, 2006).

Levinson, D., *Family Violence in Cross-Cultural Perspective* (London: Sage Publications, 1989).

Liddle, A., "Feminist Contributions to an Understanding of Violence against Women – Three Steps Forward, Two Steps Back", *Canadian Review of Sociology and Anthropology* 1989 26(5), 759-776.

Martin, D., *Battered Wives* (San Francisco: Volcano Press, 1976).

Melton, H. and J. Belknap, "He Hits, She Hits: Assessing Gender Differences and Similarities in Officially Reported Intimate Partner Violence", *Criminal Justice and Behavior* 2003 30(3), 328-348.

Mirrlees-Black, C., *Domestic Violence: Findings from a New British Crime Survey Self-completion Questionnaire* (London: Home Office Research Study No. 191, 1999).

Nazroo, J., "Uncovering Gender Differences in the use of Marital Violence: The Effect of Methodology", *Sociology* 1995 29(3), 475-494.

Okun, L., *Woman Abuse: Facts Replacing Myths* (New York: SUNY Press, 1986).

Olsen, F., "The Myth of State Intervention in the Family", *University of Michigan Journal of Law Reform* 1985 18(4), 835-864.

Pagelow, M., *Woman-Battering: Victims and Their Experiences* (London: Sage Publications, 1981).

Pahl, J., "Violent Husbands and Abused Wives: a Longitudinal Study" in J. Pahl (ed), *Private Violence and Public Policy: The Needs of Battered Women and the Response of the Public Services* (London: Routledge and Kegan Paul, 1985).

Pence, E. and M. Paymar, *Education Groups for Men who Batter: The Duluth Model* (New York, Springer Publishing, 1993).

Piispa, M., "Complexity of Patterns of Violence against Women in Heterosexual Partnerships", *Violence Against Women* 2002 8(7), 873-900.

Pizzey, E., *Scream Quietly or the Neighbours will Hear* (London: Penguin, 1974).

Ptacek, J., "Why do Men Batter their Wives?" in K. Yllö and M. Bograd (eds), *Feminist Perspectives on Wife Abuse* (California: Sage Publications, 1990).

Radford, J., L. Kelly and M. Hester, "Introduction" in M. Hester, L. Kelly and J. Radford, *Women, Violence and Male Power: Feminist Activism, Research and Practice* (Buckingham: Open University Press, 1996).

Ramazanoglu, C., "Sex and Violence in Academic Life or You Can Keep a Good Woman Down", in J. Hanmer and M. Maynard, *Women, Violence and Social Control* (Basingstoke: Macmillan, 1987).

Reece, H., "The End of Domestic Violence", *Modern Law Review* 2006 69(5), 770-791.

Reece, H., "Feminist Anti-violence Discourse as Regulation", in S. Day Sclater, F. Ebtehaj, E. Jackson and M. Richards (eds), *Regulating Autonomy: Sex, Reproduction and Family* (Oxford: Hart Publishing, 2009).

Reece, H., "'Unpalatable Messages'? Feminist Analysis of United Kingdom Legislative Discourse on Stalking 1996-1997", *Feminist Legal Studies* 2011 19(3), 205-230.

Smart, C., *The Ties that Bind: Law, marriage and the reproduction of patriarchal relations* (London: Routledge & Kegan Paul, 1984).

Stark, E. and A. Flitcraft, *Women At Risk: Domestic Violence and Women's Health* (London: Sage Publications, 1996).

Stark, E., "Commentary on Johnson's 'Conflict and Control: Gender Symmetry and Asymmetry in Domestic Violence'", *Violence Against Women* 2006 12(11), 1019-1025.

Straus, M., "Sexual Inequality and Wife Beating" in M. Straus and G. Hotaling (eds), *The Social Causes of Husband-Wife Violence* (Minneapolis: University of Minnesota Press, 1980).

Straus, M., "State-to-State Differences in Social Inequality and Social Bonds in Relation to Assaults on Wives in the United States", *Journal of Comparative Family Studies* 1994 25(1), 7-24.

Tauchen, H., A. Witte and S. Long, "Domestic Violence: A Nonrandom Affair", *International Economic Review* 1991 32(2), 491-511.

Walby, S. and A. Myhill, "New Survey Methodologies In Researching Violence Against Women", *British Journal of Criminology* 2001 41(3), 502-522.

Walby, S. and J. Allen, *Domestic Violence, Sexual Assault and Stalking: Findings from the British Crime Survey* (London: Home Office Research Study No. 276, 2004).

Wilson, E., *What is to be Done about Violence against Women?* (Harmondsworth: Penguin, 1983).

Yllö, K., "Through a Feminist Lens: Gender, Power and Violence" in R. Gelles and D. Loseke (eds), *Current Controversies in Family Violence* (California: Sage Publications, 1993).

The Spirit and the Corruption of Cricket

Peter Alldridge
Queen Mary, University of London, UK

This is part of an enquiry prompted by recent high-profile cases of fixing specific events in cricket matches to cheat gambling markets. In many ways the issues are as for financial conduct, regulation of the press, or many other issues. Should there be statutory or self-regulation, single agencies for single vices or each sport to itself? At what point is the criminal law to be involved? The answer to this last question seems to be, in the UK at the moment, that cheating to win an event, even when it carries prize money or the opportunity to earn more money later by advertising and endorsements, is principally a regulatory matter for the sport involved, but that the criminal law is legitimately involved when sportspeople underperform deliberately as part of a gambling fraud. That is, that the person who is trying to win the game by cheating is in a different position from the person who is trying to fix the game so as to win money by gambling, even though both fall within scope of the criminal prohibition, because at least s/he is trying to 'play the game'.

One simple answer to corruption in cricket is to adopt whatever is regarded as best practice in other games that are relatively successful in dealing with corruption. Over and over again, however, the cricket literature embodies the idea that cricket is unique, different and nobler, because it has a 'spirit'. In many ways, these claims are like the arguments that the City of London was different and more honourable and needed to be protected from the vulgarity of explicit rules and intrusive regulators. This essay will suggest that the 'spirit' is an impediment to proper regulation.

The 'Spirit' of the Game and the Idea of 'Not Cricket'

Cricket was established in many areas of the British empire (Kaufman and Patterson, 2005). It was used to contribute to the civilising myth of empire (Malcolm, 2002; Stokvis, 2005; Holden, 2008). The last 50 years have seen enormous change in its administration from the cosy 'amateurs' of the MCC (Riordan, 2006) to the global government of a sport whose administrative centre is now in Dubai but whose financial centre is in India (Speed, 2011; Bose, 2006; Wadhwaney, 2005; Guha, 2002; Astill, 2013). The same era has seen huge changes in the regulation and organisation of gambling,

A. Diduck, N. Peleg, H. Reece (eds.), Law in Society: Reflections on Children, Family, Culture and Philosophy
 ISBN 978-90-04-26148-8. pp. 331-346.

driven by some of the features of globalisation, notably the advent of online betting, giving the possibility of a bet being made at internet speed in a jurisdiction of choice. The introduction of one-day formats, and in particular the T20 format, in many respects designed to make cricket more like baseball, so that spectators can watch a match in an evening, with every ball 'counting', enhances the possibilities for corruption.

During the 1932-33 'Bodyline' series (Fraser, 2005: 357 *et seq.*), England used 'leg theory' – fast, short-pitched bowling towards the batter's body, with a leg-side field – to counter the threat posed by the Australian, Bradman, who had carried all before him in England in 1930. The Australian captain, Woodfull, famously asserted that only one side (his) was playing cricket. Diplomatic telegrams were exchanged. The expression 'not cricket' (Rae, 2001) is, used in this context, a most interesting metaphor. What it seems to mean is doing something which may be within the formal rules governing whatever activity is in point, but which is strongly though informally condemned. There was no question but that Jardine's strategy was within the then laws of cricket. There have subsequently been two legislative strategies to outlaw it. The first is the rule limiting to two the number of fielders permitted to be behind square on the leg side, so the chances of the batsman being out caught in the leg trap are reduced. The second is rules dealing with intimidatory bowling, whether by a general proscription or by a limit per over on short-pitched bowling. Protective equipment has also reduced the physical danger.

Woodfull was not appealing to rules but to a 'spirit' of cricket. Cricket does indeed pride itself (i) on having a 'spirit' evident in a set of norms distinct from its rules; and (ii) in being unique amongst games. Neither of these claims bears much examination, but what they imply about the game is important. From the time of its appropriation by English public schools in the 19th century (Sandiford, 1983), the spirit was linked to a cult of masculinity, emphasising – at least until relatively recently – the physical risk and decrying the use of protective gear (Birley, 2000). It was also invoked to reinforce class boundaries. Over the history of cricket, all kinds of things have been presented as being part of its spirit (Rae, 2001; Birley, 2000). Pelham Warner asserted that it would be contrary to the spirit of the game for a professional to captain England (Smith and Porter, 2000; Wagg, 2000) and cricket maintained the amateur/professional distinction until 1962. Attire always had to be white, as, in the West Indies, until Frank Worrall, and notwithstanding the pre-eminence of Learie Constantine and then of George Headley, did the captain (James, 1963).

One of the respects in which cricket is different from most major sports is that the element of luck is greater. Home ground and initiative are dealt with in all games by playing home and away. In cricket the toss confers a significant advantage. The rules of cricket operate to give unearned credit by leg byes, edges, misses and meteorological vicissitudes ('saved by rain'). The governing assumption seems to be that these matters even themselves out over the course of a cricket career, and that enduring a little misfortune is character-forming. The 'spirit' is partly to do with putting up with the hardship imposed by worn or wet wickets, worn or wet balls, losing the toss, adverse weather and poor decisions by umpires, and in general taking the rough with the smooth, not complaining and being a good sport.

In 2000, at the prompting of two grandees of the game and sons of empire, former England captains and MCC presidents, 'Lord Ted' Dexter and Lord (Colin) Cowdrey, the laws were amended explicitly to include the idea of a 'spirit' and this formed part of the 'Spirit of Cricket' initiative. It is, of course, significant (and would attract the attention of the German historical school) that the attempt to codify the spirit came at a time when England was losing control of the game. As a result of the Dexter/Cowdrey stand, the laws of cricket[1] now contain a preamble, as follows.

> **The Spirit of Cricket**
> Cricket is a game that owes much of its unique appeal to the fact that it should be played not only within its Laws but also within the Spirit of the Game. Any action which is seen to abuse this spirit causes injury to the game itself. The major responsibility for ensuring the spirit of fair play rests with the captains.

There are questions to be answered as to whether or not a 'spirit' could be incorporated expressly in a codified set of laws anyway, and if so when. The more explicit a spirit is made, the less it is a spirit, and the more just further rules.

Some examples are given of the sorts of things that might amount to violations of the spirit of the game. It is said to be against the Spirit of the Game:

> to dispute an umpire's decision by word, action or gesture, to direct abusive language towards an opponent or umpire or to indulge in cheating or any sharp practice, for instance:
> a) to appeal knowing that the batsman is not out[2]
> b) to advance towards an umpire in an aggressive manner when appealing
> c) to seek to distract an opponent either verbally or by harassment with persistent clapping or unnecessary noise under the guise of enthusiasm and motivation of one's own side. (Marylebone Cricket Club, 2013: preamble para. 5.)

Of course, sportspersonlike behaviour, in the sense of not taking unfair advantage, exists and is admired in many sports. The practice of snooker players or golfers, for example, to call fouls upon themselves is analogous to 'walking' in cricket. In those cases, and also self-reporting to the Serious Fraud Office (Alldridge, 2013; Serious Fraud Office, 2013), there is an element of self-interest. It is good to have a reputation

1 'Part of the punditry of Cricket is that it has laws, not mere rules like lesser games' (Birley, 2000: 16).

2 This is contentious. When the batter does not play a stroke, many bowlers appeal knowing it not to be our 'to remind the umpire' that the batter might be given out LBW. The advent of DRS (Decision Review System technology) has given rise to the common occurrence of the fielding side appealing strongly and then not exercising its right to review a 'not out' decision. Not all such choices can be explained on standard of proof grounds.

of being a 'walker', because it means that when the batter does not 'walk' s/he is indicating that s/he did not hit the ball. Likewise, elementary respect for the opposition (clapping the incoming batsman), both between opponents and between home crowd and visitors, is part of many sports. Beyond the simple requirements of courtesy, what is different ('unique') about cricket and does the spirit supersede the laws? Consider three examples.

Mankading

An example of the spirit of the game that is frequently given is the norm that it is wrong for the bowler to run out a non-striker who is 'backing up' and out of his/her ground, without first warning him/her. The laws say only that the batter is out, and if umpires are called upon to adjudicate they give the batter out. Running out a non-striker backing up is known in Australia as 'mankading', after an episode in the 1947-8 Australia-India Test series in which Vinoo Mankad ran out Bill Brown (Preston, 1950: 772. See Fraser, 2005: 133-5). Wisden records, without adverse comment, that Mankad had warned Brown about backing up out of his ground in an earlier first-class match on that tour (*An Australian XI v. India*; Preston, 1950: 769) and then had run him out when he did it again. In the Second Test Match Mankad ran Brown out in this way without warning. That is, Mankad seemed to subscribe to the rule against 'mankading' and the 'unless you warn them first' exception but thought that once one warning per batter (or per bowler per batter) had been given, the exception was satisfied, at least for that season and possibly for all time. Bradman, Brown's captain, did not object to Mankad's behaviour and just played by the rules (and had not objected on 'spirit' grounds to bodyline, which had been developed specifically against him). Mankad's idea of the rule was not that a batsman got a clean slate at the beginning of each match, but that the rule was like the operation of benefit of clergy in the late 16th century. Under a statute of 1575 (18 Eliz.I c.7.), benefit of clergy was pleaded after conviction but before sentencing (rather than, as had previously been the case, as a bar to jurisdiction) and it did not nullify the conviction. Defendants who availed themselves of the benefit once were branded on the thumb and not allowed to use it again (Blackstone IV *Commentaries* 360).[3] Mankad evidently thought that Brown was a 'repeat offender' and that by giving the warning in the earlier match he had branded Brown's metaphorical thumb, at least for that season.

The explanation given by Fraser for the prohibition on mankading, (the '... [c]learest and starkest example of the conflict between legal formalism and the idea of a game based on higher or more important "ethical" norms'. Fraser, 2005: 134) is that it is unethical – a form of sharp practice. It is sneaky and unworthy of a gentleman. A legal analogy might be winning a case by relying on legal requirements in respect of formalities or limitation periods.

3 And see 2 Henry VI IV. ii. 69-71: 'But methinks he should stand in fear of fire, being burnt i' the hand for stealing of sheep.'

> … [T]here are occasions when the lawyer rebels at pleading the Statute of Limitations or when, if peculiar circumstances seem to require it, he resorts to the statute with explanations and apologies to his adversary.… the lawyer may feel that it would be shabby to permit the client to plead the statute and thereby escape performance of a just obligation (Stevens, 1951-2: 355).

The underpinning claim is that a gentleman ought not to want to win so much as to do that. This prompts four comments. First, is a batter who backs up out of his crease, assuming that he will not be run out, not cheating? Second, even if the norm has a place in first-class cricket, where one run either way rarely matters, does it or should it in T20 where frequently it will? Third, it would be quite easy to amend the rules to cover this situation. This has not been done, we may assume, because it is more important to the administration to retain the obedience to the unwritten norm. Fourth, deceiving the opposition or catching them napping is an accepted and lauded way to win in many ball games. A googly – an off-break bowled with a leg-break action – is, of course, intended to deceive. The actions of the 'mankader' are clearly analogous to those of a baseball pitcher attempting to pickoff a runner on a base. There are rules in baseball about when the pitcher can fake a pitch throw and when he cannot (Major League Baseball Official Rules: 8.00.). An illegal fake is a balk. The difference is that in the cricket case the batter is assumed not to intend to go beyond the crease at the relevant time. In baseball, if the pitcher is about to pitch, all the players are alert and stray at their peril. A pickoff is quite legitimate and not regarded as being at all underhand. In cricket, in Hohfeldian terms, the batter who relies on the convention claims a (moral) liberty to be inadvertent and nonchalant, at least once. The bowler has no (moral) right to interfere. On this account the claim of the advertent non-striker, who concentrates on the bowler and tries to gain as much advantage as possible from backing up out of the crease, is far weaker. There are some rules whose benefits are not conferred upon advertent actors purporting to act in reliance upon them. A defendant who sees someone acquitted by reason of insanity and then claims the right to be acquitted on the grounds of being equally insane will usually be convicted. The right to be a nonchalant non-striker is like that.

Batter Accidentally Knocked Over

Second, the spirit documentation considers whether it is a violation of the spirit of the game to run a batsman out who has been knocked off his feet. The answer given in the 'Spirit of Cricket' documentation is, 'yes'.

> But, if the umpires consider the collision is accidental, then the Laws apply as though it had not happened. The umpire concerned has no option but to give the batsman out if there is an appeal. The only possible reprieve left for the batsman is for the fielding captain to ask that the appeal be withdrawn. That code of honour, the Spirit of Cricket, suggests that this should not be necessary. The 'best course of action' is for the fielding side

> not to put down the wicket in the first place. If only the Spirit of Cricket was so firmly ingrained that such gestures were the norm.

Or, if only the laws had been better drawn in the first place. If the objective of the legislator were to achieve the conclusion advocated, or the fielders not appealing or withdrawing their appeal, it would be easy to rewrite the rules so as to achieve it. This could be done by giving the umpire power to call 'dead ball' when a player is accidentally knocked over (which would have the additional advantage of preventing the question arising whether, in the case where the batter was running when knocked over, the batting side should be credited with the additional run). Somehow, it is thought better to talk of the spirit of the game. It is a general precept of sportsperson-like behaviour that one ought not to take a competitive advantage from the accidental indisposition of an opponent. This example need not be regarded as anything more significant than that.

Bowling Underarm to Prevent a Six

Third, there was much criticism of an Australian captain (Greg Chappell) ordering a bowler (his brother Trevor) to bowl underarm in a one-day international in 1981 in which the opposition (New Zealand) needed six to win off the last ball. This was greeted by universal condemnation, including condemnatory remarks by both Prime Ministers. There are many sports in which a team with the advantage will 'run down the clock' in such a way as to prevent the other team scoring before the end. Baseball has a specific pitching role for 'closers', whose job is not to concede hits in the closing innings. In those football codes where the clock still runs when the ball is in the stand it is regarded as legitimate for the team that is ahead to kick the ball into the stand to use up time. There must come a point at which giving the opposition a fair chance towards the end of the game simply becomes suicidal. The legislative analogy is the filibuster. Some legislatures allow it: some do not. Where filibusters are allowed, for example in the United States' Senate, the reason is usually that that was the only basis upon which those who agreed to this constitutional structure would sign up. The adverse reaction to Chappell's tactic is particularly strange in cricket, in which all sorts of stratagems (tying and untying shoelaces, tending to the pitch, asking for fresh equipment and so on) are deployed to waste time and do not attract censure. Again, if it were really thought desirable to prevent this sort of behaviour, it would be quite straightforward to change the rules to do it. It might well make sense to outlaw underarm bowling altogether. Cricket prefers not to change the written rule but to condemn.

Distilling the Spirit

I conclude that substantively the 'spirit of cricket' is nothing more than the elementary sporting precept that one ought not to take unfair advantage and that those who wish to argue for the uniqueness of cricket should do so on aesthetic and not moral grounds. But that does not by any means not capture its importance.

I suggest that the reasons that cricket insists so firmly on the anti-mankading rule is not so much to do with the ethics of the conduct, which can easily be contested, and which could be expressed in the Laws, but are to do with an oral tradition, venerating the unwritten rule, and its use in bonding as a community. Tolerance of and fascination by the unwritten is part of a particular type of Englishness (Fox, 2008; Wilkinson, 1962; Simons, 1996; Williams, 2003; Marqusee, 2005). Other games have unwritten rules, but do not glory in them quite in this way (Dickson, 2009). The cricketing community knows that one should not mankad, or bowl underarm to deny the opponent a chance, and bonds in condemning those who do. The substance of that rule is not nearly so important as its function. If it were not mankading it would have to be something else. I hope now to show that emphasis on the spirit, and the use of the captain as the principal compliance officer, is a major impediment to dealing with corruption in cricket.

Corruption in Sports

Wherever there is betting on outcomes, there will be attempts to fix them. Some sports, notably horse racing, baseball and boxing, have long histories of anti-corruption self-regulation, usually put in place after some scandal or other, together with occasional police investigations and prosecutions. For many the defining historical moment for corruption in sport was the 1919 (baseball) World Series – the infamous 'Black Sox' affair, and which members of the Chicago White Sox took bribes to lose (Asinof, 2000). There had been rumours of a fix, and various members of the press agreed to monitor the World Series play-by-play and make notes if they saw anything untoward. Their notes, written independently, had many points of convergence. A grand jury investigation subsequently yielded indictments and acquittals. The acquittals were followed by the sport taking the matter on itself with the instantiation of the office of Commissioner, with power to put in place lifetime bans and huge fines.

Other sports have their mechanisms for ensuring integrity. From its inception in the early 18th century, until the establishment of a regulatory structure independent of course ownership, the Jockey Club asserted jurisdiction over horse racing until 2006. This is now in the hands of the British Horseracing Authority. The British Boxing Board of Control retains control of boxing. Until recently, reported cases of fixing of football matches were rare but not unknown.[4] During early 2013, enquiries by Europol have started into the allegation that 680 Champions' League games had been fixed (BBC, 2013). In the 'Bloodgate' scandal, the Harlequins Director of Rugby, Dean Richards, was banned for three years for using fake blood to get one player off the field and a substitute on, so as to gain an advantage in a coming tie-break (Benammar, 2009). The blood was used not to win bets but to win the game and the

4 The 1997 trials of Bruce Grobbelaar, the former Liverpool goalkeeper, finally giving rise to the pyrrhic victory in the defamation case of *Grobbelaar v. News Group Newspapers Ltd* [2002] 1 WLR 3024. In 2006, Juventus were relegated from Serie A in 2006 for match-fixing.

financial gains that would have come. The matter was dealt with internally by the Rugby Football Union. Again, the events that led to Lance Armstrong being stripped of seven Tour de France titles show fairly clear evidence at least of a conspiracy to defraud, yet no criminal proceedings have been brought against him.

The earliest reference to gambling on a cricket match is in the records of a 1646 court case concerning non-payment of a wager that was made on a game at Coxheath in Kent. Curiously, the wager was for 12 candles, but the participants included members of the local gentry (Bowen, 1970: 47). In 1652, a case at Cranbrook against John Rabson, Esq. and others referred to 'a certain unlawful game called cricket'. Rabson was a member of the gentry but the other defendants were all working class (David, 2000: 15). When it first became popular, in the 18th century (Brunström and Cassidy, 2012), there was a great deal of betting on the outcome of cricket matches. The laws of cricket were established at the Artillery ground London in 1744, and were really to deal with bets (Harvey, 2011). Even the word 'draw' referred to withdrawing the stakes. As soon as there was gambling, there were scams. James Pycroft, one of the early historians of the game, recorded 'A Dark chapter in the History of Cricket' dealing with the confession of 'Silver' Billy Beldham, the finest player of his era (he played from 1782-1821), to fixing (Pycroft, 1856: 99 *et seq*).

With increased interest in gambling and the large sums involved, coupled with the shift in the centre of gravity of the game to India, in which betting is largely unlawful and therefore unregulated (Mahyera, 2012), the profits available from gambling have multiplied.[5] In times gone by there were stories of the corrupt trading, explicit or implicit, of 'We will lose this championship game if you let us win the Sunday League match.'[6] There are now out-and-out betting cheats.

Gamblers – bookmakers and punters alike – are in the business of predicting the future. Betting is a competition as to who does it best. As with any speculative investment, there are two major factors bearing on a person's success – the quality of the predictive device (usually an algorithm) and the quality (how accurate, how early and how full) of the information. There are various events and background conditions in the period before the match which bear upon the odds. These include information as to the pitch, the weather, the teams, the toss and so on. If you have a better algorithm or better information than the bookie, you will win consistently and they will stop taking your bets. At critical junctures before and during the course of the game there will be events bearing upon the odds. Consequently, the knowledge that the odds are going to be changed by an event is 'price sensitive information'.

---

5 Legal gambling in India is confined to horse-racing, while casinos are allowed only in some states. In such an atmosphere, illegal syndicates continue to thrive and Indian media estimates the amount bet on 2009 IPL Twenty20 competition at $427m (£280m) (The Guardian, 2013).

6 The former first class cricketer, Donald Topley, is believed to have reiterated to Lord Condon his allegations that in 1992 a three-day match and a one-day match between Essex and Lancashire were fixed, Lancashire to win the one-day match and Essex to win the three-day game to aid their respective championship challenges in the different competitions (Briggs, 2001).

In addition to those on the final result and its margin, there are betting markets on more specific events within cricket games. It is possible to bet on the number of runs in a session, or the outcome of the first ball or other matters unrelated to the final outcome. The more specific it is, the more susceptible it is to a fix, and the easier it is for players to explain it to themselves. Conversely, the more specific and the less inherently probable the event, the more easily will fixes be detectible. It is difficult to show that a team is losing a match, particularly a one-day match, by design. It is much easier to show that the fifth ball of the seventh over was a no-ball by design. If a gambler knows in advance of an event that it will occur and consequently the odds or the spread will change, they can bet or set odds accordingly.

Three episodes illustrate the problem of corruption in cricket. First, and most famously, on England's tour of South Africa in 1999/00, South Africa were leading the series 2-0. The final (fifth) Test (international) match at Centurion Park was heading for a draw because rain prevented play on the second, third and fourth days (out of a scheduled five). Hansie Cronje, the South African captain, engineered the possibility of decisive finish (a win for either side or even a tie) by agreeing with the England captain, Nasser Hussain, to exchange a declaration of the English first innings for forfeiture of the South African second, so that the two innings match became, in effect, a one innings match with enough time for a positive result. This is a mechanism sometimes used in some forms of cricket to generate a competitive finish but Cronje was the only Test captain to ever forfeit an innings. A Test captain would not usually risk losing a Test Match, even in a decided rubber, if s/he did not have to. At the time, Cronje was acclaimed for raising the spirit of cricket to new heights with this cavalier behaviour. Mark Nicholas described it as 'the golden age of the game'. Bob Woolmer, then South Africa coach, said: 'Hansie did the game the biggest favour imaginable at the dawn of the new century' (Hoult, 2004).As it happens, England won very narrowly. The entire episode, however, was a betting scam. The South African captain received two sums totalling R50K, plus a leather jacket from a bookmaker, to generate a result. A further promised R500K did not materialise (said Cronje). Bookmakers had taken substantial bets on a draw. Cronje's actions did not prevent a draw entirely, but reduced its likelihood from almost certain to third favourite (after wins for each side). There is no question that on the last day Cronje was playing to win, and he could explain his conduct to himself on that basis. He even bet R50 on South Africa. By reducing substantially the chances of a draw, after it had been clear favourite, he had ensured that the bookmakers won. It was the cricket equivalent of nobbling the favourite. This scam was unusual: it was not pre-planned, and it turned on the weather. It could only be accomplished by the team captain, and did not require any help within the team.

When Cronje was finally caught for bribe-taking (as a result of a newspaper 'sting'), a Commission of Enquiry was established in South Africa (King Commission (2000)). In consequence, Cronje and former Indian captain Azharuddin were investigated, found guilty of match-fixing and banned from playing cricket (for life and for five years, respectively) (Central Bureau of Investigation, 2000). They could have been subject to prosecution, but were not. Cronje made a confession to fixing specific events ('spot fixing') but not 'match-fixing'. His confession implicated various other players. Cronje died in a plane crash in 2002. By 2006 Azharuddin had pretty much been rehabilitated and on 5 November 2012 his life ban from cricket was quashed. The court criticised the BCCI for initiating arbitrary proceedings against him without following principles of natural justice.[7] He is now a member of the Indian Parliament.

In an attempt to respond to this crisis, Cricket made an attempt to regulate itself. The ICC set up an Anti-Corruption and Security Unit (ACSU) in 2000 originally under Lord Condon, and now Sir Ronnie Flanagan, both retired police chiefs. ACSU is an operating division of the ICC Code of Conduct Commission, which is chaired by Michael Beloff QC. ACSU acts in consultation with the ICC Chief Executive, Haroon Lorgat. Day-to-day operational responsibility rests with the General Manager and Chief Investigator. It does not have police powers and lacks resources. ACSU continues to monitor and investigate any reports of corruption in cricket, consider its own procedures[8] and a Code of Practice[9] has been introduced which, for example, introduced anti-corruption training,[10] reporting obligations, emphasis upon vigilance, prohibitions on betting on cricket and the use of mobile telephones in dressing rooms, contact with bookmakers and so on.[11] ACSU is short of resources, has been described by former England captain Andrew Strauss' as a 'toothless tiger', and has yet to catch anyone fixing cricket matches. In the absence of police interest, the press will probably remain a more effective investigative body.

In England, corruption gave rise to prosecutions and imprisonment and the appeals in the next two episodes, *R. v. Amir (Mohammad) R. v. Majeed,* and *R. v. Westfield* [2012] EWCA Crim 1186; [2012] 2 Cr. App. R. 18 (and see Hawkins, 2012). In each case the pleas of guilty followed rulings by the trial judge. Majeed was the agent for cricket players representing Pakistan in the Pakistan Cricket Board's 2010 tour of England. He pleaded guilty to conspiracy to give corrupt payments (Criminal Law Act 1977, s. 1(1)), Prevention of Corruption Acts 1889-1916) and conspiracy to cheat (Criminal Law Act 1977, s. 1(1), Gambling Act 2005, s. 42.) Three co-accused who also pleaded guilty to corruption offences were under a contractual duty to provide full-time services to the Board as professional cricketers which included duties of ethical behaviour and not accepting bribes. In the course of a 'sting' operation by the *News of the World,* he agreed with an undercover investigative journalist to arrange with the three co-accused for the bowlers to bowl no balls at specified times during the course of a particular test match between England and Pakistan, in return for payment. The no-balls were duly delivered. *Westfield* was a separate case of a county cricketer taking bribes to give runs away.

---

7 *Times of India*, 17 November 2012.

8 In this regard the report by de Speville was significant: http://static.icc-cricket.com/ugc/documents/DOC_704008CED784991CB529668F9EDED418_1328164590163_112.pdf.

9 As a consequence of the recommendations of a Commission: http://www.icc-cricket.com/anti_corruption/icc-code-of-conduct.php.

10 The modules are at http://www.thepca.co.uk/anti-corruption.html.

11 http://www.icc-cricket.com/anti_corruption/overview.php.

Bribes or Gambling Scams?

The cases were decided under the Prevention of Corruption Acts 1889-1916. Under the old (pre-Bribery Act 2010) law the main criterion limiting criminal liability was that the actions had to be performed 'corruptly' and a jury held that they had. There is a lingering idea in the English law of bribery that it is an attack on the relationship between, in this case, employer and employee and the court presents the offences as being against the Pakistan Board and Essex CCC respectively. The use of bribery charges treated the employers as having been the victims. The defendants were clearly in breach of contract. Each cricketer was obliged to refrain from doing anything which might damage the reputation of the team for which he was playing, or the country he represented, or the Board or Club which employed him. The point of the contracts was that the cricketer should play on behalf of the country or county to the best of his ability. The Board or Club were victims of these activities. However, not all payments to commit crimes, and certainly not all payments to breach contracts of employment, are bribes. Few forms of disloyalty or incitement to disloyalty in bilateral relationships are criminal at all.[12] Disloyal employees may be disciplined and sometimes dismissed by their employers, but do not, without more, face criminal sanctions. It is difficult to justify a further single exception for bribery, and even if it were to be justified it is difficult to see how, without more, it could be that serious. Usually, a sufficient remedy for betrayal is provided by remonstration, ostracism, divorce, dismissal or an action for breach of contract or breach of trust. If those remedies have been determined to be inadequate in these cases then significant reforms are due. Furthermore, if personal betrayal is central to the offence, it is difficult to see why the *quid pro quo* – the money (or other advantage) – should take on so much significance. Money is but one reason for disloyalty. It does not necessarily make an instance of disloyalty worse or better than the infinite range of other reasons for which people are disloyal.

Under the Bribery Act 2010, it seems that things would be more complex. The jury would be asked whether or not the agreement was that a relevant function be performed improperly within the meaning in the Bribery Act 2010. It is performed improperly if it is performed in breach of a relevant expectation. The significant one here (Condition A in section 3(3) of the Bribery Act 2010) is that the person performing the function or activity is expected to perform it in good faith. It is not enough that there be a legal obligation, but evidence of legal obligations could provide the basis for a jury finding that the contemplated performance was improper. Under the 2010 Act the issue would be whether the employee was not only in breach of the various expectations set out in the contracts and the regulations incorporated by them, but also of an expectation of good faith. Substituting 'duty' for 'expectation', as a matter of employment law, this is a tricky question. An expectation of good faith would arise from

12 Treason and the offences under the Incitement to Disaffection Act 1934 (which arises from the particular position of the soldier) are the only obvious exceptions. Inciting a police officer to disobey orders falling short of obstruction is not, without more, an offence.

a fiduciary duty, or from a contract *uberrimae fidei*, but neither circumstance obtains here. It would not necessarily arise under the implied duty of mutual trust and confidence. There is no express term either in the county or the national contract setting out a duty of good faith. Even if there is no legal duty, however, there might nonetheless be an expectation of good faith based on a moral obligation. The Law Commission was confident of the jury's ability to apply this test on the basis of the ordinary meaning of the words rather than as something that needed to be defined in the Act: '... the expectation in question is that which would be had, in the circumstances by people of moral integrity ... it will be for the tribunal of fact to decide what that expectation amounted to, in the circumstances' (Law Commission, 2008: para.3.176). It can be imagined that a jury might expect good faith of the cricketer, just as the jury held the behaviour to be corrupt. It is not obvious, however, that the new test is any clearer, or generates greater predictability.

We still need a clear, fully articulated, rationale for the crime of bribery, showing what and to whom offenders do wrong. There was a running fight throughout the efforts to reform bribery law as to whether the harm in bribery law was incitement to disloyalty (i.e. was the victim the employer?) (Alldridge, 2013: 1188 et seq). There are two bases for the offence, and they are not mutually exclusive. The first focuses on whether the defendants were disloyal (usually to employers). The second basis is that bribes interfere in the proper operation of a market, in this case a gaming market, harming the gaming industry and other gamblers betting on the fixed events.

In *Amir*, although the sentences were approved on the basis that the newspaper sting covered a betting scam (*R v Amir and another* [2011] EWCA Crim 2914 [3]) there was no evidence, and it is extremely unlikely, that there was one. That does not mean, of course, that there was no criminal conspiracy, nor that this might not have a glimpse at the tip of an iceberg. The case shows that a newspaper could pay people to breach their contracts by bowling no-balls, possibly thinking that there might be a betting scam, but nothing more than that. This is another of those regrettable cases where the conviction is for one thing and the sentence for another. The evidence did not show there to have been a betting coup. It does not really show any wrongdoing that need involve the criminal courts at all. It should have been dealt with as a disciplinary matter. In 'normal' cases arising from betting scams on cricket, prosecutors should use the gambling offence and not bribery, and where there is no gambling offence they should be circumspect about the use of bribery.[13] If anything, conspiracy to defraud, for all its faults, might have been a more appropriate charge. As a matter of labelling, it is important that the charge be the right one (Williams, 1983; Chalmers, 2008).

The crime of Westfield, an Essex county bowler, was far more typical of the problem of corruption in cricket. Allegedly recruited by his teammate Danesh Kanaria

13 4.There is a non-exhaustive definition of the offence in the Gambling Act 2005, s. 42: 'cheating at gambling may, in particular, consist of actual or attempted deception or interference in connection with—

'(a) the process by which gambling is conducted, or

(b) a real or virtual game, race or other event or process to which gambling relates.'

(Riach, 2013), he was offered and accepted £6,000 in return for agreeing deliberately to concede more than 12 runs off the first over he bowled in a limited overs match against Durham. Again, there was no significant betting market on the number of runs from a particular over. Nobody went into a bookmaker and said, 'I want to place a bet on the eighth over yielding twelve runs.' Westfield's over was the eighth. In 'spread betting', which is regulated by the Financial Conduct Authority, not the Gambling Commission, the bet pays more or less depending on how far from the spread the final result is. Suppose the bookmaker believes that in a given 10 overs, 67-73 runs will be scored. The spread ('bracket') will be set at 67-73. A gambler believes that there will be more than 73 runs, and 'buys' at £25 a point at 73. If the number of runs is 76, the gambler wins (16–13) = 3 x £25. If the number of runs is 10, the gambler loses (13–10) = 3 x £25. A 'sell' transaction is similar except that it is made against the bottom value of the spread. Often 'live pricing' will change the spread during the course of an event, allowing a profit to be increased or a loss minimised. If the bookmakers knew in advance how many runs are to be scored off (say) the eighth over of a set of ten, they could set the spread high, the punters sell and lose substantially. That was the Westfield scam. The sums of money being gambled daily on this sort of match, especially in India, are huge. In this case again the wrong charge was dropped. Westfield pleaded guilty to accepting or obtaining corrupt payments: a similar count of conspiracy to cheat was not proceeded with against him. It is the cheat charge that better describes what he did, and it is the mundane nature of the crime that makes it so dangerous.

Conclusions

That it concerned a low-profile match and low-profile cricketer made Westfield's crime the most insidious and the most difficult type to combat. What can be done? There is a range of possibilities.

(i) *Legalisation of gambling in India?* This has been suggested (Mahyera, 2012) and might help, but would only be as effective as the body that then regulated gambling.

(ii) *Better education of players?* ACSU does have in place a compulsory education scheme for professional cricketers. As a form of consciousness-raising and conveying the relevant rules avoiding misunderstandings this is helpful. Since it is the captains – the individuals singled out by Cowdrey and Dexter as the *custodes* – who have the most power to affect the matters on which betting takes place, it is them upon whom training and policing should focus.

(iii) *Greater powers to ACSU?* While ACSU might be worthwhile as an educative body, it is, as Strauss said, toothless without police powers with which to get access to phone records and similar types of evidence. Even if it had greater powers, it is so seriously under-resourced as to be, in practical terms, useless.

(iv) *Limit the range of bets that can lawfully be placed?* It is true that the availability of 'spot' betting – betting otherwise than on the final outcome of the match – has given rise to some betting scams. The accounts given by those involved in the three scams considered here all emphasise that they did not adversely affect their team's chances in the games in question – that they did not betray their team-mates. If bets could only be placed on the result, then the sorts of gambling fraud that could be justified by the players to themselves in this way would be ruled out. The argument against trying to do this has two strands. The practical one is that it is unlikely that any legal prohibition would be enforceable. All betting is illegal in India anyway. The objection of principle is that if consenting adults want to bet on insects climbing a wall, then they should not be stopped simply because of how other people might behave.

(v) *More aggressive prosecution policy?* There is nothing wrong with the current prosecution policy. The implied policy of prosecuting gambling scams when there is evidence is perfectly justifiable.

(vi) *Deployment of statistical evidence at trial.* One of the reasons that FSA/FCA has not prosecuted in a number of insider dealing cases in which the regulator thinks it is clear that insider dealing has taken place is that they say they do not have the evidence. Assume a number of trades made by an individual, of which some occur just before a significant rise in the share price, that rise coming as a result of an announcement of information which is price-sensitive. FCA does not currently prosecute without evidence of communication (phone records etc.). That is, at the moment they do not prosecute only on the probabilities. The same is true of gambling scams. It should be possible to convict without any evidence other than that of likelihood if the legitimate explanation for the events in question is sufficiently improbable.

(vii) *Captains.* It is no coincidence that two of the major wrongdoers in the cases under consideration – Cronje and Butt – were captains. It is the captain, usually when fielding, who has significantly the most power imperceptibly to diminish his side's prospects or to affect individual events. The idea in the Cowdrey/Dexter amendment that the captains should be the custodians of propriety is misplaced and smacks of snobbery. The captains are the people upon whom regulators should concentrate.

None of these is entirely satisfactory. As with any attempts to prevent market manipulation, it is difficult to police and enforce. Highly punitive responses to the few who will be caught plus more education seems to be one way forward, but this will only have limited effect while the risks of corruption are so small and the rewards so high.

The myth is that cricket is unique, partly because of its 'spirit', and is not corrupt. The reality is that it is just as much susceptible to attempts to corrupt as many other sports and, because of its complexity, is more vulnerable. Talk of the 'spirit' of the game gets in the way of action to combat corruption, and corruption is overwhelmingly the greatest threat to the game.

References

Alldridge, P., "The UK Bribery Act: The 'Caffeinated Younger Sibling' of the FCPA", *Ohio State Law Journal* 2012-3 73, 1181-1224.

Alldridge, P., "The Changing Contours of Bribery Prosecutions" in J. Horder, and P. Alldridge (eds), *Modern Bribery Law* (Cambridge: Cambridge University Press, 2013).

Asinof, E., *Eight Men Out: The Black Sox and the 1919 World Series* (NYC: Holt Paperbacks, 2000).

Astill, J., *The Great Tamasha: Cricket, Corruption and India's Unstoppable Rise* (London: John Wisden & Co Ltd, 2013).

BBC, "Match-fixing: Champions League tie played in England 'was fixed'", *BBC Sport*, 4 February 2013. http://www.bbc.co.uk/sport/0/football/21319807

Benammar, E., "Dean Richards ban: how 'Bloodgate' saga unfolded", *Daily Telegraph*, 18 August 2009.

Birley, D., *The Willow Wand* (2nd edn) (London: Aurum Press, 2000).

Blackstone's Commentaries on the Laws of England, IV, 360.

Bose, M., *The Magic Indian Cricket, Cricket and Society in India* (Revised edn) (London: Routledge, 2006).

Bowen, R., *Cricket: A History of its Growth and Development* (London: Eyre & Spottiswoode, 1970).

Briggs, S., "Match-fixing claims "unprovable"", *Daily Telegraph*, 31 January 2001.

Brunström, C., and Cassidy, T.M., "'Scorn Eunuch Sports': Class, Gender and the Context of Early Cricket", *Journal for Eighteenth-Century Studies* 2012 35, 223-237.

Central Bureau of Investigation, Report on cricket match-fixing and related malpractises, (New Dehli: Central Bureau of Investigation, October 2000). Chalmers, J. and Leverick, F. "Fair labelling in criminal law", *Modern Law Review* 2008 71, 217-238.

Dickson, P., *The Unwritten Rules of Baseball: The Etiquette, Conventional Wisdom, and Axiomatic Codes of Our National Pastime* (London: Harper, 2009).

Fox, K., *Watching the English: the hidden rules of English behaviour* (London: Nicholas Brealey Publishing, 2008).

Fraser, D., *Cricket and the Law: "The man in white is always right"* (2nd edn) (London: Routledge, 2005).

Guha, R., *A Corner of a Foreign Field: The Indian History of a British Sport* (London: Picador, 2002).

Harvey, A., "Playing by the Rules", *Sport in History* 2011 3, 330-339.

Hawkins, E., *Bookie Gambler Fixer Spy* (London: Bloomsbury, 2012).

Holden, G., "World Cricket as a Postcolonial International Society: IR Meets the History of Sport", *Global Society* 2008 22, 337-341.

Hoult, N., "Centurion 2000: Hussain still bitter about the day Cronje cheated", *Daily Telegraph*, 16 December 2004.

James, C., *Beyond a Boundary* (London: Stanley Paul, 1963).

Kaufman, J. and Patterson, O., "Cross-National Cultural Diffusion: The Global Spread of Cricket", *American Sociological Review* 2005 70, 82-110.

Law Commission, *Reforming Bribery*, Law Com. No.313, HC Paper No.928 (London: TSO, 2008).

Mahyera, R., "Saving Cricket: A Proposal for The Legalization Of Gambling In India To Regulate Corrupt Betting Practices In Cricket", *Emory International Law Review* 2012 26, 365-489.

Malcolm, D., "Cricket and Civilizing Processes A Response to Stokvis", *International Review for the Sociology of Sport* 2002 37, 37-57.

Malcolm, D., "The diffusion of cricket to America: A figurational sociological examination", *Journal of Historical Sociology* 2006 19, 151-173.

Marqusee, M., *Anyone But England: An Outsider Looks at English Cricket* (3rd edn) London: Aurum Press, 2005).

Marylebone Cricket Club, *The Laws of Cricket* 2000 Code (5th edn) (London: Marylebone Cricket Club, 2013).

Preston, H. (ed), *Wisden Cricketer's Almanac* 1949 (London: Wisden, 1950).(2nd edn)

Rae, S., *It's Not Cricket: Skullduggery, Sharp Practice and Downright Cheating in the Noble Game* (London: Faber and Faber, 2001).

Riach, J., "Danish Kaneria was subsequently banned for life: 'Panel rejects Danish Kaneria's appeal against life ban for spot-fixing", *The Guardian*, 27 April 2013.

Riordan, J., "Amateurism, sport and the left: amateurism for all versus amateur elitism", *Sport in History* 2006 26, 468-483.

Sandiford, K., "Cricket and the Victorian Society", *Journal of Social History* 1983 17, 303-317.

Serious Fraud Office, *Guidance on Deferred Prosecution Agreements* (London: Serious Fraud Office, 2013).

Simons, J., "The 'Englishness' of English Cricket", *Journal of Popular Culture* 1996 29, 41-50.

Smith, A. and Porter, D., *Amateurs and professionals in post-war British sport* (London: Routledge, 2000).

Speed, M., *Sticky Wicket: A Decade of Change in World Cricket* (London: HarperSports, 2011).

Stevens, R., "Ethics and the Statute of Frauds", *Cornell Law Quarterly* 1951-2 37, 355, 355.

Stokvis, R., "The civilizing process applied to sports. A response to Dominic Malcolm-cricket and civilizing processes", *International Review for the Sociology of Sport* 2005 40, 111-114.

Underdown, D., *Start of Play* (London: Allen Lane, 2000).

Wadhwaney, K., *Indian Cricket and Corruption* (Delhi: Siddharth Publications 2005).

Wagg, S., "'Time gentlemen please': The decline of amateur captaincy in English county cricket", *Contemporary British History* 2000 14, 31-59.

Wilkinson, R., "Political leadership and the late Victorian public school", *British Journal of Sociology* 1962 13, 320-330.

Williams, G., "Convictions and Fair Labelling", *Cambridge Law Journal* 1983 42, 85-95.

Williams, J., *Cricket and England: A Cultural and Social History of Cricket in England between the Wars. No. 8* (London: Frank Cass, 2003).

Children's Rights: Preventing the Use of State Care and Preventing Care Proceedings

Judith Masson
Bristol University, UK

Introduction

The Rights and Wrongs of Children (Freeman, 1983) captured the concerns about the role of state care in the early 1980s. Many of the worst defects of the public are system were swept away by the reforms of the Children Act 1989, the increased recognition of children as rights bearers and greater legal scrutiny of children's services departments. However, the fundamental issue of the proper role of the state in the care of children and young people remains, and with it questions about the rights of children and their parents, the obligations of the state and the processes to be used. Whilst at a theoretical level it might be possible to reach a settled agreement on these, changes in understanding of children's needs, developments in social work practice and shifts in the resources made available for children and families necessitate continual reassessment of how state care should be provided, used and arranged.

In his conclusion to chapter 5, 'Children of the State', Freeman wrote, 'Children should have the right not to be in care. Too many children are in care unnecessarily. Measures at state and local level could prevent children coming into care' (Freeman, 1983: 181). Freeman's call to prevent entry to care was clearly not a matter of 'abandoning children to their rights'. State care would continue to be necessary for some children, whose families were unable to provide an acceptable standard of care, but not *too many*. Preventing entry was not simply negative, imposing substantive or procedural barriers against state intervention. Rather, it required *measures*, positive action. Both central government and the local state needed to provide alternatives to care, which would enable children to remain with their families and receive good enough care.

This chapter explores the policy and practice of prevention of state care in the 21st century and the extent to which they support children's rights to care and not to be in state care unnecessarily. It uses the term 'care' in the broader sense, as Freeman did, of children being looked after by the state, rather than limited to those who are on care orders under the Children Act 1989. Specifically, it examines two positive approaches to prevention, the provision of family support and the use of a formalised pre-pro-

A. Diduck, N. Peleg, H. Reece (eds.), Law in Society: Reflections on Children, Family, Culture and Philosophy
 ISBN 978-90-04-26148-8. pp. 347-365.

ceedings process to divert families from care proceedings. The section on the pre-proceedings process draws on an ESRC-funded study into its operation and impact. The *Families on the Edge of Care Proceedings* study was conducted with Dr. Jonathan Dickens from the Centre for Research on Children and Families, University of East Anglia, in six local authorities between 2010 and 2012 (Masson *et al.*, 2013; Dickens *et al.*, 2013). This chapter argues that securing some children's rights to care by their family requires both the availability of family support services and processes to assist some parents to make use of these. Also, that state care remains a positive option for some children in the care of relatives, largely because of lack of financial and other support for such carers. Prevention of state care thus remains a contingent goal, which depends on the available alternatives for securing children's well-being. Finally, where the family cannot or will not provide good enough care, there should be a right to state care which enables children and young people to achieve their potential.

Too Many? The Numbers of Children in the Care System

Both the number and rate per 10,000 of children in public care declined from the early 1980s to the late 1990s (Rowlands and Statham, 2009). These reductions reflect changes in policy and practice, which have kept most young offenders out of the care system, raised the threshold for care proceedings, increasingly relied on the wider family to care for children who cannot remain at home and promoted adoption for young children in care. The high cost of care (Beecham and Sinclair, 2007), shortages of placements and the difficulties of rehabilitating children home (Bullock *et al.*, 1993; Farmer, 2012) have all encouraged local authorities to establish strong gate-keeping procedures to prevent entry to s. 20 accommodation (Packman and Hall, 2008). The emphasis in decisions in the European Court of Human Rights on care as a temporary measure (*Johansen v. Norway* (1996) 23 EHRR 33, para. 78) has encouraged this trend, with the government (and local authorities) being required to explain why children cannot return to their family (*YC v. UK* (2012) App. No. *4547/10* ECtHR).

Increases in the care population in the decade from 1999 largely reflected increases in the length of time children and young people remained in the care system (Rowlands and Statham, 2009). Two major factors have contributed to the increasing length of care careers. First, delaying young people's exit from the care system reversed a trend of abandoning young people to early independence by design (pushing children out of the care system) or by default (a lack of suitable placements for older, young people). The Children (Leaving Care) Act 2000 made local authorities, not the benefit system, responsible for supporting care leavers under the age of 18 years. In keeping with changes in wider society and recognition of the vulnerability of children who have been brought up in care (Stein, 2008), increased emphasis was put on caring for young people in state care. This has resulted in the development of better support for young people when they leave care and rights for some young people to remain in care or to return if they leave before the age of 18 years (Munro *et al.*, 2010a, 2010b). Secondly, and less positively, the increasing number and length of care proceedings meant that children spent long periods in care before decisions for placement in the care of relatives or adoption (DCA and DfES, 2006; DfE, 2012).

The Green Paper, *Care Matters: Transforming the Lives of Children and Young People* (DfES. 2006), questioned whether more children should be supported in their families with a consequent reduction in the care population. The working group set up to examine this were concerned that lower numbers of care proceedings might mean that some local authorities were failing to make applications. However, they concluded that a numerical approach to determining the size of the care population could be damaging to individual children and that more should be done to support children aged 11-15 outside the care system because of the poor outcomes for those who enter at this time (Narey, 2007).

More recently, the death of 'Baby P' (Haringey LSCB, 2009) has resulted in a very substantial increase in care proceedings and in the numbers of children in care (ADCS, 2010, 2012). In part, this increase is a result of the pressure social workers and local authorities experience in the face of a media storm following the highly publicised and hideous death of a child who had a child protection plan. It also reflects recognition of the inadequacy of family support, where professional capacity to engage families is limited and parents are not committed to working with social workers to achieve change.

Not only has there been a change in the number of children looked after by the state, there have also been changes in the circumstances of children who are looked after, and the quality of the care provided. Over time, care has come to be used differently. In the 21st century, children in care are far more likely to have been made the subject of a court order than in the 1980s and to be in care because of abuse or neglect. Entry to the care system is often the culmination of a long process during which the local authority and the court have explored alternatives to making a care order (Masson *et al.*, 2008, 2013). Young children tend to leave care for relative placements or adoptive homes, whilst those who enter later, grow up in care (Sinclair *et al.*, 2007). This underlines the role that state care has both as a place of last resort (Hunt *et al.*, 1999) and a childhood home for children and young people who can neither return to their families nor be found an adoptive family.

As a result of concerns about the quality of care and the poor outcomes for looked after children (Select Committee on Health, 1997-8) considerable efforts (and resources) have been committed to improving and ensuring the quality of the care provided. Looked after children have additional rights to education and more attention is given to their experience of the care system through children's rights services and local care councils. Local authorities are 'corporate parents' and councillors are encouraged to consider, 'If this was my child...' (DfES and LGIU, 2003). Preventing entry to care can no longer be seen as a simple protective measure, which values children's families and saves children from poor quality substitute care. However, social engineering is never acceptable; an assessment that care might be better than home can never justify a decision to remove a child from their family (*Re SB (Children)* [2009] UKSC 17, Hale B. at para. 7). Also, entry to care creates as well as resolves problems; children are often relieved to be in care but they miss their families and worry about their future (Ofsted 2009; 2012).

In the absence of any alternative sources of support such as benefits for relative carers or supported housing for children whose parents cannot, or will not, provide for them, local authority care is an essential service. For those who are cared for by relatives, the benefits of being a 'looked-after child' – financial (and other) support before and after age 18 – place young people in a markedly better position (Selwyn *et al.*, 2013). This form of state care is not something to be prevented, although the need for such support to be under the umbrella of *care* can be questioned. A more equitable arrangement would link provision of resources to need rather than placement status (Hunt and Waterhouse, 2013). If this were done, the numbers of young people in public care could be reduced. Even greater advantages would be gained by children and young people living with relatives, whose lives and futures are severely constrained by poverty. However, it seems unlikely that central government would be willing to extend the benefits system in this way, or that local authorities could extend the support provided for looked after children to the much larger number of children in the care of relatives outside the care system.

Prevention and the Children Act 1989

The Children Act 1989 sought to move away from the narrow idea of prevention in child welfare to the broader notion of 'family support'. Rather than merely using services to prevent children's entry to care (Child Care Act 1980, s. 1), local authorities were given a 'general duty' to safeguard and promote the welfare of 'children in need' and so far as this was consistent, to promote their upbringing by their families (Children Act 1989, s. 17(1)). Statutory Guidance (DH, 1991) emphasised the wide discretion that local authorities had to provide family support and the consequent need to establish priorities. The training materials developed for the implementation the Act noted that, 'Part III comes before Part IV' that is, compulsory measures of care should only be used where family support services were inadequate to protect children (DH and FRG, 1991). Within this context, (voluntary) accommodation for a child (s. 20) was seen as a service to the family at a time of acute family stress, not something that had to be prevented.

The new approach and wider powers did not come with additional resources (Masson, 1992). Rather than developing broad programmes to provide support for families, local authorities were constrained to focus their resources on the cases of greatest concern. Although they provided (or commissioned) some primary prevention services, resources were focused on secondary prevention: family support for children whose health or development were already impaired, particularly those at risk of neglect or abuse (Parton, 1997), and tertiary prevention: services to repair harm to children, including to assist with rehabilitation or re-unification. The Act supported this approach through specific duties for prevention of neglect and abuse (Sched. 2, para. 4) and to investigate cases of actual or suspected significant harm (s. 47). Local authorities retained powers to bring care proceedings; resources for preventive services were continually under pressure from the need to protect children.

In the 1990s, there was an attempt to refocus children's services away from a child protection orientation and towards provision of family services (DH, 1995; Gilbert *et al.*, 2011) but this had only limited effect. The demands of the protection system, particularly the increasing complexity and cost of legal proceedings, and the ways local authority performance was monitored and funded, made it difficult to redirect services.

Resource constraints resulted in local authorities refusing requests for services, even where families were clearly in need. Legal challenge to such decisions explored the nature of the 'general duty' and the extent of local authority children's services' responsibilities for homeless families or destitute young people, and thus rights to s. 20 accommodation or other services. The wording of s. 17 was construed as providing wide discretion to local authorities, allowing them to refuse services unless doing so breached the European Convention on Human Rights or was unreasonable (*R. (ota G) v. Barnet LBC* [2003] UKHL 57). Thus a challenge to a policy, which would separate homeless families through limiting support to care for the children in a foster home, rather than accommodation for the family together, was unsuccessful (*R. (ota W) v. Lambeth LBC* [2003] UKHL 57). The courts were more responsive when it came to the duty to accommodate young people estranged from their families, rejecting a number of approaches local authorities developed to limit their responsibilities. So, where housing was provided for young people without carers, they were held to be 'accommodated under s. 20' and were therefore owed 'leaving care' duties (*R. (ota Behre) v. Hillingdon LBC* [2003] EWHC 2075). Similarly, local authorities were no longer able to avoid their responsibilities to homeless 16- and 17-year olds, by providing only assistance on the basis that they were resourceful enough to find their own accommodation (*R. (ota G) v. Southwark LBC* [2009] UKHL 26). Nor could social workers request relatives to care for a child who needed protection and then treat the arrangement as a private, family matter rather than the provision of s. 20 accommodation through a family placement (*R. (SA) v. Kent CC* [2011] EWCA Civ. 1303). Effectively, the Children Act 1989 had created rights to care but left preventive services discretionary.

The Labour Government's focus on social exclusion gave a new impetus to family support and to primary prevention. New universal services were provided for pre-school children by *Sure Start*, in children's centres, initially in deprived areas. Early intervention services, provided largely on a voluntary basis, were developed as a way of preventing problems associated with poor parenting, which might lead to problems such as poor educational outcomes and unemployment, later. The *Every Child Matters* programme (H.M. Government, 2004) also sought to shift to prevention whilst strengthening protection, countering what might otherwise have been a greater emphasis on child protection investigation in the wake of the Victoria Climbié Inquiry (Laming, 2003). However, protection work again dominated local authority concerns following the media storm in the wake of the 'Baby P' case (Haringey, 2009).

The outlook for primary prevention appears much less positive under the Coalition government with cuts in services and reductions in the income of some of the poorest families. Although Eileen Munro's *Review of Child Protection*, set up by the Coalition government (Munro, 2011) stressed the value of 'early help' and preventive rather than reactive services, there has been little progress in developing these. Changes to the welfare system, particularly the capping of benefits, are having the greatest impact on large families. *Sure Start* is being cut back to focus on the neediest families and children centres closed; reduced budgets are resulting in major cuts to many other local authority services. Reduction of income and moving away from family and support networks as a result of the cap on housing benefit will leave some families struggling to cope. Preventive services have not completely disappeared but rarely provide the long-term support some families need (Featherstone *et al.*, 2013).

Substantial budget cuts are also forcing local authorities to rethink the use of their most expensive service – care. The Early Intervention Foundation (earlyintervention-foundation.org.uk) is promoting alternatives, including to prevent family breakdown without the need to provide full-time care. The early intervention approach emphasises intervening early, with young children and before problems become entrenched, the use of evidence-based programmes and joint working across agencies. Where alternative services truly meet children's needs they are a welcome development, strengthening preventative work. However, there are risks that a lack of evidence results in negative assumptions about services, thresholds are raised even higher, children are left without care and action is only taken where families are seen as a problem to others. There has long been recognition that there are very disadvantaged families, with multiple and complex problems who repeatedly interact with a range of public services in relation to physical and mental health, housing and benefits and their children's care and behaviour. Concerns about the costs of these families in current service provision, on local communities, and for children's futures as adults, led to the development of new approaches. Family Intervention Projects provide intensive support, either in their own homes or in separate 'core units' to help families make changes, and have succeeded in reducing some problem behaviours and improving family functioning (Action for Children, 2011). Focusing much of the rhetoric on the problems these families cause rather than those such as poverty, health and social exclusion that they experience (Levitas, 2012), the government has established the *Troubled Families Programme* (DCLG, 2012) to target such families. Local authorities are required to operate the programme in their area. This is providing forms of family support, preventing family breakdown and admission to care but the language has shifted: this is family intervention by workers who have 'a persistent, assertive and challenging approach' (DCLG, 2012: 7).

Whilst family support under the Children Act 1989 was expected to be provided 'in partnership' with families so families agreed what services they used, the reality for families at the edge of care because of child protection concerns has always involved at least the possibility of coercion. A failure to accept or use services identifies parents as 'unco-operative' and raises levels of concern, making compulsory measures more likely (Platt, 2006). Conversely, where parents are willing to work with children's services, higher levels of risk can be managed (Platt and Turney, 2013). Emergency protection powers are used where families in extreme crisis refuse to agree to placement of their child in foster care or with relatives, and offers of s. 20 accommodation sometimes make clear that they cannot really be refused (DH, 2001; Masson, 2005). Such practices highlight the problem of treating the provision of accommodation simply as a service, and family support as optional where children are in need of protection. They also raise questions about protecting rights where arrangements are not truly voluntary, and how this might be done.

Preventing Care Proceedings and the Introduction of the Pre-proceedings Process

The rationale for preventing care proceedings was more limited than for preventing entry to care. The concerns were not primarily with respecting children's right to life with their family or avoiding the damaging aspects of the care system. Rather, they were about reducing the burden that care proceedings placed on the courts, the time taken in proceedings and the cost to the legal aid system of those proceedings.

Concerns about the cost of the care proceedings system and the time taken by courts to make decisions about children led to the government establishing the *Child Care Proceedings System Review* in 2005 (DCA and DfES, 2006). The Review forecast an increase in the number of proceedings and sought to reduce the pressure on courts in a number of ways. First, it sought to prevent the need for care proceedings by encouraging parents to address the local authority's concerns. Secondly, it wanted to ensure that local authorities prepared court applications more thoroughly. Thirdly, it recommended that parents had legal advice from a specialist solicitor before proceedings were issued so that they could be helped to understand the concerns and engage with proceedings from the start. It brought these ideas together, suggesting an immediate pilot and evaluation of a scheme to establish, 'the impact of early advice on the parents' experience of and engagement with the system; the extent to which early advice can ensure that cases only reach ... proceedings when all safe and appropriate alternatives have been explored; and the impact of early advice on cases that go to court' (DCA and DfES, 2006: 5.11). The Review did not seek to explain why such a process might be effective but noted that most proceedings led to children's permanent removal from their parents and most parents praised their solicitors.

Preventing care proceedings whilst securing children's rights to protection from significant harm depends on improvement in the way the parents care for their children or parental agreement for an alternative care arrangement, either care by relatives or s. 20 accommodation. That a relatively simple intervention might be able to achieve this appeared to suggest that local authorities brought proceedings too readily, a view that was not supported by research evidence of high thresholds and cases resulting in orders (Brophy, 2006; Masson *et al.*, 2008). Where proceedings were not prevented, the intention was that the pre-proceedings process would enable proceedings to be completed more swiftly. The pre-proceedings period would provide time for the local authority to complete assessments and so there would be less need to commission expert reports in proceedings and fewer late claims by relatives to look after a child. However, achieving speedier court decision-making also required changes in court practice. Rather than conducting their own assessments of the child's needs and the parents' capacity to care, using experts appointed at the request of the parents, courts would need to focus more narrowly on examining the key issues to be decided in the local authority's case. This would involve a change of culture and more robust case management so that proceedings could be completed in the timetable for the child (President of the Family Division, 2008).

The scheme was not piloted, nor was there any discussion of its theoretical or social work practice underpinnings. Rather, the idea was taken forward with the reforms to care proceedings in statutory guidance for local authorities (DCSF, 2008). This set out the formal pre-proceedings process to be followed before proceedings were issued, unless 'the scale, nature and urgency' of safeguarding concerns meant it could not be used (DCA and DfES, 2006: para. 3.30).

What is the Pre-proceedings Process?

The process appears very simple as set out in the *Children Act 1989, Guidance and Regulations, Volume 1* (DCSF, 2008). It is triggered by the local authority's decision, taken with legal advice, that the threshold for care proceedings is met. The social worker then sends the parents a 'letter before proceedings', listing concerns about the children's care and inviting them to a 'pre-proceedings meeting' to discuss these. Under a heading, 'HOW TO AVOID GOING TO COURT' (DCSF 2008, 73), the letter warns parents of the possibility of proceedings and advises them to take the letter to a solicitor so that they can be accompanied at the meeting by a solicitor (or a paralegal). The letter before proceedings entitles the parents to free legal advice under legal aid, with solicitors paid a fixed fee (£365) for providing this service. The Guidance includes no further advice about the meeting, but states that its outcome should be explained to the parents orally and by letter. Nor does it make any links to other local authority processes such as child protection planning or looked after child (LAC) review. However, local authorities are required to file pre-proceedings documents with any subsequent applications for care proceedings (President of the Family Division, 2008). In this way, the court is made aware that the process has been used, and local authorities are made accountable if they fail to alert parents of serious concerns.

Although the guidance suggests a free-standing process and a single meeting, in practice it is part of a longer relationship between children's services and parents. In the *Families on the Edge of Care Proceedings Study*, over 80 per cent of the children whose care was considered under the pre-proceedings process were subject to child protection plans and a quarter had been on plans for a year or more (Masson *et al.*, 2013). The letter before proceedings marked a 'step up' in the local authority's action; a court order had not yet been obtained but parents in pre-proceedings were not voluntary clients. Rather, their failure to make the changes set out in the child protection plan identified them as 'highly resistant' (Fauth *et al.*, 2010).

Does the Pre-proceedings Process Work?

Although the Ministry of Justice commissioned an 'early evaluation' into the new court procedures for care proceedings (Jessiman *et al.*, 2009), there were no plans for research on the pre-proceedings process. Indeed, the only data about use of the process was the number of bills solicitors submitted to the Legal Services Commission for doing this work. These showed that nationally, over 6,200 parents obtained pre-proceedings legal advice in 2009-10, a wide variation in the numbers doing so in different local authorities and considerable change over time (Masson *et al.*, 2013). However, it was not possible to determine from these figures the proportion of cases where the pre-proceedings process was used, or the effect the process had on them. This is what the *Families on the Edge of Care Proceedings* study aimed to do. By examining the use of the process in six local authorities and comparing cases with and without pre-proceedings, it was possible to establish its effects. The quantitative study analysed local authority legal department records: 120 files where the process was used and 87 files where care proceedings were started without a pre-proceedings letter or meeting. A parallel qualitative study in the same authorities, included observations of 36 pre-proceedings meetings and interviews with those who participated in them: 24 parents, 35 lawyers (representing parents or the local authority) and 35 social workers or social work managers (Masson *et al.*, 2013).

Care proceedings were avoided in a quarter of the file cases where the pre-proceedings process was used. This was not simply a short-term effect; none of these cases had entered care proceedings within a year. A higher proportion of the observed cases had not resulted in proceedings by the end of the study but the follow up period was shorter. Out of 30 cases in the file sample where the local authority decided not to bring proceedings, parental care improved in 16 and in another 10, alternative care arrangements were made, 6 with relatives and 4 in s. 20 foster care, including one with the child's grandmother. In four other cases, the file disclosed insufficient information to be clear why proceedings had not been brought. Improved care was not the only factor which kept cases out of care proceedings; difficulties in proving significant harm because of the passage of time or the nature of the evidence contributed to local authority reluctance to start proceedings in a few cases. For example, it would probably not have been possible to satisfy the significant harm test where a young child with multiple carers had sustained non-accidental injuries; the child now appeared safe living with his father away from the rest of the family and so proceedings were not needed.

Where the process did not succeed in diverting cases from proceedings (86 cases), it was also unsuccessful in shortening the duration of care proceedings and narrowing the issues in dispute. Cases where the pre-proceedings process had been used took almost the same time as those that went directly to court, approximately 51 weeks from application to final hearing. This occurred because courts treated cases where the pre-proceedings process had been used no differently from other care cases. Judges did not manage these proceedings more robustly but continued to approve parents' requests for further assessments. Indeed, judges, who participated in a focus group for the research, said they were unaware whether the local authority had used the pre-proceedings process and were reluctant to accept its assessments. As a consequence, local authorities became more reluctant to commission expert assessments during the pre-proceedings period. Only one of the six authorities made frequent use of an external assessment service and had ceased doing so by the end of the study. The time spent in pre-proceedings meant that children waited longer for decisions where their case was not successfully diverted (Masson *et al.,* 2013).

How Does the Pre-proceedings Process Work?

The perspectives of the parents on the receiving end of the pre-proceedings process, their lawyers and the local authority professionals involved, provide the basis for explaining how the pre-proceedings process prevented care proceedings, using social work theories of parental involvement, empowerment and engagement. There is no magic in the meeting, rather the process as a whole can provide the foundation for an effective partnership between the parents and the social worker (Dickens *et al.,* 2013).

The letter gave a stark indication of seriousness of the local authority's concerns often referred to by parents and professionals alike as 'a wake up call'. It was a clear demonstration of the social worker's power to take their concerns to the court. The mention of the need to take action to 'avoid going to court' and the importance of seeing a solicitor both reinforced this message. The letter invited the parents to a meeting, indicating that they could have some involvement in decisions. Importantly, it suggested their situation was not hopeless; they *could* avoid court. The literature on working with highly resistant families (Fauth *et al.,* 2010) stresses the importance of involving families and dealing openly with the power dynamic between them and social workers. If parents are to try to make changes they need to feel that they can succeed; self-esteem, competence and hope have all been linked to parents engaging with social workers to resolve problems (Yatchmenoff, 2008).

Parents said they were 'shocked' by the letter; most responded by following the instruction to see a solicitor. Solicitors advised parents to co-operate with children's services on the basis that it would be harder for them to keep their children if proceedings were started:

> This is the last chance saloon. You either row in now or you're going to end up in court, and trying to undo it is going to be a damn sight harder than it is to stick to the contract. (Parent's solicitor.)

Such advice was not intended to produce mere compliance – lawyers told their clients that the local authority could not easily be diverted. Lawyers also provided a positive message, 'you can beat them', indicating that the solicitor had faith in the client, in their capacity to do what was necessary and the possibility of winning against children's services. This encouragement was not usually based on knowledge of the client or on an appraisal of the local authority's concerns; lawyers rarely knew enough about the circumstances to assess the strength of a case at the start of the process. Solicitors also tried to improve their client's position by making sure that clients understood what they were agreeing and social workers did not impose terms that parents could not keep, seeking adjustments in any that might be easily broken. For example, where a parent was required not to contact a specific person, usually an abusive partner or relative, lawyers raised the issue of unplanned meetings in the street, where a parent might feel obliged at least to be civil.

The solicitors' role is widely recognised as a partisan supporter (Davis, 1988). Even though most had only spoken to their lawyer once before the meeting, parents trusted that the lawyer would act in their interests:

> You know that everyone in the room is against you... and when you've got your solicitor with you, you know they're the only person who's 100% backing you up, so it helps you. (Parent.)

Support, including legal advocacy, is recognised as a means of encouraging parental participation in child protection (Darlington *et al.*, 2011). This was its effect in many of the pre-proceedings meetings observed. It was notable that most parents' solicitors said relatively little in these meetings, leaving the talking to parents themselves. This allowed parents to show that they were willing to discuss the local authority's concerns. However, lawyers were clearly listening attentively and intervened occasionally to clarify points, or to take a parent out of the meeting before they got too angry or distressed.

Parents were more willing to accept their lawyer's advice than the same advice from the social worker, a point noted by many of the local authority staff interviewed:

> Their solicitor would say to them clearly, 'this is serious stuff' – so it's not just us as a department saying it – or nagging them to death, as they might well see it – there's somebody else outside the authority actually saying to them that this needs to change. (Team Manager.)

This feeling that the lawyer was helpful to the local authority encouraged social workers and their managers to be positive about the process and to use it to promote change. Effective engagement can only occur where social worker *and* client are willing to engage (Darlington *et al.*, 2011). Some social worker managers used the meeting skilfully to harness the parents' assumed desire to do the best for their children, focusing on what the parents could do to achieve this:

> [I] try and focus on where we would like to go from here – trying to see if there are some positives, and try to hang on to those and try and move those forward.

Having a solicitor at the meeting and legal advice made a substantial difference to parents. Not only did they feel encouraged and supported, some thought that social workers moderated their behaviour because of it. Parents felt less 'picked on', were more willing to accept the social worker's proposals and were reassured by the prospect of the lawyer's assistance if the local authority did not keep to the agreement. Support and the feeling that the social worker was controlled empowered parents, redressing the power imbalance inherent in any child protection meeting. As a consequence, parents were more willing to engage with the local authority's plan for their child. Empowerment (Fauth *et al.*, 2010), redressing power imbalances and using power with parents not over them (Dumbrill, 2006) are seen as crucial for successful social work intervention. They provide a foundation for parental engagement, a state where the parent does not merely comply with the terms of the agreement but 'buys in' to the idea that they will make changes in their parenting (Yatchmenoff, 2008) and is a 'key contributor' to effective helping (Munro, 2011: para. 2.24).

Of course, these positive effects were not present in all cases. Some meetings were quite negative; some were not well prepared, held in unsuitable rooms and poorly conducted, or with two parents who were not well supported or were in conflict with each other. There were also parents who felt disempowered and did not engage, despite the presence of their lawyer. A substance misusing mother, who had already lost the care of her older children to her mother, explained why she had agreed to her new baby also being placed there, despite having told her solicitor earlier that she was opposed to this:

> ... some things I don't agree with but I feel pushed to go along with it, because in the past I have sort of said I don't agree with something and then it has been, 'Okay then, we will just go to court', so now I keep my mouth quiet about things I don't agree with ...

Overall, the pre-proceedings process has the potential to deliver key aspects of a successful intervention with highly resistant parents. It can empower parents; it limits the extent to which social workers can use power over them; and it allows parents some involvement. In this way it can provide a foundation for their engagement and an effective partnership with the social worker, sometimes a new social worker for the family. The partisan role of the lawyer is a catalyst whose presence makes the difference for the parent. This supports the provision of services for families at the edge of care proceedings; some parents engage with services they had rejected earlier. The process provides a 'last chance' for some parents to avoid care proceedings, either by improving their care or agreeing to change of the child's carer. This effect also depends on the capacity of the social work staff to use the process to establish a working partnership with the parents.

In a minority of cases, the process prevented both care proceedings and the child's entry to the care system. Where only proceedings were prevented, it helped ensure that kin care was considered before foster care, either by encouraging parents to suggest a suitable relative carer or by encouraging their agreement to a family group conference, where the family had an opportunity to make its own plan. Where the parents agreed alternative care, legal advice helped to ensure that they understood what was proposed, and their continued role. In some cases the process could be as effective as care proceedings in protecting the rights of parents.

Children's Rights and the Pre-proceedings Process

There is no special provision for children in the pre-proceedings process although in care proceedings they have representation by both a lawyer and children's guardian. The effect is to leave children's involvement in the shadows, and dependent on the beliefs, capacity and creativity of parents and social workers. Local authorities have a duty to ascertain the views of children they propose to look after (Children Act 1989, s. 22(4) but must respect 'parental sensitivity' in the pre-proceedings process (DCSF, 2008: 3.28). Lawyers have criticised the lack of representation for children, suggesting that they had no voice in the process (MacDonald, 2008; Jessiman, 2009). In response, the 'best practice guide' advised always considering children's invitation to the meeting and how to include their views; if parents vetoed attendance, children should be told how to use the complaints process (MoJ and DCSF, 2009: 13). Additionally, Cafcass piloted a form of the process where a family court adviser attended the pre-proceedings meeting. Advisers provided 'essential oversight' of the child's best interests and advice on the social work plan, largely on the basis of their expertise rather than direct knowledge of the child (Broadhurst *et al.*, 2011). Although this approach made claims to provide representation for children, or at least children's welfare, it appeared only to provide another professional view.

Being absent from the meeting or without external representation does not necessarily mean that children's views are excluded in decision making. There were examples of social workers working with children to establish their views before the meeting and ensuring that decisions took full account of these. Skilled direct work enabled Belinda Charlery (a pseudonym), aged 13, to talk to her social worker about her exceptionally difficult relationship with her mother, who had learning difficulties. At the pre-proceedings meeting, Ms Charlery accepted that she could not keep Belinda safe and agreed to her going into foster care (s. 20), without being told just how unhappy Belinda was, living at home. This approach protected Belinda's rights and provided a better prospect for repairing relationships than more direct discussion which would have been hard to control had Belinda attended the meeting.

Many other children whose care was considered in the pre-proceedings process were babies, a third of cases included a child who had not yet been born. The focus in these meetings was the children's current and future well-being; social workers sought to maintain parents' attention on this rather than on talk about parents' rights or the local authority's powers. Some children were accorded the same rights as adults in the pre-proceedings process. Where children were also parents, they had the same representation as other parents, whose care was a cause of concern. For these very young parents, lawyers' previous experience representing children was particularly valuable in enabling them to establish a rapport, take instructions and provide advice (Masson *et al.*, 2013).

Not all children had their rights adequately protected in the pre-proceedings process. None entered care inappropriately but some waited too long for the local authority to react to their parents' failure to keep to the plan and these delays were compounded by the length of care proceedings. That said, by giving the parents another chance to work with children's services and helping them to engage, the process helped some children remain with their parents or live with relatives, who would otherwise have entered care.

A Counter to Freeman – a Right to State Care

Freeman argued for a right *not* to be in state care so that preventive services would be given a higher priority. This has been done to some extent. One consequence of prioritising prevention and family care is that state care has not been valued or adequately supported. Use of state care meant failure (by the family and the worker); the quality of care was poor so care should be prevented, not improved. The consequences of the neglect of residential care homes and the young people placed within them were only two apparent in the Pindown and Leicestershire Inquiries (Levy and Kahan, 1991; Kirkwood, 1993) into abuse in care. They are also seen in foster care, where the development and support of carers has not kept pace with the increasing complexity of the children needing care, and carers are still seen primarily as volunteers who are reimbursed for their expense rather than as an integral part of the social care workforce.

Making a case for a right to be in care is not intended to place care above prevention, or to justify social engineering, but to stress that the state has obligations to care for those without adequate care elsewhere. This reflects the right to special protection and assistance in Art. 20 of the UNCRC. Viewing care as a residual service rather than a right, results in some children waiting too long for care, being returned to inadequate homes or being left without the care they need. Care is not an end in itself but must exist to enable children to reach their potential (ADCS, 2013).

Delayed entry to care is a frequent concern of Cafcass guardians (Cafcass, 2009 2012), occurring particularly where children are neglected. There were examples in the *Families on the Edge of Care Study* of cases drifting in pre-proceedings, with the local authority taking no action despite parental failure to comply with the written agreement; on average almost six months elapsed between the legal planning meeting and the care application for cases subject to the pre-proceedings system which were not diverted from proceedings. Long durations in pre-proceedings reflected indecisiveness by social workers, poor monitoring and a strong desire on the part of the local authority to avoid bringing proceedings. The majority of the children were living with the parents at home and continued to experience a lack of care until they were removed in the course of care proceedings (Masson *et al.*, 2013).

Despite recognition of the importance of continuity of care for children's development, repeated attempts are made to return children from care, which result in re-abuse. Reunification is attempted despite lack of change by parents or support, sometimes because suitable care is not available (Hunt and Macleod, 1999; Farmer, 2012). Decisions of the European Court of Human Rights that care should generally be seen as a temporary measure encourage this, valuing family reunification over continuity of care.

Poor outcomes have resulted in local authorities being reluctant to offer care for children aged 11-16 years rather than the development of more effective ways of providing care to them. This is now being challenged by the Association of Directors of Children's Services, which is arguing for the re-design of services across youth justice, health, education and children's social care to provide a continuum of support to meet the needs of troubled adolescents appropriately (ADCS, 2013).

A right to care should also mean the continuation of care for young people beyond the age of 18 years, so that the care system recognises, as families do, that young adults continue to need support. The Government's *Care Leaver Strategy* (HM Government, 2013) recognises the need for support but sees its own role largely as a 'catalyst and advocate' rather than a provider, despite the fact that major changes to the welfare state in terms of benefits, education costs and employment opportunities are a direct result of central government policies. Leaving responsibility for provision largely to local government as in the case of relative care is inadequate and unfair.

A right to care is meaningless without sufficient resources. To achieve the best for children, the right to care must be funded and exist alongside rights to other services so decisions are made on the basis of what is right for the child.

Conclusions: Problems and Possibilities in Preventing and Providing State Care

The Children Act 1989 ideal of support provided in partnership with families was never realised because of a lack of resources. The aspirational statement of a general duty to promote welfare and support families is an unrealisable sham. Local authorities gained powers to help families but were constrained by limited resources to focus on those most in need. That situation still pertains. The courts have crystallised some duties which support homeless young people and a small, select group of relative carers. However, whilst resources remain inadequate, new duties serve to limit further the possibilities of support for those with needs but not enforceable rights. Attempts to redirect resources from child protection to family support have also failed; the pressure from the media, the public and central government to secure protection has increased bureaucracy and in doing so sucked in resources. Rather than allowing local authorities to decide whom they will help and how, they are now directed to deal with 'troubled families' in specific ways. In this shift, both local authority intervention and care are stigmatised further, making it harder to encourage families to accept help.

Preventing *unnecessary* entry to care is a policy that cannot be disputed. However, preventive action has to be resourced, and delivered in ways that enable children and their families to use it. As the local state retrenches, preventive work is also being curtailed, provided only for those at the very edge of care. Not only may this mean that opportunities are missed to provide more effective help earlier, there is also increased pressure to ensure that the available help is accepted. Rather than a service to families, preventive work becomes an extension of compulsory action, where refusal will inexorably lead to proceedings. This provides a very challenging context for working with families, who need to be empowered if they are to be engaged.

When Michael Freeman promoted the idea of a right not to be in care, he was concerned about the stigma of being in care, its poor quality, the narrow horizons the state had for the children in its care and the lack of alternatives to care for parents in difficulty. Providing care was an easy option for the state but a poor one for children and families.

The right not to be in care looks rather different in the 21st century. Rights and resources for children in care have improved considerably the lives of those in care, and far more emphasis is placed on keeping children out of care and in their families through reliance on relatives. Whilst some family placements bring advantages, they often leave children poorly provided for. In assessing when entry to care is necessary, and when it should be prevented, the reality of children's lives must be considered: what care provides and what will be provided without it. The disparities in support available to children in these different care arrangements are very great, and continue as long as leaving care duties are owed, to the age of 25 years. There are children who would be better provided for if their relative carer was approved as a local authority foster carer. While none of those concerned – the child, the relative carer, the parents and the local authority – want this, such arrangements are easily prevented. Not only should relative carers be better supported but there should be rights to care for those whose relatives cannot care. A continuum of preventive and care services is required to enable all children to reach their potential.

References

Action for Children, *Intensive Family Support: The evidence* (Watford: Action for Children, 2011).

Association of Directors of Children's Services, *Safeguarding pressures Report Phase 2: Exploring reasons and the effect* (Manchester: ADCS, 2010).

Association of Directors of Children's Services, *Safeguarding pressures Report Phase 3* (Manchester: ADCS, 2012).

Association of Directors of Children's Services, *Position statement: what is care for: Alternative models of care for adolescents* (Manchester: ADCS, 2013).

Beecham, K. and Sinclair, L., *Costs and outcomes in children's social care* (London: DfES, 2007).

Brophy, J., *Research review: child care proceedings under the Children Act 1989*, DCA Research Series 5/06 (London: Department for Constitutional Affairs, 2006).

Bullock, R., Little, M. and Millham, S., *Going home: The return of children separated from their families* (Aldershot: Dartmouth, 1993).

Cafcass, *The Baby Peter effect and the increase in s31 care order applications* (London: Cafcass, 2009).

Cafcass, *Three Weeks in November, Three Years On: Cafcass Care Application Study* (London: Cafcass, 2012).

Darlington, Y., Healy, K. and Feeney, J., "Challenges in implanting participatory practice in child protection: a contingency approach", *Children and Youth Services Review* 2010 1020-1027.

Davis, G., *Partisans and mediators* (Oxford: Clarendon Press, 1988).
Department for Children, Schools and Families, *The Children Act 1989 Guidance and Regulations, Volume 1: Court Orders* (London: TSO, 2008).
Department for Communities and Local Government, *Working with troubled families,* London: DCLG, 2012).
Department for Constitutional Affairs and Department for Education and Skills, *Child Care Proceedings System Review* (London: DCA and DfES, 2006).
Department for Education, *Action plan for adoption* (London: DfE, 2012).
Department of Health, *The Children Act 1989 Guidance and Regulations, Volume 2: Family Support, day care and educational provision for young children* (London: HMSO, 1991).
Department for Education and Skills and Local Government Information Unit, *If this were my child ... A councillor's guide to being a good corporate parent* (Nottingham: DfES Publications, 2003).
Department for Education and Skills, *Care Matters: Transforming the Lives of Children and Young People* (cm. 6932) (Norwich: TSO, 2006).
Department of Health, *Child protection: messages from research* (London: TSO, 1995).
Department of Health, *Children Act Now* (London: TSO, 2001).
Department of Health and Family Rights Group, *The Children Act 1989 – working in partnership with families* (London: HMSO, 1991).
Dickens, J., Masson, J., Young, J. and Bader, K., "The paradox of parental participation and legal representation 'at edge of care' meetings", *Child and Family Social Work* 2013 (advanced access) doi:10.1111/cfs.12075.
Dumbrill, G., "Parental experience of child protection intervention: A qualitative study", *Child Abuse and Neglect* 2006 30, 27–37.
Family Justice Review, *Final Report* (London: MoJ and DfE, 2011).
Farmer, E., "Improving reunification practice: pathways home, progress and outcomes for children returning from care to their parents", *British Journal of Social Work* 2012 (advanced access) 1-19 doi:10.1093/bjsw/bcs093.
Fauth, R., Jelicic, H., Hart, D., Burton, D. and Shemmings, D., *Effective practice to protect children living in highly resistant families* (London: CE4O, 2010).
Featherstone, B., Morris, K. and White, S., "A marriage made in hell: early intervention meets child protection", *British Journal of Social Work* 2013 (advanced access) 1-15 doi:10.1093/bjsw/bct052.
Freeman, M., *The Rights and Wrongs of Children* (London: Pinter, 1983).
Gilbert,N., Parton, N. and Skivenes, M., *Child protection systems: International trends and orientations* (Oxford: Oxford University Press, 2011).
Haringey Local Safeguarding Children Board, *Serious Case Review 'Child A': Second Serious Case Review Overview Report Relating to Peter Connelly* (London: DfE, 2009).
H.M. Government, *Every child matters: change for children* (London: TSO, 2004).
H.M. Government, *Care Leaver Strategy* (London: Department for Education, 2013).
Hunt, J., Macleod, A. and Thomas, C., *The Last Resort: Child Protection, the Courts and the 1989 Children Act* (London: TSO, 1999).

Hunt, J. and Macleod, A., *The best-laid plans* (London: TSO, 1999).

Hunt J. and Waterhouse, S., *It's Just Not Fair! Support, need and legal status in family and friends care* (London: FRG/Oxford University Centre for Family Law and Policy, 2013).

Jessiman, P., Keogh, P. and Brophy, J., *An early process evaluation of the public law outline in the family courts,* MoJ research series 10/09 (London: MoJ, 2009).

Kirkwood, A., *The Leicestershire Inquiry 1992* (Glenfield: Leicestershire County Council, 1993).

Laming, H., *The Victoria Climbié Inquiry Report* (2003 cm. 5730) (London: TSO, 2003).

Levitas, R., "There May Be 'Trouble' Ahead: What we know about those 120,000 'troubled' families", *Poverty and Social Exclusion in the UK,* Policy Response Series No. 3, 2012 available at http://www.poverty.ac.uk/sites/poverty/files/attachments/WP%20Policy%20Response%20No.3-%20%20'Trouble'%20ahead%20(Levitas%20Final%2021April2012).pdf.

Levy, A. and Kahan, B., *The Pindown Experience and the Protection of Children: The Report of the Staffordshire Child Care Inquiry* (Stafford: Staffordshire County Council, 1991).

MacDonald, A., "The voice of the child: still a faint cry", *Family Law* 2008 38, 648-653.

Masson, J., "Implementing change for children: action at the centre and local reaction", *J. Law and Society* 1992 19(3), 320-338.

Masson, J., "Emergency intervention to protect children: using and avoiding legal controls", *Child and Family Law Quarterly* 2005 17, 75-96.

Masson, J., Pearce, J., Bader, K., Joyner, O., Marsden, J. and Westlake, D., *Care Profiling Study, Ministry of Justice Research Series 4/08* (London: Minstry of Justice, 2008).

Masson, J., Dickens, J., Bader, K. and Young, J., *Partnership by Law?* (Bristol: University of Bristol School of Law, 2013).

Ministry of Justice and Department for Children, Schools and Families, *Preparing for care and supervision proceedings* (London: Ministry of Justice, 2009).

Ministry of Justice and Department for Education, *Government response to the Family Justice review: a system with families at its heart,* Cm. 8273 (London: TSO, 2012).

Munro, E., *The Munro Review of Child Protection, Final Report,* Cm. 8207 (London: TSO, 2011).

Munro, E. R., Ward, H., Lushley, C. and National Care Advisory Service, *The Right2beCared4 pilots interim report, DFE RR 031* (London: Department for Education, 2010a).

Munro, E. R., Maskell-Graham, D., Ward, H. and National Care Advisory Service, *Evaluation of the Staying Put: 18+ Family Placement Pilot Programme Interim Report: Overview of Emerging Themes and Issues* (London: Department for Education, 2010b).

Narey, M., *Beyond care matters: the future of the care population* (Nottingham: DCSF, 2007).

Ofsted, *Keeping in touch* (Manchester: Ofsted, 2009).

Ofsted, *Children's rights monitor 2011* (Manchester: Ofsted, 2012).

Packman, J. and Hall, C., *From care to accommodation* (London: TSO, 1998).

Parton, N., *Child protection and family support* (London: Routledge, 1997).
Platt, D., "Threshold decisions: How social workers prioritize referrals of child concern", *Child Abuse Review* 2006 15, 1.
Platt, D. and Turney, D., "Making threshold decisions in child protection: a conceptual analysis", *British Journal of Social Work* 2013 advanced access doi:10.1093/bjsw/bct007.
President of the Family Division, *The Public Law Outline* (London, Ministry of Justice, 2008).
Rowlands, J. and Statham, J., "Numbers of looked after children in England: a historical analysis", *Child and Family Social Work* 2009 14, 79-89.
Select Committee on Health, *Looked After children* (London: House of Commons, H.C 247: 1997-8).
Selwyn, J. T., Farmer, E., Meakings , S. J. and Vaisey, P., *The Poor Relations? Children and Informal Kinship Carers Speak Out: A Summary Research Report* (Bristol: School for Policy Studies, University of Bristol, 2013).
Sinclair. I., Baker, C., Lee, J. and Gibbs, I., *The pursuit of permanence* (London: Jessica Kingsley, 2007).
Stein, M., "Transitions from Care to Adulthood: Messages from Research for Policy and Practice", in M. Stein and E. R. Munro (eds), *Young People's Transitions from Care to Adulthood: International Research and Practice* (London: Jessica Kingsley Publishers, 2008).
Yatchmenoff, D., "A closer look at client engagement: understanding and assessing engagement from the perspectives of workers and clients in non-voluntary child protective services", in M. Calder (ed), *Carrot or stick?* (Lyme Regis: Russell House, 2008).

IV

Law and Personal Living

Michael Freeman and the Rights and Wrongs of Resolving Private Law Disputes

Felicity Kaganas
Brunel University

Christine Piper
Brunel University

Introduction

In 1983 Michael Freeman's book – *The Rights and Wrongs of Children* – was published. Chapter 6 was entitled 'Children as victims of the divorce process'. It set out Freeman's views on the way private family law should develop and it also identified the ways in which he hoped it would not. In this chapter, we will examine some of Freeman's ideas and the extent to which they have been incorporated into the family law landscape. However, as Freeman says, 'the annals of legal history are strewn with examples of institutions and practices which have had unintended (or unproclaimed) consequences' (1983: 231) and it is on these that we will focus. We will suggest that, while Freeman was prescient in predicting some of the ways in which family law would change, and while some of his hopes have been realised, they have not always been realised in the way he intended or, indeed, in ways he could have foreseen. Some of these changes have brought about consequences detrimental to vulnerable family members but these effects, although anticipated by government, have been 'unproclaimed' and indeed minimised. In other cases the consequences of changes to the law have proved to be very different from those intended by the lawmakers. And each failure to give effect to those intentions has led the government to redouble its efforts and to seek a solution in yet more legislation.

Co-Parenting

Freeman wrote that 'surprisingly little attention [had] been focussed on the children of divorce' (1983: 191). He observed that one of the effects of the 'paucity of research' was the influence on thinking of 'truisms and myths' (1983: 192). These included the belief that the 'non-custodial parent should play a minimal role in parenting decisions' (1983: 192). This 'conventional wisdom' (1983: 209), however, was contradicted by the only longitudinal study of children in divorced families, *Surviving the Breakup* (Wallerstein and Kelly 1980). While Freeman discerned serious flaws in the research, he was persuaded that an on-going relationship with both parents promotes children's

A. Diduck, N. Peleg, H. Reece (eds.), Law in Society: Reflections on Children, Family, Culture and Philosophy
Copyright 2015 Koninklijke Brill NV. Printed in The Netherlands. ISBN 978-90-04-26148-8. pp. 369-393.

welfare (1983: 214-5). Joint custody, he said, disrupts the parent-child relationship less than other arrangements and was 'the ideal to be sought' (1983: 208). In addition, he noted that 'everyone seems agreed that access is a "good thing"'[1] but that courts were allowing access decisions to go by default, and where they were making orders, they were not enforcing them (1983: 215-6).

However, Freeman's endorsement of joint custody and liberal access was not unqualified. He said that joint custody, meaning an order giving both parents the right to make and veto decisions about their children's upbringing, could work where 'a couple is capable of reaching shared decisions in the child's best interests' and might be suitable only in a 'minority of cases' (1983: 208). Co-parenting was the 'goal' to aim for but it required commitment and financial resources, he said. He envisaged it as part of an 'amicable' divorce (1983: 208) and quoted Wallerstein and Kelly's view that joint custody would not involve a specific apportionment of time but should be seen, rather, as a 'concept of two committed parents, in two separate homes, caring for their youngsters in a post-divorce atmosphere of civilized, respectful exchange' (quoted in Freeman (1983: 214)). Freeman did not envisage co-parenting as an arrangement that would be appropriate for most divorced or separated families and he certainly did not advocate it for parents in conflict. He did suggest that 'decisions as to access are too important to be left to the custodial parent' (1983: 218) and that access visits should not be 'diminished or stopped' just because they are 'unsettling' (1983: 217). However, he also acknowledged that access could be contrary to the child's best interests and even 'positively harmful' (1983: 215). He clearly interpreted the research as showing that continuing parental involvement should be coupled with parental co-operation in order for children to benefit (1983: 216).

Since Freeman's book was published, the nature of the debate has changed and its shape has reflected changing constructions of the 'good' post separation family and of children's welfare, as well as changing perceptions of the role of the law. Far from being ignored, children's experiences of divorce or separation have become the focus of intense scrutiny on the part of researchers and policymakers. A new truism has replaced the old one: shared parenting, or at least liberal contact, is best for children in almost all circumstances, as long as it is safe. In addition, it is now asserted that litigation harms children and that parents should agree without taking their quarrels to court. This is consistent with Freeman's endorsement of co-operation, co-parenting and liberal access. Indeed he may not have foreseen the extent to which his views have become the 'new orthodoxy'.[2] But what is different is that nuance and circumspection have largely disappeared from the debate and from the law. Over the years it has become more and more difficult for resident parents to resist contact. Pressure from fathers' rights groups, together with the impact of some child welfare research studies, have combined, in a way that Freeman probably did not foresee, to make paternal involvement in their children's lives an almost unqualified 'good'.

1 With the exception of Goldstein, Freud and Solnit (Freeman, 1983: 215).

2 This term was used by Maclean and Eekelaar (1997: 50).

In contrast with the current position, the Law Commission debating joint custody in the 1980s was sceptical about what are now assumed to be the benefits of shared parenting in its various guises. The Commissioners were not persuaded by the arguments fielded in favour of joint custody, namely that joint custody might facilitate agreements (Law Commission, 1986: para 4.38) or encourage greater involvement by the parent with whom the children were not living. (paras 4.35-4.36). They concluded that the case for a presumption in favour of joint custody had not been made out (1986: para 4.46). And although the law on parental responsibility has now superseded the joint custody debate, the observations of the Law Commission are still relevant.

The Law Commission took the view that the main benefit of joint custody was symbolic and that it did not represent 'genuine sharing of parental responsibility'. To the extent that it might encourage the parent who did not have the burden of day-to–day care to 'interfere' in day-to-day matters, it was 'obviously undesirable' (1986: para 4.40). There were cases, the Law Commissioners said, 'in which the needs of the child and the custodial parent to feel secure and free from even the unlikely threat of interference must be put before the symbolic advantages of joint custody, even if this increases the risk of the child and the non-custodial parent losing touch with one another' (para 4.43). The law should promote a secure environment for the child and the security of the parent bringing up the child might be important in achieving this (para 3.7; see also paras 3.8 and 4.25). Joint physical custody was generally not practicable and, if imposed on one parent, it could cause stress and difficulty for that parent and the child.

The limits of the law were also acknowledged. It could set 'standards' (Law Commission 1986: para 4.31). However, there was little the law could do to encourage contact between children and parents. And there was little the court could do if the custodial parent or the child were opposed to contact, unless a change in custody were a realistic alternative (para 4.31).

In its subsequent report (Law Commission, 1988), the Law Commission indicated that giving both parents the equal and enduring status of parental responsibility, with court orders to deal with the allocation of the child's time after separation or divorce, was part of its strategy to encourage both parents to feel 'concerned and responsible' (para 2.10). However, it conceded that the law could not alter relationships and the best it could do was to 'lower the stakes' and reduce the opportunities for conflict (Law Commission 1988: para 4.5). These changes were embodied in the Children Act 1989 but not even the modest aim of reducing conflict and litigation was achieved. Consequently, law reform was again being considered in 2004.

A New Presumption

The Green Paper (DCA, DfES and DTI, 2004) published that year and the White Paper that followed it (DCA, DfES and DTI, 2005) show signs of the impact of both women's advocates and fathers' rights groups. The new mantra, that contact is in children's best interests 'so long as it is safe', is a response to evidence that was emerging about the prevalence and effects of domestic violence in cases where contact is in dispute

(DCA, DfES and DTI, 2004 Ministerial Foreword: 2; paras 3, 41; DCA, DfES and DTI, 2005 Ministerial Foreword: 5). But the claims of fathers' groups were also considered. The benefits of continuing relationships between children and both parents, the changing roles of fathers and mothers and the equal importance of both parents are presented as generally accepted truths in the policy documents of the time (DCA, DfES and DTI, 2004 Ministerial Foreword: 2, paras 4, 6, 35, 36; DCA, DfES and DTI, 2005 Ministerial Foreword: 6, para 2).

More significantly, there are references to fathers' dissatisfaction with the law and to the assertions of fathers' groups[3] that the law is biased in favour of mothers (DCA, DfES and DTI, 2004: para 18).[4] The government rejected this accusation (DCA, DfES and DTI, 2004 Ministerial Foreword: 1), affirmed that the existing legal position was the correct one (DCA, DfES and DTI, 2005: para 10) and concluded that a presumption that time should be shared equally between the parents would have no legal effect in practice (DCA, DfES and DTI, 2004, Ministerial Foreword: 2 para 43; DCA, DfES and DTI, 2005: para 13). In many separated families, such arrangements would not be workable. In any event, the government did not believe that an 'automatic 50:50 division' of the child's time would be in the best interests of most children and considered that it could be damaging: 'Children are not a commodity to be apportioned equally after separation .... a one-size-fits-all formula will not work' (DCA, DfES and DTI, 2004: para 42). It was not the law that needed to be changed but adult behaviour in dealing with disputes (DCA, DfES and DTI, 2004: para 43; DCA, DfES and DTI, 2005: para 8). This could be best achieved through developing 'advice, information, mediation, conciliation and enforcement processes' (DCA, DfES and DTI, 2005: para 14).

In contrast, calls from fathers' rights groups to tighten up the law on enforcing contact orders have been treated more sympathetically. The Children Act (section 11A ff) was amended (by the Children and Adoption Act 2006) to make provision for Contact Activity Directions and Conditions and to introduce new enforcement measures.[5] Yet still the perception has persisted that courts are biased and that resident mothers flout contact orders with impunity (Norgrove, 2011a: paras 5.33-5.36). The perceived failure of the law to achieve the desired effects led to further calls for law reform; even more law would be needed to solve the problem. In 2011 the *Family Justice Review* panel recommended in its Interim Report that a statement be inserted into the Children Act, emphasising the importance for children of a meaningful relationships with both parents (Norgrove 2011a: para 5.78). However, in its Final Report the panel, after considering the effects of similar legislation in Australia, withdrew its recommendation. It noted that it is already accepted in law that contact is in chil-

---

3 The most vocal groups were Families Need Fathers and Fathers4Justice. The former has moderated its stance over the years while the latter has maintained a more militant approach.

4 Concerns with allegations of such bias were also being voiced by the judiciary. See *V* v *V* (*Contact: Implacable Hostility*) [2004] EWHC Fam 1215 paras 4-10; *Re D* (*Intractable Contact Dispute: Publicity*) [2004] EWHC Fam 727 para 4.

5 These are not widely used: Norgrove, 2011a: para 5.35. Courts do not often order unpaid work: Trinder et al (2013) 43.

dren's best interests (Norgrove 2011b: para 4.37). The proposed change could risk creating a perception that parents have the right to equal time. It could lead to confusion, misinterpretation, false expectations, increased litigation and 'would do more harm than good' (Norgrove 2011b, Executive Summary: para 109; Report: para 4.29-4.40).

In its response to the Family Justice Review, the government reached a very different conclusion. It favoured a presumption of shared parenting as a way of making parents more likely to reach agreements (MoJ and DfE 2012: para 64) and, it seems, of improving compliance with court orders:

> We ... need to improve couples' compliance with decisions .... [I]t means ... making it clearer that there is no in-built legal bias towards either the father or the mother. We believe that where there are no significant welfare issues, we should reinforce the principle through law, that it is in the best interests of the child to have a full and continuing relationship with both parents. (MoJ and DfE 2012, Joint Ministerial Foreword: 3)

The Consultation document that followed stated that the aim of the Government was to 'promote clearer alternatives to legal action' (DfE and MoJ, 2012: para 2.1). Legislation to promote shared parenting, it said, was intended to 'encourage more separated parents to resolve their disputes out of court and agree care arrangements that fully involve both parents' (DfE and MoJ, 2012: para 4.3; see also Djanogly, 2012).

The result is the Children and Families Act 2014[6] which introduces a new section 1(2A) into the Children Act 1989. This applies in contested section 8 proceedings[7] and it creates a presumption 'that involvement of [each] parent in the life of the child concerned will further the child's welfare'. The presumption operates unless it can be shown that the parent concerned cannot be involved in any way without putting the child at risk of suffering harm or that the parent's involvement will be contrary to the child's welfare.[8] The purpose of this amendment, say the Explanatory Notes to the Children and Families Bill, is to 'send a clear signal to separated parents that courts will take account of the principle that both should continue to be involved in their children's lives where that is safe and consistent with the child's welfare' (para 8, See also para 92. See also DfE (2012: 4). It is not intended, however, to promote equal division, or any other apportionment, of the child's time (para 92; DfE and MOJ 2012: para 4.4).[9]

Although Freeman saw shared parenting as something to be aimed for, he did not assume it was suitable for the generality of cases and he probably did not foresee that the tide of opinion favouring parental involvement after separation or divorce would

6 The Act received Royal assent on 13 March 2014 (DfE 2014).

7 However contact and residence orders are to be replaced by child arrangements orders (s12 Children and Families Act 2014). Section 1(2A) will also apply in parental responsibility cases.

8 See *Children and Families Bill. Explanatory Notes* paras 93-6.

9 This is the import of the new s1(2B) of the Children Act 1989, inserted by the Children and Families Act, s11.

bring in a presumption promoting such involvement. Critics of the new presumption predicted that it will have negative consequences but these criticisms did not sway the government. And, in addition to these foreseeable consequences, it can be predicted also that the government's professed aims in pushing through this legislation will not be achieved and that there will be unforeseen consequences as well.

The Presumption and Court Practice

The government says that the reformed law will serve children's best interests, is intended to address the grievances of fathers' rights groups and is meant to deter parents from using the courts, Djanogly (2012):

> The amendment would serve to reinforce by way of statute the expectation that both parents should be involved in a child's life, unless of course that is not safe or not consistent with the child's welfare. The Government recognises that courts already operate on this basis, but nevertheless there is a widespread perception among those who use the courts that this is not the case. The amendment will address this... In doing so, it will encourage the resolution of agreements outside court by making clear the basis on which courts' decisions are made and by ensuring that parents' expectations are realistic when deciding whether to bring a claim to court. The Government anticipates that over time, this change will contribute to a societal shift towards greater recognition of the value of both parents in a child's life, and to a reduction of the perception of bias within the court system. (DfE 2013: para 63, Annex 1 of Annex B ; see also DfE and MoJ 2012: para 2.1; para 4.3)

However, as the government conceded, the courts were already operating on the basis of a presumption (*Re M (Contact: Welfare Test)* [1995] 1 FLR 274, 281. See Hunt and Macleod (2008: 191). See also Perry and Rainey (2007: 23) or assumption (*Re L (Contact: Domestic Violence); Re V (Contact: Domestic Violence); Re M (Contact: Domestic Violence); Re H (Contact: Domestic Violence)* [2002] 2 FLR 334 at p 364) in favour of contact. Most fathers who want it were being awarded contact (Hunt and Macleod, 2008: 19, 251, 253; see also Perry and Rainey, 2007). What is more, Hunt and Macleod found that courts awarded contact even in cases where mothers expressed multiple concerns including serious objections based on domestic violence, child abuse, the father's poor parenting, the father's mental health problems and the father's substance misuse (see Hunt and Macleod (2008: 9, 84, 16). See also Coy et al (2012). Courts were also increasingly prepared to order shared residence, even in cases where it might seem unworkable (see Harris-Short (2010) for a review of the cases).

So it may well be the case that the change will have little effect in practice (see DCA, DfES and DTI (2004) Ministerial Foreword p2, para 43. DCA, DfES and DTI (2005) para 13). Indeed, an examination of the statements emanating from government ministers suggests that the government have no intention of attempting to influence the courts by means of the new presumption (see Kaganas 2013: 259-60). For example, Tim Loughton MP, the then Minister for Children and Families, said in the House of Commons:

> [Shared parenting] may mean 10% of the time, 20% of the time, weekends, during the week, holidays, staying at grandparents-whatever. I am not interested in that; that is for the judge to determine.[10]

Yet the new law may affect outcomes in some cases and may, as a result, jeopardise the welfare and safety of mothers and children. Dewar, reviewing the effects of a similar statutory provision in Australia,[11] reports that where cases were decided by the courts, an increase in the proportion of orders for shared time suggested that children were being exposed to risk and that those parents least likely to co-operate were being ordered to do so (2010: 383-4).

In his evidence before the Justice Committee, Ryder J was of the view that the presumption in the then Children and Families Bill would not change practice in British courts (Justice Committee, 2012: para 170). However HHJ John Mitchell said that there is a 'danger that the presumption will be used by advocates and judges where they feel undecided or overwhelmed' (ibid: para 173). And the ability of resident parents (usually mothers) to rebut the presumption will no doubt be impeded by the withdrawal of legal aid from private law family disputes in terms of the Legal Aid, Sentencing and Punishment of Offenders Act 2012 (LASPO).

Focusing on Parents and Weakening the Welfare Principle

Whether parental 'involvement' is generally in the best interests of children is itself open to doubt. While there is continuing support for Freeman's view that co-operative co-parenting serves children's best interests, there is a considerable body of research pointing to the harm caused by conflict, exposure to domestic violence and even erratic visiting (see, for example, Fehlberg *et al,* 2011; Fortin *et al,* 2012; see also Justice Committee 2012: paras 169 – 170). The government, however, maintains that it is acting in children's best interests. Yet there are concerns that the existence of a presumption will undermine the paramountcy principle (see Kaganas (2013: 275-8) for discussion). For example, the Law Society (Law Society, 2012) has argued that a presumption would prioritise the relationship between the child and the parents at the expense of other considerations, such as safety. The Justice Committee (2012: para 170) said that attention in court would be directed at rebuttal of the presumption and away from children's best interests. And, in a memorandum submitted to the House of Commons Public Bills Committee, Jane Fortin and Joan Hunt stated that the

---

10 Uncorrected Transcript of Oral Evidence. To be published as HC 282-I.The operation of the Family Courts: follow-up 13 June 2012 http://www.publications.parliament.uk/pa/cm201213/cmselect/cmjust/uc282-i/uc28201.htm (accessed 25 September 2012) Q 29.

11 Family Law Act 1975 (Cth), s 60(CC)(2)(a) and (b) (as amended in 2006).

change would lead to a 'more simplistic and broad-brush' approach to cases (Fortin and Hunt, 2013: para 8. See also Hamilton, 2013 and Kaganas, 2013).

The government's other objective – to counter perceptions of bias and allegations of unfairness emanating from fathers' rights groups – may also divert attention from, or undermine, the welfare of the children involved. Certainly, the Australian presumption is thought to have had this effect. Where that presumption applies, the courts are directed to consider orders for the child to spend equal time with each parent, or, where this is not practicable or in the child's best interests, 'substantial and significant time'. However, research carried out by the Australian Institute of Family Studies (Kaspiew *et al* 2009; and see further Kaganas, 2013: 275-8) revealed that the presumption appears to have led parents and professionals to understand that it confers on parents a right to equal responsibility and equal time. This has meant that litigation and negotiation has focused more on parental rights than on children's welfare (Kaspiew *et al* 2009: 216). Legal sector professionals, in particular, expressed the belief that the consequences have included increased difficulty in working with parents to achieve child-focused arrangements (ibid, Summary: 12). In addition, the law has failed to satisfy Australian men and has even exacerbated fathers' disaffection with the legal system; fathers, expecting equal time, were unhappy when their expectations were not met (Kaspiew *et al* 2009: 216).

The UK government insists that it has avoided all the pitfalls of the Australian legislation by removing any reference in the statute to shared parenting, by refraining from using words like 'meaningful' to define the relationships the law is designed to promote, by maintaining the paramountcy principle, and by excluding the implication of equal or any other specific allocation of time (DfE and MoJ 2012: para 5.1). Indeed, the Bill was amended by the House of Lords in response to concerns expressed by the Shared Parenting Consortium about the possible effects of the presumption on the paramountcy principle, and, in order to counter the possibility that separating parents might assume that they are legally bound to share time equally, a provision was introduced to clarify the meaning of 'involvement' (Family Law Week, 2014). A new s1(2B) was inserted in the Children Act 1989 providing that, '"involvement" means involvement of some kind, either direct or indirect, but not any particular division of a child's time.'[12]

Yet the presumption in the Children and Families Act, even with the new definition of 'involvement', is unlikely to ensure that parents focus on their children's welfare rather than their own battles. And it is unlikely to achieve the aim of increasing confidence in the family justice system, not least because what is being delivered falls far short of what fathers' rights groups are demanding and what some men think it is delivering. It was already apparent from public comments on the Bill made before the amendment that it was being understood by some as giving equal rights. For example:

---

12 The provision inserted by the House of Lords, in the version of the Bill dated 30 January 2014, referred to involvement that 'promotes the welfare of the child' (http://services.parliament.uk/bills/2013-14/childrenandfamilies/documents.html, accessed 17 March 2-14). The reference to welfare has been omitted from the Act.

> This Bill will help restore fairness, and allow fathers to play a rightful and equal part in the upbringing of their child. It will also make children happier, and for them to know that their fathers and mothers are both there to support them. Many thanks.[13]

It may be that the amendment may have the effect of leaving some fathers under no such illusions. But it is also likely to inflame the ire already expressed by some men who, even before the amendment, understood the effect of the presumption correctly:

'Anything other than a presumption of 50-50 as a starting point for contact post-separation is discrimination and a prejudice against (normally) separated dads and cannot be justified'.[14]

Similar sentiments are expressed in the sole comment added to a solicitor's blog posted within 24 hours of the passing of the Act:

> It demonstrates the emptiness of the government's promise to legislate for non-resident parents, aka fathers, to remain significantly involved in raising their children after separation. These changes achieve precisely nothing to strengthen the position of fathers in private law disputes which account for by far the greater number of cases that end up in court.[15]

The Normative Function of Law

Unlike these fathers the proponents of the legislation have been predicting that it will have a considerable impact. The government claims that the presumption will lead to more agreements between parents and reduce the levels of litigation. It is assumed that the messages that 'radiate' beyond law (Dewar 2010: 385) will lead parents to change their behaviour so that they resolve their disputes out of court and agree care arrangements that fully involve them both: 'The legislation will become part of the consistent messaging that influences the starting point both for families undergoing separation, and the professionals who support them' (DfE and MoJ 2012: para 4.6).

The change in the law, then, is meant to send a message to parents and, it seems, to society generally,[16] that both parents should play a part in their children's lives.

---

13 Robert S, Children and Families Bill Public Reading: Additional Comments http://www.parliament.uk/business/bills-and-legislation/public-reading/children-and-families-bill/general-comments/?page=7 (accessed 24 April 2013).

14 Ian T, Children and Families Bill. Public Reading: Additional Comments http://www.parliament.uk/business/bills-and-legislation/public-reading/children-and-families-bill/general-comments/?page=9 (accessed 24 April 2013). See further Kaganas (2013); 'Caroline Opposes Lords' Amendment to Children & Families Bill on Shared Parenting' http://www.carolinenokes.com/uncategorized/caroline-opposes-lords-amendment-to-children-families-bill-on-shared-parenting/ (accessed 13 March 2014).

15 Paul, 'Comment' left on Marilyn Stowe Blog 'Children and Families Act given Royal Assent'.

16 'The aim of the legislative amendment is also to reinforce the expectation at societal level that both parents are jointly responsible for their children's upbringing' (DfE and

It is assumed that this message 'will make both parents take responsibility for their children and persuade each (usually mothers) to accept the other's (usually fathers) involvement in their children's lives' (Kaganas 2013: 281). This message embodies a view that has long infused English family law. Its enshrinement in legislation attests not only to its axiomatic status but also to an increasing emphasis on the symbolic and educational function of the law as a means of changing behaviour.

However law's messages are not always heard by those at whom they are directed and, even if heard, are not always understood and given effect in the ways intended; as we have seen in relation to aggrieved fathers, these messages can be misinterpreted and can have unintended consequences. Certainly, the history of family law reform does not give support to the view that the law can be fashioned to affect individual behaviour in predictable and desirable ways. For instance, the introduction of equal and enduring parental responsibility was intended to make parents take responsibility and to 'lower the stakes', so removing reasons to fight. Yet parents still 'fight': the effect of the law has merely been to shift the site of battle to the issue of contact.

Fehlberg *et al* (2011: 319), writing about the Australian presumption, pointed out that 'the evidence so far does not suggest that changing the law leads more families to enter shared time arrangements, let alone 'workable' arrangements (ie manageable for parents and appropriate for children's needs at different points in their childhood)'. Dewar in turn observed that the legislation, which was designed to promote settlement between parents, only had the effect of intensifying the pre-existing predisposition of parents to agree or disagree (2010: 381-82). And in the UK, Kaganas and Day Sclater (2004) found that the mothers opposing contact in their sample were well aware of the norm that contact is best for children. However they saw their resistance as justified since they knew that, because of paternal shortcomings, contact was not best for *their* children.

So the legislation will not please fathers' rights groups or eliminate perceptions of bias. It is unlikely to affect to a significant extent the way in which the courts approach contact disputes, although it may lead to a more simplistic approach in some cases. It is not likely to reduce conflict and litigation, although LASPO may have the effect of preventing some parents from using the courts.

Using law as the purveyor of messages in order to change hearts and minds, or at least behaviour, does not appear to be a very effective strategy. However, it seems that law's messages sometimes do have an impact where those hearing them are not in a position to resist them, particularly where these messages are used to 'reinforce popular sentiment or push popular sentiment' (Zolotor and Puzia, 2010: 242; see also Kaganas, 2013). In particular, they may influence out-of-court negotiations: parents bargain in 'the shadow of the law' and their agreements will, to some extent, be shaped by it. Dewar found that the Australian presumption has strengthened the bargaining position of men asserting their 'rights' relative to women and, in those cases, parents were less likely to take a child-centred approach (2010: 382-3). He observed a reduction in the use of lawyers after the reforms and, speculated that, while this could be

MOJ, 2012: para 3.2).

interpreted as demonstrating the success of the reforms in promoting agreement, it could also, given the prevalence of violence and abuse, be evidence of arrangements being agreed to in worrying circumstances (2010: 383; see, also, Rhoades, 2012).

It seems likely that the main effect of the British reform will be similar. The new provision might enable non-resident fathers to 'persuade' vulnerable mothers and children to agree to contact pursuant to negotiation or mediation, particularly if those mothers are told that this is what the law mandates.

The Shadow of the Law

The impact of law's messages, then, is felt primarily by those who are vulnerable and least able to resist and, so, it can exacerbate their position. We should therefore be concerned, as was Freeman, about the nature and content of the shadow cast by the courts and legislation on bargaining positions. In chapter 6 of *Rights and Wrongs* Freeman comments on the continuing importance of law: 'parents bargain in "the shadow of the law" so, whilst few cases are contested, the contribution the courts can make is not negligible' (Freeman 1983: 226). His reference to 'the shadow of the law' derives from the work of Mnookin and Kornhauser (1979) in which the authors talked of the bargaining 'endowment' that the law and the courts applying it confer: 'In other words, the outcome that the law will impose if no agreement is reached gives each parent certain bargaining chips' (1979: 968).

Freeman's comments were clearly in the context of the judicial role and the content of court orders and he urged the courts to make 'better decisions', not just to encourage different outcomes but in order to provide a better shadow (1983: 226). Earlier in the chapter he had argued that the 'courts have a role to play' in regard to contact and that, 'If the norm is to be "continued involvement" (here Freeman footnotes Richards, 1982: 146) this is what the courts should stress'. For example, he said that judges should question parental decisions not to ask for access (1983: 219). But he also said that the views of children as to whether they wanted contact or not should be better represented in contested cases (1983: 226-7).

Time has seen the fulfilment of Freeman's wish that judges give a clear message that both parents should have a continuing relationship and involvement with their children. This is an idea and ideal that is and will continue to be shared by all those working in the family justice system; the shadow of the law in this regard is clear. And it will perhaps be intensified by governmental pronouncements and the symbolic use of legislation in creating the new presumption (Kaganas, 2013). Whether the shadow of the nuanced reasoning in judgments in difficult cases will be clear is another matter. Reviewing private family law in Australia, Dewar argues that the law is complex, can only be understood by specialists, and the 'simplified messages that radiate beyond that are inaccurate and often harmful' (2010: 385). This is of concern in the context of the increase we note below in the number of new alternative advice and dispute resolution bodies whose personnel often have no legal training.

Further, if the number of cases coming before the courts decreases, the breadth and usefulness of the law from adjudicated cases may also diminish with a consequent effect on the shadow of the law. Of course, the lack of good advice from solicitors may have the opposite effect; it may lead to an increase in the number of cases reaching the courts. Research over many years has shown that solicitors do not encourage the use of litigation (see, for example, the review in Eekelaar and Maclean, 2013: 25-30) and Hunt has predicted that without lawyers to discourage unrealistic expectations and to persuade clients to compromise, there will be more litigation (Hunt, 2011: 384, 383). There is some evidence that this has in fact occurred (see eg Lawyersupportedmediation (2013) and (2014); Munby, 2014: 167) and there are certainly more litigants in person (LIPs): between April and September 2013, *almost half* (45%) of all parties involved with private family law child proceedings, were unrepresented (Lawyersupportedmediation (2014). See also *C (A Child) & Anor* v *KH* [2013] EWCA Civ 1412 para 4). However the cases which are adjudicated may not provide useful guidance for future disputants or even courts. Herring and Powell have argued that the family courts are increasingly dealing only with unusual cases and so are no longer working with presumptions which convey an easily transferable legal message:

> The courts have recognised that while it is possible to identify matters which generally benefit children, it is wrong to assume that therefore the child in the particular case will benefit from them. This is especially because, as emphasised in *Re B*, the cases that come before the court do not represent the average case (Herring and Powell 2013: 558).

If they are right, the reasoning in these unusual cases will not apply to the 'average case' because the judgments are so individualised. And in any event, parents seeking to resolve their disputes outside the courts will not be exposed to the complexity of the reasoning of the courts. Given that research indicates that about half of divorcing or separating couples seek legal advice (Barlow *et al*, 2013: 307) and that legal aid to pay for that advice is now severely restricted (see Harris, 2013; Miles, 2012), law's shadow may not reach the 'average' disputant. This will be of particular concern in relation to family law's protective function.

Law as Protector

Freeman was also concerned that encouragement of private ordering should not downgrade the ability of family law to protect the more vulnerable members of the family.

> Not the least value of a "regime of rules" (Kennedy, 1976), of the forms and rhetoric of law is that it can on occasion "inhibit power and afford some protection to the powerless" (Thomson, 1975: 266). ... We must not let our concern with the insensitivity of traditional legal mechanisms turn us away from the unqualified good in the rule of law (1983: 233).

He was referring to the child as the one who needed protection (1983: 233) and in the Preface to *The Moral Status of Children* (Freeman 1997) he wrote that in *The Rights and Wrongs of Children*, 'I underestimated the importance of giving children participatory rights'. How to make the voice of the child heard and what weight to give it in informal ordering is still an unresolved issue, notwithstanding initiatives and encouragement in relation to 'child inclusive' mediation (CIM) over many years (see, for example, National Family Mediation, 1994; Parkinson, 2012). Walker, noting the long-standing divergent arguments amongst mediators in regard to the inclusion of children, argues that '[g]iving children a voice can make a significant difference to the outcomes achieved' (2013: 192) and Australian research with high conflict families suggests CIM provides benefits which can be sustained over at least four years (McKintosh *et al* 2008), although a recent small scale study suggests otherwise (Bell *et al* 2013: 193-195). The Family Justice Review also stated that CIM 'should be available to all families seeking to mediate, provided that it is appropriate and safe and undertaken by well-trained practitioners' (Norgrove, 2011: para 4.106; see also Parkinson 2013: 209). But while CIM remains contentious, the removal of law from the resolution of private law disputes may mean that children's views will be unheard.

It is not only children who might be silenced and even placed at risk in contact disputes. In cases involving a significant imbalance of power and especially in cases involving domestic violence, it is also the vulnerable parent who may suffer. We are concerned about the effect of domestic abuse on the process and outcome of private ordering (see Piper, 2013), and this also concerned Freeman at the time of the passage of the Family Law Act 1996. That year he published an edited collection entitled *Divorce: Where next?* in which he referred to such abuse as 'not a matter which can be easily swept under the carpet' (Freeman, 1996: 2). It has in fact not been swept under the carpet in that abuse is one of the exceptions to the blanket withdrawal of legal aid in private family cases. Indeed we are not allowed – in policy and legislation – to ignore domestic violence.

However, there are unexpected consequences of this 'exceptionalising' of domestic violence. First, it is in effect used to justify excluding from the exception those private law cases with other problematic issues which make the protection of law necessary. And this overlaps with the second consequence of the way the exception has been drafted and is understood. Even with a definition of domestic violence which includes psychological abuse, the evidentiary burden insufficiently acknowledges research about the way control is exercised by the abusing partner, how this affects the vulnerable partner, and how difficult it is to provide compelling evidence of some forms of abuse (see O'Hara, 2013). The way the exception will operate also fails to take into account what is known about the victim's psychological difficulties in communicating about the abuse to those who can label the case as exceptional. For vulnerable partners to be protected all those who are gatekeepers to the availability of legal aid for them will need to be adequately trained in methods of screening for domestic violence. Otherwise, how will such professionals know there has been abuse? How will they know whether there is a risk that it will continue, that it will affect the children and that it will affect what happens in mediation or court adjudication (see Piper and Kaganas 1997)?

Research suggests that, at present, screening in many of the relevant processes is not of sufficient quality and duration. Research on in-court mediation (Trinder *et al* 2010) and on the pre-mediation session (the MIAM) for out-of court mediation (Morris, 2011; Morris, 2013; Barlow *et al* 2013) provides evidence that there is often neither the time nor expertise to screen adequately. Further, research on Parenting Information Programmes suggests that courts do not see referral to them as problematic where there is abuse and that screening before attendance at such programmes is also not adequate (Smith and Trinder 2012: 440-441).

The result – unintended though not unforeseen – of exceptionalising domestic violence is that the law may not in practice protect many who have suffered abuse. There is, however another development which reduces the capacity of law to protect, and that is how law – accurately and appropriately – is to be introduced into dispute settlement.

So far we have not contested the assumption that lawyers are more likely than other professionals to take account of the shadow of the law. However, in Freeman's edited collection of 1996, one of us argued – on the basis of available research from the USA (see, for example, Sarat and Felstiner, 1986), The Netherlands (Griffiths 1986), and England and Wales (see, for example, Davis *et al* 1994: 72) – that both lawyers and mediators worked with legal and non-legal norms (Piper 1996: 70). Research on the practice of family solicitors also suggested that solicitors themselves conflated legal and socio-political norms in their explanations of legal concepts (King 1999; Piper 1999). Overlapping with this is a normative discourse based on 'child welfare science'. As Rebecca Bailey Harris and colleagues concluded in their report on their empirical research about practitioners dealing with section 8 applications:

> 'In the absence of legal rules, other than procedural rules, disputes tend to be settled by reference to norms. These are not in essence legal norms other than in the limited sense that they are employed within a legal context. Legal knowledge is hardly relevant. It is essentially "welfare" discourse expressed as legal principle' (Bailey-Harris *et al* 1998: 27).

So for a long time we have known that it is quite difficult to isolate the shadow of law as such in relation to settling parental disputes. But parents want to know what they should do and they may not be able to distinguish between the legal and the non-legal norms being purveyed. They value 'partisan' support if using a solicitor (Davis 1988: chapters 8 and 9) but are often very anxious simply to know what is 'normal' or 'usual' – something which mediators do not always convey (Walker *et al* 1994: 92):

> 'Both Mr and Mrs Clifford found mediation helpful, but the search for norms remained unsatisfied. Mrs Clifford said: "We were trying to find out what was the norm. We wanted guidance but they said that as long as we were happy it was alright' (Walker *et al* 1994: 94).

However, if norms are, explicitly or implicitly, communicated they are, then, very powerful. Yet the development of new forms of dispute resolution is making it increasingly difficult to know what norms are being conveyed and whether they include more than the message of the new presumption.

Alternative Dispute Resolution

When Freeman wrote *Rights and Wrongs,* mediation – then conciliation – was in its infancy and he envisaged that an effective conciliation service 'could do much to smooth relations between parents and assist parents to preserve relationships with their children in the aftermath of divorce' (Freeman 1983: 219). His main fear was that a consequence of more private ordering would be a commodification of children. The empirical evidence available does not tell us whether this has occurred (Ryerstedt 2012) but we do know that the focus in mediation is often a generalised 'child' rather than the actual child, and that children are rarely part of the mediation process (see, for example, Trinder *et al* 2010).

Despite his reservations, Freeman viewed mediation as a helpful service. However he probably did not foresee that, alongside the enactment of yet more legislation to make contact 'work', there would be moves to promote mediation as well as an effort to curtail the use of the law. He did not anticipate that for those engaged in contact disputes there would be only the options of litigation in person, expensive lawyers' fees or extra-legal help. As a result of the adoption of what Eekelaar (2011: 311) has referred to as an 'attenuated concept of family justice', the court is seen as relevant only when it comes to protecting the vulnerable:

> The court's role should be focused on protecting the vulnerable from abuse, victimisation and exploitation and should avoid intervening in family life except where there is clear benefit to children or vulnerable adults in doing so. (Norgove 2011a: Annex A)

Disputes between parents about their children are private and the consequences of individual choice in this conception of the relationship between state and family, and they are not significant enough to warrant the full panoply of the family justice system: 'Where the issue is one which arises from the litigant's own personal choices, we are less likely to consider that these cases concern issues of the highest importance.'(Ministry of Justice, 2010: para 4.19.0)

However, while it is only mediation that is funded, it is not, as Sir James Munby P. has pointed out, now the only alternative to solicitor negotiation and advice or court applications – there are several other options:

> You must never forget that, as one door closes, another opens. ADR – mediation, collaborative law, arbitration, perhaps on the IFLA model or following the approach recently adopted by Baker J – will I suspect play an increasingly significant role in your professional lives (Munby 2013: 402).

The IFLA is the Institute of Family Law Arbitrators, a not for profit company whose members are Resolution, The Chartered Institute of Arbitrators and the Family Law Bar Association. By early 2014 it had trained around 100 arbitrators made up of solicitors, barristers and retired judges.[17] So those already operating as IFLA arbitrators are all legally trained and, theoretically, able to use the law to protect clients and children.

A recent case has set a precedent for referring a matrimonial case to a different kind of arbitration (see Rose 2013). In *AI v MT (Alternate Dispute Resolution)* [2013] EWHC 100 (Fam), the court had, in earlier proceedings, endorsed the use of rabbinical arbitration at the New York Beth Din (paras 15-16) and the result was upheld in the form of a consent order: 'The outcome was in keeping with English law whilst achieved by a process rooted in the Jewish culture to which the families belong' (para 37). The content of the order was deemed to be in the child's best interests and Mr Justice Baker commented that,

> 'it can be argued that arbitration is in line with the principle underpinning the Children Act 1989 that primary responsibility for children rests with their parents who should be entitled to raise their children without the intrusion of the state save where the children are suffering, or likely to suffer, significant harm' (para 32).

He warned, however, that, 'It does not... necessarily follow that a court would be content in other cases to endorse a proposal that a dispute concerning children should be referred for determination by another religious authority. Each case will turn on its own facts' (para 33). This caution is justified; where arbitration bodies are not essentially civil legal bodies then the norms used may be generated from diverse sources and disciplines and the words used – such as the 'welfare of the child' – may have different meanings (see King and Piper 1995: chapter 1).

What we now have is a proliferation of bodies to help separating parents make joint decisions but we do not know whether and how the shadow of the law features. For example, a legal qualification is not a requirement in the Law Society's latest criteria for mediators wishing to be accredited under the Law Society mediation scheme (to conduct MIAMs and publicly-funded mediation).[18] And the internet provides evidence of the existence and development of a confusing array of new groups and people offering ADR services and legal advice (see, for example, Eekelaar and Maclean 2013: 47-49; see also for telephone advice services, Smith *et al* 2013). Regulation is currently in the very early stages: although 35 organisations were recognised with the 'Help and support for separated families' (HSSF) mark during the pilot phase. The HSSF mark has been conferred on agencies that offer advice and support and that 'show that they actively work to help parents collaborate constructively to arrange things for their children'.[19] Whether all those offering these and dispute resolution services have a sufficient understanding of the protective role of law is, therefore, unknown. And there is yet another site which may draw on diverse norms, not neces-

17 See http://ifla.org.uk/what-is-arbitration.

18 See http://www.lawsociety.org.uk/accreditation/specialist-scheme/family-mediation/

19 See, for example, http://www.sortingoutseparation.org.uk/en/hub.aspx, accessed 17 March 2014.

sarily drawn from law's shadow, to inculcate the message of joint parenting. There is now education to persuade parents to do the 'right' thing.

Education

Freeman saw a role for education but not, perhaps, quite the one that it is now intended to have; it is now meant not only to inform but also to lead parents to modify their conduct. As Reece points out, in these times of what she calls post-liberalism, 'the sole purpose of providing information is to ensure that people make the right decision' (2003: 183).

Freeman said that parents have to be educated to accept that they are both responsible for and should be involved in the care of their children (Freeman, 1983: 218). He pointed to a code of visiting practices as a useful means of informing parents how to behave and how to meet their children's needs. So it seems that he saw education as a method of imparting information about what is best for children.

This process of information giving has come to be part of the educational toolkit used to teach parents how to deal with their breakup. For example, Cafcass has produced leaflets containing advice for parents and children (Cafcass, undated; Cafcass, 2010). There is now also an information hub (referred to as FISH - Family Information Services Hub or Family Information and Support Hub – in some areas, the Parenting Hub in others: see Herring 2012), the Child Maintenance Options site,[20] and the new government 'Sorting out Separation' site.[21] However, as Hunt suggests, the main impact of these sources of information is likely to be on those couples who would not litigate anyway: 'Merely *knowing* about alternative ways to resolve disputes would probably have a minimal impact on the scale of litigation' (2011: 381).

While there is little evidence that public education campaigns and information websites have the effect of altering individual behaviour (see Eekelaar and Maclean 2013: chapter 9; Kaganas 2013: 288-9) there is some evidence of limited success if a campaign takes into account factors that motivate change. A recent social marketing campaign designed to stimulate men's take-up of a new service for domestic violence perpetrators was devised in this way (Thomson *et al*, 2013). Social marketing campaigns rely on research carried out with the target population for their design and content and are aimed at 'reducing or replacing negative behaviours by promoting and encouraging positive alternatives' (Thomson *et al*, 2013: 34). In this case, focus groups were held in order to gain insight into the views of a sample of men that included perpetrators. The campaign was then devised to accommodate the finding that a strong motivation to change was the men's perception of themselves as fathers. They wanted to maintain a positive image of themselves from the perspective of their children, and were moved to change by the knowledge that violence could harm their children or lead them to lose contact (Stanley *et al*, 2012: 1312).

---

20 Child Maintenance Options <http://www.cmoptions.org/> accessed 26 May 2013.

21 Sorting Out Separation <http://www.sortingoutseparation.org.uk/en/hub.aspx> accessed 26 May 2013,

The message in this campaign was carefully crafted and it was intended to prompt men to see themselves through their children's eyes. In contrast, it appears that parents involved in contact disputes are not motivated to change; the very reason parents continue with their contact battles is because their image of themselves as good parents is tied up in the conflict. Mothers see themselves as protecting their children's best interests by resisting contact with fathers whom they see as dangerous or inadequate, while fathers persist in seeking contact so that their children will know they did not give up and abandon them (Kaganas and Day Sclater 2004).[22]

Separated Parents Information Programmes (PIPs) do not reduce conflict either, although they also include the strategy of trying to get parents to see things from the point of view of the children involved in disputes. These programmes take the form of group courses lasting 4 hours and they are the most popular contact activity ordered by the courts under s11A-E Children Act 1989 (Smith and Trinder, 2012: 429). They are intended to enable parents to see the effects of conflict through children's (albeit not their own children's) eyes:

> The course seeks to communicate to parents the child's experience of separation. In doing so, the overriding message is that conflict, especially over the children and especially expressed in front of the children, is harmful to children. The course therefore seeks to encourage some more specific behaviours, that is, parents should try to reduce ... conflicts ... for the sake of their children. As part of that, the course seeks also to encourage the use of mediation to resolve disputes.
>
> Another explicit message is the need of the child in most cases to have a relationship with both parents (Trinder *et al* 2011: 48).

Parents tend to give positive evaluations of these courses and they do appear to result in more contact taking place (Smith and Trinder, 2012: 436-7). However there is no evidence that there is any improvement in the parents' relationship and it is likely that children who are experiencing contact are not being protected from the harm that parental conflict causes (Smith and Trinder, 2012: 437). This problem may become even more apparent in future. PIPs are court mandated and are limited to those parents who are involved in litigation. Given the possibility that the legal aid cuts may reduce the number of cases going to court, PIPs may be available only to a small minority of parents and these will be high conflict cases.

Smith and Trinder say that PIPs do not address relationship conflict and attribute this to four factors: a pro-contact ethos which leads to a focus on the legal dispute and to oversimplification; a one-size-fits all approach which means that the programme is not appropriate in many cases such as those with a history of violence; resource constraints which mean that there are no other programmes and so there is a 'low intensity intervention being delivered to a high-needs population, (2012: 446); and

22 For detailed discussion of the psychosocial aspects of the divorce experience, see Day Sclater, 1999.

the self-referential nature of law that means that when cases return to court, judges return the parties to the legal dispute. They recommend a greater focus on communication and conflict resolution skills as well as a greater variety of programmes (2012: 449).

Salem *et al* are also in favour of intensive programmes but they do say that most reviews 'have concluded that there is *not yet* convincing evidence that parent education programs reduce inter-parental conflict, enhance parent-child relationships or improve children's post-divorce adjustment' (2013: 137). And the authors go on to observe that achieving these goals may 'require more extensive programs' (2013: 137) than those which are designed to impart information in a few hours. Further, these short duration courses can inflame the dispute in high conflict families (Hunt, 2011: 387). There is evidence that more intensive programmes can reduce parental conflict but these longer programmes could not be delivered to all divorcing families (Salem *et al* 2013: 139-40).

Parenting co-ordinators have also been seen by some as having positive results but, according to Hunt, there is little research on their effectiveness (2011: 386). These co-ordinators, who are legal or mental health professionals, have been introduced in the USA and Australia to work with parents in order to implement parenting plans and, if necessary, to arbitrate the dispute. Reviews referred to by Hunt are mixed, with some reports of satisfaction and some reports that there are families that do not respond well to the intervention (2011: 386; see also Fieldstone *et al* 2012).

Perhaps the most well-known comprehensive services for families that need help with post-separation arrangements are the Family Relationship Centres in Australia. These are modelled on the basis of the belief that people might need not only information and education but also services such as mediation, counselling and financial advice as well as legal advice and the option of litigation (P Parkinson 2013: 198). Information is provided but there are also individual sessions; booklets are not considered adequate to meet the needs of families requiring help (ibid: 203).

According to Parkinson this combination of services has led to reduced court involvement and he says that the services are useful for those who cannot afford to litigate and who do not qualify for legal aid (ibid: 208, 209). However such complex institutions and intensive interventions require investment and this is clearly not what our government wants. The cheaper interventions they have opted for are not backed up by any evidence of the likelihood of success and, if Hunt is right, they could make things worse.

Conclusions

Freeman's vision has, to a large extent, become reality. He recommended that the law and professionals send a message to parents about the need for cooperative parenting and that parents be educated about their responsibilities. In addition he thought that mediation should be encouraged. However it is most unlikely that he could have envisaged the withdrawal of legal aid and the move to exclude disputes about children from the legal arena. He could not have predicted that there would be a drive to replace adjudication with mediation. He could not have envisaged that, for most separating parents, all that would be left, apart from mediation or litigating in person, would be the message. Nor would he have envisaged that 'education' would be dispensed largely remotely through the use of websites and other 'outlets'. With his concern for the welfare of children and his efforts to promote respect for their views, he probably would not endorse approaches to dispute resolution that marginalise the interests and wishes of the child in question. He therefore would probably not approve of a message that put contact first or a law that contains a presumption that 'involvement' by both parents is in children's best interests.

The government's stated intention is to help children, to get parents to change their behaviour so that they reach agreement and keep out of court, and to increase respect for the legal system. There is no evidence that any of these things will happen. What is more likely is that the unintended or, at least, unproclaimed consequence will be that parents, or more likely only one of them, will agree to attend education and mediation but that the fight will continue – maybe even in court. What is of great concern is that, in some instances, vulnerable mothers will be persuaded by the combination of education, mediation and the new law – all probably giving the same simplified message – to agree to outcomes which do not include the protection they need or which leave their children in a situation which is not in their best interests. Neither mediators nor solicitors wish parents to be left without legal advice: 'Negotiating an agreement in ignorance of legal rights and entitlements would be dangerous ... Mediation needs to be combined with independent legal advice, not used as a substitute' (L Parkinson 2013: 205). Yet these concerns have not been heeded.

It may be that new sources of support and advice will emerge and will help to reduce unhappiness and conflict post-separation for all concerned. However, we fear that for the majority a simplified message about parental involvement will be purveyed, possibly combined with other, as yet unclear norms, will make settlement more difficult and even riskier.

Bibliography

Bailey-Harris, R., Davis, R., Barron, J. and Peara, J., *Monitoring Private Law Applications Under the Children Act: Research Report to the Nuffield Foundation* (Bristol: Bristol University, 1998).

Barlow, A., Hunter, R., Smithson, J., Ewing, J., Getliffe, K. and Morris, P., 'Mapping Paths to Family Justice: a national picture of findings on out of court family dispute resolution', *Family Law* 2013, 306-310.

Bell, F., Cashmore, C,. Parkinson, P. and Single, J., 'Outcomes of Child Inclusive Mediation' *Int J of Law, Policy and the Family* 2013 27(1), 116-142.

Cafcass *Putting Your Children First. A Guide for Separating Parents* (London: TSO, undated).

Cafcass *My Family's Changing* (London: TSO, 2010).

Caroline Opposes Lords' Amendment to Children & Families Bill on Shared Parenting' http://www.carolinenokes.com/uncategorized/caroline-opposes-lords-amendment-to-children-families-bill-on-shared-parenting/ (accessed 13 March 2014).

Coy, M., Perks, K., Scott, E. and Tweedale, R., *Picking up the Pieces: domestic violence and child contact* (London: Rights of Women, 2012).

Davis, G., *Partisans and Mediators: The Resolution of Divorce Disputes*, (Oxford: Clarendon Press, 1988).

Davis, G., S. Cretney and J. Collins, *Simple Quarrels* (Oxford: Clarendon Press, 1994).

Day Sclater, S., *Divorce: A Psychosocial Study* (Aldershot: Ashgate, 1999).

Dewar, J., 'Can the centre hold? Reflections on two decades of family law reform in Australia', *Child and Family Law Quarterly* 2010, 22, 377 - 386.

DCA, DfES and DTI, *Parental Separation: Children's Needs and Parents' Responsibilities* Cm 6273 (London: HMSO, 2004).

DCA, DfES and DTI, *Parental Separation: Children's Needs and Parents' Responsibilities: Next Steps* Cm 6452 (London: HMSO, 2005)

DfE, *Co-operative Parenting Following Family Separation. Proposed Legislation on the Involvement of Both Parents in a Child's Life, Summary of Consultation Responses and the Government's Response* (London: Department for Education, 2012)

DfE, 2013 Children and Families Bill 2013: Contextual Information and Responses to Pre-Legislative Scrutiny. Cm 8540, (London: Department for Education, 2013) https://www.education.gov.uk/publications/eOrderingDownload/Children%20and%20Families%20Bill%202013.pdf (accessed 10 April 2013)

DfE, Press Release 'Landmark Children and Families Act 2014 gains royal assent' (13 March 2014, https://www.gov.uk/government/news/landmark-children-and-families-act-2014-gains-royal-assent (accessed 14 March 2014)

DfE and MoJ, *Co-operative Parenting Following Family Separation: Proposed Legislation on the Involvement of Both Parents in a Child's Life.* Consultation (London: Department for Education, 2012).

Djanogly, J., *Hansard*, Westminster Hall Col 165WH 24 May 2012 http://www.publications.parliament.uk/pa/cm201213/cmhansrd/cm120524/halltext/120524h0001.htm (last visited 31 January 2013)

Eekelaar, J., '"Not of the Highest Importance": Family Justice Under Threat' *Journal of Social Welfare and Family Law* 2011, 33(4) 311 - 317.

Eekelaar, J. and Maclean, M., *Family Justice, The Work of Family Judges in Uncertain Times* (Oxford: Hart Publishing, 2013).

Eriksson, M., 'Contact, Shared Parenting, and Violence: Children as Witnesses of Domestic Violence in Sweden' *Int J Law Policy Family* 2011 25(2), 165-183.

Family Law Week '"Shared Parenting" amendment puts child welfare before presumption of equal access' (5 February 2014).

Fehlberg, B., B. Smyth, M. Maclean and C. Roberts, 'Legislating for Shared Time. Parenting after Separation: A Research Review', *Int J of Law, Policy and the Family* 2011, 25(3) 318- 327.

Fieldstone, L., M. Lee, J. Baker, J. and J. McHale, 'Perspectives on Parenting Coordination: Views of Parenting Coordinators, Attorneys, and Judiciary Members' *Family Court Review* 2012, 59(3), 441 - 454.

Fortin, J. and Hunt, J., Memorandum submitted by Jane Fortin and Joan Hunt (CF14). Submission of views to the House of Commons Public Bills Committee on Clause 11 of the Children and Families Bill Session 2012-13 (March 2013) http://www.publications.parliament.uk/pa/cm201213/cmpublic/childrenandfamilies/memo/cf14.htm (accessed 30 April 2013).

Fortin, J., Hunt, J. and Scanlan, L., *Taking a Longer View of Contact* (Sussex Law School, 2012).

Freeman, M., *The Rights and Wrongs of Children* (London: Frances Pinter, 1983).

Freeman, M., (Ed.) *Divorce: Where Next?* (Aldershot: Dartmouth, 1996).

Freeman, M., *The Moral Status of Children: Essays on the Rights of the Child* (Leiden: Martinus Nijhoff Publishers, 1997).

Griffiths, J., 'What do Dutch lawyers actually do in divorce cases?' *Law and Society Review* 1986, 20(1), 135 - 175.

Hamilton, C., Memorandum Submitted by Professor Hamilton (CF 17) Opening Statement of Professor Hamilton. Children and Families Bill Public Bill Committee Oral Evidence Session. Session 2012-13 (2013) http://www.publications.parliament.uk/pa/cm201213/cmpublic/childrenandfamilies/memo/cf17.htm (accessed 16 April 2013).

Harris, P., 'Legal aid cuts? What legal aid cuts?' *Family Law* 2012, 1267-1268.

Harris-Short, S., 'Resisting the March Towards 50/50 Shared Residence: Rights, Welfare and Equality in Post-separation Families', *J of Social Welfare and Family Law* 2010, 32(3) 257 - 274.

Herring, J., 'Divorce, Internet Hubs and Stephen Cretney' in R. Probert and C. Barton (eds), *Fifty Years in Family Law, Essays for Stephen Cretney* (Cambridge/Mortsel: Intersentia, 2012).

Herring, J. and Powell, O., 'The rise and fall of presumptions surrounding the welfare principle' *Family Law* 2013, 553-558.

Hunt, J., 'Through a Glass Darkly: The Uncertain Future of Private Law Child Contact Litigation' *J of Social Welfare and Family Law* 2011, 33(4) 379 - 396.

Hunt, J. and Macleod, A., *Outcomes of Applications to Court for Contact Orders after Parental Separation or Divorce* (London: Ministry of Justice, 2008).

Justice Committee, *Fourth Report. Pre-Legislative Scrutiny of the Children and Families Bill* (2012) http://www.publications.parliament.uk/pa/cm201213/cmselect/cmjust/739/73907.htm#a10 (accessed 29 April 2013).

Kaganas, F., 'A Presumption that "Involvement" of Both Parents is Best: Deciphering Law's Messages, *CFLQ*, 2013, 25(3), 270 - 293.

Kaganas, F. and Day Sclater, S., 'Contact Disputes: Narrative Constructions of "Good" Parents', *Feminist Legal Studies* 2004, 12(1), 1 - 27.

Kaspiew, R., Gray, M., Weston, R., Moloney, L. Hand, K. and Qu, L., *Evaluation of the 2006 family law reforms* (Australian Institute of Family Studies, 2009).

Kennedy, D., 'Form and Substance in Private Law Adjudication', *Harvard Law Review* 1976, 89, 1685-1778.

King, M., 'Being Sensible: Images and Practices of the New Family Lawyer', *Journal of Social Policy* 1999, 28(2), 249-273.

King, M. and Piper, C., *How the Law Thinks About Children* (Second Edition) (Arena: Aldershot, 1995).

Law Commission, *Family Law. Review of Child Law: Custody* Working Paper No 96 (London: HMSO, 1986).

Law Commission *Family Law. Review of Child Law. Guardianship and Custody* Law Com No 172 (London: HMSO, 1988).

Law Society, *Co-operative parenting following family separation. Response from the Law Society of England and Wales* (London: The Law Society, 2012) http://www.lawsociety.org.uk/representation/policy-discussion/co-operative-parenting-consultation-response/ (accessed 30 April 2013).

Lawyersupportedmediation 'Separating Couples Still Bypassing Mediation', 27 Oct 2013 http://lawyersupportedmediation.com/blog-posts/couples-still-bypassing-mediation (accessed 12 December 2013)

Lawyersupportedmediation 'Parents shun mediation for the courts' 8 March 2014 http://lawyersupportedmediation.com/blog-posts/parent-shun-mediation-courts (accessed 13 March 2014)

Maclean, M. and Eekelaar, J., *The Parental Obligation: A Study of Parenthood Across Households* (Hart Publishing: Oxford, 1997)

McKintosh, J., Wells, Y., Smith, B. and Long, C., 'Child-focused and child-inclusive divorce mediation: Comparative outcomes from a prospective study of post-separation adjustments' *Family Court Review* 2008, 46(1), 105-124.

Miles, J., 'Legal Aid, Article 6 and "Exceptional Funding" under the Legal Aid etc Bill 2011' *Family Law* 1003-1009.

Ministry of Justice, 2010. Proposals for the Reform of Legal Aid in England and Wales, Consultation

Paper CP 12/10.

Mnookin, R. and Kornhauser, L., 'Bargaining in the shadow of the law: the case of divorce', *Yale Law Journal* 1979, 88, 950- 997.

MoJ and DfE, *The Government Response to the family Justice review. A System with Children and Families at its Heart.* Cm 8273 (London: TSO, 2012a).

Morris, P., 'Screening for Domestic Violence in Family Mediation Practice' *Family Law* 2011, 41 649-651.

Morris, P., 'Mediation, the Legal Aid, Sentencing and Punishment of Offenders Act of 2012 and the Mediation Information Assessment Meeting' *JSW&FL* 2013, 445-457.

Munby, Sir James, 'Failure is not an Option' An address to the annual dinner of the Family Law Bar Association, Middle Temple Hall, February 2013, *Family Law* 2013, 401.

Munby, Sir James, 'View from the President's Chambers: the process of reform: where are we?' *Family Law* 2014, 167.

National Family Mediation (with the Calouste Gulbenkian Foundation) *Giving Children a Voice in Mediation: A Study of Mediation Practice* (London: National Family Mediation, 1994).

Norgrove, D., *The Family Justice Review.* Interim Report (London: The Ministry of Justice, the Department for Education and the Welsh Government, 2011a).

Norgrove, D., *Family Justice Review.* Final Report (London: The Ministry of Justice, the Department for Education and the Welsh Government, 2011b).

O'Hara, M., 'Legal Aid Cuts are Devastating to Women, Especially those Suffering Abuse, *The Guardian* 3 December 2013.

Parkinson, L., 'Adults should talk to kids more' *Family Law* 2012, 346-351.

Parkinson, L., 'The Place of Mediation in the Family Justice System', *Child and Family Law Quarterly* (2013) 25(2) 200-214.

Parkinson, P., 'The Idea of Family Relationship Centres in Australia,' *Family Court Review* (2013) 51(2) 195-213.

Perry, A. and Rainey, B., 'Supervised, Supported and Indirect Contact Orders: Research Findings', *Int J of Law, Policy and the Family* 2007, 21(1), 21-47.

Piper, C., 'Norms and Negotiation in Mediation and Divorce' in M Freeman (ed.) *Divorce: Where Next?* (Aldershot, Dartmouth, 1996).

Piper, C., 'How Do you Define a Family Lawyer?', *Legal Studies* 1999 19(1), 93-111.

Piper, C., 'Mediation and Vulnerable Parents' in Wallbank and Herring (eds), *Vulnerabilities, Care and Family Law* (Abingdon: Routledge, 2013).

Piper, C. and Kaganas, F., 'The Family Law Act 1996 s1(d): How will "they" know there is a risk of violence?' *Child and Family Law Quarterly* 1997, 9(3), 279-89.

Rhoades, H. 'Legislating to promote children's welfare and the quest for certainty' *Child and Family Law Quarterly* 2012 24(2), 158-175.

Richards, M., 'Post-Divorce Arrangements for Children: A Psychological Perspective' *Journal of Social Welfare Law*, 1982, 69, 133-151.

Rose, C., 'A new Path?' *N.L.J.* 2013, 163(7548), 153.

Ryrstedt, E. 'Mediation Regarding Children – Is the Result Always in the Best Interests of the Child? A View from Sweden' *Int J Law, Policy and the Family* 2012, 26 (2), 220-241.

Salem, P. Sandler, I. and Wolchick, S., 'Taking Stock of Parent Education in the Family Courts: Envisioning a Public Health Approach', *Family Court Review* 2013, 131-148.

Sarat, A. and Felstiner, W. 'Law and strategy in the divorce lawyer's office' *Law and Society Review* 1986 20, 93-134.

Smith, L. and Trinder, L. 'Mind the Gap: Parent Education Programmes and the Family Justice System', *CFLQ* 2012 24(4), 428-451.

Smith, M., Balmer, B., Miles, J., Denvir, C. and Patel, A., 'In scope but out of reach? Examining differences between publicly funded telephone and face-to-face family law advice', *CFLQ* 2013 25(3), 253-269.

Stanley, N., Fell, B., Miller, P., Thomson, G. and Watson, J., 'Men's Talk: Men's Understandings of Violence Against Women and Motivations for Change', *Violence Against Women* 2012, 1300-1318.

Stowe, M. Marilyn Stowe Blog 'Children and Families Act given royal assent', 14 March 2014, http://www.marilynstowe.co.uk/2014/03/14/children-and-families-act-given-royal-assent/ (accessed 14 March 2014)

Thomson, E. P., *Whigs and Hunters* (London: Allen Lane, 1975).

Thomson, G., Stanley, N. and Miller, P., 'Give me "strength to change": insights into a social marketing campaign in the North of England', *Primary Health Care Research & Development* 2013, 14(4) 350-354.

Trinder, L., Firth, A. and Jenks, C., '"So presumably things have moved on since then?" The management of risk allegations in child contact dispute resolution' *Int J Law, Policy and the Family* 2010, 24(1) 29-53, 34-38.

Trinder, L., Jenks, C. and Firth, A., 'Talking children into being *in absentia*? Children as a strategic and contingent resource in family court dispute resolution' *Child and Family Law Quarterly* 2010 22(2) 234-257.

Trinder, L., Bryson, C., Coleman, L., Houlston, C., Purdon, S., Reibstein, J. and Smith, L., *An Evaluation of the Costs and Effectiveness of the Separated Parents Information Programmes (PIP)* (London: DFE, 2011).

Trinder, L., Hunt, J., Macleod, A., Pearce, J and Woodward, H., *Enforcing Contact Orders: Problem Solving or Punishment?* (Exeter: Exeter Law School, 2013).

Walker, J., McCarthy, P. and Timms, N., *Mediation: The Making and Remaking of Co-operative Relationships* (Newcastle University: Relate Centre for Family Studies, 1994).

Walker, J., 'How can we ensure that children's voices are heard in mediation?' *Family Law* 2013, 191-195.

Wallerstein, J. and Kelly, J., *Surviving the Breakup* (New York: Basic Books, 1980).

Zolotor, A. and Puzia, M., 'Bans against Corporal Punishment: A Systematic Review of the Laws, Changes in Attitudes and Behaviours', *Child Abuse Review* 2010, 229-241.

Best Interests of the Child in Relocation: The Work and Views of Lawyers in England and Wales

Ghislaine Lanteigne*
University College London, UK

1. Introduction

In England and Wales, when a child arrangements order is in place (indicating 'with whom the child concerned is to live' and/or 'when the child is to live with any person'), a separated or divorced parent who wishes to relocate with the child outside the United Kingdom is required to have 'the written consent of every person who has parental responsibility' – in most circumstances, the other parent – or 'the leave of the court' (Children Act 1989, c. 41).[1] In contrast, this requirement does not apply to movements of a separated or divorced parent and child within the United Kingdom, and it is only in exceptional circumstances that a court would place conditions on a residence (child arrangements) order in private law as to the location where the parent should live within the United Kingdom (*In re E* (*Minors*) (*Residence: Conditions*) [1997] EWCA Civ 3084, [1997] 2 FLR 638).

Patterns of parental care for a child vary amongst separated and divorced parents; however, international relocation disputes often involve a primary carer (usually the mother) with whom the child lives, who wishes to move abroad but this is opposed by the other parent (usually the father). In some circumstances the parents might have shared care responsibilities for the child and the relocation proposal is disputed by one of them. A relocation proposal by one of the parents has the potential to bring a profound change in the life of these parents and their child and, when contested, will present challenges to be managed.

---

* PhD Candidate (Faculty of Laws, University College London), LLM, MA Linguistics, MA Sociology. The UCL Research Ethics Committee has approved the study on which this chapter is based. The study would not have been possible without the generous participation of the lawyers who took time to be interviewed and answer the demographic questionnaire. I am very grateful to them for this. With thanks to Professor Michael Freeman and the referee for constructive comments. Any omissions or errors are my sole responsibility.

1 Sections 13(1)(b), 13(4), as amended by the Children and Families Act 2014, c. 6 (hereinafter Children Act and Children and Families Act 2014).

A. Diduck, N. Peleg, H. Reece (eds.), Law in Society: Reflections on Children, Family, Culture and Philosophy
Copyright 2015 Koninklijke Brill NV. Printed in The Netherlands. ISBN 978-90-04-26148-8. pp. 395-423.

This chapter presents preliminary findings of a comparative qualitative study on the issues arising with regards to 'the best interests of the child' in England and Wales and in Canada in the preparation of relocation cases for court or in the settlement of these disputes through alternative dispute resolution (ADR). More specifically, this study aims at providing information on issues arising from factors considered by lawyers in the preparation of cases for court or by ADR practitioners in the settlement process of these disputes, as well as presenting their perspectives on the resolution process used. The focus of this chapter is on findings from the interviews and a demographic questionnaire conducted with lawyers from England and Wales based in London who acted for parents using litigation for international relocation disputes.

One qualitative study (George, 2011) presents the perspectives of judges, barristers, solicitors and social science professionals from England and Wales and from New Zealand about children's welfare in relocation disputes, using hypothetical vignettes to discuss issues and possible outcomes to these situations. The study also reports on the practitioners' experience and evaluation of relocation law in practice.[2] A few recent socio-legal studies incorporating a qualitative approach have focussed on family members' views and experience of relocation in England and Wales (Freeman, 2009), Australia (Parkinson *et al.*, 2010) and New Zealand (Taylor *et al.*, 2010). In contrast, this study centres on the practical work and views of lawyers and ADR practitioners who act as front line workers and gatekeepers, and seeks to contribute to the debate surrounding the resolution of relocation disputes.

In order to contextualise the findings from the interviews and questionnaire with the lawyers from England and Wales, first an overview of court guidelines for relocation cases in this jurisdiction will be presented, then an overview of socio-legal issues in view of the wellbeing and best interests of the child in relocation disputes. With regards to terminology used across disciplines and jurisdictions, 'wellbeing' is referred to in the social science literature reviewed while 'best interests of the child' is referred to, for instance, in legal international documents, in Canadian law, and to some extent in England and Wales case law. 'Welfare of the child' is used in England and Wales in statute and case law and is equivalent to 'best interests of the child'. Due to recent amendments to the Children Act, where appropriate in this paper the previous terminology (residence and/or contact orders) and the new one (child arrangements orders)[3] are used together with one or the other in parentheses.

---

2 The author is grateful to Rob H. George for providing before the time of writing this chapter a copy of his Chapter 4 on 'Evaluating Relocation Law in England and Wales' from his then forthcoming book reporting on his study. As findings in George's study are reported for participants as a group (incorporating the different categories of practitioners) and are in part based on hypothetical vignettes, or explore topics not covered in this chapter, comparisons between the findings of his study and those presented in this chapter are not pursued.

3 Children Act , s. 8(1), as amended by the Children and Families Act 2014 'residence order' and 'contact order' are replaced by 'child arrangements order' which regulate 'arrangements relating to any of the following— (a) with whom a child is to live, spend time or

2. Court Guidelines in England and Wales for Relocation Cases

Until fairly recently, the decision from the Court of Appeal in *Payne v. Payne* [2001] EWCA Civ 166, [2001] 1 FLR 1052 (*Payne*) determined the main guidelines in England and Wales for court decisions in international relocations. Although Dame Elizabeth Butler-Sloss P. also gave a judgment and provided a non-exhaustive list of considerations for these cases based on the paramountcy of the welfare of the child, it is part of the judgment of Thorpe L.J. that has usually been referred to as the guidance from the case. He indicated that in relocation cases, 'the welfare of the child is the paramount consideration' and that a refusal of a primary carer's reasonable proposal 'is likely to impact detrimentally on the welfare of her dependent children'.[4] He concluded that unless the application is incompatible with the welfare of the children, the primary carer's application to relocate should be granted. Thorpe L.J. advocated the following guidance: (a) establishing that the mother's proposal is genuine and well researched; (b) if so, assessing the father's opposition (is it genuine?), the extent of the detriment to him and to his relationship with the child if the application were granted, as well as the possible offset brought by the extension of the child's relationships with the maternal family and homeland; and finally (c) appraising the impact of a refusal on the mother. The evaluations in (b) and (c) are then brought into an overriding review of the child's welfare as the paramount consideration, guided as appropriate by the welfare checklist of the Children Act. Thorpe L.J. also stressed the importance of considering 'the emotional and psychological well-being of the primary carer' in an evaluation of the welfare of the child.[5]

It should be noted that the welfare checklist under Section 1(3) of the Children Act as referred to by Thorpe L.J. is not specifically fashioned for relocation disputes but is to be considered by the court when making orders related to children. The factors listed can be summarised as follows: (a) wishes and feeling of the child in view of his age and understanding, (b) his physical, emotional and educational needs, (c) likely effect on him of changes in his circumstances, (d) his age, sex, background and other relevant characteristics, (e) harm he has suffered or is at risk of suffering, (f) capability of each parent and any other relevant person to meet his needs, and (g) range of powers available to the court under this Act in the proceedings in question.

Some critiques propose that *Payne* sustained a presumption in favour of the primary carer (Perry, 2001; Duggan, 2007) and have categorised England and Wales as a pro-relocation jurisdiction (Carmody, 2007; Freeman, 2010). In 2011, the Court of Appeal brought down a decision (*K v. K (Children: Permanent Removal from Jurisdiction)* [2011] EWCA Civ 793, [2012] 2 FLR 880) (*K v. K*) which seems to have shifted the paradigm developed by *Payne*. In *K v. K*, both parents shared in the daily care of their five- and two-year old daughters. Thorpe, Moore-Bick and Black L.JJ., through individual judg-

---

otherwise have contact, and (b) when a child is to live, spend time or otherwise have contact with any person'.

4 *Payne* at para. 26.

5 *Ibid* at para. 41.

ments, indicated that the only principle to be derived from *Payne* is the paramountcy of the welfare principle and that the rest is guidance as to the factors to be considered under the umbrella of this principle.

Based on the 'practical arrangements' established by 'two equally committed carers',[6] Thorpe L.J. identified shared care cases as a type where use of the welfare checklist of the Children Act as referred to by Hedley J. (*Re Y (Leave to Remove from the Jurisdiction)* [2004] 2 FLR 330, [2004] Fam. Law 650) is warranted, while when a primary carer is identified, the guidance in *Payne* would be appropriate. However, Black L.J. preferred not to distinguish between these two types of cases within different lines of authority but rather proposed that they were 'within the framework of which *Payne* is part'[7] by which we can suppose she referred to the framework of the paramountcy of the welfare of the child. She also pointed out that *Payne* should be read as a whole, including the judgments of both Thorpe L.J. and Dame Elizabeth Butler-Sloss P. Black L.J.'s approach entails considering all cases under the welfare principle with reference to the Children Act and, depending on the nature of the case, referring to *Payne* for specific factors to be considered.

In using the guidelines provided by *K v. K,* courts could focus on Black L.J.'s approach (Scott, 2011; Eaton and Reardon, 2011) or alternatively, they could use an approach based on Thorpe L.J.'s judgment (Herring, 2011). *K v. K* has also been considered as 'lending significant support to *Payne*', which remains good law to guide lower courts in '(most) international relocation cases', with shared care being the 'limited exception' (George, 2012: 112,125). Irrespective of these possible decision pathways, the paramountcy of the welfare principle was pivotal in the court's analysis in *K v. K.* This central tenet was present in *Payne*; the court in *K v. K* reaffirmed it as the basis for relocation decisions with reference to the welfare checklist of the Children Act.

A subsequent case from the Court of Appeal helps to point the way forward. In *Re F (child)* [2012] EWCA Civ 1364, [2013] 1 FLR 645 (*Re F*), Munby L.J. (as he then was) reviewed *Payne* and its interpretation in *K v. K* to underline that in cases governed by section 1 of the Children Act, '[f]rom beginning to end the child's welfare is paramount',[8] and is to be determined with reference to the welfare checklist. He refers to a similarity of views between Moore-Bick and Black L.JJ. in *K v. K* to also stress that the guidance in *Payne* is not determinative of a case but is nevertheless valuable and can be referred to depending on individual circumstances.

3. Socio-legal Issues in Relocation Disputes

3.1 *The Voice of the Child*

Current approaches in social sciences and socio-legal studies view children as agents capable of shaping their own lives, expressing their views and influencing the lives

6 *K v. K* at para. 57.
7 *Ibid* at para. 144.
8 *Re F* at para. 37.

of others, particularly those in their own family (Smart *et al.*, 2001; Butler *et al.*, 2002; Parkinson and Cashmore, 2008). Their views in decisions affecting them, such as those resulting from parental separation disputes, are seen as important in that children are perceived as 'the most reliable witnesses of their own experience' (Butler *et al.*, 2002: 99). However, a concern about involving children in such decisions is the extent to which this represents too large a responsibility by placing the child in possible loyalty conflicts within the interparental dispute. Within this view, the *voice* of the child is to be heard and taken into account but the *choice,* i.e. the decision, is left to parents and/or dispute resolution professionals (Parkinson and Cashmore, 2008). Some children themselves report wanting to be consulted while some prefer not to participate in decisions concerning them in post-separation arrangements (Smart *et al.*, 2001; Buchanan and Hunt, 2003; Parkinson and Cashmore, 2008) and in relocation circumstances (Gollop and Taylor, 2012). Consultation was also strongly supported by young adults in a study focussing on their perspectives on post-separation contact arrangements they had experienced as children (Fortin *et al.*, 2012).

In England and Wales, when parents resort to litigation for their relocation dispute, the court may make, vary or discharge an order related to child arrangements (previously: 'residence' and 'contact') and shall have regard to 'the ascertainable wishes and feelings of the child' considering 'his age and understanding', this being part of the statutory welfare checklist.[9] Research shows that although it is hard to establish rigid age frames for when a child can effectively provide his or her wishes and feelings, supportive environments can greatly extend their capabilities (Taylor, 2006). Within this perspective, the child is usually consulted by a social science professional as part of the preparation of a welfare report. This report can be ordered by the court at the first hearing of an application concerning 'any question with respect to a child under this Act',[10] including a relocation dispute. The report would be provided by a CAFCASS officer (Children and Family Court Advisory and Support Service) or by an independent service jointly chosen by the parents, these professionals usually being social workers.

3.2 Use of Litigation

The research presented in this section reports on the effects of interparental conflict on children, and on parents' experience and views in using litigation for family disputes. An important body of research concerning the effects of interparental conflict on children presents data on the consequences of separation and divorce for children. It is indicated that interparental conflict before and after separation and divorce (the marital dissolution unfolding over time) can affect the wellbeing of a child. (Amato and Keith, 1991; Emery, 1999; Amato, 2001; Hetherington and Kelly, 2002; Grych, 2005;

---

9 Children Act s. 1(3)(4), as amended by the Children and Families Act 2014.

10 *Ibid* s. 7.

Harold and Murch, 2008; Amato, 2010).[11] Conflict that is frequent, intense, child related and poorly resolved is particularly detrimental (Harold and Murch, 2008).

In a study on divorce litigation, the majority of parents involved reported that the legal process was distressful, it had raised the level of conflict with the other parent and they felt left out of the decision making (Pruett and Jackson, 2001). In a study on disputed contact cases, although in the court proceedings violence was cited as an issue for a quarter of the cases, suggesting an already existing high conflict situation for these parents,[12] the researchers indicate that many of the parents' reports suggest that the proceedings themselves were significant in 'fuelling the flames and maintaining high stress levels over a prolonged period' (Buchanan and Hunt, 2003: 379).

Most of the parents involved in a New Zealand study on relocation disputes also viewed the court process as very stressful with a negative impact on their relationship with their ex-partner (Taylor, *et al.*, 2010). Many of these parents were also strongly dissatisfied with the cost of litigation, with some of them reporting serious financial difficulty, including mortgagee sales. Distress about the high costs of litigation was also reported by parents involved in relocation disputes in England and Wales (Freeman, 2009; Taylor and Freeman, 2010) and in Australia (Parkinson *et al.*, 2010). Although the legal costs varied considerably for parents in the Australian study, the average cost for a parent choosing litigation was $74,250 AUD while an average salary at around the time of the first interviews in 2007 was about $55,600 per year, A number of parents reported having to sell properties, including the family home, with others borrowing or accepting gifts of money from family to meet their legal costs.

Two studies, one of which is mentioned above (Buchanan and Hunt, 2003; Trinder *et al.*, 2008), reporting on the relationship between litigated contact disputes and child adjustment, indicate poorer adjustment in children, particularly for boys, as compared to community norms.[13] Correlation between the wellbeing of the parent and that of the child is also reported. Trinder hypothesises that this could be linked to the emotional state of the parent who reports on the wellbeing of the child or to a diminished capacity to parent in times of distress. Wallerstein and Kelly (1980), in discussing this latter aspect, indicate that following separation or divorce, a parent might need to focus on their own concerns, hence for a period of time offer less support to their child.

---

11 In a review of 92 studies, variables used in the studies fall under the following categories: academic achievement, conduct, psychological adjustment, self-concept, social adjustment, mother-child relations, father-child relations, and other (Amato & Keith, 1991).

12 Physical violence was reported as existing at some point in the relationship in 56% of cases.

13 The tests included the General Health Questionnaire (GHQ) and the Strengths and Difficulties Questionnaire (SDQ) which were administered around the time of the court proceedings with follow-up at a one year interval for the first study, and at six month and two year intervals for the second study. Parents in the second study also reported interparental violence or abuse, and this was indicated as a reason for the separation by almost 30% of them.

Moreover, for a child, a relocation proposal by one parent can represent another edition of the original disruption that happened in the marital dissolution (Wallerstein and Tanke, 1996). Consequently, in view of the above research, interparental conflict in the context of a contested relocation proposal can affect the wellbeing of the child.

3.3 Diversion from Litigation

It has been argued that law is 'too blunt an instrument with which to address the profound emotional forces that underlie family litigation' (Day Sclater and Kaganas, 2003: 157). Families facing personal and stressful decisions which they cannot resolve on their own, will be drawn into a legal system operating within a highly structured problem-solving framework (Miller *et al.*, 2013) accompanied by the possible emotional and financial turmoil described above. Some of the shortcomings identified with using the adversarial system in family disputes include, as documented above, intensification of conflicts (Bream and Buchanan, 2003; Emery *et al.*, 2005; Pruett *et al.*, 2005; Firestone and Weinstein, 2008), along with disempowerment and dehumanisation of participants, rights over interests, zealous advocacy, delays and expenses (Firestone and Weinstein, 2008). In particular, it has been suggested that the adversarial system with its oppositional and binary thinking does not work as well in complex and fluid situations as is required under the best interests of the child principle (Menkel-Meadow, 1996).

In the light of limitations to the adversarial system such as those listed above, mediation, as the best known form of ADR, is well established in England and Wales with institutionalised groups of practitioners, involvement of the legal profession and government support (Roberts and Palmer, 2005). More extended use of mediation was part of the recommendations of the final report of the Family Justice Review 2011. Further support includes the Children and Families Act 2014 which makes it mandatory under Section 10 to attend a Mediation Information and Assessment Meeting before an application in relevant family matters is made to court. The Child Arrangements Programme under Practice Direction 12B has replaced the Private Law Programme and is a streamlined court case management approach for disputes concerning arrangements related to children. There is also an emphasis on exploring out of court settlement for these disputes.

However, in spite of the above critiques of the adversarial system and endorsement of mediation, several parents in England and Wales participating in a study on relocation mentioned being reticent in using mediation, mostly due to their and the other parent's polarised positions on the question of the proposed relocation. (Freeman, 2009). Research with parents involved in relocation disputes indicates that in Australia, 59 per cent of the disputes studied were resolved by judicial determination (Parkinson *et al.*, 2010) while in New Zealand, this was the case for 51 per cent of the disputes analysed (Taylor *et al.*, 2010). In contrast, the first study indicates that 6 per cent of all family disputes in Australia are resolved by a court judgment.

Considering the above issues in the socio-legal literature surrounding the use of litigation for relocation disputes, the current study aims in part at exploring lawyers' work and views as advisors and advocates to parents using litigation for these disputes.

4. Methodology and Participants' Background

This study uses a phenomenological approach with a focus on 'the quality and texture of the participant's experience' (Willig, 2012: 69). Purposive sampling procedure was used in sending invitations by email to approximately 95 solicitors and barristers from different firms in London, identified through lists of professional associations and websites of firms as having experience in relocation. Twelve lawyers with experience of relocation disputes in the last five years were selected (nine lawyers responded to emails while three lawyers were invited based on snowball sampling). Semi-structured, in-depth interviews of an average of 40 minutes each were held at their place of work between September 2012 and January 2013, where lawyers had been invited to talk about their experience in using either litigation, negotiation or collaborative law with relocation disputes. The interviews were taped, transcribed and then reviewed in detail using the software NVivo to help achieve a thematic analysis. Demographic data was collected before the interviews through an online questionnaire using the software Opinio.[14]

Eleven of the 12 lawyers from England and Wales who were interviewed decided to talk about preparing cases for court and parts of their interviews are presented in this chapter.

One lawyer talked about her experience as a collaborative lawyer and this is not included in the findings reported here. Prior to this chapter being submitted, the findings and analysis on which it is based were presented to each of the 11 lawyers who participated in this part of the study and as a result, slight adjustments were made to add to the preservation of anonymity in the reported data.

Among the lawyers from England and Wales who participated in this part of the study, seven were solicitors and four were barristers: six women and five men. They all had long-standing experience with relocation cases: 9 lawyers had more than 15 years of experience (one lawyer had more than 25 years of experience; 4 lawyers had 21-25 years of experience and 4 lawyers had 16-20 years of experience) while 2 lawyers had 11-15 years of experience. Apart from experience in litigation, the lawyers had experience with relocation cases in the following fields: negotiation (9), mediation (6) and collaborative law (2). Two additional lawyers also acted as mediators but did not have experience in mediating relocation disputes. Two lawyers (one solicitor and one barrister) also acted as arbitrators in family law in financial and property matters, and one barrister acted as a Recorder in a county court. Nine lawyers indicated repre-

14 A similar procedure was used to interview 12 lawyers in Toronto, Canada and 6 mediators each in London and Toronto and those findings (part of a work in progress) are not presented here. These cities, being the largest in each country/jurisdiction, were chosen as the locations for the interviews to maximise variety of representation in the samples and to enable an eventual comparison between them.

senting most often either parent, while one lawyer indicated mainly representing the parent wishing to relocate and another one mainly representing the opposing parent.

The lawyers were part of groups of various sizes offering services in family matters in their firms/chambers: 3 solicitors were from groups with less than 10 practitioners; 4 were from groups of 10-19 practitioners and the 4 barristers were in chambers with 50 and more practitioners. Services other than litigation in relocation disputes offered by the firms/chambers to which the participants belonged were as follows: negotiation and mediation (9 firms/chambers), collaborative law (8 firms/chambers), Early Neutral Evaluation (one chamber) and support with self help (one firm).

Lawyers were invited to talk about their general experience in litigation over the last five years with completed relocation cases. Topics covered during the interviews included the following: common factors in the decision to litigate, common factors in preparing cases for court, involvement of the child, and use of litigation and of ADR in relocation disputes. For the second and third topics listed above, challenges and advantages were also explored. Two other topics were also covered during the interviews but are not presented in this chapter: 'views on court guidelines for relocation cases' and 'professional and personal challenges' in working with relocation cases. Also not presented in detail are suggestions spontaneously made by lawyers about issues they identified in relocation disputes.

The legal terminology used by lawyers in this study is within the previous framework of the Children Act (prior to amendments brought by the Children and Families Act 2014) in particular regarding 'residence' and 'contact'. This terminology will also be used in introducing and summarising findings.

5. Findings

5.1 *Choosing a Dispute Resolution Process*

What brings parents to choose litigation for their relocation dispute? All of the lawyers interviewed indicated that what brings a parent to consult them on the issue of relocation is linked to the difficulty in reaching an agreement with the other parent and that the issue is a crucial and deeply emotional one as illustrated in the following:[15]

> Going back to Australia or staying here is seismic, completely seismic, it's that moment in your life when – like with the sliding doors film – it either pans out one way or a completely different way and, you know, 'I'm only in this country because I fell in love with you, I always wanted to go home, I thought we were going to go home and now you're

15 Expressions used to indicate the range of occurrences under a theme, apart from 'all' and 'one', are as follows: 'almost all' and 'most of' cover comments by 9-10 lawyers, 'a few' covers comments by 2-4 lawyers, otherwise approximate sample portions are used, e.g. 'about half' to cover comments by 5-6 lawyers. See Howitt (2010) for the possibility in qualitative research of quantifying occurrences of comments by different participants under a theme.

> stopping me from going home. Oh my God'! So, people's ability to negotiate is much lower over this stuff than any other area of work. (Male solicitor.)
>
> If the mother says, 'No, no, I want to move right now!' It's the all or nothingness of it that causes people to litigate because they don't see that discussing it [could help]. (Female barrister.)[16]
>
> If one parent has a desperate desire to relocate elsewhere now ... and the other parent opposes the move because they believe it will fracture their relationship with their children or they just don't want to give in to what their former spouse wants, then the only viable mechanism in most people's minds is litigation. (Male solicitor.)[17]

The difficulty for a parent who is not able to agree to a relocation proposal is seen as being linked to that parent's attachment to the child and deep concern over the situation. For example:

> The real problem is that it's very hard for the parent on the receiving end of the request to agree to allow their child to go and live in another country because they know it's going to impact their relationship with the child and a lot of the cases that I deal with I get the sense that it's because the parent wants to be able to say, 'I didn't want you to go and I tried to keep you here and I thought you were better off here and I fought my hardest because I didn't want you to go and live abroad, I wanted you to be near me'. And I think that's often why the cases don't settle, because the parent feels the need to demonstrate that they really don't want this to happen and that they fought for their child. (Female solicitor.)
>
> I know very few parents who have just litigated because they didn't like the other parent. Certainly my clients have had their children in the forefront of their minds but it was not a decision they could make. It was a decision that a third party would have to make. (Female solicitor.)

Situational factors influencing the choice of a dispute resolution process were mentioned by a few lawyers:

---

16 Based on their overall experience, some of the lawyers refer to the parent who proposes to move as 'the mother' while 'the father' is referred to as the opposing parent.

17 When a sentence or part of it has been removed from a quote for clarity or brevity, this is indicated with three dots: ... ; when two or three sentences have been removed from a quote or the text within a quote is taken from two paragraphs in the transcript, this is indicated by two oblique bars: //; inserted clarifications of the meaning of a quote are within square brackets: [ ].

> Generally people come when they are either already in the process of proceedings, i.e. they've been served with an application to relocate or they're thinking about relocation and they don't know how to go about it. (Female solicitor.)

> Very often we would get the proceedings going anyway because there's this woman who is saying, 'Well, I've got to move by such and such a date, I have this job opportunity, it will only be held open for me for so long', so we issue the proceedings. (Female solicitor.)

> In the cases that I have dealt with this is usually as a result of child abduction initially and so it means it is an emergency, so the beginning of the case is done usually very quickly. (Male solicitor.)

Almost all of the lawyers mentioned that they consider alternatives to litigation with the parent towards the beginning of the case. Their views on the use of ADR for these disputes will be explored in Section 5.5 below.

5.2 *Preparing for Court – Common Factors and Challenges*

To illustrate the common factors focused on in preparation for court, lawyers referred mainly to their representing the parent wishing to relocate (usually the mother) as these factors constitute the framework of the case. When representing the opposing parent, a few lawyers reported briefly that they focus on questioning the relocation proposal, including the contact arrangements. In their representing the parent who wishes to relocate, all of the lawyers indicated reviewing the relocation proposal extensively. This requires preparing detailed information so as to build a picture of the child's life in the other location, 'a life book' as one female solicitor called it. Items to be part of this dossier include: the income and/or possibility of employment for the parent wishing to relocate, housing, schools, child care, support network, health care (doctor, dentist), leisure possibilities in the area, the child's familiarity with the new country including language and other amenities relevant to the child.

All of the lawyers indicated also focusing on the future contact arrangements with the non-relocating parent and this was underlined as a crucial factor by about half of them. These arrangements include direct contacts (such as visiting and holiday arrangements) and indirect contact (such as Skype and emails) and cover the feasibility of the planned arrangements, i.e. financial, logistical and timing aspects. Distance was mentioned by a few lawyers as being critical. For instance:

> One [factor] is how far away the relocation is – to what extent will it be possible to put together a package of contact which is likely to work, and that in turn brings in a question of finance. (Male barrister.)

A few of the lawyers said they use the welfare checklist of the Children Act to frame details of the child's life in the other location and the future contact arrangements. About half of the lawyers explained that providing detailed living and contact arrangements had the benefit of reassuring the other parent, the officer preparing a welfare report and the court so that, as indicated by one female solicitor, it can be seen that 'it isn't just sort of something that's been cooked up overnight; it's been well thought out and well researched, and is logical'.

Most of the lawyers stated that they explore with the parents the rationale given for wishing to relocate. An important factor considered by one male solicitor was domestic violence and this was present in 'nearly all' of his cases and therefore emergency measures were necessary, i.e. in one occurrence, a non-molestation order in view of threats to life.

When lawyers were asked about the challenges met in the preparation of cases, one of the most common themes was a well-researched dossier, prepared by the lawyer and the parent wishing to relocate, which could mean sometimes encouraging participation from that parent. If acting for the opposing parent, it could mean finding particular information about the new location, for instance, in one case a city which had an economy and level of crime that could be considered difficult. The next most common theme in representing the parent wishing to relocate was ensuring adequate contact arrangements, as explained below:

> I also ask the client to think about how they are going to promote contact with the left-behind parent. I mean, that's very important. ... How are you going to maintain contact with someone who is not going to see the child on the regular basis they have been up to now? (Female solicitor.)

> If there is any real doubt about the mother's commitment and if there's any suspicion that part of her motivation is to try and diminish the relationship with the father, then that is a highly relevant factor which the court has to be concerned about and which, if I get that feeling when I'm acting for a mother, it sends a red warning signal. If I get that feeling when I'm acting for a father then it's a matter that I will play on because it is a factor which is likely to lead the court to refuse to grant permission. (Male barrister.)

According to a few lawyers, a parent's rationale for wishing to relocate needs to be satisfactory, as one stated:

> The starting point has to be, what's your motivation? Why do you want to leave this country when you came here happily, one assumes, and you have happily had children here and you have raised your family here, what is it that now makes you say, 'I no longer want to be here and I want to take my children with me?' If you're given a satisfactory reason by the client, the rest of it tends to fall into place because they will probably be quite a reasonable person and they will therefore have actually thought it through. (Male solicitor.)

Other challenges mentioned by a few lawyers relate respectively to the emotional state of the parent who wishes to relocate, how a parent will deal with the welfare officer's investigation, and safety (only one lawyer mentioned 'security'):

> The one that's challenging is the showing that the parent is struggling. If somebody is very depressed, for example, that would be psychiatric evidence but people don't get very depressed, they don't tend to go to psychiatrists about it. They are just very down because they can't, obviously, go off and go home or their feelings are unsupported. That's a challenge because I think sometimes the court or the other parent might think they're putting it on just to sort of show the court that they can't survive here anymore. (Female barrister.)

> I would always much rather meet the client before the client has met the CAFCASS officer so that I can go through the matters which are likely to be concerning to the CAFCASS officer and discuss with the client how he or she is going to be dealing with those. (Male barrister.)

> Security: not for just the client and the child but also for us as well, to be honest, as we have been threatened, yes. We have got CCTV because people here have been threatened by parties to cases. (Male solicitor.)

5.3 *Involving the Child*

As referred to in the literature review and in the previous section, one way to seek the wishes and feelings of the child in family law cases is through a welfare report. The findings of the interviews presented here centre on this professional consultation with the child.

5.3.1 Age and Understanding of the Child

According to all of the lawyers interviewed, there is some fluidity about the youngest age at which a child will be consulted but most of them reported along the lines indicated by the following lawyer in terms of age of consultation and weight accorded by the court to the reported data:

> Obviously if it's a baby their wishes and feelings aren't sought, [and] two, three, four year olds. Once they get over that age they will be spoken to by a CAFCASS officer. How much weight is put on their views depends on their age and understanding of the issue. So between sort of five and ten, eleven, they will have their views taken into account in the sense of they'll be sought, they'll be included in the report but they won't necessarily be given a lot of weight when deciding what's best for the child. As a child gets over eleven - twelve, thirteen, fourteen, that sort of age - then their opinions do count for a lot and the court does take them into account but it isn't the only factor. The court is looking at the child's welfare, what's in the child's best interests and even if the child isn't necessarily keen on moving the court may still think it's in the child's best interests to do so if they're staying with their primary carer and it is probably the only reasonable plan for that child's day to day care. (Female solicitor.)

However, the following comments add details on the balancing task of the court in this area:

> The difficult age is between five and eleven because obviously children of that age vary in terms of maturity and their ability to express their feelings. You know, sometimes I've done a case where a nine year old is very, very clear and intelligent and mature. (Male barrister.)

> I don't think I've ever seen a relocation succeed with a child over eleven unless the child really wants to go. (Female solicitor.)

This last perspective is similar to one indicated in an Australian study on family law disputes where in a sub sample of 15 lawyers interviewed, it is reported that 'many lawyers expressed the view that making orders which go against the wishes of teenagers is futile' (Parkinson and Cashmore, 2008: 99).

5.3.2 The Welfare Report

In summarising the view of a few lawyers about CAFCASS, one female and one male barrister indicated respectively that it 'does the best that it can do' and that 'they're usually very good at it'. On the other hand, as one male solicitor put it, 'because of variability of quality and because of speed' he would employ independent social workers, as a few other lawyers also indicated. For those using CAFCASS, it means a wait period which, according to a few lawyers, can vary between 4 and 12 months and hence the timing of the litigation process is influenced not only by the wait time for court hearings but also for the CAFCASS welfare report.

One advantage of a professional consultation with the child, as viewed by one female barrister, is that it is 'the only way' to involve them since 'any more would be overburdening them and any less would have them not involved at all'. Other advantages respectively mentioned by a few lawyers are that it provides a voice for a child caught in the middle and can help parents reach a decision either based on what their child has indicated, or on the professional's assessment, as indicated in the following:

> Provided you've got a [independent] social worker who is prepared to report in a timely way, you can compromise the case on the back of the report if it's a pretty sturdy report which says 'yes' or 'no'. Then it's likely that the litigation will come to an end without the horrors of three days of cross-examination of both parties. (Male solicitor.)

5.3.3 Importance of the Voice of the Child

Most of the lawyers were of the view that in principle it is important to give a proper space to the voice of the child. As one lawyer remarked:

> I only do children work and I think in all of my litigation my lament is adults speak on behalf of their children, and you'll have two perfectly sensible parents in court with diametrically opposed views both saying, 'This is in my child's best interests'. So, it's really difficult and I often think, 'Well, where is the child in all of this'? And you [as a barrister] speak of how 'he' [the father] feels and 'she' [the mother] feels and not how 'they' [the children] might feel. (Female barrister.)

However, some concerns were expressed about seeking the wishes and feelings of the child, for instance, consequent pressure for the child, as indicated by about half of the lawyers and summarised below:

> I think going through the whole facade of trying to elicit children's wishes and feelings, where it's very difficult, they're in an almost impossible situation. Their loyalties are to both parents. It exposes them to the possibility of their parents putting pressure on them, maybe not consciously, but putting pressure on them to provide a specific response if asked a question by this lady who's going to come and visit or, 'When you go to court to say what I want you to say'. (Male solicitor.)

The above views resonate with the perspectives of most of the Australian lawyers in the Parkinson and Cashmore (2008) study, who also considered it important that the voice of the child be heard in interparental disputes but with slightly more than half of them expressing concerns about parental pressure on the child.

Finally, one lawyer referred to the level of responsibility required of the child and another one questioned altogether the process of ascertaining the wishes and feelings of the child in relocation disputes as currently litigated:

> I think it's a really complicated issue and I think often the children are spoken to for an hour by the CAFCASS officer and that will be it. And then, the burden of managing this falls on them because if, for example, Mum goes to live in Argentina and the child was twelve and they decide between them that three times a year she or he will be brought to England. It's the child whose life is disrupted because they are living in one place, going to school in one place and then when they have holidays and they should be spending it with their peers in that country, they're here. But then, the paternal family might be here and they need to see them. I think it's difficult and the burden falls very heavily on the children. (Female barrister.)

> Of course in the real world you would engage with kids properly but we're in Alice in Wonderland [referring to possible adversarial strategies used by parents concerning the interim contact from the beginning of litigation to the final hearing]. Who does involving kids in something this toxic? Is that good for them? I'm not sure. I don't know. (Male solicitor.)

5.4 *Using Litigation*

Questions asked to lawyers included: What do you think of the use of litigation in relocation disputes? In your opinion, does it serve the best interests of the child? The themes touched upon by the lawyers when discussing the use of litigation included: necessity, costs and time requirement, case strategy, emotions and the co-parenting relationship, the best interests of the child, and benefits. It is worth noting that descriptors about relocation litigation (other than those appearing in the quotes of this section) used respectively by different lawyers point to the turbulent dynamics present in this type of litigation: 'stressful', 'out of control', 'scary', 'struggle', 'bloodshed – not real bloodshed', 'painful', 'damaging'.

5.4.1 Necessity, Costs and Time Requirement

As indicated in section 5.1 above, all of the lawyers were of the view that in the absence of interparental agreement, litigation becomes a necessary option. One lawyer commiserated with parents facing a difficult choice:

> I can see why people can't compromise or don't wish to compromise. It's the sort of case where you need a third party to make that terrible decision. ... The relocation decision is the hardest because it has such profound effects on family life. (Male barrister.)

Two female solicitors indicated that litigation was a 'last resort' while two male solicitors were respectively of the view that it was 'awful' and 'the wrong environment' altogether for dealing with most children's issues.

Although not queried about the costs of relocation litigation, most of the lawyers found these high or, in the words of a male solicitor, 'eye-watering'. Lawyers' comments include the following:

> The cases have got to be prepared properly on both sides and it is very expensive. (Female solicitor.)

> How these cases are litigated probably depends on how wealthy the parents are because they're quite expensive to litigate if you do them properly, and most people of average financial backgrounds probably can't litigate them. (Female solicitor.)

The possibility of some clients having to ask their parents for financial help or to sell their own property in order to meet litigation expenses was mentioned by one female solicitor. Finally, a few lawyers indicated that the whole litigation process can take about nine to twelve months.

5.4.2 Case Strategy

Although not asked directly about their case strategy, about half of the lawyers offered information on this aspect as they presented their experience with relocation cases. As one female solicitor put it: 'it's all tactics; every single hearing is tactical'. The strategies underline the adversarial nature of litigation and some of these strategies seem fair play while others appear assertive and sharp. Used by the legal team, they are to ensure that, in view of the relocation proposal, the hopes of one of the parents are realised. However, as indicated by a few lawyers, these strategies will have negative effects on members of the divided family. Information from lawyers regarding strategies is categorised under the themes set out below.

Exchanging information about the relocation proposal:

> It is advantageous from the client's point of view because they need to know at an early stage whether or not they've got prospects of success, and if they don't have prospects of success, if it was a purely free standing application. Then, we would tend to look at the other issues surrounding the breakdown of the family to see whether it's possible to negotiate through a settlement on global terms.
>
> [A possible scenario mentioned would be an attempt to negotiate a divorce settlement for a wealthy client to enable extended periods of stay in the country of origin for the mother who wished to relocate but where the children of the couple could continue residing in England with their father for these periods of time and also have holiday time with their mother in her county of origin]. (Male solicitor.)

> It's a very different type of case to other sort of cases where you don't necessarily put all your cards on the table. [In relocation cases], you put them all in terms of your positive plan for the future and the distress you'd have if you weren't able to carry through that plan. You put that all down as quickly as you can to ensure that your client has the best possible chance of getting the other side to agree, and the court indicating that an agreement [an order allowing relocation] is likely. So again, you have tried to avoid the full blown litigation. (Female solicitor.)

Overall strategy of the parent wishing to relocate:

> If you're acting for the mother you've got to demonstrate that she will indeed co-operate and ensure that the children continue to have a good relationship with the father. (Female solicitor.)

> Our strategy here if we're representing the relocating parent is: throw everything at the other side in a positive fashion. We don't want to fight because we're really not trying to do anything awful, we just need to move. That's the strategy and you throw absolutely everything, and then you let the other side become the real nasty bully and you effectively encourage that. (Female solicitor.)

Court procedures:

> Statement prepared with the parent, based on child centred language and avoidance of attacks on the other parent. (Female barrister.)
> Application by the opposing parent for a residence order (child arrangements order for the child to live primarily with that parent). (Female solicitor.)
> Agreement by the relocating parent to a mirror order and security to ensure contact. (Female solicitor.)

Cross-examination:

> We destroyed her when she was cross-examined because we were able to show that actually she wasn't bothered really whether this child kept in touch with her Dad or not and she couldn't be trusted to ensure that that happened if she got permission. (Female solicitor.)

> I think to be skilled at cross-examining you need to have a real sense of what the family are like so I would spend a lot of time with any client whether they're going or not, to find out how they ticked as a family, to find out the nuances that may not necessarily be in a statement, to use that to cross-examine and I think the effect of that can be quite devastating to the person hearing it because I'd only know that because I've been told that. So, in terms of where it leaves the family at the end of the process it's not a very good place. (Female barrister.)

Consolidating positions:

> The problem with litigation is that you can't concede anything or worse than that, the people who are running the case on a day by day basis are too scared to concede anything because it's the barristers who decide the case at the end of the day and they say, 'Ah, hang on, as it's happened you shouldn't have conceded that because look, we're now in this place and now there's no time, no place back from that'. So what you end up with is during that nine month period you multiply the number of areas and you escalate the difficulty of all of them. It is like an arms race in World War I, isn't it? It's like you are building up more and more battlements. (Male solicitor.)

Micromanagement and gloss during the period of litigation:

> One of the big challenges is the need to micromanage everything. ... He has to send five emails a day to show how centrally involved he is with these kids. He's consulting his lawyers just to make sure he gets each of those emails spot on and does absolutely everything. So we are literally micromanaging every single piece of parental communication for nine months because the delays at court are so bad. That's what goes on. And ... we have to manage these huge great statements ... where Mum says why 'I want to go' and Dad says, 'Oh no, you can't' and then Mum responds. ... We also probably have a disagree-

> ment over contact because Mum can't concede all that he wants or she's going to be 'a shared care Mum' and she's lost her case. So he does his statement about why he wants to have more contact on the interim basis and she has her statement about why not. So then we have to have the first hearing to decide to structure the case, we have a hearing to decide the interim contact arrangements and then we have the final hearing which goes on for three days or more because we've got to look at loads of stuff. We've got to do a compare and contrast of every aspect of their lives in the new country versus every aspect of their lives here. (Male solicitor.)

Finally, one lawyer commented on the intensity of relocation cases due to the inevitable adoption of sharp strategies if one party starts 'the fight', added to the fact that it is difficult to predict the outcome of a case:

> There's this real division as a pathway splits in two: the brave parents who can find a way of holding on to their humanity, their parenthood and their responsibility and those parents who get lured into a fight, and I think that it just needs one parent to be doing the fight to mean that both parents will. Because if someone is being strategic and evil and undermining, it's so difficult not to do that stuff. And it's really uncomfortable. On top of that, you've then got the factor that you don't know which judge you're going to be in front of. You don't, until two weeks before the hearing, even know what the social worker or the CAFCASS officer is going to say and therefore you end up having to fight these cases all the way through to the door of the court, if not to the end of the hearing to really have any ability to guess how it's going to go. (Male solicitor.)

5.4.3 Emotions and the Co-parenting Relationship

All of the lawyers underlined the high level of distress that accompanies the litigation of relocation disputes. A few lawyers pointed to the history of the parental relationship or the profound parent-child attachment, as illustrated by the following:

> Often the litigation is an extension [of] how they they've behaved in the marriage. So if the mother has felt bullied, being told 'she can't go' is an extension of being bullied. If the father is felt walked over by the mother who thinks she's in charge, saying 'she's going' will be more of the same. 'Oh look, now she's decided to live across the world and she thinks she can just take the children!' There's a lot of emotional response to the application and not clear thinking. (Female barrister.)

> Although we tell them that litigation is going to be costly not just financially but emotionally, it's a rollercoaster ride! 'You don't know what the judge is going to say, you'll be cross-[examined]'. You do tell them the pitfalls but at the end of all of that advice I frequently hear them say, 'I don't care. This is my child or my children and I don't want them to go to Australia, instead I want to be able to pick them up from school as I do now, spend the weekend with them', and I understand that. That's a sort of a human kind of instinct, really. (Female barrister.)

With regards to the consequences of litigation, a few lawyers considered that it is harmful to the co-parenting relationship in view of the mistrust and disappointment that spring from it, as pointed out below:

> Whether they stay here or one of them goes, they are still parents and they've got to be able to work together but it's very destructive of that. ... It's a very acrimonious process, a very destructive process for parents. // Where I have remained in contact with parents post this type of litigation, always things are more difficult between them in terms of the arrangements that they make. (Female solicitor.)

> We've got a system to resolve conflicts that paradoxically makes the conflict worse. ... What it actually does is it destroys the parental relationship. Not only have you got the disappointed parent whichever one it is, but you've also got the fractured relationship because of the dishonesty of the preparation of the case. Each of them feels deeply abused by the lies because they know that what's presented isn't true and it's been probably as untrue on each side. (Male solicitor.)

5.4.4 The Best Interests of the Child

Lawyers had a range of opinions when asked whether litigation serves the best interests of the child. For instance, one lawyer was positive about the approach of the legal system and saw his role in part as an agent for the child:

> I think the English court is geared towards putting the child's interests first. I do think that. Definitely. Everyone, almost everyone, even I, who act for parents, I am saying, 'Well, think about your child, think about your daughter, look at it from your child's point of view'. All the time, I'm saying that. I must have said that this week ten times to clients. (Male solicitor.)

Another lawyer explained how, in her view, the court deals with the best interests of the child while also enabling parents to have a voice:

> Does it serve the best interests of the child? Not always. I think it's more about the adults when you get to the litigation stage because especially if they're very young, if you've got a three year old and a one year old for example ... although the factors for the court are 'the welfare of the child as their paramount consideration' and I think the court does that, the court performs its role and its function. But the hearing, the litigation I think is about helping the adults to tell the court, for example, somebody who is on the receiving end of an application, for them to have their voice to say, 'I don't want this to happen. I love my child'. ... So I think it is a lot about managing adult expectations. But I don't want to minimise the fact or completely deter people from the fact that when I speak as a lawyer, when the judge speaks and we're all speaking, it's about the children so although it may be about your clients in the way that they want to have their voice, for us, as I tell my clients, 'We're here for the children and, if a judge does a good judgement and takes

> into account all the factors – here's your evidence, here's the other party's evidence, the CAFCASS report – you know, you may never like the idea but we have gone through the process of fairness, if you like, where the judge has heard everything and made a decision that he or she thinks is in the best interests of the child'. (Female barrister.)

About half of the lawyers pointed out the very difficult role of parents in navigating the litigation adversarial process to their advantage, also in possibly co-opting their child in their effort to influence the court, as explained below:

> Of course, it's not good for children to see the discord that divorce and litigation brings at all. It takes a superhuman effort on the part of the parents who need to keep reminding themselves that they need to put their children first when dealing with it. (Female solicitor.)

> When litigation becomes very intense everyone is scrabbling around, you know, like a balancing machine. Even for the little weights it probably helps if, even the seven year old says, 'Oh', he 'really wants to go' or even if the seven year old has a little book talking about Canada like, 'My Life in Canada', brilliant, we'll have some of that! And so, Mum and Dad are trying to harvest all this stuff off the kids because it might help a bit. It might just kind of trigger something in the judge because we don't know what the judges are going to do, what's going to work for them so we're harvesting stuff all the time and so, yes the kids are becoming involved but they're becoming polarised within this process, possibly being polarised with Mum, when they're with Mum and polarised with Dad, when they're with Dad. It's incredibly toxic isn't it? (Male solicitor.)

The other few lawyers had mixed responses referring to the necessary function of the legal system in dealing with relocation disputes but also to some downsides, for instance, with the child becoming aware of the dispute, as presented by this lawyer:

> I think I could answer by saying that litigation by parents never serves the interests of a child. Litigation is always a disaster. It polarises attitudes, it's expensive, it's stressful and children above quite a young age almost invariably have some idea of what's going on and the fact of the litigation has an effect on them. They often take a degree of responsibility, they feel that they are somehow at fault for the fact that litigation is taking place. So litigation is never a good idea but the problem is with relocation that for the reasons I gave [entrenched positions with a binary outcome] there's really no other way of reaching a solution. So, in a sense it's not in the best interests of the child but it's the least bad outcome. I mean, there is almost never a good outcome for a relocation dispute. The court is concerned with a balance of harm test. (Male barrister.)

5.4.5 Benefits

One female solicitor indicated that a benefit of litigation is 'that at the end of the day ... there will be an outcome ... so it will not drag on'. A few lawyers mentioned that for some parents there is a benefit in being able to refer this difficult decision to an authority, as in the following:

> Once the responsibility for not making the decision is out of the client's hands, although the upset is still there, the relief at not having had to make a decision to say goodbye to your child out of the jurisdiction works better for some. (Female solicitor.)

A few lawyers indicated procedural benefits to litigation such as reality-testing through cross-examination of a parent with optimistic plans and the granting of an order by the court:

> If you have someone who is moving because ... they've met a man in Spain, and over a couple of years' relationship they want to go and live in Spain, they might speak in superlatives, 'It's all going to be wonderful, the children love him, they love Spain!' That's what they might say in a statement and then under scrutiny you might engage with them and they might see the pitfalls. (Female barrister.)

> It [a court order] establishes ... what the plans are, and who is going to see who and when, and which country has the jurisdiction when habitual residence will move. // I don't think litigation generally does [serve the best interests of the child] but the court order does. (Female solicitor.)

5.5 Use of Alternative Dispute Resolution

Lawyers were asked if in their experience parties involved in relocation disputes were willing to consider alternative dispute resolution processes. In response, a few lawyers pointed to the anguish experienced by the parent opposing the relocation proposal and how this affects their perspective on a dispute resolution process:

> I think they are so terrified of losing their child that they find it really difficult and I think often, things like, 'Let's go to mediation' means 'Somebody's going to put pressure on me to agree to this and I don't agree to it'. ... You know, some people say, 'My life will be over if my child leaves the country because I'll never see that child again' – very difficult for them to see: 'Look, go and sit round a table and talk about it'. They can't, they can't get to that point. (Female solicitor.)

> Mediation doesn't really work because one parent doesn't feel able to agree. ... There's too much at stake. Too much at stake for them to just say like [with] other things we do, contact hearings, 'Yes I agree to that'. I don't think I've ever had a case where it's been agreed, ever. (Female barrister.)

Most of the lawyers spoke about the inherent polarisation of positions between parents when dealing with a relocation proposal and how this is not amenable to ADR. For example:

> When I talk about money or when I talk about how to bring up 'our kids', it's much more focused. It can be much more focused on higher aspirations about 'Look we're trying, we're in this together, how can we make this good? How can we make it work for you as well as working for me? How can we make it work for our kids? How can we go on being the family that we'll be proud of?' But you step into leave to remove and it's brutal. (Male solicitor.)

> Well, that one is something that normally there is no negotiation over. ... I don't know of any case that has been negotiated on a leave to remove [apart from] one or two, where they were in Europe, the time difference was an hour ahead, the flying time was maybe two and a half hours, there was enough family wealth so that flying would not be an issue. (Female solicitor.)

As indicated earlier, almost all of the lawyers stated that they provided information to their client about the possibility of ADR, as illustrated in the following:

> My first port of call is never court. (Female barrister.)

> The first instinct is to try and put the plan to the other party and see if there can be some consensus ... [about] what's best for the children and how to make it work. (Female solicitor.)

> If they [the parents] cannot resolve issues between themselves, I always recommend and actively support referrals for family mediation and I have seen seemingly intransigent cases resolved in this way. (Female solicitor.)

> The fundamental issue, in my experience, is very difficult to mediate and we do try. I would say most of my recent cases try mediation but it's almost like going through the motions because if someone really wants to go and someone really doesn't want them to go how do you mediate it? How do you avoid going to court? (Male barrister.)

A willingness to suggest mediation, particularly with regards to child-related matters, was also reported by many of the solicitors in England and Wales who participated in a study about their work in divorce situations (Eekelaar *et al.*, 2000). In the current study, about half of the lawyers (including solicitors and barristers) pointed out that they were themselves trained mediators and/or collaborative lawyers and therefore very open to ADR. However, as one barrister mentioned, also amounting to a summary of the others' position, although he would 'always look for alternatives to litigation if possible ... this is one category of cases where that's usually difficult'.

6. Discussion

The interviews with the lawyers in England and Wales touch on two realities: the lawyers' work and views as advisors and advocates to parents involved in a relocation dispute and the situation they describe concerning parents and child. Summaries of the lawyers' work and views, and the situation of parents and child will first be presented followed by a discussion of the implications for the best interests of the child.

The lawyers interviewed indicated that part of their work with a parent wishing to relocate was to prepare detailed evidence on the proposed child's living arrangements in the other location along with adequate contact arrangements with the opposing parent. On the other hand, work with the opposing parent involves questioning the relocation proposal. This is in keeping with the requirement in England and Wales of considering the child's welfare in court decisions with respect to the upbringing of a child, as presented in Section 2 above. Most of the lawyers viewed it as important to consider the voice of the child in relocation cases, with about half of them also expressing concerns for the child. As gatekeepers to information on dispute resolution processes, almost all of the lawyers indicated informing parents about mediation but reported reluctance from them in opting for this ADR. With regards to their work as advocates, all of the lawyers were of the view that relocation litigation is distressing for parents and almost all of them expressed concerns about possible negative effects for the child. On the whole, in their work as front line workers to the legal system, the lawyers' narratives showed concerns about the parents' choice of litigation in their relocation dispute but saw it as necessary in view of the parents' polarised positions.

The comments provided by the lawyers interviewed point to a highly stressful situation for the parents involved in relocation litigation. Based on the lawyers' accounts, this requires that parents help with preparing evidence concerning the proposed relocation, have their child consulted (depending on age and understanding), probably participate in competitive strategic moves in preparation of court hearings and spend a large amount of money in an attempt to realise their respective goals, whether it be to relocate with the child or continue the relationship with the child in the current environment. The situation can also prove stressful for a child as he or she will be consulted (depending on age and understanding). Nonetheless, the child might also get caught in the parents' relocation dispute. The time requirement for this model of dispute resolution can be up to a year. Damage is possible to the co-parenting relationship which should ideally continue post-litigation.

The findings of this study as summarised above are the results of a qualitative study with a small sample, hence carry limited possibilities for extrapolation. However, these findings, because they are the results of interviews with practitioners with long-standing litigation experience in relocation, carry some weight. Although not reported by parents themselves, the findings constitute an account by practitioners who work closely with parents in their struggle to resolve relocation disputes through litigation. These findings could be read as hypotheses to be tested against other findings or as raising questions about the use of litigation for relocation disputes.

The findings point to a dichotomy between the factors taken into account at the substantive level in preparing evidence for court (based on the welfare checklist supplemented by guidelines from the Court of Appeal) and the strategies relied on to reinforce the parents' positions in view of court hearings. The decision of the court, based on substantive law and evidence, helps protect the best interests of the child and assure as reasonable a decision as possible. However, in the lawyers' views, as parents rely on the tactical possibilities of litigation to present their evidence, this can become arduous and depleting of their resources as well as possibly those of their child. More specifically this can drain the parents' emotional and financial resources, damage their co-parenting capabilities post-litigation and risks the possibility of the child being co-opted into the dispute.

Some of the lawyers' perspectives indicated above are echoed in research on parents' use of litigation for family disputes and on interparental conflict, as examined in Section 3.2 above. Parents have reported that litigation is a source of high stress and fuels interparental conflict (Pruett and Jackson, 2001; Buchanan and Hunt, 2003), and this is also the case in relocation litigation (Taylor *et al.*, 2010). Interparental conflict, in turn, can affect a child's wellbeing (Amato and Keith, 1991; Emery, 1999; Amato, 2001; Hetherington and Kelly, 2002; Grych, 2005; Harold and Murch, 2008; Amato, 2010). Moreover, correlation of parent and child wellbeing has been found in litigated contact disputes (Buchanan and Hunt, 2003; Trinder *et al.*, 2008), where in this last study, the notion of diminished capacity to parent was referred to as one interpretation for the correlation (Trinder *et al.*, 2008). It should be noted however that in the last two studies, violence was reported for a proportion of parents. Finally, the lawyers' concerns over the depletion of the parents' financial resources also resonate with the voice of parents involved in research about relocation, some of which is from England and Wales (Freeman, 2009; Taylor and Freeman 2010; Parkinson *et al.*, 2010; Taylor *et al.*, 2010).

This raises the question of the role of the adversarial system with regards to the best interests of the child in the preparation of relocation cases for court, which is an integral part of the litigation process. From the perspectives of the lawyers in this study and parents in other research mentioned above, the demands of relocation litigation on parents are seen overall as stressful and as fuelling interparental conflict. The cost of relocation litigation is also seen as a source of high stress. Interparental conflict is reported in other research as affecting the wellbeing of children and furthermore, from the lawyers' perspective in this study, there is a risk that the child could be co-opted in the dispute. Apart from the crucial benefit of a resolution to the dispute, crystallised in a court order, the views of the lawyers interviewed raise the question of the adequacy of the adversarial system in sufficiently supporting the best interests of the child during the preparation of relocation cases for court.

Although some alternatives to litigation are discussed with parents, mediation being a common one, the interviews with lawyers indicate that because of the parents' emotional turmoil and the binary outcome to relocation disputes, the possibility that these alternative dispute resolution processes are chosen is much reduced. A reticence on the part of parents to choose mediation is also reported in other research on relocation in England and Wales (Freeman, 2009). In view of the demanding and difficult process reportedly experienced by parents and possibly their child in relocation litigation, ADR models need to be explored further.

Since the decision *per se* about a relocation proposal does not seem conducive to collaboration by parents, this could be a factor in shaping alternatives. For instance, processes favouring a third party intervener who had some form of authority or control in a flexible dispute resolution process could help parents present their positions without the collaboration needed in mediation or collaborative law and without the full range of weaponry that litigation provides. Among suggestions provided by some lawyers concerning issues raised in their interviews (but not reported in the findings) were the use of arbitration and Early Neutral Evaluation as possible alternatives to litigation, mediation, collaborative law and lawyer negotiation. It is hoped that arbitration, for instance, could offer a more flexible procedure, thus possibly reducing time and expenses. However, as of now, in England and Wales, arbitration in family law 'does not apply to disputes directly concerning the care or parenting of children'.[18] Early Neutral Evaluation presented by a knowledgeable legal person offers parents at an early stage of the dispute a possible outcome regarding a court decision, without having to go through litigation. It is not possible within the range of this chapter to discuss these options in detail but that they were mentioned points to the fact that the lawyers in this study are well aware of the limits of litigation and ADR such as mediation, collaborative law and lawyer negotiation, and are reflecting on alternatives for relocation disputes.

7. Conclusion

The findings of this qualitative study with lawyers in England and Wales highlight a situation that is unique in private family law: the possibilities for compromise in relocation disputes are limited while at the same time the outcome can profoundly affect the established parent-child relationships. Litigation then appears as a difficult but necessary choice. In choosing this dispute resolution process, parents need to prepare evidence to convince a court that their individual proposal for their child is the best for that child. Inevitably, this will pit them against one another. The best interests of the child principle helps ensure that reasonable decisions are rendered by courts. However, based on the comments of lawyers interviewed, apart from the resolution of the dispute and the court order, the question remains as to the adequacy of the adversarial litigation process in protecting sufficiently the best interests of the child as parents engage in the preparation of their case for court. Alternatives providing parents with a range of decision-making processes need to be looked at so that the tribulations of litigation can possibly be avoided. Each child of parents involved in a relocation dispute deserves to have his or her best interests taken into account not only in a third party's decision but also in any dispute resolution process used to reach a decision.

---

18 Institute of Family Law Arbitrators, Arbitration Rules (2014), art. 2.3(c).

References

Amato, P. R., "Children of Divorce in the 1990s: an Update of the Amato and Keith (1991) Meta-Analysis", *Journal of Family Psychology* 2001 15(3), 355-370.

Amato, P. R., "Research on Divorce: Continuing Trends and New Developments", *Journal of Marriage and Family* 2010 72, 650-666.

Amato, P. R. and B. Keith, "Parental Divorce and the Well-Being of Children: A Meta-Analysis", *Psychological Bulletin* 1991 110(1), 26-46.

Bream, V. and A. Buchanan, "Distress among Children whose Separated or Divorced Parents cannot Agree Arrangements for them", *British Journal of Social Work* 2003 33, 227-238.

Buchanan, A. and J. Hunt, "Disputes Contact Cases in the Courts", in A. Bainham, B. Lindley, M. Richards and L. Trinder (eds), *Children and their Families: Contact, Rights and Welfare* (Oxford: Hart, 2003).

Butler, I., L. Scanlan, M. Robinson, G. Douglas and M. Murch, "Children's Involvement in their Parents' Divorce: Implications for Practice", *Children & Society* 2002 16, 89-102.

Carmody, The Hon. T., "Child Relocation: An Intractable International Family Law Problem", *Family Court Review* 2007 45(2), 214-246.

Day Sclater, S. and F. Kaganas, "Contact Mothers, Welfare and Rights", in A. Bainham, B. Lindley, M. Richards and L. Trinder (eds), *Children and their Families: Contact, Rights and Welfare* (Oxford: Hart, 2003).

Duggan, The Hon. W. D., "Rock-Paper-Scissors: Playing the Odds with the Law of Child Relocation", *Family Court Review* (2007) 45(2), 193-213.

Eaton, D. and M. Reardon, "*K v K*: The End of the Road for *Payne*?", *International Family Law* 2011, 308-312.

Eekelaar, J., M. MacLean and S. Beinart, *Family Lawyers: the Divorce Work of Solicitors* (Oxford: Hart, 2000).

Emery, R. E., "Postdivorce Family Life for Children: an Overview of Research and some Implications for Policy", in R. A. Thompson and P. R. Amato (eds), *The Postdivorce Family* (London: Sage Publications, 1999).

Emery, R. E., D. Sbarra and T. Grover, "Divorce Mediation: Research and Reflections", *Family Court Review* 2005 43(1), 22-37.

Family Justice Review, Final Report (UK Government, 2011), online: https://www.gov.uk/government/uploads/system/uploads/attachment_data/file/217343/family-justice-review-final-report.pdf, last accessed 28 July 2014.

Firestone, G. and J. Weinstein, "In the Best Interests of Children: A Proposal to Transform the Adversarial System", in J. B. Singer and J. C. Murphy (eds), *Resolving Family Conflicts* (Aldershot: Ashgate, 2008).

Fortin, J., J. Hunt and L. Scanlan, *Taking a Longer View of Contact: The Perspectives of Young Adults who Experienced Parental Separation in their Youth* (Brighton: Sussex Law School, 2012), online: https://www.sussex.ac.uk/webteam/gateway/file.php?name=nuffield-foundation-final-report-16nov2012.pdf&site=28, last accessed 28 July 2014.

Freeman, M., *Relocation: The reunite Research*, (reunite International Child Abduction Centre, 2009), online: http://www.reunite.org/edit/files/Library%20-%20reunite%20Publications/Relocation%20Report.pdf, last accessed: 28 July 2014.

Freeman, M., "Relocation and the Child's Best Interests", *International Family Law Journal* 2010, 247-254.

George, R. H., "Practitioners' Views on Children's Welfare in Relocation Disputes: Comparing Approaches in England and New Zealand", *Child and Family Law Quarterly* 2011 23(2), 178-202.

George, R. H., "Reviewing relocation? *Re W* (*Relocation: Removal Outside Jurisdiction*) [2011] EWCA Civ 345 *and K v. K* (*Relocation: Shared Care Arrangement*) [2011] EWCA Civ 793", *Child and Family Law Quarterly* 2012 24(1), 110-129.

Gollop, M. and N. Taylor, "New Zealand Children and Young People's Perspectives on Relocation Following Parental Separation", in M. Freeman (ed), *Law and Childhood Studies* (Oxford: Oxford University Press, 2012).

Grych, J. H., "Interparental Conflict as a Risk Factor for Child Maladjustment: Implications for the Development of Prevention Programs", *Family Court Review* 2005 43(1), 97-108.

Harold, G. T. and M. Murch, "Inter-parental Conflict and Children's Adaptation to Separation and Divorce: Theory, Research and Implications for Family Law, Practice and Policy", in A. Bainham (ed), *Parents and Children* (Aldershot: Ashgate, 2008).

Herring, J., "Family: Moving Forward?", *New Law Journal* 2011 161, 1011-1013.

Hetherington, E. M. and J. Kelly, *For Better or for Worse* (New York: W. W. Norton, 2002).

Howitt, D., *Introduction to Qualitative Methods in Psychology* (Harlow: Pearson Education, 2010).

Institute of Family Law Arbitrators, *Family Law Arbitration Scheme, Arbitration Rules* (2014), online: http://ifla.org.uk/cms/wp-content/uploads/2014/02/Rules-2014-3rd-edn-final.pdf, last accessed 28 July 2014.

Menkel-Meadow, C., "The Trouble with the Adversary System in a Post-Modern, Multi-Cultural World", *Journal of the Institute for the Study of Legal Ethics* 1996 1, 49-77.

Miller, M. K. and B. H. Bornstein, *Stress, Trauma and Well-Being in the Legal System* (New York: Oxford University Press, 2013).

Parkinson, P. and J. Cashmore, *The Voice of a Child in Family Law Disputes* (Oxford: Oxford University Press, 2008).

Parkinson, P., J. Cashmore and J. Single, "The Need for Reality Testing in Relocation Cases", *Family Law Quarterly* 2010 44(1), 1-34.

Perry, A., "Case Commentary: Leave to Remove Children from the Jurisdiction", *Child and Family Law Quarterly* 2001, 455-462.

Pruett, M. K. and T. D. Jackson, "Perspectives on the Divorce Process: Parental Perceptions of the Legal System and its Impact on Family Relations", *The Journal of the American Academy of Psychiatry and the Law* 2001, 29(1) 18-25.

Pruett, M. K., G. M. Insabella and K. Gustafson, "The Collaborative Divorce Project: A Court-Based Intervention for Separating Parents with Young Children", *Family Court Review* 2005 43(1), 38-51.

Roberts, R. and M. Palmer, *Dispute Processes: ADR and the Primary Forms of Decision-Making* (Cambridge: Cambridge University Press, 2005).

Scott, T., "The Retreat from *Payne*: *MK v CK*", *Family Law Journal* 2011 41 (Aug.), 886-889.

Smart, C., B. Neale and A. Wade, *The Changing Experience of Childhood: Families and Divorce* (Cambridge: Polity, 2001).

Taylor, N., "What Do We Know about Involving Children and Young People in Family Law Decision Making? A Research Update", *Australian Journal of Family Law* 2006 20, 154-178.

Taylor, N. and M. Freeman, "International Research Evidence on Relocation: Past, Present, and Future", *Family Law Quarterly* 2010 44, 317-339.

Taylor, N., M. Gollop and M. Henaghan, *Relocation Following Parental Separation: The Welfare and Best Interests of Children* (Dunedin: Centre for Research on Children and Families and Faculty of Law, University of Otago, 2010), online: http://www.otago.ac.nz/cic/pdfs/Relocation%20Research%20Report.pdf, last accessed 28 July 2014.

Trinder, L., J. Kellet and L. Swift, "The Relationship between Contact and Child Adjustment in High Conflict Cases after Divorce or Separation", *Child and Adolescent Mental Health* 2008 13(4), 181-187.

Wallerstein, J. S. and J. B. Kelly, *Surviving the Breakup: How Children and Parents Cope with Divorce* (London: Grant McIntyre, 1980).

Wallerstein, J. S. and T. J. Tanke, "To Move or not to Move, Psychological and Legal Considerations in the Relocation of Children Following Divorce", *Family Law Quarterly* 1996 30(2), 305-332.

Willig, C., *Qualitative Interpretation and Analysis in Psychology* (Maidenhead: Open University Press, 2012).

Surrogacy Law: From Piecemeal Tweaks to Sustained Review and Reform

Amel Alghrani
Liverpool University, UK

Danielle Griffiths
Manchester University, UK

Margaret Brazier*
Manchester University, UK

Introduction

'The time is opportune for a new Surrogacy Act.' (Freeman, 1999: 20)

The opening quotation from Michael Freeman's seminal paper in 1999 is as valid today as it was then. The situation has become even more complex and 'the law governing surrogacy remains confused, incoherent and poorly adapted to the specific realities of the practice of surrogacy' (Horsey and Sheldon, 2012: 67). In celebrating the academic scholarship of Freeman, one of the many areas in which his writings and work show great foresight is surrogacy. The practice of surrogacy, whereby a woman gestates a child for others, has evolved very differently than was envisaged when the legislation which governs this contentious practice was first drafted in 1985. Despite the United Kingdom being one of the first countries in the world to legislate on research upon embryos and to implement a regulatory framework to govern assisted reproductive technologies (the Human Fertilisation and Embryology Acts 1990 and 2008), one area in which the UK has fallen short in offering effective regulation or protection is when it comes to the use of surrogate mothers to assist individuals or couples to found a family.

Born amidst controversy, the principal statute governing such arrangements, namely the Surrogacy Arrangements Act 1985, was primarily concerned with removing financial incentives for people to assist or partake in this method of founding a family. In 1998, the government commissioned an inquiry, chaired by Margaret Brazier, to review aspects of the regulation of surrogacy in the United Kingdom (the Surrogacy Review 1998). The report has mouldered on the shelves ever since.

* This paper is part of a wider Wellcome Strategic Programme in the Human Body, Its Scope, Limits and Future. We thank all those who attended and commented on earlier presentations of this paper at the Wellcome Trust 'Motherhood: All Change' Conference held on 9 and 10 September 2013, Manchester, UK and in particular Professor Michael Freeman, whose seminal works have proved the inspiration behind this paper.

A. Diduck, N. Peleg, H. Reece (eds.), Law in Society: Reflections on Children, Family, Culture and Philosophy
 ISBN 978-90-04-26148-8. pp. 425-451.

Freeman, whilst supporting the case for regulation, criticised the government's position and the Surrogacy Review's recommendation that payment to surrogate mothers be prohibited, stating:

> Surrogacy will continue; it will probably grow as infertility increases; it will go underground and the fees will become larger. We cannot stop women exercising their autonomy, nor can we persuade them that being paid aggravates their exploitation, when common sense tells them the reverse. (1999)

Time has proved Freeman right, as Brazier now agrees. In the almost three decades which have passed since the enactment of the statute, it is clear that a crude ban on payments is no longer sustainable and the law is in dire need of reform. The 1985 Act is outdated, and piecemeal changes made by the Human Fertilisation and Embryology Acts 1990 and 2008 have served to saddle the law with much incoherence, confusion and uncertainty. As increasing numbers resort to the use of international surrogates or so-called 'Do-It-Yourself arrangements', reform is now imperative if the law is not to become obsolete.

In this chapter we endeavour to move the debate forward and suggest proposals for reforming the regulation of this practice. What we are suggesting is a four-stage process beginning with very modest suggestions:

1. Identify simple measures that may help couples and surrogates avoid some of the pitfalls of current practice (discussed below) that could be implemented without changes in legislation, e.g. improving access to information (including legal advice), better record-keeping, greater scrutiny of agencies, better advice regarding websites that advertise foreign surrogacy services and above all better data collection. Unless there is reliable evidence about the forms and extent of surrogacy in the UK, proposals for more radical reform cannot sensibly be formulated.
2. Carefully consider making minor but potentially contentious changes to the Surrogacy Arrangements and the HFE Acts, permitting a moderate fee to be paid to the surrogate for her services. Such potential changes could only be made in response to research collected as part of Stage 1, namely gathering empirical data which considers, for example, the incidence of full as opposed to partial surrogacy, and the motivations and views of surrogates and commissioning couples regarding the issue of payment and expenses.
3. Create a Committee of Inquiry to review the present legal, ethical and social concerns surrounding surrogacy so as to facilitate the introduction of a wholly new Act. Many factors including the rising demand and increasing use of foreign surrogates has meant concerns have changed since 1985.
4. The UK government should take steps to press for an International Convention addressing transnational surrogacy, something akin to the 1993 Hague Intercountry Adoption Convention which governs international adoptions. Whilst surrogacy is permitted in the UK under strict (and arguably ineffective) regulation, matters are compounded by the increasing recourse to international sur-

rogates. The lack of international standards or regulation in this domain rightly raises 'serious child protection concerns' (Hutchinson, 2012: 9) and the 'legal status of children born of international surrogacy arrangements is complex and uncertain' (ibid: 2). Thus our last recommendation considers whether it is possible and indeed desirable to work towards an international convention regulating international surrogacy arrangements. We examine the contention put forward by Anne-Maree Hutchinson that 'with so many children born by way of surrogacy arrangements, the time has now come for the establishment and implementation of international standards by way of a multi-lateral convention' (ibid: 2).

Before we embark on those proposals, we first place the discussion in context through a brief but necessary background discussion.

Background

i. *Public and Judicial Opinion*

In 1985, in the case of *Re C*, Kim Cotton attracted much attention when it was reported that she had carried a baby for a foreign couple in exchange for payment. Hearing the case, Latey J. reflected on the difficulties the practice engendered, referring to the 'difficult and delicate problems of ethics, morality and social desirability raised by surrogacy' (*Re C* [1985] FLR 846, 846). Media headlines such as 'baby-for-cash deal' (BBC, 1985) were much more hostile. Such hostility was explicit in the earlier case of *A* v *C* ([1985] FLR 445),[1] where the judges were unanimous and damning in their condemnation of surrogacy. Ormrod L.J. commented that the surrogacy arrangement was a:

> simple, logical but totally inhumane proceeding ... this was a wholly artificial situation from the beginning which should never have happened and which no responsible adult should ever have allowed to happen. (8.17)

Similarly the Report of Committee of Inquiry into Human Fertilisation and Embryology (the Warnock Committee), set up in 1982 to 'examine the social, legal and ethical implications of recent and potential developments in the field' (Warnock, 1984: 4), condemned the practice as 'totally ethically unacceptable' (46). It was amidst this climate that the restrictive Surrogacy Arrangements Act 1985 was drafted. Seeking to outlaw any form of commercial surrogacy, the Act was ill considered, and in its narrow focus reflected the Warnock Committee's view that surrogacy would gradually disappear.

To the contrary, however, surrogacy as a method of founding a family continues. In an analysis of the case law, infrequency of judicial condemnation may be taken to

1 Note this case was decided in 1978 but not reported until 1985.

reflect a shift in attitudes towards the practice. In *Re P (Minors) (Wardship)* ([1987] 2 FLR 421 (Fam) 426), a case which arose when the surrogate declined to hand over the twins she had gestated, it was noted by Mason and Laurie that 'there was no criticism of either commissioning parents or of the surrogate for having entered into a surrogacy agreement' (2006: 111). In its 2006 White Paper discussing reform of the Human Fertilisation and Embryology (HFE) Act 1990, the government conceded that 'professional opinion has shifted to a position where surrogacy is recognised as an appropriate response to infertility in some circumstances' (Review of the Human Fertilisation and Embryology Act 2006: 6989: 2.64). In 2012 in *Re T* ([2011] EWHC 33 (Fam)), Baker J. noted how 'surrogacy ... has been *accepted* as a method of enabling childless couples to experience the joy and fulfilment of parenthood' (33).[2] Yet it is a practice that remains contentious, and Van Den Akker suggests that public attitudes may not have shifted too much and that whilst surrogacy may be occurring more openly within the UK, social support for the practice is still lacking (2006). For those struggling in their reproductive endeavours, surrogacy may provide the only method by which they may attain a 'family'. Infertility may influence how socially acceptable the practice is viewed as. In 2012, it was estimated that one in six couples in the UK are infertile and that this number was increasing (Ramskold, 2013). Same sex couples and single people who may not be infertile but for obvious reasons require assistance in forming a family are also increasing (Nordquist and Smart, 2014). These factors have increased the demand for surrogacy. Whilst opinion and demand might have changed in the last two decades, notwithstanding minor amendments to the Human Fertilisation and Embryology Act 1990 in 2008, the law governing surrogacy fails to meet the needs of all those who are involved in a surrogacy arrangement.

ii. The Legal/Regulatory Landscape

> The UK became in 1985, the first country to legislate when it passed an ill-considered and largely irrelevant panic measure, which in essence criminalised commercial surrogacy (Freeman, 1989: 165).

The Surrogacy Arrangements Act 1985 was enacted in response to the public outcry to the Kim Cotton case (*Re C* [1985] FLR 846) and the recommendations of the Committee of Inquiry into Human Fertilisation and Embryology in 1984 reflecting its concern with the 'risk of commercial exploitation of surrogacy' (para. 8.18). The Committee recommended that:

> legislation be introduced to render criminal the creation or the operation in the UK of agencies whose purposes include the recruitment of women for surrogate pregnancy or making arrangements for individuals or couples who wish to utilise the services of a carrying mother. (para. 8.18)

2 Our emphasis.

Amidst the well-rehearsed arguments on concerns regarding commodification and exploitation (Warnock, 1984; Brazier 1998; Freeman, 1989), the 1985 Act prohibited commercial involvement in the initiation and negotiation of surrogacy arrangements. The publication or distribution of advertisements indicating a willingness to take part in a surrogacy arrangement was also made a criminal offence (s. 2). Surrogacy arrangements would not be enforceable, by or against any of the parties making it (s. 1B). Whilst the statute delineated prohibitions and erected barriers to initiating surrogacy arrangements, it did not prevent such arrangements being made.

Appearing to 'accept the need for reform' (Jackson, 2013: 846) in response to the *Karen Roche* case (Cooper, 1997) and a US agency seeking to operate in the UK (Brazier, 2011), the government in 1998 commissioned The Surrogacy Review. None of its recommendations was ever implemented. The report proposed a new Surrogacy Act backed by a Code of Practice which would set out a model of good practice for couples and surrogates including discouragement of multiple surrogacy and a frank exchange of information to all involved. The parties should agree a Memorandum of Understanding. Underpinning the recommendations was the central proposal that there should be a continued prohibition of any payment to surrogate mothers other than compensation for specific expenses actually incurred as a result of the pregnancy. In response to this recommendation, Freeman commented:

> the [Surrogacy Review] fails to appreciate that withdrawing remuneration from surrogates will only drive potential surrogates away from regulated surrogacy into an invisible and socially uncontrolled world where the regulators will be more like pimps than adoption agencies. (1999: 10)

Later changes were made to the Human Fertilisation and Embryology Act 1990 by the 2008 Act to permit non-profit making bodies to charge a reasonable fee to recoup their costs. Provision was also made for ascribing 'legal parenthood' to children born through assisted conception.[3]

At present, English law works on a strict 'two-parent' model for legal parenthood and a child cannot have more than two legal parents. The surrogate mother is regarded as the child's legal mother,[4] and if the surrogate is married her partner will be the legal father of the child (HFE Act 2008, s. 38), unless a lack of consent to treatment can be shown on his part. If a commissioning couple wish to become a child's legal parents following a successful surrogacy arrangement, they must either adopt the child or apply for a parental order. The latter is governed by section 54 of the

---

3 The Human Fertilisation and Embryology Authority (HFEA) on 20 March 2013 acted to update the guidance it provides UK fertility clinics on surrogacy. The major change is to guidance given on legal parenthood; in particular if the surrogate is unmarried, then it is now possible for the intended father who provided the sperm (who was formerly treated as a gamete donor and excluded from the birth certificate) to be named on a birth certificate with surrogate. The changes came into force on 1 October 2013.

4 Human Fertilisation and Embryology Act 2008, s. 33.

Human Fertilisation and Embryology Act 2008, which replaced section 30 of the HFE Act 1990 and extended the categories of persons who could apply for a parental order so as to include civil partners and couples in an 'enduring family relationship', in addition to married couples, but not single people. [5] Finally, the Human Fertilisation and Embryology Regulations 2010 make the welfare of a child the paramount concern when considering an application for a parental order and introduce a welfare checklist setting out matters that the court must take into account. An application for a parental order cannot be applied for until the child is at least six weeks old. Colin Rogerson points out that:

> In reality it is not uncommon for the parental order process to take anywhere between 6 to 12 months before a parental order is made. Thus there will be a significant time in a child's life where the parents caring for it are not recognised by law as being the child's legal parents. (2012: 3)

In only permitting a strict two-parent only model, the UK is not without criticism, particularly in surrogacy cases where both the commissioning couple and the surrogate may wish to continue formally to play a role in the child's life. Moving beyond the two-parent family model may, as Mianna Lotz argues, benefit a child economically, emotionally and practically. Canada offers an alternative example of a legal framework which recognises more than two parents. The British Columbian (BC) Family Law Act (2011) has made it possible for a child to have more than two parents where ART is used to conceive the child. In the context of surrogacy and donor conception, section 30 (1) stipulates that the birth mother (the surrogate) and donor(s) can be named as a parent alongside the intended parent or parents. A condition to there being more than two legal parents is a pre-conception agreement among all of the prospective parents. BC family law recognises that removing the two-parent limitation so as to allow a broader range of contributions to a child's well-being has the potential substantially to promote the welfare of the child, parents and society. It also recognises that parenthood is not determined solely by genetics – gestational links and intentions also play an important role.

Reform 1: Information and Data Provision

Our first category of reforms involves minor measures that could be implemented without changes in legislation but might improve practice. Such reforms verge on

5 Section 54 provides '(1) On an application made by two people ("the applicants") the court may make an order providing for a child to be treated in law as the child of the applicants if— (a) the child has been carried by a woman who is not one of the applicants, as a result of the placing in her of an embryo or sperm and eggs or her artificial insemination, (b) the gametes of at least one of the applicants were used to bring about the creation of the embryo, and (c) the conditions in subsections (2) to (8) are satisfied. These provisions came into force on 6 April 2010 following the Human Fertilisation and Embryology Act 2008 (Commencement No. 3) Order 2010 No. 987.

'tinkering at the edges' but as well as being steps that can be taken swiftly, they are crucial and foundational to the more thorough reforms we propose later.

i. *Incidence and Data Gathering*

Ascertaining exact information about surrogacy arrangements in the UK is difficult, and there are massive discrepancies in the data available. Records of Parental Orders (POs) which transfer legal parentage from the surrogate (and her husband if she has one) to the commissioning couple are routinely kept and at present provide us with the only official data. Research undertaken by Crawshaw *et al* analysing data from parental orders confirm the practice of surrogacy is on the rise. Their research charted the number of POs granted in the UK and noted there had been an increase from 52 POs granted in 1995 to 149 in 2011 (2012). In 2012, this figure rose to 192.[6] Crawshaw *et al* acknowledged that numerous factors could explain the increase, in particular recent legislative changes in the HFE Act 2008 which enabled same sex couples and couples in an 'enduring family relationship' to apply for POs, along with increasingly greater recourse to international surrogates. Yet, they argue, neither alone fully accounts for the increase. They contend that the increasing social acceptability of the practice (driven by infertility rates) has also contributed to the increasing incidence of surrogacy.

Yet much remains unknown, and the data from POs reveals a very partial and limited picture. Crawshaw *et al* concede that none of the actual data on POs includes important information such as whether it was a full or partial surrogacy, characteristics of the commissioning couple and surrogate (sexuality, social class etc.), whether donor gametes were used, the country of origin of the gamete progenitors (if used) and whether a surrogate mother was used due to medical necessity. Nor do the POs provide information on how many surrogacy arrangements are unsuccessful, for instance where the surrogate or the commissioning couple has reneged on the agreement.

Despite general recognition of an increase in the use of foreign surrogates, Crawshaw *et al* (2012) found limited information about the country of origin of the different parties involved in these arrangements. There is no legal requirement in the UK to record country of origin or citizenship of the adults involved. Data collected by Crawshaw *et al* showed that there has been an increase in the use of surrogate mothers abroad. The General Registry Office reported that 64 of the 111 babies involved in POs made in 2012 (58 per cent) were born outside the UK compared to 26 per cent in 2011. Crawshaw *et al* argue that the figures understate the true scale of the 'trade' which is driven by agencies operating in countries such as India to which intending parents are drawn by the number of potential surrogates, a lack of red tape and the absence of regulation (Ramskold and Posner, 2013). There is a marked discrepancy between the official figures and other estimates. According to a recent media report:

6 Many thanks to Eric Blyth for giving us this most recent 2012 figure.

> It is estimated that 2,000 births to surrogate mothers took place [in India] last year [2011], with most experts agreeing that Britain is the biggest single source of people who want to become parents in this way. Britain may account for as many as 1,000 births last year in India. (Bhatia, 2012)

It is unclear where between 64 and 1,000 the true figure lies. Whilst it is apparent that the use of surrogates is on the increase and it has not disappeared as Warnock (2002) may have predicated in the 1980s, the lack of meaningful data creates real cause for concern. This concern is particularly acute in the context of foreign surrogacy arrangements where there is higher potential for exploitation and risk of things 'going wrong', even to the extent of children being stateless and abandoned. Any attempt to develop proper and effective regulation must protect the interests of those involved, but in particular the children, and must be based on sound knowledge and information. In particular, better record keeping and provision of sound advice is necessary to ensure the child's welfare is the paramount concern.

ii. Provision of Sound and Accurate Advice to Commissioning Couples and Surrogates

The Surrogacy Arrangements Act 1985 makes it illegal for a commercial organisation to set up a surrogacy arrangement in the UK. Non-profit making volunteer organisations that provide matching services are permitted and a number of agencies such as Surrogacy UK and COTS[7] assist and guide those who wish to found a family with the use of a surrogate. The Surrogacy Review recommended that such agencies should be subject to a system of accreditation, regulation and inspection in order to ensure that their services are of a suitable standard. At present such organisations remain completely unaccredited and unmonitored. In *Re G* (*Surrogacy: Foreign Domicile*) ([2007] EWHC 2814 (Fam)) MacFarlane J. condemned the absence of 'any statutory or regulatory umbrella' which leaves the role of facilitating surrogacy arrangements to 'groups of well-meaning amateurs' (at para. 29). MacFarlane J. recognised that the ban on commercialisation meant that these agencies are operating in a very restrictive environment. Emily Jackson notes that this case illustrates how 'surrogacy arrangements are not properly regulated and agreements are often made without legal advice, with potentially disastrous consequences' (2013: 846).

Reform introduced by the HFEA 2008 allowed these organisations to recoup 'reasonable payment' to cover costs associated with providing guidance and assistance in facilitating surrogacy arrangements; yet as highlighted by Horsey and Sheldon (2012), this is a limited change which has offered little improvement to the provision of such services. Crucially it fails to offer a means to monitor and regulate the services these organisations provide. The lack of accredited specialist agencies helping members of

7 Childlessness Overcome through Surrogacy , COTS and Surrogacy UK are Voluntary Organisations working in the UK. For more information see: http://www.surrogacy.org.uk/About_COTS.htm http://www.surrogacyuk.org/.

the public seeking the use of a surrogate mother is further compounded by the inconsistencies in provision of advice and services, particularly by clinics. Gamble of Natalie Gamble Associates, the UK's only firm of solicitors to specialise exclusively in fertility and parenting law, highlighted some of the present inadequacies of information given by clinics:

> As surrogacy professionals, we often see that the quality of advice given to surrogacy patients by clinics is variable, and sometimes downright wrong. Common errors include advising patients that they need a legally binding surrogacy agreement, giving incorrect information about how much can be paid to a surrogate, or giving a misleading picture about the risks of the surrogate changing her mind and what happens if she does. There is also often confusion about how consent and other HFEA forms should be completed. This is perhaps not surprising given the complexity of the law and the fact that surrogacy is still relatively rare for many clinicians. But it is not good enough. As surrogacy is becoming more common, we need to make sure that it is handled consistently and professionally, and that everyone involved (most importantly the intended child) is protected as far as possible. (2013)

A proper system of accreditation and regulation of surrogacy agencies would aid the provision of sound and accurate advice. This is imperative in light of the prevailing increase in the use of foreign surrogates, where there are clear gaps between laws in different jurisdictions creating much confusion and in *X* v *Y* (*Foreign Surrogacy*) ([2008] EWHC 3030 (Fam)) resulting in children being 'marooned stateless and parentless' (para. 10). While the 1985 Act bans any advertising, foreign surrogacy websites are subject to less restriction, thus it is imperative that proper warnings and advice are given to intending parents.

Natalie Gamble Associates have now launched 'Brilliant Beginnings', a non-profit making UK surrogacy and egg donation agency. Similar to COTS and Surrogacy UK, it promises to help create UK families through surrogacy and egg donation. It differs to the extent that it is being run by legal experts with sound knowledge and experience in this area and has pledged to reinvest resources into campaigns to promote change and raise awareness (Gamble and Prosser, 2013). But is this really a Brilliant Beginning? This agency and others such as COTS will be working within the same legal landscape, and until real reform is affected through the law little will change. We propose that reform one would be an interim measure that would ease some of the current difficulties while a broader review takes place. Only with the implementation of our next three will we be ready for a truly 'brilliant beginning' (Alghrani and Griffiths, 2013).

Reform 2: Make 'Minor' Legislative Changes to Permit Payment of a 'Moderate Fee' to Surrogate Mothers

i. Does the Prohibition on Payment to Surrogate Mothers Remain Sustainable?

Our second proposal involves making minor but potentially contentious legislative changes to permit payment of a 'moderate fee' to the surrogate mother for her services. We should be clear, however, that as we developed this proposal we found unexpected levels of complexity bedevilling the question.

Freeman disputed the idea that women need protection from entering into surrogacy arrangements, arguing that women should have the right to make decisions about their own bodies. In response to concerns around the child that payment to a surrogate may raise he asserted:

> The money is paid to the surrogate not to compensate her for giving up the child, nor to 'buy' the child. The money is payment for her services; it is compensation for the burden of pregnancy. The child may have a right not to be sold, but that is a distortion of what is happening, even in cases of commercial surrogacy. (Freeman, 1989: 178)

Whilst the 1985 Act makes it a criminal offence for any third party to initiate, negotiate or take part in a surrogacy arrangement for profit (SAA 1985, s. 2), surrogate mothers are entitled to receive reimbursement for expenses in connection with a surrogacy arrangement. Whilst payment over and above reasonable expenses is not a criminal offence in principle, it may prevent the commissioning couple from obtaining a parental order transferring legal parentage to them. The Human Fertilisation and Embryology Act 2008, s. 54 (formerly s. 30 of the HFE Act 1990) provides that a Parental Order will only be granted if (1) *no money or other benefit (other than for expenses reasonably incurred) has been given or received by either of the applicants for or in consideration of the making of the order;*[8] (2) the child is already in the care of the commissioning couple and the surrogate has consented (Human Fertilisation and Embryology Act 2008, s. 54); and (3) the surrogate has consented to a parental order within six weeks of the birth of the child (Human Fertilisation and Embryology Act 2008, s. 54(7)). The Human Fertilisation and Embryology Regulations 2010 have now mandated that the welfare of the child be *the* paramount concern when making parental orders.

A 'reasonable sum' paid to the surrogate to cover expenses as permitted by the HFE Act 2008 (s. 2A) will be a matter of fact in each case but Surrogacy UK and COTS

---

8 HFEA 2008, s. 54 (8): 'The court must be satisfied that no money or other benefit (other than for expenses reasonably incurred) has been given or received by either of the applicants for or in consideration of— (a) the making of the order, (b) any agreement required by subsection (6), (c) the handing over of the child to the applicants, or (d) the making of arrangements with a view to the making of the order, unless authorised by the court'.

estimate this at present to range between £7,000 and £15,000 (Surrogacy UK). Emily Jackson notes that 'while ostensibly surrogacy arrangements should not be made on a commercial basis in practice things are rather different' (2013: 832). Payments made which have exceeded 'reasonable expenses' have been retrospectively authorised by the courts in at least seven cases in the last five years (*Re X and Y (Foreign Surrogacy)* ([2008] EWHC 3030 (Fam)); *Re S (Parental Order)* ([2009] EWHC 2977 (Fam)); *Re L (Commercial Surrogacy)* ([2010] EWHC 3146 (Fam)); *Re IJ (Foreign Surrogacy Agreement Parental Order)* ([2011] EWHC 921 (Fam)); and *Re X and Y (Parental Order: Retrospective Authorisation of Payments)* ([2011] EWHC 3147 (Fam)). In the most recent, *J* v *G* ([2013] EWHC 1432 (Fam)) the applicants, a British civilly partnered male couple, commissioned a surrogate in California and made payments totalling £35,650 – almost twice what is at present usually deemed to be reasonable expenses - and yet the parental order was granted. The reason for this gap between theory and practice is that courts are in an impossible position. Whilst the HFE Act 2008 makes it clear that a PO will only be granted if (1) no money or other benefit (other than for expenses reasonably incurred) has been given or received by either of the parties, this conflicts with changes in the Human Fertilisation and Embryology (Parental Orders) Regulations 2010[9] which make the child's welfare the paramount consideration throughout the child's lifetime. Their impact was highlighted by Hedley J. in *Re L (a minor)* ([2010] EWHC 3146 (Fam)) when he said:

> The effect of the 2010 Regulations (s. 1 2010/986) is … welfare is no longer merely the court's first consideration but becomes its paramount consideration. The effect of that must be to weight the balance between public policy considerations and welfare decisively in favour of welfare. *It must follow that it will only be in the clearest case of the abuse of public policy that the court will be able to withhold an order if otherwise welfare considerations support its making. It underlines the court's earlier observation that, if it is desired to control commercial surrogacy arrangements, those controls need to operate before the court process is initiated i.e. at the border or even before.* (Our emphasis) (paras 9 and 10)

This provision makes it unlikely courts will ever refuse retrospectively to authorise payment and grant a PO when the child/children are resident with the commissioning parents, especially where the surrogate mother resides outside the jurisdiction. The courts declaring expenses to be grossly disproportionate would bar a parental order being granted, which could leave a child parentless and in some cases stateless.

---

9 Regulation 2 provides: 'The provisions of the 2002 Act [that is to say, the Adoption and Children Act 2002] set out in column 1 of Schedule 1 have effect in relation to parental orders made in England and Wales and applications for such orders as they have effect in relation to adoption orders and applications for such orders, subject to the modifications set out in column 2 of that Schedule.' The effect of this provision is, *inter alia*, that section 1 of the 2002 Act applies to the making of parental orders in the following terms: '(1) This section applies whenever a court is coming to a decision relating to the making of a parental order in relation to a child. (2) The paramount consideration of the court must be the child's welfare, throughout his life'.

This would not be in a child's best interests, especially when there are two perfectly capable parents who have already expended so much financially and emotionally to create the child. Hedley J. acknowledged this in *Re L* in the quotation just above. The reluctance of the judiciary to endorse foreign arrangements where excessive payments have been made was made clear by Hedley J. in *Re X and Y* (*Foreign Surrogacy*) ([*2008*] *EWHC 3030* (*Fam*)) who described the process as 'most uncomfortable' (para. 28). However, until there is intervention prior to the court process, there is understandable unwillingness to sacrifice the child's welfare for a point of principle. And thus the law casts doubt on that very principle.

The 1985 Act is not working. Even if the premise that paid surrogacy is exploitative has credence, couples continue to seek to found a family through commercial surrogacy, paying women abroad (who may be more vulnerable to exploitation than women in the UK) and contracting with commercial agencies set up to facilitate such agreements in other jurisdictions.

The climate in which such legislation is operating has altered dramatically since it was enacted. We live in an age of the internet where the use of the World Wide Web to facilitate private arrangements or international surrogacy is finger tips away. As Gamble and Prosser note:

> The landscape for opportunities to bring up a family through surrogacy and egg donation in the UK has changed – though not as fast as it has internationally. We live in a globalised world in which commercial surrogacy is a reality. If parents cannot build their family in the UK, they will, and do, look abroad to countries like India, the Ukraine and the USA which provide commercial surrogacy and egg donation services. (2013)

Recent case law demonstrates that couples are resorting to the 'murky waters' (*Re T* (*a child*) (*surrogacy: residence order*) ([2011] EWCH 33 (Fam) (para. 38)) of the web to find willing surrogate mothers, and in some cases these women are being paid far *less* than 'reasonable expenses'. In *Re T* an informal agreement was made by the commissioning couple and the surrogate over the internet: pursuant to their agreement, the commissioning couple gave the surrogate mother one payment of £2,000 and a further sum of £2,500 along with maternity clothes and other items. This is much less than the amount COTS deem reasonable expenses. *Re T* demonstrated some of the pitfalls of the present legislation. Private agreements hold dangers not only because of the lack of vetting of individuals entering into such agreements but also because there is no guidance or counselling in place. Throughout the judgement in *Re T* it was clear that the couple and the surrogate had not grasped the enormity of what they were undertaking (Alghrani, 2012). Such counselling is crucial, and Baker J. noted that 'inevitably ... the advent of the internet has facilitated the making of informal surrogacy arrangements between adults. In such cases, those entering the arrangement do not have the advantage of the advice, counselling and support that the established agencies provide' (*Re T* (para. 2)).

Stephen Wilkinson (2003) has argued that whilst there may be good reasons to believe commercial surrogacy may be exploitative, particularly if the practice will attract a large number of poor women motivated through financial necessity, the ban on paying surrogate mothers is inconsistent if we still allow low paid cleaning work for example, or some forms of sex work. Banning commercial surrogacy, despite potential exploitation, simply displaces exploitation. For Wilkinson, the risks of exploitation should be reduced in other ways besides banning payment, for example by ensuring that surrogate mothers are well paid.

Echoing Wilkinson, we would add that banning commercial surrogacy in the UK has been counterproductive and has led to exploitation being shifted to other countries such as India, where the surrogates have fewer rights and face more dangers. Concern has been raised about Indian surrogates during their contracted pregnancies where they are often subject to strict surveillance and control (Bailey, 2011), and there is higher risk to a surrogate's health (Deckha, 2013). Thus for those who are of the view that commercial surrogacy *should* be prohibited, the law is failing to achieve this aim, and demand is driving commissioning couples overseas or to the uncertain terrain of the internet where the potential for exploitation is higher.

ii. How Much is a 'Moderate' Payment?

The provisions in the 1985 legislation which prevent the commercial involvement in the negotiation and setting up of surrogacy arrangements along with the ban on advertising which impedes willing surrogate mothers and commissioning parents from finding each other in the UK is 'largely ineffective and potentially dangerous' (Anderson, 2012: 43), as increasing numbers go abroad where commercial surrogacy is permitted, then return to the UK. As demonstrated above, parental orders have been granted where the fee paid has exceeded 'reasonable expenses'. We suggest one possible way forward is to reconsider lifting the ban on advertising so as to facilitate those who wish to enter into such arrangements, permitting payment to agencies to cover their fees, and allowing a 'moderate fee' to be paid to surrogate mothers in addition to 'reasonable expenses'. The surrogate would be recompensed for her labour and not simply the financial costs of pregnancy.

Permitting a 'moderate fee' to surrogate mothers will raise the question of how such a reform would translate into practice. One option suggested is to permit payment to the surrogate of the minimum wage for her service: a nine-month pregnancy calculated at the price of the current minimum wage gives us a sum in the region of £40,300.[10] Pregnancy is hard work and a risky enterprise; allowing payment of a minimum wage allows for formal recognition of the valuable services surrogates provide; it is this service that is being remunerated and not the purchase of a baby. But this might be on top of the fee paid to an agency to cover the expenses of introducing the couple and facilitating the agreement. And at first blush £40,300 looks more than moderate recompense and exceeds payments made in many US states. An alternative might be to treat surrogacy as akin to a full-time job and pay up to a maximum

10 We are grateful to Professor Susan Bewley for this comment at the Wellcome Trust 'Motherhood: All Change' conference held on 9 and 10 September 2013, Manchester, UK.

of the minimum wage of £6.31 for 37.5 hours over the 40 weeks of pregnancy, adding up to a fee of £9,465. We could, instead, consider paying the living wage which takes account of the cost of living in the UK. At £7.65 for 37.5 hours over 40 weeks, this would amount to £11,475. As the last few weeks of pregnancy are the hardest, we could perhaps consider paying more during this time. Paying the minimum wage for every hour of pregnancy during the last six weeks would amount to £6,360. Such payments would be subject to tax and national insurance.

Why not allow the market to set the fee? We suggest restricting payment to a 'moderate sum' in part to avoid pricing many commissioning couples out of the market, which would mean that only those of considerable means would have this method of founding a family open to them. Courts retrospectively authorising payments have been keen to ensure the amount paid has not been so much as to 'overbear the will of the surrogate' (*A* v *another and others* ([2011] EWHC 1738 (Fam))). Hedley J. in *Re S (Parental Order)* ([2009] EWHC 2977 (Fam)), a case which involved a Californian surrogacy arrangement in which USD $23,000 was paid, said:

> … (3) The court should be astute to ensure that sums of money which might look modest in themselves are not in fact of such a substance that they overbear the will of a surrogate. (para. 7)

Set the UK fee too high and couples will still resort to jurisdictions like India where a surrogate's services can be obtained for less. Set it too low and the change in the law may not produce more willing surrogates and thus couples again will still look abroad. We need more research investigating whether or not surrogates are content with 'reasonable expenses', would want to be paid an additional 'moderate fee' and what sort of sums they would deem reasonable.

Whether such payment will increase the number of willing UK surrogates is unclear: due to the paucity of data there is no accurate profile on the motivations and characteristics of women who undertake surrogacy in the UK. Imrie and Jadva (2013) suggest that some UK surrogates are happy with the current system of expenses, fearing that allowing payments will mean that only the very rich can afford to found a family in this manner and that it will subvert the altruistic motives of many surrogates. Other evidence in the UK and USA demonstrates a shift in the nature of women who act as surrogates. In *J v G* ([2013] EWHC 1432 (Fam)), Theis J. noted that the parental order reporter recorded the following in her report about the surrogate mother:

> She explained that to be a surrogate in California a woman needs to be financially independent and emotionally secure … I did not sense that the respondent surrogate was vulnerable to financial or other exploitation. Indeed it was she who set the sum she required and was paid … (para. 22)

When examining surrogates' motives, it is a false dichotomy to choose between a purely altruistic choice and a financial one. Having altruistic motives does not rule out financial motives. Nurses are seen as pursuing a vocation caring for the sick and yet it is not suggested they should work unpaid. Furthermore, whilst women may consider being a surrogate for altruistic reasons, many could be put off by the added costs associated with pregnancy which 'reasonable expenses' may not cover. Whilst only some couples can afford to pay a surrogate, only some women can financially 'choose' to be a surrogate. 'Reasonable expenses' may cover the basics; other factors may exclude some women from becoming surrogates. For example, while maternity rights are enshrined in law, many women get only very basic maternity pay and suffer a delay in career progress once they have children. A surrogate may only need to take a minimal time off work as she will not be caring for the infant, but she will still lose money.

Permitting moderate payment may increase the number of willing surrogates in the UK, lessening the need for commissioning couples to look abroad or to the internet where the potential for exploitation and harm to either parties or the resulting child is higher. Money may well be or become a motivating factor, but to argue that this eradicates all other altruistic motives ignores the complexity of why women choose to become surrogates. This is reflected in a comment made by Kim Cotton, the woman at the centre of *Re C*: she was a married, 'stay at home' mother of two when she agreed to act as a surrogate for a foreign couple in exchange for £6,500; she explains how both money and a desire to help others influenced her decision:

> I was a young mum at home with my kids when I saw a television programme about surrogacy. I was always looking for ways to earn money and when I saw this I thought, 'This is ridiculous. I'm pregnant at home anyway and I can be paid for it. Excellent.' I loved my two kids and I didn't realise so many people had difficulty conceiving, so I wanted to help. I told my husband about it. He thought it was a great idea, but he would never have allowed me to do it for nothing, and I felt the same. We viewed it as a job; the childless couple got something and I got something (O'Connell, 2002).

Excessive payments may lead to an unbalanced shift towards more financial motivations; a moderate payment which would fully compensate the surrogate for her 'work' is a sensible way forward in terms of promoting the availability of surrogates in the UK and ensuring a fair recompense, whilst also preserving the altruistic motives which many surrogate mothers have.

iii. What Will Payment Mean for Surrogate?

> Surrogacy is not an assembly line for producing androids; it is the collaborative creation of a human being ... Genetic parents needs to be aware that they are collaborating with a woman not with a womb. (Wallbank, 2002: 294)

If moderate payment is permitted openly and lawfully, what does that mean for the surrogate and how may it alter her role once her services are rendered? Under the current model of 'reasonable expenses', research has shown that a UK surrogate is most often viewed as a woman helping a family and not just as a womb for rent, with no connection with the resulting child. Research conducted at the Centre for Family Research in Cambridge examined whether, and how, surrogacy affects family relationships (Jadva *et al*, 2003). A largely positive picture of the relationships between the surrogate and her own family and between these individuals and the families created through surrogacy emerged. The study found that surrogates stayed in touch with the majority of the surrogacy children (77 per cent) and with most of the parents (85 per cent of mothers, 76 per cent of fathers). Of the surrogates who had chosen to maintain contact with the surrogacy families, most would meet in person once or twice a year. Jadva stated: 'our research shows that in the majority of cases, relationships formed as a result of surrogacy are valued and enjoyed by surrogates and sustained over time' (Jadva *et al*, 2013).

The research looked at the experiences of surrogacy from a range of perspectives, including that of the partners and children of surrogates as well as surrogates themselves. It was based on in-depth interviews with 34 surrogates, 36 children of surrogates and 11 partners of surrogates. Twenty of the surrogates had been interviewed by Jadva more than ten years ago in a previous project which looked at the psychological wellbeing and experiences of surrogates one year after the birth of the surrogacy child. The participation of these women allowed the researchers to track relationships over time, adding a valuable dimension to the study. Most of the surrogates' own children (86 per cent) had a positive view of their mothers' involvement in surrogacy. Almost half (47 per cent) were in contact with the surrogacy child all of whom reported a good relationship with him or her. A significant number of surrogates' children referred to the child as a sibling or a half sibling (Jadva *et al*, 2013).

Recognising this link to the surrogate mother, legal motherhood is vested in the woman who gestates and gives birth to a child until she formally relinquishes this title and a parental order is granted. In law at least, the emphasis is on gestation. Commenting on this, Baroness Hale stated in *Re G* (*Children*) ([2006] UKHL 43):

> the fact that in English law the woman who bears the child is legally the child's mother recognises a deeper truth: that the process of carrying a child and giving him (which may well be followed by breastfeeding for some months) brings with it, in the vast majority of cases, a very special relationship between mother and child, a relationship which is different from any other. (para. 34)

In this manner the gestational link between surrogate mother and child is implicitly recognised. This can be contrasted with the position in India where gestational ties made through surrogacy are not formally acknowledged. Amrita Pande's (2009) ethnography with Indian surrogates highlighted how the surrogate mothers fostered kinship ties through shared bodily substances (blood and breast milk) and the labour of gestation and birth. The women were seeking to have their role acknowledged: that they went beyond merely providing a service or womb for nine months. Yet in Indian surrogacy houses, once the child is handed over, this link is often not acknowledged or extended. In a recent BBC news report, a UK-based commissioning couple commented about two Indian surrogates who were both pregnant with their genetically related twins: 'she's doing a job for us, how often do you communicate with your builder or your gardener?' (Taneja, 2013). It is clear here that the surrogacy arrangement is reduced to a purely economic transaction.

If we were to permit a moderate fee in the UK, would the 'special relationship' placed on gestational ties and the way we view it change as it potentially becomes more of a transaction? The recent Irish case of *M.R. & Anor* v *An tArd Chlaraitheoir & Ors* ([2013] IEHC 91) raised the question of what role gestation should take when ascribing motherhood. The Irish High Court ruled that it was the genetic mother of the twins who had been born through a surrogate that should be recognised as the 'legal' mother of the children. The judge was not convinced on the role of epigenetics, stating that it was 'most unlikely that epigenetics will ever trump the deterministic quality of chromosomal DNA' (para. 98). Such emphasis placed on genetics is worrying, and leaves little consideration for the gestational surrogate. Increasing research and information on epigenetics may necessitate reconsideration of the role (if any) a surrogate could have after the birth, particularly if we allow payments. Will the surrogate become, as is often the case in the USA, simply a 'gestational carrier' and not in any sense a mother? Lyndon Shanley (2004) argues that medical and legal discourses encourage a view of surrogacy as a contractual agreement between families, and fails to capture the complexity of the relationships created among the surrogate, intending parents and child. Here the failure to acknowledge gestational links in law and culture once a parental order has been made does not capture the nature of the complex relationships that surrogacy entails and wrongly shoehorns these complex relationships into the two-parent nuclear model.

There are some surrogates who are happy to gestate the child and have no further links to the commissioning couple or child. There are some who wish to have a distant role in the child's life. There is no 'one size fits all' remedy but it must be recognised that this is an area fraught with difficulty and emotion. If, as we advocate, moderate payment is permitted, we must ensure it is not viewed as a totally commercial transaction, so as to ensure the surrogate's reproductive links with the resulting child are recognised. Recognition could take the form of a more pluralistic account of parenthood in this context as advocated by Wallbank (2003).

While the issue of payment to surrogates is in many ways so significant as to warrant a separate debate and a swifter change in law, ultimately the issue will be tied up with our reform three, that is, any change to payment should eventually be part of a new Surrogacy Act.

Reform 3: Set up a Warnock-type Review to Consider a New Surrogacy Act Creating a System of Pre-conception Regulation

> ... the best way to control the damage that surrogacy could potentially cause is through the process of regulation. (Freeman, 1989: 166)

Freeman was supportive of the regulation of surrogacy despite recognising the pitfalls of the restrictive scheme offered by the 1985 Act. Our third proposal recommends the creation of a Committee of Inquiry, to review the present legal, ethical and social issues raised by surrogacy so as to facilitate the creation of a wholly new Act.

Below we suggest some items that such a committee of inquiry should consider in a bid to move towards a more permissive and facilitative regulatory framework.

i A Pre-conception Regulatory Framework

Surrogacy regulation is ineffective and only comes into play when things go wrong or when the commissioning parents acquire legal parenthood for the child who is normally already in their care. One way of avoiding this and arguably offering greater protection to any children born through such arrangements, as well as surrogate mothers and commissioning couples, is to establish a pre-conception regulatory framework. At the centre of such a framework should be the child's welfare as the paramount consideration. This would bring this method of family formation in line with other statutes governing children: section 1 of the Children Act 1989 makes the welfare of the child the paramount consideration in any court proceedings about his/her care and upbringing. Section 1(2) of the Adoption and Children Act 2002 makes the welfare of the child throughout his life the paramount consideration of both the court and the adoption agency in adoption proceedings. The Human Fertilisation and Embryology Act 1990 (as amended) makes it a condition of any licence to provide treatment services that a woman must not be provided with those services unless account has been taken of the welfare of any child who may be born as a result of the treatment and of any other child who may be affected by the birth (section 13(5)). A pre-conception regulatory framework should be designed with any child/children created with the aid of a surrogate as the paramount concern.

Residence requirements for both surrogate and commissioning couple/individuals could be mandatory, stipulating that all must be resident in the UK. This would avoid the problems raised by international surrogacy arrangements where complex immigration laws may bar entry of a child, causing them to be marooned stateless and parentless as in the case of *Re X* v *Y* (*Foreign Surrogacy*) (Beaumont and Trimmings, 2012).

Regulation could entail judicial pre-approval to meet the lack of 'before the fact' regulation, but an obvious drawback could be that it may prove too time-consuming to be feasible. Alternatively, a system for prior approval by a regulatory board or authority could be put in place, just as it is for those seeking the use of assisted conception services such as IVF.[11] The Human Fertilisation and Embryology Authority is responsible for licensing and monitoring fertility clinics, which are mandated by law to consider the welfare of a child prior to offering treatment (HFE Act 1990, s. 13(5) as amended by the HFE Act 2008). Similarly, the Human Tissue Authority as set

---

11 Cf Harris (2000): we respectfully note Harris's arguments that the interests or welfare of the child are rightly central to any discussion of the ethics of reproduction and his contention that this legitimate concern is misunderstood in The Surrogacy Review and at least one of the provisions of the Human Fertilisation and Embryology Act 1990.

up by the Human Tissue Act 2004[12] has specific panels to ensure that directed living donations are free from duress or undue influence and that no unlawful payments have been made.[13] In the context of adoption and fostering, prospective parents are thoroughly vetted and the guiding principle throughout the Adoption and Children Act 2002 is that the child's welfare is paramount. Whilst the lengthy bureaucracy, duplication and delay in the adoption process has been criticised, it does offer a thorough vetting process of prospective parents. Singer and Wells advocated that just as private adoptions are illegal, so too should be private surrogacy arrangements (1985: 126). Instead they suggested the creation of a State Surrogacy Board which would be responsible for finding and screening suitable surrogates and matching them to commissioning couples. They state:

> We do not claim that a Surrogacy Board will bring about problem-free surrogacy, but we do think it has the capacity greatly to reduce the incidence of problems in this area. It is clearly preferable to unregulated surrogacy, whether illegal or legal, and also preferable to attempts to enforce contracts against surrogates. While a prohibition on private surrogacy arrangements will always be difficult to enforce, the availability of officially regulated surrogacy would eliminate most of the motivation for private agreements. Regulation is therefore preferable to any other alternative that has been proposed or that we are able to suggest. (1985: 211)

An illustration of a comprehensive preconception regulatory scheme for approving surrogacy arrangements can be found in Israel where much focus is placed upon the suitability of the surrogate mother (Surrogate Motherhood Agreements (Approval of Agreement and Status of Newborn) Law; Schuz, 2003). This suitability is by professional assessment (both medical and psychological) and an Approvals Committee. There are various restrictions introduced by the Approvals Committee which reflect its general views on suitability: a surrogate mother must be older than 22 and younger than 40, must not have given birth more than five times and, whilst not officially published, it is expected that she will have given birth at least once (and she will not be allowed to serve as a surrogate more than once.) A further restriction is that relatives of the intended parents are not allowed to serve as surrogate mothers. Once deemed 'suitable' the surrogate mother is fully informed of all the risks and the nature of the commitment, and must seek independent legal advice. Physical health is examined, and provisions for mental health are also made available throughout the entire process to ensure that the real danger to the mental health of the surrogate mother is addressed (Anderson, 2012). Once these conditions are met, Israeli law denies the

---

12 The HTA has been responsible for regulating living organ donation since 1 September 2006. This is when the Human Tissue Act 2004 came into force.

13 All living donors are assessed by an Independent Assessor (IA), who is required to conduct an interview and specifically look for evidence of coercion, payment or reward. The HTA must be satisfied that there is no evidence of payment or reward and that valid consent has been given before it can approve a donation.

surrogate mother the right to renege on the arrangement unless circumstances have substantially changed or the welfare of the child is at serious risk. There are certain aspects of the Israeli regulation system that we would not endorse as appropriate for the UK, namely the restriction of surrogacy as a method of family formation to heterosexual couples. Banning men and women without partners and same-sex couples has resulted in an increase in individuals from these cohorts seeking the assistance of international surrogates (Lior, 2013).

In looking for an alternative preconception regulatory framework tailored to the needs of the UK, we submit that any suggested changes must have at its core a drive to find a system which can secure the best outcomes for children born through such arrangements. A preconception regulatory scheme could allow for the immediate transfer of legal parentage (no six week delay as currently mandated). Emily Jackson notes: 'the complexity of the rules governing the transfer of legal parenthood undoubtedly deters some commissioning parents from acquiring a formal relationship with "their" child and this is clearly not in a child's best interests' (2013: 846). But if the child is at birth to become in law the child of the commissioning couple, such a scheme forces us to revisit the thorny issue of enforceability of surrogacy arrangements.

ii Revisit the Issue of Enforceability of Surrogacy 'Contracts' in the Context of Pre-approval Scheme

The law at present stipulates that surrogacy 'contracts' are not enforceable by or against any of the parties making them (section 1A of the Surrogacy Act 1985 inserted by section 36 of the Human Fertilisation and Embryology Act 1990):

> it does not matter by what means the child was created, be it sexual intercourse, donor insemination or IVF, the arrangement is not an enforceable contract. (Brazier, 2011: 381)

Research conducted into the experience of commissioning couples reported that many perceived the surrogacy arrangement as a positive one (Mullock et al, 2003). In practice, cases where surrogates renege on agreements often attract much publicity but it is thought that such cases are rare. According to COTS, 98 per cent of arrangements involving COTS members have reached successful conclusions. Similarly, in 1997 the Surrogacy Review noted evidence to suggest that in only a handful of cases (perhaps 4 – 5 per cent) do surrogacy arrangements prove unsuccessful (Brazier Report, 1998: para. 3.38). To date there have been six published cases where surrogates have refused to relinquish the child.[14]

Nonetheless the lack of enforceability at present may deter commissioning couples from entering into surrogacy arrangements in the UK and provide an incentive to

---

14 *Re P (Minors)* [1987] 2 FLR 421; *Re MW* [1995] 2 FLR 7159; *C and C* [1997] Fam Law 226; *W and W* v *H* [2002] 2 FLR 252; *Re P (Surrogacy: Residence)* [2008] 1 FLR 177; *Re T (a child) (surrogacy: residence order)* [2011] EWCH 33 (Fam); *Re H* [2002] 2 FLR 252; *Re P (Surrogacy: Residence)* [2008] 1 FLR 177.

commission surrogates abroad. The insecurity inherent in surrogacy arrangements in the UK adds validity to Warnock's concern nearly two decades ago that surrogacy is risky(Warnock, 2002). Yet such inherent uncertainty and risk arguably stems from the very fact that such arrangements are not enforceable or legally binding. Emily Jackson argues that 'the law's failure to enforce surrogacy contracts inevitably contributes to their insecurity' (2010: 853). She goes further to state:

> It could even be argued that their complete unenforceability may persuade women to become surrogates even if they are not sure they want to give up the child after birth. (2013: 853)

Gamble (2012) notes: 'there is something a little condescending, even Victorian, about the law's presumption that a woman cannot make an informed rational decision to carry a child for someone else, and to bear the consequences of that decision'. Others such as Rosemarie Tong favour retaining the stance that such 'contracts' are unenforceable:

> The value of a change of heart period is important from a feminist point of view. First it acknowledges a parental relationship whose moral significance traditional philosophy has ignored – namely the gestational relationship ... A second advantage of the 'change of heart' period is that it challenges the notion that contracts must be honoured no matter what – as if contracts were more important than people ... (1994: 67)

A change in the regulation of surrogacy to make surrogacy contracts enforceable would offer more security to commissioning couples and may incentivise individuals to find surrogates located within the UK. It may offer greater certainty in relation to parental status and thus solve the problem that international surrogacy is creating children left stateless and parentless. But should society take that step of forcing any surrogate in full or partial surrogacy to surrender the child against her will? We cannot agree among ourselves.

iii Access to Surrogacy as a Method of Founding a Family

The HFE Act 2008 sought to widen the categories of those who could apply for a parental order, opening it from solely husband and wife to civil partners and two people living together in an 'enduring family relationship' (the Human Fertilisation and Embryology Act 2008, s. 54). One group who are not eligible to apply for parental orders are those who are single. In the spirit of broadening our conception of the family, we argue that consideration should be given to this cohort of individuals who may also wish to found a family through surrogacy.[15] As single people cannot at present apply for a Parental Order, they are prevented from obtaining legal parenthood over children created through surrogacy arrangements who may already be in their cus-

15 This omission/exclusion has also been mentioned by Horsey and Sheldon (2012).

tody. Refusal to grant legal parental status to the appropriate person who is looking after the child on a daily basis is potentially dangerous and does little to ensure a child's interests are paramount.

This restriction is also out of sync with reality and changes to legislation in other spheres. First, single people who are naturally fertile are free to found a family through sexual intercourse. Secondly, single people in the UK can legally adopt children (Adoption and Children Act 2002). Thirdly, there have been changes to assisted reproduction in the form of s. 13(5) of the Human Fertilisation and Embryology Act 2008, which removed the justification for clinicians to discriminate against women without male partners.[16]

The present restriction which bars this cohort from attaining legal parenthood through surrogacy lacks persuasive justification. There is no guarantee as to the stability of marriage relationships or so called 'enduring family relationships'. The latest census figures from 2011 reveal that 16.1 per cent of all families in the UK are now headed by a lone parent, 90 per cent of which are headed by a single woman (Macrory, 2012). Furthermore, evidence to suggest that children raised by single parents fare worse are tenuous given the inextricable link with poverty. As Jackson notes:

> while there are numerous studies which appear to show some correlation between single parenthood and poor outcomes, these often reflect the poverty and greater mobility that often accompany divorce, separation or unplanned single parenthood. (2013: 772).

She further notes that there is a difference between those who choose single parenthood and those who have it thrust upon them. Extending parental orders or access to single individuals in any preconception framework warrants serious consideration. The risk is that at present such individuals are creating children through surrogates privately commissioned, either here or abroad, and raising those children without the appropriate legal parenthood. This is arguably a far greater danger to the welfare of a child than the speculative unsubstantiated fears revolving around permitting the acquisition of legal parenthood in a formal manner.

Reform 4. International Surrogacy Arrangement – the Need for a Global Approach

An international surrogacy arrangement has been described as 'one which involves more than one country of habitual residence, nationality or domicile of the commissioning parents, donors and the gestational mother' (Hutchinson, 2013: 3). Hutchinson notes that 'there are currently no international laws which make provision for rights of parentage either from the perspective of the commissioning parents, gestational mothers or most importantly the child' (*ibid*: 3). As case law testifies, such transnational arrangements have given rise to the most significant problems in surrogacy.

16 Section 13(5) removed the requirements that clinicians take account of the welfare of any child born 'including the need of that child for a father'.

Katarina Trimmings and Paul Beaumont undertook research from 2010-2012 funded by the Nuffield Foundation on the growing social phenomenon of international surrogacy and how it could be regulated at global level. In co-operation with the Hague Conference on Private International Law[17] they explored the possible types of international regulation of surrogacy arrangements and proposed a model of regulation of international surrogacy arrangements at the international level.

Similarly, the European Parliament funded a project entitled 'A Comparative Study on the Regime of Surrogacy in Member States' (2013), which provided an overview of the wide range of policy concerns relating to surrogacy as a practice at national, European and Global level. The study concluded that whilst it was impossible to indicate a particular legal trend across the EU, all Member States appeared to agree on the need for a child to have clearly defined legal parents and civil status. They emphasised the importance of understanding surrogacy as a 'global phenomenon' (2013: 193) and argued 'that while the EU remains a relevant place for action given the existing differences between Member States, the multiplication of questions sent to the ECHR and the *sui generis* effective legal order that the EU proposes, it may not necessarily be the most appropriate level at which to regulate'. Rather, they deemed that the 'territorial limitations of a purely intra-EU regime signal the desirability of a more global response' (2013: 193).

That a global response is needed is acknowledged by many. The Council on General Affairs and Policy of the Hague Convention noted how artificial it would be to address challenges in private international law regarding the status of children generally, separately from those faced by the general community in relation to international surrogacy cases. Following an acknowledgment of the 'complex affairs of private international law and child protection arising from the growth in cross border surrogacy arrangements' (Permanent Bureau Report), on 10 March 2011 the Permanent Bureau of The Hague Conference on Private International Law published a preliminary note entitled, 'Private International Law Issues Surrounding The Status of Children, Including Issues Arising from International Surrogacy Arrangements'. The Hague Conference's Council mandated the Permanent Bureau to gather information on the matter and its Questionnaires have been drafted and sent to all Members of the Hague Convention for the purpose of gathering 'information on the practical needs in the area, comparative developments in domestic and private international law, and the prospects of achieving consensus on a global approach' (Permanent Bureau Report). Those questionnaires are now posted on the organisation's website, and The Hague Conference on Private International Law is currently continuing its work looking into the problems which might arise for families and in particular for children, as a result of the differing laws in States concerning who is/are the legal parent(s) of a child, as well as looking into the broader concerns which might arise in cases involving international surrogacy arrangements.

Attention is now being given to the problem, and it is clear that in light of growing numbers resorting to the web to commission private and international surrogates,

17 See http://www.hcch.net/index_en.php?act=home.splash.

coupled with the rise in the use of international surrogacy agencies, regulation on an international scale is needed. Supporting the calls for global regulation in this context, Hutchinson argues that 'the debate in relation to the need for a Convention governing international surrogacy arrangements, akin to the 1993 Inter-country Adoption Convention which governs international adoptions, is long overdue' (2013: 3). We agree with Hutchinson's (2013: 16) contention that 'the time has come to unify the various efforts to deal with the issues surrounding international surrogacy into a multi-lateral convention, providing a framework for the growing number of international surrogacy arrangements being entered into'. How exactly we go about creating such a convention/framework is the key question here, but alas it is an issue which is beyond the scope of the present chapter.

Conclusion

Freeman's contribution to the debate on surrogacy remains as valid now as it was in 1999. As he predicted, surrogacy has not gone away and the problems have exacerbated. The question is how we now move forward. Sensitive and sensible reform is long overdue. As the demand for surrogacy increases and large numbers look to surrogates or commercial agencies abroad or on the web, there is little (if any) vetting of the parties involved. The welfare of the child must be the paramount concern and at the centre of any regulation: it is imperative that the government is able accurately to identify and attribute parenthood and parental responsibility for a child so as to secure its welfare. Increasing evidence that individuals are resorting to private or international arrangements, and then raising those children without the appropriate legal parenthood, is a dire concern which the government cannot ignore. The UK needs a better legal framework, one which is fit for purpose and which provides certainty and clarity for all those involved, ensuring that the most vulnerable members in our society are protected. Reform in this area is long overdue, and endeavours should be made towards 'prospective, facilitative, enabling and liberal regulation' (Jackson, 2013b) as opposed to the after-event in theory restrictive but in practice ineffective framework we currently have. We end with the words of Philip Anderson:

> Surrogacy is not going to go away, and as such it is important that steps are taken to protect the vulnerable parties involved. Gone must be the early legislation characterised by ambivalence, and in its place a well thought out and reasoned attempt at tackling the many problems and risks currently faced alone by those entering into surrogacy arrangements. (2012: 20)

References

Alghrani, A., "Commentary – Surrogacy: 'A Cautionary Tale'", *Medical Law Review* 2012 20(4), 631-641.

Alghrani, A. and Griffiths, D., "Surrogacy: What is so brilliant about 'Brilliant Beginnings'?", *Bionews* 2013 724(October).

Anderson, P., "An Evaluation of Surrogacy Law and its Potential Development in the UK; Is There A Clear Way Forward?", *Kings Student Law Review* 2010 2(2), 37-51.

Bailey, A., "Reconceiving Surrogacy: Toward a Reproductive Justice Account of Indian Surrogacy", *Hypatia* 2011 26(4), 715-741.

BBC "1985: Inquiry over 'baby-for-cash' deal" [online] available at http://news.bbc.co.uk/onthisday/hi/dates/stories/january/4/newsid_2495000/2495857.stm (1985) (accessed 23 July 2013).

Beaumont, P. and Trimmings, K., "Regulating International Surrogacy Arrangements", *International Family Law* 2012, 125-128.

Bhatia, S., "Indian surrogacy industry: we could never have imagined we'd be parents", *Daily Telegraph,* 26 May 2012.

Brazier Report, *Surrogacy: Review for Health Ministers of Current Arrangements for Payments and Regulation* (London: Department of Health, 1998).

Brazier, M. and Cave, E., *Medicine, Patients and the Law* (London: Penguin Books, 2011).

University of Cambridge "Family bonds: how does surrogacy impact on relationships?" (online) (2013), available at http://www.cam.ac.uk/research/news/family-bonds-how-does-surrogacy-impact-on-relationships (accessed 29/07/2014).

Cooper, G., "Doctors Demand Tighter Laws on Surrogacy" (online) available at http://www.independent.co.uk/news/doctors-demand-tighter-laws-on-surrogacy-1261713.html (accessed 3/08/2013).

Crawshaw, M., Blyth, E. and Akker, O. "The changing profile of surrogacy in the UK – Implications for national and international policy and practice", *Journal of Social Welfare and Family Law* 2012 34(3), 265-275.

Deckha, M., "Prioritizing a Postcolonial Feminist Ethic in Regulating Transnational ARTs: The Case of Commercial Gestational Surrogacy", Presentation given at *Motherhood: All Change* Conference, Manchester, September 2013.

Department of Health, *Review of the Human Fertilisation and Embryology Act Proposals for revised legislation (including establishment of the Regulatory Authority for Tissue and Embryos)* (London: The Stationery Office, 2006).

European Parliament, Directorate General for Internal Policies, *A Comparative Study on the Regime of Surrogacy in Member States,* available at http://www.europarl.europa.eu/studies.

Freeman, M., "Is Surrogacy Exploitative?", in S. McLean (ed), *Legal Issues in Human Reproduction* (Aldershot, Dartmouth: 1989).

Freeman, M., "Does Surrogacy have a Future after Brazier", *Medical Law Review* 1999 7(1), 1-20.

Gamble, N., "Should surrogate mothers still have an absolute right to change their minds?", *BioNews,* 22 October 2012.

Gamble, N., "The HFEA gets into gear on surrogacy", *BioNews,* 7 May 2013.

Gamble, N. and Prosser, P., "The 'Brilliant Beginnings' of surrogacy reform in the UK", *BioNews,* 27 August 2013.

Harris J., "The Welfare of the Child", *Health Care Analysis* 2000 8(1), 27-34.

Horsey, K., "Challenging presumptions: legal parenthood and surrogacy arrangements", *Child and Family Law Quarterly* 2010 22(4), 449-474.

Horsey, K. and Sheldon, S., "Still hazy after all these years: The law regulating surrogacy", *Medical Law Review* 2012 20(1), 67-89.

Hutchinson, A., "The Hague Convention on Surrogacy: Should we agree to disagree?", *ABC Section of Family Law* 2012 Fall CLE Conference, Philadelpia, October 2012, p. 9.

Imrie, S. and Jadva, V., "Surrogacy law: a call for change?", *BioNews*, 5 August 2013.

Jackson, E., *Medical Law: Text, Cases and Materials* (Oxford: OUP, 2013).

Jackson, E., *DIY Surrogacy*, presentation given at *Surrogacy Revisited* seminar, Manchester, June 2013.

Jadva, V., Murray, C., Lycett, E., MacCallum, F. and Golombok, S., "Surrogacy: the experiences of surrogate mothers", *Human Reproduction* 2003 18(10), 2197-2204.

Lior, I., "Israeli couples being forced overseas in search for surrogate mothers" (online), available at http://www.haaretz.com/news/national/.premium-1.532242 (accessed 23/07/2013).

Lotz, M., "The Two-Parent Limitation in ART Parentage Law: Old Fashioned Law for New Fashioned Families", in D. Cutas and S. Chan (eds), *Families Beyond the Nuclear Ideal* (London: Bloomsbury, 2012).

Macrory, I., "Measuring National Well-being – Households and Families" (online) available at http://www.ons.gov.uk/ons/dcp171766_259965.pdf (accessed on 23/08/2013).

Mason, J. K. and Laurie, G., *Mason and McCall Smith's Law and Medical Ethics* (Oxford: Oxford University Press, 2013).

Mullock, F., Lycett, E., Murray, C., Jadva, V. and Golombok, S. "Surrogacy: The Experience of Commissioning Couples', *Human Reproduction* 2003 18(6), 1334-1342.

Nordqvist, P. and Smart, C., *Relative Strangers: Family life, genes and donor conception* (Basingstoke: Palgrave Macmillan, 2014).

O'Connell, D., "What Happened next?" (online) available at
http://www.guardian.co.uk/theobserver/2002/jun/30/features.magazine97 (accessed 23/07/2013).

Pande, A., "'It may be her eggs but it's my blood': Surrogates and everyday forms of kinship in India", *Qualitative Sociology* 2009 32(4), 379-397.

Permanent Bureau of The Hague Conference, *Private International Law Issues Surrounding The Status of Children, Including Issues Arising From International Surrogacy Agreements*, available at http://www.hcch.net/upload/wop/genaff2011pd11e.pdf.

Ramskold, L., "Commercial Surrogacy: how provisions of monetary remuneration and powers of international law can prevent exploitation of gestational surrogates", *Journal of Medical Ethics* 2013 39(6), 397-402.

Rogerson, C., "Surrogacy and Employment law: when it's not your pregnancy is it your leave of absence?", http://www.dawsoncornwell.com/en/documents/ABA_CR.pdf.

Schuz, R., "Surrogacy in Israel: An Analysis of the Law in Practice" in R. Cook, S. Day Sclater and F. Kaganas (eds), *Surrogate Motherhood: International Perspectives* (Oregon: Hart Publishing, 2003).

Shanley, L., *Making Babies, Making Families* (Boston: Beacon Press, 2004).

Taneja, P., "The couple having four babies by two surrogates" (online) available at http://www.bbc.co.uk/news/uk-24670212 (accessed 23/07/2013).

Tong, R., "Feminist Perspectives and Gestational Motherhood: The Search for a Unified Legal Focus", in J. Callahan (ed), *Reproduction, Ethics and the Law: Feminist Responses* (Indiana UP: Bloomington and Indianapolis, 1994).

Van den Akker, O., "Psychosocial aspects of surrogate motherhood", *Human Reproduction Update* 2006 12(2), 91-101.

Wallbank, J., "Too Many Mothers: Surrogacy, Kinship and the Welfare of the Child", *Medical Law Review* 2002 10, 271-294.

Warnock, M., *Report of the Committee of Inquiry into Human Fertilisation and Embryology* (HMSO, London 1984).

Warnock, M., *Making Babies: Is There a Right to Have Children?* (Oxford University Press, Oxford, 2002).

Wilkinson, S., "The Exploitation Argument against Commercial Surrogacy", *Bioethics* 2003 17(2), 169-187.

The Right to Responsible Parents? Making Decisions about the Healthcare of Young and Dependent Children

Jo Bridgeman*
Sussex Law School, University of Sussex, UK

Introduction

Over the course of his academic career, Michael has critically analysed a wide range of issues concerning the legal regulation of medicine: adolescent decisions about birth control (Freeman, 1983); decisions about the medical treatment of severely disabled newborns (Freeman, 1983); the exercise of responsibility in the planning of parenthood (Freeman, 2008); end of life decisions (Freeman, 2002); *Gillick's* 'false dawn' (Freeman, 1997a, 2005), the rights of the child born after medically assisted conception (Freeman, 1997a); 'saviour siblings' (Freeman, 2006); sterilisation of women with learning disabilities (Freeman, 1988); surrogacy (Freeman, 1999); renouncing maternity (Freeman, 2012). I am sure that is not a comprehensive list! In his examination of these topics, all of which are of enormous significance for the individual and their families, Michael explored the extent to which the rights, and the dignity, of the individual were respected. This chapter explains, and further reflects upon, two aspects of Michael's work on the rights of young and dependent children and the responsibilities of their parents in relation to healthcare decision-making. First, I explain the context in which Michael argued that important decisions about the healthcare of children require independent and principled review. I examine the extent to which, in recent cases, the courts have fulfilled this responsibility. Then, I take up Michael's argument, that children have the right to responsible parents, in order to ask what, in the context of decisions about the health of children, it might mean to 'act in a parentally responsible manner'.

Rights, Interests and Responsibilities

Michael has, as a number of the chapters in this volume amply testify, been both a pioneer and a champion of children's rights. Michael has also been at the forefront

* I would like to thank the anonymous referee for their insightful and helpful comments on an earlier draft of this chapter.

A. Diduck, N. Peleg, H. Reece (eds.), Law in Society: Reflections on Children, Family, Culture and Philosophy
Copyright 2015 Koninklijke Brill NV. Printed in The Netherlands. ISBN 978-90-04-26148-8. pp. 453-468.

in presenting the arguments for conceptualising the parent/child relationship in terms of parental responsibility rather than parental rights (Freeman, 2008: 21). He has argued that, given their particular vulnerabilities, children must be understood as rights-holders if their integrity and dignity is to be protected but that, at the same time, children need to be cared for (Freeman, 1992: 55-6):

> [W]e have to recognize the moral integrity of children. We have to treat them as persons entitled to equal concern and respect and entitled to have both their present autonomy recognized and their capacity for future autonomy safeguarded. And this is to recognize that children, particularly younger children, need nurture, care and protection. Children must not... be 'abandoned' to their rights (Freeman, 1992: 66 references omitted).

I believe that Michael's earliest thoughts on the moral and legal responsibilities of parents and of the state in relation to the healthcare of children are to be found in his seminal 1983 book, *The Rights and Wrongs of Children* (Freeman, 1983). In the final chapter, concerned with state intervention into family life, Michael considered the, then recent, cases of *Re D* – in which the court was asked to determine whether the proposed sterilisation of an 11-year old girl who had Sotos Syndrome was in her best interests – and *Re B* – in which the court was asked to authorise an operation on Baby Alexandra to clear an intestinal blockage, Alexandra also had Down's Syndrome (*Re D (a minor) (wardship: sterilisation)* [1976] Fam 185; *In Re B (A Minor) (Wardship: Medical Treatment)* [1981] 1 WLR 1421). In 1983, when Michael wrote and in the preceding years in which these cases were decided, medical law as a discipline was in its infancy. There were very few decided cases in English law and certainly not a body of law, requiring Michael to consider many examples from US case law. It was a time when medical paternalism reigned; when patients were more inclined to defer to the medical profession than challenge them. Respect for patient autonomy had not yet become the guiding principle of the legal regulation of medical practice that it is today. *Gillick*, which would recognise children as rights-holders and parents as under duties to fulfil their responsibilities to their children, had not yet been decided (*Gillick v. West Norfolk and Wisbech AHA* [1986] AC 112). It was from this small but expanding field that these two cases were selected as 'central' to the debate around children's rights. Both offered examples of the imposition of 'restraints on the power of parents to make decisions on their children's behalf and, in so doing, control their lifestyles' (Freeman, 1983: 244).

Furthermore, whilst reflecting upon these cases, Michael offered a critique of the arguments advanced against state intervention into family autonomy by Goldstein, Freud and Solnit in their then recent books, *Beyond* – and *Before* – *The Best Interests of the Child* (Goldstein *et al.*, 1979a, 1979b). Presenting the case for non-intervention, they identified six exceptional circumstances when, they considered, state intervention could be justified, the sixth of which was parental failure to obtain medical care.[1] But

1 (Freeman, 1983: 250-255). The others being: where a parent asks the court to determine the residence of a child; adoption or care by non-parental caretakers; where the child's

not in all cases. State intervention was not justified where failure to secure medical treatment may result in non-fatal harm, only if it threatened death; where medical treatment was novel or experimental, only where there was consensus; and, only in those circumstances when treatment was aimed at giving the child 'a chance for normal healthy growth or a life worth living' (Freeman, 1983: 255, quoting Goldstein *et al.*, 1979a: 91). Whether Goldstein *et al* would have considered justified the intervention which saved the life of Baby Alexandra turns upon interpretation of this final criteria. I return to this case below. I first consider *Re D* and judicial scrutiny of proposals to sterilise children with learning difficulties.

Independent, Principled Review of Proposals to Sterilise Children?

In the view of Goldstein *et al.* there would be no justification for state intervention to prevent, or even review, the proposed sterilisation of 11-year old D; the procedure would not result in her death (*Re D (a minor) (wardship: sterilisation)* [1976] Fam 185). In contrast, Michael argued that the case demonstrated the need for independent, principled, review of decisions concerning the healthcare of children. On this point, the facts bear some repeating. D's parents had formed the view, when D was a very young child, that D should undergo a sterilisation procedure. Heilbron J. observed that D's 'caring and devoted' mother (D's father having died) genuinely believed that D would not be able to marry or care for a child: she refused to accept the views of others involved in D's care that D's behaviour, social skills, academic performance and ability to care for herself had improved (*Re D (a minor) (wardship: sterilisation)* [1976] Fam 185, 188). Her Ladyship accepted the view of the child psychiatrist who had discussed with D her problems at school that her mother was over-protective: 'To be over-zealous in looking after a handicapped child is a very understandable attitude from a very devoted mother' (*Re D (a minor) (wardship: sterilisation)* [1976] Fam 185, 197, 188-9). D's mother was supported in her decision by D's consultant paediatrician, Dr Gordon, who shared the mother's concerns, understood the difficult circumstances in which D's mother was providing the best possible care for D and her sisters and had a favourable attitude towards sterilisation. The gynaecologist who agreed to perform the operation did so after speaking to D's mother and Dr Gordon but not to D herself, and after very little 'independent consideration to the wider implications of this operation'. Legal proceedings were initiated by an educational psychologist from the local education authority whose 'courage, persistence and humane concern' for D was commended by her Ladyship (*Re D (a minor) (wardship: sterilisation)* [1976] Fam 185, 192). Heilbron J. noted the exemplary fashion in which the professionals and services, including schools, social workers and psychologists, co-operated in the care of D (*Re D (a minor) (wardship: sterilisation)* [1976] Fam 185, 188), but lamented the inability of Dr Gordon to appreciate that 'others, whose duties, training and skills were directed to

parents have died or disappeared without making suitable arrangements for the child; conviction of a sexual offence against the child; infliction, or attempted infliction, of serious bodily injury and failure to prevent infliction of such injury.

the assessment and amelioration of many of these problems, had much to contribute in the formulation of a decision of this gravity' (*Re D* (*a minor*) (*wardship: sterilisation*) [1976] Fam 185, 192). This was a case, her Ladyship concluded, for the court to 'throw some care around this child' (*Re D* (*a minor*) (*wardship: sterilisation*) [1976] Fam 185, 194 quoting from *Wellesley v. Duke of Beaufort* (*1827*) 2 Russ 1, 20). Heilbron J. concluded that the proposed sterilisation would have violated 'a basic human right, namely the right of a woman to reproduce' (*Re D* (*a minor*) (*wardship: sterilisation*) [1976] Fam 185, 193). Furthermore, there was the prospect that D herself may, at a future date, be devastated by the realisation of what had been done to her and the court would not risk causing harm to a child but, rather, sought to prevent harm being done (*Re D* (*a minor*) (*wardship: sterilisation*) [1976] Fam 185, 197, 194). Whilst the mother was genuinely seeking to do her best for her daughter, others involved in her care were able to contribute to an assessment of what this might involve and independent review by the court was required to secure consideration of their informed opinions. Independent review was required of the proposed sterilisation which was not simply a medical matter, it was also a social matter, a question of care and of human rights.

A decade later, the House of Lords considered an appeal against the authorisation of a sterilisation operation upon a ward, 17-year old Jeanette. Lord Templeman expressed the opinion that, in all cases, proposals to sterilise a child without her consent should be reviewed by the court:

> A court exercising the wardship jurisdiction emanating from the Crown is the only authority which is empowered to authorise such a drastic step as sterilisation after a full and informed investigation.... No one has suggested a more satisfactory tribunal or a more satisfactory method of reaching a decision which vitally concerns an individual but also involves principles of law, ethics and medical practice (*Re B* (*A Minor*) (*Wardship: Sterilisation*) [1987] 2 WLR 1213, 1218B-C, E).

Yet, dismissive of her rights and without offering principled guidance for determination of best interests in such cases, the House of Lords upheld the judgment of the lower court as applying the right criteria in consideration of all the evidence. Sterilisation was justified as offering protection to the freedom of a vulnerable individual. That decision, which Michael has also subjected to detailed critique (Freeman, 1988), was followed in the last decade of the 20th century by judicial approval of proposals brought to the court to sterilise children with learning difficulties without their consent as in their best interests:[2] proposals which were not subjected to rigorous scrutiny but justified in terms of imagined alternative scenarios and informed by the views of experts or dominated by medical assessments rather than by the knowledge and ex-

2 And even more cases approving the sterilisation of women, although approval was frequently sought when the young woman was 17 so that the court could authorise the procedure. The court cannot consent to the sterilisation of an adult but merely declare the procedure to be in her best interests and hence lawful in the given circumstances, *In Re F* (*Mental Patient: Sterilisation*) [1989] 2 W.L.R. 1025.

perience of those involved in the child's daily care and support or with reference to rights, integrity or dignity (*Re M (A Minor) (Wardship: Sterilization)* [1988] 2 FLR 497; *Re P (A Minor) (Wardship: Sterilization)* [1989] 1 FLR 182; *Re HG (Specific Issue Order: Sterilisation)* [1993] 1 FLR 587).

Approval of the court was required; as Peter Singer QC said, 'one of the responsibilities incorporated into the definition of parental responsibility is a responsibility to bring before a High Court judge the question whether your child should be sterilised' (*Re HG (Specific Issue Order: Sterilisation)* [1993] 1 FLR 587, 595). Although Sir Stephen Brown P. in the Family Division of the High Court, in *Re E*, held that where surgery upon a child was proposed for medical reasons, which would have the effect of sterilisation, it was not necessary for the court to give consent, thus drawing a distinction between therapeutic and non-therapeutic sterilisation (*Re HG (Specific Issue Order: Sterilisation)* [1993] 1 FLR 587, 595). No independent, principled, scrutiny of the former is required by law. In such circumstances, doctors can proceed with consent from the child's parents, in the exercise of their parental responsibility, having formed the view that the procedure is in the best interests of the child. Whilst the BMA advises that unless sterilisation is a 'necessary consequence' of therapeutic treatment, legal advice should be sought as 'virtually' all cases require court approval, we do not know the extent to which sterilisations are performed without consent from the court, justified on the basis that the procedure is therapeutic.

However, from the turn of the century and led by two Court of Appeal decisions concerning adults, the courts do now demonstrate greater willingness to question sterilisation proposals.[3] Detailed consideration of the cases concerning adults is beyond the scope of this chapter, aside from noting that the court will now consider whether contraception is necessary because the individual is engaging in consensual sexual activity and whether less invasive methods have been attempted.[4] Together

---

3 *Re A (medical treatment: male sterilisation)* [2000] 1 FLR 549, in which the sterilisation of a male with Down's Syndrome was determined not to be in his best interests and *Re SL (adult patient: medical treatment)* [2000] 2 FLR 452 in which Butler-Sloss P. held that the least invasive option was in SL's best interests. The evidence was that it was likely that a better contraceptive method would be found for SL within five years and thus the IUD should be tried first. Although in the context of the relationship between *Bolam* and best interests with respect to decisions concerning the sterilisation of adult patients, use of the least invasive method must equally be in the best intererts of children.

4 *A Local Authority v. K* [2013] EWHC 242, and give greater weight to the expressed wishes of the individual. Having concluded that Mrs A lacked the capacity to make a decision about contraception as she was unable to weigh up information about contraception, which she could comprehend, due to the coercion she was under from her husband not to use contraception, Bodey J. in *A Local Authority v. A* [2010] EWHC 1549 [73] declared that it would be in her best interests to use contraception if she consented but refused to order that she should be provided with it. And, in *An NHS Trust v. DE and others* [2013] EWHC 2562, DE was considered to be competent to consent to sexual relations, he had a long-term girlfriend – a relationship which had been disrupted due to her pregnancy – experience of becoming a father, expressed a clear wish to have no further children and the increased supervision was placing severe restraints upon his freedom.

these considerations should preclude proposals to sterilise a child. Whilst there are no reported cases since in which court authority has been sought for sterilisation of a child, the history of case law demonstrates that reference to best interests alone is insufficient. Procedures which threaten to violate the integrity and dignity of the individual through a concern to protect and care need to be reviewed by an independent body according to principled guidance. The courts, caring parents and compassionate professionals will be better able to achieve their shared goal of securing the best for children with learning difficulties in their care with further guidance as to the factors relevant to determination of best interests.

Parental Refusal of Consent: Subjected to a Principled Examination?

The second example which Michael considered in *The Rights and Wrongs of Children* was the first occasion upon which the English courts were asked to authorise an operation upon a child whose parents were refusing to give their consent. In *Re B,* the court was asked whether surgery to relieve an intestinal blockage was in the best interests of Baby Alexandra, born with Down's Syndrome (*In Re B* (*A Minor*) (*Wardship: Medical Treatment*) [1981] 1 WLR 1421). The procedure, which was necessary if Alexandra was to live, would have been performed without question on a child who did not have Down's Syndrome. Templeman L.J. noted that the parents had refused their consent with 'great sorrow' and in the 'genuine belie[f]' that it was in her best interests (*In Re B* (*A Minor*) (*Wardship: Medical Treatment*) [1981] 1 WLR 1421, 1422-1423). His Lordship met the submission that the views of 'responsible and caring parents' such as these should be respected with the response that the decision was now for the court. In light of the evidence and the views of her parents and doctors, the court decided that Alexandra's future was not 'demonstrably going to be so awful that in effect the child must be condemned to die' and authorised the procedure as in her best interests (*In Re B* (*A Minor*) (*Wardship: Medical Treatment*) [1981] 1 WLR 1421, 1424B). Alexandra recovered and, Michael informed us, at the age of ten months returned to the care of her parents. Her life was saved by the independent review of the court; the decision taken out of the hands of those most directly involved. Yet, Michael argued that whilst both parents and the healthcare professionals caring for the child have an interest which precludes a 'rational decision',[5] the courts are 'far from an ideal forum for decision-making'. He suggested that a 'code of principles' was required for such cases.[6] Over time, with development, testing and evaluation, there would be less of a need to refer cases to court for application of the principles.

5 Although, as Priscilla Alderson has argued, emotional responses are also important to such decisions, Alderson, 1990: 61.

6 Michael also observed that the case was considered in the alternatives presented by the choice between intervention or non-intervention – between allowing the parents to decide that the child should be allowed to die and 'imposing' the child upon them. Whilst a third option, to operate and terminate the parental relationship, was not considered, Freeman, 1983: 262.

Re T provided a further opportunity for reflection upon the rights of children and the responsibilities of their parents and the court (*Re T* [1997] 1 FLR 502; Freeman, 2000). Whereas Alexandra's parents and doctors had been in agreement, 18-month old T's parents were refusing consent to a liver transplant proposed by his consultants. Parents, Michael argued, may not have the resources or objectivity to judge and sick children have a right to a 'rational', 'principled, and reasoned, determination' (Freeman, 2000: 267-8). The role of the court, as Butler-Sloss L.J. explained, was not to decide whether the decision of the child's parents was reasonable but to undertake an independent assessment of the welfare of the child in a balancing exercise which assessed the relevance and weight of factors which would be considered by a reasonable parent. On the facts of the case this included the seriousness of the proposed operation, the benefits of major invasive surgery and post operative treatment, the danger of short and long term failure, the possibility of further transplants and C's life expectancy with and without the operation. However, the Court placed enormous weight upon the evidence of consultant paediatrician, Dr P, who would not perform the operation against the wishes of the child's mother, informing the court that he considered that 'total commitment of the caring parent' was 'essential to the success of the treatment'. But in the attempt to acknowledge the importance of his mother's care and recognise her knowledge of her son, the judgment slips from the best interests of the child in relation to the prospect of major transplant surgery to the ability of the mother to cope with the care of her child following surgery to which she was opposed.[7] As Jean McHale and Marie Fox have argued of this case, whilst the Court of Appeal attempted to recognise the contribution of those in caring relationships to understanding the interests of the child, greater clarity is required:

> [I]f a paradigm of caring is to function as a framework for deciding such cases the courts need to be explicit about what this means. .... Certainly, in cases involving young children, judicial guidance and clarification would be necessary as to the meaning of caring and the weight to be ascribed to the views of carers. In *Re T* itself, reference is made to the importance of caring without such articulation and there are unanswered questions as to why such stress was laid in this particular case on the part played by the 'caring parents (Fox and McHale, 1997: 708).

On this occasion, Michael was critically examining the case in light of the arguments in the revised and consolidated, Goldstein, Solnit, Goldstein and Freud, *The Best Interests of the Child: The Least Detrimental Alternative* (1996; Freeman, 1997b). *Re T,* Michael suggested would, on their criteria, be a case for intervention but, he suggested, the Court of Appeal drew on similar ideology to inform the conclusion that refusal of the mother was in the best interests of the child (Freeman, 2000: 262). Adopting a

7 In the subsequent case of *Donald Simms and Jonathan Simms v. An NHS Trust and Secretary of State for Health; PA and JA v. An NHS Trust and Secretary of State for Health* [2002] EWHC 2734, [60] her Ladyship identified, as distinct considerations, the interests of the child, the views of the parents and family and the impact upon both.

critical view of the decision, a view shared by the majority of commentators on this unusual case,[8] Michael concluded that allocation of decision-making to them was an endorsement of parental rights (Freeman, 2000: 259). In contrast to Baby T, Michael was of the view that conjoined twins, Jodie and Mary, 'had the right to expect a thorough investigation of their plight by a neutral decision-maker' and 'they got it' (*Re A* [2000] 4 All ER 961).[9] And the decision, taken out of the hands of their parents, 'subjected to a principled reasoning' (Freeman, 2001) traverses the principles of English law venturing across family, medical, criminal and human rights law, with consideration of intention, act/omission, necessity, 'quasi self-defence', personhood, quality of life and worthwhileness of treatment, best interests and parental responsibility. Despite all of this resulting in a very lengthy legal judgment, I suggest that the Court of Appeal judgment does not give sufficient consideration to the parental concerns about their ability to care for Jodie, who after surgery was expected to have serious ongoing healthcare needs, given the facilities and resources available to them in their home island of Gozo. The Court should have addressed their concerns grounded in their knowledge of the resources and services available to them in their home country, as well as the attitudes towards disability to which she would be exposed. I am not suggesting that more careful scrutiny by the Court of Appeal of the concerns of the parents would, or should, have changed the outcome, but it would have recognised that they bring very specific knowledge and that whilst the primary responsibility for the care of children rests with their parents, they depend upon the support, advice and care of professionals and upon services to support them in the care of their child. Independent review has to be comprehensive as well as principled.

The responsibilities of parents, professionals and the court in relation to the healthcare of children was recently considered in the judgment of Bodey J concerning the post-operative treatment for malignant brain tumours of seven-year old Neon Roberts. The case was brought to court because of a disagreement between Neon's parents about his post-operative treatment. Neon's mother was objecting to conventional post-operative radiotherapy and chemotherapy which offered an 80-86 per cent success rate but carried risks of serious side-effects including intellectual and cognitive impairment, effects upon growth hormone, thyroid and sub-, or in-, fertility. His mother wished him to receive alternative, complementary, treatments which she considered would avoid or reduce the long-term side effects. Bodey J. acknowledged that, as his father was consenting, Neon's doctors could have administered radiotherapy and chemotherapy. However, the Trust's application to court was understandable in light of the disagreement between the parents, the seriousness of

8 It is more usual for the court to give consent to treatment proposed by the caring professionals as in the best interest of the child, *Re C (A Child) (H.I.V. Testing)* [2000] 2 WLR 270, *Re MM (Medical Treatment)* [2000] 1 FLR 224, *An NHS Trust v. A* [2007] EWHC 1696.

9 Expressing agreement with the outcome but finding the reasoning of Robert Walker L.J., that it was in the best interests of both babies that they be separated, more compelling than the majority view. Employing his rights framework: 'The decision is one which upholds dignity: the right of Jodie to live with dignity, the right of Mary to die with dignity. Perhaps even the right of Mary to confer life upon her sister', Freeman, 2001: 279.

the child's condition and the disadvantages which accompanied the benefits of the post-operative treatment (*An NHS Trust v. SR* [2012] EWHC 3842, [2]). Having given the mother's views careful consideration, Bodey J. concluded that the evidence was not there to enable the court to prefer the alternative to standard mainstream treatment, which would require 'identification of a clinician experienced in treating children aged about 7 having this kind of brain cancer; a clinician with the access to the necessary equipment and infrastructure to put the suggested treatment into effect and able and willing to take over medical care of and responsibility for N' (*An NHS Trust v. SR* [2012] EWHC 3842, [25]): treatment which was studied, tested, reported and peer-reviewed and offered a comparable prognosis to the conventional treatment (*An NHS Trust v. SR* [2012] EWHC 3842, [25]).

Bodey J. then gave a comprehensive set of orders to ensure the medical treatment of Neon in accordance with his judgment of Neon's best interests. Bodey J. made a declaration that the treatment package proposed was lawful, with the 'minimum dosages' of radiotherapy and chemotherapy 'to produce maximum survival rates' (*An NHS Trust v. SR* [2012] EWHC 3842, [23], [15]). The complementary techniques preferred by his mother could be used in conjunction with mainstream therapy as long as they did not conflict or disrupt the main treatment (*An NHS Trust v. SR* [2012] EWHC 3842, [21]). Orders were made permitting the administration of ancillary care, authorising clinicians to act upon the consent of the father alone and making a residence order in favour of the father to offer security during Neon's treatment (*An NHS Trust v. SR* [2012] EWHC 3842, [27-9]).

Bodey J. expressed the hope that, 'when she has had time to stand back and reflect upon his best interests', Neon's mother would accept the court's decision as 'N clearly needs both his parents to be pulling together alongside the treating team and nothing could be worse than for him to pick up on any sense of maternal opposition to the treatment' (*An NHS Trust v. SR* [2012] EWHC 3842, [22]), In sum, whilst the court was not able to draw upon a principled set of guidance, seven-year old Neon had a comprehensive, independent, review of his plight. Bodey J. gave careful and serious consideration to the preference of Neon's mother for alternative approaches to conventional post-operative treatment whilst recognising the responsibilities of Neon's father with respect to his son's health and the medical evidence. The responsibility of the court to undertake a thorough, careful, independent review of the treatment and objections to it was fulfilled and a comprehensive set of orders made to ensure the best treatment of the child.

Independent and Principled Review?

Re B has provided the basis for determination of a further stream of cases and it is from these cases, I suggest, that a more developed set of guidance now exists which could be further explicated to provide a principled set of guidance by which the courts could undertake independent review of decisions concerning children's healthcare. This has not always been the case. On a number of occasions, the court has been asked whether doctors may lawfully withhold or withdraw treatment from a severely disabled child contrary to the wishes of the child's parents.[10] *Re B* is not strictly speaking analogous; the procedure to be withheld in that case was an unexceptional operation upon a child with learning difficulties. And in comparison with the decision of the Court of Appeal in her case, there are, I suggest, too many cases in which the declaration of the court that a proposal to withhold or withdraw medical treatment from a severely disabled child was lawful must have left parents feeling that the future of their child had not been subjected to rigorous, principled, scrutiny. Very different assessments of the best interests of the child were the reason for application for judicial review of future medical treatment in *Re C, Royal Wolverhampton Hospital NHS Trust v. B, A National Health Service Trust v. D,* and Luke Winston-Jones (*Re C (a minor) (medical treatment)* [1998] 1 FLR 384; *Royal Wolverhampton Hospital NHS Trust v. B* [2000] 1 FLR 953; *A National Health Service Trust v. D* [2000] 2 FLR 677; *Re L (Medical Treatment: Benefit)* [2004] EWHC 2713 (Fam)). In all of these cases, the court gave the order sought by the hospital declaring lawful the withdrawal or withholding of treatment resulting in the death of the child. In each of these cases, the court focused upon the medical evidence and gave very little consideration to the views of the parents as to the best interests of their child, of other professionals or wider considerations; an unbalanced determination which would in all possibility leave parents not being 'personally persuaded that this course of action is the best for their child' (McHaffie in association with Fowlie *et al.*, 2001: 397).

Whilst the Court of Appeal review of the care of Charlotte Wyatt, in 2005, was by no means the end of judicial involvement,[11] I think it is here that we can see the court

10 There are further cases in which the view of the court has been sought in the absence of a clear dispute between parents and treating doctors. The child's interests and rights in a principled review is the same: *Re C (a minor) (wardship: medical treatment)* [1989] 2 All ER 782; *Re J (a minor) (wardship: medical treatment)* [1990] 3 All ER 930; *Re C (a baby)* [1996] 2 FLR 43: *K (a minor)* [2006] EWHC 1007; *Re B* [2008] EWHC 1996; *Re RB* [2010] 1 FLR 946; *An NHS Trust v. KH,* 5 October 2012. A developed set of principled guidance would assist in the determination of cases in the hospital wards and identification of those cases which require independent determination.

11 Hedley J. five times on the issue whether it would be lawful to withhold artificial ventilation if her condition deteriorated to require mechanical ventilation to prolong her life: *Portsmouth NHS Trust v. Wyatt & Wyatt, Southampton NHS Trust Intervening* [2004] EWHC 2247 (7 October 2004); *Portsmouth Hospitals NHS Trust v. Wyatt and others* [2005] EWHC 117 (Fam) (28 January 2005); *Wyatt v Portsmouth NHS Trust and Wyatt (By her Guardian) (No 3)* [2005] EWHC 693 (Fam) (21st April 2005); *Re Wyatt* [2005] EWHC 2293 (Fam) (21 October 2005); Unreported 23 February 2006. The Court of Appeal twice on the same question – Unreported [2005] EWCA Civ 185 (9 February 2005); *Re Wyatt (a child) (medical treatment: continuation of order)* [2005] EWCA Civ 1181 (12 October 2005). In November 2004, Hedley J. made an order permitting the administration of diamorphine to relieve the pain of a fractured leg (due to brittle bones), her parents having refused fearing that it would depress her breathing and in December 2004 made declarations giving directions in relation to palliative care. As well as orders granting anonymity to expert witnesses (13 September 2004) and forbidding identification of expert witnesses in the media (16 September 2004), later extended to all experts who gave evidence with regard to her care. Details of the unreported cases are set out in the Court of Appeal judgment

drawing together principles from earlier cases in a form which can offer a guide to decisions whether life-prolonging treatment should be provided, withheld or withdrawn:

1. It has to be decided which course of action is in the best interests of the child, in which the welfare of the child is paramount and determined from the assumed perspective of the child (*Re J*);
2. Best interests is given a wide definition including medical, social and other factors (*Re A*) – this requires careful consideration of the facts of the individual case;
3. There is a strong, but not irrebuttable, presumption in favour of prolonging life (*Re J*);
4. Determination of best interests must balance the relevant factors (*Re J*), which may be achieved though a balance sheet of certain and possible benefits and disadvantages (*Re A*).
5. Whether life would be intolerable was a guide in the assessment of best interests.

The 'propositions' from *Wyatt* were delineated and applied by Holman J. in his consideration of whether it was lawful to withdraw artificial ventilation and provide palliative care to 18-month old MB who suffered from the degenerative and progressive condition, spinal muscular atrophy (*An NHS Trust v MB* [2006] EWHC 507, [16]). Despite the unanimous opinion of 14 consultants, including both those involved in his care and independent experts, Holman J. concluded that it was not currently in MB's best interests for ventilation to be discontinued but neither should his treatment be escalated. In a judgment focused upon the best interests of the individual child given his condition at that point in time, Holman J. carefully balanced the benefits and burdens, in doing so placing more weight than is usual upon MB's mother's evidence about the quality of his life. Holman J. thus recognised the particular expertise which MB's mother had gained through her attentive care of her child, of his quality of life, of what brought him pleasure and pain and of his ability to cope with his condition and necessary medical interventions. Consideration of the partial, personal views of those who continuously cared attentively to the needs of the child is as important, to a comprehensive determination of the best interests of the child, as the impartial, clinical view of those with medical expertise.

The *Wyatt* 'propositions' were accepted as the 'discipline' by which to determine whether ventilation should be withdrawn and palliative care provided to nine-month old OT, who suffered from a mitochondrial condition of genetic origin (*Re OT* [2009] EWHC 633, permission to appeal was refused, *T and another v. An NHS Trust and another* [2009] EWCA Civ 409). And, most recently, these principles were carefully applied in a structured manner in the sensitive, comprehensive judgment of Hedley J. in *NHS Trust v. Baby X* (*NHS Trust v. Baby X and others* [2012] EWHC 2188). Baby X had sustained profound and irreversible brain damage in an accident at home. The

---

Re Wyatt (a child) (medical treatment: continuation of order) [2005] EWCA Civ. 1181, [17-25]. There have since been family proceedings regarding the care of Charlotte.

professionals caring for him considered that there had been no improvement in his condition and that continued artificial ventilation was futile. Removal would be soon followed by his death. His parents disagreed, believing that they had seen signs of improvement and wanted their son to be given every chance. Hedley J. stressed that the welfare principle was the 'lodestar' and the process for determination was as set out by the Court of Appeal in Charlotte Wyatt's case, together giving the court 'all the requisite legal authority and guidance for the formulation of its decision' (*NHS Trust v. Baby X and others* [2012] EWHC 2188, [6]). Hedley J. then considered the medical evidence of the treating doctors, expert medical evidence, the baby's condition and prognosis, the parental understanding of their duties and assessment of his welfare, listed the benefits and burdens, and all the relevant welfare considerations from the assumed point of view of the baby. His Lordship stressed that the baby was a 'human being of unique value: body, mind and spirit expressed in the unique personality that is X' (*NHS Trust v. Baby X and others* [2012] EWHC 2188, [24]). Having considered all these factors, Hedley J. concluded that X's welfare required his removal from ventilation to palliative care and expressed the hope that his parents and professional carers would work together in the future provision of care to Baby X.

Here, I suggest is a starting point from which principled guidance can be developed for independent and comprehensive determination of the best interests of the child. Guidance must direct the decision-maker to consider the child as an individual, including the individual child's experiences – observed or otherwise communicated – of their condition, of medical treatment and ability to cope with interventions. Respect for the individual, their rights, integrity (bodily, mental and personal) and dignity must inform such decisions. Decisions about medical treatment must be informed by the knowledge of all involved in the care of the child arising from parental and professional responsibilities. Careful consideration must be given to the parental views of their child's best interests, given their primary responsibility, their attachment to, care of, concern about and love for their child. Beyond the clinical expertise of doctors, the particular knowledge of other healthcare professionals such as nurses and community care workers arising from their professional expertise and responsibilities must be considered. Wider concerns about provision of care to the child must be acknowledged and addressed in ensuring the best interests of the child. Guidance should explain what would be required before a court could conclude that novel, experimental or alternative treatments were in the best interests of the child. Further elucidation would result from application, testing and evaluation.

Generally, parents will make the decision about their child's healthcare according to what is best for their child and informed by their unique perspective of their child. Where caring professionals reach different conclusions, the decision must be referred to court for independent scrutiny.[12] Decision-makers, whether made on the ward and in the courtroom would be assisted by principled guidance. Court intervention should not, however, be limited to consideration of treatment of children about

12 This much was recognised by the ECtHR in *Glass v. United Kingdom* [2004] 1 FLR 1019, discussed in Bridgeman, 2005.

whom there is a difference of opinion which cannot be resolved. I suggest that it is also the responsibility of the NHS Trust to refer to the court cases which raise new issues including those surrounding the medical condition of the child, novel or innovative treatment or uncertainty about the interests of the child. Development of guidelines for determination of cases will also assist in identifying those which need to be referred to court for independent determination. This must include, for example, controversial treatment of the nature proposed to be administered to Ashley X in the United States. The 'treatment plan' for Ashley X, born with brain damage and entirely dependent upon the care of others, included a hysterectomy, removal of breast buds, appendectomy and high-dose oestrogen therapy to restrict her height and weight. Her father explained that the treatment plan, guided by her best interests and maximisation of her quality of life, was approved by the hospital ethics committee at Seattle Children's Hospital which entrusted her parents to 'do the right thing' for Ashley (Kittay, 2011). She was thus denied a principled, independent review of the drastic plan for her treatment. It is surely the case that, however motivated by a view as to what is best for the child by those caring for her, such radical proposals must be subjected to independent, principled, review.

The Right to Responsible Parents?

Writing in 1997, in 'Do Children Have the Right Not to be Born?', Michael observed that it had taken a long time for the parent/child relationship to be understood in terms of parental responsibilities rather than parental rights. Now that it was, he asked, were there other respects – such as the creation of children – in which our moral reasoning could be assisted by the concept of parental responsibility?[13] Michael explored the links between children's rights, the Article 12 of the European Convention on Human Rights right to marry and found a family and responsible parenthood asking whether children had the right to responsible parents: which, he made absolutely clear, he considered children did. The focus of that essay, however, was the responsibilities of parents as a correlative of the right to have children. That is, whether 'there are any circumstances in which it would be wrong to bring a child into existence', such that potential parents would have a duty not to have a child (Freeman, 1997a: 166). In that context, Michael asked what is 'meant by acting in a parentally responsible manner'? (Freeman, 1997a: 173) He concluded,

> To exercise parental responsibility is to put the interests and welfare of children or future children above one's own needs, desires or well-being. Welfare is, it must be accepted, an indeterminate and value-laden concept and the problems inherent in this cannot be ignored. But there is an irreducible minimum content to a child's well-being,

13 Freeman, 1997a: 166. I hope that I have done something to fill the gap noted by Michael who observed that ethic of care feminists had not had much to say about parental responsibility, 178, fn 85; see, for example, in the context of children's healthcare, Bridgeman, 2007.

> and these must be satisfied by anyone carrying out the role of, or purporting to become, a parent. … Responsible parents want their children to have good and fulfilling lives. They are prepared to forgo pleasures and make sacrifices to ensure their children are able to flourish (Freeman, 1997a: 180).

This led Michael to the conclusion that there are circumstances in which potential parents are under a duty not to have a child, such as where they know that the child may be born with serious impairments.[14]

Michael suggested that a child's 'right not to be born' derived from parental duties and in this context, in contrast to others in which the focus should be firmly upon the rights of the child, the focus should be upon agents not recipients.[15] However, he continued to suggest that the 'right not to be born' could be conceived of as the 'right to responsible parents'. This, I suggest, has the benefit of directing attention to both recipient and agent, to children's rights and parental responsibilities: to the relationship between them. And to the role of the state in support of it. Parental responsibility is to be exercised in the performance of duties to children; it is the 'normative standard by which to judge the decisions and actions of parents' (Freeman, 2008: 33) but one which must then have a call upon the state for support in the fulfilment of it. In reaching his conclusion, Michael acknowledged that the right he asserted was 'inchoate', 'ill-defined' and unrecognised in domestic, European or international rights instruments (Freeman, 1997a: 184; Freeman, 2008: 34). But, it was 'relatively uncontentious' to view 'procreation as a huge responsibility rather than as a right or a privilege' (Freeman, 2008: 27):

> To view the problem through the lens of parental responsibility… is to recognize the commitment involved in bringing a child into the world. It is to acknowledge that having children is an exercise of autonomous will and is (or certainly should be) a commitment to love, nurture and care. It is to accept that parents should want the best for their children. To exercise parental responsibility – I use the term normatively rather than descriptively – is to plan parenthood sensibly and with empathy for the needs of the child (Freeman, 1997a: 183).

Raising children, like having them, is a great responsibility. Parents have legal obligations to their children, but the responsible parent will go beyond their legal duties in the care of their child (Lind *et al.*, 2011: 13). Parents, 'acting in a parentally responsible manner' with respect to children's healthcare will respect their child's individuality, the changing needs of the child, the contribution of others to their child's care and

14 Michael limited his analysis to the decision to conceive a child and did not consider the morality or legality of abortion, although he did say that there may be cases where the decision to terminate may be 'thought an appropriate exercise of parental responsibility', Freeman, 1997a: 182.

15 Which is the argument he has had with Onora O'Neill. Freeman, 1992, responding to O'Neill, 1988.

the importance of independent review of decisions with grave consequences for the child's future.

Responsible parents will respect their child as a separate individual, connected to them but separate from them. They will recognise that what is required of them in fulfilling their responsibilities will change with the age and circumstances of the child. The responsible parent will understand that in fulfilment of their responsibilities they will need the support of professionals who will bring their professional expertise to the child's care. The responsible parent will also recognise that there are some decisions about a child's future, including serious healthcare decisions with grave consequences for their child, which should be entrusted to an independent body making decisions according to a set of clear, comprehensive and developed principles. Children and their parents are surely entitled to decisions which are made by an independent body, comprehensive and principled; protective of rights, responsibilities and care.

References

Alderson, P., "Consent to Children's Surgery and Intensive Medical Treatment", *Journal of Law and Society* 1990 (17), 52-65.

BMA, *Consent Tool Kit*, http://bma.org.uk/practical-support-at-work/ethics/consent-tool-kit

(last accessed 15 July 2013).

Bridgeman, J., "Caring for Children with Severe Disabilities: Boundaried and Relational Rights", *The International Journal of Children's Rights* 2005 13, 99-199.

Bridgeman, J., *Parental responsibility, young children and healthcare law* (Cambridge: Cambridge University Press, 2007).

Feder Kittay, E., "Forever Small: the Strange Case of Ashley X", *Hypatia* 2011 (26), 610-631.

Fox, M. and McHale, J., "In whose best interests?", *Modern Law Review* 1997 (60), 700-709.

Freeman, M. D. A., *The Rights and Wrongs of Children* (London: Pinter, 1983).

Freeman, M., "Sterilising the Mentally Handicapped", in M. Freeman (ed), *Medicine, Ethics and Law* (London: Stevens, 1988).

Freeman, M. D. A., "Taking Children's Rights More Seriously", *International Journal of Law and the Family* 1992 (6), 52-71.

Freeman, M., "Do Children Have the Right Not to be Born?", in M. Freeman, *The Moral Status of Children: Essays on the Rights of the Child* (Leiden: Martinus Nijhoff, 1997a).

Freeman, M., "Removing Rights from Adolescents", in M. Freeman, *The Moral Status of Children: Essays on the Rights of the Child* (Leiden: Martinus Nijhoff, 1997a).

Freeman, M., "The Rights of the Artificially Procreated Child", in M. Freeman, *The Moral Status of Children: Essays on the Rights of the Child* (Leiden: Martinus Nijhoff, 1997a).

Freeman, M., "The Best Interests of the Child? Is *The Best Interests of the Child* in the Best Interests of Children?", *International Journal of Law, Policy and the Family* 1997b (11), 360-388.

Freeman, M., "Does surrogacy have a future after Brazier?", *Medical Law Review* 1999 (7), 1-20.

Freeman, M., "Can we leave the best interests of very sick children to their parents?" in M. Freeman (ed), *Law and Medicine, Current Legal Issues 2000* (Oxford: Oxford University Press, 2000).

Freeman, M., "Whose Life is it Anyway?", *Medical Law Review* 2001 (9), 259-280.

Freeman, M., "Denying Death its Dominion: Thoughts on the Dianne Pretty Case", *Medical Law Review* 2002 (10), 245-270.

Freeman, M., "Rethinking *Gillick", International Journal of Children's Rights* 2005 (13), 201-217.

Freeman, M., "Saviour Siblings", in S. McLean (ed), *First Do No Harm* (Aldershot: Ashgate, 2006).

Freeman, M., "The Right to Responsible Parents", in J. Bridgeman, H. Keating and C. Lind (eds), *Responsibility, Law and the Family* (Aldershot: Ashgate, 2008).

Freeman, M. and Margaria, A., "Who and What is a Mother? Maternity, Responsibility and Liberty'", *Theoretical Inq L* 2012 (13), 153-178.

Goldstein, J., Freud, A. and Solnit, A., *Beyond The Best Interests of the Child* (New York: Free Press, 1979).

Goldstein, J., Freud, A. and Solnit, A., *Before the Best Interests of The Child* (New York: Free Press, 1979).

Goldstein, J., Goldstein, S., Solnit, A. and Freud, A., *The Best Interests of the Child: The Least Detrimental Alternative* (New York: Free Press, 1996).

McHaffie, H. E., Fowlie, W., Hume, R., Laing, ,Lloyd, and Lyon, *Crucial Decisions at the Beginning of Life: Parents' experiences of treatment withdrawal from infants* (Abingdon: Radcliffe Medical Press, 2001).

Lind, C., Keating, H. and Bridgeman, J., "Introduction: Taking family responsibility or having it imposed: recognising law's limitations?", in C. Lind, H. Keating and J. Bridgeman (eds), *Taking Responsibility, Law and the Changing Family* (Aldershot: Ashgate, 2011).

O'Neill, O., "Children's Rights and Children's Lives", *Ethics* 1988 (98), 445-63.

The Abuse of Parents by Children

Jonathan Herring
University of Oxford, UK

Introduction

Michael Freeman is one of the pioneer writers on the abuse of women and children. His ability to combine academic rigour with passionate advocacy marks him out as one of the greats of legal academia. His searing indictments of the failures of the law to deal with abuse ring out as loudly today as they ever did. In this chapter I do not propose to discuss his writing, rather I propose to unworthily follow in his footsteps, and address an area of abuse where the law has failed to respond appropriately, namely the abuse of parents by their children.

Parentline was a telephone help service set up to advise parents facing difficulties. Staff were trained on the issues likely to arise: children who would not eat vegetables; babies who kept waking in the night; bedwetting. But a large portion of the calls were about something completely different. 27 per cent of parents complained of children abusing them. As the Parentline (2003: 2) report put it:

> Children shouting, swearing, spitting, pushing, kicking, punching even threatening with or using weapons against their parents and other family members is the shocking reality facing many families today.

The vision of the home as a haven in a heartless world has long been tarnished. Awareness of domestic violence and child abuse means the home is talked about as much as a site of violence as it is a haven for comfort. 'The *home* is in fact the *most dangerous place* in modern society', Antony Giddens (1989: 408) informs us. I am afraid this article adds to that picture, with a discussion of parent abuse, an issue which has not received adequate legal or social attention. As Rachel Condry (2010: 1) points out:

> Adolescent-to-parent violence does not fall within official definitions of domestic violence and the problem has remained largely unarticulated within the fields of youth justice, domestic violence, policing and criminology, particularly in the UK.

A. Diduck, N. Peleg, H. Reece (eds.), Law in Society: Reflections on Children, Family, Culture and Philosophy
 ISBN 978-90-04-26148-8. pp. 469-487.

One of the primary aims of this article is to explore why it is that parental abuse has been so ignored. In part this is because the practice challenges our pre-conceptions about childhood, parenthood and families. In part it is also because the issue falls between the stools of legal categories of domestic abuse, child abuse and criminal behaviour.

Parental abuse can be horrific. 'The terrorist in my home' is how one mother described her experiences (Holt, 2011). A study of online reporting found parents being bitten, kicked, battered, thumped and punched (*ibid*). The violence sometimes moved on to the siblings and property. Notably these were rarely 'one off' events but 'formed part of the daily tapestry of their lives' (*ibid*). Interestingly, many parents in describing their experiences focussed on the emotional impact rather than the physical injury. Fear and guilt are particularly prevalent. Amanda Holt (*ibid*) notes in her study how many parents felt there was no one who could assist because the problem was unrecognised: 'we are desperate and there just seems to be no help – where do we turn next?' As Valerie Outram (quoted on BBC News (2009)) has put it, 'It's like domestic violence was 20 or 30 years ago. It's hushed up, brushed under the carpet and no one talks about it.' The experiences of parents and the lack of official recognition or response produced an overarching narrative among victims of 'powerlessness and loss of hope' (Holt, 2011: 463).

Statistics

Prevalence

Amanda Holt (2012) in her overview of the research finds its prevalence varies from 7-29 per cent of parents. Reliable data is hard to find (*ibid*) first, because most of the research has to rely on self-reporting and so there is likely to be considerable under-reporting, and second, because there is no consistent definition of parent abuse (Condry and Miles, 2012).

Examples of the kind of statistics that we do have are the following. Parentline (2012) found between June 2008 and June 2010 27 per cent of calls to their helpline involved aggression. Of these, 62 per cent were about verbal aggression and 8 per cent physical aggression. A study of data for the Metropolitan Police found 1914 cases reported to the police across London in one year (Condry and Miles, 2012).

Gender of Victims

Nearly all studies find that mothers are more at risk of being abused than fathers (see e.g. Evans and Warren-Sohlberg, 1998; Hong, 2011; Holt, 2012, for an overview). In the leading UK study, Condry and Miles (2013) found that 77 per cent of victims of cases of parent abuse reported to the police in their sample were women. Lone mothers are particularly prone to parental abuse (Howard, 2008). International evidence also suggests that mothers are more likely to be victims than fathers (Bobic, 2008). Where the father is the victim, then the abuse is predominantly caused by sons (Howard, 2008).

Gender of Perpetrators

Most studies find higher levels of parent abuse by sons rather than daughters (Boxer, Gullan and Mahoney, 2009). Jo Howard's (2008) major review of the issue suggested about a third of perpetrators are female. Condry and Miles (2013) found that 87 per cent of suspects of cases reported to the police in their sample were male. This issue is a familiar one for those who have looked at the gender issues in relation to domestic violence. In part the answer may be that much depends on the nature and extent of the behaviour. Where we are discussing serious levels of violence used as part of a campaign of control, it is universally carried out by men (Howard, 2008).

Age

It is generally agreed that the peak age for violence is between 15 and 17 (Bobic, 2008), although the research from Parentline (2010) found cases starting from 13.

Definitions

Until recently, UK policy documents have excluded parental abuse from the definition of domestic abuse, which had been restricted to incidents involving those over 18 (Wilcox, 2012). The Government extended the definition to those over 16 in late 2012 (HM Government, 2012), but that still means much parental abuse falls outside the definition. That is not necessarily a bad thing, because, as will be argued below, there are unique features of parental abuse which are not found in domestic violence. However, it does contribute to its invisibility.

How can we define parental abuse? Jo Howard (2008: 2) provides a very helpful definition. It is:

> an abuse of power perpetrated by adolescents against their parents, carers and/or other relatives including siblings. It occurs when an adolescent attempts physically or psychologically to dominate, coerce and control others in their family.

There are a number of notable and helpful features of this definition. The first is it is limited to adolescents who abuse. This makes it clear that a toddler throwing a tantrum, for example, is not covered. Such behaviour is harmful, but it raises different issues to the one discussed here. Second, the definition covers abuse to siblings and carers as well as parents. Third, it emphasises that the central feature of parental abuse is that it is designed to coerce or control. This is an important point because it pinpoints the nature of the harmful behaviour. It cannot be understood as simply a series of acts. It can only be understood as a course of behaviour (Herring, 2011). The new UK Government (2012: 1) definition of domestic violence captures this by referring to 'Any incident or pattern of incidents of controlling, coercive or threatening behaviour, violence or abuse between those aged 16 or over who are or have been intimate partners or family members regardless of gender or sexuality.'

Howard's definition provides a very helpful starting point, but I want to bring out some particular issues which are key to any detailed definition.

Unjustified Harmful Acts

One of the difficulties in defining parent abuse is to draw the line between justified and unjustified acts (National Clearinghouse on Family Violence, 2003). Tension between parents and children is hardly unknown. Difficult teenage behaviour is expected by parents. It may even be a healthy and normal aspect of child development as the teenager establishes her or his own identity and separateness. This is why it is helpful to use the theme of conduct used to control or coerce behaviour as part of the definition of parental abuse. It helps mark out the difference between child misbehaviour and unacceptable behaviour. As one report (National Clearinghouse on Family Violence, 2003: 4) suggests:

> Parent abuse is any act of a child that is intended to cause physical, psychological or financial damage to gain power and control over a parent.

It is important also to exclude behaviour which is self-defensive. As we shall see there are strong links between cases of parental abuse and domestic violence. Some cases of apparent parental abuse may, on further inspection, be acts seeking to prevent a man abusing his partner or child. A son might, for example, have reached an age where he seeks to protect his mother from the father's violence.

Violence or Abuse

The definition from Jo Howard (2008) mentioned earlier made it clear that the abuse does not need to contain violence. There has been much debate amongst those writing on domestic violence over whether violence is an essential element of domestic violence (e.g. Johnson, 1995). At first sight it seems obvious that violence should be at the heart of domestic violence. The clue is in the name. Indeed, it is noticeable that in most academic literature, as in this article, the term 'domestic abuse' has been relied upon rather than 'domestic violence', to capture the fact that a broader concept is intended. It is interesting that the Supreme Court in *Yemshaw v LB Hounslow* [2011] UKSC 3 has held that domestic violence under the Housing Act is not limited to assaults (discussed further in Herring, 2011).

The argument against restricting parental abuse to physically violent acts is as follows. The experiences of victims of domestic abuse, including parental abuse, show that it is best understood not simply as a series of violent or abusive acts, but rather as a programme of 'coercive control' (to use Evan Stark's (2007) phrase) or 'patriarchal terrorism' or 'intimate terrorism' (to use Michael Johnson's (2005) phrase). Michael Johnson (2005) distinguishes intimate terrorism from what he calls 'situational couple violence' or 'mutual violence'. Patriarchal terrorism is 'violence enacted in the service of taking general control over one's partner' (Johnson, 2005: 43). By contrast, in the situational couple violence or mutual violence case, there is violence but there is no attempt to control the relationship. Rather, there is an incident of violence that arises in a moment of conflict during an intimate relationship which is not generally marked with inequality. It involves a lashing out in self-defence, anger or frustration, rather than an attempt to exercise control. As this distinction shows, it is not whether or not there is violence which matters so much as whether there is a pattern of control. That is particularly helpful in the case of parental abuse as it helps provide a reasonably clear distinction between the 'stroppy teenager' being awkward, who may engage in isolated acts of abusive behaviour, and the perpetrator of parent abuse who is using abuse to exert control.

The controlling intent of parental abuse can only be understood by looking at the relationship between the parties as a whole. Psychologist Mary Ann Dutton (2003: 1204) explains:

> Abusive behaviour does not occur as a series of discrete events. Although a set of discrete abusive incidents can typically be identified within an abusive relationship, an understanding of the dynamic of power and control within an intimate relationship goes beyond these discrete incidents. To negate the impact of the time period between discrete episodes of serious violence – a time period during which the woman may never know when the next incident will occur, and may continue to live with on-going psychological abuse – is to fail to recognize what some battered woman experience as a continuing 'state of siege'.

The aim of the behaviour of the abuser is to dominate the victim and diminish her sense of self-worth. This is done by: restricting the victim's access to work; isolating her from friends; manipulating the victim emotionally; taking advantage of the mother's feelings of inadequacy in her role; and using physical attacks. Physical violence, then, is but one tool used in the relationship to keep the parent inferior (Rachmilovitz, 2007). From this perspective, it is intimidation, isolation and control which should be the hallmarks of parental abuse rather than the means to achieve them, which may, or may not, involve violence (Jacobson and Gottman, 2007).

Understanding parent abuse as coercive control has important implications. In order to determine whether it exists it is necessary to examine the whole relationship between the parties, rather than assessing the severity of individual attacks. Incidents which might appear trivial can be seen as having a significant impact when appreciated in their broader context. Coercive control abuse may involve physical attacks, and often does, but the abuser may not need to resort to those. The abuser intimidates, isolates and controls through a range of means. These effects, rather than physical violence, should be seen as the hallmarks of parental abuse.

The Significance of Parenthood

The fact the abuse takes place by a child on their parent adds a special dimension to parent abuse, as compared with other forms of family abuse. In saying that, I understand parenthood in a broad way to include anyone who is providing significant levels of care to a child. Why is the fact that the abuse is to a parent significant? One factor is that in cases of parental abuse the ability of the victim to escape from the violence is restricted (Reece, 2006). Not only might this be true in physical terms: the parent may have nowhere to go apart from their home with the child; it is also a psychological issue. There are powerful emotional bonds that make it very hard for a parent to leave a child. Abandoning a child is commonly regarded as the ultimate betrayal of the mothering role and the ultimate admission of one's failure as a parent.

Another feature of parental abuse that makes it particularly severe is that it involves a breach of trust (Herring, 2011). Parenthood involves becoming physically and emotionally vulnerable. The trust which is central to close relationships creates special obligations not to misuse that vulnerability. Intimate relationships rely on trust so that we can flourish (Eekelaar, 2007: 44-47). Parenthood is for many people central to their identity and sense of self (Rachmilovitz, 2007). Parent abuse strikes at the very conception of the self for the victim. It turns what could be a tool for self-affirmation and self-identification into a tool for alienation and self-betrayal (Arnault, 2003).

Act Perpetuating Structural Disadvantage

Parental abuse is an act which perpetuates structural disadvantage and takes advantage of it. Michelle Madden Dempsey (2009: 112) explains the meaning of structural disadvantage:

> Structural inequalities are functions of social structures, the 'sets of rules and principles that govern activities in the different domains of social life'. When social structures sustain or perpetuate the uneven distribution of social power, they can be understood as structural inequalities.

Madden Dempsey's point is that abuse within the relationship can be a tool used to maintain the dominance of one party in the relationship, usually the man. It typically does this by taking advantage of existing societal disadvantages. Madden Dempsey (2007) argues domestic violence is linked to inequalities within the relationship and within society more widely. She explains:

> the patriarchal character of individual relationships cannot subsist without those relationships being situated within a broader patriarchal social structure. Patriarchy is, by its nature, a social structure – and thus any particular instance of patriarchy takes its substance and meaning from that social context. If patriarchy were entirely eliminated from society, then patriarchy would not exist in domestic arrangements and thus domestic violence in its strong sense would not exist... Moreover, if patriarchy were lessened in society generally then *ceteris paribus* patriarchy would be lessened in domestic relationships as well, thereby directly contributing to the project of ending domestic violence in its strong sense. (Madden Dempsey, 2007: 938).

The same is true for parental abuse. It not only impacts on the parents and child themselves. It reinforces and relies upon power exercised by men over women in society more generally and reinforces the disadvantages of mothers in particular. As the Parliamentary Assembly, Council of Europe, Committee on Equal Opportunities for Women and Men (2002, para 12) puts it:

> Violence against women is a question of power, of the need to dominate and control. This in turn is rooted in the organization of society, itself based on inequality between the sexes. The meaning of this violence is clear: it is an attempt to maintain the unequal relationship between men and women and to perpetuate the subordination of women.

Abuse towards parents reflects this. As Wilcox (2012) suggests, verbal intimidation, abuse and misogyny are commonly found in school playgrounds. The abuse at home in some cases is a reflection of that. The attitude of adolescent male abusers towards women generally is reflected in their treatment of mothers. The response of adolescents in their abuse can reflect the law of worth placed on mothers and the blame that is laid at their feet for any failures in the family.

Parental abuse often rests on an attitude of contempt held towards the mother. This may be reflected in the abuser's attitudes, but is also received by the victim as a confirmation of the message sent out by society to mothers more widely. Society sends a double social message to mothers: a mother's work is worthless and yet is indispensable. Mothers are held responsible for anything in the home that is not as it should be. Anti-social behaviour interventions under the Anti-Social Behaviour Act 2003 and parenting orders under the Crime and Disorder Act 1998 disproportionately fall on mothers (Henricson and Bainham, 2005). Recent responses to youth offending have focussed on 'problem families' and 'parenting deficit' (Condry and Miles, 2012), explicitly blaming mothers for the sins of their children. Yet at the same time the government encourages mothers to take up paid employment and use low paid child care as an appropriate substitute for mother care. Mothering is of so little value that it can be performed by anyone. Notably in David Cameron's 2013 announcement of a tax break for married couples, the tax advantage is only to be offered in cases where both parents are tax payers. The 'full time' mother gets nothing. As is often noted, however, the mother cannot win because the working mother with her 'latch key kids' may feel her children are missing out if she is not available to them every non-school hour.

The lack of respect shown by teenagers towards mothers and the blame for teenagers' behaviour that is laid at their mothers' feet by the adolescents themselves and by the state is but a reflection of their broader social status. Barbara Cottrell and Peter Monk (2004) found in their studies that:

> Service providers and parents consistently described that among adolescent boys, abusive behaviour was influenced by the role modelling of masculine stereotypes that promote the use of power and control in relationships.

This all explains why the state finds it hard to respond to the adolescent violence: there is no room in the mothering discourse for the mother to be the victim. She is either worthless and invisible, or she is the cause of problem families. Either way, she cannot be the victim of abuse by her children.

These broader social attitudes impact on the attitudes of victims and perpetrators towards what is happening. Hence it is that some mothers seek to 'downplay' the violence used, describing it as playfulness or 'mucking around' (Howard, 2008). Cottrell and Monk (2004) make an interesting observation about the attitude of female adolescent abusers:

> In contrast, aggression by female youth was noted as a paradoxical response used to create distance from the 'feminine ideals' that were often ascribed to them. Furthermore, ongoing shifts in traditional female stereotypes have led to more examples being portrayed throughout society where women embody a masculine image of power. Some illustrations that were given included female television and movie characters who use extreme violence in response to situations of personal conflict.

In some cases the girls recognised their mother as weak and powerless and used the abuse to distance themselves from what they regarded as a 'female vulnerability' (Howard, 2008).

The Links between Parent Abuse and Domestic Violence

There are clear links between domestic abuse and parental violence (Wilcox, 2012). These include: that there is coercive control through a family relationship; that there is a strong gendered element; that the behaviour interacts with, reinforces and reflects broader social harms. The behaviour causes isolation from the world, exacerbating its impact.

However there are some differences between domestic violence and parental abuse. As Paula Wilcox (*ibid*) points out, parents have an ongoing legal and social responsibility to the child which makes leaving the relationship far from straightforward. The social stigma attaching to a victim of domestic violence leaving her partner is different to that of a mother leaving her child. Second, the power relationship is not necessarily straightforward. The parents have access to greater financial and social resources than the child, although the abuse may well restrict access to those (Wilcox, 2012). Sometimes the abuse of the teenager is a response to violence against him, be that in terms of child abuse, corporal punishment or witnessing child abuse (Edenborough et al., 2008).

Explanations

There are a range of explanations for parental abuse.

1. *Child Abuse Leads to Parent Abuse*

The links between child abuse and abuse of a parent are well established, but complex. In one Australian Study, 32 per cent of young people who abused parents had themselves suffered past maltreatment (Biehal, 2012). According to Roger Levesque (2011):

> A large proportion of children and adolescents who perpetrate parent abuse have been physically or sexually abused by their parents, or have witnessed domestic violence.

The link between child abuse and parent abuse could operate in several ways:

1) It may be that some cases of what appear to be parental abuse are better understood as self-defence, where the child is now sufficiently large to be able to defend him/her-self from an abusive parent.
2) It may be that the abuse is better understood as revenge by the child for the abuse they suffered as a child.
3) It may be that the family relationships are all characterised by violence and the child is just reflecting the violent nature of the family.

The link between the child abuse and parental abuse must be treated with some caution (Heyman and Smith, 2002). Of course, there are cases of parental abuse where there was earlier child abuse, but there are plenty of cases where there is not. Similarly, there are cases of child abuse where the child does not in due course respond with violence. Interestingly, where there is a link between child abuse and parental abuse, the violence is often directed towards the non-abusive parent (Howard, 2008: 7).

There is some evidence of links between parental abuse and corporal punishment. That is something I know would interest, but not surprise, Michael Freeman. The evidence suggests that where the child is beaten by one parent, he responds with abuse of the other (Hong et al., 2013).

2. *Links with Domestic Violence and Witnessing It*

As already mentioned, there is a link between witnessing domestic abuse between parents as a child and parental abuse (Paterson et al., 2002; Wilcox, 2012). Indeed, Jo Howard (2010) suggests:

> The most significant determinant for adolescent violence in the home is a child's and mother's experience of family violence

As Brown (1977) puts it:

> What seems to be happening is that young men, having seen their fathers beat their mothers, learn that she is an appropriate victim

It is well established that witnessing domestic abuse causes a range of harms in children. There is evidence that boys witnessing domestic violence have negative views about women and a greater acceptance of violence towards women (Tew and Nixon, 2011). Of particular interest in this chapter, the negative views include the view that violence towards mothers is appropriate (Bobic, 2008). Indeed Cottrell and Monk (2004) found that parent abuse often starts when an abusive father leaves the home. This behaviour seems to be influenced by 'a combination of direct male role modelling, idealisation of the abuser and anger at the mother for failing to protect the family' (Hong et al., 2013). To the mother, the son takes over where the father left off.

3. *Parenting Styles Have Been Found as a Link Too*

To some commentators parental abuse is linked to parenting style. It has been suggested that parents who are overly authoritarian or unduly permissive are more prone to abuse by their adolescent children (Levesque, 2011). Parental abuse, it is said, is caused by the failure to draw clear boundaries in the relationship (Cottrell, 2011) or where the child feels unable to assert their own identity (Howard, 2008). After all, adolescence is meant to be a time to separate from parents (Browne and Hamilton, 2008).

This explanation is a controversial one. It is easy for it to become a reason for blaming parents. This is revealed in a quotation in a talk given to parents:

> Children are not adults. They are dependent, vulnerable persons, requiring protection and leadership. The relationship between parents and children is not equal: it is a protective, unequal relationship of an adult with a dependent child. The relative balance between dependence and independence is not static and changes with the age of the child, but essentially equality is not achieved until adulthood. In a positive parent-child relationship, the parent has accountability and responsibility to provide reasonable authority over the child. The relationship is dysfunctional when the reverse is true, and carries with it the potential for abuse. (Jacqueline Barkley, in a talk to parents, 1999, quoted in Howard, 2008: 32)

I will return later to the assumption in this quotation that it is the parents who have power and the children who are vulnerable.

4. *Social Attitudes*

Another explanation for parental abuse lies with broader social attitudes about women and parents (Hong et al., 2013) Boys learn to exercise power over women and play out masculine stereotypes of power and control over women (Cottrell and Monk, 2004). A Canadian report puts it this way:

> In our society, violence and aggression are commonly used to achieve goals and maintain control. Parents shout at their children, the police pepper spray protesters, and

> Hollywood's good guys shoot and kill to save the world. Aggression and violent images invade most corners of our lives. In some families or communities, physical, emotional or verbal abuse is an accepted method of communication. If it has been occurring for years or generations, it may have become customary behaviour (National Clearinghouse on Family Violence, 2003: 11).

Interestingly the Report even sees this as part of the explanation of where girls use violence:

> Some professionals report that girls express hatred toward their mothers for being submissive, and for subjecting themselves and their children to the violence of their husband or partner. ... One mother reports that her teenage daughter contemptuously yelled at her, 'You're nothing but a coward!' Strategies such as submission, which women use to cope with abuse, often lead to further victimization (National Clearinghouse on Family Violence, 2003: 11).

It is these social attitudes which mean that some abusers even feel justified in use of violence (Howard, 2010).

5. *Mental Health and Substance Abuse*

Mental health issues for adolescents can be linked with violence (Biehal, 2012). ADD/ADHD (Ghanizadeh and Jafari, 2010), depression (Calvete et al., 2013) and other behavioural and personality disorders can be linked with violent behaviours in adolescents (Cottrell and Monk, 2004). Some commentators are cautious about medicalising abuse. They are worried especially by terms such as 'conduct disorder' or 'oppositional defiant disorder' where that is a description of and not an explanation for anti-social behaviour, offering pseudo medical explanations for abuse (Gallagher, 2004).

Substance abuse has also been correlated with parental abuse (Kennair and Mellor, 2007). Particularly well established are the links with alcohol and drug use (Holt, 2012).

Conclusion on Causes

It is clear there is no single cause of parent abuse. In many cases there is a complex interplay of different factors. As is often the case in explaining human behaviour, it can be difficult to isolate causes from correlations.

Perhaps the most controversy surrounds the extent to which social factors are an explanation. Helen Baker (2012: 266) is worried by theories which simply see adolescent violence as reflecting broader social attitudes:

> Such theories are also problematic, however, because they do not attribute any agency or choice to children to determine their lives, viewing them as passive reactors to violence and acting in a pre-determined way. Children are however, active agents in their own

> lives, and able to make choices. Therefore these theories make generalisations about the futures of *all* children who experience violence, treating them as a homogenous group rather than as distinct individuals.

She is concerned that such approaches 'construct children as mere receptacles for adult behaviour' (*ibid*).

I, however, find the social reasons persuasive. This seems to be how those involved understand what is happening. A study of teenage boys who abused their parents found that none of the boys blamed themselves. They blamed their mothers or siblings. The study referred to one boy who said: 'They looked at me the wrong way so it's their fault that I hit them'. Another explained that his abuse was caused by his mother 'frustrating him and nagging him'. Mothers often blamed themselves too and excused the abusers as inheriting traits from their fathers (Howard, 2008). Nearly all the mothers felt blamed by others for what had happened. Many blamed themselves. One mother explained that she was a target of her son (Bradley)'s violence because:

> 'perhaps my backbone may have not been strong enough... I think I'm a soft target... sort of, for peace in the house... I might give in a lot easier... just to shut him up. I didn't have that sort of back up to... reinforce things with him.' She explained: 'Like a good mother, I was bottling it [the stress] inside... I doubt myself as a good mother... feeling worthless as a person... always thinking... could I have done this better and... blaming myself.' Bradley also does 'the blame game' (Howard, 2008: 48).

These understandings of the behaviour by the parties involved only really make sense when they are seen against the backdrop of broader social attitudes about violence against women and the status of mothers discussed earlier.

Legal Jurisdictions

The law has struggled to deal with the problem of parental abuse. Amanda Holt and Simon Retford (2009) in interviewing frontline practitioners found they certainly recognised the problem of parent abuse, but did not know how to respond to it. They found ad hoc solutions because there was no national guidance. They 'made do' as best they could. There are some boxes that practitioners might readily use:

- Child protection
- Domestic violence
- Child abuse

None of these is satisfactory.

One possibility is to treat parental abuse as a straightforward crime to be reported to the police and pursued under the criminal justice route. That is a popular route with those who see parental abuse as a form of domestic violence and take the view that violence in the home must be taken as seriously as violence in the street.

The criminal approach has difficulties. The outcomes may not be those which the parent wants. Most parents would be willing to go to great lengths to avoid seeing their children prosecuted. Further, the legal response to youth crime is ill-designed to combat parental abuse. This is because under the youth justice regime parents are increasing seen as responsible for the way the young offender acts. Holt (2012) refers to one case where a son was violent to his mother. He was prosecuted under the criminal justice procedure and was fined. The son did not pay, but the bailiffs were able to recover the money from the mother! In another case a mother was fined because her son had failed to attend school, even though her efforts to persuade him to attend school resulted in the son abusing her. As Condry and Miles (2012) point out, many of the youth justice parenting interventions are premised on the assumption that parents control their children. This is the very assumption which is challenged by parental abuse.

Hunter and Piper (2012) found in their studies that parental abuse most commonly came to the attention of public authorities through the police. Indeed, they suggest that the criminal and youth justice are the 'dominant response' to the issue. There is some scope in the system to respond more appropriately to the issue (Holt, 2009). The Youth Justice Board when dealing with young offenders is required to investigate a family's circumstances and that might well reveal the abuse. Under the Crime and Disorder Act (CDA) 1998, s. 37(1), help or punishment can be offered. There is also the possibility of youth conditional cautions (CDA, s. 66A) which might be used. Perhaps more usefully the court can order the child lives elsewhere (Criminal Justice and Immigration Act (CJIA) 2008, s. 1(i) and (j) and Schedule 1, para. 17) for up to six months, but only if:

> the behaviour which constituted the offence was due to a significant extent to the circumstances in which the offender was living (CJIA, Schedule 1 para 17(3)(a)).

That provision seems to presume that the case is one where the parenting caused the child to offend. It may, therefore, be seen as a misuse to use it in a parental abuse case.

Hunter and Piper (2012: 226) conclude:

> There are ... clear disadvantages, notably the criminalisation of the young person. Whilst there is some merit in attaching to parent abuse the symbolic – and possibly deterrent – value of being treated as an offence, criminalisation is not in the best long-term interests of children and is also likely to lead to unhelpful feelings of guilt in the parent. The addition of parenting orders also stigmatises the parent.

ASBO

An alternative would be to use Anti-social Behaviour Orders (ASBOs), which are available to those aged ten or over. These can be imposed by a criminal court following a conviction for an offence or through a civil jurisdiction on application by the police, housing associations or local authority. The definition of anti-social behaviour in the

CDA 1998 is relevant to the parent abuse issue: it is behaving 'in a manner that caused or was likely to cause harassment, alarm or distress' (CDA 1998, s. 1(1)(a)). However, ASBOs are only available if the behaviour relates 'to one or more persons not of the same household as himself' (CDA 1998, s. 1). That would appear to rule out the use of ASBOs in parental abuse, unless a third party was impacted.

Domestic Violence Legislation

Turning to the civil law, a victim of domestic abuse could seek to use occupation and non-molestation orders under the 1996 Family Law Act (FLA). However, the legislation appears to prohibit the making of occupation orders or non-molestation orders against those under 18 (see FLA, ss. 33 and 62(3)(d)). Further, the emphasis in the legislation on protecting children from significant harm means it would be unlikely to exercise its jurisdiction to remove an abusive child.

Inherent Jurisdiction

Perhaps the most likely source of a jurisdiction for an order requiring an abusive child to leave the home would be the inherent jurisdiction. In *DL v A Local Authority* [2012] EWCA 999 the court acknowledged a jurisdiction to protect vulnerable adults from abuse. This jurisdiction is still in its infancy, and there would be a number of difficulties in using it in a parental abuse scenario. It would be necessary to show that the victim was a vulnerable adult. The court has been reluctant to offer a precise definition of a vulnerable adult, but it would need to be shown that the impact on the victim was such that she was unable to exercise or severely impaired in exercising autonomy. Even if this was shown it would be surprising if the court were willing to use the jurisdiction to do something as interventionist as force the removal of a child from her home.

Child Protection

In cases where the parental abuse is seen to constitute a case needing child protection, it is highly unlikely that a care order or supervision order would be sought. It is, perhaps, not impossible to imagine a child benefiting from a supervision order. It would be necessary to satisfy the threshold criteria in section 31, which require proof that the child is suffering significant harm. That may be problematic in some cases, although a sensitive reading of the concept of harm might include the fact that the child is abusing others. More likely, sections 17 and 20 of the Children Act 1989 could be used. This imposes a general duty on local authorities to assist children in need and a duty to accommodate children in need. However, that jurisdiction may only be used with the consent of the child, which is unlikely in a case of parental abuse.

Conclusion on the Legal Jurisdiction

One of the problems with using the law to tackle cases of parental abuse is that by the time the behaviour has reached the attention of the authorities it may have escalated to such a level that all solutions are unsatisfactory. It is normally too late to make the kind of low level interventions which a court might be able usefully to make such as a supervision order. By the time the abuse has become sufficiently serious to reach court, only the drastic options of imprisoning the child or forcibly removing him from the home are left. This is often not wanted by the parties, but might be appropriate in the most severe cases. More attractive solutions are available at the early stages, normally before the court gets involved. These might involve therapy and relational advice; empowering parents with strategies with which to respond to abusive behaviour; and challenging the behaviour of the adolescent (National Clearinghouse on Family Violence, 2003).

Discussion

Parent abuse has proved enormously difficult for the law to respond to. In part this is because the practice of parent abuse undermines so many societal and legal assumptions.

First, there is the assumption that parents have responsibility for and control over their children. Family law is premised on the assumption that parents have responsibilities for their children and can make decisions based on the child's best interests. True, there is discussion over the extent to which parents should have responsibilities for or rights towards their child, but nowhere in that discussion is there an awareness that parents might need protecting from their children.

Second, there is the series of contradictory attitudes about mothers. When children commit crimes against others, parents are held responsible for them. As Henricson and Bainham (2005: 103) have said:

> the attribution of blame to parents for their children's behaviour up to the age of 16 underestimates children's independence and overestimates the ability of parents to control the behaviour of young people as they grow older.

This is not just a legal assumption, but one that is widely held in society. Parents feel great stigma when they feel abused, especially when the abuse is perpetrated by girls (Tew and Nixon, 2010). There is a danger that:

> In these circumstances, the very status of 'mother' may, rather than confer any real power, serve to trap women within abusive relationships – their ongoing responsibility to parent often preventing them either leaving the abusive relationship or even seeking help to stop the violence (Kennair and Mellor, 2007).

Third, as mentioned earlier, there is, quite rightly given our increasing understanding of child abuse, an acknowledgement of the vulnerability of children. Understandably with the spectre of child abuse, the picture is commonly painted of the powerful adult and the vulnerable child. However, we need to acknowledge the vulnerability of parents. No one can make you cry like your child can. Parents will do anything for their children. Parents expect and strive to be the ideal parents, boosted often by unreal expectations in the media (see Reece, 2013). Parenthood involves opening oneself up to risk of pain, expense and hurt. Of course, parents hope it is all worth it, but we must acknowledge the power that children have over parents.

Fourth, this issue shows the love of lawyers for their legal categorisations. We have seen in this chapter complaints that parent abuse does not neatly fall within categories and that professionals must find ad hoc responses. Neither of these is a bad thing. The complexity of parental abuse and the fact that it can cover such a range of cases mean that only an ad hoc response is justified. Quite rightly it does not fit into one of the prepared boxes, even though there might be individual cases that do. We should support this uneasy position of this complex phenomenon. I think there are cases of the most serious kind where the right of the mother to protection from torture or inhuman or degrading treatment requires state intervention (see Herring, 2013, for further discussion). If the violence is below that level lawyers can do no better than say that each case is to be dealt with on its own special facts. That is not a get-out but an acknowledgement of the complexity of human relationships.

Conclusion

The issue of parental abuse challenges some of the basic legal and social assumptions about the nature of childhood and parenthood. It is not surprising that it has, therefore, not fitted neatly into any pre-existing category. This chapter has sought to explore the reasons behind parental abuse and why the law has struggled to find an appropriate response. It has, in fact, concluded that the complexity of the issue means that the law should not produce a set response. I would argue that the best the law can do is to say that in cases where the violence the mother is facing is such as to amount to torture or inhuman or degrading treatment she must be protected from that, regardless of the impact on the abuser. In less serious cases I would join with Caroline Hunter and Christine Piper (2012) in suggesting that interventions need 'to balance safeguarding the adult parent with providing an outcome that is in the best interests of the child.' This is not an area for a set policy or formula to be used. Each case is so very different. Complexity, confusion and ad hoc-ery is, in fact, greatly to be welcomed.

References

Arnault, L., "Cruelty, Horror, and the Will to Redemption", *Hypatia* 2003 18, 155-176.

Baker, H., "Problematising the Relationship between Teenage Boys and Parent Abuse: Constructions of Masculinity and Violence", *Social Policy and Society* 2012 11(2), 265-276.

BBC News, "Abused by Their Own Children", www.bbc.co.uk/2/hi/8366113.stm (last accessed 30 September 2013).

Biehal, N., "Parent Abuse by Young People on the Edge of Care: A Child Welfare Perspective", *Social Policy and Society* 2012 11(2), 251-263.

Bobic, N., *Adolescent Violence Towards Parents* (Melbourne: Australian Domestic and Family Violence Clearinghouse, 2008).

Boxer, P., Gullan, R., and Mahoney, A., "Adolescents' Physical Aggression Towards Parents in a Clinically Referred Sample', *Journal of Clinical Child and Adolescent Psychology* 2009 38, 106-16.

Browne, K. and Hamilton, C., "Physical Violence Between Young Adults and Their Parents: Associations with a History of Child Maltreatment", *Journal of Family Violence* 1998 13(1), 59-79.

Calvete, E., Orue, I. and Gámez-Guadix, M., "Child-to-Parent Violence: Emotional and Behavioral Predictors", *Journal of Interpersonal Violence* 2013 28(4), 755-772.

Condry, R., *Investigating Adolescent Violence Towards Parents* (London: ESRC, 2010)

Condry, R. and Miles, C., "Adolescent to Parent Violence and Youth Justice in England and Wales", *Social Policy and Society* 2012 11(2), 241-250.

Condry, R. and Miles, C., "Adolescent to Parent Violence: Framing and Mapping a Hidden Problem", *Criminology and Criminal Justice* 2014 14(3), 257-275.

Cottrell, B. and Monk, P., "Adolescent-to-Parent Abuse: A Qualitative Overview of Common Themes", *Journal of Family Issues* 2004 25(5), 1072-1093.

Dutton, M., "Understanding Women's Response to Domestic Violence", *Hofstra Law Review* 2003 21, 1191-1204.

Edenborough, M., Jackson, D., Mannix, J. and Wilkes, L., "Living in the Red Zone: The Experience of Child-to-Mother Violence", *Child and Family Social Work* 2008 13(4), 464-73.

Eekelaar, J., *Family Law and Personal Life* (Oxford: Oxford University Press, 2007).

Evans, D. and Warren-Sohlberg, L., "A Pattern Analysis of Adolescent Abusive Behaviour Towards Parents", *Journal of Adolescent Research* 1998 3, 210-16.

Gallagher, E., "Youth Who Victimize their Parents", *Australian and New Zealand Journal of Family Therapy* 2004 25(2), 94-105.

Ghanizadeh, A. and Jafari, P., "Risk Factors of Abuse of Parents by their ADHD Children", *European Child Adolescent Psychiatry* 2010 19, 75-78.

Giddens, A., *Sociology* (Cambridge: Polity Press, 1989).

Henricson, C. and Bainham, A., *The Child and Family Policy Divide: Tensions, Convergence and Rights* (London: Family and Parenting Institute, 2005).

Herring, J., "The Meaning of Domestic Violence", *Journal of Social Welfare and Family Law* 2011 33, 297-314.

Herring, J., "The Serious Wrong of Domestic Abuse and the Loss of Control Defence", in A. Reed and M. Bohlander (eds), *Loss of Control and Diminished Responsibility* (Aldershot: Ashgate, 2011).

Heyman, R. and Smith, A., "Do Child Abuse and Interparental Violence Lead to Adulthood Family Violence?", *Journal of Marriage and Family* 2002 64(4), 864-870.

HM Government, *New Definition of Domestic Violence* (London: HM Government, 2012).

Holt, A., "(En)Gendering Responsibilities: Experiences of Parenting a 'Young Offender'", *The Howard Journal* 2009 48(4), 344-356.

Holt, A., "'The terrorist in my home': teenagers' violence towards parents – constructions of parent experiences in public online message boards", *Child and Family Social Work* 2011 16, 454-463.

Holt, A., "Researching Parent Abuse: A Critical Review of the Methods", *Social Policy and Society* 2012 11(2), 289-298.

Holt, A., *Adolescent-to-Parent Abuse* (Bristol: Policy Press, 2012).

Holt, A. and Retford, S., "Practitioner Accounts of Responding to Parent Abuse – A

Case Study in *Ad Hoc* Delivery, Perverse Outcomes and a Policy Silence", *Child and Family Social Work* 2013 18(3), 365-76.

Hong, J., Kral, M., Espelage, D. and Allen-Meares, P., "The Social Ecology of Adolescent-initiated Parental Abuse: A Review of the Literature", *Child Psychiatry and Human Development* 2013 43(3), 431-454.

Howard, J., *Adolescent Violence in the Home, The Missing Link in Family Violence Prevention and Response* (Monash: Monash University, 2010).

Howard, J., *It All Starts At Home* (Monash: Monash University, 2008).

Hunter, C. and Piper, C., "Parental Abuse: Can Law Be the Answer?", *Social Policy and Society* 2012 11(2), 271-227.

Jacobson, N. and Gottman, J., *When Men Batter Women: New Insights into Ending Abusive Relationships* (New York: Simon & Schuster, 2007).

Johnson, M., "Patriarchal Terrorism and Common Couple Violence: Two Forms of Violence against Women", *Journal of Marriage and Family* 1995 57, 283-305.

Johnson, M., "Apples and oranges in child custody disputes: Intimate terrorism vs. situational couple violence", *Journal of Child Custody* 2005 2, 43-64.

Kennair, N. and Mellor, D., "Parental Abuse: A Review", *Child Psychiatry and Human Development* 2007 38(3), 203-219.

Levesque, N., *Encyclopaedia of Adolescence* (New York, Springer, 2011).

Madden Dempsey, M., "What Counts as Domestic Violence? A Conceptual Analysis", *William and Mary Journal of Women and the Law* 2006 12, 301-376.

Madden Dempsey, M., "Towards a Feminist State: What Does 'Effective' Prosecution of Domestic Violence Mean?", *Modern Law Review* 2007 70, 908-938.

Madden Dempsey, M., *Prosecuting Domestic Violence* (Oxford: Oxford University Press, 2009).

National Clearinghouse on Family Violence, *Parent Abuse: The Abuse of Parents by Their Teenage Children* (Ottawa: Government of Canada, 2003).

Parentline Plus, *There's a War Going On! Aggression and Violence in Children* (London: Parentline, 2003).

Parentline Plus, *When Family Life Hurts: Family Experience Of Aggression In Children* (London: Parentline, 2012).

Parliamentary Assembly, Council of Europe, Committee on Equal Opportunities for Women and Men, *Domestic Violence* (Brussels: Council of Europe, 2002).

Paterson, R., Luntz, H., Perlesz, A. and Cotton, S., "Adolescent Violence towards Parents: Maintaining Family Connections When The Going Gets Tough", *Australian and New Zealand Journal of Family Therapy* 2002 23(2) 90-100.

Rachmilovitz, O., "Bringing down the bedroom walls: Emphasizing substance over form in personalized abuse", *William and Mary Journal of Women and Law* 2007 14, 495-524.

Reece, H., "The End of Domestic Violence", *Modern Law Review* 2006 69(5), 770-796.

Reece, H., "The Pitfalls of Positive Parenting", *Education and Ethics* 2013 8(1), 42-54.

Stark, E., *Coercive Control* (Oxford: Oxford University Press, 2007).

Tew, J. and Nixon, J., "Parent Abuse: Opening Up a Discussion of a Complex Instance of Family Power Relations", *Social Policy and Society* 2010 9, 579-589.

Wilcox, P., "Is Parent Abuse a Form of Domestic Violence", *Social Policy & Society* 2012 11(2), 277–288.

An Unnatural Union? – British Conservatism and the Marriage (Same Sex Couples) Act 2013

Andrew Gilbert
Anglia Ruskin University; PhD Candidate, Faculty of Laws, UCL

This paper started out with the title *Towards a Conservative Theory of Family Law*, and was presented under that name at the Law and Michael Freeman colloquium. The original title was a deliberate hat tip to Michael Freeman's 1985 inaugural lecture *Towards a Critical Theory of Family Law* (Freeman, 1985). However, on reflection, I felt that the paper's aims are far more modest than an attempt at a large scale assessment of conservatism and family law, the use of the expression 'conservative theory' is problematic for the reasons set out below and it was too much of a contortion to continue with it merely for the sake of a witty reworking of Freeman's inaugural title. Despite the title change, this work is no less inspired by the spirit and letter of that lecture which contained the, now axiomatic, claim that 'family law cannot be understood if it is assumed to operate neutrally, ahistorically or cocooned from the indices of power' (Freeman, 1985: 155). This paper also rests on the premise that, generally, 'law is politics, all the way down' (Tushnet, 1991: 1526) and that, particularly, '[f]amily law is, in short, inescapably political' (Collier, 1995: 49). Despite these claims, it is surprising that a lot of the work on family law does seem to escape detailed politico-legal analysis, and this paper aims to make a modest contribution to addressing this deficiency.

It also aims to address another lacuna, namely that relating to discussion of British conservatism and family law. There are studies which have synthesised family law and Conservative Party politics (e.g. Douglas, 1990; Durham, 1991; Abbott and Wallace, 1992; Fox Harding, 1999; Reece, 2003) but I am not aware of any which have sought to situate it against a backdrop of the political philosophy of British conservatism.[1] In doing so, this article also aims to counteract a dearth of academic interest in conservatism and law in general. In 1995 Paddy Ireland wrote that 'there remains remarkably little in the way of systematic academic analysis of conservatism, nor of

1 Although work has been done in relation to housing policy (e.g. King, 2001); the concept of same-sex marriage and conservatism generally (e.g. Wax, 2005; Rauch 1996, 2004; Sullivan 1989, 1995); Cameron and the family (e.g. Hayton, 2010); and public law and the work of Oakeshott (Gee and Webber, 2013).

A. Diduck, N. Peleg, H. Reece (eds.), Law in Society: Reflections on Children, Family, Culture and Philosophy
 ISBN 978-90-04-26148-8. pp. 489-508.

its importance to our understanding of law' (190). A search of Google Scholar reveals that Ireland's article has been cited just nine times, the most recent of which was in 2005, and none in regard to family law. So whilst there are many excellent analyses of the relationship between family law and the political process, it is submitted that this remains a relatively underexplored and undertheorised area in the context of British conservatism.

The intellectual provocation for this paper came from some words of Prime Minister David Cameron in his 2011 Party Conference Speech:

> And to anyone who has reservations, I say: Yes, it's about equality, but it's also about something else: commitment. Conservatives believe in the ties that bind us; that society is stronger when we make vows to each other and support each other. *So I don't support gay marriage despite being a Conservative. I support gay marriage because I'm a Conservative*' (Cameron, 2011, emphasis added)

These words were greeted by (mostly) enthusiastic applause in the conference hall, but one wonders if, in drawing rooms across the English shires, could be heard the quieter sound of party membership cards being torn up and thrown on the fire (Holehouse, 2013). My point is that the Prime Minister clearly believes that an argument *can* be made from conservatism *for* same-sex marriage, and it is this argument which I explore below. Conservatism is, admittedly, often connected with contrarian arguments around same-sex marriage, chief among which are the New Natural Law theory of Finnis (1993, 1997) and Lee and George (1997), and the Hegelian offensive of Scruton (1986, 2006, 2013). Most 'conservative' arguments in favour seem to be either conservative/libertarian or are otherwise only partially theorised. The conservative/libertarian position rests on a classical liberal reading of Mill's harm principle, and this is one of the most common and compelling arguments for same-sex marriage. It is not, however, a *conservative* argument as I and others would see it (Carey, 1998). The other strand of conservative support for same-sex marriage tends to construct gay *men* in particular as the problem which can be fixed through assimilation into, and civilisation through, the institution of marriage, which in turn strengthens marriage (Rauch, 1996, 2004; Sullivan, 1989, 2005). This emphasises – as does Cameron – conservative family values such as commitment and stability. Rauch helpfully discusses the conservative problem of change from a Hayekian perspective but, as Wax (2005) argues, Hayek is less apposite here – there is nothing he says which Burke and Oakeshott do not cover more fully and with a broader socio-economic vista. So in part one of this paper I seek to construct what might be a conservative argument for same-sex marriage by drawing on conservative political thought. And then in part two I use discourse analysis of the parliamentary debates concerning the Marriage (Same Sex Couples) Bill to see if this argument has been deployed.

Throughout my work I take 'British conservatism' to mean an amalgam containing the British manifestation of the political philosophy of conservatism and the political activity of the Conservative Party. Although they could be considered to be close siblings, they are certainly not identical twins. As we shall see, the Conservative Party is not simply a conduit through which the pure ideological waters of conservatism flow, and this distinction between conservative theory and Conservative practice pervades this paper. I will use the word 'conservative' (small 'c') to denote the political philosophy, and 'Conservative' (big 'C') to refer to what the British Conservative Party says or does, or to members of the parliamentary party. As O'Hara observes (2011: 14), this taxonomy helps us to make sense of a world where not all Conservatives are conservatives, and not all conservatives are Conservatives.

Part One

What is Conservatism?

Finlayson considers that conservatism is 'one of the hardest [political theories] to describe philosophically' and 'to seek a singular essence of conservatism would be to misunderstand it from the start' (Finlayson, 2003: 155). This definitional uncertainty is partly a result of some conservatives eschewing the task of drawing verbal boundaries around their political beliefs. To define conservatism would be to risk it being seen as an ideology, with all the baggage the term 'ideology' carries with it of grand visions of society and utopian social planning. But it is also because conservative thought is often articulated against a prevailing political and social context, meaning that it 'must be mined from the particular and historical ore' (Muller, 1997: xiv).

Notwithstanding the reluctance of some conservatives positively to self-define, O'Gorman credits Edmund Burke with being the first to express British conservatism as a coherent corpus of principles (O'Gorman, 1986). Burke published his famous *Reflections on the Revolution in France* in 1790 in response to the violent socio-political upheavals taking place across the English Channel. *Reflections* reads primarily as an extended, impassioned exercise in political rhetoric, a warning against all those (in Britain) who might wish to tear down centuries of tradition in the name of abstract Enlightenment notions such as liberty, equality and fraternity. O'Gorman identifies four recurring themes in Burke's work: a pessimistic belief in the inherent evil of humankind; an organic theory of society (which rejects universal theories about the organisation of government and society, and which points to a pragmatic form of governance which 'goes with the grain' of societal development); the importance of historical tradition, of continuity and stability of key institutions (monarchy, church, parliament, family etc.); and conservation of the existing structures and power relationships within society (O'Gorman, 1986: 1-2). It was to these institutions that citizens owed their loyalty, not to individuals or abstract ideologies. Burke's thesis could be accurately summed up in the words of Scruton: 'conservatism is not about freedom, but about authority' (Scruton, 2001: vii).

Conservatism is unusual as a political philosophy in that it is not defined by its ends (Brennan and Hamlin, 2004). Liberalism is concerned with the freedom of the individual to pursue the good life, socialism is directed towards equality in socio-economic relations, but conservatism has no end in mind and 'may be defined without identifying it with the policies of any party' (Scruton, 2001: 4). Conservatism is a procedural doctrine and, with no foundational substantive content, it subscribes to no particular beliefs about the world or human conduct (Oakeshott, 1991). It encapsulates a limited style of politics, with statecraft being a government's raison d'être, as Oakeshott (1991: 60) puts it:

> Men sail a boundless and bottomless sea; there is neither harbour for shelter nor floor for anchorage, neither starting-place nor appointed destination. The enterprise is to keep afloat on an even keel; the sea is both friend and enemy; and the seamanship consists in using the resources of a traditional manner of behaviour in order to make a friend of every hostile occasion.

There have been a number of attempts to elucidate the principles of conservatism (e.g. O'Gorman, 1986; Norton, 1996; Hayek, 1999; Finlayson, 2003; Quinton, 2006) and there is some disagreement over the characteristics of the conservative gene, but I think that O'Hara does well to focus on two core principles, summed up as the knowledge principle and the change principle (O'Hara, 2011).

Knowledge Principle

Conservatism approaches the world with an epistemological modesty and scepticism (Oakeshott, 1991; Muller, 1997). It sees human society as so complex and dynamic that our understanding of it must necessarily be limited, and it sees human beings as fallible and unpredictable. This leads conservatives to be suspicious of grand utopian theories, universal principles (such as liberty and equality), and sweeping prescriptions for the curing of society's ills. As Burke wrote:

> I cannot stand forward, and give praise or blame to any thing which relates to human actions, and human concerns, on a simple view of the object, as it stands stripped of every relation, in all the nakedness and solitude of metaphysical abstraction ... The circumstances are what render every civil and political scheme beneficial or noxious to mankind. (Burke, 2004: 89)

What mattered, Burke argued, was not acontextual concepts such as rights and liberty but the experience of history: what works? The conservative respect for institutions flows from this. Institutions have developed over time; they endure because they work, and because they work they demand our respect and protection: 'For the conservative, the historical survival of an institution or practice – be it marriage, monarchy, or the market – creates a prima facie case that it has served some human need' (Muller, 1997: 7). It is not of central importance why the institution endures or indeed whether those reasons are known at all, as the conservative interprets its survival as due to its embodying valuable social knowledge (Scruton, 2001). In contrast to liberals, conservatives are more concerned with institutions than individuals:

> The individual depends for his freedom and his happiness on the institutions which form and protect him, and because institutions are more easily formed than created, the conservative remains hostile to the liberal attempt to put every institution, and every authority, in question, for the sake of a freedom whose form and limits are never defined. (Scruton, 1988: 9)

The emphasis on the importance of tradition means conservatism is more nationally specific than any of the other major political philosophies. As philosophies which are defined chiefly by their ends, liberalism and socialism are in essence universalist in their prescriptions and therefore variations at a theoretical level tend not to be driven by geographical factors. Conservatism, on the other hand, is shaped by historical developments in specific countries (see particularly O'Sullivan, 1976), which helps explain why conservative parties across the West represent a fairly broad church of political opinion.

All of this leads to a pragmatism at conservatism's core, which has been elegantly described by Michael Oakeshott thus:

> To be conservative ... is to prefer the familiar to the unknown, to prefer the tried to the untried, fact to mystery, the actual to the possible, the limited to the unbounded, the near to the distant, the sufficient to the superabundant, the convenient to the perfect, present laughter to utopian bliss. (Oakeshott, 1991: 408)

Conservatism and the Family

Conservatism, in both theory and practice, is often associated with a defence of the family, usually the married, heterosexual family. However, I would argue that the Conservative focus on family form over function is a departure from the root of the conservative commitment to the family, which is because 'it is the vehicle for the transmission of values and civilities which make it possible for us to get along together in society' (David Willetts MP quoted in Barton and Douglas, 1995: 237). So, if it is being true to its ontological roots, conservatism does not value family for any normative reasons but because of its importance as an institution. O'Hara agrees that it is a 'misperception that conservatives must favour traditional family structures over newly emerging forms' (O'Hara, 2011: 172). A conservative argument for same-sex marriage would not be driven by naked appeals to universal principles of equality and fairness, but viewing the family primarily from a functional perspective would state that if a family headed by a same-sex couple functions like a family headed by a heterosexual one then it should be given equal recognition.

Conservatism and Orthodoxy

This leads on to the important distinction between conservatism and orthodoxy. Orthodoxy defends institutions because of 'a belief in their correspondence to some ultimate truth' (Muller, 1997: 4), which may rest on religious or secular foundations but either way it transcends merely historical or contingent justifications. And it is such justifications which are the hallmark of conservatism proper: institutions (e.g. monarchy, church, family) are defended because they have proved themselves over time and too great a risk is posed by their diminution or destruction. Arguing that conservatism is actually a creature of the Enlightenment, Muller writes, 'What makes social and political arguments *conservative* as opposed to *orthodox* is that the critique of liberal or progressive arguments takes place on the enlightened grounds of the search for human happiness, based on the use of reason' (Muller, 1997: 5, his emphasis). It is apparent that orthodoxy looms large in much Conservative argument over same-sex marriage. I therefore classify below arguments from Conservative MPs as orthodox (and not therefore conservative) which argue against same-sex marriage based on a metaphysical appeal to the inviolability of the heteronormativity of marriage, without more.

Change Principle

Change is. Therefore, as conservatism claims to be amongst the most realistic of political theories, it would be untenable for it to be opposed to change. Any presumption that conservatism holds to a kind of timeless moral order slips into the error of orthodoxy identified above. Change, though, is a problem for the conservative. It represents a 'threat to identity, and every change is an emblem of extinction' (Oakeshott, 1991: 410). So for change to be acceptable it must also represent continuity: maintaining the social ecology, rather than rending its delicate fabric (Scruton, 2001). As Wax puts it, 'The periphery might be altered, but the core should remain intact' (Wax, 2005: 1071).

Not only are conservatives not opposed to change but there are times when it will be seen as the best way forward. In Burke's famous words, 'A state without the means of some change is without the means of its conservation' (Burke, 2004: 106). Burke advocates here the use of change as a sort of socio-political pressure release valve. He interprets events in France as being the destruction of an ancient society and its many organising institutions through an explosive release of popular energy. His prescription for Britain is to avoid such a catastrophe through evolutionary change which would bleed off stirrings of revolutionary zeal. Conservatism then is concerned with the *management* of change and how change can be reconciled with established societal structures. And the conservative's cautious disposition towards change is a necessary corollary of her scepticism towards human understanding of the operation of society.

If conservatism is open to the possibility of change, how does it determine which change is desirable and which should be resisted? A reading of conservatism's most influential thinkers elicits the following guiding principles.

First, the burden of proof is on the innovator to show that the benefits of the change outweigh its costs (O'Hara, 2011; Oakeshott, 1991). In practical terms this poses two significant, perhaps insurmountable, problems for conservatives. The first is that liberalism (broadly defined), as the dominant paradigm, gets to decide who has the burden of any proof, and indeed, whether any such proof is required. Protest all it likes, conservatism simply does not have the standing in British polity to insist that its opponents shoulder the burden of proof. What it could insist on, however (and this has relevance to the Marriage (Same Sex Couples) Act), is that fellow conservatives who advocate change discharge this evidential standard. But this still leaves open the possibility that not all Conservatives are conservatives, and this expectation might not be respected. The second problem is that for most, if not all, changes, the effects are necessarily prospective. Wax sums up this point thus: 'The consequences of unprecedented shifts in law, custom, or practice have, by definition, not yet been realized' (Wax, 2005: 1083). If a change has already taken place in another country (as was the case with same-sex marriage) then evidence might be tendered of its impact there, but such evidence would be treated with circumspection by conservatives and non-conservatives alike due to locally specific factors which might not translate commensurately across cultures. The effect of this principle is that conservatives will often find themselves fighting battles they are destined to lose and that, at best, their creed might act as 'a politics of delay' (Scruton, 2006: ix), and as a challenge to liberalism to think carefully about the impact of change before proceeding.

Second, the change must be in response to a felt need, rather than in pursuit of a utopian vision (Oakeshott, 1991: 412). It is not for the conservative to indulge in blue-sky thinking; in steering the ship of state, he has no particular destination in mind and is concerned only with keeping the vessel afloat. Change must be demand driven, not emerging from above and imposed on an unwilling society. What weight to attribute to this principle is a problem for the conservative, because to give it too much weight would place the conservative entirely at the mercy of societal shifts. Muller says that the dilemma here for the conservative is 'when to declare the battle for a particular institution definitively lost' (Muller, 1997: 423). To go on fighting in the face of defeat is characteristic of reactionary conservatism – the defence of lost causes, prevalent in the work of Scruton (Scruton, 2001; 2006; Scruton and Blond, 2013). It is a curious feature of the Act that the degree to which the 'need' for same-sex marriage was 'felt' was highly contentious. Many of the contributions from Conservative MPs expressed bemusement that there was no apparent groundswell of public opinion calling for the legal recognition of same-sex marriage, although there was evidence of increasing public support but not amongst Conservative voters (Clements, 2013).

Third, in terms of scale and rate of change, the change should be incremental and evolutionary (Burke, 2004: 117). O'Hara observes, without criticism, that 'cluelessness is a standard state for governments' (O'Hara, 2011: 25). Conservatism is at ease with this cluelessness and sees it as a reality which should result in polities making changes slowly and steadily. Any change should not occur at such a speed and scale that the socially valuable qualities in the object of change are lost. Burke's notion of evolutionary change is analogous to what Darwin was later to propose in the field of biology: natural selection leads to an accentuation of advantageous characteristics and a diminution or elimination of disadvantageous ones. Burke captured a similar idea in *Reflections*: 'Thus, by preserving the method of nature in the conduct of the state, in what we improve we are never wholly new; in what we retain we are never wholly obsolete' (Burke, 2004: 120). He continues this theme throughout his work, concluding with his statement that he 'would make the reparation as nearly as possible in the style of the building' (Burke, 2004: 375). Scruton's idea that for change to be acceptable it must represent continuity also conveys an organic view of society (Scruton, 2011: 11). It might be argued, therefore, that same-sex marriage is consonant with this principle: same-sex couples were permitted to adopt children following the Adoption and Children Act 2002; civil partnerships were introduced in 2005; the Human Fertilisation and Embryology Act 2008 significantly enhanced the status of same-sex couples using artificial reproduction services; so could same-sex marriage be seen as the next incremental step?

Fourth, the change should be rigorously evaluated before the next incremental step. Support for this is found in O'Hara (2011) and in Burke: 'By a slow but well-sustained progress, the effect of each step is watched; the good or ill success of the first, gives light to us in the second' (Burke, 2004: 281). In evaluating a proposal to allow same-sex marriage, a British conservative might examine the impact on families of the legislation cited in the above paragraph. A conservative in favour of the change must show at least that institutional harm has not resulted, although they would be faced with perhaps insurmountable empirical challenges in doing so.

And fifth, change should be reversible where possible (O'Hara, 2011: 88). This is a development of the previous principle. If, on evaluation, it transpires that the change has been a mistake, then ideally there should be a way to return to the *status quo ante*. The reality is, of course, that in a liberal society once a freedom has been granted it is difficult to reverse. It is inconceivable that the permissive legislation of the 1960s relating to abortion, divorce and homosexuality could be repealed in an attempt to return to an earlier moral settlement. And this would surely be the case with the legalisation of same-sex marriage, as it would confer the legally, fiscally, socially privileged status of marriage. Once released, the genie could not be put back in the bottle.

How a conservative perceives a proposed change affects the likelihood that they will support and promote it. Does same-sex marriage *change* the concept of opposite-sex marriage, or do they just exist alongside each other, with each one catering for the needs of a different constituency? I would argue that where on a revolutionary/evolutionary scale of change a Conservative MP perceived the legalisation of same-sex marriage affected how willing they were to support the Bill. Those who constructed it as a radical change – a redefinition of marriage – tended to oppose it, whereas others who saw it as merely extending the marriage franchise to same-sex couples approached it as an evolutionary change which could be accommodated within their conservative mindset.

So, how might insights from the knowledge and change principles inform an argument in favour of same-sex marriage? In summary the argument might run something like this:

> We value marriage because of its functional benefits and not for metaphysical reasons. We therefore have no objection on normative grounds to same-sex marriage and we recognise that in order to conserve the institution of marriage it might be necessary for it to change. But any change carries risks that marriage and society may be, somehow, dam-

> aged. In arguing for this change therefore we need to show that institutional and societal damage will not ensue.

In analysing the discourse in the parliamentary debate, I have looked for evidence that Conservative MPs have used this argument, or at least elements of it, in their speeches.

Part Two

The next part of the paper briefly considers the background to the Bill and its main provisions before going on to examine how Conservative support and opposition were constructed in the parliamentary debates.

Background to the Bill

For such a radical piece of legislation it could be said that the Marriage (Same Sex Couples) Bill almost 'rose without trace'. While Cameron had long sent inclusive messages towards the lesbian and gay community (e.g. Cameron, 2006), there was no mention of the reform in the 2010 general election manifestos of either the Conservative or Liberal Democratic parties which went on to form the coalition government, and the subsequent Coalition Agreement was also silent on the matter. However, the following statement can be found in 'A Contract for Equalities' which was launched on 3 May 2010: 'We will also consider the case for changing the law to allow civil partnerships to be called and classified as marriage' (Conservative Party, 2010, 14). If they were unaware in May 2010, by July Conservative MPs would have realised something was going on in Whitehall when Simon Hughes MP, the deputy leader of the Liberal Democrats, announced that the government was planning a consultation on 'taking civil partnerships to the "next level"' (Peev, 2010), and that the new law would be in place before the next general election in 2015.

'Equal civil marriage: a consultation', was published by the government in March 2012. The consultation was open for 12 weeks and was framed in terms that suggested the government had already decided to legislate for same-sex marriage but just wanted views on how best to do it. The opening sentence of the Executive Summary reads: 'This consultation is about how the ban can be lifted on same-sex couples having a marriage through a civil ceremony' (Government Equalities Office, 2012: 3). Not surprisingly this presumptive tone upset many of the Bill's opponents.

The Bill was given its First Reading in the House of Commons on 24 January 2013 and completed its Commons stages on 21 May 2013. The House of Lords First Reading was on the same day and the Bill finished its Lords stages on 10 July 2013, before receiving Royal Assent on 17 July 2013. Many of the discursive themes in the debates echoed those from the Civil Partnership Bill in 2003-4.

Main Features of the Bill

The Bill ran to 18 sections and seven lengthy schedules, which mostly concerned amending existing legislation or setting out the position regarding religious rites and same-sex marriage. Section 1(1), however, proved to be amongst the most controversial in the history of family law-making: 'Marriage of same sex couples is lawful.' Perhaps the main area of tension, given the often religious nature of marriage ceremonies, was the position of religious bodies in relation to conducting, or not conducting, same-sex weddings. So concerned was the government to uphold religious conscience that it devised the so-called 'quadruple lock'. This meant that: (1) no religious organisation or minister could be compelled to marry same-sex couples or to permit such a marriage on their premises; (2) religious organisations which wanted to conduct same-sex marriages would have to *opt in* in order to do so; (3) the Equality Act 2010 would be amended so that (1) was not unlawful; and (4) there was no duty on the Church of England to marry gay couples under common law.

Four further aspects of the Bill are worth noting here. First, paragraph 5(2) of schedule 3, part 2, makes an interesting statement about change and tradition. By setting out that 'husband' includes a man married to another man, and 'wife' a woman married to another woman, it embraces the fundamental change at the heart of the Bill but holds to the established heterosexist nomenclature of 'husband' and 'wife'. Second, paragraph 3 of schedule 4, part 3, inserts a new section 1(6) into the Matrimonial Causes Act 1973: 'Only conduct between the respondent and a person of the opposite sex may constitute adultery for the purposes of this section.' This caused a divergence of opinion in parliament, with some suggesting this meant that same-sex married couples would be treated differently with regard to using adultery as a basis for divorce (e.g. H.L. *Hansard*, 19 June 2013, cols. 375-382). In one sense, same-sex and opposite-sex couples will be treated the same in that only penile/vaginal penetrative sex amounts to adultery, with extra-marital homosexual sex founding a divorce under the behaviour fact. But on the other hand, there is a clear double standard here as the implied fidelity expectation in opposite-sex marriage is not extended to gays and lesbians in a way that is consonant with their sexual orientation. (Eekelaar overlooks this point (2014: 16)). It seems paradoxical that the government felt able radically to revise the meaning of marriage but not adultery.[2] Third, paragraph 4 of schedule 4, part 3, deals with non-consummation, amending s.12 of the Matrimonial Causes Act 1973 to make clear that the non-consummation grounds do not apply to same-sex marriage. There is not space here to consider these provisions in detail but what was written by many feminist and queer theorists about the Civil Partnership Act 2004 seems to apply in whole or part. (For a helpful discussion see Crompton, 2013). The 'continuing centrality of penetrative intercourse' (Stychin, 2006: 83) in the construction of conjugality is likely to mean that same-sex marriage will be 'conservative,

2 Although Butler-Sloss did attempt to introduce same-sex adultery (H.L. *Hansard*, 8 July 2013, col. 142). Contrast this with Mackay's amendment to remove conjugality and allow sibling marriage (H.L. *Hansard*, 24 June 2013, col. 635).

rather than either transgressive or transformative' (Barker, 2013; 2012; 2006: 249), especially given the dominant assimilationist discourse around the Bill. Finally, section 12 and schedule 5 make important changes to the law regarding trans people, specifically providing a means to avoid the upsetting situation where a person in transition is forced to choose between obtaining a full gender recognition certificate and continuing with their marriage or civil partnership. This provision attempts to balance the interests of the trans person and their spouse/civil partner, and was considered in parliament (e.g. H.L. *Hansard*, 10 July 2013, cols. 295-301; H.C. *Hansard*, 21 May 2013, cols. 1123-1148).

Analysis of the Debates

An Overview

Space does not permit a detailed examination of the Bill's entire parliamentary passage, so instead I will give an overview of the discursive terrain. The House of Commons Second Reading was taken up with debate over the merits and impact of same-sex marriage and the robustness of the quadruple lock, particularly whether it would withstand legal challenge under human rights law. The Public Bill Committee comprised 21 MPs, of whom only four voted against the Bill at Second Reading (Burrowes, Kwarteng, Loughton, Shannon). These four were nicknamed 'team marriage' by Burrowes (H.C. *Hansard*, 7 March 2013, col. 427). Were it not for the dogged determination of Burrowes in particular, and his Labour foil, Chris Bryant, the Bill would have almost evaded scrutiny. The proposed amendments in Committee were largely of a probing nature and covered changing the word 'marriage' to 'union' (H.C. *Hansard*, 7 March 2013, col. 425), as well as statements on the moral purpose of marriage (H.C. *Hansard*, 26 February 2013, col. 187). The Bill completed the Committee stage unamended. By the time the Bill was back before the full House at Report stage, the concerns over religious liberty at an institutional level appear to have been largely assuaged, but some amendments were tabled covering individual religious liberties which would have allowed registrars, for example, to conscientiously object to conducting same-sex marriages (H.C. *Hansard*, 20 May 2013, col. 926). A new strategy emerged at this stage: one of the Bill's long-standing opponents, Tim Loughton, seemingly overwhelmed by a spirit of egalitarianism, tabled an amendment extending civil partnership to different-sex couples (H.C. *Hansard*, 20 May 2013, col. 990). The world then momentarily turned upside down with the Daily Telegraph calling it a wrecking amendment (Hodges, 2013), whilst Peter Tatchell came out in support (Eaton, 2013). The amendment was heavily defeated but the matter was clearly not going to go away. Many of the Third Reading speeches were expansive and impassioned (e.g. Abbott, H.C. *Hansard*, 21 May 2013, col. 1167; Donaldson, H.C. *Hansard*, 21 May 2013, col. 1160), capturing the historic nature of the occasion.

The Bill was sponsored in the Lords by Baroness Stowell who reported that the Bill's consultation prompted the largest ever response of its kind (H.L. *Hansard*, 3 June 2013, col. 939). She stated her belief that the institution of marriage will be strengthened the more 'it reflects modern society' (H.L. *Hansard*, 3 June 2013, col. 939). Her speech echoed the assimilationist tones of her Commons counterpart; the love and commitment of gays and lesbians were 'no different from that of opposite-sex couples' (H.L. *Hansard*, 3 June 2013, col. 941; also 17 June 2013, col. 47; 8 July 2013, col. 32). In contrast, although not presenting as a radical feminist/queer theorist, Baroness Cumberlege urged gay people 'to be bold, to be confident and eschew the institutions of others, to build their own and be themselves' (H.L. *Hansard*, 3 June 2013, col. 968), which prompted gay Conservative Lord Black to respond: 'we do not want different institutions; we want the same institutions' (H.L. *Hansard*, 3 June 2013, col. 988). The arguments at Second Reading covered much the same ground as in the Commons but there was a sense that resistance was futile (and unconstitutional) given the overwhelming support the Bill received in the lower chamber. In Committee there were a number of creative suggestions to change reference to 'marriage' in the Bill to 'union' (H.L. *Hansard*, 17 June 2013, col. 11), 'espousal' (col. 14), 'matrimony' (col.15), 'matrimonial marriages' (col. 17), 'marriage (same sex couples)' (col. 23), 'traditional marriage/same sex marriage' (col. 28), or 'ancient marriage/modern marriage' (col. 28) all of which ultimately fell away, but they stand as evidence of a discursive strategy to prevent the (mis)appropriation of the word 'marriage'. When the Lords did divide on the Bill, it attracted overwhelming support (e.g. H.L. *Hansard*, 4 June 2013, col. 1109).

The remainder of the paper focuses on the House of Commons Second Reading, which ran for six hours on 5 February 2013. I have focussed on this debate because: first, the speeches tended to be more concerned with the broad themes of the Bill (particularly arguments pro and contra same-sex marriage) rather than with specific detail, and as such I believe that the speakers' ideas and beliefs are made plainer; and second, the Commons, as an elected chamber, has a more party political character and contains a higher concentration of Conservatives, making it a superior 'sample' to one drawn from the House of Lords. I divided my detailed analysis into two, and considered the arguments of Conservative MPs in favour of the Bill and those against. A total of 115 members of parliament spoke in the debate, of whom 56 were Conservative. Speeches were limited to four minutes, which typically amounted to about 600 words of text. At the end of the debate the House voted – it was a free vote – in favour 400 to 175, with Conservatives voting 136 against, 127 in favour, and 40 abstentions.

Before proceeding to a discussion of the arguments put forward by Conservatives on both sides of the debate, it is worth mentioning the influence of religious belief. The words 'Christ', 'Christian', 'Christianity' and 'God' occurred 77 times, 28 times by Conservatives and 49 times by others (but this includes the Northern Irish MPs who significantly inflated the figure!). Occasional reference was made to other faiths such as Islam and Judaism, but Christianity dominated. A religious narrative permeated the entire Second Reading, although it was an unreliable indicator of a speaker's party allegiance or voting behaviour: Christianity was prayed in aid by members of all main parties and by the Bill's supporters and opponents alike. The words 'free' and 'freedom' were used 83 times, and 'liberty' 10 times, mostly by Conservatives, and almost always when voicing concern over the Bill's perceived threat to religious liberty, i.e. almost never as an argument *for* same-sex marriage ('equal'/'equality' did the work there). This supports the view that Conservatives opposed the Bill for two main reasons: it would harm the institution of marriage and restrict religious freedom both to speak out against same-sex marriage and to refuse to conduct same-sex marriage ceremonies.

Conservative MPs in Favour of the Bill

I have noted that a large minority of Conservative MPs voted in favour of the Bill. Analysis of this group shows that the majority were female and that younger MPs and those elected to parliament in 2010 were also more likely to support the Bill. Conservatives used the word 'institution' (in relation to marriage) on 34 occasions (non-conservatives: 21 occasions) and 'tradition'/'traditional' on 20 occasions (non-conservatives: 21 occasions). Non-conservative MPs made 67 references to the words 'equal', 'equally' and 'equality' in their arguments in favour of the Bill while Conservative supporters referred to the same terms 41 times. The former group used 'fair' or 'fairness' only twice but the latter made seven references to it. This is a crude indicator of the discursive strategies employed in parliament, but it does give a sense that Conservatives used a broadly similar lexicon to non-Conservatives in framing their arguments.

The Second Reading motion was moved by the Conservative minister, Maria Miller. Her speech was a hybridised defence of the Bill's central provision, drawing on both conservative and liberal ideas. She begins by seeming to plant her flag firmly on liberalism's lawn ('Parliament should value people equally in the law, and enabling same-sex couples to marry removes the current differentiation and distinction.' (H.C. *Hansard*, 5 February 2013, col. 125)), but then moves into familiar conservative territory with a Burkean argument that marriage has evolved over time:

> Some say that the Bill redefines marriage, but marriage is an institution with a long history of adaptation and change ... Suggestions that the Bill changes something that has remained unchanged for centuries simply do not recognise the road that marriage has travelled as an institution. (H.C. *Hansard*, 5 February 2013, col. 126)

She draws again on both political traditions in the conclusion to her speech, although she makes no attempt to adduce any evidence to establish her claim about supporting marriage:

> [T]his Bill is about one thing – fairness. It is about giving those who want to get married the opportunity to do so, while protecting the rights of those who do not agree with same-sex marriage. Marriage is one of the most important institutions we have; it binds families and society together, and it is a building block that promotes stability. This Bill supports and cultivates marriage, and I commend it to the House. (H.C. *Hansard*, 5 February 2013, col. 133)

A similar hybrid approach is seen in Margot James' contribution, although her words are more remarkable for her denunciation of the social conservatism of the American Republican Party. Despite her attempt to distance her own views from those held by those in what is often considered to be the Conservatives' sister party, she demonstrates some awareness of her party's anxieties about the Bill's impact on tradition. It is doubted that her assurance will have satisfied sceptical colleagues as no attempt is made to discharge the burden of proving that the measure's benefits will outweigh its societal costs:

> My party should never flinch from the requirement to continue this progression [towards treating people equally]; otherwise we may end up like the Republican party, which lost an election last year that it could have won were it not for its socially conservative agenda. … I can assure hon. Members that this will not undermine tradition. (H.C. *Hansard*, 5 February 2013, col. 164)

Others also seem to depart from the way change is understood within the conservative ontology. John Howell switches the burden of proof and places it on those opposing same-sex marriage: 'No compelling case has yet been made against the change' (H.C. *Hansard*, 5 February 2013, col. 216). But he then goes on to mention Spain's introduction of same-sex marriage in 2005 and his view that since then 'life has gone on as normal', perhaps thereby implicitly acknowledging that it is not just for opponents to establish a contrarian case.

On the other hand, some contributors demonstrated an understanding of both the inevitability of change and the conservative imperative that change should also be continuity as far as possible:

> I am by nature a small 'c' conservative. I do not like change … For conservatism to work, we have to accept that the world changes. If we do not, we become an anachronism. What we have to do as Conservatives is to shape that change and try to preserve the best of what we inherited. (Barwell, H.C. *Hansard*, 5 February 2013, col. 218)

Nick Herbert highlights how today's heresy is often tomorrow's orthodoxy with a statement which also belongs to the evolutionary conservative school:

> I believe that many who do not share that view nevertheless have a principled concern that gay marriage would mean redefining the institution for everyone, yet Parliament has repeatedly done that. If marriage had not been redefined in 1836, there would be no civil marriages. If it had not been redefined in 1949, under-16-year-olds would still be able to get married. If it had not been redefined in 1969, we would not have today's divorce laws. All those changes were opposed. (H.C. *Hansard*, 5 February 2013, col. 155)

As stated above, how conservatives understand the magnitude of a proposed change on a revolutionary/evolutionary scale is an indicator of whether they will go on to support it. For those MPs who perceived same-sex marriage as a positive broadening of the marriage franchise which would increase the sum total of human happiness, it was then a small step for them to endorse the measure, and even more so if they were satisfied that no damage would ensue to opposite-sex unions. The following two contributions demonstrate this point:

> My starting point in this debate is that if we can extend to some people rights that will bring them great joy and happiness, without damaging the rights of other people or institutions, that is a good thing. I believe that that is what the Bill sets out to do. (Ellison, H.C. *Hansard*, 5 February 2013, col. 206)
>
> Essentially, we are asking whether we can remove the barriers that stop same-sex couples enjoying the commitment – the 'at one' meaning – of marriage. That is what the Bill comes down to. It does not redefine marriage; it just takes away barriers. (Bottomley, H.C. *Hansard*, 5 February 2013, col. 212)

It was unusual for parliamentarians – especially Conservative ones – actually to make explicit reference to political philosophers, and even rarer for them to quote them. Given conservatism's antipathy towards liberalism,[3] it was surprising that Andrea Leadsom (who abstained) quoted Mill's harm principle and esteemed him as one of her political heroes (H.C. *Hansard*, 5 February 2013, col. 221). There are numerous examples of other supporters making naked appeals to liberal values in their arguments, with little or no attempt to place them in a conservative framework. Mike Freer, reflecting on his own civil partnership, said:

> I am not asking for special treatment; I am simply asking for equal treatment ... I ask my colleagues, if I am equal in this House, to give me every opportunity to be equal. Today, we have a chance to set that right and I hope that colleagues will join me in voting yes this evening. (H.C. *Hansard*, 5 February 2013, col. 179)

At most, speeches made in support of the Bill sometimes contained a partial appeal to conservative principles, but there were no examples of wholesale adoption of my model argument.

Conservative MPs against the Bill

The conservative knowledge and change principles were more apparent in the discourse of those MPs who spoke against the Bill, and some MPs in particular articulated them with clarity and precision. However, there were a number of examples of the error Muller identifies in his discussion of conservatism and orthodoxy. It is sometimes a fine line in practice between tradition and orthodoxy, but Muller is clear that, 'The orthodox theoretician defends existing institutions because they are meta-

---

3 It is worth stressing that I am here referring to conservatism as ideology rather than the praxis of the Conservative Party. There is, of course, a long history of liberal Conservatism in British politics. For a helpful discussion, see O'Hara (2011),chapter 7.

physically *true*' (Muller, 1997: 4). An example of an orthodox, rather than a conservative, defence of marriage can be seen in Sir Roger Gale's contribution:

> It is not possible to redefine marriage. Marriage is the union between a man and a woman. It has been that historically and it remains so. It is Alice in Wonderland territory – Orwellian almost – for any Government of any political persuasion to try to rewrite the lexicon. It will not do. (H.C. *Hansard*, 5 February 2013, col. 152)

Others thought that it was 'impossible' for the sponsoring minister to change the meaning of the word 'marriage' through legislation (Gillan, H.C. *Hansard*, 5 February 2013, col. 174; see also Leigh, H.C. *Hansard*, 5 February 2013, col. 161 and Howarth, col. 185). These are all at root semantic arguments about the immutability of the word 'marriage', which are founded neither on the reality of parliamentary supremacy nor on conservative doctrine.

Turning to consider examples of well-framed conservative arguments, the knowledge principle was evident in Edward Leigh's speech:

> We must get away from the idea that every single thing in life can be forced through the merciless prism of equality. I am a Conservative. I believe we should be concerned with equality, but not at the expense of every other consideration – not at the expense of tradition. We should be in the business of protecting cherished institutions and our cultural heritage. Otherwise, what is a Conservative party for?' (H.C. *Hansard*, 5 February 2013, col. 161)

And he concludes with, 'I will vote tonight to proclaim my support for the future of our children and for the essence of traditional marriage.' These words are reminiscent of Burke's social contract theory. Burke rejected Rousseau's theory but believed in a social contract based on the enduring link of intergenerational responsibility: '[A] partnership not only between those who are living, but between those who are living, those who are dead, and those who are to be born' (Burke, 2004: 194).

Aspects of the change principle are clear in this excerpt from Angie Bray's speech: 'I would like to make it clear that, although I am not implacably opposed to change, I need to be convinced that it is necessary and has been properly thought through' (H.C. *Hansard*, 5 February 2013, col. 174). She insists that change must arise from a felt need and its likely effects evaluated prior to implementation. Sir Gerald Howarth also questions the mandate for 'this massive social and cultural change' (H.C. *Hansard*, 5 February 2013, col. 130).

Democratic Unionist MP Ian Paisley (conservative, but not Conservative), took a similar, but more detailed line, although still stymied by the causation issue:

> [T]he facts paint a very different picture. Since same-sex marriages were introduced in Portugal, Spain and the Netherlands, the number of mixed-sex marriages has decreased considerably – indeed, by tens and tens of thousands – [*Interruption.*] The facts are clear. When they were introduced in Spain, 208,000 people were married in mixed-sex mar-

> riages, whereas last year 161,000 people were married in mixed-sex marriages, so the numbers are declining, not increasing. (H.C. *Hansard*, 5 February 2013, col. 136)

Hirschman (1991) identified three principal conservative stances towards change: the perversity thesis (action to improve an aspect of social life will only make that aspect worse); the futility thesis (the proposed change will not work); and the jeopardy thesis (the change threatens to harm a previous, precious accomplishment). The jeopardy thesis, in particular, was evidenced in the oft-heard argument that same-sex marriage would undermine opposite-sex marriage. It is not worth quoting examples of this claim from opponents because it is never developed beyond a mere assertion. The claim was, however, countered in a rather mocking fashion by a number of the Bill's proponents:

> The other argument against the Bill is that it would undermine marriage. Mrs Barwell suffers enough as a result of my job, and if I thought it likely that I would go home tonight only to be accused of undermining my marriage by voting for the Bill, I would not vote for it. However, no one has yet come up with a credible explanation of how it would undermine marriage. (Barwell, H.C. *Hansard*, 5 February 2013, col. 218)

Concluding Remarks

First, whether MPs thought a positive conservative case could be made or not, it is clear that the majority of Conservative MPs did not agree with David Cameron that support for same-sex marriage should follow from being conservative. This was underlined at Third Reading, when 133 voted against and 117 in favour. My analysis of the debate indicates that conservative ideology was more readily articulated in *opposition* to the Bill, rather than in favour of it. This is perhaps unsurprising, given that conservatism is more easily deployed as a politics of opposition and stasis. So while it is possible to construct a theoretical argument for same-sex marriage, the Oakeshottian insistence on proof that change would bring a net benefit effectively means that conservatism often lacks a practical theory of progressive change.

Second, Conservative MPs in favour of the Bill almost all conceptualised their support (in so far as they did conceptualise it) in hybridised terms, drawing from liberal or post-liberal (communitarian?) ideas, established conservative arguments (e.g. Rauch, Sullivan) and elements of what I have argued here. They tended not to construct their support exclusively from conservative political theory, in an apparent departure from their party leader's boast that he was a supporter of same-sex marriage *because* he is a conservative. The findings of this case study do not go as far as Barnes' conclusion that conservative ideology 'arguably plays very little part in shaping the way the party actually operates' (Barnes, 1994: 318), but conservatism's influence is certainly diluted and might be further diminished as a result of the Act's passage. I suggest that this lack of reliance on a conservative conceptual framework might be for three reasons:

1. Conservatives are simply more comfortable conforming to the dominant liberal narrative of equality and fairness. Perhaps they perceive that this makes them

(seem) more in touch with the *Zeitgeist* and therefore more electorally attractive; or
2. They are not familiar enough with their own identifying ideology to be able to construct an argument from it in favour of same-sex marriage; or
3. They are aware of the arguments in support but were simply not able to deploy them because they could not produce any evidence to satisfy the change principle's burden of proof (because the changes had not yet happened). Wax identifies this probative problem as 'a war that conservatives are destined to lose' (Wax, 2005: 1083).

Third – and no surprises here – the liberal paradigm dominates family law making, which is consistent with Scruton's claim that liberalism is 'the official ideology of the Western world' (Scruton, 2001: 182). The contemporary relevance of conservatism (and post-liberalism) is primarily, I would argue, as an important critique of the liberal monolith. Its privileging of tradition, caution towards change and insistence that the drive for human happiness be contextualised can all provide a valuable check on liberalism's tendency to be 'essentially revisionary of existing institutions' (Scruton, 2001: 186). Ultimately though, family law reform is most likely to succeed when it is consonant with practices in family life, regardless of the prevailing political wind (see, for example, Glendon, 1989).

References

Abbott, P. and Wallace, C., *The Family and the New Right* (London: Pluto Press, 1992).
Barker, N., "Sex and the Civil Partnership Act: The Future of (Non)Conjugality?", *Feminist Legal Studies* 2006 14(2), 241-259.
Barker, N., *Not The Marrying Kind: A Feminist Critique of Same-Sex Marriage* (Basingstoke: Palgrave Macmillan, 2012).
Barker, N., "Two Myths about Same-Sex Marriage", in A. de Waal (ed), *The Meaning of Matrimony* (London: Civitas, 2013).
Barnes, J., "Ideology and Factions", in A. Seldon and S. Ball (eds), *Conservative Century: The Conservative Party since 1900* (Oxford: Oxford University Press, 1994).
Barton, C. and Douglas, G., *Law and Parenthood* (London: Butterworths, 1995).
Brennan, G. and Hamlin, A., "Analytic Conservatism", *British Journal of Political Science* 2004 34(4), 675-691.
Burke, E., *Reflections on the Revolution in France* (London: Penguin, 2004).
Cameron, D., Speech to Conservative Party Conference, Bournemouth, 4 October 2006.
Cameron, D., Speech to Conservative Party Conference, Manchester, 5 October 2011.
Carey, G. (ed), *Freedom and Virtue: The Conservative/Libertarian Debate* (Wilmington: Intercollegiate Studies Institute, 1998).
Clements, B., "Partisan Attachments and Attitudes towards Same-Sex Marriage in Britain", *Parliamentary Affairs* 2014 67(1), 232-244..
Collier. R., *Masculinity, Law and the Family* (London: Routledge, 1995).

Conservative Party, *A Contract for Equalities* (London, 2010).
Crompton, L., "Where's the Sex in Same-Sex Marriage", *Family Law* 2013, 564-573.
Douglas, G., "Family Law Under the Thatcher Government", *Journal of Law and Society* 1990 17(4), 411-426.
Durham, M., *Sex and Politics* (Basingstoke: Macmillan, 1991).
Eaton, G., "Equality Campaigners Divided over 'Wrecking' Amendment to Gay Marriage Bill", *New Statesman*, 20 May 2013.
Eccleshall, R., *Political Ideologies: An Introduction*, 3rd ed. (London: Routledge, 2003).
Eekelaar, J., "Perceptions of Equality: The Road to Same-Sex Marriage in England and Wales", *International Journal of Law, Policy and the Family* 2014 28(1), 1-25.
Finlayson, A., "Conservatisms", in A. Finlayson (ed), *Contemporary Political Thought: A Reader and Guide* (Edinburgh: Edinburgh University Press, 2003).
Finnis, J., "Law, Morality, and 'Sexual Orientation'", *Notre Dame Law Review* 1993 69, 1049-1076.
Finnis, J., "The Good of Marriage and the Morality of Sexual Relations: Some Philosophical and Historical Observations", *American Journal of Jurisprudence* 1997 42, 97-134.
Fox Harding, L., "'Family Values' and Conservative Government Policy: 1979-1997", in G. Jagger and C. Wright (eds), *Changing Family Values* (London: Routledge, 1999).
Freeman, M., "Towards a Critical Theory of Family Law", *Current Legal Problems* 1985 38(1), 153-185.
Gee, G. and Webber, G., "Rationalism in Public Law", *Modern Law Review* 2013 76(4), 708-734.
Glendon, M.A., *The Transformation of Family Law* (Chicago: The University of Chicago Press, 1989).
Government Equalities Office, *Equal Civil Marriage: A Consultation* (London: HM Government, 2012).
Hayek, F., *The Constitution of Liberty* (London: Routledge, 1999).
Hayton, R., "Conservative Party Modernisation and David Cameron's Politics of the Family", *The Political Quarterly* 2010 81(4), 492-500.
Hirschman, A., *The Rhetoric of Reaction* (Cambridge, MA: The Belknap Press of Harvard University, 1991).
Hodges, D., "The Tory Rebels Think Gay Marriage is an 'Infestation'. If Labour Helps Them Wreck the Bill, it Will be a Disgrace", *Daily Telegraph*, 20 May 2013.
Holehouse, M., "'Dire' Fall in Tory Membership a Threat to Election Victory", *Daily Telegraph*, 9 August 2013.
Ireland, P., "Reflections on a Rampage Through the Barriers of Shame: Law, Community, and the New Conservatism", *Journal of Law and Society* 1995 22(2), 189-211.
King, P., "Was Conservative Housing Policy Really Conservative?", *Housing, Theory and Society* 2001 18, 98-107.
Lee, P. and George, R., "What Sex Can Be: Self-Alienation, Illusion, or One-Flesh Union", *American Journal of Jurisprudence* 1997 42, 135-157.
Muller, J., *Conservatism* (New Jersey: Princeton University Press, 1997).

Norton, P., "The Principles of Conservatism", in P. Norton (ed), *The Conservative Party* (London: Prentice Hall – Harvester Wheatsheaf, 1996).

O'Gorman, F., *British Conservatism: Conservative Thought from Burke to Thatcher* (London: Longman, 1986).

O'Hara, K., *Conservatism* (London: Reaktion Books, 2011).

O'Sullivan, N., *Conservatism* (London: Dent, 1976).

Oakeshott, M.J., *Rationalism in Politics and Other Essays* 2nd ed. (Indianapolis: Liberty Fund, 1991).

Peev, G., "We Will Allow Gay Couples to Get Married, Says Top Lib Dem", *Daily Mail*, 20 July 2010.

Quinton, A., "Conservatism", in R. Goodin and P. Pettit (eds), *Contemporary Political Philosophy* 2nd ed. (Oxford: Blackwell, 2006).

Rauch, J., "For Better or Worse?", *The New Republic*, 6 May 1996, 18-23.

Rauch, J., *Gay Marriage: Why it is Good for Gays, Good for Straights, and Good for America* (New York: Henry Holt, 2004).

Reece, H., *Divorcing Responsibly* (Oxford: Hart, 2003).

Regan, M., *Family Law and the Pursuit of Intimacy* (New York: New York University Press, 1993).

Scruton, R., *Sexual Desire: A Philosophical Investigation* (London: Weidenfeld and Nicolson, 1986).

Scruton, R., *The Meaning of Conservatism* 3rd ed. (Basingstoke: Palgrave, 2001).

Scruton, R., *A Political Philosophy* (London: Continuum, 2006).

Scruton, R. and Blond, P., *Marriage: Union for the Future or Contract for the Present* (London: ResPublica, 2013).

Stychin, C., "Not (Quite) a Horse and Carriage: The Civil Partnership Act 2004", *Feminist Legal Studies* 14(1), 79-86.

Sullivan, A., "Here Comes the Groom: A Conservative Case for Gay Marriage", *The New Republic*, 28 August 1989, 20-22.

Sullivan, A., *Virtually Normal: An Argument about Homosexuality* (London: Picador, 1995).

Tushnet, M., "Critical Legal Studies: A Political History", *Yale Law Journal* 1991 100(5), 1515-1544.

Wax, A., "The Conservative's Dilemma: Traditional Institutions, Social Change and Same-Sex Marriage", *San Diego Law Review* 2005 42, 1059-1103.

V

Law and International Living

The Family Law World of Michael Freeman

Sanford N. Katz
Libby Professor of Law, Boston College Law School

The Federal Government and Child Welfare Reform

Unlike Great Britain, where Parliament is the source of laws regulating the family, in America the family is regulated by the individual States. The federal Congress is rarely involved except where interstate commerce, broadly defined, the federal Constitution, or funding certain programs are involved.[1]

During the 1960s and 1970s, the Children's Bureau of the then US Department of Health, Education, & Welfare (now the Department of Health & Human Services) conducted studies on the condition of dependent children in the United States. Instead of the usual White Paper, something more tangible was the result: model laws for the states to consider and, ideally, enact. These acts were the Model Child Abuse Mandatory Reporting Act, the Model Act to Free Children for Permanent Placement, and the Model Subsidized Adoption Act. All three had an important impact on the protection of children in the United States and reflected the tension between promoting the rights of children, which was one of Michael Freeman's major contributions, and the rights of parents.

Marriage and parenthood, discussed below, are two enormously important and legally secure institutions regulated by state law. Once a couple marries, only they

---

1 For example, Congress enacted the Defense of Marriage Act in 1996. That Act had two major provisions: one that limited the Full Faith and Credit Act in the Federal Constitution so that one state would not 'be required to give effect to any public act, record, or judicial proceeding of any other State, territory, possession, or tribe respecting a relationship between persons of the same sex that is treated as marriage under the laws of such other State, territory, possession, or tribe, or a right or claim arising from such relationship.' The other provision defined marriage and spouse for all federal acts to exclude same-sex relationships. It stated, 'the word "marriage" means only a legal union between one man and one woman as husband and wife, and the word "spouse" refers only to a person of the opposite sex who is a husband or a wife.' In 2013 The US Supreme Court found section 3 of the Act to be unconstitutional under the Due Process Clause of the Fifth Amendment (*United States v Windsor* 570 US).

A. Diduck, N. Peleg, H. Reece (eds.), Law in Society: Reflections on Children, Family, Culture and Philosophy
 Printed in The Netherlands. ISBN 978-90-04-26148-8. pp. 511-520.

– and not the state – may terminate their relationship. There is no such thing as involuntary divorce. Likewise, once a child is born, the mother takes the child home from the hospital and rears it without any state interference unless, of course, she abuses him. Indeed, state intervention into the parent-child relationship was relatively rare until the 1960s, when the terms 'child abuse' and 'child neglect' entered the American legal lexicon (see Katz, 1971).

The laws that were enacted in response to these phenomena demonstrate that a child's being raised by parents who advance his or her well-being by providing shelter, safety, security and emotional support is an important value in American culture (Goldstein *et al.*, 1973). Depriving a child of his or her well-being in any of these regards violates a parent's legal obligations, which are ordinarily defined by state statutes.

The first child welfare cases usually involved injuries from physical punishment that were severe enough to require medical attention. The major defense of the parent was 'parental immunity', which invoked the principle that a parent has a right to raise his child according to the parent's ideology and religious values, which may involve corporal punishment, free from governmental intrusion. At this stage, such conduct was not regarded as family violence.[2]

The spike in inexplicable injuries to children brought into hospital emergency rooms happened in the early 1960s. A concerned Dr. C. Henry Kempe and his associates in Colorado decided to investigate the phenomenon, and their findings were published in a seminal article that introduced the phrase, 'battered child syndrome'(Kempe *et al.*, 1962; see also Myers, 2006: 84-86; Guggenheim, 2005: 183 for further discussion; and Gardner and Durpe, 2012 for relevant case law). That was the impetus for the federal government's response and the drafting of the Model Mandatory Child Abuse Reporting Act (Children's Bureau, 1963).

At the time of its drafting, the Act was the subject of intense criticism because it sought to regulate certain relationships thought to be immune from governmental intrusion.[3] Specifically, parental rights groups complained that the Act interfered with the parent-child relationship and violated family privacy. As stated earlier, parents viewed their responsibility to their children as one that involved inculcating values like respect through discipline, which many thought was supported by Scripture (Greven, 1990: 48) or justified by their particular culture (Freeman, 1998: 289). Whether such discipline resulted in injuries was thought secondary to the principle reason for the punishment. Thus, parents believed that assault and battery were excusable acts.

One of the major issues for the drafters was the identification of mandated reporters. It was thought that those adults who come in contact with children, like pediatricians, nurses, day care operators, and school teachers and administrators should all be included in the list. Physicians were reluctant to conform because doing so would breach doctor-patient confidentiality. Another major stumbling block was mandat-

---

2 It is interesting to observe that about 30 years later 'family violence', especially violence against women, was recognised as a major social issue. See Schneider, 2008.

3 I was a member of the working group that developed the Act.

ing clergy. Ultimately, Roman Catholic priests were exempted because it was believed that mandating them to report abuse that they heard about during confession was an unacceptable intrusion into the Church's affairs.

Ironically, the issue of mandatory reporting returned to the public consciousness 36 years later because of abuse perpetrated by Roman Catholic clergymen, not because of abuse that priests merely learned of during confession. According to a study commissioned by the United States Conference of Catholic Bishops, from 1999-2002, nearly 4,392 priests were thought to have sexually abused some 10,000 children. Through 2006, nearly 5,000 priests were implicated in more than 12,000 credible victim reports, and an additional 3,091 abusive clergy and 4,568 victims were identified from 2004 through 2009. The statistics both for children and clergy are incredible (statistics as cited in Katz, 2007: 310-11).

In addition, the civil law suits against individual clergy and the Church have resulted in staggering costs. By 2006, the Church had spent over $1.38 billion on sexual abuse settlements. Overall, the costs have ranged between two billion to three billion dollars. Perhaps more important than the cost of the abuse to the Church was its attitude. The Church hierarchy, including bishops and cardinals, wronged the victims by choosing to conceal the scandal and protect its reputation (Katz, 2007: 310-11).

Model Act to Free Children for Permanent Placement

Child neglect came into public view in the 1970s because of the high number of children in foster care. During the 1970s, an estimated 500,000 children in the United States were living in foster care, almost a third more than in the 1960s. Policymakers in Washington, D. C. saw a crisis particularly because foster care was costly both to the federal government and the states. This was the impetus for the Model Act to Free Children for Permanent Placement (Howe, 1979).

The aim of the Model Act was to help the states reduce the number of children in foster care by streamlining the judicial procedure for terminating parental rights and freeing children for adoption. To achieve that goal, the Act had to balance the right of parents to rear their children with the right of children to be raised in an environment that advances their best interests. Importantly, because both groups' rights had constitutional dimensions, the balancing process itself had to be fair to parents on the one hand while promoting the child's best interests on the other.

The name of the Act illustrated the policy behind it. Rather than naming the Act an Act to Terminate Parental Rights, the framers wanted to emphasis that the goal was to secure a permanent home for the child. Thus, the framers emphasised placement and not termination. This was based on the latest social science research, which revealed that successful child development required stability and, specifically, continuity of care. It was found that children who were placed in multiple foster homes suffered psychologically and struggled to develop trusting, lasting relationships later in life. Such children suffered intellectually because of the interruption in education associated with every move from one foster environment to another. While the Act did not receive the same acceptance by the states as the Model Mandatory Child Abuse

Reporting Act, it nonetheless served to guide the states in developing their own version of an act that would terminate parental rights and promote the placement of children. In a way, the Model Act to Free Children for Permanent Placement inspired a partnership between the law and social services that remains to this day.

The Model Subsidized Adoption Act

In addition to cumbersome termination of parental rights statutes, financial considerations also impeded the placement of foster children with adults who wished to adopt them. The likely candidates for adoptive parenthood were the foster parents themselves. However, these parents, who received foster care payments while foster children were in their care lost that payment once they adopted their foster child. Subsidised adoption was introduced to remedy this and other situations where finances prevented an otherwise desirable adoption (Katz and Gallagher, 1976).

Subsidised adoption was intended to provide a subsidy to the hard-to-place foster child, either because that child had physical or emotional difficulties which needed attention, was an older child, or was part of a group of siblings that needed to be placed together. The amount of the subsidy was determined by the special needs of the child, not the financial status of the adoptive couple. Today, all states have some sort of subsidised adoption programme (see Katz and Katz, 2012: 77-80), which is funded under the Federal Adoption Assistance and Child Welfare Act of 1980.

The Impact of Social Changes on Family Law

During the 1970s, two state supreme court cases changed family law. Both were based on the recognition of the reality of the time. One was *Posner v. Posner* (233 So.2d 381 (1970)), a 1970 Florida Supreme Court case that validated antenuptial agreements, and the other was the 1976 California Supreme Court case, *Marvin v. Marvin* (557 P.2d 106 (1976)), which validated contract cohabitation.

In *Posner*, Justice Roberts wrote:

> With divorce such a commonplace fact of life, it is fair to assume that many prospective marriage partners whose property and familial situation is such as to generate a valid antenuptial agreement settling their property rights upon the death of either, might want to consider and discuss also – and agree upon, if possible – the disposition of their property and the alimony rights of the wife in the event their marriage, despite their best efforts, should fail. (*Posner v. Posner*, 233 So.2d 381: 384)

Although this reasoning seems self-evident today, it was not so in 1970; by then, only a few cases had upheld prenuptial agreements on 'reasonableness' grounds. What made *Posner* so important was that, before 1970, except in certain cases, couples contemplating marriage could only contract away their inheritance rights, not their marital rights. The permanence of marriage was thought to be such a fundamental value in American life that to recognise formally the possibility of divorce might not only have a negative impact on the provision, but might also make the entire agreement unenforceable.

All that has changed since *Posner* and today antenuptial agreements regulating the allocation of marital property upon divorce or death are generally enforced. One major reason for their use relates to changes in the laws regulating the assignment of property upon divorce. Under the traditional title theory, which held that title to property determined ownership even upon divorce, judicial discretion was limited. However, with the advent of equitable distribution, judicial discretion was only limited by the interpretation of statutory guidelines and thus the outcome of marital property disputes grew more unpredictable. An enforceable antenuptial agreement allowed couples to determine how they wanted to allocate the distribution of their assets upon the termination of their marriage, rather than leaving such an important decision to a judge.

The guiding principle for antenuptial agreements is that they must be substantively and procedurally fair; whether such fairness must exist at the time of the agreement's drafting or the time of divorce depends on the jurisdiction. The Commonwealth of Massachusetts, for example, has adopted 'the second look' approach, which allows the judge to examine the antenuptial agreement and determine whether it is fair at the time of signing and also at the time of divorce (*Osborne v. Osborne*, 428 N.E.2d 810 (1981)). This approach can be criticised as undermining the stability of the antenuptial agreement (see further Katz, 2003: 30-34).

The major issue today, however, is whether antenuptial agreements should be treated like commercial agreements or considered as special contracts with certain limitations because of the relationship of the parties to each other.[4] That relationship of trust is not necessarily present in commercial relationships.[5] Some states regulate prenuptial agreements either judicially or through a statute by requiring, among other things: that they meet the requirements of the Statute of Frauds; that they are entered into no earlier than a certain amount of time before the wedding; that both parties are represented by counsel; and that both parties reveal the approximate value of their estate. These are hardly the requirements of a commercial contract, in which freedom to contract is the core principle. While commercial contracts and antenuptial agreements both require that the process of entering the agreement be free from misrepresentation, fraud and coercion, the idea that the terms must be fair at the time of making is not necessarily a requirement in a commercial contract, which is based on the principle of private autonomy. Adhesion contracts – standard form take-it-or-leave it contracts – are the only other type of contract that may be reviewed for unfairness or disparity of bargaining power.

---

4 In *Simeone v. Simeone*, 581 A.2d 162.165 (1990), the Supreme Court of Pennsylvania stated '[p]renuptial agreements are contracts, and, as such, should be evaluated under the same criteria as are applicable to other types of contracts.'

5 In *Rosenberg v. Lipnick*, 389 N.E.2d 385 (Mass. 1979), the Supreme Judicial Court of Massachusetts discussed how parties to an antenuptial agreement do not deal at arms length, but rather in an atmosphere of mutual trust.

One of the major issues in antenuptial agreement enforcement is whether a woman can contract away all her property rights without any consideration beyond the marriage itself. This has been a controversial issue in which some courts have stuck to the conventional approach that if the woman is a competent adult, has been represented by counsel, and is aware of her future husband's assets, she should be able to contract away her economic rights, including alimony. Others have said that a woman's waiving all her rights is simply against public policy because doing so risks rendering her a 'public charge', who is dependent on welfare.

Contract Cohabitation

In 1976, the California Supreme Court decided *Marvin v. Marvin* (557 P.2d 106 (1976)), the famous case of the actor Lee Marvin and his live-in girlfriend, which held that Michelle Marvin might have an action against her lover if she could prove a cohabitation contract. Two footnotes in the opinion provided alternative remedies to contract if certain facts could be established. After the case went up and down the California courts, Michelle ultimately ended up with nothing.

I raise *Marvin* to illustrate that the California Supreme Court recognised social mores when the opinion was written:

> [W]e believe that the prevalence of nonmarital relationships in modern society and the social acceptance of them, marks this as a time when our courts should by no means apply the doctrine of the unlawfulness of the so-called meretricious relationship to the instant case. As we have explained, the non-enforceability of agreements expressly providing for meretricious conduct rested upon the fact that such conduct, as the word suggests, pertained to and encompassed prostitution. To equate the nonmarital relationship of today to such a subject matter is to do violence to an accepted and wholly different practice. (557 P.2d 106: 122)

The court went on to say:

> We are aware that many young couples live together without the solemnization of marriage, in order to make sure that they can successfully later undertake marriage. This trial period, preliminary to marriage, serves as some assurance that the marriage will not subsequently end in dissolution to the harm of both parties. We are aware, as we have stated of the pervasiveness of nonmarital relationships in other situations. (557 P.2d 106: 122)

Marvin broke new ground by holding that individuals may enter into a contract concerning their private relationship or have a contract judicially superimposed on them whether both intended it or not. The decision was not immediately accepted nationally. Appellate courts in at least 26 states and the District of Columbia have approved of the relational contract claims between cohabitants, with five states – Illinois,

Mississippi, Georgia, Louisiana and Michigan – disapproving of all forms of relief for a disappointed cohabitant.

What seems to me to be important about *Marvin* is that the supreme court of the most populous state in the United States recognised that there are alternative forms of family relationships. A couple need not go through a formal ceremony either in a city hall or in a house of worship or live together with the intent to be married as is the case in common law marriage to be legally recognised as a couple. However, it is important to emphasise that contract cohabitation, whether expressed through writing or conduct, is not considered legal marriage unless the couple themselves have defined their relationship, particularly with regard to financial obligations. For example, in the Supreme Judicial Court of Massachusetts case of *Wilcox v. Trautz* (693 N.E.2d 141 (1998)) Justice Greaney emphasised that contract cohabitation is different from marriage, and that marriage remedies do not apply upon the termination of the cohabitation. He wrote:

> Social mores regarding cohabitation between unmarried parties have changed dramatically in recent years and living arrangements that were once criticized are now relatively common and accepted. 'As an alternative to marriage, more couples are choosing to cohabit. These relationships may be of extended duration, sometimes lasting as long as many marriages. In many respects, these cohabitation relationships may be quite similar to conventional marriages; they may involve commingling of funds, joint purchases of property, and even the birth of children' … With the prevalence of nonmarital relationships today, a considerable number of persons live together without benefit of the rules of law that govern property, financial, and other matters in a marital relationship. Thus, we do well to recognize the benefits to be gained by encouraging unmarried cohabitants to enter into written agreements respecting these matters, as the consequences for each partner may be considerable on termination of the relationship or, in particular, in the event of the death of one of the partners. 'In recent years, increased attention has focused on the advisability of unmarried couples entering into cohabitation contracts in which they … detail the financial consequences of dissolution.' … This may be especially important in a jurisdiction like Massachusetts where we do not recognize common law marriage, do not extend to unmarried couples the rights possessed by married couples who divorce, and reject equitable remedies that might have the effect of dividing property between unmarried parties.' (693 N.E.2d 141: 144-145)

To me, *Marvin* made domestic partnerships and civil unions possible.

The California court took nonmarital partners living in an intimate relationship out of the closet, and with one opinion made them legal. Using 'rights' talk, the court gave each partner rights to pursue a remedy whether in law or in equity.

Over 30 years of experience with contract cohabitation has provided social science researchers with enough material to make comparisons with marriage. According to Professor Garrison's survey of that research, 'married individuals typically live longer, happier, and healthier lives than the unmarried. Married men and women do better economically than their unmarried counterparts; they have a higher savings rate and thus accrue greater wealth than the unmarried.' (Garrison, 2008: 326)

Professor Garrison reported that cohabitants generally come from a different social class than married people. They tend to be younger and poorer than married couples, less educated than married couples, less likely to support their partners and, compared with married couples, more likely to value independence. Reading Professor Garrison's studies, one comes away convinced that marriage, not contract cohabitation, is the preferred status if one values a monogamous life-long relationship based on love, loyalty and mutual dependence.

During the late 1960s and 1970s, the United States Supreme Court decided three cases that had a profound impact on Family Law. Interestingly, all three cases involved a challenge to established law. In *Stanley v. Illinois* (405 U.S. 645 (1972)), the Court held that a father of illegitimate children whom he had raised with the children's mother should be given notice and an opportunity to be heard in a proceeding which would determine the custody of his children. The Court did not limit its requirement to dependency hearings and in a now famous footnote extended that right to adoption proceedings (405 U.S. 645: 657; see further Katz, xxxx:153-157).[6] Thus, in one line the Court brought the father of illegitimate children into the adoption process, where he had previously been a non-factor. In *Orr v. Orr* (440 U.S. 268 (1979)),the Court held that both husbands and wives were entitled to alimony upon divorce, and that to exclude husbands from obtaining alimony violated their equal protection rights. Thus, the decision in *Orr v. Orr* was another step toward equality in marriage. In *Loving v. Virginia* (388 U.S. 1 (1967)), the Court struck down a state anti-miscegenation statute and declared that marriage was a fundamental right protected by the US Constitution.

It is my belief that both *Orr v. Orr* and *Loving v. Virginia* paved the way for *Goodridge v. Department of Public Health* (798 NE2d 941 (2003)) decided by the Massachusetts Supreme Judicial Court in 2003. *Orr*'s impact may not be as obvious as *Loving*'s, but its shift away from antiquated gender roles removed gender as an important characteristic of marriage. *Orr* implicitly asked: if two people are equal in a relationship, what difference does gender make? The relevance of *Loving* is more readily apparent. If, as the United States Supreme Court held, marriage is a fundamental right, then a state must show extraordinary reasons for restricting it. In *Goodridge*, the Massachusetts court found that the state failed to make such a showing.

The 60 years in which Michael Freeman played a dominant role in shaping family law in Great Britain marked a period of transformation in which, in the United

---

6 Footnote 9 reads:

> We note in passing that the incremental cost of offering unwed fathers an opportunity for individualized hearings on fitness appears to be minimal. If unwed fathers, in the main, do not care about the disposition of their children, they will not appear to demand hearings. If they do care, under the scheme here held invalid, Illinois would admittedly at some later time have to afford them a properly focused hearing in a custody or *adoption proceeding.* (emphasis added). *Ibid.* at 657.

The *Stanley* case and its impact on adoption laws in the United States is fully discussed in Katz, 2003: 153-57.

States, the laws regulating family life began reflecting reality, rather than trying to mould families into outmoded archetypes. Interestingly, John Eekelaar has expressed the transformation over that period in similar terms. Comparing family law cases reported in 2011 with those reported in 1959-60, he concludes that the earlier law was based on a constructed vision of the world, one in which people lived, or were expected to live, according to the neat moral and behavioural categories imagined by the law. Essentially, the law tried to maintain, or even create, a type of social structure, and was designed to reward conformity with that structure, and penalise aberrations from it. Put another way, upholding that actual, or imagined, structure took precedence over the well-being of individuals (Eekelaar, 2013).

Eekelaar particularly noted the modern prevalence of 'public law' cases (largely concerning the powers of welfare authorities regarding vulnerable children) which were absent from the earlier cases, indicating not only a growing state involvement in child welfare, but also greater legal control over the exercise of state powers, similar to the developments in the United States described earlier. Likewise, he also noted the growing influence of social science and empirical evidence. Eekelaar also notes the changed legal response to 'illegitimacy', so that the reality of personal relationships became more important than their compliance with social convention. In both countries, however, the legal response to unmarried cohabitation has been to rely on traditional legal devices, like contract and trusts. The English Law Commission has proposed going further (Law Commission, 2007), but Eekelaar suggests there is 'little appetite for reform'. The United States has, however, gone much further in permitting the 'equitable' disposal of property and financial issues upon divorce to be regulated by antenuptial contracts. This was given a boost in England and Wales by a Supreme Court decision in 2010 (*Radmacher* v. *Granatino* [2010] UKSC 42; see also Law Commission, 2011). Finally, the issue of permitting same-sex couples to enter a legally recognised union came to a head in both countries around the same time, though in the UK this has been achieved in a two-step process. First, same-sex couples were permitted to enter civil partnerships, which were legally almost identical to marriage (Civil Partnership Act 2004). Later, Parliament enacted the Marriage (Same Sex Couples) Act 2013 allowing same-sex couples to marry in England and Wales (Eekelaar, 2014).

References

Children's Bureau, U.S. Department of Health, Education, & Welfare, *The Abused Child-Principles and Suggested Language for the Reporting of the Physically Abused Child* (1963).

Eekelaar, J., "Then and Now – Family Law's Direction of Travel", *Journal of Social Welfare and Family Law* 2013 35(4), 415-425.

Eekelaar, J., "Perceptions of Equality: The Road to Same-sex Marriage in England", *International Journal of Law, Policy and the Family* 2014 28(1), 1-25.

Freeman, M., "Cultural Pluralism and the Rights of the Child" in J. Eekelaar and T. Nhlapo (eds), *The Changing Family: Family Forms and Family Norms* (Oxford: Hart, 1998).

Garrison, M., "Nonmarital Cohabitation: Social Revolution and Legal Regulation", *Family Law Quarterly* 2008 42(3), 309-331.

Goldstein, J., Solnit, A. and Freud, A., *Beyond the Best Interests of the Child* (New York: Free Press, 1973).

Greven, P., *Spare the Child: The Religious Roots of Punishment and the Psychological Impact of Physical Abuse* (New York: Alfred A. Knopf, 1990).

Guggenheim, M., *What's Wrong with Children's Rights* (Cambridge, MA: Harvard University Press, 2005).

Howe, R. A. W., "Development of a Model Act to Free Children for Permanent Placement: A Case Study in Law and Social Planning", *Family Law Quarterly* 1979 13(3), 257-344.

Katz, S. N., *When Parents Fail* (Boston: Beacon Press, 1971).

Katz, S. N., *Family Law in America* (Oxford: Oxford University Press, 2003).

Katz, S. N., "Protecting Children Through State and Federal Laws" in B. Atkin (ed), *The International Survey of Family Law* (Bristol: Jordan, 2007).

Katz, S. N., "Five Decades of Family Law", *Family Law Quarterly* 2008 42(3), 295-307.

Katz, S. N. and Gallagher, U. M., "Subsidized Adoption in America", *Family Law Quarterly* 1976 11(1), 1-54.

Katz, S. N. and Katz, D. R., *Adoption Laws in a Nutshell* (St. Paul, MN: West, 2012).

Kempe, C. H., Silverman, F. N., Steele, F. N., Droegemueller, W. and Silver, H. K., "The Battered Child Syndrome", *Journal of the American Medical Association* 1962 18(1), 17-24.

Law Commission, *Cohabitation: The Financial Consequences of Relationship Breakdown* Law Com No. 307 (London: TSO, 2007).

Law Commission, *Marital Property Agreements* CP 198 (London: TSO, 2011).

Myers, J. E. B., *Child Protection in America: Past, Present, and Future* (Oxford: Oxford University Press, 2006).

Schneider, E. M., "Domestic Violence Law Reform in the Twenty-First Century: Looking Back and Forward", *Family Law Quarterly* 2008 42(3), 353-363.

The Contribution of the South African Constitutional Court to the Jurisprudential Development of the Best Interests of the Child

Meda Couzens*
School of Law, University of KwaZulu-Natal, Durban, South Africa

This contribution contains an analysis of the 'best interests of the child' jurisprudence of the Constitutional Court of South Africa (the Court), in as far as this jurisprudence reflects the position of the Court that the constitutional provision of the best interests of the child recognises a self-standing right. The jurisprudence of the Court is not analysed from a critical perspective, but rather with a view of establishing what is, in the Court's view, the independent legal content of the constitutional provision of the best interests of the child. A brief comparative analysis will show that the Court is not alone in viewing the best interests of the child as creating a self-standing right, and shares this position with the Committee on the Rights of the Child and other national courts. The analysis of the Court's relevant case-law shows that certain entitlements and obligations can be sourced to the application by the Court of the constitutional provision of the best interests of the child. In this manner, the Court created various positive obligations for the state, which, arguably, could not have been created by relying exclusively on other constitutional rights which the children enjoy. While more conceptual clarity is needed in terms of how the best interests of the child operates as a self-standing right, the recognition of the best interests of the child as a self-standing right indicates nonetheless the position of the Court that children need child-focused legal institutions to respond to their needs as legal subjects.

1. Introduction

There is an abundant literature on the rights of children in South Africa and especially in relation to the consequences of their constitutionalisation in section 28 of the Constitution of the Republic of South Africa 1996 (the Constitution) (Sloth-

* I would like to thank Professor Michael Freeman for giving me the opportunity to contribute to this conference. Thank you for your confidence in me, Professor Freeman. Mr David Barraclough has assisted with the editing of this contribution.

A. Diduck, N. Peleg, H. Reece (eds.), Law in Society: Reflections on Children, Family, Culture and Philosophy
 ISBN 978-90-04-26148-8. pp. 521-549.

Nielsen, 1996; Bonthuys, 2005; Proudlock, 2009; Skelton, 2009).[1] South Africa has a supreme Constitution (section 2 of the Constitution) and the Bill of Rights (Chapter 2 of the Constitution), of which section 28 is a part, 'applies to all law, and binds the legislature, the executive, the judiciary and all organs of the state' (section 8(1) of the Constitution). An important consequence of this heightened protection granted to the rights of children is that the courts, as the guardians of constitutional supremacy, may invalidate law or conduct (administrative, executive or judicial) which is inconsistent with section 28 of the Constitution. In terms of the substance of section 28, sub-section (3) defines a child as a person under the age of 18, and sub-section (1) provides for child-specific constitutional rights, such as the right to a name and nationality; the right to family and parental care, or to appropriate care when removed from the family environment; the right to basic necessities; the right to be protected against abuse and exploitation in various settings; rights when coming in conflict with the law; the right to legal representation in certain cases; and rights during armed conflict. Section 28(2), which is the focus of this contribution, reads: 'A child's best interests are of paramount importance in every matter concerning the child.'

This contribution has a narrow scope, and explores the constitutional jurisprudence in as far as it refers to the constitutional provision of the best interests of the child as a self-standing right.

Section 28(2) is widely applied by the Constitutional Court (hereafter 'the Court'), and its jurisprudence indicates that it has three functions: being a tool for the interpretation of section 28(1) of the Constitution, when sections 28(1) and 28(2) are read together; a tool for establishing the scope of other constitutional rights and their potential limitations; and a self-standing right (Friedman et al, 2009). Section 28(2) creates 'a right for children *as children* – because they are especially vulnerable and because we think they are precious and because their interests have all too often given way to the interests of others' (Friedman et al, 2009: 47-45). Although section 28(2) 're-iterates the common-law standard of the best interests of the child', a distinction is made between the common-law standard, which is applied by high courts as the upper guardians of children, and the constitutional standard of the best interests of the child, which applies to '"every matter concerning the child"' (Friedman et al, 2009: 47-40).

An unusual aspect of the Court's jurisprudence is that of approaching section 28(2) as containing a self-standing right, although, unlike section 28(1), section 28(2) does not include the term 'right' (Visser, 2007). Whether such an approach is justifiable in the light of the Court's own lack of clarity on the issue, has been queried (Bonthuys, 2006). Bonthuys (2006) argues that despite rhetorically referring to section 28(2) as a right, the Constitutional Court does not treat it as such. For example, it does not analyse its content, as it does with other rights and seldom uses the limitation inquiry

1 Notably, the constitutional rights of children are not limited to the child-specific rights in section 28, although certain age-related restrictions apply regarding certain rights. For example, the right to vote and to be elected is reserved for adults (section 19(3) of the Constitution).

in relation to section 28(2). Bonthuys also points out that in most cases in which the Court referred to section 28(2) as a self-standing right, it was not necessary for it to do so, since the matter fell within the ambit of other constitutional rights (Bonthuys, 2006; also Malherbe, 2008). For other authors, however, this is not significant, and it 'does not mean that the principle is superfluous or useless', because 'the principle serves as a check, even a safeguard, on official action…' (Malherbe, 2008: 285). Generally, the approach of the Constitutional Court has been embraced as a positive development (Skelton, 2008; Gallinetti, 2010).

Although many of the intricacies of approaching section 28(2) as an independent right have not yet been adequately explored,[2] this contribution does not approach this issue from a critical perspective. Instead, the purpose of this contribution is to identify the potentially independent and enforceable legal content of section 28(2), as reflected in the jurisprudence of the Court. I will depart from two assumptions, which make it unnecessary to explore the justification of approaching section 28(2) as a self-standing right. First, I will assume that the Court, which is well versed in the application of human rights law, was correct to decide that it was necessary to approach section 28(2) as an independent right because the more specific rights of children were not able, by themselves, to grant sufficient protection to children (for a similar view, see Visser, 2007: 459). Secondly, I will assume that with proclaiming section 28(2) as an independent right, the Court intended to assign it a legal content, which is to be reflected in its judgments.

The ultimate purpose of this contribution is to show that section 28(2) can be regarded as a source of legal entitlements and obligations, which give contour to an independent legal content. I will try to show that section 28(2) has been relied on to develop certain child-focused legal obligations – especially incumbent on the state – which, arguably, could not have been created otherwise. These obligations respond to the special position of children as rights holders, and allow courts to treat children as children in law.

Whilst the analysis focuses on the South African jurisprudence, it also has relevance for children's rights advocates elsewhere. There are significant similarities between section 28(2) of the Constitution and article 3(1) of the UN Convention on the Rights of the Child (the CRC).[3] The versatility of article 3(1) of the CRC has influenced the South African Constitutional Court in terms of recognising full potential to section 28(2), in that the Court applied this section beyond the confines of branches of law traditionally associated with children. Furthermore, in its General comment No. 14 (2013) on the right of the child to have his or her best interests taken as a primary

2 Does s. 28(2) meet the criteria to be considered an independent right? What is the difference between the best interests when applied as a principle and as a self-standing right? When should s. 28(2) be used as an independent right, and when should it be used in conjunction with other constitutional rights?

3 Article 3(1) of the CRC reads: 'In all actions concerning children, whether undertaken by public or private social welfare institutions, courts of law, administrative authorities or legislative bodies, the best interests of the child shall be a primary consideration'.

consideration (art. 3, para. 1) (the General Comment no. 14), the Committee on the Rights of the Child (CRC Committee) seems to take the same approach as the South African Constitutional Court, endorsing the status of the best interests of the child as a self-standing right. It might be useful for courts in other jurisdictions to learn about the benefits (and the traps) of approaching article 3(1) of the CRC (or corresponding national provisions), as containing a self-standing right, as recently advocated by the CRC Committee.

This contribution is structured as follows: Part two is a brief review of comparative and international sources which engage with the legal status of the best interests of the child – primarily article 3(1) of the CRC and its normative value. Part three reviews selected decisions of the South African Constitutional Court which, in the view of the author, may give contour to the independent legal content of section 28(2). In part four, the entitlements and obligations arising from the application of section 28(2) by the Court, are reviewed, and then further analysed in part five. In conclusion, I reflect on the factors which facilitated the approach of the Court, the potential and dangers of this approach, and the comparative value of its jurisprudence.

2. International and Comparative Perspective

As mentioned above, approaching the best interests of the child as a self-standing right has occurred infrequently.[4] One concern seems to be that the best interests of the child are better used as a tool to guide the discretion of the decision-makers, rather than being approached as an individual right whose application leads to a predictable outcome (Van Heerden, 1999; Cockrell, 2000). Internationally, the early literature on article 3(1) of the CRC referred to it as a guiding principle, rather than a right. Van Bueren (1998: 46) explicitly states that article 3(1) 'does not create rights or duties, it is only a principle of interpretation which has to be considered in all actions concerning children' (1998: 46). Alston concurs, when he writes that: 'Article 3(1) does not seek to impose specific duties, but rather to state a general principle that should inform decision-making in relation to "all actions concerning children"' (Alston, 1994: 15). Freeman also points out that article 3(1) 'enunciates the best interests principle' (2007: 25), but it does so in 'an unadorned normative statement' (2007: 31). The CRC Committee has, until recently, approached the best interests of the child as a general principle of the CRC and has not referred to article 3(1) as creating an independent right. However, in various concluding observations, instead of invoking more specific articles of the CRC, the Committee remarked that state laws or policies have disregarded article 3(1) (Freeman, 2007: 32).[5]

4 Some authors have suggested that art. 3 of the CRC can be construed as creating a right for the child to have his/her welfare protected. See Schuz (2002).

5 See, for example: *Concluding Observations of the Committee on the Rights of the Child, Bulgaria*, CRC/C/15/Add.66 (1997), para. 15, expressing concern that the legislation on adoptions is not compatible with art. 3; *Concluding Observations of the Committee on the Rights of the Child Norway*, CRC/C/15/Add.23 (1994), para. 12, concluding that the absence

In what might have been a preview to the Committee's reasoning in General Comment No. 14, Zermatten indicates that the expression, 'the best interests of the child shall be a primary consideration', contains three important elements (Zermatten, 2010). First, it contains a rule of procedure, which requires that the decision-maker assesses the impact of a decision on a child or children and that such impact is given due importance. Second, it is the foundation of a substantive right, which guarantees that individual children or children generally have their best interests assessed. Thirdly, it is an 'interpretive legal principle, developed to limit the unchecked power over children by adults' (Zermatten, 2010: 485).

In its General Comment No. 14, the Committee unequivocally states that article 3(1) contains a right, which the Committee phrases as being 'the right to have his or her best interests assessed and taken into account as a primary consideration in all actions or decisions that concern him or her, both in the public and private sphere' (General Comment No. 14, paras. 1 and 6). In addition to being a right in itself, in the interpretation of the Committee, the best interests of the child is also an interpretive legal principle, and a rule of procedure.[6] According to the Committee (General Comment No. 14, para. 14), article 3(1) creates the following obligations for the states:

(a) The obligation to ensure that the child's best interests are appropriately integrated and consistently applied in every action taken by a public institution, especially in all implementation measures, administrative and judicial proceedings which directly or indirectly impact on children;
(b) The obligation to ensure that all judicial and administrative decisions as well as policies and legislation concerning children demonstrate that the child's best interests have been a primary consideration. This includes describing how the best interests have been examined and assessed, and what weight has been ascribed to them in the decision.
(c) The obligation to ensure that the interests of the child have been assessed and taken as a primary consideration in decisions and actions taken by the private sector,

---

of a *de jure* recognition of the right to health and education of children whose asylum requests had been rejected, is contrary to arts. 2 and 3 (same position in *Concluding observations of the Committee on the Rights of the Child: Denmark*, CRC/C/15/Add.33 (1995) para. 14); *Concluding observations of the Committee on the Rights of the Child: Paraguay* CRC/C/15/Add.27 (1994), para. 7, expressing the opinion that legislation concerning age vis-à-vis military service, and non-validity of child testimony in sexual abuse cases, raises issues regarding its compatibility with the best interests of the child as being a primary consideration in all matters concerning children.

6 Paragraph 6 (b) of the General Comment No. 14 defines the value of the best interests as an interpretive principle, in that, 'If a legal provision is open to more than one interpretation, the interpretation which most effectively serves the child's best interests should be chosen.' As a rule of procedure, art. 3(1) requires an evaluation of the possible impact of a decision on a child/children; an indication of how the best interests of the child were considered in the decision-making, what criteria have been used, and the weight given to the interests of children against other considerations (para. 6(c)).

including those providing services, or any other private entity or institution making decisions that concern or impact on a child.

From a comparative perspective, the French and the Norwegian jurisprudence warrant attention. In France,[7] up until May 2005, the Court of Cassation (the apex of judicial jurisdiction) considered that the CRC created obligations for the state, and not individual rights[8] that could be applied directly by the courts (case no. 91-11.310 of 19 March 1993 and case no. 91- 18735 of 15 July 1993). (For criticism, see Monéger, 2006; Bonnet, 2010; and Bureau (2005). Strikingly, when the Court of Cassation decided to break with this approach, it did so by recognising the direct effect of a very unlikely candidate – article 3(1) of the CRC (case no. 02-20.613 of 18 May 2005; case no. 02-16336 18 May 2005) (See discussion of these cases, Ancel, 2011; Bureau, 2005; and Gouttenoire, 2012). In the decision which turned the tide, the Court decided that article 3(1) of the CRC could serve as the legal grounds for the decision of a lower court.[9] This is a subtle acknowledgment of the past reluctance to engage with article 3(1) on the basis that it constitutes an enforceable legal standard and, at the same time, is an indication that the enforceability of the above article is now beyond contestation. Currently, the two supreme jurisdictions apply article 3(1) of the CRC directly, albeit without qualifying it as a principle or as a right.

In Norway,[10] a recent decision of the Supreme Court raised questions about the normative value of article 3(1) of the CRC (*A, B, C and the Norwegian Association for Asylum Seekers (NOAS) (third party intervener) v. The State, represented by the Immigration Appeals Board* HR-2012-02399-P (case no. 2012/1042)). The case concerned a challenge to a decision by Norwegian authorities to expel a family of illegal immigrants to their country of origin. The applicants requested, *inter alia*, a declaratory judgment to the effect that the removal of the child concerned from Norway was in conflict with arti-

7 France is a monist state, whose Constitution allows the courts to rely directly on ratified international treaties, and gives them priority over ordinary national laws. According to art. 55 of the 1958 Constitution, '[t]reaties or agreements duly ratified or approved shall, upon publication, prevail over Acts of Parliament, subject, with respect to each agreement or treaty, to its application by the other party.' The effect of such direct application is a finding that art. 3 has been breached, followed by the granting of a remedy (i.e. setting aside of a lower court judgment, and annulation of an administrative decision or administrative act).

8 Conseil d'Etat (the apex of the administrative jurisdiction) took a different position. In 1995 it decided that art. 16 of the CRC is directly applicable by the administrative courts (case no. 141083 of 10 March 1995). In 1997 it decided that art. 3(1) has direct effect and can be directly relied on to invalidate individual administrative decisions (case no. 161364 of 22 September 1997).

9 In the case no. 02-16336 18 May 2005, the Court of Cassation acquiesced to the fact that a lower court which relied on article 3(1) of the CRC 'has justified its decision *in law*' (my translation; my emphasis).

10 Norway is a dualist state which incorporated the CRC. The Human Rights Act of 1999 was amended in 2003 (Act 86 of 1 August 2003), in order to add the CRC to the international human rights treaties which are recognised with the status of national law.

cle 3 of the CRC (paras. 20 and 26). The state counter-argued that no declaratory judgment can be given for breach of article 3 of the CRC, because this article constitutes 'only a guideline for the exercise of discretion and does not establish individual rights' (para. 34). Writing for the majority, Justice Matningsdal recalled the conditions set in the national law for the declaratory judgment sought by the applicants – that a '"legal claim" must exist', and that there must be 'a "genuine need" to have the claim decided"' (para. 89). For Justice Matningsdal, article 3 cannot give rise to a legal claim, since the best interests of the child will not necessarily be the decisive element in the decision-making process (para. 100). The position of the majority can thus be understood as being a rejection of the idea that article 3(1) can create individual rights.[11] The dissenting judges, however, found that article 3(1) of the CRC imposes obligations on the state towards the individual child, and that it is a self-executing norm which can be applied directly by the courts. For Justice Matheson (with two judges concurring), article 3(1) gives rise to certain legal claims, such as 'a claim in law for such an assessment in actual fact being conducted, as well as the norm of the Convention being respected in the actual evaluation' (para. 141). Justice Bårdsen (with four other judges concurring) took a slightly different view – pointing out that the normative force of a legal provision is not diminished by its vague or general formulation: 'the actual linguistic formulation naturally does not deprive the norm established on the basis of the wording of its nature of being legally binding for the State' (para. 118).

The brief review above shows that, like the South African Constitutional Court, the CRC Committee and courts in other jurisdictions engage with the best interests of the child concept on the basis that this may/could constitute an independent source of rights and obligations, which can be enforced by courts. While these developments do not *per se* validate the position of the South African Constitutional Court, they show an emerging engagement with article 3(1) of the CRC on the basis that it has an independent normative force. The jurisprudence presented below should thus be seen as part of an on-going search for maximising the impact of the best interests of the child as a legal standard.

3. Review of the Constitutional Court's Jurisprudence

A brief review of selected Constitutional Court cases relevant to this contribution is now presented. In some cases, the Court has applied section 28(2) independently, while in others, this section was applied in conjunction with other constitutional provisions, especially those in section 28(1). The latter cases are discussed, because, in the view of this author, certain entitlements and obligations can be linked to the application of section 28(2) by the Court, in the respective case.

The number of cases in which the best interests has been applied as a self-standing provision is relatively small, and the Court itself is not consistent with the terminol-

11 The majority makes the point, however, that 'breaches of this Convention can be examined by a review of the validity of the relevant decision' (para. 93).

ogy it uses to refer to section 28(2).[12] The trend started in *Minister for Welfare and Population Development v. Fitzpatrick and Others* 2000 (7) BCLR713 (CC) (*Fitzpatrick*), where the Court stated (para. 17):

> Section 28(1) is not exhaustive of children's rights. Section 28(2) requires that a child's best interests have paramount importance in every matter concerning the child. The plain meaning of the words clearly indicates that the reach of section 28(2) cannot be limited to the rights enumerated in section 28(1) and section 28(2) must be interpreted to extend beyond those provisions. It creates a right that is independent of those specified in section 28(1).

The Court found that this position was not incompatible with its earlier decision in *Fraser v. Naude and Others* 1998 (11) BCLR1357 (CC) (*Fraser*), where the Court refused leave to appeal against an adoption order in a protracted litigation, because '[c]ontinued uncertainty as to the status and placing of the child cannot be in the interests of the child' (para. 9). The Court's position in *Fitzpatrick* was a strong rebuttal of the position expressed by the High Court in *Jooste v. Botha* 2000(2) SA 199 (T), where it was held that section 28(2) 'is intended as a general guideline' (210D). The Constitutional Court did not define the content of this independent right, however, and approved of the fact that the standard 'has never been given exhaustive content' because '[i]t is necessary that the standard should be flexible as individual circumstances will determine which factors secure the best interests of a particular child' (para. 18, fn omitted). The court found that the statutory provisions prohibiting intercountry adoptions were 'too blunt and all-embracing', and to this extent they did not 'give paramountcy to the best interests of children and are inconsistent with the provisions of section 28(2) of the Constitution and hence invalid' (para. 20). In an *obiter* statement, the Court declared itself prepared to apply the constitutional limitation clause[13] to section 28(2) had such argument been made by the parties (para. 20). Despite its reluctance to assign a legal content to section 28(2), two aspects of the judgment are relevant for defining its normative value: that a law affecting children must not create obstacles to making decisions in the best interests of individual children, and that section 28(2) – in its newly-declared capacity as an independent right – is capable of being limited under section 36 of the Constitution.

Perhaps encouraged by what was said in *Fitzpatrick*, up until *S v. M (Centre for Child Law as Amicus Curiae)* 2008 (3) SA 232 (CC) (*S v M*) – which is discussed further below

12 In *Fitzpatrick* (see below), after declaring s. 28(2) an independent right in para. 17, in para. 18 the Court referred to the best interests as being 'a standard'.

13 Section 36(1) reads: 'The rights in the Bill of Rights may be limited only in terms of law of general application to the extent that the limitation is reasonable and justifiable in an open and democratic society based on human dignity, equality and freedom, taking into account all relevant factors, including (a) the nature of the right; (b) the importance of the purpose of the limitation; (c) the nature and extent of the limitation; (d) the relation between the limitation and its purpose; and (e) less restrictive means to achieve the purpose'.

– the Court made little deliberate effort to establish the legal content of section 28(2). The Court avoided spelling out general legal obligations of sufficient abstraction, which are capable of being separated from the context in which they were formulated. This, however, does not mean that the jurisprudence on the best interests of the child did not evolve, or that the legal potential of section 28(2) remained unutilised. A few aspects were developed. Section 28(2) continued to be used independently as a benchmark to assess the constitutionality of legislation and findings of incompatibility resulted in the invalidation of the offending legal provisions. In *Du Toit and Another v. Minister of Welfare and Population Development and Others* (*Lesbian and Gay Equality Project as Amicus Curiae*) 2003 (2) SA 198 (CC) (*Du Toit*), for example, the two applicants, who were living in a permanent same-sex relationship, challenged the constitutionality of the legislation which prohibited them from jointly adopting two children. The Court decided that '[e]xcluding partners in same sex life partnerships from adopting children jointly where they would otherwise be suitable to do so [is] in conflict with the principle enshrined in s 28(2) of the Constitution' (para. 22), because it 'defeats the very essence and social purpose of adoption which is to provide the stability, commitment, affection and support important to a child's development, which can be offered by suitably qualified persons' (para. 21). Thus, the law which deprived children 'of the possibility of a loving and stable family life as required by s 28(1)(*b*) of the Constitution' (para. 22), failed to give paramountcy to the best interests of the children and was in conflict with section 28(2).[14]

The Court then started using section 28(2) in developing child-centred, effective, judicial remedies. In *Bannatyne v. Bannatyne* 2003 2 SA 363 (CC) (*Bannatyne*), the failure of the Supreme Court of Appeal (SCA) to take into consideration that the legislative remedies provided for in the maintenance legislation, were not effective remedies in the case at hand, meant that the court did not give paramount consideration to the best interests of children. The SCA should have considered other available legal remedies to ensure an effective protection of the rights of children.[15] Section 28(2) obliges the courts to assess the effectiveness of statutory remedies and if such are found to be ineffective, to use alternative remedies provided in the law, or even create

14 The Court also found that the statutory provisions were contrary to the applicants' s. 9(3) (equality) and s. 10 (dignity) rights (paras. 23-29).

15 In the view of the SCA, 'the applicant had not pursued her remedies under the Act "fully and diligently"' (para. 18). Acknowledging that the legislature has created the legal infrastructure for protecting the rights of children to maintenance, by drafting the Maintenance Act of 1998 (para. 25), 'despite the good intentions of this comprehensive legal framework specifically created for the recovery of maintenance, there is evidence of logistical difficulties in the maintenance courts that result in the system not functioning effectively' (para. 26). The practical challenges experienced by children and their mothers in recovering maintenance, showed that the legal remedies provided for by the Maintenance Act were not always effective, and '[w]here legislative remedies specifically designed to vindicate children's rights as efficiently and cost-effectively as possible fail to achieve that purpose, they do not provide effective relief' (para. 31).

new remedies.[16] In *Sonderup v. Tondelli and Another* 2001 (1) SA 1171 (CC) (*Sonderup*) – a case on international child abduction – the Court, relying on section 38 (the right to an appropriate remedy) read with section 28(2), included child-centred requirements in its order of immediate return of the child to her country of habitual residence (para. 51). These conditions were aimed at safeguarding the child's interests and attenuating the limitations to the child's short-term interests arising from the order of immediate return.[17]

The Court then seized the opportunity offered by the *obiter* statement in *Fitzpatrick* (para. 20), and started exploring the application of the limitation clause to section 28(2). In *Sonderup* the applicant argued that the statute which required the courts to authorise the immediate return of a child to the country wherefrom he/she was abducted by one parent,[18] obliged the courts to act in a manner which did not recognise the paramountcy of the best interests of children (para. 26). The Court assessed the impugned statute against section 28(2) and conceded that the manner in which it regulated the application of the best interests of the child to jurisdictional proceedings, might make the statute 'inconsistent with the provisions of s 28(2) of the Constitution which provide an expansive guarantee that a child's best interests are paramount in every matter concerning the child' (para. 29). However, the limitations to the application of the best interests of the child in jurisdictional matters, were justified under section 36 of the Constitution (para. 29). As indicated above, the Court 'compensated' for the limitations imposed to the short-term best interests by attaching certain conditions to the order of return. In *Du Toit*, the Court found no constitutional justification for the limitations imposed to section 28(2) by legislation which did not allow same-sex partners, in a permanent relationship, jointly to adopt children (paras. 31, 37). In *De Reuck v. Director of Public Prosecutions* (*Witwatersrand Local Division*) *and Others* 2003 (12) BCLR 1333 (CC) (*De Reuck*), the court dealt with

---

16 Paragraphs 19 and 20 suggest that the courts may design new remedies to suit the needs of children. In *Bannatyne,* a new remedy was not necessary, because a common law remedy was available.

17 For example, the Court made the child's return to Canada conditional on the father obtaining a court order from the Canadian courts that criminal procedures against the mother would be dropped (para. 52), and that the child would remain in the interim custody of the mother (para. 53). Furthermore, the Court ordered the father to arrange accommodation for the mother and the child, to pay maintenance for the child, and school expenses, and to provide a roadworthy vehicle for the mother to use in Canada. The approach of the Court is a precursor to *S v. M* (below), where it required that if an inevitable interference by the state in the relationship between children and parents occurs, the courts must take reasonable steps to mitigate the impact of the interference. Although in *Sonderup* the Court's interference did not result in a separation of a child from a parent, certain potentially negative consequences arose from the intervention of the state (the order of immediate return). To pre-empt these, the Court crafted a remedy which sought to limit the impact of the order on the child.

18 The Hague Convention on the Civil Aspects of International Child Abduction Act 1996, which incorporated at the time the Hague Convention on the Civil Aspects of International Child Abduction.

a constitutional challenge against legislation which prohibited the possession and distribution of child pornography. In its decision, the Court relied on the duty of the state to protect the dignity of children, and to prevent harm (para 67), rather than on section 28(2) independently. It, however, reinforced its earlier position that section 28(2), 'like the other rights enshrined in the Bill of Rights', does not 'trump' other constitutional rights and 'is subject to limitations that are reasonable and justifiable in compliance with section [section 36]' (para. 55).

The 'Rosetta stone' of section 28(2) is, however, the case of *S v. M*, which was decided in 2007. Here, the Court overcame its reluctance to assign a fixed content to the above section, and clarified the meaning of 'giving paramountcy to the best interests of children'. The case dealt with the duties of judicial officers vis-à-vis children, when sentencing primary caregivers. The underlining concern in such cases is that a custodial sentence would deprive children of parental care to which they are entitled under section 28(1)(b) of the Constitution. The Court discussed comprehensively section 28(2) and re-iterated its view that it contains a self-standing right (para. 14). The Court did not rely exclusively on section 28(2), however. Instead, it applied sections 28(1)(b) and 28(2) together. Although the litigation did not involve the children directly, section 28(2) provided the legal justification for the Court legitimately to introduce children's rights into the balancing act. As stated by Gallinetti, the approach of the Court 'underscores the need to mainstream the best interests principle in all legal arenas where children are involved even where established legal rules or principles have never given regard thereto previously' (Gallinetti, 2010: 115). According to *S v. M,* section 28(2) requires of the courts 'first, *consideration* of the interests of children; second, the *retention* in the inquiry of any competing interests because the best interests principle does not trump all other rights; finally, the *apportionment* of *appropriate* weight to the interests of the child' (Gallinetti, 2010: 115; *S v. M* paras 33, 26 and 32). Thus, the courts must be sufficiently informed to assess the impact of various sentencing options on children (paras. 35-36, 39). Furthermore, when law enforcement action against the primary caregivers could result in negative consequences for the children, the rights and interests of children must be considered independently of the connected rights of their primary caregiver,[19] in a deliberate effort to avoid children 'paying' for the faults of their parents.[20] Finally, the courts should 'take reasonable

---

19 This has not always been the attitude of the Court. Cases such as *President of the Republic of South Africa and Another v. Hugo* 1997 (6) BCLR 708 (CC), and *Government of the Republic of South Africa and Others v. Grootboom and Others* 2001 (1) SA 46 (CC) (*Grootboom*), show that in the past, the Court was reluctant to 'use the best interests of children in order to award rights or privileges to their parents' (Bonthuys, 2006: 34).

20 As poignantly put by the Court: 'The unusually comprehensive and emancipatory character of section 28 presupposes that in our new dispensation the sins and traumas of fathers and mothers should not be visited on their children' (para. 18). This was reinforced in *Van der Burg* (below), where the Court held that, 'The failure of parents to emphasise the interests of their children, or the possible manipulation of the children's situation to suit the objectives of parents, may not be held against children' (para. 68).

steps to minimise' the adverse effects on children of a legitimate and inevitable interference of the state with their right to parental care (para. 42).[21]

What came out very strongly from *S v. M*, is that the courts are enjoined by section 28(2) to have an active role in ensuring that in all matters concerning children, their best interests are given the importance they deserve. This aspect was further developed in subsequent cases. In *Van der Burg and Another v. National Director of Public Prosecutions and Another* 2012 (2) SACR 331 (CC) (*Van der Burg*) the Court dealt with an appeal against a forfeiture order of a residential property, which was used as an illegal pub by the parents of three minor children. Acting as *amicus curiae*, the Centre for Child Law argued that 'the Constitution obliges a court to consider the best interests of the applicants' children before a final determination can be made on the forfeiture' (para. 3). Although the Court disagreed with the *amicus* that a curator was needed to inform the Court about the children's situation, it nonetheless considered the interests of children, pursuant to section 28(2). The fact that the interests of children were only formally raised before the Constitutional Court and then by an *amicus*, begged the question as to who should raise the issue of such interests in the course of litigation. The Court indicated that it is expected that this will be done by the parents, but should they fail to do so, it is the duty of the court to consider the interests of the children. There is also an expectation that other state agencies involved (the National Prosecuting Authority in this case) will assist with all the information at their disposal (para. 68). Like in *S v. M*, the Court indicated that '[t]he failure of parents to emphasise the interests of their children, or the possible manipulation of the children's situation to suit the objectives of parents, may not be held against the children' (para. 68). The Court considered that children's interests need to be assessed separately, not just in order symbolically to assert their independence, but also because 'the interests of the children may require steps to be taken independently of the conclusion reached on forfeiture at the end of the proportionality enquiry' (para. 70).

In *Director of Public Prosecutions, Transvaal v. Minister of Justice and Constitutional Development, and Others* 2009 (2) SACR 130 (CC) (*DPP*), the Court was called on to confirm a declaration by the High Court that certain provisions of the Criminal Procedure Act of 1957 – which were intended to protect child victims and child witnesses – were inconsistent with section 28(2). The Court was prepared to assess the statutory provisions against section 28(2) alone, although in the end it found that the challenged provisions could be interpreted so as to avoid the inconsistency with section 28(2) (para. 84). The documentation available to the Court, however, raised serious concerns about the effectiveness of this legislation. The question then arose

21 In *S v. Howells* 1999 (1) SACR 675 (C) (*Howells*) (prior to *S v. M*) – applying the best interests of the child as being the upper guardian of all children – the High Court requested social workers to ensure that children are adequately cared for during their mother's incarceration, and that contact be maintained between the incarcerated parent and the children. After *S v. M*, in *S v. S* (Centre for Child Law as *Amicus Curiae*) 2011 (7) BCLR 740 (CC), the Court ordered the correctional services to ensure that social workers visit the children every month, and to report on whether they are in need of care and protection.

as to whether the Court should investigate the matter *mero motu*,[22] and grant an appropriate remedy (para. 190). Faced with a 'disturbing state of affairs', which was 'inconsistent with the constitutional promise that the child's best interests shall be of paramount importance in all matters concerning the child' (para. 198), the Court decided that it should address the matter. Responding to the extreme vulnerability of child-victims (para. 200), the Court designed a supervisory order to respond to these exceptional circumstances, which required urgent attention in order to avoid further violations of the rights of child-complainants (para. 205).

A similar approach has been used in *C and others v. Department of Health and Social Development, Gauteng and Others* 2012 (2) SA 208 (CC) (*C v. Department of Health Gauteng*) and *Head of Department, Department of Education, Free State Province and Welkom High School and Others* [2013] JOL 30547 (CC) (*Welkom High School*), where section 28(2) emboldened the Court to 'scratch the surface' (para 130) and acknowledge the real impact on children of the challenged statute or policy. In *C v. Department of Health Gauteng*, certain sections of the Children's Act 38 of 2005 were challenged for making no provision for the automatic judicial review of emergency removals of children, within a reasonable period of time. The absence of the automatic review would have potentially resulted in the separation of children from their parents for up to 90 days. In the absence of an automatic judicial review, the parents and children were not, however, completely deprived of remedies, which included criminal sanctions against those who wrongfully removed the children, and administrative action against the removal. According to Yacoob J., although strict statutory provisions existed for the emergency removal of children, 'there exists always the possibility that a removal would be wrongly made' (para. 76), and '[i]t is in the interests of children for any law that effects the removal of children to provide, at the same time, for proceedings in which the correctness of the removal is tested by a Children's Court in the presence of the child and parents' (para. 79). Implied in the position of the majority, is that the law may take no chances in a scenario where a child could be wrongfully removed from the family environment, without such removal being challenged. People most likely affected by such removals – children, the indigent, and possibly uneducated parents – would be unable to use the existing legal remedies,[23] which made such remedies inaccessible and ineffective in such cases. The majority also viewed as contrary to section 28(2) the fact that children and their parents were not properly listened to in the emergency removal decisions. For Skweyiya J., who wrote a concurring judgment, section 28(2) requires that an appropriate degree of consideration be given to the interests of children, and that this requires that '[a]s

22 Interestingly, the Court asked whether it should investigate these issues as the upper guardian of all children, and not as an effect of s. 28(2).

23 The position of the majority and concurring judges contrasts with that of the minority. For minority judges, the fact that the law provided criminal sanctions for those wrongfully removing children from their family environment, was sufficient (para. 124). In these judges' view, the law should not be invalidated because those charged with its implementation make mistakes. See discussion of this case in Couzens (2013).

a minimum, the family, and particularly the child concerned, must be given an opportunity to make representations on whether removal is in the child's best interests' (para. 27). The majority then found, that the absence of an automatic judicial review within a reasonable period of time in the presence of the children and their parents, was contrary to section 28(2) and section 34 (paras. 27 and 77). The Court also considered the interests of the children when crafting the judicial remedy. Although it had several options,[24] it settled for reading-in, a remedy which allowed the Court to insert words in the challenged provisions, so as to bring them in line with the Constitution. The other options were excluded by the Court, as being insufficiently protective of children's interests (para. 88).

Section 28(2) had a strong impact on the Court's design of an appropriate remedy in *Welkom High School*. Here the Court dealt with the power of the Department of Education to instruct the principals of two schools not to exclude pregnant learners from school for a period of up to two years, in disregard of the schools' pregnancy policy. Although the Court was not called on to decide on the unconstitutionality of the schools' policies, it did not overlook the negative impact of the policies on pregnant girls. In an *obiter* statement, the majority took the view that 'by operating inflexibly, the policies may violate section 28(2) of the Constitution, which provides that a child's best interests are of paramount importance in every matter concerning the child' (para. 116).[25] Although, technically, no violation of rights was established, the Court nonetheless decided to order the schools governing bodies to review their pregnancy policies in the light of the Court's judgment and to report to the Court on the steps taken to do so (para. 125). In the opinion of the Court, such an order was justified by section 172(1)(b) of the Constitution, which authorises the courts to grant a just and equitable remedy (para. 119 fn omitted):

> The considerations in favour of granting such an order in this case can be characterised as follows: the rights of children are implicated and section 28(2) of the Constitution requires that their best interests be of paramount importance in deciding the appropriate relief; if relief is not granted in this matter, there may be potentially far-reaching effects on children who are not party to these proceedings, who might never independently challenge these or similar policies; and there is a need for clarity on what the

24 Simply to declare the challenged provisions to be constitutionally invalid, or to declare the invalidity of the relevant section and then suspend the order of invalidity in order to allow Parliament to remedy the defect in the law.

25 Detailing on the consequences of such inflexibility, the majority of the Court (per Kampepe J.) further indicated in para. 116: 'The policies require that pregnant learners must leave school for the remainder of the year in which they give birth without regard to the health of the learner, the point in the school year at which she gives birth, arrangements she has made for appropriate care for her newborn, the wishes of the learner and her parents or her capacity to remain in school. The policies are designed in such a way as to give the school governing bodies and principals no opportunity to consider the best interests of pregnant learners.' Ironically, the dissenting judges would have reached a more child-focused decision – without even considering the best interests of the child.

Constitution and the Schools Act do and do not allow with regard to the content of pregnancy policies in schools.

Thus, section 28(2) justified the crafting of a remedy in somewhat unusual circumstances, when a human rights violation has not been fully established. Such a drastic remedy was nonetheless necessary because of the serious impact on children of the school policies. The remedy was envisaged to have a pre-emptive effect – rather than an *ex post facto* remedial impact.

This departure from technical legal rigidity in the name of the best interests of the child is also seen in *AD v. DW (Centre for Child Law as Amicus Curiae; Department for Social Development as Intervening Party)* 2008 (3) SA 183 (CC) (*AD v. DW*).[26] The Court looked into how section 28(2) should be interpreted in relation to the principle of subsidiarity, which applies to intercountry adoptions. The trenchant position of the Court was that despite the importance of the principle of subsidiarity it cannot be 'the ultimate governing factor in inter-country adoptions' (para. 49), because '[d]etermining the best interests of the child cannot be circumscribed by mechanical legal formulae or through rigid hierarchical rankings of care options' (para. 50). Furthermore, because '[c]hild law is an area that abhors maximalist legal propositions that preclude or diminish the possibilities of looking at and evaluating the specific circumstances of the case' (para. 55), the subsidiarity principle is subsidiary to the paramountcy principle. In the view of the Court, '[t]his means that each child must be looked at as an individual, not as an abstraction. It also means that unduly rigid adherence to technical matters ... should play a relatively diminished role ...' (para. 55).

The jurisprudence reviewed above shows that section 28(2) is justiciable, and that it was applied by the Court in a variety of cases.[27] In some cases, where section

---

26 There is common-law precedent for this position, however, but the Court based its arguments on s. 28(2).

27 The Court, however, is not always consistent or predictable in its use of s. 28(2). In some cases which are central to the Court's jurisprudence on the rights of children – *Grootboom, Minister of Health and Others v. Treatment Action Campaign and Others* 2002 (5) SA 721 (CC), *MEC for Education: KwaZulu-Natal and Others v. Pillay* 2008 (1) SA 474 (CC) – the Court has not engaged formally with s. 28(2). In a few recent delict cases, the much flaunted best interests played no role despite ample space for such (*Le Roux and Others v. Dey (Freedom of Expression Institute and Restorative Justice Centre as amici curiae)* 2011 (3) SA 274 (CC) which concerned an action for defamation by a teacher against four teenage school children); and *F V Minister of Safety and Security and Others* 2013 (2) SACR 20 (CC), which concerned the 13-year-old victim of a rape committed by an off-duty police officer, who sought to hold the Minister vicariously liable). It might be illustrative, that in his dissenting judgment in *Le Roux* (above), Yacoob J. criticised the majority for ignoring that they were dealing with children, while in *F v. Minister of Safety and Security* (above) he himself 'forgot' that the victim was a child. Judges gave no explanation for not considering s. 28(2) in these cases. The Court seems more inclined to utilise s. 28(2) when the subject matter deals with one of the rights in s. 28(1) – which raises concerns that the Court is willing to be child-centred in only a limited number of cases. If this is

28(2) was applied independently, it was not always necessary for the Court to do so.[28] Section 28(1) rights – substantive and more specific rights – were engaged in most of these cases[29] and, in fact, applying section 28(2), the Court has protected the substance of those rights. This raises concerns that section 28(2) is over-used, to the detriment of the jurisprudential development of other rights of children.[30] The themes in the Court's jurisprudence on section 28(2) seem to be: the need for flexible laws which accommodate individual needs; a demand that consideration be given to children's interests in matters concerning them; the need for child-focused remedies and procedural flexibility when dealing with children's rights matters.

I will now establish whether entitlements and obligations can be linked to the application by the Court of section 28(2), which, arguably, would have been more difficult to develop other than relying on this section.

4. Normative Themes in the Court's Approach

Although the Court has embraced section 28(2), it has been reluctant 'to define with any precision the content of the right to have the child's best interests given paramount importance in matters concerning the child' (*DPP*, para. 73; see also *Fitzpatrick*, para 20). However, certain elements of the emerging, independent, legal content of section 28(2) can be gleaned from the jurisprudence of the Court.

According to the Court, section 28(2) 'imposes an obligation on all those who make decisions concerning a child to ensure that the best interests of the child enjoy paramount importance in their decisions' (para. 73). This is a twofold obligation: to consider (take into account) the interests of children, and to give 'appropriate weight ... in each case to a consideration to which the law attaches the highest value, namely, the interests of children who may be concerned' (*S v. M*, para 42).

---

the case, then the limited jurisprudential development of s. 28(1) rights may have adverse consequences on the scope of the application of s. 28(2).

28 Bonthuys remarked this in 2006 (at 27), and her observation remains valid in the light of the more recent jurisprudence. *Du Toit*, *Bannatyne* and *C v. Department of Health, Gauteng* involved the right in section 28(1)(b), but the Court preferred to render its decision relying on s. 28(2).

29 In cases such as *Fitzpatrick*, *Du Toit* or *AD v. DW*, the lack of substantial engagement by the Court with s 28(1)(b) – the right to parental care – might have stemmed from the Court's concern that its position could be interpreted, so as to support the idea that children have a positive right to be provided with a family, or to be adopted.

30 The approach of the majority in *C v. Department of Health, Gauteng* might be illustrative. The majority judgment gave no explicit attention to the right to parental care in s. 28(1)(*b*) of the Constitution, although it was directly relevant in the case. Yacoob J., for the majority, decided that '[i]t is neither necessary nor appropriate to enter into a mechanical comparison' to illustrate how the impugned provisions of the Children's Act seek to give effect to s. 28(1) of the Constitution (para. 75). Thus the constitutionality assessment was based on ss. 28(2) (and 34) of the Constitution. The majority seems to have favoured s. 28(2), to the detriment of other constitutional rights of children.

The obligation to consider the interests of the children concerned requires the courts to enquire into the potential impact of court decisions on children. The courts need to have sufficient information at hand, in order to assess the impact of their decisions on the children who are directly or indirectly affected. In some cases, this will require the appointment of a curator *ad litem*,[31] or there could be a request by the court to the officers of the court to make available the relevant information, which they might hold (in *Van der Burg*, para. 68; *S v. M*, para. 36). In other cases, giving adequate consideration to the best interests of children requires listening to children and their parents (*C v. Department of Health, Gauteng*). In cases pertaining to law enforcement directed at the parents, the obligation to consider the children's interests requires that such interests be assessed independently of those of their parents. This ensures that children have their dignity respected as individual human beings, and also makes it possible to intervene timeously should the children be in need of protective measures following the justified interference of the state in the parent-child relationship (*S v. M*; *Van der Burg*).[32] This is what the Court did in *S v. S* (*Centre for Child Law as Amicus Curiae*) 2011 (7) BCLR 740 (CC), where a majority of the Constitutional Court decided that a custodial sentence needed to be imposed on the primary caregiver of two minor children. The Court ordered that social workers visit the children monthly and provide the competent authorities with information on their well-being (para. 66).

Section 28(2) demands that the best interests of children are considered in all matters concerning them, whether such matters involve the children directly or only affect them. Arguably, in cases such as *S v. M* and *Van der Burg*, section 28(2) was the legal justification for including the children's interests in the legal inquiry – since such decisions did not involve them directly. Also, as a result of section 28(2), a court must *ex officio* consider the interests of children should the parents/guardians/legal representatives of children fail to defend such interests. Although the common law institution of upper guardianship empowered the courts *ex officio* to establish what is in the best interests of children, courts acted as upper guardians primarily in liti-

31 In *Van der Burg*, for example, the *amicus* relied on s. 28(2) to request the appointment of a curator *ad litem*, for the children concerned. In *Du Toit*, however, the appointment of the curator *ad litem* was linked to section 28(1)(h) (para. 3).

32 This does not mean that similar outcomes could not have been achieved through the Court applying other legal norms. In *Howells, Johncom Media Investments Ltd v M and Others* 2009 (4) SA 7 (CC) (*Johncom Media*) and *DPP*, for example, the courts did not rely on s. 28(2), but on its powers as the upper guardian of all children.

gation pertaining to family and child-protection issues,[33] with some exceptions.[34] Reliance on section 28(2) allowed the Court to require, when necessary, *ex officio* consideration of children's best interests in all matters concerning children and not just family law or child protection matters. This ensures that children's interests are not marginalised because they are not canvassed before the court. As stated by the Court, '[c]ases involving children are pre-eminently of the kind where one must scratch the surface to get to the real substance below' (*Welkom High School,* para. 130), because 'the courts are essentially guarding the best interests of a child, not simply settling a dispute between litigants' (*AD v. DW,* para. 55).

Giving 'appropriate weight ... in each case to a consideration to which the law attaches the highest value', does not mean that the decision-makers must give primacy to children's interests at all times. Like other rights in the Bill of Rights, section 28(2) can be limited, if justifiable to do so under section 36 of the Constitution (*Fitzpatrick, De Reuck, Sonderup,* and *S v. M*). The Court's interpretation of section 28(2) requires, however, that the rights/interests of children enter the balancing act in relation to other rights with a certain advantage. As stated by other authors: 'a child's interests have a leg-up vis-à-vis other rights and values' (Friedman et al, 2009: 47-45).

In addition to the obligation to give paramount consideration to the best interests of the child, section 28(2) also gives every child the right to have his/her *individual* best interests considered. This means that relevant laws must create conditions for

33 Upper guardianship is exercised by the superior courts, mainly the High Courts. According to *Coetzee v. Meintjies* 1976(1) SA 257 (T) at 261, courts act as upper guardians when the child has no guardian, or when the guardian neglects his/her duties, or when guardians cannot agree on what is best for the child. In cases such as *H v. I* 1985(3) SA 237 (C), and *L v. H* 1992(2) SA 594 (E), the courts held that upper guardianship can also be exercised if parental power is exercised unreasonably by the natural parent. In *Nugent v. Nugent* 1978(2) SA 690 (R), the court was of the view that parental power is always subject to the right of the court to interfere with the exercise of such power, as the upper guardian of all children. However, the court does not have an unlimited right to interfere, and cannot exercise its powers as the upper guardian simply because it does not approve of the decision taken by the parents (*S v. L* 1992(3) SA 713 (E)) (from van Heerden (1999)).

34 *Howells; S v. Zuba & 23 Similar Cases* [2004] 1 All SA 438 (E) (para. 39). There is lack of clarity on the relationship between the best interests of the child as a standard applied by superior courts in exercising their responsibilities as the upper guardians of all children, and the application of the constitutional standard of the best interests. In *Van der Burg,* for example, the Court suggests that a distinction exists between the upper guardianship and the consequences arising from s. 28(2): 'The High Court is not only the upper guardian of children, but is also obliged to uphold the rights and values of the Constitution. In all matters concerning children, including applications for the forfeiture of property which provides a home or shelter to children, it is the duty of the court to consider the specific interests of the children' (para. 68). In some cases, however, the Court relies on its upper-guardian responsibilities to pursue children's best interests, rather than on s. 28(2) (*Johncom Media,* paras. 42-43; *DPP,* para. 190 per Ngcobo J., and para. 246 per Skweyiya (concurring).

their flexible application, in order to allow decision-makers to respond to the needs of individual children.[35] In *S v. M* (para. 24), the Court poignantly stated that:

> A truly principled child-centred approach requires a close and individualised examination of the precise real-life situation of the particular child involved. To apply a predetermined formula for the sake of certainty, irrespective of the circumstances, would in fact be contrary to the best interests of the child concerned.

This flexibility requirement might also justify – in certain cases – a departure from established procedural rules (*AD v. DW* and *J v. J* (2008 6 SA 30 (C), for example). Section 28(2) is in fact a guarantee that the best interests of individual children will not be sacrificed for the sake of technical legal issues.[36]

As illustrated by cases such as *Bannatyne, C v. Department of Health, Gauteng,* and *Welkom High School*, section 28(2) also demands that child-centred remedies are available in law, or crafted by the courts, and that such remedies are accessible to children and those who protect them.[37] Section 28(2) was used by the courts to construct

35 This is clear from cases such as *Fitzpatrick, S v. M, AD v. DW*, and *Welkom High School*. The Constitutional Court is, of course, not the only entity approaching s. 28(2) on the basis that it requires that law is sufficiently flexible to make allowance for the best interest of the individual child. In *Christian Lawyers Association v. Minister of Health and Others* (Reproductive Health Alliance as *Amicus Curiae*) 2005 (1) SA 509 (T), for example, deciding on a challenge to a statute allowing girls of any age to terminate a pregnancy without obtaining the consent of their parents, at 528I/J-529A, the High Court said: 'The legislative choice opted for in the Act serves the best interest of the pregnant girl child (s. 28(2)) because it is flexible to recognise and accommodate the individual position of a girl child based on her intellectual, psychological and emotional make up and actual majority. It cannot be in the interest of the pregnant minor girl to adopt a rigid age-based approach that takes no account, little or inadequate account of her individual peculiarities'.

36 Sloth-Nielsen and Mezmur rightly criticise the minority judgments in the SCA (*De Gree and Another v. Webb and Others* (*Centre for Child Law as Amicus Curiae*) 2007 (5) SA 184 (SCA)), for having overlooked the protective value of technical legal rules, designed to protect children more generally (Sloth-Nielsen, J. and B. D. Mezmur, "(Illicit) transfer by De Gree", *Law, Democracy and Development* 2007 9(2) at 81). For example, Hanke AJA, in dissent, dismissed the concerns raised by the majority regarding the appropriate court to deal with the adoption and application of the principle of subsidiarity, as 'legal niceties' (*De Gree* (above), para. 99).

37 Child-centredness may raise issues pertaining to the rule of law (or put differently, the application of the best interests provision may raise rule of law concerns). In *AD v. DW*, the majority endorsed the view of the minority in the Supreme Court of Appeal, 'in its insistence that Baby R's best interests should not be mechanically sacrificed on the altar of jurisdictional formalism' (para. 30). Sachs J. also rejected an 'unduly rigid adherence to technical matters', which disregards that 'the courts are essentially guarding the best interests of a child, not simply settling a dispute between litigants' (para. 55). The position of the Court was later relied on in *J v. J* (2008 6 SA 30 (C)), where the court regarded itself as not being bound 'by procedural strictures and legal niceties' (para. 20, referring to *AD v. DW*). In *Allpay Consolidated Investment Holdings (Pty) Ltd and Others v. Chief Executive Officer of the South African Social Security Agency and Others* [2012] ZAGPPHC 185, a pub-

judicial remedies which compensated for the court not having given priority to the best interests of the child – but which were superseded by other legitimate interests. In *Sonderup*, the Court decided that '[p]ursuant to s 38, read with s 28(2), this Court is entitled to impose conditions [to her immediate return to Canada] in the best interests of Sofia' (para. 51). A 'compensatory' order was also made by the Court in *S v. S*. More recently, in *Welkom High School*, the majority took the view that section 28(2) justified the development of a pre-emptive remedy, because not granting the relief would leave children exposed to the risk of having their rights violated by the policies, which they are highly unlikely to challenge independently (para. 119).

5. Critical Analysis of the Position of the Court

In my view, the cases discussed above show that section 28(2) is capable of independent legal content. No doubt that in applying section 28(2), the Court started from the premise that, as an enforceable provision of the Constitution, this section demands a certain conduct (action or omission), most often of the state.[38] Whether this necessarily qualifies section 28(2) as a right according to jurisprudential theories of rights, is perhaps still up for discussion.[39] However, the Court is posed to treat section 28(2) as a self-standing right. At least three elements indicate that the Court means what it says

---

lic procurement process for the payment of social grants was declared illegal and invalid by the High Court, but the Court decided not to invalidate the contract entered into by the state with the winning bidder, because the invalidation of the contract would have led to substantial delays in the payment of social grants to the beneficiaries – of which more than 11 million were children (para. 73). This latter decision (although overturned in appeal and, at the time of writing, with the Constitutional Court for a further appeal) raises concerns under the rule of law because the consideration of the children's interests led to the court refusing to invalidate an unlawful contract, which would continue to produce effects in disregard of the principle of legality. The same can be said about the unusual approach taken by the Court in *Welkom High School*, where it can be argued that because the Court did not find a violation of rights, there was no need for it to grant a remedy. Despite the potential criticism of the courts' position, such judgments might nonetheless send a judicial message that legal rules (including the rule of law) need to be developed/adapted, so as to respond to the situation of children.

38 In an exception, in *Bannatyne*, the Court declared that section 28(2) requires the parents to provide their children with proper parental care, although thereafter it declared that this section imposes an obligation on the state to create the necessary environment for the parents to fulfil their parental duties (para. 24; see also Bonthuys (2005: 619); Visser (2007: 460)).

39 It might be that the Court was concerned with the justiciability of s. 28(2), and the location of the section in the Bill of Rights offered the simple solution of approaching this section as a right in itself. On the other hand, the Court was not shy to declare equally general and vague constitutional provisions as justiciable. Examples include the rule of law (*Fedsure Life Assurance Ltd v. Greater Johannesburg Transitional Metropolitan Council* 1998(2) SA 374 (CC)), public participation (Brickhill & Babiuch (2007)) or the separation of powers (*South African Association of Personal Injury Lawyers v. Heath and Others* 2001 (1) BCLR 77 (CC)).

when it states that section 28(2) is a self-standing right. First, the entitlements and obligations read by the Court in section 28(2) are sufficiently autonomous from other constitutional rights of children, for the Court to be justified in placing them within the scope of the best interests provision. Second, breaches of section 28(2) result in judicial remedies.[40] Third, the Court treats section 28(2) as a right by implication when it applies section 36 (the limitation clause) to section 28(2), which is typical of cases where the courts have to decide whether, in concrete situations, limitations to rights are constitutionally acceptable or not. Although these latter cases hardly enrich the legal content of section 28(2), they do send a symbolic message. Like any other rights, the right to have paramount consideration given to the best interests of children cannot be brushed aside based on the discretion of the decision-maker; any limitations must be legally justifiable, under the strict test provided for in section 36.[41]

Whether one agrees with the categorisation of section 28(2) as an independent right or not, what seems clear in the jurisprudence of the Court is that section 28(2) does have an independent normative content, to which the case law now gives a fairly clear contour.[42] Much of the concern about the best interests revolves around its indeterminacy, both in terms of the factors which are to be considered in establishing such, and in terms of the outcomes of its application. In my view, the Court distances itself from this debate, and a preoccupation for unveiling the normative force of section 28(2) is apparent in the Court's jurisprudence. Unfortunately, the Court has been reluctant to issue comprehensive statements on the legal content of section 28(2), allegedly in an attempt to preserve its flexibility (*Fitzpatrick*, para. 18; *DPP*, para. 73). This might be a misplaced concern, and in my view, the Court conflates two distinct issues: the factors to be taken into consideration when deciding on the best interests of the child/children, and the potential legal obligations or rights arising from section 28(2). Keeping open the list of factors to be considered in establishing the child's best interests is not incompatible with giving contour to the legal entitlements and obligations arising from section 28(2). This would be in line with the Court's own use of

40 In *Fitzpatrick, Du Toit* and *C v. Department of Health, Gauteng* – the Court invalidated various statutory provisions which were found contrary to s. 28(2). In *S v. M,* the court developed an obligation for courts to attenuate the impact of state interference in the parent-child relationship. In *Welkom High School* the Court developed a pre-emptive remedy.

41 There is lack of clarity on this issue. In cases where the Court applied or considered applying s. 36 to s. 28(2), the effect of such application was/would have been over-riding the children's interests. But, the right in s 28(2), as phrased in *S v. M,* is a right to have paramount consideration given to the best interests of the child, and not the right to prioritise the interests of the child in all matters. It is not clear then whether s. 36 can be used also to circumscribe the scope of s. 28(2) (i.e. to justify not considering the interests of children in certain matters), or if it should only be used to justify overriding the interests of children in certain matters.

42 I borrowed the term 'normative force' from *S v. M,* para. 14. It is a neutral term which avoids controversies in the way in which s. 28(2) is referred to. It also suits the line taken in this contribution, which is not a critical review of the approach of the Court, but rather an attempt to identify its legal force.

section 28(2) – as a legal rule rather than a tool to guide the discretion of the decision-makers.

It can be argued that interpreting section 28(2) in the sense that it creates only a right to give paramount consideration to the best interests of the child, weakens, somehow, the traditional force of the principle. The formulation seems to be procedure-oriented in the sense that it requires the courts to consider, but not necessarily give priority to, the best interests of children. While some criticism may be levelled at this position,[43] perhaps the Court had little choice. To remain a viable and effective *constitutional standard* – as opposed to a family law or child protection standard – the best interests provision had to fit within the whole architecture of the Bill of Rights, which means abandoning its absolutism and accepting the possibility of giving way to other legitimate interests. As the Court put it in *De Reuck,* an absolute priority to the best interests of the child 'would be alien to the approach adopted by this Court that constitutional rights are mutually interrelated and interdependent and form a single constitutional value system' (para. 55). Arguably, this realistic approach has allowed the Court to recognise section 28(2) a wide scope rather than confine its application to areas where giving priority to children's interests was previously tested and accepted. In any case, a procedure-oriented approach should not be easily dismissed. Its primary merit is that it increases the visibility of children to the decision-makers, and this is an important step considering the marginalisation of children's interests. Furthermore, it allows the courts to scrutinise the best interests of the child in matters which do not directly involve children – but nonetheless affect them.

Section 28(2) has been used by the Court to create obligations which make the law more responsive to children's needs as rights holders. To be effective, the rights of children need to respond to their special needs as legal subjects. An important aspect of the Court's approach to the effectiveness of children's rights, are the positive obligations which the Court developed in applying section 28(2), which one does not see replicated in the jurisprudence on the rights of adults.[44] It is perhaps symbolic that rather than grounding this jurisprudence in the right to equal protection by the law (section 9(1) of the Constitution) or the right to an appropriate remedy (section 38 of the Constitution), the Court often relied on section 28(2). It seems that, for the Court, this section is quintessential for giving children the legal protection which is due to them.

---

43 An issue which has not yet been explored is the impact on the common-law principle of the best interests of the position of the Court, that s. 28(2) can be limited. This question is of importance because within the sphere of application of the common law standard of the best interests, the best interests of children always received priority over the interests of their parents.

44 The obligation of the courts to obtain information relevant for establishing the best interests of the child; the obligation of other court officers to assist the court with information; the obligation to consider the interests of the children although they are not parties to the matter, and when children might be affected by the decision of the court; the obligation to take reasonable measures to diminish the impact of the legitimate state interference with a child's right to parental care.

The Court bestowed on section 28(2) an individual focus specific to the common law standard, even in cases where it dealt with constitutional challenges against legislation. This creates a situation whereby a standard designed for application in individual cases, is transferred and applied to decisions with general impact. Concerns were raised that this could create legal chaos,[45] because this individually-focused application of the best interests of the child allows for deviations from general legal rules, in order to serve the best interests of individual children (Heaton (2009), referring to the concerns raised by Cockrell (2000)). The underlining concern is that creating general rules modeled after the needs of individual children might not serve the interests of all other children.[46] The application of section 36 (the limitation clause) to section 28(2) offers a solution, by allowing the limitation of the best interests of the individual child, in order to preserve the application of general legal rules (Heaton, 2009). Despite this possibility, the assessment of legal rules against section 28(2) still raises challenges because of the difficulties in anticipating the impact of the invalidation of legal rules on children generally, given the multitude of individual circumstances children might find themselves in.[47] However, denying the application of section 28(2) to legal rules – which might result in the invalidation of such rules (statutes, common law, policies and normative administrative acts) – would mean depriving this provision of its constitutional status, which is undeniably conferred upon it.[48]

45 Bonfils and Gouttenoire (2008) raised this concern in France, but the challenge is valid in the South African context as well. A good example is offered by *Fitzpatrick*, where the focus on the individual child led to the invalidation of a statutory provision, which prohibited intercountry adoptions. This left the authorities poorly equipped to deal with the complexities of intercountry adoptions, because of the lack of adequate structures to do so. This situation is now remedied by the entry into force of the Children's Act 38 of 2005, which incorporates the Hague Convention of 29 May 1993 on the Protection of Children and Co-operation in Respect of Intercountry Adoption, and provides for the institutional mechanisms for regulating intercountry adoptions.

46 Discussing the common law restrictions on minor's capacity, Cockrell (2000) indicates that, in individual cases, such restrictions might be contrary to the immediate best interests of the child. Cockrell then raises the question as to whether the application of s. 28(2) might have produced a different outcome, in the sense that 'common-law restrictions on capacity should never be allowed to operate contrary to the immediate best interests of a child'. He argues further that 'the answer must be in the negative, and that it would be quite contrary to principle to interpret section 28(2) as mandating the differential application of settled rules of law in an effort to promote the short-term interests of the child. The better view is that the phrase "every matter concerning the child" in section 28(2) must be taken to refer to matters which involve the exercise of discretionary powers, rather than the application of rules of law' (fn omitted; para. 3E22).

47 This is typical of constitutional litigation in which the challenge might be brought in a matter concerning an individual child, but the decision has a wider impact. In some cases, however, this potential conflict between the interests of a particular child and those of children in general is not present. See *Du Toit*, *DPP* or *C v. Department of Health, Gauteng*, where it is clear that the decision can be only beneficial for all the children.

48 Section 8(1) provides that, 'The Bill of Rights applies to all law, and binds the legislature, the executive, the judiciary and all organs of the state'.

In my view, what is needed is a more conscious effort by the courts to distinguish, in their judgments, between the application of section 28(2) (and the criteria relevant thereof) in decisions with impact on individual children and those with an impact on children generally.

6. Conclusion

The jurisprudence reviewed in part 3 of this contribution shows that section 28(2) is capable of some independent legal content. Although the Constitutional Court does not deliberately seek to clarify the legal content of section 28(2) and is, in fact, reluctant to spell out a comprehensive legal content for the section, some obligations and entitlements can be gleaned from its jurisprudence. Whilst its judgments might not be flawless, the Court relies on section 28(2), confident that this is a viable legal tool. The strongest assertion of the legal force of section 28(2) is to be found in the Court's position that section 28(2) contains a self-standing right. Whether the position of the Court in this regard is justified or not, cannot be decided here. Certainly the Court does not theorise about the potential different roles which section 28(2) could take, and what 'hat' should section 28(2) wear and when. Adequate importance could have, perhaps, been given to the best interests of the child, without declaring it a right in itself.[49] There is justified concern that over-reliance on the best interests of the child – and declaring the best interests of the chid as a self-standing right might result in such over-reliance – could be detrimental to the jurisprudential development of other rights of the child.

Disputes aside, there are positive aspects arising from the Court's position. Approaching the best interests of the child as a self-standing right has powerful symbolic value in that it asserts the need for child-focused legal institutions. It indicates that the status of the best interests of the child has radically changed and this is now a rule with an identifiable legal content, rather than just a practical tool to guide discretion in decision-making concerning children. Although scattered through many judgments, an independent legal content for the constitutional standard of the best interests of the child, is emerging. The entitlements and obligations sourced to the application of section 28(2) are geared toward responding to children's special needs as legal subjects. The position of the Court is attractive in that it integrates this unusual standard in a rights jurisprudence, preserving the essence of the principle, while considering its interaction with the rights of others and other legitimate interests. The jurisprudence of the Court reflects a distinction between the best interests of the child as a constitutional standard, and the best interests of a child as a tool for child protection and family law adjudication. It is this distinction which allowed the Court to give section 28(2) a wide scope, and to articulate it within the rights framework of the Constitution.

---

49 The principle of effective protection, for example, may be a good avenue to pursue, especially in those countries where art. 3(1) of the CRC does not apply directly, or has not received constitutional recognition. See Tobin (2009).

The South African jurisprudence shows the versatility of the best interests of the child as a legal tool.[50] This suggests that none of the characterisations utilised so far – standard, right, principle – exhausts, in isolation, the legal significance of the best interests of the child, or its potential. Perhaps trying to fit the 'best interests' into one of the available terminological 'boxes' might be unduly limiting and potentially regressive. The solution might be to accept that the best interests of the child is a multi-functional tool. As has been suggested: '[o]ne would not want to block the flexibility and growth of the law by a need for certainty and neatness' (Friedman *et al*, 2009: 47-40). This is not to say that more clarity on how the best interests be utilised is not needed. This could be achieved on a case-by-case basis, where the decision-makers acknowledge the complexity of the legal nature of the best interests, and then decide, with reasons, the manner in which they are going to employ it in a particular case.

When considering the jurisprudence of the Court from the perspective of the General Comment 14 of the CRC Committee, one can state that the Court has been visionary in its application of section 28(2). Its jurisprudence could well be useful for courts in other states, which are also faced with the application of article 3(1) of the CRC. The position of the South African Constitutional Court is fully in line with the interpretation of article 3(1), given by the Committee in General Comment 14. Indeed, the jurisprudence of the Court reflects the use of the best interests of the child, as a right to have such best interests considered, as a procedural rule, and as an interpretation principle. Whilst the courts may be concerned that the 'best interests of the child' is not equipped for application in decision-making with general impact, this need not be an insurmountable obstacle. It rests with the national courts to seize the opportunities presented by the CRC jurisprudentially, in order to develop the best interests of the child in a manner which fulfils its potential as a legal tool designed to respond to the legal needs of children.

References

Books and Monographs

Bonfils, P. and Gouttenoire, A., *Droit des mineurs* (Paris: Editions Dalloz, 2008).

Freeman, M., "Article 3: The Best Interests of the Child" in A. Alen, J. Vande Lanotte, E. Verhellen, F. Ang, E. Berghmans, M. Verheyde and Bruce Abramson (eds), *A Commentary on the United Nations Convention on the Rights of the Child* (Leiden: Martinus Nijhoff Publishers, 2007).

Van Bueren, G., *The International Law on the Rights of the Child* (Hague: Martinus Nijhoff Publishers, 1998).

50 Arguably, this is not exclusively the merit of the courts. In many cases *amicus curiae*, notably the Centre for Child Law, contributed greatly by presenting child-focused arguments to the courts.

Book Chapters

Bonthuys, E., "Children", in I. Currie & J. de Waal (eds), *The Bill of Rights Handbook* (2nd ed) (Wetton: Juta, 2005).

Brickhill, J. and R. Babiuch, "Political Rights" (2nd ed, Original Service: 03-07), in S. Woolman and M. Bishop (eds), *Constitutional Law of South Africa* (2nd ed.) (Cape Town: Juta, loose-leaf updated, 2007).

Cockrell, A., "The Law of Persons and the Bill of Rights" (last updated 2000), in *Bill of Rights Compendium* (LexisNexis Butterworth) (electronic source).

Friedman, A., A. Pantazis, A. and A. Skelton, "Children's Rights" (2nd ed, RS 1: 07-09), in S. Woolman and M. Bishop, *Constitutional Law of South Africa* (2nd ed.) (Cape Town: Juta loose-leaf updated, 2009).

Proudlock, P., "Children's Socio-economic Rights", in T. Boezaart (ed.), *Child Law in South Africa* (Claremont: Juta, 2009).

Skelton, A., "Constitutional protection of children's rights", in T. Boezaart (ed.), *Child Law in South Africa* (Claremont: Juta, 2009).

Van Heerden, B., "Judicial Interference with the Parental Power: The Protection of Children", in B. van Heerden, A. Cockrell, and R. Keightley (eds), *Boberg's Law of Persons and the Family* (2nd ed) (Kenwyn: Juta, 1999).

Articles

Alston, P., "The Best Interests Principle: Towards a Reconciliation of Culture and Human Rights", *International Journal of Law and the Family* 1994 (8), 1-25.

Ancel, J.-P., "La Convention de New York relative aux droits de l'enfant devant la Cour de cassation", *Justice & Cassation* 2011, 13-22.

Bonnet, B., "Le Conseil d'Etat et la Convention internationale des droits de l'enfant à l'heure du bilan: De l'art du pragmatism", *Dalloz* 2010 (17), 1031-1037.

Bonthuys, E., "The best interests of children in the South African Constitution", *International Journal of Law, Policy and the Family* 2006 (20), 23-43.

Bureau, D., "De l'application directe en France de la Convention de New York du 26 janvier 1990 sur les droits de l'enfant", *Revue critique de droit international privé* 2005, 679-697.

Couzens, M., "The Constitutional Court Consolidates its Child-Focused Jurisprudence: The Case of *C and Others v Department of Health and Social Development, Gauteng and Others*", *SALJ* 2013 (4), 672-688..

Gallinetti, J., "2kul2Btru: What children would say about the jurisprudence of Albie Sachs", *SAPL* 2010 (25), 108-123.

Gouttenoire, G., "L'application de la Convention internationale des droits de l'enfant", *Petites affiches* 2012 (50), 17-20.

Heaton, J., "An individualised, contextualised and child-centred determination of the child's best interests, and the implications of such an approach in the South African context", *Journal for Juridical Science* 2009 (34), 1-18.

Malherbe, R., "The constitutional dimension of the best interests of the child as applied in education", *TSAR* 2008 (2), 267-285.
Monéger, F., "Enfant (droits de l')" *Répertoire international Dalloz* Jan 2006, 1-13.
Schuz, R., "Symposium: Families and Children in International Law: The Hague Child Abduction Convention and Children's Rights" *Transnat'l L. & Contemp. Probs.* 2002 (12), 393-452.
Skelton, A., "Severing the Umbilical Cord: A subtle jurisprudential shift regarding children and their primary caregivers", *Constitutional Court Review* 2008 (1), 351-368.
Sloth-Nielsen, J., "The contribution of children's rights to the reconstruction of society: Some implications of the constitutionalisation of children's rights in South Africa", *International Journal of Children's Rights* 1996 (4), 323 -344.
Sloth-Nielsen, J. and B. D. Mezmur, "(Illicit) transfer by *De Gree*", *Law, Democracy and Development* 2007 (9), 81-100.
Tobin, T., "Judging the Judges: Are They Adopting the Rights Approach in Matters Involving Children?", *Melb. U. L. Rev.* 2009 (33), 579-625.
Visser, P. J., "Some ideas on the 'best interests of a child' principle in the context of public schooling", *THRHR* 2007 (70), 459-469.
Zermatten, J., "The Best Interests of the Child Principle: Literal Analysis and Function", *International Journal of Children's Rights* 2010 (18), 483-499.

Legislation

Constitution of the Republic of South Africa, 1996.
Children's Act 38 of 2005.
Hague Convention on the Civil Aspects of International Child Abduction Act, 1996.

International Conventions

Hague Convention of 29 May 1993 on Protection of Children and Co-operation in Respect of Intercountry Adoption
UN Convention on the Rights of the Child, 1989

Cases

South Africa

Allpay Consolidated Investment Holdings (Pty) Ltd and Others v. Chief Executive Officer of the South African Social Security Agency and Others [2012] ZAGPPHC 185.
Bannatyne v Bannatyne 2003 2 SA 363 (CC).
Christian Lawyers Association v. Minister of Health and Others (Reproductive Health Alliance as *Amicus Curiae*) 2005 (1) SA 509 (T).
De Gree and Another v. Webb and Others (Centre for Child Law as Amicus Curiae) 2007 (5) SA 184 (SCA).

De Reuck v. Director of Public Prosecutions (*Witwatersrand Local Division*) *and Others* 2003 (12) BCLR 1333 (CC).
Director of Public Prosecutions, Transvaal v. Minister of Justice and Constitutional Development, and Others 2009 (2) SACR 130 (CC).
Du Toit and Another v. Minister of Welfare and Population Development and Others (*Lesbian and Gay Equality Project as Amicus Curiae*) 2003 (2) SA 198 (CC).
F v. Minister of Safety and Security and Others 2013 (2) SACR 20 (CC).
Fedsure Life Assurance Ltd v. Greater Johannesburg Transitional Metropolitan Council 1998(2) SA 374 (CC).
Fraser v. Naude and Others 1998 (11) BCLR1357 (CC).
Government of the Republic of South Africa and Others v. Grootboom and Others 2001 (1) SA 46 (CC).
Head of Department, Department of Education, Free State Province v. Welkom High School and others (*Equal Education and another as amici curiae*) [2013] JOL 30547 (CC).
J v. J (2008 6 SA 30 (C).
Johncom Media Investments Ltd v. M and Others 2009 (4) SA7 (CC).
Jooste v. Botha 2000(2) SA 199 (T).
Le Roux and Others v. Dey (Freedom of Expression Institute and Restorative Justice Centre as *amici curiae*) 2011 (3) SA 274 (CC).
MEC for Education: KwaZulu-Natal and Others v. Pillay 2008 (1) SA 474 (CC).
Minister of Health and Others v. Treatment Action Campaign and Others 2002 (5) SA 721 (CC).
Minister for Welfare and Population Development v. Fitzpatrick and Others 2000 (7) BCLR713 (CC).
President of the Republic of South Africa and Another v. Hugo 1997 (6) BCLR 708 (CC).
S v. Howells 1999 (1) SACR 675 (C).
S v. M (Centre for Child Law as *Amicus Curiae*) 2008 (3) SA 232 (CC).
S v. S (Centre for Child Law as *Amicus Curiae*) 2011 (7) BCLR 740 (CC).
S v. Zuba & 23 Similar Cases [2004] 1 All SA 438 (E).
Sonderup v. Tondelli and Another 2001 (1) SA 1171 (CC).
South African Association of Personal Injury Lawyers v. Heath and Others 2001 (1) BCLR 77 (CC).
Van der Burg and Another v. National Director of Public Prosecutions and Another 2012 (2) SACR 331 (CC).

France

Cour de Cassation case no. 91-11.310 of 19 March 1993.
Cour de Cassation case no. 91-18735 of 15 July 1993.
Cour de Cassation case no. 02-20.613 of 18 May 2005.
Cour de Cassation case no. 02-16336 18 May 2005.
Conseil d'Etat case no. 141083 of 10 March 1995.
Conseil d'Etat case no. 161364 of 22 September 1997.

Note: The cases are accessible at: http://www.legifrance.gouv.fr/

Norway

A,B, C and the Norwegian Association for Asylum Seekers (NOAS) (third party intervener) v. The State, represented by the Immigration Appeals Board) HR-2012-02399-P (case no. 2012/1042) (English version available on the Court's website at: http://www.domstol.no/en/Enkelt-domstol/-Norges-Hoyesterett/Summary-of-Recent-Supreme-Court-Decisions/Summary-2012/ (accessed 3 September 2013).

Electronic Sources

Committee on the Rights of the Child *Concluding Observations of the Committee on the Rights of the Child Norway*, CRC/C/15/Add.23 (1994), available at: http://www.unicef-irc.org/bulletin/ConcludingObservations/download/IV/Norway/CRC-C-15-Add23.pdf accessed 6 September 2013 (accessed 6 September 2013).

Committee on the Rights of the Child *Concluding observations of the Committee on the Rights of the Child : Paraguay* CRC/C/15/Add.27 (1994), available at: http://www.unhchr.ch/tbs/doc.nsf/(Symbol)/CRC.C.15.Add.27.En?Opendocument (accessed 6 September 2013).

Committee on the Rights of the Child *Concluding observations of the Committee on the Rights of the Child: Denmark*, CRC/C/15/Add.33 (1995), available at: http://www.unicef-irc.org/bulletin/ConcludingObservations/download/IV/Denmark/CRC-C-15-Add33.pdf accessed 6 September 2013 (accessed 6 September 2013).

Committee on the Rights of the Child *Concluding Observations of the Committee on the Rights of the Child, Bulgaria*, CRC/C/15/Add.66 (1997), available at: http://www1.umn.edu/humanrts/crc/bulgaria1997.html (accessed 3 September 2013).

Committee on the Rights of the Child *General comment No. 14 (2013) on the right of the child to have his or her best interests taken as a primary consideration* (art. 3, para. 1) CRC/C/GC/14 29 May 2013, available at: http://www2.ohchr.org/english/bodies/crc/comments.htm (accessed 9 August 2013).

Assisted Reproduction and the Child's Right to Know His or Her Origins: Sweden's Response to Its International Law Obligations and New Challenges Raised by Surrogacy

Jane Stoll[1]
Faculty of Law, Uppsala University

> Society must adopt the attitude that donor insemination is not a right for unintentionally childless people but that the proposed child's best interests must always be in the forefront with an assessment of whether insemination may take place. (*SOU 1983:42: 87.*)

Introduction

All Swedish donor offspring conceived from gametes donated after 1 March 1985 have an unconditional legal right to identifying information about the donor when they are sufficiently mature. The right to information contained in the Genetic Integrity Act (SFS 2006:351) is, however, only one source of the right: the domestic source. There are strong indications that Swedish donor offspring also have a right to at least some information about the donor under international law because Sweden has ratified a number of international conventions, which provide for the right to know one's origins. It should, of course, follow that donor offspring born following surrogacy arrangements also have a corresponding right to information; but in the case of surrogacy, could the right to information about origins be based on a purely gestational connection with the surrogate mother?

This chapter briefly outlines the source and scope of a donor offspring's right to information about genetic origins under two conventions: the United Nations Convention on the Rights of the Child (CRC) and the European Convention on Human Rights (ECHR). An account is then given of the source and the scope of the right to identifying information under Swedish law. The possible scope of a surrogate-born child's right to information is briefly considered before several issues regarding the impact of domestic and cross-border surrogacy arrangements on the child's right to know about his or her origins are raised.

1 LL.D, Sweden. All translations of Swedish materials have been made by the author.

A. Diduck, N. Peleg, H. Reece (eds.), Law in Society: Reflections on Children, Family, Culture and Philosophy
Copyright 2015 Koninklijke Brill NV. Printed in The Netherlands. ISBN 978-90-04-26148-8. pp. 551-570.

Convention on the Rights of the Child

Source of the Right to Information about Origins

The source of the child's right to information about his or her genetic origins is derived from the child's right to know his or her parents (Tobin, 2004; Hodgkin and Newell, 2002; Breen, 2001; Detrick, 1999). This right can be found in Art 7(1) of the CRC:

> The child shall be registered immediately after birth and shall have the right from birth to a name, the right to acquire a nationality and as far as possible, the right to know and be cared for by his or her parents.

It should, however, be mentioned that there is no clear-cut interpretation about whether Art 7 gives a child the right to information about his or her genetic origins. Lucy Smith, for example, does not believe that the words, 'the right to know and be cared for by his or her parents', support such an interpretation. In Smith's view, these words are directed, first and foremost, to the child's right to be raised by his or her parents (Smith, 2008; Singer, 2000).

In relation to the right to know, Art. 7 of the CRC should be read together with art. 8, the right of a child to preserve his or her identity (Tobin, 2004; Hodgkin and Newell 2002).

Art. 8 of the CRC provides that:

> 1. States Parties undertake to respect the right of the child to preserve his or her identity, including nationality, name and family relations as recognized by law without unlawful interference.
> 2. Where a child is illegally deprived of some or all of the elements of his or her identity, States Parties shall provide appropriate assistance and protection, with a view to re-establishing speedily his or her identity.

Assuming donor offspring do have a right to information about the donor under Art. 7, recording and preserving identifying information about gamete donors in accordance with Art. 8 could be interpreted as necessary. The existence of such information is also a prerequisite for donor offspring to be able to trace their genetic origins.

In determining the scope of a donor offspring's right to know, two questions are fundamental:

1. Does the right to know one's parents or origins extend to donor offspring?
2. Does the right to know extend to identifying information about the donor?

In attempting to answer these questions, the starting point for this chapter is that the term 'parents', as found in the CRC, includes genetic parents. This assumption is supported, *inter alia*, by the Committee on the Rights of the Child (Stoll, 2008; Hodgkin and Newell, 2002). However, a child's right to know his or her parents is qualified by the inclusion of the words, 'as far as possible' in Art. 7, leaving it open for different interpretations by the various States Parties. To whom, then, does the right to information extend?

The Scope of the Right to Information under the CRC

The interpretation of whether the right to information about genetic origins under the CRC extends to donor offspring varies amongst different contracting states. Although there is no unified way in which this right has been interpreted and applied at national levels, there are strong indications that Art.7 applies to donor offspring.

When the CRC was drafted, a child's right to know his or her parents was principally concerned with the right of adopted children to find out about their biological parents (Hodgkin and Newell, 2002; Detrick, 1999; Freeman, 1996). Now, however, it is widely accepted that beneficiaries of the right to know include donor offspring. This is evident both from the reports of States Parties to the Committee on the Rights of the Child – where States Parties have themselves raised issues concerning donor offspring, bringing this to the attention of the Committee (SOU 1997:116) – and from statements made by the UN Committee itself regarding various States' interpretations of the child's right, as far as possible, to know his or her parents. As to the latter, the Committee has expressed concern about the possible contradiction between Art.7 and Norway's former policy in relation to anonymous sperm donors. Denmark has also been mentioned by the Committee in this regard. Moreover, the Committee's critical comments about France's policy on anonymous birth, which include references to both adoption and medically assisted procreation, not only confirm that the definition of 'parents' under Art. 7 includes genetic parents (Hodgkin and Newell, 2002); it in effect assumes that the right to know extends to donor offspring. Since the comments and recommendations of the Committee on the Rights of the Child are recognised 'as the highest authority for interpretation of the Convention' (Hodgkin and Newell, 2002: vx), these examples indicate that the right, as far as possible, to know one's parents – or genetic origins – under Art. 7 of the CRC extends to donor offspring and their right to information about the donor. Even though Art. 7 has not been interpreted in this way by all States Parties, it is clearly the view of the Committee on the Rights of the Child and to this extent difficult to disregard.

Does the Right to Know Extend to Identifying Information about the Donor?

Comments made by the Committee on the Rights of the Child in response to anonymous births and anonymous sperm donation provide a strong indication that, in the Committee's view at least, the scope of Art. 7 now includes the right to know the identity of the donor, irrespective of the original intention behind Art. 7.

Even so, it is not unusual for States Parties to attempt to justify an interpretation of Art. 7 that permits the destruction of records containing identifying information about a child's genetic parents. The qualification that a child has the right to know his or her parents 'as far as possible' has been used to rationalise practices such as anonymous gamete donation, anonymous birth and secret adoptions.

In determining the meaning of 'as far as possible', Hodgkin and Newell (2002: 117) identify three different situations that need to be distinguished. Either:

1. A parent cannot be identified;
2. A mother refuses to identify the father; or
3. A State decides that a parent should not be identified.

Whilst it is not possible entirely to prevent the first two scenarios, the third situation is different because it turns upon the will of a State Party. An example from this category is where States Parties protect the anonymity of gamete donors. According to Hodgkin and Newell, this third category 'includes the most controversial aspects of the interpretation of "as far as possible", appearing to unnecessarily breach children's right to know their genetic parents.' (Hodgkin and Newell, 2002: 117). This is in line with statements made by the Committee on the Rights of the Child, which consistently maintains its position that secrecy regarding a parent's identity is unacceptable.

The assumption that it is acceptable, under certain circumstances, to withhold information from a child about his or her genetic parents is also evident from the reservations to Art. 7 made by various States Parties. Such reservations have included the intention by States Parties to uphold the confidentiality of genetic parents in relation to ART procedures, adoption and anonymous births (Detrick, 1999).

Whether the reasons for denying a child information about his or her genetic origins stem from a State Party's reservation or from its own interpretation of Art. 7, however, makes no difference to the article's scope, which appears firmly established. The UN Committee's view about a child's right to know the identity of his or her genetic parents has been unwavering. To this end it has even been unconvinced by arguments from various States Parties which, in an attempt to justify secrecy following anonymous births and so called secret adoptions, maintain that such practices are consistent with the child's best interest. Similar arguments in relation to the secrecy of gamete donation have been no more persuasive (Hodgkin and Newell, 2002).

When it comes to donor offspring then, it is doubtful that States Parties can rely on the Art. 7 limitation 'as far as possible', in order to justify the destruction of records containing the identity of gamete donors. On the contrary, in order for a State Party to be confident that its practices are consistent with Art. 7 of the CRC, it must instead preserve, and arguably make available to donor offspring on request, information identifying the genetic parent or parents. The Committee on the Rights of the Child has unambiguously shown its hand in relation to the importance of maintaining accurate records about genetic parents in order to ensure that this information is subsequently available to the children to whom it relates. This, of course, includes securing information for donor offspring. Thus, while it is acknowledged that the limitation 'as far as is possible' in Art. 7 could be subject to different interpretations by individual State Parties, there is little room for an interpretation that permits the destruction of records about a child's genetic parents where this information is available, such as in the case of gamete donors.

European Convention on Human Rights

Source of the Right to Information about Genetic Origins

Concerning the ECHR, the source of the right to information about genetic origins is the *right to respect for private life* contained in Art. 8 of the ECHR, which provides as follows:

> 1. Everyone has the right to respect for his private and family life, his home and his correspondence.
> 2. There shall be no interference by a public authority with the exercise of this right except such as is in accordance with the law and is necessary in a democratic society in the interests of national security, public safety or the economic well-being of the country, for the prevention of disorder or crime, for the protection of health or morals, or for the protection of the rights and freedoms of others.

All four rights contained in paragraph one of Art. 8 'can be said to fall within the concept of "privacy".' (Cameron, 2006: 111)

Scope of the Right to Information under the ECHR

As early as 1989, the European Court of Human Rights in *Gaskin v The United Kingdom* (App no 10454/83, Judgment of 7 July 1989) confirmed its view that 'respect for private life [under Art. 8] requires that everyone should be able to establish details of their identity' (*Gaskin*: para. 39). Whether or not this decision is authority for a child's right to know the identity of his or her genetic parents has been debated. Forder (1993), for example, assumes it is, while Kilkelly (1999) and Van Beuren (1995) do not agree with this interpretation. However, in light of several subsequent judgments, it is now clear that the right to establish the truth regarding one's origins or personal identity – including the identity of one's parents – falls within the concept of private life under Art. 8 of the ECHR.[2]

Note also that in the UK case of *Rose and Another v Secretary of State for Health and Human Fertilisation and Embryology Authority* [2002] EWHC 1593 (Admin), 26 July 2002), it was held that Art. 8 of the ECHR was engaged with regard to both identifying information and non-identifying information sought by donor offspring. This was a case for judicial review brought under the Human Rights Act 1998 (UK). Although it has no precedent value for signatories to the ECHR, it gives a clear message about the way in which the UK has chosen to interpret the application of Art. 8, i.e., the arti-

---

2 See, for example, *Godelli v Italy* (App no 33783/09, Judgment of 25 September 2012 (final 8/03/2013): para 50); *Jäggi v Switzerland* (App no 58757/00, Judgment of 13 July 2006: para 25); *Odièvre v France* (App no 42326/98, Judgment of 13 February 2003: para 29); and *Mikulić v Croatia* (App no 53176/99, 7 February 2002: paras 54 (referring to *Gaskin*) and 64).

cle may be engaged even where donor offspring apply for information about donors where there would otherwise be no legal right to such information. This case should also be of interest to other contracting States. As Cameron has pointed out, in another context, '[c]onvention issues can arise under national law which have not (yet) arisen in the context of the Convention system. Thus, studying the case law of other jurisdictions dealing with the Convention can be of immediate benefit to one's own system ...' (Cameron, 1999: 20).

Engaging Art. 8 then, does not appear to be a problem for donor offspring. But whether the right to genetic origins under Art. 8 could ever be regarded as absolute is another question. Paragraph two of Art. 8 appears to make it possible for states to limit the exercise of the right to respect for private and family life where it interferes with 'the protection of the rights and freedoms of others.'[3] The Court is thus required to take into account competing interests in determining whether there has been a violation of Art. 8 of the Convention and a fair balance must be struck between those interests (*Godelli v Italy* App no 33783/09, Judgment of 25 September 2012; *Jäggi* v *Switzerland* App no 58757/00, Judgment of 13 July 2006).

Surrogacy and the Right to Information about Origins under the CRC and ECHR

While it seems clear that the scope of the right to information under the CRC and ECHR extends to donor offspring, it is less evident that it also includes surrogate-born children. If so, would the right to information be based on a genetic connection or a gestational connection with the surrogate mother, or could it be based on either of these factors?

As regards the CRC, if the surrogate mother's genetic materials are used, the surrogate-born child would clearly have the same right to information about the surrogate mother as any other child would have to know about his or her genetic origins since the definition of parents includes genetic parents. While this would be subject to the Art. 7 qualification 'as far as possible' – which could be open to different interpretations by the various States Parties – the Committee on the Rights of the Child has been unambiguous in relation to the importance of maintaining accurate records about genetic parents, in order to ensure that this information is subsequently available to the children about whom it relates.

3 Of those few cases that explore the nature and scope of the right to information about genetic origins, two judgments in particular, *Odièvre* v *France* and *Jäggi* v *Switzerland*, above, indicate the extent of this limitation. They also provide a realistic idea about the potential scope of the right to identifying information. These two cases are important for donor offspring because they demonstrate a marked change in the line of reasoning by the Court, both in relation to the evaluation of the scope of the right and as regards the extent of a State's perceived margin of appreciation. At the same time they offer insight about the extent to which donor offspring may be able to rely on art. 8 as a means to pursue identifying information about the donor. For a discussion of these cases and their relevance for donor offspring, see Stoll, 2008.

Most international surrogacy arrangements, however, concern gestational surrogacy where there is no genetic link between the surrogate mother and the child. In such a case, if the genetic materials came from both of the commissioning parents, for example, would, or should, the child still have a right to information about the surrogate?

Even if the surrogate is not a genetic parent, she is nevertheless a biological parent by virtue of carrying and giving birth to the child. In this situation, the surrogate-born child would have three 'biological' parents rather than two. As for the parental status of the surrogate, in most jurisdictions she is the legal mother at the time of the child's birth (Stoll, 2013). It would thus be difficult to argue that the scope of the term 'parent' for the purposes of the right to information would not extend to a gestational surrogate mother. Where it concerns records, then, for the reasons outlined above, this would also include securing information about gestational mothers for surrogate-born children.

As for the surrogate-born child's right to information under the ECHR, it is clear that the right to privacy under Art. 8(1) includes the right to establish details about one's identity; something which also includes information about one's parents. Since a gestational surrogate mother is always a biological mother, and in most cases a legal mother, it must follow that the scope of Art. 8(1) extends to the surrogate-born child's right to establish details about the surrogate mother, irrespective of whether or not the connection is genetic or gestational. A State Party could, however, limit the exercise of the right in accordance with Art. 8(2), where it interferes with 'the protection of the rights and freedoms of others' although in such a situation a fair balance must be struck between the competing interests (*Godelli v Italy*; *Jäggi* v *Switzerland*). Accordingly, the right to identifying information about a gestational or genetic surrogate mother could not be regarded as absolute.

The Right to Information under Swedish Law

Background

How, then, has Sweden interpreted its obligations to donor offspring, and what measures has it taken to satisfy them?

Since the Act on Insemination (SFS 1984:1140) came into force, the regulation of ART in Sweden has undergone several changes. Originally, the provisions governing access to identifying information applied only to sperm donation since egg donation was unlawful prior to 1 January 2003. From that date, however, the IVF Act (SFS 1988:711) was amended to, *inter alia*, permit egg *or* sperm donation in combination with IVF under certain limited circumstances. In effect, this means that all Swedish donor offspring born from gametes donated in accordance with ART legislation in force after 1 March 1985 have a prospective right to obtain identifying information about the donor; that is, assuming they were conceived either in a publicly-funded Swedish hospital or institution authorised by the National Board of Health and

Welfare to perform ART procedures (Genetic Integrity Act Ch 6:2, Insemination; Ch 7:4, IVF).[4]

On 1 July 2006, both of the above Acts were repealed and re-enacted, essentially unchanged, as individual chapters of the new Genetic Integrity Act (SFS 2006:351) which now governs all activities related to assisted human reproduction and associated research in Sweden, including access to information following donor treatment procedures. In substance, however, nothing has changed where it concerns access to information for donor offspring. Chapter Six of the Genetic Integrity Act now regulates the practice of insemination in Sweden, replacing the former Act on Insemination. In turn, the practice of IVF is now governed by Chapter Seven of the Genetic Integrity Act, replacing the repealed IVF Act. The insemination and IVF chapters of the 2006 Act have mirror provisions with respect to the right of donor offspring to obtain identifying information about the donor, although the section numbers of the corresponding chapters are different.

The table below summarises, *inter alia*, the main milestones concerning the practice and regulation of ART in Sweden to date.

4 Prior to 1985, there were approximately 230 births recorded each year following donor insemination. This figure, as predicted, dropped significantly after anonymity was abolished and in 1995 only 57 donor offspring births were recorded. By 2005, this figure had increased to 161 (Stoll, 2008). The most recently-published figures show that 204 donor offspring were born in Sweden following IVF in 2010: 118 from sperm donation and 86 from egg donation (Socialstyrelsen, 2013). This figure does not, however, reflect the total number of donor offspring born in Sweden because, since 2007, the national quality register for ART only keeps statistics on IVF treatments.

1920s	Donor insemination (DI) practised in Sweden
1953	Report of the Insemination Committee (SOU 1953:9) proposed a law to regulate insemination
1983	Children conceived by artificial insemination – main report of the Insemination Investigation (SOU 1983:42)
1985	*Insemination Act* (SFS 1984:1140) in force 1 March → best interest of child to know circumstances of conception (before CRC)
1990	Swedish Parliament gives consent to ratify CRC
1993	Office of Children's Ombudsman created
2003	*IVF Act* (SFS 1988:711) amended to permit IVF with *either* egg or sperm donation
2005	Lesbian couples given right to ART from 1 July (Prop. 2004/05:137)
2006	*Genetic Integrity Act* (SFS 2006:311) in force 1 July; repealed SFS 1984:1140 and SFS 1988:711
2010	New regulations and guidelines issued by the National Board for Health and Welfare (SOSFS 2009:32) in force 1 April; repealed the former Regulations and Guidelines on Assisted Reproduction (SOSFS 2002:13).
2013 February	A majority of the Swedish National Council on Medical Ethics find that 'altruistic surrogacy – under special conditions – can constitute an ethically acceptable method of assisted reproduction.' (SMER 2013b:21).
2013 June	The Swedish Government appoints a special investigator to lead the government investigation on: 'Increased possibilities for the treatment of infertility' (Dir 2013:70). The investigator must determine, *inter alia*, whether special rules are needed for children born following cross-border surrogacy arrangements.

Source of the Right to Information

The source of the right to identifying information about the donor can be found in Chapters 6 and 7 of the Genetic Integrity Act (SFS 2006:351). The relevant mirror provisions provide that:

> A person conceived … [as a result of a donor treatment procedure] … has, if he or she has reached sufficient maturity, the right to access the information about the donor which is recorded in the hospital's special medical record.
> If anyone has reason to suspect that he or she was conceived through … [a donor treatment procedure] … the Social Welfare Board is obliged to, on request, help them find out if there is any information recorded in a special medical record. (Ch 6:5, Insemination; Ch 7:7, IVF.)

Best Interests of the Prospective Child – Always the Starting Point for Donor Treatment Procedures

The requirement to consider the interests of the prospective child prior to commencing a treatment procedure is the cornerstone of the insemination and IVF chapters of the Genetic Integrity Act. Mirror provisions contained in these chapters provide, *inter alia*, that donor insemination or IVF '… may be performed only if it can be presumed that the prospective child will grow up under good conditions.' (Ch 6:3, Insemination; Ch 7:5, IVF)

From the wording alone it is self-evident that this sentence was inserted into the respective provisions in order to ensure that the interests of the future donor offspring would be prioritised over the needs and interests of prospective parents and donors. Its origin lies in the Insemination Committee's mandate, established as early as 1983, to protect, foremost, the interests of children born following donor insemination. The Committee's obligation to ensure that the starting point for insemination treatment was that the child would 'grow up under good conditions' (SOU 1983:42: 25) clearly meant that a donor treatment procedure could only be undertaken if it was in the best interests of the future donor offspring. With regard to the issue of access to identifying information, the Committee drew heavily on the experiences of adopted children and was convinced that it was in the best interests of donor offspring to be told the truth about their genetic origins (SOU 1983:42; Stoll, 2008). The connected presumption that openness is presumed to be a pre-condition for the child to grow up under good conditions and therefore in the best interests of the child is further reinforced in the Government Bill (prop 1984/85:2).

This focus on the best interests of the child has continued to be a common theme in virtually all subsequent preparatory works connected to donor offspring and access to information. Moreover, the wording of the respective sections of the Genetic Integrity Act (Ch 6:3, Insemination; Ch 7:5, IVF), above, and the regulations and guidelines (SOSFS 2009:32, Ch 4:11) is almost identical to the wording contained in the original directive given to the Insemination Committee. This demonstrates a history exceeding 25 years where the requirement to consider the best interests of the prospective child prior to donor treatment procedures has been well established under Swedish law. When one takes into account that the CRC was not yet in force in the 1980s, Sweden's success in firmly entrenching the best interest of the child principle in its insemination and IVF laws should be regarded as particularly significant.

Notwithstanding the focus on the child's best interests, it might be surprising that the notion of the 'best interest of the donor offspring' is not defined in the Genetic Integrity Act. Even so, there can be no doubt as to the presumed connection between best interests and the right to information. The clear view expressed in the preparatory works to the legislation was that it is in the best interests of donor offspring to have a right to information about their genetic parents (SOU 1983:42). The access to information provisions was based on this assumption. Accordingly, while there may be different interpretations about what the best interests of donor offspring could include, such interpretations have little bearing regarding access to identifying information by donor offspring in Sweden. The Swedish Parliament has made it clear that, in its view at least, it is in the best interests of donor offspring to have a right to know the identity of the donor.

Scope of the Right to Information

Swedish law is equally clear when it comes to the *scope* of the right to identifying information: The unconditional legal right applies to donor offspring conceived under the Genetic Integrity Act – or the repealed IVF and insemination Acts – from gametes donated after 1 March 1985. Moreover, in order to exercise their right to information under the Genetic Integrity Act, donor offspring must have reached 'sufficient maturity'.

It follows that donor offspring born either through 'do it yourself' inseminations arranged or carried out between private persons, or following treatment procedures carried out abroad, have no right to information about the donor under the Genetic Integrity Act. Likewise, parents and donors have no right to identifying information about each other and donors have no right to know the identity of the donor offspring.

The question of whether the parents of donor offspring should be entitled to find out the identity of the donor before the donor offspring child is 18 years old was raised by the original Insemination Committee in 1983. It could not, however, find any convincing reasons ever to permit the release of identifying information to the parents. Accordingly, it recommended that only donor offspring should have a right to this information (SOU 1983:42); something which was reinforced in the subsequent Government Bill and supported by the Swedish Parliament (prop 1984/85:2).

As to when the right to information may be exercised, the Genetic Integrity Act expressly provides that all donor offspring who have reached 'sufficient maturity' have a right to such information (Ch 6:5, Insemination; Ch 7:7, IVF).

Whether mature minors should have the right to find out the identity of the donor was also discussed at considerable length by the Insemination Committee before the Act on Insemination was proclaimed. In its deliberations, it found that even children who were younger than 18 years of age could experience a great need to find out the identity of their biological parent, particularly during the teenage years. Although the Committee believed that, in general, teenage children were not sufficiently emotionally mature to use this information in a responsible way, it nevertheless considered it appropriate that the social authorities help them work through the feelings they were experiencing – feelings which were associated with the knowledge that they had been conceived through insemination. Moreover, it considered that in exceptional cases it may be justified to give the child the possibility of finding out the identity of the donor, especially where the child is almost 18 years of age. To this end, the Committee proposed that mature minors should have the right to obtain identifying information about the donor, provided that the donor first consented to the release of the information (See SOU 1983:42; Stoll, 2008).

The Swedish Parliament had a different view, however, determining instead that all donor offspring should have an unconditional right to identifying information about the donor if they have reached 'sufficient maturity'; thereby eliminating any need for the consent of the donor. For adult donor offspring, sufficient maturity is presumed. Donor offspring who are under 18 years of age, however, must first be evaluated by the Social Welfare Board in order to establish whether or not they are sufficiently mature to know the identity of the donor. When the Act on Insemination was passed, it was anticipated that the requirements for sufficient maturity would generally be fulfilled when the child was in the upper teens (prop 1984/85:2).

Right to Information – Supporting Provisions

The Genetic Integrity Act contains several other provisions that have a direct bearing on a donor offspring's right to information and to this extent should be mentioned. The first of these concerns the requirement to preserve information about the donor. The Act stipulates that information about the donor shall be recorded in a special medical record which shall be preserved for at least 70 years (Ch 6:4, Insemination; Ch 7:6, IVF).

Before the Act on Insemination was in force, record keeping following donor treatment procedures was arbitrary and the possibility for donor offspring to discover that they were born through insemination or to find out the identity of the donor was very small. All documents concerning insemination treatment were either destroyed or inaccessible to anyone other than the responsible doctor, largely in an attempt to keep the information secret from the child (SOU 1983:42). The record-keeping provisions of the Swedish insemination and IVF laws were principally designed to preserve information about the donor for future donor offspring. To this end, they fulfill a vital support function necessary for the access to information process (Stoll, 2008).

In addition to the record keeping requirements, the Genetic Integrity Act contains two prohibitions that are particularly relevant to the best interests of donor offspring and their right to identifying information about the donor: the prohibition against the importation of sperm and the prohibition against using the gametes of dead donors. In addition, the regulations governing assisted conception prohibit the mixing of gametes in a treatment procedure.

The importation of frozen sperm into Sweden without permission from the National Board of Health and Welfare is prohibited by the insemination chapter of the Genetic Integrity Act (Ch 6:7). The origin of this prohibition was the Insemination Committee's recommendation that the unauthorised importation of sperm from other countries be prohibited in order to prevent foreign sperm banks from selling sperm by mail order to women in Sweden for the purpose of self insemination. In particular, the Committee felt that this activity would not be consistent with the best interests of the child (SOU 1983:42). In addition to promoting the best interests of donor offspring, this prohibition supports the access to information process by attempting to ensure that all Swedish donors are traceable for donor offspring who may wish to exercise their right to identifying information.

The Genetic Integrity Act also provides that eggs or sperm from a donor who has died may not be used for insemination or IVF (Ch 6:4, Insemination; Ch 7:6, IVF). This prohibition is reinforced in the regulations (SOSFS 2009:32 Ch 4:14). An important motivation behind the prohibition is that it could potentially have negative consequences for the child if the child were to discover that the donor was already dead at the time of the child's conception (prop. 2001/02:89). In addition to being in the best interests of the child, such a prohibition promotes access to identifying information by leaving open the possibility for contact between the donor offspring and the donor in the future.

Finally, the former practice of mixing gametes from different donors in the same donor treatment procedure is prohibited by the regulations which provide that insemination or IVF may not be carried out on a woman using the gametes of more than one donor in each treatment cycle (SOSFS 2009:32 Ch 4:15). The source of this prohibition also stems from the deliberations of the Insemination Committee which reported that the practice was at that time known to occur in the USA and in Norway even though there was no indication that it was a problem in Sweden. Nevertheless, since the priority of the Committee was to ensure that the identity of the donor could be established because it was in the best interests of the child, it proposed that the practice of mixing sperm from different donors in order to achieve a pregnancy should not be permitted (SOU 1983:42).

Exercising the Right to Information

Having a legal right to information does not necessarily guarantees the its realisation. In the case of donor offspring, the child must first know how he or she was conceived. The acquisition of this knowledge is, in most cases, contingent upon the parents telling the child. In addition, there must be records available about the donor.

Although Swedish donor offspring have a right to know the identity of the donor, it is now apparent that a considerable number of them will not be able to exercise this right because they do not know how they were conceived (Stoll, 2008). When the access to information provisions first came into force in 1985, the Swedish Parliament determined to leave the responsibility for disclosure about the existence of the donor with the parents of donor offspring. This decision was based on the belief that it is in the child's best interest to receive this information from its parents and on the assumption that, over time, parents would become more open with their children in relation to the child's origins. As anticipated, Swedish studies reveal that increasing numbers of parents are now making the decision to disclose (Isaksson et al, 2012; Lalos et al, 2007; Leeb-Lundberg et al, 2006). A report published in 2012, which found that 78% of parents in a multicentre study planned to disclose (Isaksson et al, 2012), confirms the trend in favour of disclosure. At the same time, it is equally clear that some donor offspring will never be told how they were conceived. It follows that these donor offspring will not be in a position to exercise their right to information if the responsibility for disclosure remains with the parents.[5]

Donor offspring who know they have a right to information, and who wish to exercise this right, may do so by turning to the Social Welfare Committee in their municipality. Donor offspring who are over 18 years of age may also contact the hospital directly.

Impact of Surrogacy Arrangements on the Child's Right to Know

If a jurisdiction's domestic law regulates surrogacy such that a surrogate-born child has a right to information about the donor or the surrogate, and the surrogacy arrangement is entered into domestically, the information would be secured, thereby making it possible for the child's right to be realised.

Where it concerns cross-border surrogacy, however, the possibility for a surrogate-born child to access information about his or her origins is less certain because it will depend on the system of record keeping in the jurisdiction in question. Even in relation to States that are signatories to the ECHR, for example, the existence and extent of records that are available or preserved, will be influenced by the way in which that State interprets and exercises its margin of appreciation.

Other factors might also make accessing information about origins more complicated following cross-border surrogacy arrangements. These include factors such as the use of anonymous donors, or possible difficulties in locating or contacting the surrogate mother or donor. Moreover, in the case of surrogacy, if the surrogate mother's spouse – presumably in the absence of a genetic connection – is recorded as the child's legal father on the original birth certificate, this could add to the confusion about origins even where records are available.

Facilitating Accurate Records and Access to Information

Assuming that it is possible to ensure that accurate records are maintained, if one accepts that surrogate-born children have a right to information about the surrogate

5 For a discussion of the Swedish studies on parental disclosure between 2000–2007, see Stoll, 2008, Chapter 4.

mother, how can access to information be facilitated, both at the national and international level?

Regarding Sweden, if surrogacy arrangements were to be supported by law, preserving and recording information about the surrogate mother would be automatic since systems for record-keeping following all assisted reproductive treatments are already well established. Even so, several additional measures that would facilitate access to information – both in general and in relation to surrogacy arrangements – could be taken domestically.

First and foremost, a central register should be created and maintained by a national body such as the National Board for Health and Welfare in order to improve and streamline the searching process and the release of information. A complementary voluntary register and/or a DNA register would make it possible for contact to be made between donors and donor offspring who would otherwise have no legal right to information. More education for the authorities in question and a dedicated, compulsory counselling and follow-up programme for prospective parents would also promote the right to information, as would more information to the public in general. These measures are all achievable (Stoll, 2008).

As regards cross-border ART and surrogacy arrangements, however, promoting access to information is more difficult since it presupposes the harmonisation of laws in relation to the way in which birth records and birth certificates are recorded and made available. Moreover, even if an international agreement about surrogacy were to exist in the future, it is reasonable to assume that not all jurisdictions would choose to become bound by it. Even so, while finding a core of common values on which to base a convention certainly poses a challenge, it is nevertheless something to strive for.

To this end, a number of projects attempting to identify and solve problems connected to surrogacy at the international level are currently underway and should be mentioned. The first of these concerns the work being carried out by the Hague Conference on Private International Law in relation to the private international law issues surrounding the status of children, including issues arising from international surrogacy arrangements. Since 2010, the Permanent Bureau has presented two preliminary reports (The Hague Conference, 2011 and 2012) and is expected to present its final report to the Council on General Affairs and Policy of the Conference in 2014.

Another project that must be highlighted is the recently-published study comprising the 2013 edition of *Studies in Private International Law* (Trimmings and Beaumont, 2013a). The topic of this volume is 'International Surrogacy Arrangements and their Regulation at the international Level'. The study is extensive and comprises three parts: Part One contains 25 national reports on surrogacy; Part Two examines international perspectives of cross-border surrogacy; and in Part Three, the editors provide a general report on surrogacy (Trimmings and Beaumont, 2013b). In the chapter by Baker (2013), the question of a possible future convention on international surrogacy arrangements is raised. In this context, Trimmings and Beaumont point to a number of fundamental principles that would have to be observed or determined if an international convention on surrogacy were to be implemented. These include the best interests of the child, the need to ensure that prospective parents are suitable and that information is preserved; and the significance of a genetic connection with one of the commissioning parents. Other issues raised include the need for a central authority in each contracting state and access to birth records by surrogate-born children (Trimmings and Beaumont, 2013b: 539-541).

A third project on international surrogacy issues that requires special mention is the European Parliament's comprehensive comparative study on surrogacy in the EU member states, which was published in May 2013. This study includes an empirical analysis, in addition to legal analyses comprising national legislation and case law, European Union law and private international law. It also contains country reports from 11 countries. An important conclusion made is that '... it is impossible to indicate a particular legal trend across the EU, however, all Member States appear to agree on the need for a child to have clearly defined legal parents and civil status.' (European Parliament, 2013: 1)

On the domestic front in Sweden, several recent public initiatives have the potential significantly to influence future Swedish policy on surrogacy arrangements and the way in which surrogacy is regulated, including the facilitation of accurate records and access to information. In February 2013, the Swedish National Council on Medical Ethics (SMER) released the report, 'Assisted Reproduction: Ethical Aspects'. In this report, the Council emphasised that it is urgent that children born following surrogacy abroad are given the same conditions as other children. An additional concern expressed by the Council was the need to guard the interests of the prospective child, i.e. always to take priority over parents. Moreover, a majority of the Council considered that 'altruistic surrogacy – under special conditions – can constitute an ethically acceptable method of assisted reproduction' (SMER 2013, p. 21). This is significant, coming 18 years after the Council's recommendation that surrogacy should not be permitted in Sweden; something which had a major impact on ART legislation at the time (SMER, 1995).

In March 2013, shortly after the release of the SMER report, the Government appointed a special investigator to examine children's rights under Swedish law. One of the tasks of the investigator is to review a selection of court and administrative decisions and to evaluate the extent to which the application of law and other regulations accord with the CRC and the optional protocols that Sweden has entered into. The scope of this investigation includes the question of CRC incorporation (Dir. 2013a).

Finally, on 19 June 2013, the Swedish Government appointed a special investigator to consider different ways to increase the possibilities through which unintentionally childless people could become parents (Dir 2013b). Of the three initiatives mentioned, it is this government investigation on 'increased possibilities for the treatment of infertility' that will most directly affect the law and policy concerning surrogacy. With a focus on the best interests of the child and the child's right to know about his or her origins, one of the tasks of the investigator is to take a position about whether special rules are needed for those children who are born following surrogacy arrangements abroad. Another task is to take a position about whether a prerequisite for ART procedures should be a genetic connection between the child and the (one or two) intended parents. The investigation in its entirety is expected to be finalised by 24 June 2015.

Conclusion

A starting point of this chapter has been that it is in the best interests of the child to have a right to information about his or her origins. Moreover, if a State has expressly conferred such a right on donor offspring, the child's interest in knowing about its origins should be afforded greater weight than any possible interest a parent or donor might have in keeping this information secret. This is consistent with long-standing Swedish policy and has strong support domestically. It also has support internationally, through art. 3(1) of the CRC which provides that '[i]n all actions concerning children ... the best interests of the child shall be a primary consideration.'

Having signed and ratified the CRC, even though it has not been incorporated or transformed into Swedish law at the time of writing, Swedish authorities and courts are required to interpret Swedish law against the background of the Convention's purpose and provisions. Regarding the specific issue of access to information for donor offspring, Sweden's domestic position – that facilitating the child's right to information is consistent with the child's best interests – was firmly grounded already before the implementation of the CRC (Stoll, 2008).

Now that more prospective parents are turning to surrogacy arrangements to build families, it is timely to consider whether more can be done to ensure that the rights of surrogate-born children are brought into line with those of donor offspring and other children. In this context, a reasonable place to start could be to take into account the surrogate-born child's need for information about his or her origins and, in particular, to consider whether it is possible to extend the right to enable surrogate-born children to know the identity of the surrogate mother, irrespective of whether or not she is the genetic or gestational mother.

References

Official Publications, Sweden

Swedish Government Official Reports (SOU):

SOU 1983:42
SOU 1997:116

Government Bills:

Prop 1984/85:2
Prop 2001/02:89

Swedish Council on Medical Ethics:

Rapport om behandling av ofrivillig barnlöshet, Statens medicinsk-etiska råd, 1995 (SMER 1995).

Assisterad befruktning – etiska aspekter, Statens medicinsk-etiska råd, 2013 (SMER 2013:1).

Terms of Reference:

Dir. 2013:35, Översyn av barnets rättigheter i svensk rätt (Dir. 2013a).

Dir. 2013:70, Utökade möjligheter till behandling av ofrivillig barnlöshet (Dir. 2013b).

Sweden's Official Statistics:

Graviditeter, förlossningar och nyfödda barn, Sveriges officiella statistik, (Socialstyrelsen, 2013).

International Publications

The European Parliament:

A comparative study on the regime of surrogacy in EU Member States, European Parliament, May 2013. Available at <http://www.europarl.europa.eu/delegations/sv/studiesdownload.html?languageDocument=EN&file=93673> accessed 1 September 2013.

The Hague Conference on Private International Law:

Preliminary Document No 11 of March 2011, 'Private international law issues surrounding the status of children, including issues arising from international surrogacy arrangements' available at <http://www.hcch.net/upload/wop/genaff2011pd11e.pdf>

Preliminary Document No 10 of March 2012, 'A preliminary report on the issues arising in relation to international surrogacy arrangements' available at <http://www.hcch.net/upload/wop/gap2012pd10en.pdf> accessed 1 September 2013.

Books and Articles

Baker, H., "A Possible Future Instrument on International Surrogacy Arrangements: Are there 'lessons' to be learnt from the 1993 Hague Intercountry Adoption Convention?" in K. Trimmings and P. Beaumont (eds), *International Surrogacy Arrangements: Legal Regulation at the International Level* (Oxford: Hart, 2013).

Breen, C., "Poles Apart? The Best Interests of the Child and Assisted Reproduction in the Antipodes and Europe", *International Journal of Children's Rights* 2001 9(2), 157-180.

Cameron, I., "The Swedish Experience of the European Convention on Human Rights since Incorporation", 48 *International and Comparative Law Quarterly* 1999 48(1), 20-56.

Cameron, I., *An Introduction to the European Convention on Human Rights* 5th edn (Uppsala: Iustus, 2006).

Detrick, S., *A Commentary on the United Nations Convention on the Rights of the Child* (The Hague: Martinus Nijhoff, 1999).

Hodgkin, R. and P. Newell, *Implementation Handbook for the Convention on the Rights of the Child* (Geneva: UNICEF, 2002).

Forder, C., "Constitutional Principle and the Establishment of the Legal Relationship between the Child and the Non-marital Father: A Study of Germany, the Netherlands and England", *International Journal of Law and the Family* 1993 7(1), 40-107.

Freeman, M., "The New Birth Right? Identity and the Child of the Reproduction Revolution", *International Journal of Children's Rights* 1996 4(3), 273-297.

Isaksson, S., G. Sydsjö, A. Skoog Svanberg and C. Lampic, "Disclosure Behaviour and Intentions among 111 Couples Following Treatment with Oocytes or Sperm from Identity-release Donors: Follow-up at Offspring Age 1-4 Years", *Human Reproduction* 2012 27(10) 2998-3007.

Kilkelly, U., *The Child and the European Convention on Human Rights* (Farnham: Ashgate, 1999).

Lalos, A., C. Gottlieb and O. Lalos, "Legislated Right for Donor-insemination Children to Know Their Genetic Origin: A Study of Parental Thinking", *Human Reproduction* 2007 22(6), 1759-1768.

Leeb-Lundberg, S., S. Kjellberg and G. Sydsjö, "Helping parents to tell their children about the use of donor insemination (DI) and determining their opinions about open-identity sperm donors", *Acta Obstetrician et Gynecologica* 2006 85, 78-81.

Singer, A., *Föräldraskap i rättslig belysning* (Uppsala: Acta Universitatis Upsaliensis, 2000).

Smith, L. "Nyere utvikling i barneretten", *Tidskrift for familierett, arverett og barnevernrettslige spørsmål* 2008 2(6), 84-94.

Stoll, J., *Swedish Donor Offspring and Their Legal Right to Information* (Uppsala: Juridiska Institutionen, 2008).

Stoll, J., *Surrogacy Arrangements and Legal Parenthood: Swedish Law in a Comparative Context* (Uppsala: Juridiska Institutionen, 2013).

Tobin, J., "The Convention on the Rights of the Child: The Rights and Best Interests of Children Conceived Through Assisted Reproduction" Occasional Paper, Victorian Law Reform Commission (2004).

Trimmings, K. and P. Beaumont (eds), *International Surrogacy Arrangements: Legal Regulation at the International Level* (Oxford: Hart, 2013a).

Trimmings, K. and P. Beaumont, "General Report on Surrogacy' in K. Trimmings and P. Beaumont (eds), *International Surrogacy Arrangements: Legal Regulation at the International Level* (Oxford: Hart, 2013b).

Van Bueren, G., "Children's Access to Adoption Records: State Discretion or an Enforceable International Right?", *Modern Law Review* 1995 58(1), 37-53.

Sometimes as a Child, Sometimes as an Adult: Children and Access to Justice in Italy

Maria Federica Moscati[1]
Sussex University

Introduction

The present study explores the extent to which children can be said to have access to justice under Italian law. It is argued that the Italian situation presents an almost comprehensive legal framework and offers important procedural guarantees for children who become involved with the law. Nevertheless, some barriers to access to justice for children still persist, in both civil litigation and the juvenile justice system. With specific reference to the involvement of children into the civil litigation system, very few steps have been taken in order to resolve disputes between children by recourse to alternative dispute resolution. The barriers appear particularly important in the juvenile justice system and especially with regard to the treatment of children who are involved in organised crime in Naples, in the far south of Italy.

This demonstrates that the Italian legislator is caught between two contrasting approaches to childhood: a *paternalistic view*, by which children are considered to be an extension of their parents and in need of protection, and an *equality ideal* or better, *a levelling idea*, by which children and adults are treated in the same way. In this study, it is argued that these two approaches to childhood have significantly influenced and shaped the procedural safeguards guaranteed to Italian children. Although more details are offered in the next sections, here it suffices to say that the *paternalistic approach* creates a number of limitations to a child who is willing to initiate a civil action. Such an action can be commenced only if the child is represented by the parents, or by a guardian. As the result of a *levelling approach* to childhood, we find that the treatment of those children involved in organised crime and willing to collaborate with the judiciary, is governed by the same law that rules on adults' conduct.

1 The author of the present paper wishes to thank Dr Roberto Gentile for all precious information on children involved in organised crime in Naples; the Italian Ombudsman for Children and Youths, Dr Vincenzo Spadafora, for his report on the situation of Italian juvenile justice; and the anonymous reviewer for the useful comments on this paper.

A. Diduck, N. Peleg, H. Reece (eds.), Law in Society: Reflections on Children, Family, Culture and Philosophy
 ISBN 978-90-04-26148-8. pp. 571-587.

Before examining the two approaches in more detail, it can be said that both ideas should be considered within the general cultural nature of Italy. In particular, this means that the different degree of acceptance of children's rights and children's participation as guaranteed by international human rights instruments, and the flexibility in the recognition, depend on contextual factors and domestic diversity. Thus, the normative level has to create a consensus between the international and national contexts. However, in this process of legislative negotiation it is possible that the basic principles lose their original shape and those international standards – in our case children's rights – bring new meanings and acquire new importance in the local social context of Italy.

Several writers have analysed the role that paternalism plays in the recognition and implementation of children's rights (Fortin, 2009), and it is not the aim of this research to look at such debates – it suffices here to clarify that the author of the present paper believes in the idea that children have rights, including procedural rights, and have the right to the exercise of those rights. Rather, here the concern is more with the reasons of paternalism with regards to rights of children in Italy. Generally speaking, it could be said that the Italian paternalistic view of childhood shifts strongly into a charitable and beneficent approach to the issues surrounding children and youths. The reasons for this approach can be found first in the role that the family plays in Italian legal culture and secondly in the strong influence that the Roman Catholic Church and its culture have on Italian politics and law. The family plays important economic, symbolic and ideological functions in Italian society and as such is a key concern of Italian political culture. In particular, Italian politics has frequently relied upon the family in delivering several important services to citizens. For instance, in Italy, although education and health are public, it is the family which provides much of the 'welfare' in terms of assistance and basic needs. In addition, the family is considered to be the basic, protective and fundamental unit for the transfer of values and culture to children – and although with less emphasis than in the past, a patriarchal approach still shapes the decision about what has to be transferred to children. This idea about the central role of family in Italian culture contributes to perpetuate a paternalistic legal culture of childhood by which children are seen as individuals to protect, more than for them to be entitled to exercise their rights.

A second factor which contributes to the paternalistic legal attitude toward childhood in Italy is the influence that the Roman Catholic Church exercises on Italian legal culture. In particular, following the signature of an agreement between the Italian State and the Holy See in 1929, the Roman Catholic Church informed and influenced public opinion through the teaching in schools and through the intellectuals (Gramsci, 1929 [2006]). With particular reference to the idea of childhood the Roman Catholic Church could instil, into popular culture and law, belief of subordination of children to the morals proper of the Holy See which recognise that the basic and fundamental instrument to transfer religious morals is the family. The family, as an institution which precedes the State, is the best community for the education and transmission of the religious values which are fundamental to society as a whole. Children are educated by families for the benefit of society (Pontifical, 2000).

The Roman Catholic Church expressly recognises that the family is instrumental in maintaining respect for all human rights instruments. And the human rights instruments should give priority to the recognition of the rights of the family (Pontifical, 1999). Children are precious gifts and the rights of the child are important, but only if they do not conflict with the primary rights of the parents. The parents have the last word regarding decisions involving religion, education, association with others and privacy.

However, the paternalistic approach is mitigated, and sometimes blurred, by a levelling approach to childhood by which children are treated as adults. As this chapter will explain further, the reference here is to the lack of specific legislation governing the involvement of children in organised crime. As for the paternalistic approach, the recourse to general Italian culture will help to understand the reasons for the levelling approach. In particular, a general reluctance and negligence of the Italian legislator to devote time and resources to the revision of criminal procedural laws, and more importantly to the reform of the law governing the management of prisons, represents the main reason for the levelling approach to childhood.

As far as access to justice is concerned, theoretically, the present study adopts a critical approach to the original meaning of access to justice, as defined by Mauro Cappelletti in the late 1970s. As Cappelletti and Garth pointed out, access to justice may be characterised as involving 'waves of legal reform aiming at making rights effective' (Cappelletti and Garth, 1978: 21).They identified three waves of legal reforms worldwide as characterising the growth of the access to justice movement. The waves have been neither static nor discrete but rather, developed alongside each other. The first wave involved legal aid to the poor; the second involved the development of so-called public interest suits for the protection of diffuse interests; and the third wave aimed at reforming civil procedure and encouraging the use of alternative dispute resolution. One of the main contributions of the access to justice movement to the study of law and dispute resolution is the focus on the parties of the dispute as being the primary protagonists and on whom, therefore, the analyst should concentrate. As a consequence, the dispute resolution process has to take into account, and be shaped according to, the characteristics and goals of the parties. As Marc Galanter has recently pointed out, the boundaries of the access to justice movement are still developing. The movement develops in a way that expands the notions of justice and injustice, the meaning and perception of wrong, and also seeks to enlarge the range of people who could take legal action (Galanter, 2010). Such developments depend on several personal and social factors including the consciousness and perceptions that individuals and groups have about the injustice they perceive themselves to be victims of (Felstiner *et al.*, 1980). In addition, many of the principles of the original Access to Justice Movement have been extended to or incorporated into international human rights law – amongst others by the United Nations Convention on the Rights of the Child (1989, hereinafter UNCRC) and the European Convention on the Exercise of

Child's Rights (1996).[2] While the phrase access to justice is not mentioned explicitly in the two Conventions, the several rights listed therein must be included in our general understanding of access to justice. In particular, Art. 12 of the UNCRC states that

> the child shall in particular be provided the opportunity to be heard in any judicial and administrative proceedings affecting the child, either directly, or through a representative or an appropriate body, in a manner consistent with the procedural rules of national law.

In addition, with regard to criminal cases in which a minor is accused of breaking the law, Art. 40 of the UNCRC provides for the right to legal assistance and fair treatment in the juvenile justice system. In particular, member states are required to set a minimum age for criminal liability and to provide minimum guarantees for fair and prompt resolution of judicial or alternative proceedings. The Convention, furthermore, includes protection from cruelty for those children who are in detention (Art. 37).

In the European context, the European Convention on the Exercise of Child's Rights (1996) crucially emphasises procedural rights of children and their exercise (Art. 1) including the right to be informed and to express his or her views in proceedings (Art. 3) and the right to apply for the appointment of a special representative (Art. 4). In addition, the Convention specifies that, 'Parties shall consider granting children additional procedural rights' which might include the right to appoint their own representative (Art. 5). This aspect is particularly interesting in the Italian context where the principle of granting procedural rights to the children does not extend

---

2 There are other international instruments, which, although they do not have the same strength of the UNCRC, nevertheless offer protection to children into the juvenile justice system. First, the UN Standard Minimum Rules for the Administration of Juvenile Justice (The Beijing Rules,1985), and in particular rule 11 on diversion and rule15.1 addressing the right to be represented by a legal adviser or apply for free legal aid. Second, the Committee on the Rights of the Child: 2007 General Comment No.10: a child in conflict with the law must be guaranteed legal or other appropriate assistance in the preparation and presentation of his/her defence. Third, the Lilongwe Declaration on Accessing Legal Aid in the Criminal Justice System in Africa: 2004.Fourth, the UN Guidance Note of the Secretary General: UN Approach to Justice for Children (2008) – promoting child-sensitive procedures and methods that ensure the child's fully-fledged participation in a judicial, administrative and community-based approach. Fifth, the UN Guidelines on Justice in Matters involving Child Victims and Witnesses of Crime adopted by the Economic and Social Council: resolution 2005/20 of 22 July 2005, in para.22 establishes that child victims and witnesses should have access to assistance. Finally, United Nations Rules for the Protection of Juveniles Deprived of their Liberty (Havana Rules) which provided guarantees for children who have been restricted and deprived in their liberty, and the Guidelines for Action on Children in the Criminal Justice System (Vienna Guidelines). Among regional instruments, particular important is article 17 (2) (iii) of the African Charter on the Rights and Welfare of the Child (1999) by which children shall be afforded legal and other appropriate assistance in the preparation and presentation of their defence.

so far as to include the right to choose and nominate such a representative. There is still a system in which the intervention of parents or public prosecutor is expected. This conservatism is rooted in the still paternalistic perspective that childhood has in the Italian society. A specific application of the Strasbourg Convention is made with regard to family proceedings and member states are required by the Convention to select and choose at least three types of family proceeding to which the minimum standards of the Convention apply. In addition, the Council of Europe adopted in 2010 the 'Guidelines on Child-Friendly Justice' which represent a practical tool for governments in all cases in which children come to be involved in the justice system. The rights to access to justice are protected before, during and after the proceedings (Kilkelly, 2010).

In the light of the above mentioned legislation, the present paper is concerned with analysing to what extent the three waves of the Access to Justice Movement have been influential in Italy and in addition considers other examples of access to justice for children including the right to be heard, the right to legal assistance in civil cases and the right to specific laws aimed at protecting children involved in organised crime. This chapter argues that both the theoretical and methodological framework used to understand and overcome barriers to justice in the civil justice context – as conceptualised by Cappelletti – might be easily adapted to the criminal justice system.

This chapter, as noted above, is divided in three parts and it relies on empirical data which, amongst others, has been collected through interviews with the Italian Ombudsman for Children and Youths and an Italian public prosecutor. The chapter first address the development of Italian norms addressing the right to access to justice of children. In doing so, the chapter considers whether and to what extent the Italian legislation adheres to international standards. In addition, Part I is dedicated to an explanation of the separation of jurisdiction over disputes involving children between the Juvenile Court (*Tribunale per i Minorenni*), the Civil Court (*Tribunale Ordinario*) and the Tutelary Judge (*Giudice Tutelare*). Then, in Part II, the chapter examines examples of procedural rights of children in the context of civil litigation procedure. In particular, Part II looks at whether and to what extent the three waves of the Access to Justice Movement are implemented in the Italian legal scenario. Then Part II moves on to considering the right to participation and the right to legal assistance for children. Part III focuses on barriers to access to justice in the criminal law, considering the use of children by organised crime in Naples in the south of Italy, and the law governing the protection of children who decide to collaborate with the judiciary. The case study is based on original research materials primarily collected through local newspapers and a semi-structured interview with an Italian Public Prosecutor, Roberto Gentile,[3] who works at the juvenile court of Naples.

---

3 In particular an interview on 11 October 2013.

Access to Justice of Children in Italy: National Framework

Italian legislation includes several principles and norms aimed at protecting the rights of children. Such protection starts in the Italian Constitution with the provisions which rule that it is a duty of the Republic to remove all obstacles to the correct development of each individual (Art. 2) and, in particular, to protect children and youths (Art. 31). More specifically, on the protection of procedural rights, it could be said that the procedural rights of children fall within the requirement of provision of a fair trial (Art. 111), and the norm ensuring legal representation during court proceedings (Art. 24).[4] The Constitutional framework is reinforced by the ratification of several international conventions, which protect the rights of the child, including Art. 24 of the Lisbon Treaty protecting the rights of the child in court proceedings. With particular reference to the Strasbourg Convention, family proceedings are now governed by such laws as those on parental authority (Art. 145, Civil Code); natural affiliation (Arts. 244, 247, 264 and 274, Civil Code); and a son's opposition to certain facts regarding the administration of property resulting from the conduct of his parents (322 and 323, Civil Code). The signature and ratification of the UNCRC by means of Law 27/5/91 no. 165 led to enactment of new legislation regulating the prevention of criminal misconduct by children (Law 19/7/91, no. 216) and on support strategies for young people (Law 28/8/97, no. 285). The influence of the UNCRC, and in particular of Art. 12, has encouraged a new vision of the child within civil proceedings and in particular it has contributed to the development of the idea that participation in court proceedings is now a right of every child. As a result, the participation of the child is now considered to be necessary during the proceedings concerning separation and divorce and those related to the dissolution of cohabitation.[5] However, as the present paper will show further, implementation of the principle of participation is still something of puzzle in Italy (Ruo, 2012). This might be explained in view of the protective attitude toward childhood still present within Italian culture. Indeed, the idea that a child is an extension of the parents and is in need of protection emerges from the lan-

---

4 Article 24 of the Italian Constitution states:

1 Anyone may bring cases before a court of law in order to protect their rights under civil and administrative law.

2 Defence is an inviolable right at every stage and instance of legal proceedings.

3 The poor are entitled by law to proper means for action or defence in all courts.

4 The law shall define the conditions and forms of reparation in case of judicial errors.

5 See further in the essay, the new art. 155 of the Civil Code introduced by law n.54/2006. With Law 15 January 1994, no. 64, Italy has signed and ratified the Hague Convention on the Civil Aspects of International Child Abduction and the European Convention on the Repatriation of Minors, which both provide provisions aimed at hearing a child during court proceedings. However, the Italian legislator has subordinated the hearing to the evaluation and discretion of the judge.

guage used by the Italian legislator which continues to prefer to use the terms *'minor' and 'son'*, instead of child.

In order to meet the needs of children in conflict with the law and to realise the re-education and empowerment of a child rather than the punishment, the Italian legislator in 1988 issued Presidential Decree 448 of 1988 (Hereinafter: Law 448/1988). This is a specific law on juvenile criminal proceedings, formulated in line with the directions of the main sources of international law and the principles of the Italian Constitution. Unlike ordinary criminal procedures, Law 448/1988 provides for a procedure that facilitates a rapid release of the child from the criminal track. As a consequence, a quick resolution of the proceedings and the use of mediation between minor offender and victim have been introduced into the Italian juvenile justice system. Notwithstanding such requirements, the legal framework on juvenile justice and, in particular, criminal juvenile justice, is not completely adequate to meet the specific needs of children in conflict with the law. In fact, there are still a few areas which are not governed by Law 448/1988, but by the general norms of the Italian Criminal Code (Royal Decree of 19 October 1930, no. 1398), its subsequent revisions and other general legal statutes dealing with criminal law. As a result, there are situations, as the present paper shows further, in which children and adults are treated alike creating inevitable barriers to access to justice for children.

As far as the application of procedural guarantees is concerned, all judges dealing with children in court proceedings, mainly in juvenile justice, must respect the principles of the law. Under Italian law the expression 'juvenile justice' is not obvious and not easy to grasp. It can be said that not all proceedings in which a child is involved are included in the so-called system of ' juvenile justice'. The Italian Constitutional Court has stated that juvenile justice includes all those court proceedings which are concerned with both personal and patrimonial issues which directly, and sometimes indirectly, affect the interests of the child.[6] Although vague, nevertheless such definition indicates that the core of the juvenile justice system is the protection of the interests of the child. Therefore juvenile justice is concerned with all those court proceedings involving those rights and interests of the child which in order to be protected necessarily require the intervention of the judiciary (Tommaseo, 2007). This means that juvenile justice represents a practical implementation of the principle contained in Art. 2 of the Constitution, according to which the State has the duty to remove all obstacles to the complete fulfilment of the rights of individuals.

The need to create a justice system adequate to meet the needs of children has inspired the enactment of Royal Decree n.1404/34, the law establishing specialised juvenile courts (*Tribunale per i Minorenni*). The juvenile court is a collegial body composed of four judges, two professional judges and two lay judges chosen from among experts in biology, psychiatry, criminal anthropology, pedagogy or psychology (Art. 2). It has jurisdiction in criminal, civil and administrative matters, and is meant to handle cases in the spirit of the realisation of the child's best interests. In criminal cases the juvenile court has exclusive jurisdiction on all crimes committed by a per-

---

6 Constitutional Court, Decision 30/12/1997.

son under 18 years of age, even if committed together with adults. It is not uncommon in Italy that a trial takes place after a long delay, and therefore the person in trouble is already adult by the time of the court proceedings. Nevertheless, the rules of juvenile criminal procedure contained in Law 448/1988 apply in such cases.

In civil matters, issues concerning the protection of children are decided by both the juvenile court and ordinary courts. The juvenile court has jurisdiction in cases of care and exercise of parental responsibility including maintenance, upbringing and education (article 147 Civil Code). The court may impose limits on the exercise of parental authority, issuing instructions to the parents of the child and activating the intervention of health and social services to support and monitor the living conditions of the child in the family (Art. 333 of the Civil Code). It may also remove the child from the family house (Arts. 330-333 and 336 Civil Code) and accommodate the child with another family, an institution or a single person (Arts. 2 and 4 of Law, n. 184/83). In serious cases, when the child is considered to be in a situation of moral and material abandonment, the juvenile court can declare a 'state of adoptability' (Art. 8, Law no. 184/83) allowing the child to be 'adopted out' regardless of parental wishes.

The civil jurisdiction of the juvenile court includes measures concerning the custody of children of unmarried parents and disputes with regard to the exercise of parental authority (Art. 317, section 2 of the Civil Code). The juvenile court, in addition, has the power to decide to add the surname of the father who has not recognised the child at birth (Art. 262, Civil Code) and cases brought before the court for the assessment and declaration of natural fatherhood and motherhood (Art. 269, Civil Code). It may also authorise, for in serious cases, a minor who has reached 16 years of age to get married (Article 84, Civil Code). The juvenile court also decides on issues relating to international adoptions.

Moreover, the juvenile court exercises administrative powers regarding educational interventions in favour of troubled teens (Article 25 of the Royal Decree 1404/34). In all matters under its jurisdiction, an important feature of juvenile justice is to secure the cooperation of social services, shelter and health care institutions which often provide accommodation and courses for troubled children.

Together with the juvenile court, the ordinary court and the tutelary judge have some forms of jurisdiction in cases involving children. More specifically, the ordinary court deals with issues of separation and divorce and, since the enactment of Law 219/2012, which abolished in law all differences between children born in and out wedlock, it handles disputes arising between unmarried partners in which a child is involved. The tutelary judge has jurisdiction over uncontentious issues such as management of properties belonging to children.

Notwithstanding the creation of specialised courts for cases involving children, nonetheless an important barrier to access to justice is found in the system of the juvenile courts. Juvenile courts in Italy face several financial problems and have limited numbers of staff, which in turn slows down court proceedings and forces the judiciary to rely heavily on the support of the police.[7] Moreover, as the Ombudsman for Children and Youths points out, it often happens that when children are heard during civil proceedings, the information given to them is not exhaustive as it should be and their voice is not taken into consideration for the final decision, or courts do not have enough rooms equipped for the protected hearing of those children who have been victims of abuse.[8]

Access to Civil Justice

As far as the three initial waves of the Access to Justice Movement are concerned, Italian law provides legal aid for children in criminal cases. As the present study shows further, for civil litigation cases in which children are involved, the law is still not clear as to whether and how a lawyer who is representing a child will be paid. With regard to the second wave aimed at protecting diffuse interests, children are not allowed to file public interest litigation. Finally, with reference to the third wave of the Access to Justice Movement which emphasised the use of extra-judicial mechanisms for the resolution of disputes, alternative dispute resolution is used very rarely to solve disputes in which children are the disputants. Mediation has been introduced as a possibility for the resolution of intra-family disputes by Law 54/2006 on share parenting; however, it is still not commonly used. In criminal cases involving children as offenders, the advantages and merits of mediation are recognised and therefore a few juvenile courts adopt mediation. However, there is not a specific law providing for terms and modality of mediation in criminal cases.

Among the developments of access to justice in civil litigation within the Italian scenario, the participation of children during court proceedings and the right to a lawyer have generated fervid debate. Generally speaking, the approach adopted in Italy is the result of an ongoing balancing exercise between international norms and national culture on the idea of childhood, and between autonomy of and assistance to the child. For instance, although by law children might ask for a guardian to start a legal action on his or her own (Art. 79, Civil Procedure Code), in practice, this happens in very limited circumstances. As a result the position of children within civil litigation is still limited and fragile (Tommaseo, 2007).

With regard to participation of the child in court proceedings concerned directly and indirectly with the interests of a child, it must be said that the issue has been regulated mainly by international legal standards. Indeed, Italian law still lacks a comprehensive legal statute governing to what extent and in what ways a child must be involved in court proceedings. The Italian legislator has developed the law on a piecemeal basis adopting only individual norms which, on the one hand, do not offer a complete protection to the needs of the child in court proceedings and on the other

7 For example, the Prosecutor's Office at the Juvenile Court of Naples, in Southern Italy, has a duty to control all the shelters for children in trouble with the law in the region. However, there is just one car which can be used for such work.

8 Interview with the Ombudsman on 14 October 2013.

hand, provide significant leeway for the judges to exercise their discretion. However, after long debate, it seems that the discretion of the judge to decide whether to hear the child has now been limited. First, the Supreme Court of Cassation[9] clarified that it is the right of a mature and capable child to participate in proceedings and to be listened to. Second, with the revision and introduction of new Art. 155 in the Italian Civil Code, the participation of the child is clearly provided for in cases of separation and divorce.

It has been pointed out in Italian academic discourses that the Italian legislator is inconsistent in its use of terminology when considering the participation of a child in court proceedings, thus creating in this way different models of participation (Domanico, 2008). In particular, in criminal proceedings in which a child is the offender, the term used is *'examined'* which brings with it all the procedural guarantees of a fair trial as framed by Law 448/88. Implicit in the use of such terminology is the fact that the child must receive all the information about the procedure and about his or her rights and the participation of a child within the juvenile justice is active. In cases in which a child is victim of a crime, then he or she is heard through a protected hearing in which the judge or the psychologist does not ask direct questions and is in the position of listening to what the child says spontaneously (Domanico, 2008). Thus, in civil cases the child is *'heard' or 'listened to'*. Both terms have a differing impact on the way children participate in the proceedings. Only in the second instance does it appear that the right to be listened to is put into effect.

The theme of listening to the child, although much debated over the past 20 years, has received legal recognition only after the entry into force of Law 54/2006, which has introduced shared custody between parents. The new law provides that the judge organises the hearing of a child who has reached the age of 12, or of a younger child who is considered to be mature enough to understand what happens during and after the proceedings (Art. 155). With the new Art. 155, the participation of the child became mandatory and is no longer a matter to be left to the discretion of the judge. This norm applies to court proceedings of separation, divorce and nullity of marriage and to disputes involving children of unmarried parents. The move to considering the participation and hearing of the child as a duty has been encouraged by several interventions by the Supreme Court of Cassation. In its judgement 22238/2009, the Court of Cassation stated that the failure to hear minor children violates the principle of due process, because those children carry interests which are different from those of their parents and therefore children must have the opportunity to express their view. For the judges of the Supreme Court, hearing the child in judicial proceedings became mandatory as a result of the Strasbourg Convention. The failure to hear a child thus constitutes an infringement of Ar. 6 of the Strasbourg Convention, unless participating in the proceedings damages the fundamental interests of the child. Accordingly, the Court declared, the possible lack of discernment that justifies the failure to audition should be subject to specific justification.

9 Supreme Court of Cassation, decision 10/06/20111, no. 12739.

In addition, within the Italian law there are certain rules within the Civil Code which provides for the participation of the child in some specific disputes. Art. 145, which considers the intervention of the court for the determination of the family home when spouses disagree, states that the judge can consider hearing the opinions expressed by children living at home who have reached 16 years of age. Listening to children is provided for by Art. 284 for the purposes of legitimating a child born out of wedlock. In turn, Art. 250 provides that the recognition of a child born out of wedlock has no effect unless it has the consent of the child who has reached the age of 16. Where there is opposition to the recognition, the court decides after hearing the child and the parent who opposes the recognition and with the intervention of the prosecutor.

In addition, Art. 316, paragraph 4, regarding the exercise of parental rights, provides that in case of conflict between the parents the court will hear the child in making its decision. Art. 371, paragraph 1, with regard to the measures which the probate judge must give about the education of the child subject to protection, requires the hearing of the child of ten years of age, before deciding on the place where he or she is to be raised. Moreover, a child of 16 years of age shall be consulted before the appointment of a guardian (Art. 348).

Multiple references to listening to the child are contained in the law of 4 May 1983 184 (amended by Law 8, March 2001) in the field of foster care and adoption. For instance, Art. 7, paragraph 2, provides that a minor who has reached the age of 14 cannot be adopted unless he or she gives consent. Art. 10 reiterates the need of the child to be heard when the court confirms, amends or revokes the urgent measures taken previously. Art. 22 provides that the 14-year old child, and even younger if he has adequate capacity, should give consent to pre-adoptive custody with the chosen couple. Art. 25 also provides that the children of the adoptive couple will be heard with regard to the intention of their parents to adopt.

There are situations which are exempt from hearing the child including when the child does not have the capacity to understand the real consequences of the proceedings and when the hearing is not in his interests or could cause him injury. In any case, when the judge decides to exclude hearing the child, her decision must be adequately motivated and supported.

The manner in which the judge organises the meeting with the child and hears his or her views and expectations constitutes a particular issue in which procedural rules and psychological knowledge interact and intertwine. The hearing can be carried out directly by the judge or indirectly by other professionals. During the hearing, the judge may be assisted by an expert who has an auxiliary role. Taking into account the age and personality of the child, the court may choose an indirect hearing by delegating the hearing to an expert as suggested by Art. 12 UNCRC. In the absence of a national regulatory framework provision, which expressly provides rules and modality of the indirect hearing, Art. 12 of the UNCRC finds direct application.

For the definition of the concrete modalities of the hearing and the precautions that must accompany the hearing of a child during court proceedings, many protocols have been created. The protocols are intended to define a set of rules agreed between lawyers and judges with the support of associations of experts. The protocols have local significance and have no binding effect. However, the protocols may effect the single proceeding once the judge adopts the protocol, with the agreement of the parties, as the mode of procedure that will be used for listening to the child. However, the Supreme Court of Cassation in relation to proceedings in the field of international child abduction, clarified that it is part of the discretional powers of the judge to decide whether and how to listen to the child.[10]

Linked to the participation of the child in court proceedings are the right to be represented and the right to a lawyer. The Strasbourg Convention recognises the child has the right to ask personally or through other persons or bodies for the appointment of a special representative in judicial proceedings relating to his or her upbringing. In Italy, the procedural representation of the child is guaranteed in the first place by its parents as legal representatives of the child (Art. 320 Civil Code). If both parents are missing or have been deprived of parental responsibility, the child must be appointed a guardian (Art.343 Civil Code) whose functions also include the procedural representation of the child. In cases of conflict of interest between the child and the parents, the law provides for the appointment of a guardian *ad litem* to represent the minor during the court proceedings. In some cases, such as the action for disavowal of paternity, the child who has turned 16 has the right to ask the court to appoint a guardian *ad litem*, otherwise the guardian *ad litem* will be appointed by the court or at the request of the public prosecutor. There is, however, a lack of general provision allowing the appointment of a guardian *ad litem* in all cases of conflict between the child and parents. The Constitutional Court seems to recognise that when Italian law does not present any specific norm, then Art. 12 of the UNCRC is suitable to integrate the lack of legislation in the Civil Code.[11]

Law n. 149/2001, recently implemented (1 July 2007), expressly reaffirms the obligation of the defence and procedural representation of children, in particular in court judgments concerning adoption (Art. 8) and in those relating to parental responsibility (Art. 37). The scope of this provision is innovative, however, it has remained without objective implementation in practice, since currently the legislative requirements have not been followed by a proper delineation of its application and methods. Therefore, in the absence of common guidelines, different juvenile courts are adopting different interpretations of the law 149 /2001. As suggested by Domanico (2008), from a national survey on the application of that law, carried out by the National Union of Juvenile Chambers, it is evident that there are various guidelines and practices, which try to deal with several issues including: the distinction between the role of the lawyer of the child and the role of the guardian *ad litem*, the specific requirements a lawyer must possess in order to take these appointments, remuneration arrangements for curators and/or lawyers and any expert witnesses appointed during the proceedings. These are just some of the many problems encountered in implementing the established principle of the defence of the child that the juvenile courts

10 Supreme Court of Cassation, decision 4 April 2007, no.8481.

11 Constitutional Court, decision 30 January 2002, no.1.

have faced. In particular, the juvenile court of Milan interprets the law 149/2001 in a restrictive manner, meaning that the presence of a lawyer is mandatory and provides for the appointment of a lawyer in the case of clear conflict of interest between parents and child, without suspension of parental authority. The juvenile courts of Milan, Turin, Ancona and Palermo have created lists of lawyers for children and require specific skills and professional experience, gained in the context of family law and child law, in the background of those lawyers appointed to the list.

These initiatives are interesting but Italian practice is well away from a coordinated and well-developed model of lawyering in civil disputes which enhances access to justice of children. Many uncertainties exist in fact with regard to the powers and obligations of lawyers representing children, and their interaction with other professionals, such as social workers and psychologists; the appropriateness of specific training, as well as the remuneration arrangements in respect of the provision of professional work. The difficulty in implementing the legislative requirements, the absence of common guidelines, the absence of clarification by the legislature, all represent barriers to a full implementation of the principle of access to justice of children.

Access to Criminal Justice: Children in Organised Crime

This section addresses a specific example of barriers to access to justice in the juvenile justice system, namely the involvement of children in organised crime in Naples – so called Camorra[12] – and the inadequate legislation which applies when such children decide to collaborate with the justice authorities and become *pentiti* (collaborators with the police and justice).[13] It could be said that this is the subject in which the Italian legislator has approached childhood in a *levelling* manner, treating children and adults in the same way – or as has been suggested,[14] this is a case of '*carelessness*' (*trascuratezza*) of the Italian institutions.[15]

12 It is not the aim of this paper to offer a detailed account of organised crime in Italy. However, it suffices to say here that In Italy organised crime is very heterogeneous and possesses varied characteristics. The case study in this paper is concerned with children who are involved with the Camorra. The Camorra is typical of the Campania Region and its origin can be traced back to the 18th century (Barbagallo, 2011).For an historical account, see Biblioteca Digitale sulla Camorra, available at: http://www.bibliocamorra.altervista.org/index.php?option=com_content&view=category&id=37&Itemid=68 (retrieved 30 September 2013). For an analysis of the business of Camorra, see Saviano, 2008. For research published in English on the relation between Camorra and Italian politics, see Allum, 2006.

13 A first item of news on this phenomenon in Naples was published, on 14 July 2013, by a local newspaper 'Il Mattino', at http://www.ilmattino.it/napoli/cronaca/a_napoli_l_rsquo_emergenza_dei_baby_pentiti_rino_14_anni_e_sentinella_della_cosca/notizie/304114.shtml (retrieved 30 September 2013).

14 Interview with Dott. Roberto Gentile.

15 Ibid.

Before analysing the legal framework, a few words are needed on the characteristics of the children – many children[16] – who are recruited by criminal circles in Naples. It has been pointed out that these children are easy to recognise in the sense that they all present the same characteristics (Priore and Lavanco, 2007). Until a few years ago, the children involved in general criminal activities in Naples were mainly part of disadvantaged families with serious financial problems.[17] However, during the past few years, even children from families with better financial resources have started to become involved in criminal activities. The children though, who are recruited by the organised crime – Camorra – and become members of a criminal *clan* or so-called *family* (Saviano, 2006) come exclusively from very poor and marginalised families which to some extent already have links with the clan. The new kind of recruit typically decides to become part of organised crime because it offers several appealing lifestyle alternatives. For instance, immediately after the recruitment children receive money and expensive goods – designer clothes and shoes, and motorbikes – which represent status symbols and which give them a certain *social respect* (*rispetto*) within the community. And respect is a fundamental value within the local community. It is not easy, however, to gain acceptance by the organised crime circles. In order to be recruited, children must give evidence that they are *reliable* (*affidabili*), and *tough* (*resistenti*) so that they can resist the pressure of the police in cases where they are apprehended by the authorities. As a result, children are *tested* through an escalation of criminal actions starting with bag-snatching, then moving to unarmed robbery, then robbery with a knife and eventually robbery with a gun. After passing these tests of reliability, children might be accepted as being ready for membership in the gang, then become involved in still more major criminal activities including drug smuggling.[18] The involvement of children in such organised crime has many advantages for the clans. Indeed, amongst other reasons, during investigation and court proceedings the words and evidence of a child are easier to confute and disprove than the testimony of an adult criminal.

Notwithstanding the appealing aspects of being involved in organised crime, some children decide to leave and to collaborate with the judiciary. The reasons for the collaboration include a reduction in likely punishment upon conviction and in reduced length of the court proceedings. In addition, some children decide to leave the criminal life after they have been through a re-education programme and benefitted

---

16 As the President of the Court of Appeal of Naples has reported during his speech for the beginning of judicial year, the number of children recruited by organised crime has increased during the past few years, creating a real emergency for police and judiciary. Available at: http://www.ilsole24ore.com/art/norme-e-tributi/2013-01-26/procedimento-giuridico-complesso-lento-105435.shtml?uuid=Ab1olLOH (retrieved 30 September 2013).

17 The Italian Nation TV has produced an interesting documentary which shows the places where these children live and who their families are. The documentary is available at: http://www.youtube.com/watch?v=y-gq-SkU5NY (retrieved 30 September 2013).

18 http://www.ilmattino.it/napoli/cronaca/camorra_binocolo_e_trasmittente_prese_le_baby_vedette_della_droga/notizie/244642.shtml (retrieved 30 September 2013).

from the help of experts, thus coming to understand the negative effects of being part of organised crime.

These children face access to justice issues resulting from a lack of relevant legislation. There is no a specific legislation providing for situations in which children decide to collaborate with the judiciary and to leave the criminal organisation of which they have been a part. Although Law 448/88 governs the criminal proceeding in which a minor is involved as the perpetrator of a crime, nevertheless such legislation does not include any provision for the so-called *pentitismo* (collaboration with the police and judiciary) of children. As a result, the general rules which regulate cases in which adults decide to collaborate with the authorities apply.[19] This normative framework is not adequate to meet the needs of the children during witness examination and hearing. Already at the end of 1990s the public prosecutors of the juvenile court of Caltanissetta, in Sicily, called for the enactment of a specific law for dealing with children involved in the organised crime.[20] As a result of the legislature's lack of response, prosecutors in different juvenile courts have adapted the legislation for adults better to suit the needs of children. For instance, children who decide to collaborate are still interrogated, but using protective measures such as video-conferences at unknown localities which are not revealed during the hearing.

More inadequate, however, is the legal framework for prison management and organisation.[21] The same system applies to both adults and children in trouble with the law, thus making the protection of minors very difficult to achieve. Italian prisons, which already present severe problems of overcrowding,[22] are simply not equipped for the protection of those children who decide to leave a criminal organisation and who are keen to collaborate with the judiciary. As Public Prosecutor Gentile has pointed out, a child who decides to collaborate represents a danger for a criminal organisation; various actions, including the threat of violence against members of the collaborators' family, will be used in order to stop him or her talking – in order to *convince* him or her not to collaborate. One technique is that the leaders of the organisation ensure the arrest of another child who, once in prison, will bring warning mes-

19 The law governing cases of collaboration with the judiciary is Law 13 February 2001, 'Modifica della disciplina della protezione e del trattamento sanzionatorio di coloro che collaborano con la giustizia nonchè disposizioni a favore delle persone che prestano testimonianza' (Revision of the norms on the protection of those who collaborate with the justice system). This law has modified Law 15 March 1991, no. 82, as the first law on the protection and sanctioning of treatment of offenders, involved in organised crime, who decide to collaborate.

20 See: http://ricerca.repubblica.it/repubblica/archivio/repubblica/1997/02/22/baby-killer-pentiti-confessano-33-delitti.html (retrieved 30 September 2013).

21 Law 26 Luglio 1975 n. 354 ('Norme sull'ordinamento penitenziario e sulla esecuzione delle misure privative e limitative della liberta') (Norms on the penitentiary organisation and on punishment).

22 See, *Torreggiani and Others v. Italy* (application no.43517/09) in which the European Court of Human Rights has dealt with the issue of overcrowding in Italian prisons and has called on the Italian authorities to put in place remedies for such issues which represents a violation of article 3 of the European Convention on Human Rights.

sages from the outside organisation, or commit violent acts against the child who has decided to collaborate. In addition, because children and adults share the same premises, it is easy for adults to contact the children who collaborate and try to stop them. These limitations show a complete negligence on the part of the Italian legislator. Indeed, when the law on the management of prisons was enacted, it provided that the same norms would apply to children in trouble with law, only for the time in which a specific law on juvenile prisons was not enacted (Art. 79). However, this specific law never came into force, leaving children today in a potentially dangerous situation. In order to compensate for these limitations in the system, together with several decisions of the Italian Constitutional Court which has tried to re-shape law in a manner which could better meet the needs of child-offenders (Deantoni and Scivoletto, 2001), several public prosecutors' offices at the juvenile courts have signed agreements with the ordinary criminal courts providing general principles for all cases in which children are involved in criminal activities with adults.

Conclusion

This chapter has located its analysis in the principles of access to justice of children in Italy, arguing that although several measures have been adopted by the Italian legislator, several important barriers persist. In particular, this study has investigated selected barriers to access to justice in both civil and penal litigation involving children. With specific regard to the involvement of children in civil litigation, emphasis has been put on the participation of children in court proceedings related to their upbringing and their right to legal representation. It has been shown that although the principles of participation and legal defence as encapsulated in the UNCRC and the European Convention on the Exercise of Children's Rights are now part of Italian legislation, their implementation is still limited. In particular, obstacles are manifested by a lack of coordinated norms governing the procedures by which a child is heard in the proceedings and by which a lawyer is nominated.

In looking at barriers within the juvenile criminal justice, the present study has dedicated attention to the lack of specific legislation protecting those children who have been involved in organised crime in Naples and decide to collaborate with the judiciary. An additional barrier is represented by Italy not having a law on juvenile prison institutions. Finally, several limits to the an efficient juvenile justice system come from the scarce financial and structural resources that juvenile courts face generally in Italy.

Two approaches to childhood might be considered reasons for the persistence of limitations to access to justice: a *paternalistic view*, by which children are considered to be an extension of their parents and in need of protection, and *a levelling ideal* by which children and adults are treated in the same way. However, a deeper investigation within Italian culture brings one to the conclusion that all barriers to access to justice of children in Italy show just a certain degree of negligence of the Italian legislator towards the needs of children – 'there is the feeling that Italy lacks a real strong wish to plan and enact a comprehensive reform of juvenile justice aimed at eliminating barriers to access to justice for children.'[23]

References

Allum, F., *Camorristi, Politicians, and Businessmen: The Transformation of Organised Crime in Post-War Naples* (Leeds: Northern University Press, 2006).
Barbagallo, F., *Storia della Camorra* (Roma: Laterza Edizioni, 2011).
Cappelletti, M. and Garth, B., "General Report", in M. Cappelleti and B. Garth (eds), *Access to Justice. A World Survey,* Vol. I (Milano: Giuffre' Editore, 1978).
Deantoni, L. and Scivoletto, C., "L'inesistente ordinamento penitenziario minorile nella giurisprudenza della Corte Costituzionale", *Minori e Giustizia'* 2001 2, 146-159.
Domanico, M. G., "L'ascolto Del Minore Nei Procedimenti Civili", *Minori e Famiglia* 2008, available at: http://www.minoriefamiglia.it.
Felstiner, W., Abel, R. L. and Sarat, A., "The Emergence and Transformation of Disputes: Naming, Blaming, Claiming", *Law & Society Review* 1980-81 15, 631-654.
Fortin, J., *Children's Rights and the Developing Law* (Cambridge: Cambridge University Press, 2009).
Galanter, M., "Access to Justice in a World of Expanding Social Capability", *Fordham Urban Law Journal* 2010 37, 115-128.
Gramsci, A. and E. Fubini (ed), *Il Vaticano e l'Italia* (Roma: Editori Riuniti, 1929 [2006]).
Kilkelly, U., *Guidelines on Child-Friendly Justice. A Summary* (at www.coe.int/child-justice, 2010).
Long, J., *Il Diritto Italiano alla Prova delle Fonti Internazionali* (Milano: Giuffre', 2006).
Pontifical Council for the Family, "Family and Human Rights" (1999) www.vatican.va/roman_curia/pontifical_councils/family/index_it.htm.
Pontifical Council for the Family, "Family, Marriage and de facto Unions" (2000) www.vatican.va/roman_curia/pontifical_councils/family/index_it.htm.
Priore, R. and Lavanco, G., *Adolescenti e Criminali. Minori e Organizzazioni Mafiose: Analisi del Fenomeno e Ipotesi d'Intervento* (Milano: Francoangeli Editore, 2007).
Ruo, M. G., "Riferimenti Normativi e Giurisprudenziali e Prospettiva della Difesa" in UNICEF Italy (ed), *L'Ascolto dei Minorenni in Ambito Giudiziario,* (Roma: Stampa Arti Grafiche Agostini, 2012).
Saviano, R., *Gomorrah* (Milan: Mondadori, 2006).
Tommaseo, F., "Rappresentanza e Difesa del Minore nel Processo Civile", *Famiglia e Diritto* 2007 4, 409-415.

23 Interview with the Italian Ombudsman on Children and Youths.

The Application of the United Nations Convention on the Rights of the Child in Dutch Legal Practice

Coby de Graaf
University of Amsterdam, The Netherlands

Introduction

The central question in this study is:

How does the Dutch court apply the UN Convention on the Rights of the Child in its case law? The period that will be examined begins on 1 January 2002 and ends on 1 September 2011.

In the Dutch justice system a convention need not be incorporated into national legislation to be binding. The Netherlands has what is known as a monistic system, which means that a convention as such is applied in national legislation and regulations. In other words, once it has been ratified, a convention becomes part of the Dutch legal order (Nollkaemper, 2011: 488).

Whether a provision has a direct effect is irrelevant in this respect, although this is decisive for determining whether citizens are able to invoke a provision from the convention in court (Jans et al: 2011, 57).

In principle, therefore, if a convention is binding in the Netherlands, it is the law. In the Netherlands, however, the standard practice prior to ratifying a convention is to examine first whether national legislation conforms to it, and to ask whether any amendments are necessary (Nollkaemper, 2011: 494). This has been examined in detail with respect to the UN Convention on the Rights of the Child (CRC) and has led to the Sanctioning Act (*Goedkeuringswet*) for the CRC. The Sanctioning Act was submitted to the Dutch House of Representatives on 2 October 1992 and was adopted on 2 November 1994. The Convention became effective in the Netherlands on 8 March 1995 (*Tractatenblad.* 1995, 92).

During the deliberations in the House of Representatives and the Senate, the effect of the CRC was discussed at length. Remarkably, the explanatory memoranda to the Sanctioning Act do not mention the intrinsic relevance of the Convention. Overall, the process – including documents subsequently exchanged by the government – comes across as rather "defensive", including the statement:

A. Diduck, N. Peleg, H. Reece (eds.), Law in Society: Reflections on Children, Family, Culture and Philosophy
 ISBN 978-90-04-26148-8. pp. 589-602.

> As becomes clear in the sections on individual articles in the explanatory memorandum, we are of the opinion that Dutch law meets the requirements set by the International Convention on the Rights of the Child, including with regard to draft bills previously submitted ... (*Kamerstukken II* 1993/94, 22 855 (R1451), No. 6, p. 7.)

Could the ministers involved in the Sanctioning Act at the time have been overly cautious in adopting this position? It gave rise to critical questions from the House of Representatives at the time – referring to the strong influence of the European Convention on Human Rights (ECHR) on Dutch family law (*Handelingen II* [proceedings] 1993/94, 81, p. 5560.). The present study on how the CRC is applied in Dutch case law addresses this matter in greater detail.

Van Emmerik and Mijnarends have also emphasised the importance of the CRC as such. Van Emmerik argues that, regardless of the direct effect, "not only the court but also the government and the legislature are bound by the provisions from the CRC" (Emmerik, 2005). Mijnarends, who has examined how the CRC has affected juvenile criminal law, suggests that: "Ratification entails legal and moral commitment to accept the Committee's monitoring powers, pursuant to Article 43ff CRC to which every state may be held" (Mijnarends, 2000: 81-91)

The explanatory memoranda to the Sanctioning Act do, however, include a fairly lengthy section on the direct effect of the CRC. Provisions have a direct effect, if, given their "nature, content and intent", they are eligible as such; this is the standard formula, as is also used in the explanatory notes to the Sanctioning Act. Article 93 of the Dutch Constitution mentions provisions that by virtue of the content may be universally binding. Whether a universally binding provision has a direct effect is to be decided at the court's discretion. The legislature may, of course, facilitate the judiciary in this, as expressed in the explanatory notes to the Sanctioning Act (*Kamerstukken II*, 22 855 (R1451), No. 3, p. 8.). In this context, the explanatory notes list the Articles from the Convention previously set forth in provisions from other human rights conventions – the ICCPR and the ECHR – based on which direct effect "is to be deemed possible or already determined". These would be Article 7 (1), first clause, Article 9 (2), (3) and (4), Article 10 (1), second complete sentence, Article 12 (2), Article 13, Article 14, Article 15, Article 16, Article 30, Article 37 and Article 40 (2). Several articles cannot be ruled out as having a direct effect, and this definitely holds true, for example for Article 5, Article 8 (1) and Article 12 (1) (*Kamerstukken II*, 22 855 (R1451), No. 3, p. 9).

How has this subsequently been addressed in legal practice? Does this reflect a different practice and are other articles designated as being directly applicable, in addition to the ones listed above? One important question, for example, concerns the direct effect of Article 3, CRC, in which the best interests of the child is a primary consideration; this article is not identified as being directly applicable in the explanatory memorandum. Pulles concludes here that the same court does not provide a straightforward answer as to whether this article has a direct effect and therefore calls for a consistent line in case law (Pulles, 2011).

The period examined in this study began on 1 January 2002 and ended on 1 September 2011. In total, 1,028 rulings have been reviewed. The investigation into the rulings and the processing of these have been performed by M. M. C. Limbeek, N. N. Bahadur and N. van der Meij.

The discussion of the rulings is structured by area of law. The first section consists of person, family and civil juvenile cases. These 324 rulings are numerically a strong second, after immigration law. In a subsequent chapter, the application of the CRC in the remaining civil cases will be discussed. This includes rulings that do not concern person, family or civil juvenile cases, such as housing cases (which are the largest group here) (N. N. Bahadur).

The law on aliens is addressed next. In these rulings, the CRC is applied the most frequently, as was already clear from the study by Van Emmerik. The other areas of administrative law, such as social security law and other administrative law, will be discussed as well (M. M. C. Limbeek).

Finally, application of the CRC in criminal cases is reviewed. Previous studies have already revealed that the CRC is less prevalent in criminal law than in legal practice concerning the law on aliens and individual, family and civil juvenile cases. This study also reveals that the CRC is applied relatively infrequently in criminal law (N. van der Meij).[1]

Results and Observations

The research objective was to identify the effects of the CRC on the administration of justice in the Netherlands. What has been the added value of the Convention?

The Convention has in any case been applied more than the legislature discloses in the discussion of the Sanctioning Act of the CRC. This position of the legislature surfaced not only in the discussion of the direct effect of the articles from the Convention but is also apparent from the virtual absence of any review of how national law is interpreted and applied according to the Convention. The study makes the added value of the Convention perfectly clear.

What can be inferred from the research results? Can any general conclusions be reached or, in other words, are general trends and differences discernible from the effects of the Convention, depending on the area of law, and what determines such a difference? On these two questions I want to elaborate more specifically, starting with general trends visible throughout the different areas of law. According to the sequence presented in this study, these areas are: family law, aliens law, social security law and criminal law.

First, district courts are more inclined to apply the CRC than are courts of appeal and definitely more so than the Supreme Court. The Supreme Court is hardly ever inclined to apply the CRC. This is particularly striking in criminal law, as will become apparent below in the discussion of several specific results relating to criminal law. The same also holds true – albeit to a lesser extent – for the highest administra-

---

1 The whole study is available in Dutch under the title: "De toepassing van het Internationaal Verdrag inzake de Rechten van het Kind in de Nederlandse rechtspraak", J. H. de Graaf, M. M. C. Limbeek, N. N. Bahadur, N. van der Meij, Nijmegen: Ars Aequi Libri 2012.

tive court: the Administrative Jurisdiction Division of the Council of State (*Afdeling Bestuursrechtspraak van de Raad van State*, hereafter: Division) and the Central Appeals Tribunal (*Centrale Raad van Beroep*).

Another general point is that application according to the Convention turns out to be greatly preferred over direct application. This was mentioned previously in the introduction and may be clearly determined in these closing observations. In several cases the court has taken a highly creative approach. The inventory of terms used here by courts covers a wide variety, including, for example, "in light of the Convention" or "include consideration for".

In all areas of law, courts rule very differently on whether certain articles have a direct effect. This holds true, for example, for Article 3, CRC in general, and for Article 40, CRC in criminal law in particular. Sometimes these articles are considered to have a direct effect, sometimes they are not, as Pulles has also observed and is visible throughout the present study as well (Pulles, 2011). On the other hand, articles may also be identified as having a direct effect that were not listed as such in the Explanatory Memorandum to the Sanctioning Act, such as Article 8, CRC and the right to an identity.

If the court labels an article as having a direct effect, then this need not be stated clearly in so many words. The court may also – as regularly turned out to be the case in the study – simply exclude application of the provision from national law, without mentioning that the article in the Convention has a direct effect.

Determining that an article in the Convention does not have a direct effect does not derive from any standard rationale. Once again, various formulations are used. The Division generally uses the formulation that "given the formulation, [an article] does not comprise a norm directly applicable as a review standard by the court, because the provision is insufficiently specific to be applied in this manner and therefore requires further elaboration in national legislation" (*ABR v S* Division 9 April 2009, *LJN* BC9087). The Central Appeals Tribunal sometimes does this differently and argues, for example, with respect to Article 18, CRC that this article comprises, "generally described social objectives, from which no unconditional and accurately identifiable objective right consisting of an – enforceable – entitlement to care may be inferred" (*CR* v *B* Appeals Tribunal 20 October 2010, LJN BO3580).

The Convention has clearly had a positive effect, especially in distressing situations, i.e. situations that a convention on human rights and therefore, also, on children's rights, is intended to address. This concerns a general point that surfaces in all areas of law, with the exception of criminal law.

The following observation relates to this general point as well. The majority of cases where the Convention is invoked concern alleged violations of children's rights, based on measures taken by the authorities. In the cases discussed here, these are believed to infringe on the rights formulated in the Convention. The question that arises from the rulings is whether infringing on that right or those rights of the child will pass a critical review, and whether weighing the interests will sway the outcome of such a review in favour of invoking the corresponding right from the Convention.

Generally, this might entail weighing interests according to Article 8, ECHR. This list serves as a foundation for considering whether the specific categories described in the second section may justify infringing on the individual right of the person " to respect for his private and family life ". These specific categories may be designated concisely as the "general interest" category. Highlighting individual categories may be worthwhile, however, because they may offer a context for answering the previous question as to whether differences are perceptible in the extent to which the Convention has a direct effect in each area of law and what determines those differences. It has just been mentioned, for example, that invoking the Convention is hardly meaningful in criminal law. One possible explanation is that in criminal cases the general interest, and more specifically prevention of "disorder or crime", as the second section specifically formulates, seems eminently justifiable, with respect to infringement of the rights specifically at issue here from, e.g., Article 3 and Article 40, CRC. What about the other areas of law? What is the outcome there of this consideration in the event of a supposed violation of the Convention?

In family law, applying the Convention turns out to have yielded a positive score relatively more frequently than in the other areas of law, aside from criminal law, immigration law and social security cases. In the context of the consideration to be made in these areas of law, the general interest in its different manifestations prevails more often than it does with the application of the Convention in family law. Are the categories formulated in Article 8 (2), ECHR, attributed so much more importance in these areas of law that infringement is more easily justifiable here than in family law?

In this context, referring to the way the ECHR formulated this weighing of interests in the case, *Pretty* v *UK* is enlightening (2346/02, ECtHR 29 April 2002). This case was about a seriously ill woman who invoked, *inter alia,* Article 8, ECHR to terminate her life in the manner of her choice, assisted by her husband. The court considered in this case that however understandable this desire was, upon weighing interests in this context – also with regard to the vulnerability of people during their final stage of life – the general interest of protecting health and safety nevertheless prevailed over the right of the woman to protection of her "private and family life", in this case the right to terminate her life. The court considered: "The more serious the harm involved the more heavily will weigh in the balance considerations of public health and safety against the countervailing principle of personal autonomy." So this is about weighing personal autonomy against "public health and safety" considerations, and the court allowed the latter to prevail. The same pattern is discernible in the considerations by the court in the rulings examined in the course of this study.

But this pattern is only part of the key to explaining the differences in how the CRC is applied in the various areas of law. In this study of the application of the CRC, the complicating factor of parental responsibility is very important as well. Parents are pivotal in realising the rights of the child. Articles 5 and 18, CRC, in particular attest to this (Graaf, 2008). In the law on aliens and social security cases, however, parental responsibility is often specifically the problem. How can parents, who as a consequence of their status as refugees have lost control over their lives, exercise their parental responsibility? In these cases, parental responsibility is often the opposite.

In this respect, however, important positive development is identifiable over the course of nearly ten years covered by this study.

To clarify these points, some relevant cases will be discussed for each area of law. The consideration arising from the list compiled for Article 8 ECHR will be elaborated as well.

Family Law

In family law, the right to protection of private and family life in Article 8, ECHR is the leading principle. It is therefore not surprising that with 324 rulings family law – after aliens law with 430 rulings – ranks a respectable second, numerically. The majority of family law cases directly concerns alleged unjustified interference by the authorities in the 'private and family life' of the child concerned, violation of the rights of the child and therefore what is generally referred to as a negative obligation. In such a case the authorities are to refrain from taking a certain decision. In this area of law, however, the authorities may also have a positive obligation to intervene in 'private and family life.' These cases require weighing the rights of the parent and those of the child. Based on such consideration, the authorities may interfere in the 'private and family life' of the parent and allow the rights of the child to prevail over those of the parent. Once again, the list compiled for Article 8, ECHR is a useful frame of reference. This is also the last specific category of Article 8 (2), which calls for intervention by the authorities to protect the rights and freedoms of others. Numerically, however, these cases are distinctly in the minority.

Several positive examples are available for both types of obligations, starting with a negative obligation of the authorities to refrain from intervention.

Negative Obligation

The first noteworthy example here would be cases relating to Article 1, CRC – the defining provision concerning the age limit of 18 – with respect to placement in a secure institution. As a consequence of a rigid interpretation of this article, the provision in the Juvenile Care Act, allowing for placement of young adults between 18 and 21 in a secure institution, was excluded from application by the court based on Article 5, ECHR (Rotterdam district court 19 February 2009, LJN BH5398; 's-Hertogenbosch district court 27 February 2009, LJN BH4397; Roermond district court 8 April 2009, LJN BI0864; The Hague court of appeal 8 October 2009, LJN BK2806). Another clear illustration of the positive effect of the Convention is Article 2, CRC, regarding matters concerning the nationalities issue. The lower court ruled here that based on Article 2, CRC – the non-discrimination principle – distinguishing between children recognised before and after birth was unjustified (Arnhem court of appeal 13 June 2006, LJN AY5575; Arnhem court of appeal 8 May 2007, LJN BA4885; Leeuwarden court of appeal 2 July 2008, LJN BD6294). The nationality consequence was applied only after some time for children recognised after birth, whereas it was effective immediately for children recognised before birth. This ultimately led to a legal amendment (Staatsblad

2008, 270). In another interesting example, Article 3 was invoked with respect to the Passport Act (Maastricht district court 5 August 2005, LJN AU1654). Referring to the interests of the child, application of the relevant provision in the Passport Act was excluded.

While efforts to invoke the Convention are clearly more likely to succeed in distressing situations, these lines of argument also stand a better chance of approval when the article invoked is strong or comprises a clearly circumscribed standard, as well as a subject that clearly merits protection. Some such articles are Article 7, the right to a name and nationality, and Article 8, the right to respect for identity. While Article 7 (1) has also been designated as having a direct effect in the Explanatory Memorandum to the Sanctioning Act of the CRC, Article 8 has not. Based on the Explanatory Memorandum to the Sanctioning Act of the CRC, the Zutphen district court has even applied Article 7 as a matter of course (Zutphen district court 13 March 2008, LJN BC8019). The court has referred to Article 7 to exclude application of Article 1: 207 (2) in the Dutch Civil Code.

Article 7 is not always assumed to have a direct effect. The study revealed that in five cases this could be inferred – not including the application as a matter of course by the Zutphen district court – and in three cases no position was taken, including by the Supreme Court (Hertogenbosch court of appeal 23 June 2005, LJN AV6603; Rotterdam district court 8 February 2007, LJN BA0238; The Hague district court 26 July 2010, LJN BN2775; Maastricht district court 24 November 2010, LJN BO4992; Groningen district court 2 August 2011, LJN BS7594. No position taken: The Hague court of appeal 16 February 2005, LJN AS6769; Supreme Court 14 April 2006, LJN AU9239; The Hague court of appeal 22 September 2010, LJN BN8164). This case is especially remarkable, in part because Article 7, CRC closely resembles Article 8, ECHR. Should the Supreme Court not simply have resolved these different interpretations by referring to the Sanctioning Act to the CRC?

The discussion of the rulings in the category, "Interpretation and application according to the Convention", also reveals the direct effect of Article 7. Referring to Article 7, CRC and Article 8, ECHR, the court found that a minor is entitled to a surname from birth and in two cases even provisionally determines the surname, pending the Royal Decision in the matter (The Hague court of appeal 15 October 2003, LJN AL9057; Amsterdam district court 12 April 2006, LJN AY8188).

Two other examples aptly illustrate the application of Article 12, CRC, the right to be heard and the right to participate in any judicial and administrative proceedings. These are a ruling by The Hague district court and another by The Hague Court of Appeal. The district court refers to the intention of the legislature in its decision that even in cases where both parents (already) have parental authority, minors have an informal right to bring proceedings, despite the absence of a reference in Article 1:337g Civil Code to Article 1:253a Civil Code. After all, according to the district court: "depriving minors of this right would be at odds with the provision in Article 12 of the Convention on the Rights of the Child" (The Hague district court 20 March 2009, LJN BN0299). This case illustrates once again how closely direct effect and application according to the Convention may resemble one another, another important general observation that arises from the study. The other example concerns the ruling by The Hague appeals court, in which the court of appeal considered that the instruction in Article 809b, Code of Civil Procedure, concerns the right of minors to be heard and is therefore not an obligation (The Hague court of appeal 18 August 2010, LJN BN5164). After all, the court of appeals states:

> the demand by the mother that the children be questioned by the court of appeal is at odds with the principle that also arises from Article 12 of the CRC, which states that every child has the right to express his opinion freely in matters concerning the child, and that the opinion of the child is to receive appropriate consideration.

Positive Obligation

Although Article 8, CRC, the right to respect for identity, was not identified as having a direct effect in the explanatory Memorandum to the Sanctioning Act, it is nonetheless "strongly" applied by the court. This is illustrated in a ruling by the Den Bosch court of appeal, which interprets Articles 7 and 8, CRC as a parental obligation to notify a minor about his or her identity from an early age ('s-Hertogenbosch court of appeal 23 June 2005, LJN AV6603). Parents who delay it are violating the rights of the child, argued the court of appeal. This case therefore involves weighing the interests between parent and child, thereby allowing the right of the child to know from whom he or she is descended to prevail.

Another important cluster of cases in this category consists of rulings, where the court relieved the parent of authority after a period of custodial placement. The ruling by the Groningen district court is exemplary (Groningen district court 19 January 2010, LJN BL0204. Cf. Groningen district court 19 January 2010, LJN BL0217). The court considers here that "the right of both children to be raised in a situation of continuity and uninterrupted bonding ... prevails over the interest of the parent in restoring family life between the parent and the children". Both Articles 9, 3 and 20, CRC are relevant in these cases. Article 20 is invoked here to support the right to continuity of care and is used to perpetuate the residence of the minor with the foster parents. In many cases it is applied in the context of interpretation and application according to the convention.

The ruling by the Almelo district court based on Article 16, CRC pertains to the same category (Almelo district court (sub-district section) 15 October 2009, LJN BK0555). In this case the mother filed interlocutory proceedings to demand the removal of several photographs and videos of the minor that the father had posted online. The mother argued that the father was violating the personal privacy of the minor and abusing his parental authority by this action. The interlocutory proceedings court agreed and granted the claim.

Not all examples concerning family law are positive. The study also reveals negative examples of applications of the Convention. Pursuant to Article 18 (1), CRC, for example, the Groningen district court granted a claim by the mother to oblige her son's school to release information about him (Groningen district court 25 March 2009,

LJN BI6947). After all, the court found, *inter alia*: "Being involved in the educational progress of their child is an entitlement that parents may in principle derive from this provision in the Convention." The Convention may thus be used to guarantee a claim from the parent, a claim that the court granted in this case. This is in contrast to the ruling by The Hague court of appeal that was discussed above.

Immigration Law

The study reveals that the number of rulings (430) relating to the law on aliens exceeds those in family law and criminal law by a wide margin. This also corresponds with the remark at the start of these closing observations that the Convention has been particularly relevant in distressing cases. After all, decisions in the law on aliens have far-reaching consequences for children.

Still, the CRC is considerably less influential in aliens cases than in family law. The study reveals that the court – and especially the Division – is generally reluctant to apply the CRC. Motions to invoke the Convention are not granted in most cases, especially not those invoking the direct effect of the Convention, although recent case law reflects a cautiously positive trend. The court provides several explanations for this reluctance.

In some cases this is attributed to the formulation that the CRC does not create any obligations beyond what is already set forth in national legislation and regulations. Sometimes it is also argued that the CRC does not extend beyond the obligations already created by Article 8, ECHR, as is raised for example in reference to invoking Articles 9, 10 and 16, CRC (*ABR v S* Division 25 January 2006, *JV* 2006/109; *ABR v S* Division 2 May 2011, 201011016/1/V1). The most common formulation, however, is that the relevant provision from the Convention stipulates only that the interests of the child should receive consideration.

Likewise, impressions from the law on aliens may vary as to whether articles from the CRC have a direct effect. Article 2 (1), CRC exemplifies this. While the Division is cautious about this – although it addresses the substance of Article 2 (1), CRC, it does not mention whether it has a direct effect – the lower court does consider Article 2 (1) to have a direct effect in many cases. Just as with Article 7, CRC in the context of family law, where interpretations also varied as to whether this article had a direct effect, the undesirability of these different interpretations is noteworthy here as well. This is certainly true with respect to such an essential article as the non-discrimination principle in Article 2, CRC.

Here, however, the more complex matter of parental responsibility clearly shows. Aliens policy targets the parents, but the legal status that the parents have in these cases applies to their children as well. Whether this is justified is highly questionable. Should the sins of the parents be "visited" on the children, if in this case there are any "sins" of the parents? Article 2 (1), CRC appears to conflict with this as well, since it stipulates that the State is expected to guarantee the interests of "every child within its jurisdiction, without any type of discrimination at all", including based on national origin. Justification for any such infringement would clearly need to be attributed to the categories listed in Article 8 (2), ECHR, especially the worthiness of protection formulated as "public safety or the economic well-being of the country".

Gradually, however, children are starting to be recognised as having an independent position. In the past, for example, no entitlements pursuant to Articles 3, 6 and 24 existed for children whose parents were not allowed to reside in the Netherlands, according to a ruling by The Hague district court from 2003 (The Hague district court 13 November 2003, *Algemene Wet Bestuursrecht*, hereafter AWB 02/58873). This was a standard consideration, as was used by the Division as well. As we read in the summary and conclusion from Chapter 3, "Applying the CRC in aliens cases', this standard consideration has "fortunately" been abandoned since 2005. This does not mean that this practice ceased at that point. The distinction has in a sense shifted to children of parents that fulfil their obligation to cooperate and children of parents who do not, as has become clear from a Division ruling from 2007 (*ABR v S* Division 15 February 2007, LJN AZ9524). If parents fail to cooperate with their departure from the Netherlands, they – parents and children alike – lose their right to shelter.

The recent Supreme Court ruling of 21 September 2012 may be regarded as a milestone in this trend (Supreme Court 21 September 2012, LJN BW5328). Here, the Supreme Court – referring, *inter alia,* to Article 3 CRC – upheld the judgment by the Court of Appeal,

> that the decision by the mother not to cooperate with the return to Angola may not be attributed to the children (nor may the children be held accountable), since they had no say in this.

That means that in this case the right of the children to shelter should continue to be guaranteed. The children therefore are guiding rather than following, and their mother follows them.

The cases where the court aims to interpret and apply according to the Convention reveal the positive influence of the CRC more than direct effect of the Convention does. In the law on aliens, the Convention has a noteworthy added value. The Convention may be used in this context to elaborate on the general principles of good governance, as set forth in Article 7:12 AWB. This is especially the case with respect to Article 3, CRC, as is clear from the discussion of a great many rulings on Article 3 CRC in the category, "Interpretation and application according to the Convention". Lower courts are particularly inclined to apply the CRC in this manner. Article 3 relates primarily to review of the substantiation principle, the requirement of due care and the proportionality principle. The ruling by The Hague district court nicely illustrates this context (The Hague district court (zp. Assen) 25 January, AWB Act 04/1294, 04/12988, 04/12991, 04/12995, 04/12999). Here the court applied Article 3 not only by reviewing the substantiation principle of Article 7:12 General Administrative Law Act, but also considered whether the respondent may reasonably have reached his decision. In this respect, the court determined regarding the effect of Article 3, briefly stated, that even though the view of the Division is that Article 3, CRC does not have a direct effect, a concept that may be interpreted in various ways, such as "exceptional case of extreme unfairness", even if Article 3 has no direct effect, action should be in accordance with the Convention.

Social Security Law

Especially in social security cases, the influence of the Convention is surprising in the subject of independence of children from their parents. In this field, the court makes a particularly noteworthy effort to mitigate aliens policy for children through application in accordance with the Convention. The Convention has been applied primarily via the non-discrimination principle of Article 2, CRC. In social security cases the court refines this, weighing up the interests to be protected of the vulnerable groups of "illegal" children. The observation expressed previously that the Convention serves especially to protect children in distressing situations clearly surfaces here (Minderhoud, 2012). Previously, parental responsibility has been more qualified in this area than in the law on aliens. In a previous stage, this seems to have "carried over" less here than in the law on aliens. This is aptly illustrated by a case from 15 July 2011, in which the Central Appeals Tribunal recognised the individual right of the child to receive child benefits (*CR* v *B* Central Appeals Tribunal 15 July 2011, LJN BR1905). Here, the Central Appeals Tribunal reconsidered earlier case law and found that the justification for the Benefit Entitlement (Resident Status) legislation did not apply to parents of children with extended legal residence in the Netherlands. As stated:

> The Central Appeals Tribunal does not disregard that parents are primarily responsible but in this case considers it relevant that child benefits are intended to support the cost of living of their children. In this respect, particular importance is to be attributed according to the Central Appeals Tribunal to the individual interests of the child in this benefit, given the purpose of the General Child Benefit Act.

Criminal Law

On the other hand, far fewer positive results are identifiable in criminal law. A possible explanation for why the CRC is so rarely applied in criminal law was offered above. While a few positive examples are available, the overall application of the Convention is minimal in this area. One positive example here is that the Roermond district court disallowed the Public Prosecution Service in the "kissing kindergarteners" case. The court barred the prosecution because of infringement of the principles of due process and Article 3 and Article 40 (1), CRC (Roermond district court 16 February 2009, LJN BH7427; Roermond district court 16 February 2009, LJN BH7431). In this case the suspects were very young. The court refers in particular to the principle set forth in Article 40 (1), CRC that –

> every child alleged as, accused of, or recognized as having infringed the penal law to be treated in a manner consistent with the promotion of the child's sense of dignity and

> worth, which reinforces the child's respect for the human rights and fundamental freedoms of others and which takes into account the child's age.

In other cases, the court has also been inclined to consider the CRC but has been reversed by the Supreme Court.

Especially in criminal cases, the role of the Supreme Court is remarkably cautious. This concerns two specific categories of cases, namely those in which taking DNA samples is at issue and those concerning consequences associated with exceeding of reasonable time limits. Contrary to the judgment by the district court in some cases, the Supreme Court ruled that no general exception to taking DNA samples from minors could be inferred from the Convention (Supreme Court 13 May 2008, LJN BC8231; Supreme Court 13 May 2008, LJN BC8234). Unlike the Procurator General, the Supreme Court does not even weigh the interests in this matter. The Procurator General does refer to Articles 3 and 40 in his claim, but neither one makes any difference (Dutch Supreme Court 13 May 2008, LJN BC8231 (concl. P-G Fokkens); Dutch Supreme Court 13 May 2008, LJN BC8234 (concl. P-G Fokkens)). Regarding Article 40, CRC, it is argued that –

> weighing the interests of the minor and the general social interest in preventing, tracing, prosecuting and trying criminal offences by a minor... cannot be based on Article 40 (1), CRC.

With respect to Article 3, the Procurator General is of the opinion that "applying the act on DNA examination for convicted persons to convicted minors does not violate the interests of the child as meant in Article 3 CRC".

Regarding the legal consequences associated with exceeding a reasonable time limit, The Hague court of appeal – referring to a ruling by the Supreme Court – does follow the position of the lower court that the Public Prosecution Service has forfeited its right to prosecute, based on the time that has elapsed between the offence and the criminal prosecution (The Hague court of appeal 7 January 2011, LJN BP1548).[2] The lower court justified its decision in a case such as this one that a prosecutorial response would be pedagogically counterproductive (Amsterdam district court 12 May 2010, LJN BM5290; Amsterdam district court 12 May 2010, LJN BM5292; Amsterdam district court 20 May 2010, NBSTRAF 2011/14). It may be inferred from the Supreme Court ruling of 30 March 2010 that like in the adult criminal justice system, exceeding the reasonable time limit may lead the Public Prosecution Service to be disallowed (Supreme Court 30 March 2010, LJN BL3228 (concl. A-G A.J.M. Machielse)). In this ruling the Supreme Court does not address the CRC, although the Advocate General does so in this case, by concluding that when the reasonable time limit is exceeded, Article 40 (2) (b) (iii), CRC does not lead to legal consequences in juvenile cases different from those in other criminal cases (Supreme Court 30 March 2010, LJN BL3228 (concl. A-G

---

2 The court of appeal infers this from a ruling by the Supreme Court, even though only the Advocate General addresses this in the case.

A.J.M. Machielse, sub 3.3)). In another case, the Advocate General, unlike the Supreme Court, is of the opinion that pursuant to Article 40 (2), CRC, the formulation "without delay" means a shorter term, i.e. shorter than 16 months, than is the case with the "reasonable time" formulated in Article 6, ECHR and Article 14, ICCPR (Supreme Court 16 December 2003, LJN AL9062 (concl. A-G W.H. Vellinga)). The Supreme Court does not accept this argument and applies a term of 16 months for juvenile suspects, although the Supreme Court does appear to accept that this article has a direct effect.

The answer to the question as to why the CRC has had so little effect in criminal law is not that these cases are not distressing. What seems decisive here is that the general interest prevails, especially the specific category stated in Article 8 (2), ECHR, "for the prevention of disorder or crime", over the individual interest of the minor. An additional aggravating factor here is the absence of parental responsibility. The protective layer of the legal arrangement of parental responsibility between government and minor is lacking in criminal law. The minor is held criminally liable for the offences committed. The minor is assumed to be chiefly responsible for the situation that has arisen.

In criminal law this parental responsibility function is thus lacking with respect to the offence of the minor, at least formally so. In material respects, the parental responsibility and the youth of the minor are, of course, impossible to overlook. Nor are they disregarded in the CRC, on the contrary. Articles 37 and 40, CRC, which apply to juvenile criminal law, clearly concern the youth of the minors, carefully highlighting legal safeguards to be incorporated in the criminal proceedings. More than with adults, the criminal-procedural safeguards are clearly stipulated in the CRC, taking into account the youth of the suspect. This receives insufficient consideration in legal practice.

Conclusion

Generally, invoking the Convention needs to be based on substantiating facts and circumstances to serve its purpose. The study has revealed repeatedly that efforts to invoke the Convention fail for lack of proper substantiation. Adequate substantiation is therefore an important condition for successfully invoking the CRC. This provides important guidance for lawyers.

Courts seem to attribute the added value of the study mainly to the opportunities to interpret and apply the Convention accordingly, to which this study so clearly bears witness.

Overall, the Convention seems to offer more opportunities for application than initially believed and also than presently assumed to be the case. It therefore seems justified to expect that the study, in its present form, offers legal practice – as well as the legislature and the government – valuable links for applying the Convention and inspires them to do so. It may provide a significant foundation for reaching decisions largely on principle, when fundamental rights of children are at stake.

That family law courts are more likely to identify links than are courts in the other areas of law discussed here, has been an important aspect of consideration in these closing observations and has been attributed in part to the horizontal relationships between parents and children that figure in some of these cases. Unlike in cases concerning immigration law, social security cases and criminal cases, the interest is less paramount. In these (other) areas of law, the interest in its different manifestations, such as public order and safety, reduce the freedom of the court to apply the Convention, although in aliens cases, a trend is discernible (as has been the case earlier in social security cases) in which the court uses the Convention to observe the fundamental rights of the child.

References

Emmerik, M. Van, "Toepassing van het Internationale Kinderrechtenverdrag in de Nederlandse rechtspraak", *NJCM-Bulletin* 30(6) (2005) 700-716.

Graaf, J. H. de, "Rechten van het kind en ouderlijke verantwoordelijkheid, een inleiding", in: J. H. de Graaf, C. Mak, F. K. van Wijk, *Rechten van het Kind en ouderlijke verantwoordelijkheid*, Nijmegen: Ars Aequi Libri 2008.

Jans, J. H., Prechal, S.and R. J. G. M. Widdershoven, *Inleiding tot het Europees Bestuursrecht*, Nijmegen: Ars Aequi Libri 2011.

Mijnarends, E. M., "De betekenis van het Internationale Kinderrechtenverdrag in de Nederlandse rechtspraak", *Ars Aequi* 2 (2000) 82-91.

Minderhoud, P. E., "Scheurtjes in de Koppelingswet", NTM/JCM-Bulletin (2012) 37/4, 391-407.

Nollkaemper, A., *Kern van het internationaal publiekrecht*, The Hague: Boom Juridisch uitgevers, 2011.

Pulles, G.J., 'Onduidelijkheid over de rechtstreekse werking van de kernbepalingen van het VN-kinderrechtenverdrag', *NJB* 4 (2011) 231-234.

Michael Freeman and International Family Justice

The Rt. Hon. Sir Mathew Thorpe
Former Lord Justice of Appeal, Associate Member 1 Hare Court Chambers

International family law is a speciality which has richly rewarded those who have chosen it over the course of the last 20 years at least. As a judge I am convinced of that. I am confident that the practitioners would share that conviction. I cannot speak for the academics, although throughout those years I have been a member of the International Society of Family Law and attended most of its major conferences. My impression is that those who teach international family law are in good demand.

The mood of those who practice in this specialist field is generally dynamic and optimistic. This is because these years have been years of sustained development of new law and practice which has had the effect of improving and simplifying remedies and practices to meet the challenge of the increasing mobility of people and the complexity of legal and practical problems created by cross cultural and cross border relationship breakdown.

I focus first on the development of law and remedies throughout this period. The monumental law is the 1980 Hague Abduction Convention. Of course it was already strongly in place at the outset of the two decades that I am reviewing. But how the Convention has burgeoned in these last 20 years! In 1993 there were 30 States party to the Convention. Now there are 90. This threefold increase is evidence of the success of the Convention but it also marks a very significant increase in the Convention's strength and efficacy. Any Convention is selective in the sense that it provides a remedy only between those states who have given the Convention the force of law by domestic legislation. We in this jurisdiction, having ourselves legislated the Convention in 1985, can now expect summary return orders from no less than 68 states whose accessions we have recognised. Higher still would be the total were it not for the European Commission's claim to external competence and its threat of refraction and penalty to be imposed on any member state recognising an accession unilaterally. I am not alone in regarding the Commission's claim as exorbitant and frustrating in its interference with the expansion of what is a global rather than a European instrument. Whilst this restriction may not bear hard upon smaller European jurisdictions, it adversely affects the United Kingdom more than any other member state

A. Diduck, N. Peleg, H. Reece (eds.), Law in Society: Reflections on Children, Family, Culture and Philosophy
Copyright 2015 Koninklijke Brill NV. Printed in The Netherlands. ISBN 978-90-04-26148-8. pp. 603-606.

as a result of our particular relationship with Commonwealth and common law jurisdictions. Presently we are prevented from recognising the accession of Trinidad, Sri Lanka and Singapore. Unless this embargo is successfully challenged we will find ourselves in the ridiculous position of achieving nothing from future accessions which we have lobbied so hard to achieve. Japan is about to ratify, India is strongly anticipated and Pakistan may well accept the force of our persuasion. The position that the Commission has taken, and our response, are highly political issues which should not distract from a proper recognition of the achievements of the European Union in creating regional family law and in maintaining a court of justice which has proved itself innovative and effective in its rulings on the construction and application of the Brussels Regulation.

Indeed the performance of the Court of Justice of the European Community seems particularly praiseworthy when compared with the performance of the Strasbourg Court. In its recent judgments on cases in which a citizen has asserted that the grant or refusal of a return application under the Hague Convention has violated his or her rights under the ECHR, it has left a wake of alarm and confusion.

My admiration for Regulation Brussels II bis rests on both its framework and its performance in the eight years of its operation. Article 11 operates as a protocol to the 1980 Hague Convention to which all European member states must subscribe. The content of art. 11 as negotiated by the member states reflects criticisms of the Convention itself after 20 years of its operation. The measures introduced by art. 11 are intended to fortify the Convention and better to achieve its primary objective, namely the return of the abducted child by expeditious summary procedure.

Much of the general provisions of the Brussels Regulation relating to parental responsibility are modelled on the Hague 1996 Convention. Thus in both respects there is a synergy between Conventions and Regulations. The same synergy is visible in the Regulation and in the Convention providing for the reciprocal enforcement of maintenance orders.

Given the common ground covered by the Child Protection Convention of 1996 and the Brussels Regulation it is understandable, and to me acceptable, that the European Commission laid claim to external competence, which prevented member states from ratifying or acceding to the 1996 Convention. In this instance the claim has operated to the benefit of the Convention when, ultimately, Europe decreed that all member states should legislate the 1996 Convention into domestic law by June 2010. Although compliance with this requirement proved to be patchy, every member state has now ratified and incorporated the 1996 Convention with the exception of Italy, a familiar laggard. Thus Europe, all or none, can be a real aid to a Convention if the European policy decision proves to be positive. The arrival of what will soon be 29 jurisdictions has a major impact on the global spread of a Convention (Croatia joins and Denmark abstains). Thus within my period of review we see global or regional law covering inter-country adoption of children, child protection, fortified provisions to combat abduction and reciprocal enforcement of maintenance orders.

What has not been achieved is the desired Regulations covering first marriage, second marital property regimes and the property consequences of the ending of a marriage and, third, succession. The failure of the first results from the diversity of traditions and belief concerning marriage salvaged by a concord amongst a smaller European group under the provisions of Enhanced Co-operation. However the regulations governing Marital Property Regimes and Succession will result in a Regulation binding member states with the probable exception of the United Kingdom, Ireland and Denmark.

Our election to decline these two Regulations results from fundamental differences between legal tradition in common law states and in civilian jurisdictions. In my perception the civilian majority have been insufficiently prepared to make concessions to recognise our difference. Equally unresolved is the difference between our preference for *forum conveniens* and the civilian preference for applicable law provisions. In the round, although more might have been achieved, at least much new law has emerged for the benefit of the many families that combine more than one nationality and culture.

Turning now from law to practice, the great development in the period under review is the growth of direct judicial communication and collaboration. It was obvious to me that there would be no progress without formalities, guidance and institutionalisation. Hence my proposal to the 1998 de Ruwenberg Conference that the states party to the 1980 Convention should each appoint a judge to an international Network to be administered by the Permanent Bureau.

Although the acceptance of the judicial Network to complement the co-ordinating role of the Central Authorities was initially limited to Common Law jurisdictions, subsequent growth and development has been recorded in the recommendations of the Special Commissions in and after 2000. Now we have the Guide to Good Practice in Direct Judicial Communication in its final form.

Through these years Michael Freeman has given the International Family Law Committee (launched in October 1993) his support and guidance. Particularly in the early days, he attended our meetings, he helped shape our responses to consultations and he stimulated our discussions. When the Blair Government was, very briefly, committed to the reform of our ancillary relief law he helped us, at the Edinburgh Seminar, to present our law and practice and to understand the Scottish system. Given the diversity of his specialisations as a legal scholar we are indeed fortunate that he included international family law within his extraordinary range.

Many legal scholars could have offered this academic support. What made Michael's contribution unique and exceptional was his capacity to relate developments in international family justice to developments in neighbouring territories: for example, the rights of the child. Above all I admired Michael's ability to challenge, indeed often deliberately to provoke. He had little regard for the conventional wisdom and the unfailing courage to present his own views, so particularly his own views, with tenacity and conviction. No discussion was ever flat or arid if Michael was in earshot and then drawn into the flow of ideas.

References

European Council, *Council Regulation (EC) No 2201/2003 concerning jurisdiction and the recognition and enforcement of judgments in matrimonial matters and the matters of parental responsibility, repealing Regulation (EC) No 1347/2000*, 27 November 2003, Official Journal L 338 , 23/12/2003 P. 0001 – 0029

Hague Conference on Private International Law, *Hague Convention on the Civil Aspects of International Child Abduction*, 25 October 1980, Hague XXVIII

Hague Conference on Private International Law, *Hague Convention on Jurisdiction, Applicable Law, Recognition, Enforcement and Co-operation in respect of Parental Responsibility and Measures for the Protection of Children*, 19 October 1996, Hague XXXIV

Thirty Years of the Hague Abduction Convention: A Children's Rights' Perspective

Rhona Schuz
Sha'arei Mishpat Law School, Israel

I. Introduction

This paper analyses the Hague Convention on the Civil Aspects of International Child Abduction 1980 ("the Abduction Convention") and the way in which it has been implemented in the light of the doctrine of children's rights, of which Michael Freeman has been perhaps the most influential advocate over the past four decades. Back in the 1970s, Michael refused an invitation to participate in the drafting of the Convention because he saw it as anti-children and anti-women.[1] Now 30 years since the Convention came into force (in December 1983), it might well be asked whether Michael's stance was justified.

On the one hand, as will be seen below, the Abduction Convention's automatic return mechanism and the way in which its provisions have been interpreted and applied over the years can be seen as incompatible with children's rights ideology in a number of ways. It is of particular note that one of the main criticisms of the operation of the Convention has been that insufficient account is taken of domestic violence perpetrated by the left-behind parent against the abductor (Bruch, 2004; Kaye, 1999; Weiner, 2000; Hoegger, 2003; Brown Williams, 2011). Michael's pioneering work on domestic violence (1979) was published a year before the signing of the Convention; but at that time the scope of the phenomenon, the relationship between domestic violence and child abduction and the extent of the adverse effect on children of being exposed to domestic violence (Edelson and Lindhorst, 2010) were not yet documented.[2]

On the other hand, since the beginning of the current century, when I first addressed the issue of the rights of abducted children (2002), courts and policy-makers have become more aware of the need to ensure that children's rights are protected in Abduction Convention cases and have taken some steps in this direction. In particu-

1 Personal communication to author from Michael Freeman.
2 Although Michael himself does seems to have understood the connection, id.

A. Diduck, N. Peleg, H. Reece (eds.), Law in Society: Reflections on Children, Family, Culture and Philosophy
Copyright 2015 Koninklijke Brill NV. Printed in The Netherlands. ISBN 978-90-04-26148-8. pp. 607-633.

lar, in a number of decisions over the last few years, some of them very recent (see IIC2 below), the UK Supreme Court has adopted a more child-centric approach.

Thus, it is appropriate in a volume marking Michael Freeman's amazing academic career and achievements to analyse these developments and consider how we might better protect children's rights within the existing framework of the Abduction Convention. This issue has become more critical now that the proposal to negotiate a protocol to the Abduction Convention has been dropped from the agenda of the Hague Conference on Private International Law.[3]

In this paper, I will concentrate on three aspects of children's rights: (1) the child as a subject and not an object; (2) the child's right to participate and (3) the obligation to treat the child's best interests as a primary consideration. In relation to each of these aspects, I will first illustrate the various ways in which the Convention and the manner in which it has been applied over the years in a number of leading jurisdictions are inconsistent with children's rights ideology and then go on to consider steps which have already been taken and those which might be taken in the future to resolve these inconsistencies.

A number of preliminary clarifications should be made. Firstly, whilst the United Nations Convention on the Rights of the Child (the 'CRC') provides a relatively comprehensive list of the rights which children are recognized as holding, it should not be seen as the final word on children's rights (Freeman, 2002: 98) and so this paper is not restricted to discussing compatibility between the Abduction Convention and the CRC, but rather takes a broader approach to the concept of children's rights. Accordingly, even though the US has not ratified the CRC, US Abduction Convention case-law can legitimately be used to demonstrate consistency or inconsistency with the ideology of children's rights.[4] Similarly, the examination here is not limited to the question of whether the outcome of cases violates children's rights, but includes consideration of whether the legal discourse in Abduction Convention cases is consistent with the language of children's rights.[5]

Secondly, this essay is not attempting to provide a comprehensive analysis of how the Convention has been applied in all, or even most, of the 92 Contracting States, which is an impossible feat. Rather, the paper aims to demonstrate that in applying the Convention, there exists a real risk of violation of children's rights and inconsistency with children's rights ideology, and to explain how this risk has already been and can be further reduced. Examples are brought from the case-law of a number of jurisdictions, including the US and the UK, the two States which receive the most applications under the Convention (Lowe, 2011: 34).

---

3 See Guide To Part II Of The Sixth Meeting Of The Special Commission And Consideration Of The Desirability And Feasibility Of Further Work In Connection With The 1980 And 1996 Conventions [Guide to Part II], Prel doc no. 13 of 2011, www.hcch.net/upload/wop/abduct2012pd13_e.pdf. and generally Schuz (2013:441-442).

4 For the view that because of its widespread acceptance, the CRC has become part of customary international law and so may be used in US courts, see Elrod (2010-2011: 672).

5 For the relevance of the language of rights, see e.g. Freeman (1997: 17).

Finally, it is necessary to refute at the outset the claim that a children's rights analysis of the Abduction Convention is irrelevant because the Convention is intended to be a procedural vehicle to determine jurisdiction and enforce foreign court judgments with rapidity, and that the real issue is whether the substantive domestic custody and access orders were issued in accordance with the CRC. This claim itself is fundamentally incompatible with the philosophy of children's rights because it treats the child as the mere object of a technical jurisdiction determination and completely ignores the fact that Abduction Convention decisions have fateful implications for the lives of children both in the short-term and often also in the long-term.[6] Moreover, in many cases there has not yet been a domestic custody or access decision and in some cases, if the child is returned, there may not be one, because the abductor is not in a position to instigate proceedings in the country of origin. Moreover, as already mentioned, some courts are now recognising the relevance of the CRC to Abduction Convention cases. Accordingly, it is certainly appropriate to analyse to what extent the Abduction Convention and the way in which it has been applied are consistent with the most significant elements of children's rights ideology.

II. The Child as a Subject

A. The Concept of Treating the Child as a Subject

Perhaps the most fundamental aspect of the doctrine of children's rights is its recognition not only that children are not owned by their parents, but that their separate independent identities should be recognised by the law. In other words, they are subjects and not simply the objects of disputes between their parents.

One of the consequences of treating the child as a subject is that issues affecting him have to be viewed through his eyes and not paternalistically from the viewpoint of adults. The implications of this perception go further than giving mature children the right to be heard and have weight accorded to their views. In addition, findings concerning children of all ages have to take into account the situation from the viewpoint of the child. In the context of the Abduction Convention, this conclusion is particularly pertinent in relation to the crucial findings as to whether there has been a wrongful removal or retention and the place of the child's habitual residence, as well as in relation to the question of whether the child has become settled in his new environment for the purposes of the exception in Article 12(2).

---

6 The Ontario Supreme Court in *AMRI* v *KER* [2011] O.J. No. 2449 [128] referred to the "life-altering effect" of Hague Convention applications.

B. *Inconsistencies*

1. Definition of "Wrongful"

Under the Abduction Convention, the obligation to return the child to the country of origin is triggered by the finding that there has been a wrongful removal or retention. Article 3 provides that a removal or retention is to be treated as wrongful where it is in breach of the rights of any person or institution. Defining wrongful removal or retention in terms of rights of adults, usually those of the parents, treats children as an object. The message given is that the victim of the abduction is the left-behind parent and that the breach of his rights in relation to his child enables him to request return of the child, in much the same way as an owner who has been dispossessed of his property would request its return.[7]

No recognition appears to be given to the fact that the child is the primary victim and that his rights, in particular his right to contact with both parents, have been violated. Thus the Abduction Convention does not protect abducted children in cases where the left-behind parent did not have rights of custody under the law of the place of origin. Whilst many Western countries do now recognise that unmarried fathers have parental rights, there are still countries where these rights are not acquired automatically and are dependent on registration, agreement or court order. Where none of the required procedures has been carried out, the child will not be returned under the Convention (e.g. Israeli Supreme Court decision in RFamA 9941/12 *AAK* v *CHSB* (17.2.13),[8] even where the father had been actively involved in bringing up the child (*Re J (A Minor) (Abduction: Custody Rights)* [1990] 2 AC 562) and even where the separation from his father was damaging to him.[9]

---

7 The reference to the child as "it" in the Convention might be seen as lending support to this analysis: see Art. 12(2) ("its environment"); Art. 13 ("its return") and Art. 13(2) ("its views"); cf. Article 13(1)(b) which refers to "his or her return".

8 The father had not registered his rights as required by Dutch law. The fact that he had applied to the Dutch court for custody rights before the wrongful removal was found not to be relevant.

9 See comment of Barron J in his dissenting judgment in Supreme Court of Ireland in *HI* v *MG* [2000] 1 IR 110: "I am quite satisfied that the purpose of the Convention is to protect the interest of the child from harmful effects of an improper removal or retention. There can be no doubt but that to take a child of five from the only home he has ever known in which he has lived with his mother and father and to deprive him both of the security of that home and the presence of his father is a failure to protect the very interest of the child which the Convention is designed to protect. A removal in such circumstances defeats the purpose of the Convention. In my view, unless the Convention is coercive to the contrary, which it is not, it should be construed to apply to that child."

2. Determining Habitual Residence

A pre-condition to the obligation to order return under the Abduction Convention is that the child was habitually resident in another Member State immediately before the wrongful removal or retention (Article 4). This requirement reflects the reciprocal and international nature of the Convention which only applies as between Contracting States and only where the child was abducted to a State other than that of his habitual residence. Difficult questions as to the habitual residence of the child at the date of the wrongful removal or retention arise inter alia in cases of relatively recent emigration and travel abroad for the purpose of studies, employment, sabbaticals or for a trial period.

The drafters of the Abduction Convention declined to define the concept of habitual residence because they saw it is a question of fact and wanted to avoid it becoming a technical term of art. However, they do not seem to have appreciated the inherent difficulty involved in determining the habitual residence of children as opposed to adults, and that is that children are usually not in a position to decide where they live. Accordingly, in the UK and most other common law jurisdictions, the courts have, at least until recently,[10] determined the habitual residence of the child in the light of the intentions of the parent(s) who has/have the right to determine where he should live (e.g. *Re J (A Minor) (Abduction: Custody Rights)* [1990] 2 AC 562, 579; *Re N (Abduction: Habitual Residence* [2000] 2 FLR 899).

This approach (which I have referred to as the "parental rights" or "parental intention" model (2001)) is inconsistent with the recognition that the child is a subject, an independent actor with his own interests and rights because it bases the determination of the child's habitual residence on the intention of his parent(s), without any inquiry as to whether this is either necessary for, or even consistent with, the child's interests and without any consideration of the child's perspective.[11] In particular, according to the jurisprudence in some US Circuits, a child's habitual residence will not change so long as his parent(s) have not abandoned the former habitual residence, even though the child may no longer have any connection at all with the latter country (e.g. *Mozes* v *Mozes* 239 F3d 1067 (9th Cir 2001); *Gitter* v *Gitter* 396 F3d 124 (2nd Cir 2005); *Ruiz* v *Tenorio* 393 F3d 1247 (11th Cir 2004)).[12]

---

10 See C2 below.

11 The argument here is that this model treats the child as an object and not as a person in his own right and so the existence of the child objection exception does not provide an answer. Moreover, ignoring the child's perspective in determining habitual residence may lead to a finding that the Convention does not apply, in which case there will be no opportunity to consider the child's views in the Convention proceedings. Furthermore, even where return is refused on the basis of his objections, a finding that the child was habitually resident in an EU country may be critical because it will allow the court in that country to make a decision on the merits which may trump the no-return order, under the Brussels II bis Regulations (Re LC (Children) [2014] UKSC 1 at para. 21).

12 For analysis of the misconception which led to this approach, see Schuz (2013: 188-189).

It should be added that this approach is also inconsistent with the rationale behind the choice of the connecting factor of habitual residence, which was seen by the drafters as a pure issue of fact and not one that was technical and legalistic (Perez-Vera, 1982: 66). Moreover, it does not give effect to the intention of the drafters that the Convention should protect a child who had been removed "from the social and family environment in which *his* life has developed" (ibid: 11, emphasis added).

3. Interpretation of Settlement

The exception in Article 12(2) of the Convention will be established where one year has passed between the date of the wrongful removal or retention and the commencement of proceedings and the child has become settled in his new environment.

Some courts have taken a very stringent approach to the concept of settlement. Thus, for example, Purchas LJ stated that what was required under Article 12(2) was a "long-term settled position" (*Re S (A Minor) (Abduction)* [1991] 2 FLR 1) and Bracewell J explained that this phrase involved demonstrating "that the present position imports stability when looking at the future, and is permanent insofar as anything in life, can be said to be permanent" (*Re N (Minors)(Abduction)* [1991] 1 FLR 413, 418). This approach tests the child's attachment to a place in the light of adult perceptions rather than in the light of the child's sense of time, which does not usually include long term future planning (Schuz, 2008a).

Similarly, some judges have taken the view that a child cannot usually become settled where he is being concealed or the abducting parent is a fugitive from justice. In the words of Thorpe LJ, 'A very young child must take its emotional and psychological state in a large measure from that of the sole carer. An older child will be consciously or subconsciously enmeshed in the sole carer's web of deceit and subterfuge' (*Canon* v *Canon* [2004] EWCA Civ 1330 [57]). With respect, this is a generalisation that cannot be true in all cases and that fails to recognise that the child is an independent actor with his own separate feeling and emotions, not simply an adjunct to his parent. Furthermore, treating a child as not settled where the abductor is a fugitive from justice, or returning a settled child so as not to reward the abductor, is effectively punishing the child for the sins of the parents (*Canon* v *Canon* [2004] EWCA Civ 1330 [38]).

Finally, I would argue that the approach which allows the court discretion to order return of a settled child, even where the Article 12(2) exception is established (upheld in *Re M (Abduction: Zimbabawe)* [2007] UKHL 55), is inconsistent with a child-centric approach. Where a long period of time has elapsed and the child has become settled, the only way to give proper weight to his interests is by a full investigation of the merits of the case. Indeed, the danger that a court will return a settled child because of considerations relating to the behaviour of the parents and not those of the child is well illustrated by the decision of the High Court and Court of Appeal (*Re M (Children)* [2007] EWCA Civ 992) in the case of *Re M (Abduction: Zimbabwe)* itself.[13]

---

13 See also the New Zealand case of *Secretary of State for Justice* v *HJ* [2007] 2 NZLR 289, which overruled a first instance decision, in which the court had exercised its discretion

C. *Positive Developments*

1. Wide Interpretation of Parental Rights

Courts in general have held that the concept of parental rights should be defined broadly and this increases the chance that the removal or retention has been wrongful. This approach may be seen as giving indirect recognition to the child's right to contact with both of his parents. The most significant example of broad interpretation is the now almost universal treatment of the right of the non-custodial parent to veto removal of the child from the jurisdiction (*ne exeat* right) as a custody right (*Abbott* v *Abbott* 130 S. Ct. 1983 (2010)). Reference should also be made to the English doctrine of inchoate rights (*Re B* (*A Minor*) (*Abduction*) [1994] 2 FLR 249) and the willingness of some judges to hold that courts, seized of a claim for custody, themselves have custody rights while the proceedings are pending (*Re H* (*A Minor*) (*Abduction: Rights of Custody*) [2000] 2 AC 291; *Secretary, Attorney-General's Department* v *TS* (2001) FLC 93-063). The most extreme example of broad interpretation is the New Zealand jurisprudence which treats pure rights of access as custody rights (*Fairfax* v *Ireton* [2009] NZFLR 433).

2. Child-centric Interpretation

In the 1990s, some US Courts adopted an objective model to determining the habitual residence of the child, under which the child's habitual residence is determined on the basis of the quality of his connections with the country in question, independently of the parents' intentions (e.g. *Feder* v *Feder-Evans* 63 F3d 217 (3rd Cir 1995); I have referred to this model as the child-centred model (2001), since it recognises that the child is an autonomous individual and that the focus is on the degree of his acclimatisation in the country concerned. The independent approach is also adopted in some European countries, such as Austria, Germany and Switzerland (Schuz, 2013: 192).

In 2001, I argued that a proper application of the independent approach involved taking into account the parents' intentions in so far as they are relevant to the child's daily life and the quality of the connections he forms with the people and institutions around him (16). In recent years, courts in a number of countries, including the US (*Silverman* v *Silverman*, 338 F.3d 886 (8th Cir. 2003), Israel (RFamA 7784/12 *LS* v *GS*), New Zealand (*SK* v *KP* [2005] 3 NZLR 590; *Punter* v *Secretary for Justice* [2007] 1 NZLR 40) and Australia (*LK* v *Director-General Department of Community Services* [2009] HCA 9), have taken on board this hybrid approach, making clear that the parents' intentions are relevant but only as a fact to be taken into account in determining the

---

to order return of a settled child, even though the reason for the removal and concealment seems to have been the father's violence. Very recently, Justice Alito in the US Supreme Court case of *Lozano v Alvero* 134 S. Ct. 1224 at 1238-1239 has argued that abductors should not normally be allowed to benefit from their inequitable action in concealing children.

quality of the child's residence in the particular place, from his perspective. Similarly, the ECJ case-law concerning the meaning of habitual residence of a child in the Brussels II bis Regulation (Council Regulation (EC) No. 2201/2203) has also adopted a hybrid approach (*In Proceedings brought by A*, Case C523/07 [2009] ECR 1- 2805, [38]; *Mecredi* v *Chaffe*, Case C – 49710PPU [2012] Fam 22).

Most significantly, in the first of a very recent trilogy of cases involving habitual residence of children, the UK Supreme Court held that the ECJ test is to be preferred to that adopted early by the English courts since, in the words of Lady Hale, it is "focussed on the situation of the child, with the purposes and intentions of the parents being merely one of the relevant factors (*In the Matter of A Children (AP)* [2013] UKSC 60: [54]). Applying this approach in the second case, Lady Hale expressly considered the question of habitual residence from the point of view of the child (*In the Matter of KL (A Child)*) [2013] UKSC 75: [27]). Finally, in the third case (*In the Matter of Re LC (Children)* [2014] UKSC 1), it was recognised that the state of mind of children may be relevant to the determination of their habitual residence (as I suggested (2001: 17)).

D. The Way Forward

1. Rights of Custody

The message that the child is an object, rather than an independent rights-holder, which is conveyed by treating breach of parental rights as the trigger for return, cannot be adequately countered without amending the Convention. Even the most child-centred domestic rules for determining the substantive dispute cannot change the fact that the Abduction Convention's return mechanism is predicated on violation of an adult's custody rights in relation to the child and not upon a breach of that child's rights.

However, efforts can be made to limit the damage caused by the Convention's focus on parental rights. For example, courts can make a point of mentioning the fact that there has also been a breach of the child's right to contact with his parents and can emphasise that the return remedy is designed to protect that right. Since the problem identified here is of perpetuating a message which is inconsistent with the ideology of children's rights, rather than an actual breach of those rights, appropriate children's rights language can go some way to minimising the damaging impact of the formal regime, which treats the child as an object.

In addition, there is room to interpret the concept of custody rights even more broadly. Thus, for example, the doctrine of inchoate rights could also be applied to cases where an unmarried father was caring for the child together with the mother, and the New Zealand approach to access rights could be adopted. Such an approach can clearly be justified in the light of the Preamble to the Abduction Convention[14]

14 Which provides that "The States signatory to the present Convention, Firmly convinced that the interests of children are of paramount importance in matters relating to their custody, Desiring to protect children internationally from the harmful effect of their

and Article 31 of the Vienna Convention on the Law of Treaties (adopted 23rd May 1969, entered into force 27 January 1980, 1115 UNTS 331), which provides for purposive interpretation.

The main disadvantage of the latter approach, and also of the treatment of *ne exeat* rights as custody rights, is that return to a non-primary carer in support of an access right may well cause the child harm because he will not be returned to the environment in which he was living beforehand (Freeman, 2000: 50; Bruch, 2011: 241). However, it must be remembered that the obligation of the court is to order return to the country of habitual residence, not to the left-behind parent, and the limited evidence available suggests that the abducting primary carer will usually return with the child.[15] Of course there will still be cases, in particular where the abducting parent has suffered violence at the hands of the left-behind parent, in which the abducting parent cannot reasonably be expected to return with the child, even with the protection of undertakings or conditions. However, the better solution in such cases is to invoke the Article 13(1)(b) grave risk defence[16] and not to deny that there has been a wrongful removal or retention in the first place. In other words, the fact that there will inevitably be some cases where return of a child, who has been removed or retained by the custodial parent in breach of an access right or even a *ne exeat* right, will cause the child harm rather than protect him is not a reason not to treat the removal or return as wrongful in the first place. Rather, in determining whether one of the exceptions is established, the nature of the relationship between the child and the left-behind parent should be relevant.[17] Thus, interpreting the exceptions more flexibly in cases of breach of *ne exeat* rights and pure access rights is more likely to promote the rights of children than blocking claims completely in these cases.

An alternative method of giving effect to the child's right to contact with both parents in cases where the left-behind parent does not have custody rights is for Central Authorities and courts to give teeth to the access provisions in the Abduction Convention, so that left-behind parents will be able to benefit fully from the procedural and institutional advantages of the Convention and to enforce their access rights speedily.[18]

---

wrongful removal or retention and to establish procedure to ensure their prompt return to the State of their habitual residence.....".

15 See Report by the Reunite Research Unit, 'The Outcomes for Children Returned Following an Abduction' (2003), www.reunite.org/edit/files/Library%20-%20reunite%20Publications/Outcomes%20Report.pdf., 35.

16 E.g. Austrian decision OGH May 2, 1992 2 OB 596.91 [INCADAT CITE: HC/E/AT375], in which a travel restriction was held to be a custody right but the grave risk defence was held to apply.

17 The relevant exception will usually be the grave risk exception. However, the fact that the left-behind parent did not play any real role in a mature child's life should be taken into account in determining the weight to be given to the child's objections. Similarly, where a year has passed since the abduction, such a fact is likely to make it easier to show acclimatisation in the new country.

18 For analysis of the operation of the access provisions, see Schuz (2013: 423-429).

2. Child-centric Interpretation

It is to be hoped that the more child centric approach to habitual residence described above (at C2) will be universally adopted. Yet, the decision of the majority of the UK Supreme Court in the recent case of *In the Matter of LC (Children)* [2014] UKSC 1, according to which the state of mind of only adolescent children should be taken into account in determining their habitual residence, does not go far enough because children's rights ideology is not limited to mature children (Freeman, 1983: 57). Accordingly, Lady Hale's view that the perceptions of even younger children are a relevant factor in determining the quality of their residence (at [58]) is clearly to be preferred. Indeed, her comment that "the relevant reality is that of the children and not of the parents" (at [87]) is to be welcomed as recognition that the child is the subject and not the object of the Abduction Convention proceedings. Moreover, the implications of her Ladyship's words go beyond the issue of habitual residence and are relevant also inter alia to the question of separate representation for children (discussed below at IIIB1) and interpretation and application of the exceptions.

In particular, it is clear that the question of settlement for the purposes of the exception in Article 12(2) has to be determined from the child's perspective (Schuz, 2008a). Moreover, if there is to be discretion to order return of settled children, it must be exercised with extreme caution, on the basis of the child's interests and not those of the parents or the community at large.[19] As Lady Hale pointed out, in settlement cases the primary objective of prompt return cannot be achieved and so little weight can be given to Convention considerations (*Re M (Zimbabwe)*: [47]).

Finally, soft-law methods might be used to encourage more judges to adopt a child-centric approach to interpreting and applying the Convention and to ensure greater uniformity. These might include conferences, training and perhaps even a Practice Guide, similar to those already prepared by the Permanent Bureau of the Hague Conference.

III. Child's Right to Participate

A. The Rationale for and Scope of the Right to Participate

The child's right to participate, which includes both his right to be heard and his right to have appropriate weight attached to his views in accordance with his age and maturity (Article 12, CRC), is derived from the recognition of children's autonomy (Freeman, 1997: 34-37). As a human being, who has a personality, existence and views of his own, independent and distinct from those of his parents or other adults, he has the right to have a say in the shaping of his life, and his views are deserving of respect. Furthermore, non-inclusion of the child in decisions relating to him is effectively to

19 Cf. the view of the Supreme Court of New Zealand in *Secretary for Justice* v *HJ* [2007] 2 NZLR 289 that the deterrent policy of the Convention may prevail over the welfare of the child in this context.

treat him as the passive victim of his parents' dispute rather than as a moral and social actor in his own right (Fortin, 2009: 234).

Michael Freeman's claim that children have a capacity to participate in decision-making concerning their lives (1997: 36) is now supported by empirical research, which shows that children often have clear views which they are able to express articulately and cogently about their living arrangements and other matters affecting them, and that sometimes they even suggest creative solutions to disputes which had not occurred to the adults (Smart, 2006; Raitt, 2007). Furthermore, most children do want to be consulted about arrangements which will have a major impact on their lives, and feel dissatisfied and hurt when they are excluded from decision-making (Smart, 2006; Raitt, 2007; Parkinson and Cashmore, 2007).

Two central questions relating to the scope of the right to participate are particularly relevant in the child abduction context. The first is the method of hearing the child. Are the child's participation rights adequately realised if he is heard indirectly by a welfare officer or other expert? I and others have argued that true participation in decision-making involves access to the ultimate decision-maker and that the child's right to be treated as an individual is only fully realised if he is given the opportunity to be heard directly by the judge deciding the case (Schuz, 2008b; Piper, 1999; Raitt, 2007; Potter, 2008). Moreover, in some types of cases, the only way to ensure that the child's voice is properly heard by the court is to order separate legal representation of the child (Eitzen, 1985; Fortin, 2007).

The second relates to the situation where the child's participation rights appear to conflict with his welfare. This dilemma can arise both in relation to hearing the child's views and the weight to be placed on the child's views. In relation to the former, the solution is to devise means to ensure that, in the pithy phraseology of Parkinson and Cashmore (2008: 219), children are protected "in participation", rather than to seek to protect them "from participation".

In relation to the latter, Freeman's (1983: 54-60) reconciliation, which he labels 'liberal paternalism', would appear to be the most acceptable and authoritative. In his view, interventions in children's lives are justified where they are to protect them from irrational actions, which should be defined as actions that would undermine future life choices or impair interests in an irreversible way. However, he and others such as Eekelaar (1994) emphasise the need to limit paternalism to a minimum. Accordingly, the independent views of mature children should be respected unless it is manifestly clear that these views will cause them real harm.

B. *Inconsistencies*

At first sight the Article 13(2) child objection exception, which allows the court to refuse return where the child objects thereto and the Court considers that "the child has attained an age and degree of maturity at which it is appropriate to take account of his or her views", appears to have been ahead of its time and to recognise the child's right to participate. However, this exception was not motivated by acceptance of the ideology of children's rights, but rather by the pragmatic concern that forcible return of mature teenagers would give a bad name to the Convention (Beaumont and McEleavy 1999: 177-178). Furthermore, as will be explained below, the potential inherent in this provision, as a vehicle to realise the child's participation rights, has not always been exploited.

1. Failure to Hear Children

There is no provision in the Abduction Convention itself requiring courts to ascertain the views of children. Thus, traditionally their views were only heard where the abductor raised the defence of the child's objections. Accordingly, there have been cases where the child's strong objection to return has only been discovered after return has been ordered, for example when he creates such a scene that he has to be taken off the plane (*Re M (A Minor)(Child Abduction)* [1994] 1 FLR 390) or when he requests separate representation so that he can appeal against a return order to which the abducting mother consented (*AJJ v JJ & Others* [2011] EWCA Civ 1448). Similarly, in the Canadian case of A.M.R.I. v K.E.R [2011] O.J. No. 2449, return of a 14 year old girl was ordered in an uncontested hearing, she was taken from school by the police without prior notice and despite her protests handed her over to her mother who took her back to Mexico. The girl subsequently fled, and eventually found her way back to Canada.[20]

The policy of not hearing children routinely in abduction cases, which still applies in many jurisdictions, [21] seems to stem from the concern that this will cause delay in what is designed to be a summary process (Silberman, 2000: 244) and from the perception that there is no point in hearing the children's views if they will not influence the decision.[22] However, it is clear that neither of these reasons can justify violating the child's right to be heard (per Baroness Hale in *Re D (Abduction: Rights of Custody)* [2006] UKHL 51, [57]), especially in view of the fact that the CRC right to be heard is considered an independent right and not purely instrumental (Hodgkin and Newell, 1998).

In addition, in many, probably most, Contracting States, abducted children are not routinely provided with separate representation (Schuz, 2013: 390-391; Pitman, 2009). The danger of the child's interests being represented by the abducting parent, who is usually perceived by the court as morally blameworthy, can be seen clearly from the UK case of *Re M (Abduction: Zimbabwe)*. At first instance and in the Court of Appeal (*Re M (Children)* [2007] EWCA Civ 992), where the children were not separately represented, the issues were analysed more from the parents' perspective than from that of the children and thus return was ordered even though the Article 12(2) settle-

20 The appeal against their return order was allowed on the basis that the girl had been granted refugee status, because her mother was abusive.

21 E.g. Australia, Canada and US (Trimmings, 2013: 214, 226 and 229). It is significant that the Permanent Bureau's 2010 Questionnaire www.hcch.net/index_en.php?act=publications.details&pid=5291&dtid=33) para. 7.3 only asks about methods of hearing children where the objection defence has been raised.

22 The claim that the child's right to be heard is realised provided that he is heard in the substantive proceedings has already been refuted above at I.

ment exception was established. In contrast in the House of Lords (*Re M* (*Abduction: Zimbabwe* [2007] UKHL 55), where the children were separately represented, their counsel emphasised child-centric considerations and in particular the impact that the return order would have on the children, and the appeal against the return order was allowed.

Similarly, in two later UK cases the children's interests were not adequately protected at first instance because the request for separate representation was refused. In the case of *AJ* v *JJ* [2011] EWCA 1448, the court accepted the mother's offer to return with the children to Poland, thus effectively abandoning her reliance on the objections of the 15 year old minor and his siblings, without taking into account the views of the children. More recently, in *The Matter of LC* (*Children*) [2014] UKSC 1, the 13 year old girl's perspective about the quality of her five month stay in Spain was not considered. In both cases, the children were later joined on appeal.

2. Insufficient Weight Attached to Children's Views

Some courts have interpreted the child objection exception narrowly (Schuz, 2008c; Elrod, 2011), inter alia by imposing stringent tests of age and maturity (e.g. *Re S* (*Abduction: Acquiescence*) [1994] 1 FLR 819, 827); *Beatty* v *Schatz* [2009] B.C.J. No. 1054 upheld in [2009] B.C.J. No. 1557) ; by setting a high threshold for validity and strength of objections (e.g. *W* v *W* [2004] SC 63; RFamA 672/06 *TAE* v *PR*, PD 61(3) 24 (Isr)) and by readily assuming that the child's views have been influenced by those around him (e.g. *Winters* v *Cowen* [2002] NZFLR 927; *TAE* v *PR ibid*). In addition, even where the defence has been established, courts may still exercise their discretion to order return on the basis of Convention considerations (e.g. *JPC* v *SMW* [2007] EWHC 1349; *Tsui Yai Yung* v *Fu-Chang Tshui* 499 F3d 279, Cir 2007; *Re LC* (*Children*) [2013] EWHC 1383 (Fam), subsequently overruled on this point in [2013] EWCA Civ 1058). These may include concern "not to send the wrong message" that it is acceptable to retain a child who says that he or she does not want to return (*Beatty* v *Schatz* [2009] B.C.J. No. 1054 upheld in [2009] B.C.J. No. 1557).

Perusal of the literature and cases cited above suggests that there are two main explanations for the reluctance of some courts to refuse to return children on the basis of their objections. The first is a lack of understanding of the significance of the child's right to participate and/or a paternalistic worldview about the capacity of children. The second is the belief that the policy of mandatory return and the need for international comity override the child's right to have his views respected.[23] Both of these explanations appear to be reflected in an Israeli case concerning the objections of 13 and 11 year old siblings, who had been re-abducted to Israel by the father (according to him, at their request), after the Italian court had refused his application for return, following the original abduction by the mother (RFam A 672/06 *TAE* v *PR*, PD 61(3)

23 The rationale behind this approach, that the interests of children generally in preventing abductions takes precedence over the interests of particular children (Greene, 2005: 109) will be discussed below in the context of the best interests standard.

24). Whilst paying lip service to the rights of the child and even mentioning Article 12 of the CRC and an article of mine advocating recognition of the participation rights of abducted children (the Hebrew version of Schuz, 2002), the Israeli Supreme Court then proceeded to hold that the child objection exception has to be interpreted narrowly, so as not to undermine the Convention, and to approve the paternalistic view taken by the District court in relation to the children's views. The children had been found to lack the necessary maturity (even though they were not considered immature for their age by the expert) and had been influenced by the fact that the father's family in Israel "had enveloped them with everything good". In addition, the Supreme Court set a very high threshold for establishment of the exception by requiring that the child's objections be "dominant and of special force".

In summary, it can be seen that the weight attached to the views of the children in the case-law discussed in this section is inconsistent with the approach of Freeman and Eekelaar (discussed at A2 above), under which the wishes of mature children should be respected unless this will manifestly cause them real harm.

C. *Positive Developments*

1. The Right to be Heard

Overall, children seem to be participating more in Abduction Convention proceedings, although there are still considerable differences between countries (Schuz, 2013: 375-380). Perhaps the most significant development is the enactment of Brussels II Revised Regulation (EC) no. 2201/2003 Article 11.2 which requires that the child is given the opportunity to be heard in Abduction Convention proceedings, unless this appears inappropriate having regard to his or her age or degree of maturity. Whilst this provision does not require direct hearing by the judge, there is some limited evidence of growing judicial recognition of the importance of such direct hearing both inside the EC (e.g. *AJJ* v *JJ & Others* [2011] EWCA Civ 1448, [38])[24] and in other jurisdictions (e.g. Israeli Supreme Court case, RFamA 5579/07 *RB* v *VG* (*7.8.07*)).

In addition, there are some limited signs of greater recognition of the need for separate representation of abducted children. Switzerland[25] and South Africa[26] have enacted legislation mandating appointment of a separate representative for the child in Abduction Convention cases, and in New Zealand there are judicial guidelines[27]

24 Thorpe LJ rejected counsel's argument that the Guidelines for Judges Meeting Children who are subject to Family Proceedings, Practice (published by the President of the Family Division April 2010, www.fnf.org.uk/downloads/Guidelines_for_Judges_Meeting_Children.pdf) do not apply to Abduction Convention cases.

25 Art. 9(3) of the Swiss Federal Act on International Child Abduction of 2007.

26 Section 279 of the South African Children's Act 38 of 2005.

27 www.justice.govt.nz/courts/family-court/practice-and-procedure/practice-notes/practice-note-hague-convention-cases-new-zealand-family-court-guidelines-on-the-appointment-of-lawyer-for-the-child-counsel-to-assist-specialist-reports-and-on-views-of-the-child.

requiring judges to consider appointing an independent lawyer for the abducted child inter alia where one of the defences is pleaded. Similarly, in the UK, whilst the Supreme Court has continued to insist that separate representation should not be ordered routinely in Convention cases or even cases involving particular issues (*Re LC (Children)* [2014] UKSC 1) (with the exception of settlement cases: *Re M (Abduction: Zimbabwe)* [2007] UKHL 55), there is some evidence of a greater willingness by the lower courts to join children as parties, so that they can be independently represented (Freeman and Hutchinson (2007); e.g. *JPC* v *SMW* [2007] EWHC 1349 (Fam); *De L* v *H* [2009] EWHC 3074 (Fam); *In the Matter of M (A Child)* [2010] EWCA 178).[28]

2. The Weight to be Attached to the Child's Views

Some judges have been prepared to take the child's right to participate very seriously in abduction cases. For example, Justice Gillen in *Re S, N, and C* [2005] NI Fam 1 explained: "if this court is to pay more than vacuous lip service to the contents of Article 12 of the UNCRC then I must take the child's views firmly into account when reaching my decision." In a similar vein, see the words of Judge Doogue in *Hollins* v *Crozier* [2000] NZFLR 775: "The Court has a duty not to pay just lip service to this requirement. The Court has a duty to listen to Joshua, to take into account his emphatic objections to being returned. The Court has a duty to see him as a person in his own right."[29]

Moreover, in the UK following the decision in *Re M (Abduction: Zimbabwe)*, courts seem to have taken a more child-centric approach not only to the exercise of discretion in cases of children's objections (Trimmings, 2013: 202-210), but also to the determination of whether the exception requirements are established. For example, some courts have been prepared to treat children's views as genuine, even where there is evidence of influence (e.g. *X* v *Y and others* [2012] EWHC 2838 (Fam));[30] and the approach to age and maturity seems to have become more liberal (e.g. *Re W (Minors)* [2010] EWCA Civ 520, [19]).[31]

---

28 However, as seen above (at B2), this trend is by no means universal (see also e.g. *Re F (Abduction: Removal Outside Jurisdiction* [2008] EWCA 842).

29 Likewise, Justice Asulin in the Family Court in the Israeli of case of *PR* v *TAE*, FamC14830/05 tak-mish 05(4), 266 (2005) (which was subsequently overruled by the Supreme Court, as noted above) commented that adopting a narrow approach to maturity and independence of the child's views would make the child objection exception redundant and make the child's right to have his views respected an empty declaration.

30 See also e.g. the US decision in *De Silva* v *Pitts* 481 F3d 1279 (10th Cir 2007) holding that the father's largesse did not prevent the child's views being independent.

31 It is noteworthy that here Wilson LJ expresses concern that this trend might erode the high level of achievement of the Convention's objective.

D. *The Way Forward*

Children's participation rights can only be fully respected if they are given the opportunity to be heard directly by the judge,[32] and, in many cases, only if they are provided with separate representation.[33] Thus it is to be hoped that judicial interviews will become more common, that more jurisdictions will follow the lead of Switzerland and South Africa in mandating separate representation in Abduction Convention cases, and that, in the meantime, courts will exercise their discretion to appoint a guardian ad litem or independent children's lawyer more liberally.

In addition, in order to ensure that judicial reference to participation rights of abducted children is not merely lip service, it is necessary for judges to internalise the scope of these rights and the rationale behind them and to interpret and apply the Article 13(2) defence accordingly. Whilst the more child-centric approach now being applied by the English courts to the children's objections exception is clearly to be welcomed, the decision of Lady Hale in *Re M* (*Abduction: Zimabawe*) [2007] UKHL 55, which seems to have been the inspiration for the change of approach, does not go far enough. In particular, I would take issue with the view expressed there that in exercising the discretion whether to return a mature objection child, it is legitimate to take into account "the various aspects of the Convention policy" (at [43]).[34] With respect, I would argue that the so-called policy of the Convention is an extraneous consideration in determining the appropriate weight to be given to the views of particular child and cannot justify violating the participation rights of mature children who genuinely object to return. Indeed, the exceptions should be considered as part of the policy of the Convention because in enacting them, the drafters recognised that there are values which override the mandatory return mechanism. This idea was eloquently expressed, with reference to the child objections exception, by US District Court Judge Lasnick: "The purpose of the mature child exception is to give voice to a child who has attained a certain age and maturity, even if those wishes run counter to the lofty public policy purposes for which the Convention was adopted" (*Vujicevic* v *Vujicevic* 2013 US. Dist. Lexis 82110, 11th June 2013).

Finally, it should be appreciated that concerns that a wider approach would lead to reliance on children's objections becoming the rule rather than the exception (Sobal and Hilton, 2001; Nanos, 1996: 463) are exaggerated inter alia because most abducted children are too young for their views to be taken into account, even on a more liberal approach (36% of children are under four and a further 41% are aged between five

32 Where the child wants to talk to the judge, this is unlikely to cause him harm. For empirical research into the views of children about direct hearing, see references cited at A above.

33 For detailed consideration of the arguments for and against separate representation of children in Abduction Convention cases, see Schuz (2013: 396-403).

34 See also the comment of Wilson LJ in *Re W* (*Minors*) [2010] EWCA Civ 520 that the objective of the Convention is "a powerful factor militating in favour of a return".

and nine (Lowe, 2011: 19), and because many abducted children do not object to return to the country of origin and cannot be manipulated into objecting to return.

IV. Best Interests of the Child

A. *The Status and Scope of the Best Interests Principle*

Article 3 of the CRC mandates treating the best interests of the child as a primary consideration in decisions relating to children. Commentators have addressed the question of the status of the best interests principle within the doctrine of the rights of children in general (Wolfson, 1992; Breen, 2002: 67-77) and within the CRC in particular (e.g. Alston, 1994; Parker, 1994; Van Beuren, 1995). I have suggested that Article 3 should be treated as conferring a right on the child that his best interests are treated as a primary consideration (Schuz, 2002: 401-402).[35] Nonetheless, for current purposes it is not necessary to determine whether Article 3 confers a right on the individual child since a scheme which violates the best interests principle as expressed in Article 3 of the CRC can be taken as being inconsistent with the ideology of children's rights.

However, it is necessary to consider briefly the implications of the formulation in Article 3. Firstly, the article appears to have a collective focus because it refers to all actions concerning children in the plural. This would mean that decisions concerning children have to take into account the best interests of children generally and not only the best interests of the particular child in relation to whom the decision is being made.[36] However, it seems that the reason for the use of the plural form is that legislatures and some of the other institutions referred to in the article make decisions about groups of children. Accordingly, where a court is making a decision about a specific child, the individual standard should be adopted, as suggested by the use of the singular form in the phrase 'best interests of the child' at the end of Article 3 (Alston, 1994).

Secondly, the phrase "primary consideration" in Article 3 is preceded by the indefinite and not the definite article. In other words, there is no requirement that the best interests of the child are the sole or even *the* principal consideration as long as they are *one* of the main considerations (ibid, 1994: 12-13; Parker, 1994: 208). This formulation gives considerable discretion to courts and other decision-makers to determine what weight to give to the best interests of the child viz-a-viz other considerations. Thus, the Article 3 standard allows the court to give less weight to the interests of the child than does the traditional paramountcy principle.[37]

---

35 This approach seems to have been adopted by the Children Rights committee in its General Comment 14 (2013) on the right of the child to have his or her best interests taken as a primary consideration, CRC/C/GC/14, available at http://tbinternet.ohchr.org/Treaties/CRC/Shared%20Documents/1_Global/CRC_C_GC_14__7202_E.doc.

36 Id at para. 32.

37 Although it should be noted that the scope of the decisions covered by Art 3 is wider than the scope of the decisions covered by the paramountcy principle in domestic law (Freeman, 2000).

B. *Inconsistencies*

1. Lack of Consideration of Best Interests

The Abduction Convention scheme appears to be fundamentally inconsistent with the requirement to treat the child's best interests as a primary consideration. Whilst the assumption which underpins the Convention is that the best interests of the child require immediate return, it is abundantly clear that there will be cases where this assumption is not correct. Nonetheless, it will not be possible to identify such cases since the judge is not allowed to assess what are the interests of the child in each individual case. The reasoning behind this prohibition is the belief that carrying out such an investigation will necessarily cause delay, which will prevent speedy return of the child and thus postpone the restoration of the status quo, substantially undermining the deterrent effect of the Convention.

I have previously shown that various judicial attempts to reconcile the Convention scheme with the best interests standard are not persuasive (2002: 436-440). Furthermore, the potential inherent in the grave risk of harm exception in Article 13(1)(b) as a means of protecting children's interests has not been realised because most courts have consistently interpreted and applied that exception extremely narrowly (Schuz, 2013: 273-289; Weiner, 2008b).

Indeed some commentators have openly recognised that "the best interests of individual children are occasionally sacrificed in the more general interests of the wider class of children in the international community" (Bainham, 1998: 582). However, it seems to me that the word "occasionally" is an understatement, since we now know that the likelihood that return will not be in the best interests of the child is considerably greater than originally expected, because in practice the stereotype case is abduction by the primary carer or joint primary carer (73% of cases (Lowe, 2008: 47), usually the mother (69% of cases (*ibid*: 14)), and not by the non-custodial father, as envisaged by the drafters of the Convention (Schuz, 2013: 55). Nonetheless, paradoxically, this very fact seems to be one of the reasons that courts have interpreted the grave risk of harm exception in Article 13(1)(b) so restrictively, heeding the Rapporteur's warning that a liberal approach to this exception will turn the Convention into a dead letter (Perez-Vera, 1980: 16). Yet the very fact that the paradigm has changed means that this narrow approach does not reflect the intentions of the drafters. Indeed, there is evidence that the drafters envisaged that the defence in Article 13(1)(b) would cover the situation where the mother was fleeing from domestic violence (Proceedings of 14th Session of Hague Conference on Private International Law (Oct 1980 Vol III), Proces-verbal No 8, 302; Weiner, 2008: 293).

More fundamentally, the question arises whether sacrificing the interests of even a few children in order to protect other children can be justified. Freeman (1997: 34-35) has claimed that utilitarianism is inconsistent with the normative values of autonomy and equality. I agree and would argue that the apparently utilitarian approach adopted in much of the Convention case-law[38] is morally indefensible and inconsistent with the Kantian principle that a person should always be treated as an end in himself, rather than a means to an end. These arguments are even more powerful in light of the fact that the deterrent effect of the Convention is unproven and not provable. Moreover, I have shown by reference to general deterrence literature that the Convention sanction is unlikely to deter many abductions (2013: 98-102).

3. Separating Siblings

A recent Israeli Supreme Court case provides a concrete and interesting example of lack of consistency with the best interests principle. The case of *DZ* v *Y.V.A.M. VD* RFamA 2270/13, 30.5.13) involved two children (aged 3 and 5) born to an Israeli woman and a Dutch man who had lived together in Holland, where both the children were born. Under Dutch law, an unmarried father does not have custody rights in relation to his children, unless he registers them. In this case, the father registered himself in relation to the older child, but not the younger. Shortly after the relationship broke down, the mother brought the children to Israel. The District court accepted the mother's claim that the Abduction Convention did not apply in relation to the younger child, but rejected her claim that ordering return of the older child alone would expose him to a grave risk of harm or place him in an intolerable situation within Article 13(1)(b) of the Convention. This holding was upheld by the Supreme Court, which refused to commission an expert opinion on the impact of separation between the siblings.

The Supreme Court distinguished the case-law from other jurisdictions, in which the grave risk defence had been invoked in order to prevent separation of full siblings (e.g. *B* v *K* [1993] 1 FCR 382; *WF* v *RJ* [2010] EWHC 2909; *State Central Authority* v *Hotzner* (*No* 2) [2010] Fam 1041, CA; *Sec for Justice* v *Penney* [1995] NZFLR 827; *Ramirez* v *Buyauskas, 2012 U.S. Dist. LEXIS 24899*). In the court's view, in the current case there was no objective reason why the mother could not return with both children to Holland, whereas in the foreign cases the reason for the potential separation was the fact that the other sibling objected or that return would cause harm to the other sibling because of specific circumstances relating to him. Thus, whilst paying lip service to the importance of the sibling connection, the court took the view that any other result would reward the mother for abducting the older child.

---

38 This approach is evidenced inter alia by reference to the need to interpret and apply the exceptions narrowly so as not to reduce the deterrent effect of the Convention. Whilst Lady Hale in *Re M* (*Abduction: Zimbabwe*) [2007] UKHL 55 at [54] specifically stated that the children in that case should not be made to suffer for the sake of general deterrence of abduction worldwide, the reason given is that in the light of the delay involved, the primary objective of the Convention could not be achieved and thus her comment seems to be limited to settlement cases. Indeed, as seen above, in the same case (at [43]) her Ladyship does state that the policy of the Convention is a legitimate consideration in exercising discretion where an exception has been established. Thus it is not clear that she is rejecting the utilitarian approach.

With respect, the Israeli Supreme court's claim that any separation would be caused by the mother and not by its decision is difficult to accept. The court was fully aware of the mother's claims about the difficulties associated with return to the country of origin in which she did not have any status or support, including evidence of violence against her and the children. Even if these did not meet the very high threshold of the Article 13(1)(b) exception, there was a real question as to whether the best interests of the younger child lay in staying in Israel or returning with the older sibling. Thus, since the mother was surely obliged to take into account the best interests of the younger child as well, it is too simplistic to say that there was no objective reason for her not to return with both children and naïve to assume that she would do so. Indeed, in the end she returned with the older child and left the younger child in Israel with her parents.[39]

Thus it is difficult to see how a court which had treated the interests of the older child as a primary consideration could have ordered return, without at least examining the implications for him of being returned without his younger brother. Furthermore, no consideration was even given to the interests of the younger child, which were inevitably affected by the decision.[40]

C. Positive Developments

Some courts do now appreciate the relevance of the interests of children in Abduction Convention cases. For example, some judges have shown awareness of the harm caused to children by being exposed to domestic violence (e.g. *Van De Sande* v *Van De Sande*, 431 F.3d 567, 570–71 (7th Cir). 2005; *Baran* v *Beaty*, 526 F.3d 1340, 1346 (11th Cir). 2008). Moreover, there has been increasing recognition of the need to put in place protective measures to ensure the safety of returning children (e.g. *Re E* [2011] UKSC 27) and a few courts have started to understand the importance of ensuring that such measures are enforceable (e.g. *Danaipour* v *McLarey* 286 F.3d 1 (1st Cir, 2002); *Simcox* v *Simcox* 511 F3d 594 (6th Cir, 2007); generally Schuz, 2013: 294-296).

Perhaps the most striking and controversial example of the recognition of the need to take into account the interests of children in Abduction Convention cases can be found in the jurisprudence of the European Court of Human Rights (ECtHR) in a line of cases, starting with *Neulinger* v *Shuruk and Switzerland* App no 41615/07 6.7.10). In these cases, the ECtHR stated that a child's return cannot be ordered automatically or mechanically without consideration of the child's best interests. Unsurprisingly, this approach has attracted considerable criticism (e.g. from the UK Supreme Court

39 The Dutch courts held that they did not have jurisdiction in relation to the younger child since he was habitually resident in Israel and after six months allowed the mother to relocate to Israel with the older child (personal communication from mother's lawyers).

40 In two English cases, courts recognised the right to respect for family life of older step-siblings who did not wish to return but held that these could not prevail over the rights of the father and abducted child, *S* v *B & Y (Abduction: Human Rights)* [2005] EWHC 733 (Fam) and *Re E* [2011] UKSC 27 at [50].

in *Re S* (*A Child*) [2012] UKSC 10; Lowe (2012); Silberman (2013)) because it appears to undermine the very foundation of the Abduction Convention's mechanism of mandatory summary return without a full investigation into the merits of the case.

The recent decision of the Grand Chamber of the ECtHR in *X* v *Latvia* (*Application no. 27853/09*, 26.11.13) represents an attempt to find middle ground, by clarifying that in return cases the best interests of the child have to be evaluated in the light of the exceptions in the Convention, i.e. more narrowly than in custody cases. The focus of the decision, which was accepted also by the minority judges, is the need to take seriously claims of risk of harm. This approach represents a much better attempt to reconcile the Abduction Convention's mandatory return mechanism with the best interests principle than that in *Neulinger* and should prevent a head-on clash between Strasbourg and national courts. Nonetheless, the new approach is too vague. Indeed, the knife-edge majority of 9-8, caused by the lack of agreement among the Grand Chamber judges themselves as to whether the new standard had been adhered to in this case, would seem to testify to the inherent lack of clarity.

D. The Way Forward

As seen from the above discussion, there is still a need to find a *via media* which will allow for the child's interests to be given appropriate weight without carrying out a full-blown best interests assessment, and which provides clear guidance to courts. It seems to me that the distinction between short term interests of children and their long-term interests made by Thorpe LJ in *Re E* [2011] EWCA Civ 361 [69] (also in *Sonderup* v *Tondelli* 2001 (1) SA 1171 (CC)) provides a workable basis for a reconciliation between the Abduction Convention and the best interests principle. The court in the requested State has to consider only the short-term interests of the child. Where there is a grave risk of real harm to the child's interests in the short term, then return should be refused on the basis of the grave risk exception. However, where this is not the case, issues relating to long term interests should be left to the court of habitual residence and so return should be ordered.

In addition, in order to ensure that children are protected without causing delay, it is necessary to adopt appropriate expedited procedures for identifying risk of harm and for enabling children to express their views. Only in cases where this preliminary investigation reveals that one of the exceptions might apply is it necessary to take more time to check things out thoroughly. This will not have any effect on the majority of cases, in which it can be ascertained relatively quickly that exceptions do not apply and return can be ordered.

Finally, it is essential that courts become more aware of the need to 'reality test' undertakings and other measures ordered to protect the returning child, by checking that they are actually enforceable in the requesting State and will provide adequate protection. Otherwise, in the words of Marilyn Freeman (2001: 146), such measures will be little more than 'sophisticated forms of judicial conscience appeasement'.

V. Conclusion

The discussion in this essay shows that Michael Freeman's concerns about the proposed Abduction Convention being anti-children and anti-women were indeed justified. It seems that the choice of a trigger based on parental rights, combined with the warning of Professor Perez-Vera (1982: 16) as to the dangers of wide interpretation of the exceptions, conveyed the message that the Abduction Convention was primarily designed to protect the rights of adults and give effect to adult policies,[41] despite the express declaration in the Preamble that the objective of the Convention is to protect children from the harmful effects of abduction. Accordingly, during the first twenty years of implementation, many examples of incompatibility with children's rights ideology can be found in the Abduction Convention case-law.

However, there is room for optimism in the light of the positive developments outlined throughout this paper. Over the last decade, some courts in a number of jurisdictions, including the UK Supreme Court, have started to take a more child-centric approach to the interpretation and application of various aspects of the Abduction Convention. This welcome trend seems to have been inspired by a number of factors including: increasing awareness of the CRC and its implications; increasing recognition of the human rights of children and abductors by the ECtHR and other courts;[42] the Brussels II bis regulations which require children to be heard; and academic writings.

Nonetheless, there is still a long way to go. In particular, the prevailing restrictive interpretation of the Article 13(1)(b) grave risk exception means that children's interests are not being given adequate weight, especially, although not exclusively, in situations where there has been violence and harassment. Whilst more courts are recognising the need to protect returning children, in practice they often do not take steps to ensure that protective measures are enforceable (e.g. Re E [2011] UKSC 27).[43]

I submit that the real key to making the Convention compatible with children's rights ideology lies in a more child-centric approach to the objectives of the Convention. Firstly, I suggest that the expressed 'object' of prompt return (Article 1 of the Convention) should be seen as the method of achieving the broader underlying objective of protecting children from the harmful effects of wrongful removal and retention, recited in the Preamble, rather than as an objective in its own right. Moreover, it needs to be recognised that an essential corollary of protecting children from the harmful effects of abduction is to protect children from the harmful effects of mandatory return, which is itself a consequence of the abduction. Accordingly,

---

41 Such as preventing the abductor from obtaining an advantage from his wrongdoing (Perez Vera, 1980: 71).

42 See for example the pronouncement of the Ontario Court of Appeal in *AMRI* v *KER* [2011] O.J. No. 2449 at [125] that "expediency can never trump fundamental human rights".

43 In this case, in which there were allegations of serious psychological abuse, the court did not check that the undertakings would be enforceable in Norway, and the psychiatrist's recommendation that the father should not be given the mother's address was ignored.

where there are no protective measures which can prevent the harm which will result from return, the objective of protecting the child will require that he not be returned, even though this result may well conflict with other Convention objectives, such as deterrence, justice between the parents/ the rule of law and hearing the dispute in the *forum conveniens*.[44]

I would suggest that treating the objective of protecting children as the primary focus of the Convention, which overrides the other objectives in case of conflict, will help to dispel the misconception, which appears still to be held by many judges, that the policy of the Convention always militates in favour of return. Rather it is has to be understood that the policy of the Convention is only to return children whom the Convention requires to be returned and that the policy of immediate return is based on the assumption that this will protect the child from the harmful effects of abduction. The establishment of one of the exceptions automatically casts doubt on the truth of the assumption in the particular case. Thus to rely on the objective of returning children in interpreting the scope of the exceptions or in exercising discretion to return children, where an exception has been established, is to resort to circular reasoning. Accordingly, the grave risk and child objection exceptions should be interpreted in light of the child protection and participation rights that they reflect, which should also be seen as part of the policy of the Convention. Similarly, in exercising discretion, where an exception is established, the interests of the child should be the most important consideration.

Furthermore, in order to ensure that children's interests are given priority, it is necessary to ensure that those interests are properly and objectively presented to the court. This will often require independent representation for the child and providing the opportunity for children, who are old enough to express their views and perceptions, to talk directly to the judge.

Moreover, the doctrine of international comity (in any of its senses: see Schuz (2013: 132-136))[45] cannot justify violating the protection, participation or any other rights of a child (cf. *JPC* v *SMW & Another* [2007] EWHC 1349). Refusing to return a child where one of the exceptions applies is not a breach of reciprocity or even a breach of judicial courtesy viz-a-viz the State of origin, because this is one of the situations in which the Convention envisaged that it might not be appropriate to return the child.

Finally, we might well ask whether the Abduction Convention has done more harm than good. In order to be able to answer this question, we need far more empirical research into the aftermath of return. Nevertheless, some examples of cases where the return order has clearly been harmful to the child can be found in the law reports and literature. The most extreme that I am aware of is an Israeli decision in 2008 ordering a 9 year old boy to return to his father in Belgium against his clear wishes and despite a psychological report warning of the catastrophic consequences of his returning alone. On the day on which the boy was supposed to meet his father

44 For discussion of these objectives, see Schuz (2013: 96-107).

45 For detailed consideration of the role of comity in Abduction Convention cases, see Schuz (2014).

at the airport, of which he and his mother were given only 24 hours notice, the boy disappeared and has not been since. The mother was later convicted of criminal child abduction (CrA 5463/11 *RB* v *State of Israel* (26.2.13)) and sentenced to 5 years in prison – currently on appeal – although it was not proven that she knows where the child is or was directly involved in his disappearance (CrC 8150/08 (16.6.13)).

On the other hand, there are clearly very many cases in which the Convention's mechanism has prevented considerable harm to children by ensuring swift return to their country of origin, and no doubt there are also cases where knowledge of the Convention has deterred potential abductors. It might be argued that tears in some cases are the price which has to be paid for protecting most children (Waite J in *W* v *W* [1993] 2 FLR 211: 220). However, as stated above, this line of reasoning is inconsistent with the Kantian principle that a person should always be treated as an end in himself and not only as a means to an end, which surely applies equally to children and adults. In addition, it has too readily been assumed, without any evidence, that wider interpretation and application of the exceptions will undermine the Convention. Thus I would argue that by adopting a child-centric approach to interpretation and application of the Convention and by protecting the rights of individual abducted children, we can minimise the cases in which there are "tears", without losing the benefits of the return mechanism.

I will end by expressing the hope that courts will give heed to Lady Hale's powerful warning in *Re D (A Child) (Abduction: Foreign Custody Rights)* [2006] UKHL 51: [52]: "No one intended that an instrument designed to secure the protection of children from the harmful effects of international child abduction should itself be turned into an instrument of harm."

References

Alston, P., "The Best Interests Principle: Towards a Reconciliation of Culture and Human Rights", in P. Alston (ed), *The Best Interests of the Child: Reconciling Culture And Human Rights* (Oxford: Clarendon Press, 1994).

Bainham, A., *Children: the Modern Law* (2nd ed) (Bristol: Jordan Publishing Limited, 1998).

Beaumont, P. and McEleavy, P., *The Hague Convention on International Child Abduction* (Oxford: Oxford University Press, 1999).

Breen, C., *The Standard of the Best Interests of the Child: A Western Tradition in International and Comparative Law* (The Hague: Nijhoff, 2002).

Brown Williams, K., "Fleeing Domestic Violence: A Proposal to Change the Inadequacies of the Hague Convention on the Civil Aspects of International Child Abduction in Domestic Violence Cases", *John Marshall Law Journal* 2011 4(1), 39-84.

Bruch, C., "The Unmet Needs of Domestic Violence Victims and their Children in Hague Child Abduction Convention Cases", *Family Law Quarterly* 2004 38(3), 529-545.

Bruch, C., "The Promises and Perils of a Protocol to the 1980 Convention on the Civil Aspects of International Child Abduction", *Festschrift Fur Ingeborg Schwenzer* 2011 1, 237-249.

Edelson, J. and Lindhorst, T., *Multiple Perspectives on Battered Mothers and their Children Fleeing to the United States for Safety, A study of Hague Convention Cases, Final Report* (2010), www.haguedv.org/reports/fmalreport.pdf.

Eekelaar, J., "Interests of the Child and the Child's Wishes: The Role of Dynamic Self-Determinism", in P. Alston (ed), *The Best Interests of the Child: Reconciling Culture and Human Rights* (Oxford: Clarendon Press, 1994).

Eitzen, T., "A Child's Right to Independent Legal Representation in a Custody Dispute", *Family Law Quarterly* 1985 19(1), 53-77.

Elrod, L. D. ,"Please Let Me Stay": Hearing The Voice Of The Child In Hague Abduction Cases", *Oklahoma Law Review* 2010-2011 63(4), 663-690.

Fortin, J., "Children's Representation Through the Looking Glass" *Family Law* 2007 37(June), 500-509.

Fortin, J., *Children's Rights and the Developing Law* (3rd edn) (Cambridge: Cambridge University Press, 2009).

Freeman, M., "Rights of Custody and Access under the Hague Child Abduction Convention – "A Questionable Result?"", *California Western International Law Journal* 2000 31(1), 39-51.

Freeman, M., "Primary Carers and The Hague Child Abduction Convention", *International Family Law* 2001(September), 140-150.

Freeman, M. and Hutchinson, A. M., "Half-Price for Children? The Voice of the Child and the Child's Fight for Party Status in Cases on International Child Abduction", *International Family Law* 29(November), 177-181.

Freeman, M. D. A., *Violence in the home* (Farnborough: Saxon House, 1979).

Freeman, M. D. A., *The Rights and Wrongs of Children* (London: Frances Pinter, 1983).

Freeman, M. D. A., *The Moral Status of Children: Essays on the Rights of the Child* (Dordecht: Martinus Nijhoff, 1997).

Freeman, M. D. A., "Images of Child Welfare in Abduction Appeals", in J. Murphy (ed), *Ethnic Minorities, Their Families and the Law* (Oxford: Hart Publishing, 2000).

Freeman, M. D. A., "Children's Rights: Ten Years after Ratification", in B. Franklin (ed), *The New Handbook on Children's Rights* (London: Routledge, 2002).

Greene, A. M., "Seen and Not Heard?: Children's Objections Under the Hague Convention on International Child Abduction", *University of Miami International and Comparative Law Review* 2005 13(1), 105-162.

Hodgkin, R. and Newell, P., *UNICEF Implementation Handbook for the Convention on the Rights of the Child* (Geneva: UNICEF, 1998).

Hoegger, R., "What If She Leaves? Domestic Violence Cases Under the Hague Convention and the Insufficiency of the Undertakings Remedy", *Berkeley Women's Law Journal* 2003 18(1), 181-210.

Kaye, M., "The Hague Convention and the Flight From Domestic Violence: How Women and Children are Being Returned by Coach and Four", *International Journal of Law, Policy and the Family* 1999 13(2), 191-212.

Lowe, N., *A Statistical Analysis of Applications Made in 2008 under The Hague Convention of 25 October 1980 on the Civil Aspects of International Child Abduction, Part I Global Report,* Preliminary Document 8 (November 2011), available at http://www.hcch.net/upload/wop/abduct2011pd08ae.pdf.

Lowe, N., "A Supra-National Approach to Interpreting the 1980 Hague Child Abduction Convention – a Tale of Two European Courts: Part 1: Setting the Scene", *International Family Law* 2012 (March), 48-52.

Nanos, R., "The Views of a Child: Emerging Interpretation and Significance of the Child's Objection Defense under the Hague Child Abduction Convention", *Brooklyn Journal of International Law* 1996 22(2), 437-466.

Parker, S., "The Best Interests of the Child: Principles and Problems", in P. Alston (ed), *The Best Interests of the Child: Reconciling Culture and Human Rights* (Oxford: Clarendon Press, 1994).

Parkinson, P. and Cashmore, J., "What Responsibility do Courts have to Hear Children?", *International Journal of Children's Rights* 2007 15(1), 43-60.

Parkinson, P. and Cashmore, J., *The Voice of a Child in Family Law Disputes* (Oxford: Oxford University Press, 2008).

Perez-Vera, E., "Explanatory Report", in *Hague Conference on Private International Law, Acts and Documents of the 14th. Session* Vol 3 (1982), available at http://www.hcch.net/upload/expl28.pdf.

Piper, C., "Barriers to seeing and hearing children in private law proceeding", *Family Law* 1999 26 (June), 394-398.

Potter, M., "The Voice of the Child: Children's Rights in Family Proceedings", *Family in Law Review* 2008 2, 15.

Raitt, F., "Hearing Children in Family Law Proceedings: Can Judges Make a Difference?", *Child and Family Law Quarterly* 2007 19(2), 204-224.

Schuz, R., "Habitual Residence of Children under the Hague Child Abduction Convention – Theory and Practice", *Child and Family Law Quarterly* 2001 13(1), 1-23.

Schuz, R. "The Hague Child Abduction Convention and Children's Rights", *Transnational Law & Contemporary Problems* 2002 12(2), 393-452.

Schuz, R. "In Search of a Settled Interpretation of Art 12(2) of the Hague Child Abduction Convention", *Child and Family Law Quarterly* 2008a 20(1), 64-80.

Schuz, R. "The Voice of the Child in the Israeli Family Court", in B. Atkin (ed), *International Survey of Family Law 2008 Edition* (Bristol: Jordan Publishing Limited, 2008b).

Schuz, R. "Protection Versus Autonomy: The Child Abduction Experience", in Y. Ronen and C. Greenbaum (eds), *The Case for the Child: Towards a New Agenda* (Antwerp: Intersentia, 2008c).

Schuz, R., *The Hague Child Abduction Convention: A Critical Analysis* (Oxford: Hart Publishing, 2013).

Schuz, R. "The Doctrine of Comity in the Age of Globalization: Between International Child Abduction and Cross-Border Insolvency", *Brooklyn Journal of International Law* (forthcoming).

Silberman, L., "The Hague Child Abduction Convention Turns Twenty: Gender Politics and Other Issues", *New York University Journal of International Law and Politics* 2000 33(1), 221-250.

Silberman, L., "The Hague Convention on Child Abduction and Unilateral Relocations by Custodial Parents: Has the European Court of Justice Overstepped Its Bounds?" (unpublished lecture delivered at London Metropolitan University on 3.7.13).

Smart, C., "Children's narratives of post-divorce family life: from individual experience to an ethical disposition", *The Sociological Review* 2006 54(1), 155-170.

Sobal, B. B. and Hilton, W. M., "Article 13(b) of the Hague Convention Treaty: Does it Create a Loophole for Parental Alienation Syndrome – an Insidious Abduction", *International Lawyer* 2001 35(3), 997-1026.

Taylor, N., Morag, R. T., Bajpai, A. and Graham, A., "International Models of Child Participation in Family Law Proceedings following Parental Separation / Divorce", *International Journal of Children's Rights* 2012 20(4), 645-673.

Trimmings, K., *Child Abduction within the European Union* (Oxford: Hart Publishing, 2013).

Van Bueren, G., *The International Law on the Rights of the Child* (Dordecht: Martinus Nijhoff, 1995).

Weiner, M., "International Child Abduction and the Escape from Domestic Violence", *Fordham Law Review* 2000 69(2), 593-706.

Weiner, M., "Half-Truths, Mistakes and Embarrassment: the United States Goes to the Fifth Meeting of the Special Commission to Review the Operation of the Hague Convention on the Civil Aspects of International Child Abduction", *Utah Law Review* 2008a (1), 221-314.

Weiner, M., "Intolerable Situations and Counsel for Children: Following Switzerland's Example in Hague Abduction Cases", *American University Law Review* 2008b 58(2), 335-401.

Wolfson, S., "Children's rights: The Theoretical Underpinning of the 'Best Interests of the Child'", in M. D. A. Freeman and P. Veerman (eds), *The Ideologies of Children's Rights* (Dordrecht: Nijhoff, 1995).

VI

Law and Michael Freeman

Thinking about Children's Rights Sociologically

Michael Freeman
Professor Emeritus, Faculty of Laws, UCL

Origins

Sociology and children's rights can both be traced, roughly, to the middle of the 19th century, but neither Auguste Comte (Pickering 1992-2003) nor Jules Vallès (2005) have much of an impact to-day. In 1900 Ellen Key predicted the 20th century would be the 'century of the child' (1909); the social sciences ensured it was the century of the child welfare professional (Stafseng, 1993, 77; Rose, 1989). There is now happily a revival of interest in the first child professional to show a commitment to children's rights, Janusz Korczak (2007; and see Eichsteller, 2009). It is doubtful whether any of those social scientists whose construction of childhood is responsible for our seeing childhood 'through' the lens of adulthood, 'interpreting everything children do, or have done to them, in terms of how this will affect their journey towards adulthood', (Lee, 2001) had heard of, let alone read, Korczak, or Eglantyne Jebb (1929; on whom see Mulley, 2009). Piaget (1932), Parsons (1957), Margaret Mead (1948), Ruth Benedict (1949), the list could go on, had an image of children which precluded any perception that they might have rights. It did not enter their imagination.

There was hardly any discussion of children's rights by anyone else either between 1924, when the Declaration of Geneva was formulated in the aftermath of the 1st World War, and 1959 when a similar Declaration emerged from the United Nations. And nothing very much then happened until the 1970s. This was the decade of the short-lived children's liberation movement, spearheaded by Paul Adams (1971), Richard Farson (1974), John Holt (1974), Howard Cohen (1980) and a few other bold spirits. The whistle had been blown on child abuse (Kempe, 1962), though not yet on the sexual abuse of children – in fact it had, but it hadn't been convenient to listen (Smart, 1999). We now know that children did not inhabit an idyllic world of, what Holt cynically called, 'Happy, Safe, Protected, Innocent Childhood' (Holt, 1974: 22-23), an image reflected in calling pre-school the 'kindergarten', with all that gardens are associated with.

The paradigm shift (Kuhn, 1972), which occurred in the 1980s, thus needs to be accounted for. Why did we get, in 1989, the Convention on the Rights of the Child?

A. Diduck, N. Peleg, H. Reece (eds.), Law in Society: Reflections on Children, Family, Culture and Philosophy
 ISBN 978-90-04-26148-8. pp. 637-652.

Why was it ratified so swiftly and almost universally? The Victoria Gillick challenge, in 1984,[1] is readily explicable in terms of the conventional attitude to children and to parent-child relationships, but the House of Lords' decision, in 1985, projected an image of childhood (or at least adolescence) which revealed the English judiciary in the vanguard of new thinking – hardly what most of us expected, even those who had followed the *Gault* (Melton, 1989) or *Tinker* cases in the United States.[2]

There is no easy answer. Certainly, by the 1980s we began to know more about childhood. Revelations about child abuse ensured that we understood the victimisation of children. There was some concern also about child labour and renewed interest in child criminality. But these were not active sources of any thinking that children had rights. The world pronounced 1979 the International Year of the Child (Freeman, 1980), and, although this became a catalyst for the Convention, I doubt if more than a few in 1979 thought such a normative statement was a likely result. It did, of course, take another 10 years of debate and compromise before the Convention emerged (Johnson, 1992).

It is about this time that within the academy a critique of the conventional understanding of childhood developed. Piaget's work was challenged (by inter alia, Gilligan 1982). Children's thinking was shown to be more complex and sophisticated than his work had indicated. For the first time children began to be seen as social actors (though it must be noted that progressive thinkers like Korczak had recognised this 50 or more years before). But it was not Korczak who was rediscovered, but the Soviet psychologist, Lev Vygotsky (1986; see King, 1981). The structural-functionalism of Talcott Parsons also came under attack: its emphasis on the role of social structures and institutions marginalised the individual's contribution in shaping their own lives. It was Charlotte Hardman who was one of the first – in a famous article in 1973 (Hardman, 1973) – to see the significance of this in relation to children. They, as well as adults, were capable of inhabiting a 'self-regulating', autonomous world which does not necessarily reflect early development of adult culture', in which they could be seen as social actors. A striking illustration is the work of Myra Bluebond-Langner. Her account (published in 1979) of the private worlds of dying children revealed 'structure' and 'action' at play, and described the ways children were active in the scripting of death on a cancer ward. Children who were going to die engaged their doctors and parents in a game of mutual pretence. All participants in this game knew the truth, but none let on (Bluebond-Langner, 1979).

Another seminal text was Ariès's *Centuries of Childhood* (1962). Though much of his work has been discredited (see Pollock, 1983), his underlying thesis that childhood

1 *Gillick v West Norfolk and Wisbech Area Health Authority* [1986] AC 112.

2 *In re Gault* 387 US 1 (1967) is a decision of the US Supreme Court which held that juveniles accused of crimes had rights of due process including the right of timely notification of charges against them, the right to confront witnesses and the right to counsel. In *Tinker v. Des Moines Independent Community School District*, 393 U.S. 503 (1969) the US Supreme Court defined the constitutional rights of students in US public schools, particularly First Amendment rights..

is a social construction retains its significance. Children's lives are deeply shaped by constructions of childhood. Ariès's thesis was the trigger for establishing childhood as a social construction formed by, as James and James explain, 'the complex interweaving of social structures, political and economic institutions, beliefs, cultural mores, laws, policies and the everyday action of both adults and children' (James and James, 2000: 9).

One cannot date the beginning of childhood studies or the sociology of childhood with any precision, but there is general consensus that the discipline emerged in about 1990. It was in 1990 that Alan Prout and Allison James published their edited collection, *Constructing and Reconstructing Childhood.* Chris Jenks had published a collection much earlier in 1982 (*Sociology of Childhood*) but this had much less impact. A central idea which emerged was that children were 'beings' in their own right, rather than pre-adult 'becomings'. It is unnecessary to dichotomise in this way – children are both beings and becomings. And so, it may be added, are adults. This is reflected in the Convention on the Rights of the Child: two of the key principles of which recognise the importance of decisions being taken in children's best interests (Article 3), and children's agency, expressed in the Convention in forms of participation (in Article 12 and the articles which follow). It is in part because children were seen as 'incomplete' (as 'becomings') that they have been deprived of rights, of a 'voice', of citizenship (Lister, 2009; Cockburn, 2013; Cohen, 2009). It is also because they are thought to occupy a private space. Rights discourse belongs to the public sphere. The family – the site of childhood – is the quintessentially private space. Classical liberal theory – though this was challenged by John Stuart Mill (1859) – limits the role of government to the management of public life: the state has no right to intrude upon the privacy of the family. That this is rhetoric rather than reality is testified to by Donzelot's *The Policing of Families* (1979) and Nikolas Rose's *Governing The Soul* (1989). Rose describes childhood as the 'most intensively governed sector of personal existence'. He refers to a 'strategy of family privacy'. No longer, he says, 'do experts have to reach the family by way of the law or the coercive intrusion of social work. They interpellate as through the radio call-in, through the weekly magazine column, through the gentle advice of the health visitor, teacher or neighbour, and through the unceasing reflective gaze of our own psychologically educated self-scrutiny'. (Rose, 1989: 27.)

The illusion of privacy was exposed by feminism. Feminists pointed to the ways in which the state protected the privacy of some – particularly men – rather than others and how non-intervention into the family was a form of intervention (Olsen, 1984-85). The examples of domestic violence and the marital rape immunity – the former only 'discovered' in the '70s (Pizzey, 1974), the latter surviving until 1991 in England (*R v R*[1992] 1 A C 599) were frequently cited. But feminists had little to say about children's rights – Shulamith Firestone (1971) being a notable exception (see also Burman 2012, Jaggar, 1983 and Thorne, 1987). But the privacy argument played a role both in marginalising women's rights, in particular within the family, and in doing the same for children. It may have been worse for children because it was assumed that their best interests were adequately taken care of by their parents. Feminism also gave us 'standpoint theory' (Bartlett, 1990). Why not therefore 'child standpoint theory'? And

Berry Mayall, in her 2002 book on the lives of London children over a 10 year period, has indeed argued for this (Mayall, 2002: 112-139). There are problems with women's standpoint theory – it is essentialist and can overlook the ways in which women's experiences are mediated by race, class, age and sexual orientation and the same applies to children's standpoint theory. But the problem for children is aggravated by the likelihood that the researchers working with children are themselves adults. This is not inevitable – indeed, the prospect of child researchers is something we should anticipate with relish.

A combination of all these factors goes some way towards explaining the paradigm shift. There is no doubt as a result we *professionals* look at children and childhood differently from the way it was looked at 20 years ago (Young-Bruehl, 2012). The same cannot necessarily be said about the population as a whole. Think of responses by *vox populi* to child criminality – the age of criminal responsibility, for example (Scraton, 1997) – or to corporal punishment of children – the New Zealand experience is striking evidence of this. Nevertheless, there is an abundance of research now into children's lives, their experiences, their views. The Convention offers opportunities for audits; the dialogue between the UN Committee on the Rights of the Child, States Parties who are obliged to put in regular reports on the compatibility of their laws and practices with the norms in the Convention, and NGOs offer important challenges to those concerned to improve the status of children. The new Third Optional Protocol which offers children or their representatives a procedure to bring communications or complaints before the UN Committee (operative from April 2014) will potentially also offer feedback on a state's compliance with the Convention. It will, it is hoped, offer new insights from the bottom-up of failures by the institutions of governance to address and redress the injuries from which children continue to suffer.

Disciplines

In 1998 I published an article with the title 'The Sociology of Childhood and Children's Rights.' I noted that 'the growth of sociological (and anthropological) interest in children ha[d] coincided broadly with the development of the modern children's rights movement' (Freeman, 1998: 433). I also noted that there had been little dialogue or collaboration between children's rights advocates and those working in children's studies. I pointed to the existence of two journals – of course there are others – one firmly rooted within the sociology of childhood (*Childhood*), the other deliberately dedicated to children's rights issues, though with a broad remit (*International Journal of Children's Rights*, which I have edited since its inception in 1993). *Childhood* commenced publication in 1994. Berry Mayall published an article in 2000 in the International Journal of Children's Rights (Mayall, 2000) – I commissioned it – with virtually the same title ('The Sociology of Childhood in relation to Children's Rights'). Since then, only a little has been written on the relationship (Lenzer, 2002 is an example). Most recently (in 2010) Leena Alanen wrote an editorial in *Childhood* with the title 'Taking Children's Rights Seriously' (Alanen, 2010). In this she makes a number of points, including reiterating Bühler-Niederberger and Van Krieken's observation about a 'fluctuation between an analytical and a normative register' (Bühler-Niederberger and Van Krieken, 2012, 2008: 148) in childhood sociology. I think she overplays the contribution that the sociology of childhood has made to the advancement of children's rights, but that is not my principal concern here.

Towards a Sociology of Children's Rights

I intend instead to take up a challenge she offers to those focused on what a sociology of children's rights might look like. I do so in the belief that in this way childhood studies is more likely to advance children's rights, though I think it is also likely that this will achieve conceptual advances in childhood studies too. The latter is not my concern in this paper.

What is a Child?

A sociology of children's rights will necessarily ask many of the same questions as those working within the children's rights field. But it may have different insights. Clearly, both need to know what we mean by 'child'. The Convention gives us a straightforward, and deceptively simple, answer: 'every human being below the age of eighteen years unless, under the law applicable to the child, majority is attained earlier' (Freeman, 2015). This statement was the product of considerable debate and political compromise.

There was, unsurprisingly, a body of opinion which says the beginning of childhood is at conception. There were no sociologists or anthropologists (or for that matter philosophers) present at the drafting debates which produced Article 1. Had they been able to present their evidence and debate, we might have been discomforted by the knowledge that it is not just Roman Catholic belief that life begins at conception. Moskowitz's study of Taiwan, *The Haunting Fetus* (2001), is a case in point. He reports that fetuses are thought to grow into small children in the afterlife. The only way to extirpate these 'hauntings' is to pay large sums of money to temples that perform exorcisms to placate the children. He concedes that the 'appeasement' is financially exploitative, but it provides 'psychological comfort' to those involved in the choices that lead to abortion (2001: 6). The concept of 'spirit children' stretches the category of 'unborn' even further. These are those children who are believed to exist in the supernatural world and are waiting to be born as embodied children. Such beliefs are found in many communities: the Yoruba, the Akan, the Meande (all West African societies) and the Aborigines of the Kimberleys. As Heather Montgomery recognises: 'The links between newly born children and the spirit world are so strong that it is impossible to study the former without reference to the latter' (2009: 156). Apparently, children themselves are well aware of the links between their lives as spirit children and their current existences. Phyllis Kaberry (1939, see also 2008) describes how Aboriginal children of 8 or 9 were 'interested in the fact that they had once been a fish, bird, reptile, or animal prior to the entry of the spirit child into the mother' (1939: 44). Twins are also a 'problem' case, less so now because ideas about twinship and the status of twins has been changed by the impact of colonial intervention, globalisation, missionary work and other factors. But they were treated in parts of the world as anomalies. Amongst the Labwor of Uganda, for example, they had to be treated alike, so that if one was rewarded, so was the other (Abrahams, 1972). The same applied to punishment. I've come across no literature on triplets etc, but I assume such multiple births will have caused disquiet too.

But, if the beginning of childhood raises questions, so does the end of it. The Convention controversially permits the recruitment of children into armies at 15 – there is now an Optional Protocol fixing the age at 18 – and does not lay down a minimum age for marriage or for criminal responsibility. Should it do so? The sociology of childhood can offer insights here. This tells us that children's lives are shaped by the social and cultural expectations adults and their peers have of them in different times and places. The evidence from neuroscience has a contribution to make too, but that is not within the remit of this paper.

Childhood is thus socially constructed, but it also has universal characteristics (Smith, 2012, Brems, 2001). Children have similar needs and limitations. All babies and infants are dependent. They have to be fed, though who feeds them varies from culture to culture. Two hundred years ago, wet-nursing was a widespread and acceptable practice. It became less acceptable when ideas changed about what the baby ingested with the mother's milk. In much of the world children take on adult activities, for example work, at ages well below 18. The Convention ignores adolescence: persons are either children or adults. And it fixes the commencement of adulthood at 18. I think it is interesting that Senegal would have extended the concept of child 'until' at least the age of 18 years: given what we now experience as the prolonged dependence of many 'children', and also the evidence from neuroscience, is there a case for extending the ambit of the Convention beyond 18 years, and, if so, to what? It has been so argued, for example by Sonja Grover (2004) that 25 might be an appropriate cut-off point.

What Rights?

Sociology may also offer insights into what rights children should have. It is interesting that most discussion of children's rights today takes the list in the Convention as a definitive agenda. In an article I wrote in 2000 ('The Future of Children's Rights') I pointed to gaps: for example, the failure to address citizenship rights, including the right to vote. I also pointed to groups of children neglected by the Convention: disabled children (Sabatello, 2013), gay children, girl children, refugee and asylum-seeking children, indigenous children, street children, IVF children. The Convention communicates a particular vision of childhood: it lumps all those under 18 together. It protects children from adulthood. It stresses that childhood is a protected special space. It emphasizes that the appropriate place for children is at home with their families or at school. Children are accorded a right to education, not a right not to attend school. Education is privileged over work, family life over street life. The Convention implicitly assumes that children have parents, and parents who are responsible (Freeman,

2008). Indeed, parental responsibilities are laid down in the Convention (in Article 5) before any children's rights are articulated. The image of the child is of an inheritor of the liberal tradition associated with the Enlightenment. Sociologists and anthropologists by studying 'other' children can draw our attention to this incomplete image, and by raising problem cases – street children, child prostitutes, children in slavery or brutal labour, child soldiers, refugee children, children affected by war or HIV/AIDS – make us aware of the complexity of childhood and the supposedly universal characterisation of childhood spelt out in the Convention.

That childhood is a combination of the global (Katz, 2004) and the local can be brought out if we examine one child right, which we all know is in the Convention if this is properly interpreted, but is not stated as such (Burman, 1992). I refer to the child's right to be free from physical chastisement. For both lawyers and sociologists, the line between legitimate corporal punishment and child abuse is difficult to draw but sociologists of childhood can bolster the moral and legal case. Sociologists such as David Gil (1970) and Murray Straus (1974) have made it clear why a child should have this right (see also Newell, 1989). The reciprocity of the relationship between sociologists of childhood and children's rights advocates is also important here, since it was only with the development of a children's rights perspective that the corporal punishment of children began to be challenged at all. Did anyone think there was anything wrong with the practice until the early 1990s? Certainly, not in England! (I exclude from this, of course, early advocates of children's rights like Kate Douglas Wiggin (1898), Ellen Key (1900) and Janusz Korczak (2009). But even Korczak did not come out explicitly against hitting children.

Anthropology also is particularly useful in this context. The Human Relations Area Files[3] show that, whilst the physical punishment of children is common, it is not universal. Thus, David Levinson (1989) found that in 16 out of 90 societies it was rare or non-existent. He also found a close relationship between the corporal punishment of children and domestic violence against women as well as sibling aggression. To understand physical punishment of children one needs to see it in terms of power imbalance. It has always been a badge of inferiority that a person is the object of physical chastisement (Freeman, 1979). Thus, the work of the Emblers is useful. Using some of the same data as Levinson, they concluded that 'parents think ... that corporal punishment is a dramatic way to convey the discrepancy in power between themselves and their children' (Embler and Embler, 2005: 614). Also, significantly, the perception of this imbalance by the child will 'generalize to an acceptance of power inequalities later on when the child grows up', which has important consequences for the ordering of society. Anthropologists have also investigated more directly why parents hit their children (Montgomery, 2009). They get answers such as 'if not beaten the children would grow up lazy and discontented', 'in order to learn about pain', 'to learn that life is a struggle' etc (Bledsoe, 1990). Gottlieb (2004) found that among the Beng of West Africa a child was spanked if it started to walk too early. Their folk belief is that it is

3 An education and research centre established at Yale University in 1949 dedicated to the cross cultural study of human culture, society and behaviour. See: http://hraf.yale.edu/

taboo for a child to walk before the age of one. Sociologists too have tried to explain why corporal punishment is used (see Saunders and Goddard, 2001).

Of course, it is easy – I am unconsciously doing this – to look at child-rearing practices, including punishment in non-Western societies in the light of our Western pre-occupation with child abuse. This is all the more so, now that we are attuned to a children's rights agenda. If we do this, we overlook indigenous theories of child-rearing and socialisation and their methods of discipline. But cultural relativity can be taken too far. There is a danger that we trivialise non-Western child abuse. Within their context a brutal beating of a child may not be abusive. But if a culture can only be judged by endogenous value judgements, and moral principles which derive from outside their culture have no validity, morality has become a slave to custom, and the 'ought' has relinquished any transcendental power that it may have had to critique the 'is'. The argument for any practice must be more than that the practice exists, or is thought appropriate by its participants. And, often, that so-called dominant understanding is in reality the understanding of the dominant. A good example is female genital mutilation which turns on the interpretation of a dominant male elite, with a consensus having been engineered to cloak the interests of a section of society (Freeman, 1995).

Rights – Universal or Particular?

The global/local binary leads one to another question posed by a reading of the work of those within childhood studies. Could it be that children in different societies need different rights? It is common to divide the rights agenda in the Convention into rights of protection, provision and participation (Archard, 2004) – it has almost become a mantra (John, 2003; Quennerstedt, 2010). The ideal may be that children in all societies should get the complete package; there is, after all, a non-discrimination principle in Article 2. It is also true that we are unlikely to succeed in protecting children if we do not respect their agency. Underlying both protection of children and protection of their agency rights is an understanding of their dignity, personhood, and humanity. I note that Bühler-Niederberger and Van Krieken (2008) make much the same point. Commenting on a collection of articles drawn from a section of the *World Congress of Sociology*, they observe, 'While the authorities dealing with African childhoods examine the very basic rights of children and the extent to which they are recognized, the articles dealing with European childhoods are concerned with the possibilities for self-expression and self-realization, and therefore with the problems characterizing a more individualized society' (152). To explain: There is an article on corporal punishment in South African schools (Payet and Vijé Franchi, 2008). This institution was outlawed in the wake of the demise of apartheid, but it persists (though interestingly not in the former 'white' school in the study, even though 80% of the pupils in this school are now black). It appears that corporal punishment is accepted by the pupils, as long as they interpret it as an attempt to express 'care', and despite notions of children's rights that they believe in more generally. One way of interpreting this would be to view the issue of caning as less important to these children than other problems they encounter in to-day's South Africa – poverty, AIDS, violence on the streets. Payet and Vijé Franchi's explanation includes, but goes beyond, this. They argue: 'An educational ethos based on the protection of the rights of the child contrasts sharply with the idea of childhood and of education that was historically imposed on "Black" children under apartheid' with the result that 'the child inside the educator may continue to want to find reason and benevolence where only racism and hatred prevail' (167). A similar point is made in the case study on Ethiopia in the same collection which emphasizes the need to tackle child poverty (Woldehanna et al, 2008). Until this is done more effectively, questions of whether children work or go to school will remain and the answer will be inevitable. This article is also a useful illustration of another insight that sociology can offer children's rights thinking: it draws attention to the gender dimension. It would appear that the cultural definition of particular work activities as girls' or boys' work excludes rural children in particular from school attendance, and girls more so than boys.

A very different picture of childhood is found in the studies in this collection from Europe. Children are concerned with choosing clothes as self-expression (König, 2008, Pilcher, 2011), in classroom interactions (Baraldi, 2008), with participation in legal proceedings (Eriksson and Nasman, 2008), with the development of a moral consciousness (Bosisio, 2008), an understanding of justice with their appreciation of child-centred research (Powell and Smith, 2009, Lundy and McEvoy, 2012), and with their perceptions of domestic violence (Överlien and Hydén, 2009). These studies are from Germany, Italy and Sweden. Is the lesson that we should think of children and their rights differently in highly individualized societies? Are global solutions possible? What light does the life experiences of the developing world throw on the Convention? Does it matter that it is Eurocentric (Harris-Short, 2003)? It is worth observing how close the African Charter on the Rights and Welfare of the Child is to the 1989 Convention. But neither the Convention nor the Charter employed the insights of childhood studies or of children, which of course is what the 'new' childhood studies is largely about – the data simply weren't there in 1989 or 1990. There is evidence also that children themselves emphasise different rights in different cultures (Ruck and Peterson-Badali, 2006).

Those of us who work within children's rights need the insights sociology and other social sciences can offer for several reasons.

In particular, I would draw attention to the neglected aspects of childhood explored by sociologists and overlooked by, for example, lawyers. Recognising that there are different forms of abuse is an example (Bakan, 2013 ; Wild, 2014). Secondly, it offers us ways of explaining the social order. Think of the 'classics', Marx, Durkheim (see Cotterrell, 1999), Weber, Ehrlich (see Hertogh, 2009), Foucault (see Gallagher, 2008, Smith 2012), Bourdieu and, thirdly, this is not just of academic interest, but offers us a knowledge base to fight to right the wrongs from which children suffer. To take an obvious example, lawyers didn't discover or explain child abuse. But legal responses would not have been possible without the insights of the social sciences.

It is coming to be accepted that we need to rethink children's rights, if only to plug gaps in the thinking of the 1980s and to pay greater attention to groups then marginalised such as girl children, gay and transgendered children, children with disabilities, refugee and asylum-seeking children. But, can we rethink children's rights without first rethinking childhood? Here is where lawyers need sociology, but the greatest barrier to doing this is, Berry Mayall reminds us, is 'the set of labels we are taught to associate with the idea of childhood' (Mayall, 2000: 246). Elisabeth Young-Bruehl (2012) puts it more strongly, arguing that prejudice exists against children as a group, and that this is comparable to racism, sexism and homophobia. This prejudice – she calls 'childism' (see also Pierce and Allen, 1975 and Westman, 1979) – legitimates and rationalises a broad continuum of acts that are not in the 'best interests' of children, including child abuse and neglect. She convincingly maintains that reform is only possible if we address the motives and cultural forces that nourish childism. We need a fuller understanding of childhood than we have had up to now. We need to appreciate that adults deny who is a child. I was a child until I reached the age of 21: the border today tends to be drawn at 18, but now that children of 16 have voted in the Scottish referendum, there will be pressure to bring down voting rights and in due course citizenship. Neuroscience may frustrate this but the implications of this cannot be explored in this paper. Suffice to note that the reasoning of the US Supreme Court in *Roper v. Simmons* at the very least problematises child autonomy.[4]

We cannot rethink children's rights without also rethinking childhood. The sociology of childhood has begun the process from which different understanding of childhoods may emerge. In particular, it will provide evidence of how and why childhood varies from society to society, and across time. A result is that we are coming to take children seriously, a *sine qua non* to taking children's rights seriously (Freeman, 1988), or 'more seriously' (Freeman, 1997). Taking children seriously involves moving them from being objects of intervention and concern to being social actors, 'agents interacting with the structures surrounding their lives' (Mayall, 2000: 248). And this can mean transforming such structures, rewriting the conditions of their own childhoods. There are many examples of this within sociology of childhood literature. The work of Priscilla Alderson on consent to surgery (Alderson, 1993), her remarkable work with premature babies (Alderson, Hawthorne and Killen, 2003), the pathbreaking work of Myra Bluebond-Langner (1978) of the 'scripting'work on a paediatric cancer ward, and Nieuwenhuy's exploration of how children in India understand work (1994). A consequence of this work is the realisation that we must no longer take it for granted that we can rely on adults' definitions of children's needs, but listen to what children themselves have to say, their wishes and their perceptions of their needs. This connects with the UNCRC of course, with Article 12, but to take Article 12 more seriously is to accept the importance of a bottom-up approach (Liebel, 2012; but see Lenzer, 2015).

We need not be dogmatic about this. There is still space for input by adults.

4 *Roper* v. *Simmons*, 543 U.S. 551 (2005). The US Supreme Court held that it is unconstitutional to impose capital punishment for crimes committed under the age of 18.

Conclusion

Those of us who espouse children's rights have a vision of a better world for children and through this a better world for all of us. This requires us to acquire a better understanding of the lives of children, of what is important to them, how they perceive and construct their social worlds. We need to know how they perceive their education (Pollard and Filer, 1997), work, play (Strandell, 1997), friendship (James, 1996). How they acquire national consciousness (Hengst, 1997), their understanding of what is abusive (Saunders and Goddard, 2001), their perceptions of risk (Kelly, Mayall and Hood, 1997), etc.

An Editorial in *Childhood* some years ago (1998) pertinently asked: 'Given our proliferating insights into the very different sorts of childhood worlds, how can we conceptualise universal conditions of children's welfare that would constitute legitimate foundations for international children's rights activism?' (*Childhood*, 1998: 131).

This is a challenge to which those concerned to advance children's rights must rise. We cannot ignore the dimensions of class, gender, race or disability, but nor can we allow ourselves to take refuge in a relativism which ultimately will only fudge moral questions.

This challenge can be met. Finding ways of meeting it must become a prominent goal. To that end a dialogue between scholarships is called for. Nothing will be gained by a confrontation.

References

Abrahams, R., 'Spirit, Twins and Ashes in Labwor, in J. La Fontaine (ed), *The Interpretation of Ritual*, (London: Routledge 1972, reprinted 2004).

Adams, P. et al., *Children's Rights: Toward the Liberation of the Child* (New York: Praeger, 1971).

Alanen, L., 'Taking Children's Rights Seriously' *Childhood* 2010 17, 5-8.

Alderson, P., 'Young Children's Human Rights: A Sociological Analysis' *International Journal of Children's Rights* 2012 20, 177-195.

Alderson, P., *Children's Consent to Surgery* (Buckingham: Open University Press, 1993).

Alderson, P., J. Hawthorne and M. Killen, 'The Participation Rights of Premature Babies' *International Journal of Children's Rights* 2005 13, 31-50.

Alston, P (ed.), *The Best Interests of The Child* (Oxford: Clarendon Press, 1994).

Alston, P., S. Parker and J. Seymour, *Children, Rights and the Law* (Oxford: Clarendon Press, 1992).

Archard, D., *Children: Rights and Childhood* (London: Routledge, 2004).

Ariès, P., *Centuries of Childhood* (New York: Vintage Books, 1962)

Bakan, J., *Childhood Under Siege* (London: Vintage Books,2012).

Baraldi, C., 'Promoting Self-Expression in classroom interactions' *Childhood* 2008 15, 239-257.

Bartlett, K., 'Feminist Legal Methods' *Harvard Law Review* 1990 103, 829.

Benedict, R., *Patterns of Culture* (London: RKP, 1961).

Bledsoe, C., 'No success without a struggle', *Man. (N.S.)* 1990, 25, 70 – 88.
Brems, E., *Human Rights: Universality and Diversity* (Dordrecht: Martinus Nijhoff, 2001).
Bluebond-Langer, M., *The Private World of Dying Children* (Princeton: Princeton U.P, 1978).
Bosisio, R., '"Right" and "not right": Representations of Justice in Young People' *Childhood* 2008 15, 276-294.
Bühler-Niedererger, D. and R Van Krikken, 'Persisting Inequalities: Childhood between Global Influences and Local Traditions' *Childhood* 2008 15, 147-155.
Burman, E.,'Deconstructing Neoliberal Childhood', *Childhood* 2012 19, 423-438.
Burman, E., 'Local, Global or Globalised? Child Development and International Children's Rights', *Childhood* 1992 3, 45 – 66.
Cockburn, T., *Rethinking Children's Citizenship* (Basingstoke: Palgrave Macmillan, 2013).
Cohen, E., *Semi-Citizenship in Democratic Politics* (Cambridge: CUP, 2009).
Cohen, H., *Equal Rights For Children* (Totowa, N.J: Littlefield, Adams, 1980).
Cotterrell, R., *Emile Durkheim: Law in a Moral Domain* (Edinburgh: Edinburgh University Press, 1999).
Donzelot, J., *The Policing of Families* (New York, Random House, 1979).
Eichsteller, G., 'Janusz Korczak – His Legacy and Its Relevance for Children's Rights Today', *International Journal of Children's Rights* 2009 17, 377-391.
Embler, C. and M. Embler, 'Explaining Corporal Punishment of Children: A Cross-Cultural Study', *American Anthropologist* 2008 107, 609-619.
Eriksson, M. and Näsman, E., 'Participation in Family Law Proceedings' *Childhood* 2008 15, 259 – 275.
Farson, R., *Birthrights* (New York: Macmillan, 1975).
Firestone, S., T*he Dialectics of Sex* (London, Jonathan Cape, 1971).
Fortin, J., *Children's Rights and the Developing Law* (London: Lexis Nexis, 2003).
Freeman, M., *Violence in the Home – A Socio-Legal Study* (Farnborough: Saxon House, 1979).
Freeman, M., 'The Rights of the Child in the International Year of the Child', *Current Legal Problems* 1980 37, 1.
Freeman, M., *The Rights and Wrongs of Children* (London, Frances Pinter, 1983).
Freeman, M., 'Taking Children's Rights Seriously' *Children and Society* 1988 1,299-319.
Freeman, M., 'Taking Children's Rights More Seriously' (in *The Moral Status of Children*, The Hague, Kluwer, 1997).
Freeman, M., 'Why It Remains Important to take Children's Rights Seriously' 2007 15 *International Journal of Children's Rights* 5-23.
Freeman, M., 'The Future of Children's Rights', *Children and Society* 2000 14, 277-293.
Freeman, M., *Article – What is a Child?* (Leiden, Brill, 2015, forthcoming).
Freeman, M., 'Children's Rights and Parental Responsibilities' (forthcoming 2016a).
Freeman, M., 'Even Lawyers were Children Once' (Hamlyn Lectures, 2015, forthcoming in Cambridge, CUP, 2016b).

Gallagher, M., 'Foucault, Power and Participation', *International Journal of Children's Rights* 2008 16, 395-406.
Gil, D., *Violence Against Children* (Cambridge: MA, Harvard U.P., 1970).
Gilligan, C., *In a Different Voice* (Cambridge: Mass, Harvard U. P., 1982).
Gottlieb, A., *The Afterlife is Where We Come From: the Culture of Infancy in West Africa* (Chicago: University of Chicago Press, 2004).
Gross, B. and R. Gross, *The Children's Rights Movement* (New York: Anchor, 1977).
Grover, S., 'On Recognizing Children's Universal Rights: What Needs to Change in the Convention on the Rights of the Child' *International Journal of Children's Rights* 2004 12, 259-271.
Guggenheim, M., *What's Wrong With Children's Rights* (Cambridge, MA: Harvard University Press, 2005).
Hall, G. S., *Adolescence* (New York, Appleton, 1904).
Hardman, C., 'Can there be an Anthropology of Childhood?' *Journal of the Anthropological Society of Oxford* 1973 4, 85-99.
Harris-Short, S., 'International Human Rights Law: Imperialist, Inept and Ineffective? Cultural Relativism and the UN Convention on the Rights of the Child' *Human Rights Quarterly*, 2003 35, 130-181.
Hengst, H., 'Negotiating "Us" and "Them": Children's Constructions of Collective Identity' *Childhood*, 1997 4, 43-62.
Hertog, M., *Living Law* (Oxford: Hart Publishing, 2009).
Holt, J., *Escape From Childhood* (Harmondsworth: Penguin Books, 1975).
Jaggar, A. M., *Feminist Politics and Human Nature* (Brighton: Harvester Press, 1983).
James, A., Jenks C. and Prout A., *Theorizing Childhood* (Cambridge: Polity, 1998, London: Falmer, 1990).
James, A. and James A. L., *Constructing Childhood* (London: Macmillan, 2004).
James, H., 'Learning To Be Friends', *Childhood* 1996 5, 313-330.
Jebb, E., *Save the Child! A Posthumous Essay, edited by D F Buxton* (London: Weardale Press, 1929).
Jenks, C., *Childhood* (London: Routledge, 1996).
John, M., *Children's Rights and Power* (London: Jessica Kingsley, 2003).
Johnson, D., 'Cultural and Regional Pluration in the Drafting of the UNCRC' in Freeman M. and Veerman, P. (ed.), *The Ideologies of Children's Rights* (Kluwer: Dordrecht, 1992, 95-114).
Kaberry, P., 'Spirit Children and the Spirit Centres of North Kimberly' *Oceana* 1937 53, 313-329.
Katz, C., *Growing up Global* (Minneapolis: Univ. of Minnesota Press, 2004).
Kelley, P., Mayall B. and Hood S,, 'Children's Accounts of Risk' *Childhood* 1997 4, 305-324.
Kempe, C. H.,"The Battered Child Syndrome" *JAMA* 1962 181, 17.
Key, E., *The Century of The Child* (New York: Putnams, 1909) (in Swedish, 1900).
King, M., *Childhood, Welfare and Justice* (London: Batsford, 1981).
King, M. and Piper C., *How The Law Thinks About Children* (Aldershot: Arena, 1995).

Koester, D., 'Childhood In National Consciousness and National Consciousness in Childhood' *Childhood* 1997 4, 125-142.
König, A., 'Which clothes suit me? The presentation of the juvenile self' *Childhood* 2008 15, 225-237.
Korczak, J., 'Loving Every Child – The Words of Janusz Korczak' in S. Joseph (ed.) *Loving Every Child – Wisdom for Parents* (Chapel Hill, NC: Algonquin Books of Chapel Hill, 2007).
Kuhn, T., *The Structure of Scientific Revolutions* (3rd edition, Chicago: University of Chicago Press 1996).
Lee, N., *Childhood and Society* (Maidenhead: Open University Press, 2001).
Lenzer, G., 'Children's Studies and the Human Rights of Children: Toward a Unified Approach' in K. Alaimo and King B. (eds), *Children as Equals: Exploring the Rights of the Child* (Lanham, MD: University Press of America, 2002, 207-225).
Lenzer, G., 'The Vicissitudes of Children's Rights' *International Journal of Children's Rights* 2015 23, forthcoming.
Levinson, D., *Family Violence in Cross-Cultural Perspective* (Newbury Park: Sage, 1989).
Liebel, M., *Children's Rights From Below* (London: Palgrave Macmillan, 2012).
Lister, R., 'Why Citizenship: Where, When and How Children?' *Theoretical Inquiries in Law* 2007 8 (2) 693-718.
Lundy, L. and MacEvoy, L., 'Children's Rights and Research Processes: Assisting Children to (In)Formed Victims' *Childhood* 2011 19, 129 – 144.
Mayall, B., "The Sociology of Childhood In Relation to Children's Rights", *International Journal of Children's Rights* 2000 8, 243-259.
Mayall, B., *Towards a Sociology for Childhood* (Maidenhead: Open University Press, 2002).
Mead, M., *Coming of Age in Samoa* (New York: Harper Collins, 1973).
Melton, G., 'Children's Rights: Where are the Children?' *American Jourral of Orthopsychiatry* 1982 52, 530-538.
Mill, J. S., *On Liberty* (Harmondsworth: Penguin Books, 1974) (1st published in 1859).
Montgomery, H., *An Introduction To Childhood: Anthropological Perspectives on Children's Lives* (Chichester: Wiley-Blackwell, 2009).
Moskowitz, M., *The Haunting Fetus: Abortion, Sexuality and the Spirit World in Taiwan* (Honolulu, University of Hawaii Press, 2001).
Mulley, C., *The Woman who Saved the Children* (London: One World Publications, 2009).
Newell, P., 'The Fine Line Between Physical Punishment and Child Abuse", *The Independent*, July 12, 1989.
Nieuwenhuys, O., *Children's Lifeworlds* (London: Routledge, 1994).
Olsen, F., "The Myth of State Intervention in the Family", *University of Michigan Journal of Law Reform* 1984-85 18, 835-865.
O' Neill, O., 'Children's Rights and Children's Lives' *Ethics* 1988 98, 445.
Överlien, C. and Hydén, M., 'Children's Actions When Experiencing Domestic Violence' *Childhood* 2009 16, 479 – 496.
Parsons, T., *The Social System* (London: Routledge, 1951).

Payet, J. P. and Franchi V., 'The Rights of the Child and the Good of the Learners ... Corporal Punishment in South African Schools" *Childhood* 2008 15, 157-176.

Piaget, J., *The Language and Thought of the Child* (London, Routledge, 1939).

Pickering M., *Auguste Comte: An Intellectual Life* 1992-2003, 4 vols (Cambridge, CUP).

Pilcher, J. , 'No Logo: Children's Conceptions of "Fashion"' *Childhood* 2011 18, 128 – 141.

Pizzey, E., *Scream Quietly or the Neighbours will Hear* (Harmondsworth: Penguin, 1974).

Pollard, A., D. Thiessen and A. Filer, *Children and their Curriculum: The Perspectives of Primary and Elementary Schoolchildren* (London: Falmer, 1997).

Pollock, L., *Forgotten Children: Parent-Child Relations from 1500 to1900* (Cambridge: CUP, 1983).

Powell, M. and Smith, A. B., 'Children's Participatory Rights in Research' *Childhood* 2009 16, 124 – 142.

Prout, A and James A., *Constructing and Reconstructing Childhood* (London: Routledge, 1990).

Quennerstedt, A., 'Children, but not Really Human – Critical Reflections on the Hampering Effect of the three Ps' *International Journal of Children's Rights* 2010 19, 464-487.

Rose, N., *Governing The Soul* (London: Routledge, 1989).

Ruck, M. and Peterson-Badali M., '"Youths" Perceptions of Rights in Youth Activism: An International encyclopaedia' in Sherrod L., Flanagan C., and Kasimir R. (eds) (Westport CT: Greenwood Publishers, 2006).

Sabatello, M., 'Children with Disabilities: A Critical Appraisal', *International Journal of Children's Rights* 2013 21, 464-487.

Saunders, B.J. and Goddard C., "The Textual Abuse of Childhood in the English-Speaking World: The contribution of Language to the Denial of Children's Rights" *Childhood* 2001 8, 443-462.

Scraton, P., (ed.) *Childhood in 'Crisis' (London*: Routledge, 1997).

Smart C., 'A History of Ambivalence and Conflict in the Discursive Construction of the 'Child Victim' of Sexual Abuse', *Social and Legal Studies* 1999 8, 391-409.

Smart, C., B. Neale and A. Wade, *The Changing Experience of Childhood: Families and Divorce* (Cambridge: Polity, 2001).

Smith, R., *A Universal Child?* (London, Palgrave Macmillan, 2010).

Stafseng, O., 'A Sociology of Childhood and Youth – the Need of Both?' in (ed.) J Qvortrup, et al, *Childhood as a Social Phenomenon*, (Vienna, European Centre for Social Policy adn Research, 1993).

Starr, K., 'From Fraser to Frederick: Bong Hits and the Decline of Civic Culture', *UC Davis Law Review* 2009 42, 661-677.

Strandell, H., 'Doing Reality With Play', *Childhood* 1997 4, 445-464.

Thorne, B., 'Re-visioning Women: Where are the Children?' *Gender and Society* 1987 1, 85-109.

Todres, J., 'Women's Rights and Children's Rights: A Partnership with Benefits for Both', *Cardozo Women's Law Journal* 2003-2004 14, 603-624.

Twum-Danso, A., 'Reciprocity, Respect and Responsibility: the 3 Rs Underlying Parent-Child Relationships in Ghana and the Implications for Children's Rights' *International Journal of Children's Rights* 2008 17, 415-432.

Vallès J., *L'Enfant* (New York: New York Book Reviews, 2005).

Van Bueren, G., *The International Law on the Rights of The Child* (The Hague: Martinus Nijhoff, 1995).

Vygotsky, L., *Thought and Language* (Cambridge, Mass: MIT Press, 1986).

Wells, K., *Childhood in a Global Perspective* (Cambridge: Polity Press, 2009).

Westman, J. C., *Child Advocacy* (New York: Free Press, 1979).

Wiggin, K. D., *Children's Rights* (New York: Houghton, Mifflin and Co, 1898).

Wild, J., (ed) *Exploiting Childhood* (London: Jessica Kingsley 2013).

Woldehanna T., Jones N., and Tefera B., 'The Invisibility of Children's Paid and Unpaid Work: Implications for Ethiopia's National Poverty Reduction Policy' *Childhood* 2008 15, 177-201.

Young-Bruehl, E ., *Childism* (New Haven: Yale University Press 2012).

Law and … Michael Freeman: The Scholar, the Man, the Modern Renaissance Humanist

Carrie Menkel-Meadow
Chancellor's Professor of Law and Political Science, University of California, Irvine, USA; A.B. Chettle Jr. Professor of Law, Dispute Resolution and Civil Procedure, Georgetown University Law Center, USA

> Jurisprudence, like other social studies, may well be just as interested in diversity, as uniformity.
>
> M.D.A. Freeman, Lloyd's Introduction to Jurisprudence, 8th ed. (2008:15)

We have now heard two full days of talks and papers inspired by the work of our dear friend and colleague, Professor Michael Freeman, on subjects ranging from his signature fields of children's rights, medical and health care law and ethics, domestic violence, law and culture, family law, cricket, law and literature, crime and policing, law and religion, law and neuroscience, private law and contract, legal theory, jurisprudence and law and policy.

This is the man who has shepherded through over 17 volumes of 'Law and …' conference volumes, and a total of 82 books on topics ranging from law and language, law and neuroscience, law and sociology, anthropology, culture, geography, philosophy, psychology, science, bioethics, global health, childhood studies, and law and literature and popular culture, mind and brain studies, John Austin, public health and human rights, and social welfare law, amongst others.

Also serving as long-term editor of the 'Current Legal Problems/Issues' volumes of lectures and papers presented at UCL on legal topics, the long-serving editor of the *International Journal of Children's Rights,* general editor of several volumes in the Ashgate International Library of Legal Theory Series (e.g., *Medicine, Family Law, Alternative Dispute Resolution* (where we first met), and with me, as editor of the *International Journal of Law in Context*, Michael has devoted his life to the interdisciplinary and behavioural study of 'Law and …', recognising that law is situated and embedded in, as well as constitutive of, culture, society, legal institutions, families, hospitals, schools, countries and, I might add, scholarship and friendship. In short, law is not autonomous – it is interwoven with and constructed by the people and the institutions that create it, enforce it and sometimes deflect or ignore it. Law may be necessary for human order but it is not sufficient and it needs nudging and pushing to meet human needs. Law always has a context and often many contexts. Its purpose is

A. Diduck, N. Peleg, H. Reece (eds.), Law in Society: Reflections on Children, Family, Culture and Philosophy
Copyright 2015 Koninklijke Brill NV. Printed in The Netherlands. ISBN 978-90-04-26148-8. pp. 653-666.

to further and service *human* needs, not the purely logical or abstract analysis of law in service to law or analytic purity.

As Michael refused to follow his father into a more conventional English solicitor's practice, he has also refused to be the conventional doctrinal legal scholar and teacher, recognising that law's situatedness in so many different places – not only the law books, but the courts, legislatures, the legal profession, lawyer's offices, the prison,[1] the police station, and the family, among other places – required a broadening of both law school classes and legal scholarship. Michael has been one of those rare legal scholars who has been concerned with how law is theorised, made, interpreted, but also practised and experienced (by those 'acted upon' in law). Michael has asked when human needs should be assimilated to old legal categories, but more importantly, he has also focused on when new categories need to be created and recognised in law, as in recognition of children's rights (somewhat assimilated to older human rights) or domestic violence (creating new categories of legal knowledge, as well as legal liability). Legal epistemology is to follow and serve human 'problems' and needs. Knowledge is created and is necessary to improve (not just discipline or police) human's treatment of other humans. In his classic text on jurisprudence Michael tells us that modern legal scholars have learned to ask about the *purposes,* as well as the *effects* of law (Freeman, 2008). He has been able to teach and write with attention to the empirical and actual, as well as the philosophical and the political, often noting both the convergences and divergences in their interactions.

He has long studied fields initially ignored by others, asking how law can create more justice (for children, for victims of violence and for religious and ethnic 'minorities') and what happens when law fails to meet its promise of justice. His work is full of great insights at every level of intellectual engagement, drawing examples from history, art, literature and music and always concrete analysis of cases and 'facts on the ground' – or in Parliament, the High Court, international conferences, streets or sites of legal policy making. His sources for analysing law range among all fields of human endeavor – science, medicine, children's literature, sports, opera, religion and ethics, amongst other fields and he looks beyond Anglo culture to do so.

He is interested in *who* makes legal decisions about *what* and *whom* for *what reasons.*

He has written and taught eloquently about the importance of teaching law students to think critically, not to accept the dogma of law as handed down in practice or just because that is the way things 'are done'. He is no stranger to the big debates in law – whether we are governed best by positivist rules or by paying some attention to the deeper 'fundamental principles of justice' – whether located in natural law, Dworkinian jurisprudence or feminist legal theory. Is justice actually coterminous with equality and democracy, as we obsess about it on both sides of the pond? How do we know a *just* law from an *unjust* law? How do we know if an interpretation of law cre-

1 Michael reported to me that when he and some students discussed offering a course in prison law some years ago, one of his more conventional colleagues said, 'what do prisons have to do with law studies?'.

ates or diminishes justice in practice? See Michael's treatment of these big questions in his concrete analyses of *Oppenheimer v. Cattermole* [1976] A.C. 249 as to whether or not to recognise revoked German citizenship of a Jewish Holocaust survivor for tax purposes in the UK, and the *Grundnorm* cases (e.g. *Madsimbamuto v. Lardner-Burke,* [1968] 2 S.A. 284 and [1969] 1 A.C. 645), dealing with issues of what constitutes a legal system after an anti-colonial revolution. He asks us to question the assumptions of lawmakers, interpreters and enforcers and to consider the 'acted upon' in law, as well as those who can exercise more agency with respect to law (law students, lawyers, judges, legislators, politicians). He asks us to consider the morality of law, not only philosophically, but also socially. He asks us to consider legal method – is law and law study science, social science, humanistic, literary or hermeneutic analysis?

In doing all these things and asking all these questions, he has left all of us who work with him, are taught by him, or read him, far richer in our understandings of both law and life. Law is made by people, interpreted by people, and enforced (or not) by people and we learn to exercise our more educated 'agency' over law and legal institutions by learning from Michael's work, with all its breadth, scope and diversity of method and subject matter.

It has been one of the great pleasures of my academic life that for some ten years or so Michael and I were co-editors of the *International Journal of Law in Context.* Actually, Michael was the editor – my 'co-editing' consisted of providing some eyes and ears from 'across the pond' to drum up some reviewers for papers, to pass on new topics, papers, authors and board members for consideration. For two marvelous years it also involved sponsoring lectureships (thank you Roger Cotterrell and Mark Tushnet) on both sides of the pond to consider some cross-cultural and interdisciplinary 'takes' on 'Law and...' studies, including the role of cultural analysis in legal decision making (Cotterrell, 2008) and the comparative constitutional politics of emergency powers and separation of powers in an age of terrorism (Tushnet, 2007), with spirited debate and commentary both in writing (see, *International Journal of Law in Context* (*IJLC*), volumes 3(4) December 2007 and 4(4) December 2008) and at symposia hosted at UCL and Georgetown law faculties respectively. The *IJLC* was founded by the ideas and efforts of one William Twining (whom I have long admired as a serious jurisprudent and evidence scholar who has also taken legal education seriously (Twining, 2002)) to encourage (along with the wonderful book series 'Law in Context') both an *interdisciplinary* (socio-legal) and *international* (dare I say '*globalised*' (Twining, 2000) and comparative) focus on legal scholarship.

'Beyond doctrine, what makes law interesting?' – its institutions, its people, its variations in different legal regimes, its interactions with other disciplinary fields and its pluralism, in both legal and social senses of that term. Working with Michael on the *IJLC*, and becoming his friend, helped deepen my own interdisciplinary understanding of law and legal phenomena, as we extended the reach of the journal to new subject matters, e.g. euthanasia, gay partnerships, new countries and most importantly new authors.

As I worked with Michael on so many different texts and topics I came to appreciate 'Michael – the Modern Renaissance Man'. In addition to all of the formal scholarship and contributions we are honouring in this programme, Michael knows so much about so many things. His curiosity, generosity and kindness to so many of us have enabled us to learn not only from his erudition, but also from his humanity. So I want, in these comments, to reflect not only on the more formal teaching, learning and collaboration, but on the museums, music, concerts, travel advice, history, Jewish history, jokes and humour, and basic humanity that Michael has shared with so many of us. Michael is a true 'humanist' in both the Enlightenment and Renaissance sense of that term, putting humans, in all their variety and humanity, at the center of his interests, study and interpersonal interactions.

To get a sense of the breadth of Michael's knowledge, demonstrating what the true scholar is master of, one could begin with the introduction to any of the 'Law and…' volumes (or to his many editions of 'Introduction to Jurisprudence',[2] or indeed, to any of his scholarship). I here choose *Law and Popular Culture* (Freeman, 2004) (to which I contributed an essay [see Menkel-Meadow, 2004]) to illustrate both the erudition and the humanity of Michael Freeman. In introducing a volume of very diverse essays on the treatment of law, lawyers and legal institutions in all forms of popular culture (including novels, films and TV shows), Michael begins (perhaps with too 'Western' a start for such a well-travelled and studied man) with the Bible and the story of Abraham and Isaac, drawing our attention to the jurisprudence of Genesis – good and evil, punishment, guilt, free will and determinism, fairness and equity, familial obligations and faith. But in exploring the story of patriarchy and obligation, Michael quickly segues to treatments of the Abraham story in Jewish, Muslim and Christian religions and then illustrates its important legal themes and processes of negotiation, trial, familial and religious fealty, obligations, judgment and justice with references to art (Rembrandt, Chagall), poetry (Wilfred Owen), music (Stravinsky, Benjamin Britten, Bob Dylan), film (Woody Allen) and modern novels (Neil Gordon), science and linguistic analysis, while excavating his own interpretations of what Freud *might* have said about the parental dilemma (Freeman, 2004: 2). As if referring to cultural sources that have dealt with the Abraham/Isaac sacrifice is not evidence enough of his interdisciplinary experience of stories, Michael goes on to interrogate what more modern jurisprudential, philosophical and political treatments of the story might teach us. What would a feminist make of the story? Would a mother do what a father did? How should we react to the demands to adhere to an unjust law? How shall we respond to tests of our commitments, faith and loyalty? How much should we resist authority (especially when it is unjust as in the Holocaust)? And even this biblical story has relevance for Michael's great interest in the medical profession – how much should we trust it (especially in pediatric care, (Freeman, 2004:2))?

From the Biblical sources Michael turns next to the famous (or infamous?) Greek plays to remind us that jurisprudential themes emerged early in public enjoyment of the arts. Who can talk about law and justice without reference to Creon and Antigone,

---

2 Where each edition reflects new revisions or interpretations of older and more traditional jurisprudential thought, as well as additions of new schools and theories of law.

Agamemnon, Iphigenia[3] and Clytemnestra, with their treatments of the letter of the law, higher 'natural' law, religion, and the arguments for duties to states, gods and persons. Michael mines these plays for treatments of legal positivism, politics (crypto-or actual fascism), legal realism and critiques of law (in society and community) and reminds us how these themes have reappeared in more modern sources (Fugard in South Africa, Anouilh in Vichy France, Brecht in German Fascism, and Tom Paulin in Northern Ireland); Euripides, Sophocles, Homer, Aeschylus as exemplars of 'popular' culture writers exploring the meaning of justice, even as Michael notes the absences of those acted upon by 'man-made' law by asking where are the women and children.[4]

Even in his turn to the obvious treatment of law in the popular culture of Shakespeare, Michael recognises that though the opposition of mercy (and equity) to crude textual justice is most often attributed to *Merchant of Venice* (even if not actually realised, see e.g. Menkel-Meadow, 1985; Yoshino, 2011), it is in *Measure for Measure* that Shakespeare really explores the rule of law and its effects. Like a modern audience analysis scholar, Michael mines Shakespeare not only for how we read the texts (and many modern interpretations of these classic plays) but how the actual audiences of the 16th century would have read the master playwright's demonstrations of the meanings of law and justice in their own times. He wants to know how Elizabethan and Jacobean audiences might actually have reacted to the tropes of justice, law and the facts of familial and amorous relationships and their discipline by law, fathers and kings. Michael reads *King Lear* as one of the most interesting and underrated 'trial' plays, signaling the importance of the drama of the trial in so many modern treatments of law and legal process.

Lest you think this 'Modern Renaissance Man's'perspective is too Anglo-American, he stops to reflect on the teachings of Dostoevsky, Tolstoy, Thomas Mann, Herman Melville, Nathaniel Hawthorne, John Steinbeck, and Isaac Bashevis Singer for questions of law and treatments of miscarriages of justice in the modern novel. And as Abigail Adams reminded her American presidential husband, John Adams, Michael does 'remember the ladies,' touching on the treatments of justice issues (and first references to unwanted pregnancies, abortions and domestic violence) in the works of George Eliot, the Bronte sisters and Margaret Drabble, as well as pointing out the less than laudable treatment of such issues among such classic great writers as Thomas Hardy, D.H.Lawrence and Ernest Hemingway.

In what has to be one of the most touching and important interventions in law and literary studies, Michael's essay reminds us that children's (and adolescent's[5]) literature is an important source of reflections on and formations of justice concepts, and generally underrepresented in the law and literature canon, as he reviews Maurice Sendak's award-winning, *Where the Wild Things Are* (1963) with its contributions to children's sense of permissible boundaries, deference to parental authority and lying.

---

3 For a modern use of the Greek reference in analysing a notorious trial, see Malcolm, 2011.

4 I acknowledge that they were more 'present' in *Lysistrata* and *Medea*.

5 Michael's own daughter is a successful writer of young adult novels. I have read several of them. See e.g. Freeman, 2006, 2013.

He does not avoid the now *de rigueur* cite of *Harry Potter* and what it tells us about good and evil, rules, norms and institutions. In the US, serious commentators on law in popular culture now focus on both book and filmic versions of Suzanne Collins' *Hunger Games* (2008) series, demonstrating that a focus on children's literature is essential to any modern understanding of how notions of justice are learned by young people, framing their understandings of legal institutions.

Equally important in understanding Michael's breadth and depth of knowledge and sensitivity to all sources of learning about law, is that he does not shy away from so called 'low' culture (including among the invitees and authors to this volume), treatments of science fiction, mystery writers, pulp novels, comics (and today would include graphic novels and popular music as well), not to mention fantasy, romance and sexually based works (would *50 Shades of Grey* make it into a new volume?). No film (including, of course, American blockbusters, little 'foreign films', and Bollywood extravaganzas) or TV show with possible legal relevance is banished from this volume for our consideration. Michael uses this volume (as all others) of 'Law and…' (here Popular Culture) to broaden, not narrow, both the sources from which we derive our learning about law and legal concepts, and what those important concepts actually are. Here we learn that legal reelism produces legal realism as an integral part of what we come to understand as law's relevance to our lives.

In this one example, as in all others, Michael uses his erudition not to impress (though I am impressed) but to remind us that 'there is nothing new under the sun' (if you are well enough educated and experienced of life), but also that there could be much more new under the sun if we took account of unrepresented voices (children, women, abused, hurt, subordinated people, religious and ethnic minorities, the disabled and ill and so many less powerful souls). If law is for justice, than its purpose must be to aid the powerless.

I have chosen this one effort and essay of Michael's (there are so many others) to demonstrate the breadth and depth of his 'Law and…' knowledge, but that is only a beginning. In the years we have worked together I have been as impressed by his humanity, combined with his deep knowledge. To take the full measure of the man – there is commitment to justice for the powerless (probably based on his own experience) at the hands of elders, both his father (who wanted to prevent him from a university education and to follow on in his own office) and very early appearances in the law courts; extraordinary commitment to his students (some now famous, such as Nicola Lacey and Davina Cooper, as two that I know of, but many more, from all over the world, are now lawyers, legal academics and other people who make important contributions to the world); commitment to his family (through many struggles and hard times), friends and colleagues, and even to the strangers whose papers we must read, revise and sometimes reject. All of this done with kindness, and, I might add, a wonderful touch of humor as well.

His former student Davina Cooper wrote at the time of his retirement that Michael combined a 'kind of *knowingness*' (what a wonderful word!) that 'stunningly combined new ideas with humor' so that she could be both intellectually challenged, through his 'wry engagement' and his personal connection to students. Davina commented that for a hugely prolific scholar and writer, Michael conveyed that writing, 'while fun, important and engaging' was not all that mattered. Davina's own political activity was in part inspired by the work that Michael showed all of us in his advocacy for the rights of children, women, the battered and abused, the disabled and the ill, those not conventionally popular, but deserving of care, respect and human dignity. She comments that learning about the Scandinavian Housemaids Act and regulation of marriage in Israel from Michael demonstrated both what law could and could not do (Cooper, 2012). So law must be accompanied and pushed by the human agency of politics.

Michael taught by ranging through many different legal systems and demonstrated that law is *chosen*, not given, by different legal regimes. He has taught English law, jurisprudence, family law, medical law, bioethics and so much more in both mandatory and seminar-writing courses and has supervised countless master's and doctoral theses on so many subjects. I have known just a few such persons in my life – people whom I consider to be 'One-Person Law Schools'. Michael, could, if required, teach all of the subjects of a modern legal education. This was recently borne out when, as a relatively old and almost retired law professor of 40 years, I joined a Roman law reading group in the United States (never formally studied in my own legal education) and Michael told me the story of how he was asked not to return to his own Roman law class by Professor Valentine Korah for having mastered all the material when she preferred to chastise and embarrass those unprepared undergraduates who studied with Michael. I was then treated to a brief transatlantic review of all I needed to know to understand my copy of Gaius' *Institutes*.

Though I was Michael's colleague as editor, I often feel like his student – there is no subject about which I could not learn something from him. Indulge me in a few examples:

At one of my first visits to UCL, Michael took me for the *de rigueur* visit to see Jeremy Bentham—what a sight! And cheerfully informed me that like most ignorant American legal academics who thought only of Oxbridge (and maybe LSE), UCL was actually the first law faculty in England to admit Catholics, Jews, women and other 'undesirables' (like our own Oberlin and Antioch Colleges in the US – first to admit African-Americans and women in the middle 19th century). I became an immediate convert to UCL as the leading institution in the UK (now borne out by recent international ranking systems) and I now come here every time I am in London.

Whenever I come to town (joyfully for several years to attend Board of Editors meetings for our journal, and most happily for a year of residence in 2009-2010 as director of Georgetown's Center for Transnational law in Chancery Lane), Michael always has a ticket waiting for me – a special exhibition of Egyptian art, accompanied by a thorough review of the Elgin Marbles dispute at the British Museum; a concert of Elgar (and an accompanying DVD set of music for his untutored American friend) at the Barbican, a theatre ticket at the National Theatre (I am now a member) of *Our Class* (Slobodzianek, 2007) (where even a child of Holocaust survivors learned more shocking facts of man's inhumanity to man),[6] an opera ticket or an invitation to a lecture here at UCL. As educated and 'cultured' as a girl from New York and Columbia University can be, there has been no trip to London in the last 15 years in which I have not learned something important, new or wonderful from Michael.

When, as a mostly non-observant, but increasingly self-identifying, Jew (we prefer to say we are Jew-ish!) I was invited to Passover Seder at Michael and Vivien's a few years ago, I knew I would learn something – but I expected a traditional patriarchical Haggadah reading. I should have known better. As we all read our portions at a full table of at least four generations ranging from late 80s (early 90s?) to Michael's young grandchildren, interspersed with great humour (I was introduced to Michael's granddaughter as 'the lady who lives near Hannah Montana' – in my current academic home I live not far from Disneyland), celebrating the escape from slavery of the Jews from Egypt, Michael, in his wry and perfect teacherly manner informed us all that the Jews had in fact used slaves themselves to build the Second Temple.[7]

When I tried to reciprocate this wonderful generosity in Washington DC and invited Michael and Vivien to a Shabbat dinner at the home of my colleague Professor Vicki Jackson, Michael and her son engaged in a lengthy Talmudic and textual exegesis and discussion of whether ostrich 'meat' is kosher![8] Though I don't think the question was definitely resolved (both Jews and Muslims have been considering this issue for hundreds of years – see Wikipedia, 'Is Ostrich kosher?'), what I saw was a model of Talmudic and Socratic teaching and learning as Michael and young Jake Taylor interrogated this question, by jointly reading texts and posing questions and issues to each other, with humour and committed knowledge.

When, as always when I come to London, in search of books, Michael can tell me where I might find either a particular copy of something, or more importantly some still surviving old bookseller. (For those of you who know his old room in Bentham House, we had a long-running competition over whose was worse – at Georgetown I could not be seen at my desk behind the disarrayed piles of books and files. In this I had met my academic 'bookmate' and match. A sign on my door, which easily could have been on Michael's, read 'Einstein or Frankenstein?')

Many years ago when I was perusing British jurisprudence texts in a local bookshop, I was surprised to encounter Michael's *Lloyd's Introduction to Jurisprudence*

---

6 Where Jews tortured, tormented and killed by their Polish classmates avenged themselves with similar cruelty in the post- world Communist regimes, see Tadeusz Słobodzianek's play, *Our Class*, 2007. (Based on true events described in Jan Gross' book, *Neighbors*.)

7 I never knew this and it matched my horror at learning that my very successful relatives, responsible for my family's migration from Hitler's Germany to the United States, the Lehman family, were in fact, slaveholders in the 1840s on their cotton plantation in the South.

8 See my contribution to the 'non-con con' book, 'Michael Freeman: The Man and the Mysteries', 'To Eat or Not to Eat: That is the Question—Is Ostrich Kosher? A Philosophical, Talmudic, Textual and Social Reading' by Michael Freeman and Dr. Jacob Taylor (a.k.a. C. Menkel-Meadow). During the Law and Michael Freeman conference, we were informed that there was, in fact, a kosher ostrich farm in South Africa. Thank you Tamara Tolley.

(what edition would it have been?) and was surprised to see not only a whole section devoted to the modern controversies in then American feminist jurisprudence (including some citations to some of my own more obscure work), as well as law and society, pragmatism, critical legal studies, critical race theory and postmodern legal theory, long before these schools were treated seriously in American jurisprudence materials. I knew I had discovered the sort of scholar who loves learning, finding new theories and takes on the old saws, and who was open to hearing new voices and new legal theories. I had a similar experience at what I think was our first encounter – when Michael asked me for permission for one of my articles in one of his many Ashgate edited series in the International Library of Essays in Law and Legal Theory – this one on Alternative Dispute Resolution (Freeman, 1995). No one yet in the United States was really taking the field all that seriously, especially as a theoretical challenge to more conventional conceptions of legal procedure (except for that great jurisprudent, Lon Fuller) and practice. I knew this was a legal scholar who was not afraid of new ideas or new institutional designs in law and from that wonderful beginning Michael introduced me to Ashgate and my happy collaboration on many interdisciplinary books.[9]

In our eight years of co-editing the *International Journal of Law in Context*, there has not been a single subject from water rights in India, to Islamic divorce, to comparative criminal punishments, to parental surrogacy, to partnership rights, that Michael has not known something about. He has had the highest standards of quality, in scholarship, editing and always honesty and respect with and for authors, and demanding and receiving high quality peer reviews (many American journals have dispensed with many of these rigorous publication standards). Michael has not only known his subjects and the big picture ideas, he has personally line-edited virtually every piece in the journals. To watch him work has taught me (and I suspect others who have worked with him) the care, patience, rigour and depth of scholarly commitment that I fear will soon be gone from our world. Michael also sought out new and younger scholars to publish and to support, and, like our journal's 'founder', William Twining, has always been concerned that the 'international' and 'global' in our legal studies should be real – a real commitment to what we in the US call 'diversity' – not only of demographics, but of ideas and disciplinary commitments.

In my years of knowing, reading, speaking to and working with Michael Freeman, I have come to know that rarest of individuals who, from his own experiences as a child who wanted more agency over his life than his parents might have allowed, learned to love learning, the law, music, culture, difference, his religion, other religions, his countries, other countries, his family, his friends and his students, other people's work, other people's children and life itself. Always with time for a coffee or a

9 I am especially thankful to Michael and Ashgate and a few other British publishers who continue to believe, as I do, in the published *book*. I fear that one of the few things Michael has learned from me is that American scholars now depend almost entirely on electronic sources and SSRN (Social Science Research Network) which is destroying just the kind of books and journals that Michael (and I) like to write, edit and read.

meeting with a student, or a colleague, even if no room in his room, whether at school or at home – always time for a droll story (I have censored this chapter but there actually are some racy stories too[10]) to illustrate some foible of humanity or some point of law. Michael has spent his life working with, and fighting for, people dispossessed, younger, sicker, and less abled than himself. He has been aided and supported in his life by many admiring colleagues, mentees, friends, students, and his wonderful wife, Vivien, whom I am proud to call a friend.

As I think of what we have all learned from Michael, it is not only children's rights, comparative legal treatments of family law and children's issues, quality and morally delivered medical and other services, legal theory and the schools of jurisprudence that frame how we understand law, how to think, write and edit; mostly what we have learned is that this man is truly a Renaissance Man, by way of the Enlightenment – smart, educated, deep, witty, knowledgeable about subjects vast and well beyond his technical and formal knowledge in law, but mostly, a deep humanist – who puts the effects law has on people before the 'purity' of legal doctrine. If there is one theme to all the 'Law and ...' conferences that Michael has conceived of and coordinated, it is really 'Law and People' and so it seems only fitting that we, your people, of many classes, articles, conferences, meetings, and books, should now present you with a 'Law and Michael Freeman' volume of your own.

Mazel tov and thank you, dear Michael. May I add the subtitle for our volume – Law and love.

References

Collins, S., *The Hunger Games* (New York: Scholastic Inc., 2008).

Cooper, D., "With Thanks", email from Davina Cooper to Michael Freeman, 13 June 2012.

Cotterrell, R., "The Struggle for Law: Some Dilemmas of Cultural Legality", *International Journal of Law in Context* 2008 4(4), 373-384.

Freeman, H., *Loving Danny* (London: Piccadilly Press, 2006).

Freeman H., *The Boy From France* (London: Piccadilly Press, 2013).

Freeman, M. D. A., *Lloyd's Introduction to Jurisprudence* (8th edn) (London: Sweet & Maxwell, 2008).

Freeman, M., "Law in Popular Culture", in M. Freeman (ed), *Law and Popular Culture* (Oxford: Oxford University Press, 2004).

Freeman, M. (ed.), *Alternative Dispute Resolution* (Aldershot: Ashgate, 1995).

Gaius, *Institutes,* O. F. Robinson & W. M. Gordon, trans. (London: Duckworth, 1997).

Gross, J., *Neighbors: The Destruction of the Jewish Community in Jedwabne* (New York: Penguin, 2002).

James, E.L., *50 Shades of Grey* (New York: Vintage, 2012).

10 Well, there is the time Michael was stopped and searched in the Soviet Union, suspected of espionage (carrying contraband books and printed materials) when travelling to represent Jewish refusniks.

Lundy, L., (ed.) *Law and Michael Freeman: The Mysteries behind the Man* (London: Not the Conference Publication, 2013).

Malcolm, J., *Iphigenia in Forest Hills: Anatomy of a Murder Trial* (New Haven, Conn: Yale University Press, 2012).

Menkel-Meadow, C., "Legal Negotiation in Popular Culture: What Are We Bargaining About?", in M. Freeman (ed), *Law and Popular Culture* (Oxford: Oxford University Press, 2004).

Menkel-Meadow, C., "Portia in a Different Voice: Speculations on a Women's Lawyering Process", *Berkeley Women's Law Journal* 1985 1, 39-52.

Słobodzianek, T., *Our Class* (2007).

Sendek, M., *Where the Wild Things Are* (New York: Harper Collins, 1963).

Tushnet, M., "The Political Constitution of Emergency Powers: Parliamentary and Separation of Powers Regulation", *International Journal of Law in Context* 2007 3 (4), 275-288.

Twining, W., *The Great Juristic Bazaar: Jurists' Text and Lawyers' Stories* (Aldershot: Ashgate, 2002).

Twining, W., *Globalization and Legal Theory* (Cambridge: Cambridge University Press, 2000).

Yoshino, K., *A Thousand Times More Fair: What Shakespeare Tells Us About Justice* (New York: Ecco, 2011).

Books by Michael Freeman

Lloyd's Introduction to Jurisprudence, 3rd edn, 1972.

The Legal Structure, 1974.

The Children Act 1975 – A Concise Commentary, 1976.

Law students' Companion to Family Law, 1976.

The Domestic Proceedings and Magistrates' Courts Act, 1978.

Violence in the Home, 1979.

Lloyd's Introduction to Jurisprudence, 4th edn., 1979.

The Matrimonial Jurisdiction of Magistrates' Courts, 1980.

The Child Care and Foster Children Act 1980, 1980.

British Nationality Act 1981, 1982.

Cohabitation without Marriage, 1983.

The Rights and Wrongs of Children, 1983.

The Law of Residential Homes and Day Care Establishments, 1984.

State, Law and the Family: Critical Perspectives, 1984.

A Guide to the Matrimonial and Family Proceedings Act 1984, 1984.

Lloyd's Introduction To Jurisprudence, 5th edn., 1985.

The Police and Criminal Evidence Act 1984, 1985.

The Law and Practice of Custodianship, 1986.

Essays in Family Law 1985, 1986.

Medicine, Ethics and the Law, 1988.

Dealing with Domestic Violence, 1989.

Critical Issues In Welfare Law, 1990.
The Ideologies of Children's Rights, 1992.
Children, their Families and the Law, 1992.
Current Legal Problems, vol. 46, 1993.
Lloyd's Introduction to Jurisprudence, 6th edn., 1994.
Current Legal Problems, vol. 47, 1994.
Alternative Dispute Resolution, 1995.
Current Legal Problems, vol. 48, 1995.
Children's Rights – A Comparative Perspective, 1996.
Divorce – Where Next?, 1996.
Family Law Act 1996, 1996.
Current Legal Problems vol. 49, 1996.
Legislation and the Courts, 1997.
Law and Opinion at the End of the Twentieth Century, 1997.
The Moral Status of Children, 1997.
Current Legal Problems vol. 50, 1997.
Science in Court, 1998.
Current Legal Problems, vol. 51, 1998.
Current Legal Problems, vol. 52, 1999.
Family, State and Law, vol. I, 1999.
Family, State and Law, vol. II, 1999.
Law and Literature, 1999.
Law and Medicine, 2000.
Current Legal Problems, vol. 53, 2000.
Ethics and Medical Decision Making, 2001.
Lloyd's Introduction to Jurisprudence, 7th edn., 2001.
Current Legal Problems, vol. 54, 2001.
Jewish Family Law in the State of Israel, 2002.
Current Legal Problems, vol. 55, 2002.
Current Legal Problems, vol. 56, 2003.
Sweet and Maxwell's Family Law Statutes 2003/04, 2003.
Children's Rights, vol. I, 2004.
Children's Rights, vol. II, 2004.
Current Legal Problems, vol. 57, 2004.
Sweet and Maxwell's Family Law Statutes 2004/05, 2004.
Children, Medicine and the Law, 2005.
Law and Popular Culture, 2005.
Law and Sociology, 2006.
Children's Health and Children's Rights, 2006.
Law and Psychology, 2006.
Article 3 UNCRC – The Best Interests of the Child, 2007.
Law and Philosophy, 2007.
Understanding Family Law, 2007.
Law and Bioethics, 2008.

Lloyd's Introduction to Jurisprudence, 8th edn., 2008.
Domestic Violence, 2009.
Law, Mind and the Brain, 2009.
Law and Anthropology, 2009.
Family Values and Family Justice, 2010.
The Ethics of Public Health, vol. I, 2010.
The Ethics of Public Health, vol. II, 2010.
Conflict of Laws, 2010.
Law and Neuroscience, 2011.
Children's Rights – Prospects and Perspectives, 2011.
Article 1 UNCRC: The Definition of a Child, 2012.
Law and Childhood Studies, 2012.
Law and Language, 2012.
John Austin and His Legacy, 2012.
Law and Global Health, 2013.
Lloyd's Introduction to Jurisprudence, 9th edn., 2013.
The Human Rights of Children, 2013.

About the Contributors

Priscilla Alderson

is Professor Emerita of Childhood Studies at the Institute of Education, University of London. She has published widely on children's rights, children and ethics, children and health care, and education. Her books include *Young Children's Rights* (2008) and *Childhoods Real and Imagined* (2013).

Amel Alghrani

is Senior Lecturer in Law at the University of Liverpool. She qualified as a Barrister in 2003, having been awarded the Yarborough Anderson Benefactors and Scholarship Award. She completed a Master's degree in Healthcare Ethics & Law and a PhD (University of Manchester) examining the creation of families through the use of assisted reproductive technologies. Amel subsequently worked on a prestigious AHRC funded project headed by Professor Margaret Brazier as a Research Associate examining *The Impact of the Criminal Process on Health Care Ethics and Practice*. Following this she was awarded a Research Fellowship on a Wellcome funded project led by Professor John Harris titled *The Human Body—Its Scope, Limits, and Future* at the Institute for Science, Ethics, and Innovation.

Peter Alldridge

worked at Cardiff Law School from 1979-2003 before being appointed Drapers' Professor of Law at Queen Mary, University of London. He was Head of Law at QM from 2008-2012. He writes on criminal law, especially financial crime, evidence, and disability law and is the author of numerous publications including *Relocating Criminal Law* (2000) and *Money Laundering Law* (2003) and editor (with C Brants) of *Privacy, Autonomy and Criminal Law* (2003). He was specialist adviser to the joint Parliamentary Committees on the draft Corruption Bill (2003) and the draft Bribery Bill (2009).

Natasha Blanchet-Cohen

is Assistant Professor in the Department of Applied Human Sciences, Concordia University, Montreal, Canada. Her research centres on community youth development with a focus on rights-based approaches to programs and services, culture, and eco-citizenship, particularly as it relates to immigrant and indigenous young people. She is author of over 20 articles, reports and chapters on children's and youth rights, participation and citizenship.

Margaret Brazier

has taught at the University of Manchester since 1971 and became Professor of Law in 1990. She was Director of the University's Centre for Social Ethics and Policy until 2010. She was principal investigator on an AHRC funded project 'The Impact of the Criminal Process on Health Care Practice and Ethics' and a follow on project to produce recommendations for better practice in relation to death or injury consequent on serious medical error. She edited the Medical Law Review until July 2011. The fifth edition of her book *Medicine, Patients and the Law* (with Emma Cave) was published in August 2011. From 1996 to 1998 she chaired a review into the laws relating to surrogacy. From 2001 to 2004 she chaired the Retained Organs Commission, and from 2004 -2006 she chaired a Nuffield Council Working Party on critical care decisions in fetal and neonatal medicine. She was elected a fellow of the Academy of Medical Sciences in 2007 and appointed QC (honoris causa) in 2008.

Jo Bridgeman

is Professor of Healthcare Law and Feminist Ethics at the University of Sussex where she teaches Healthcare Law and Ethics, Family Law and Tort. Jo has researched and published in the field of healthcare law including work on the healthcare of teenagers, analysis of the issues arising from the Bristol Royal Infirmary Inquiry and, in *Parental Responsibility, Young Children and Healthcare Law* (CUP, 2007), a critical analysis of moral, social and legal responsibilities for the healthcare of babies, infants and young children.

Roger Cotterrell

is Anniversary Professor of Legal Theory at Queen Mary, University of London, and a Fellow of the British Academy. His books include *Living Law: Studies in Legal and Social Theory* (2008), *Law, Culture and Society: Legal Ideas in the Mirror of Social Theory* (2006), *The Politics of Jurisprudence: A Critical Introduction to Legal Philosophy* (2nd edn, 2003), *Emile Durkheim: Law in a Moral Domain* (1999), *Law's Community: Legal Theory in Sociological Perspective* (1995), *The Sociology of Law: An Introduction* (2nd edn, 1992), and the edited collection *Emile Durkheim: Justice, Morality and Politics* (2010).

Meda Couzens

is a Romanian lawyer, living and working in South Africa. Meda is currently a PhD candidate with Faculty of Law, Leiden University. She currently works as a senior lecturer in the School of Law at University of KwaZulu-Natal, Durban (UKZN), where she teaches Constitutional law and is involved in a Multidisciplinary Master in Child Care and Protection. Meda's research covers inter-country adoptions, child-headed households, local authorities and children, best interests of the child, child participation in governance and, more recently, the judicial application of the UN Convention on the Rights of the Child and legal aspects pertaining to the situation of children living in prison with their incarcerated parents in South Africa.

Coby de Graaf

is Senior Lecturer and Research Associate in Family and Child Law at the University of Amsterdam and the University of Leiden. She is the founding director at the Centre for Children's Rights Amsterdam (CCRA). She is responsible for the interdisciplinary lecture program 'Rights of the Child'. In 1999 she received her PhD for her doctoral research thesis 'Compulsory education and the right to an education'. Her recent publications include a book on the implementation of the International Convention on the Rights of the Child in Dutch jurisprudence and a book titled *The rights of the child and dignity*.

Dympna Devine

is Associate Professor in the School of Education, University College Dublin. She is Deputy Director of the newly established Childhood and Human Development Research Centre in the Geary Institute. Her specialist field is sociology, with an interest in childhood studies/children's rights and identities and their educational well-being. She was recently nominated by the Minister for Children and Youth Affairs to the National Advisory Council for Children and Young People: Better Outcomes, Brighter Futures (2014 - 2020). She has published widely in the areas of children's voice and citizenship, including *Immigration and Schooling in the Republic of Ireland* (2011), *New Managerialism in Education: Commercialisation, Care and Gender* (with Kathleen Lynch and Bernie Grummell, 2012) co-edited (with Wendy Luttrell, CUNY) a special inter-disciplinary issue on *'Children and 'value': education in neo-liberal times'* published in the journal *Children & Society (2013)*.

Alison Diduck

is Professor of Law at UCL. Alison's research interests are in the field of Child and Family Law, Legal Theory, gender issues and feminist perspectives in law and Legal History. She has published widely in these areas including with Felicity Kaganas *Family Law, Gender and the State* (2012), with Katherine O'Donovan *Feminist*

Perspectives in Family Law (2006) and as sole author *Law's Families* (2003). She sits on the editorial boards of *The International Journal of Law in Context, Social and Legal Studies* and *Current Legal Problems.*

John Eekelaar

FBA, retired in 2005 as Fellow and Tutor in Law, Pembroke College, Oxford and Reader in Family Law, Oxford University. He continues to research as Co-director, Oxford Centre for Family Law and Policy. John is author, co-author or editor of over 100 books and articles on family law, jurisprudence and socio-legal studies, including *Regulating Divorce* (1991), *Family Law and Social Policy* (1984), *Family Law and Personal Life* (2006), and with Mavis Maclean, *The Parental Obligation* (1997), *Family Lawyers: The Divorce Work of Solicitors* (2000), *Family Law Advocacy: How Barristers Help the Victims of Family Failure* (2009) and *Family Justice: The Work of Family Judges in Uncertain Times* (2013).

Lucinda Ferguson

is Associate Professor of Family Law, University of Oxford; Tutorial Fellow in Law, Oriel College, Oxford; and Director of Studies (Law), Regent's Park College, Oxford. She lectures and researches in the areas of Financial Provision upon Relationship Breakdown, Children's Rights, Child Protection, and Parenthood. She has published her work on financial arbitration, children's law, particularly children's rights theory and designing frameworks for making legal decisions that affect children. She is currently working on a major inter-disciplinary project with colleagues in the Department of Education looking at youth inclusion.

Michael Freeman

FBA, is Emeritus Professor of English Law at UCL. He is the Founding Editor of the *International Journal of Children's Rights*; Editor of the *International Journal of Law in Context*, General Editor of *International Library of Medicine, Ethics and Law* and of the *International Library of Family, Society and Law* and former Editor of the *Annual Survey of Family Law* and *Current Legal Problems.* He has published more than one hundred books and articles in the areas of Family Law, Child Law and Policy, Children's Rights, Medicine, Ethics and the Law and Medical Law, Jurisprudence and Legal Theory, and other areas of law and policy.

Lawrence M. Friedman

is the Marion Rice Kirkwood Professor of Law at Stanford University, Stanford, California. His specialties are legal history, and law and society. He is the author or editor of more than 30 books, including *A History of American Law* (3rd edition, 2005); *The Legal System: A Social Science Perspective* (1975); and *The Human Rights Culture* (2011). He is a member of the American Academy of Arts and Sciences, and the Society of American Historians and is a past President of the Law and Society Association, the American Society for Legal History, and the Research Committee on the Sociology of Law.

Andrew Gilbert

is a principal lecturer in law at Anglia Ruskin University in Cambridge and PhD candidate at the Faculty of Laws, UCL. His thesis, entitled 'British Conservatism and the Legal Regulation of Domestic Adult Relationships, 1983-2013', is being supervised by Professor Alison Diduck and Professor Michael Freeman. Andrew is a former family law solicitor and failed Conservative parliamentary candidate.

Danielle Griffiths

is a Research Fellow in interdisciplinary bioethics within the institute for Science, Ethics and Innovation (iSEI) at the University of Manchester. She worked on an AHRC funded project as a Research Associate examining *The Impact of the Criminal Process on Health Care Ethics and Practice* before she was awarded a Research Fellowship on a Wellcome funded project within iSEI entitled *The Human Body—Its Scope, Limits, and Future.* Danielle has particular responsibility for developing the reproduction strand of the project. She has published in international journals on issues relating to gender and reproduction and medical and criminal law and together with Professor Andrew Sanders edited *Medicine, Crime and Society*, published in 2013.

Mark Henaghan

is Dean and Professor of Law, University of Otago. Mark specialises in family law and is a Barrister and Solicitor of the High Court of New Zealand. He is co-author of *Family Law Policy in New Zealand* (4th ed 2013) and joint author of *Family Law in New Zealand*, (15th ed 2012). Mark is the joint author of *Relationship Property on Death* (2004 which won the 2005 J F Northey prize for the best published law book in New Zealand) and *Relationship Property Consolidated Legislation and Analysis* (2001). He is sole author of *Care of Children* (2005) and *Health Professionals and Trust* (2012 Routledge). He is an author and member of the editorial board for LexisNexis Family Law Service and the New Zealand Family Law Journal and author of a number of articles on family law. Mark is on the editorial boards of *Child and Family Law Quarterly* and *The International Journal of Human Rights*. Mark was the principal investigator of the Human Genome Project – Ethical and Legal Implications – funded by the New Zealand Law Foundation.

Jonathan Herring

is a fellow in law at Exeter College, Oxford University and Professor of Law at the Law Faculty, Oxford University. He has written on family law, medical law, criminal law and legal issues surrounding old age. He has written over forty books including: *Caring and the Law* (2013), *Older People in Law and Society* (2009); *European Human Rights and Family Law* (2010) (with Shazia Choudhry); *Medical Law and Ethics* (2010); *Criminal Law,* (4th ed) (2012); *Criminal Law: Great Debates* (2nd ed) (2011) and *Family Law* (4th ed) (2011).

Bernard S. Jackson

holds degrees from Liverpool (LL.B. Hons), Oxford (D. Phil.), Edinburgh (LL.D.) and Hebrew Union College, Cincinnati (D.H.L., honoris causa). He has held professorial posts at the Universities of Kent, Liverpool and Manchester (Co-Director of the Centre for Jewish Studies, 1997-2009; Director of the Agunah Research Unit, 2004-2009), and Visiting Appointments in Jerusalem, Oxford, Harvard, Paris, Bologna and Brussels. He is now (part-time) Professor of Law and Jewish Studies at Liverpool Hope University. His research interests (ten single authored books, including *Semiotics and Legal Theory* (1985), *Wisdom-Laws* (2006) and *Essays on Halakhah in the New Testament* (2008)) are in the semiotics of law and the history and philosophy of Jewish law.

Felicity Kaganas

is a Reader in Law at Brunel University. She teaches Family Law and Children and the Law and she has published widely in these fields and in feminist theory, including work on domestic violence and children's. She is joint author, with Alison Diduck, of *Family Law, Gender and the State* (2012), now in its third edition.

Sanford N. Katz

holds a Doctor of Laws degree from the University of Chicago Law School. He is the inaugural holder of the Darald & Juliet Libby Millennium Professor Law Chair at Boston College Law School. Prof. Katz has served as President of the International Society of Family Law, Chairman of the American Bar Association Family Law Section and Editor-in-Chief of the Family Law Quarterly. He is author of numerous publications including *Family Law in America* (2003) and (with D.R Katz) *Adoption Laws in a Nutshell* (2012).

Heather Keating

is professor of Criminal Law and Criminal Responsibility at the Sussex Law School, University of Sussex. She is a founder member of the child and family research group and the Centre for Responsibilities, Rights and the Law. She is co-author (with Chris Clarkson and Sally Cunningham) of *Criminal Law: Text and Materials* (7th ed., 2010). She was co-editor (with Craig Lind) of a special issue of the *Journal of Law and Society, Children, Responsibilities and the State,* published in 2008 which was simultaneously published by Blackwell as a book); joint editor of and contributor to *Responsibility,*

Law and the Family (2008); *Taking Responsibility: Law and the Changing Family* (2011) and *Regulating Family Responsibilities* (2011). She has written widely on issues of both criminal law and child law. She is currently writing is a monograph on children, responsibility and the criminal law.

Ghislaine Lanteigne

is a PhD Candidate in Family Law at UCL doing research on issues in the application of the 'best interests of the child' principle in relocation (comparison of law and practitioners' perspectives in England and Wales, and Canada). She completed previous studies in Law at Coventry (LLB Hons.), Moncton (LLB Canadian Equivalence) and LSE (LLM). She also holds Masters degrees in Sociology (Aix-en-Provence) and Translation Studies - Linguistics (Birmingham). She has been admitted as a solicitor in New Brunswick and Ontario (Canada) and in England and Wales (currently not practicing). She has worked as a lecturer in Law and solicitor for several years in Canada. Previous work experiences have been in teaching and research in Sociology and Applied Linguistics for governments and universities.

Laura Lundy

is a Professor of Education Law and Children's Rights and the Director of the Centre for Children's Rights at Queen's University Belfast. Her research interests are in children's rights with a particular focus on education and children's participation and she is author, co-author or editor of over 50 publications in these areas. She is currently collaborating with Natasha Blanchet-Cohen, Dympna Devine, Lacey Elizabeth Peters, Kylie Smith, Elizabeth Swadener, and Elizabeth Welty on a project researching rights-based approaches to engaging children in research.

Judith Masson

is Professor of Socio-legal Studies at the Bristol University, specialising in Child Law. She has undertaken numerous studies on law in social work including: step-parent adoption; representation of children: *Out of Hearing* (1999); partnership with parents of looked after children *Lost and Found* (1999); and emergency intervention: *Protecting Powers* (2007). In 2007-8, Judith directed a project examining 400 child protection cases which resulted in court proceedings – *Care Profiling Study* (Ministry of Justice, 2008). This was followed by an ESRC-funded qualitative study on the representation of parents in such proceedings, Pearce et al, *Just following Instructions*? (2011). She has recently completed another ESRC-funded study on the operation and impact of the pre-proceedings process in the PLO, *Partnership by law*? Judith has been a specialist adviser for Parliamentary Committees and a member of the Judicial Studies Board. From 2004-2011 she was the academic member of the Family Justice Council.

Anne McGillivray

is a Professor of Law at the University of Manitoba. Her research centres on childhood, children's rights, and the right to live free of all forms of violence. Her publications include *Black Eyes All of the Time: Intimate Violence Aboriginal Women and the Justice System* (1999), *Governing Childhood* (ed. 1997), and over 50 chapters, scholarly articles and reports on childhood, rights, corporal punishment, parens patriae, Aboriginal childhood, child protection, violence against women, and the child in literature. She serves on the boards of *The International Journal of Children's Rights*, the *Canadian Journal of Human Rights*, and *Mosaic: A journal for the interdisciplinary study of literature.* She served on the 1997 CIDA Children's Rights Delegation to Cuba and the Health Canada Steering Committee for the Canadian Incidence Study on Child Abuse and Neglect Part II.

Carrie Menkel-Meadow

is Chancellor's Professor of Law and Political Science, University of California Irvine Law School, and A.B. Chettle Jr. Professor of Law, Dispute Resolution and Civil Procedure at Georgetown University Law Center. She is the author or editor of over 10 books, including *Complex Dispute Resolution* (3 volumes: *Foundations, Multi-Party Disputes, Democracy and Decision Making,* and *International Dispute Resolution*), *Dispute Resolution: Beyond the Adversarial Model,* (2nd ed. 2011), *Law and Popular Culture* (2nd ed. 2012), and *What's Fair: Ethics for Negotiators* (2004) and over 200 articles on subjects ranging from dispute resolution, feminist jurisprudence, legal ethics, legal education to civil procedure and the sociology of the legal profession. She recently won the first ever awarded American Bar Association Award for Outstanding Scholarship on Dispute Resolution. She was co-editor with Michael Freeman of UCL of *the International Journal of Law in Context* from its founding until 2013, and with Mark Tushnet of Harvard Law School of the *Journal of Legal Education* from 2004-2009.

Maria Federica Moscati

is Senior Teaching Fellow in the School of Law, SOAS, University of London. She teaches and researches on access to justice and dispute resolution, religion and the law and law and LGBT rights. Her most recent book is *Pasolini's Italian Premonitions: Same-Sex Unions and the Law in Comparative Perspective* (2014).

David Nelken

is Distinguished Professor of Legal Institutions and Social Change at the University of Macerata in Italy and Distinguished Research Professor of Law at Cardiff University, UK. He is also the Visiting Professor of Criminology at Oxford University's Centre of Criminology. He is author or editor of numerous books on legal cultures, criminal law and comparative law, including *Beyond the Study of 'Law in Context'* (2009),

Comparative Criminal Justice: Making Sense of Difference (2010) and *Using Legal Culture* ed., (2012).

Noam Peleg

is Lecturer at the Faculty of Law, University of New South Wales, Australia. He was formerly Postdoctoral Associate at the Hebrew University of Jerusalem where he taught children's rights in international law, and Postdoctoral Fellow at UCL. His research is in children's rights and international human rights law, family law and education law. Noam has worked in a number of human rights organizations, and has extensive experience in representing children in courts, and in litigation before the Supreme Court of Israel. He has also worked for Israel's National Committee on the Rights of the Child and has taught at the LSE and Tel Aviv University. He is a member of the editorial board of the *International Journal of Children' Rights*.

Christine Piper

is a Professor in Brunel Law School and Fellow of the Academy of Social Sciences. Her research and teaching interests are focused on family and child law and policy, sentencing and youth justice. She is a member of the Editorial Board of the *Child and Family Law Quarterly* and a supporter of the charity Action for Children. Her books include: *Investing in Children, Policy, Law and Practice in Context* (2008), (with S. Easton) *Sentencing and Punishment: The Quest for Justice* (3rd ed. 2012), *The Responsible Parent* (1993) and, with M. King, *How the Law Thinks About Children* (1990, 1995).

Helen Reece

is Reader in Law at London School of Economics and Political Science. She has written extensively on Family Law in general and violence against women in particular, notably 'Rape Myths: Is Elite Opinion Right and Popular Opinion Wrong?' (2013) *OJLS* and 'The End of Domestic Violence?' (2006) *MLR* and *Divorcing Responsibly* (2003). She was taught by and later taught with Professor Michael Freeman.

Robert Reiner

is Emeritus Professor of Criminology, Law Department, LSE. His books include *The Politics of the Police* (2000), *Law and Order: An Honest Citizen's Guide to Crime and Control* (2007, and *Policing, Popular Culture and Political Economy: Towards a Social Democratic Criminology* (2011).

Bernadette J. Saunders

is a Senior Lecturer in Social Work, in the Faculty of Medicine, Nursing & Health Sciences, Monash University, Victoria. She was a Senior Research Fellow at Child

Abuse Prevention Research Australia, Monash University from 2006-2010. Her research, teaching and publications predominantly focus on children, child abuse, children's rights, and legal and ethical knowledge for social workers. Her book, with Chris Goddard: *Physical Punishment in Childhood: The Rights of the Child*, was published in 2010. She regularly engages with the Australian media in relation to the issue of 'smacking' children.

Rhona Schuz

is Senior Lecturer and Co-Director of the Centre for the Right of the Child and the Family at the Sha'arei Mishpat Law School in Israel. She was formerly a lecturer in law at Nottingham University, the London School of Economics and Bar Ilan University. Dr Schuz's publications in the areas of Family Law and Private International Law include *A Modern Approach to the Incidental Question* (1997) and *The Hague Child Abduction Convention: A Critical Analysis* (2013) and many articles in English and Hebrew. She served as an adviser to the English Law Commission on the Ground for Divorce and was appointed by the Israel Minister of Justice as a member of the Shifman Committee on the Reform of the law relation to Child Support. She represented the International Society of Family Law at the Hague Conference's Sixth Special Commission on the operation of the 1980 Child Abduction Convention and the 1996 Child Protection Convention (2011-2012). She is co-editor of The Family in Law Journal, a peer-reviewed interdisciplinary journal (in Hebrew).

Kylie Smith

is a Research Fellow and Senior Lecturer at the Youth Research Centre located in the University of Melbourne's Graduate School of Education. Her research looks at how theory and practice can transform the classroom and community (how social justice curricula might look and the effects of this for fairer spaces for children and adults to live and speak in), Children's Rights and Citizenship, the early childhood curriculum, children's participation, research with children, children's voices and transition to school.

Jane Stoll

is a member of the Faculty of Law, Uppsala University, Sweden. She holds a Licentiate of Laws (Civil Law) from Uppsala and is currently completing her Doctorate of Law. Her licentiate thesis "Swedish donor offspring and their legal right to information" was published in 2008 and her doctoral thesis concerns parenthood following surrogacy arrangements in Sweden, England & Wales and Israel. Jane completed her Bachelor of Laws and Bachelor of Commerce degrees at Griffith University, Queensland. She is also a Registered Nurse, and holds a postgraduate Diploma in Health Science from Flinders University, South Australia. She is a Solicitor of the Supreme Court of New South Wales and has practiced in both law and nursing. Her teaching and research interests include family law, medical law and bioethics, and alternative dispute resolution.

Beth Blue Swadener

is Professor of Justice and Social Inquiry and Associate Director of the School of Social Transformation at Arizona State University. Her research focuses on internationally comparative social policy, with focus on sub-Saharan Africa, impacts of neoliberal policy on local communities, and children's rights and voices. She has published ten books, including *Reconceptualizing the Early Childhood Curriculum* (2014); *Children and Families "At Promise"* (1995); *Does the Village Still Raise the Child?* (2000); *Decolonizing Research in Cross-Cultural Context, Power and Voice in Research with Children* (2011), and *Children's Rights and Education* (2013). Swadener serves as associate editor of the *American Educational Research Journal*

Sir Mathew Thorpe

was Called to the Bar, Inner Temple in 1961, was appointed Queen's Counsel in 1980, and a judge of the High Court, Family Division in 1988. He was liaison Judge for the Western Circuit between 1991 and 1995. Sir Mathew was appointed a Lord Justice of Appeal in 1995, and retired from the Court of Appeal in July 2013. During his distinguished judicial career he gave the leading judgment in the majority of family appeals, particularly appeals concerning international family law, matrimonial finance, mental capacity and the protection of vulnerable adults. In 2005 Sir Mathew was appointed Head of International Family Justice for England & Wales and since then has travelled widely as the judicial representative of the UK.

John Tobin

is Professor at the Melbourne Law School, University of Melbourne. He teaches and researches in the area of human rights especially children's rights. Among his many publications in these areas is *The Right to Health in International Law* (2012) and he is currently working with Professor Philip Alston on the preparation of a *Commentary to the UN Convention on the Rights of the Child.*

Elizabeth Welty

is a research assistant in the Centre for Children's Rights in the School of Education at Queen's University Belfast. She is originally from California and worked in the area of conflict transformation in both the United States and the United Kingdom. She is specifically interested in building the capacity of young people to be successful agents in their lives, encouraging them to be effective advocates for issues important to them. This was the underlying theme of her doctoral research in citizenship education, and the focus for building practical skills in research, facilitation and education.